ALTERNATIVE INVESTMENTS AND FIXED INCOME

FA® Program Curriculum
016 • LEVEL II • VOLUME 5

CFA Institute | WILEY

Please visit our website at
www.WileyGlobalFinance.com.

FSC
www.fsc.org

MIX
Paper from
responsible sources
FSC® C005928

CONTENTS

indicates an optional segment

indicates an optional segment

◙ indicates an optional segment

indicates an optional segment

How to Use the CFA Program Curriculum

Congratulations on reaching Level II of the Chartered Financial Analyst (CFA®) Program. This exciting and rewarding program of study reflects your desire to become a serious investment professional. You are embarking on a program noted for its high ethical standards and the breadth of knowledge, skills, and abilities it develops. Your commitment to the CFA Program should be educationally and professionally rewarding.

The credential you seek is respected around the world as a mark of accomplishment and dedication. Each level of the program represents a distinct achievement in professional development. Successful completion of the program is rewarded with membership in a prestigious global community of investment professionals. CFA charterholders are dedicated to life-long learning and maintaining currency with the ever-changing dynamics of a challenging profession. The CFA Program represents the first step toward a career-long commitment to professional education.

The CFA examination measures your mastery of the core skills required to succeed as an investment professional. These core skills are the basis for the Candidate Body of Knowledge (CBOK™). The CBOK consists of four components:

- A broad outline that lists the major topic areas covered in the CFA Program (www.cfainstitute.org/cbok);
- Topic area weights that indicate the relative exam weightings of the top-level topic areas (www.cfainstitute.org/level_II);
- Learning outcome statements (LOS) that advise candidates about the specific knowledge, skills, and abilities they should acquire from readings covering a topic area (LOS are provided in candidate study sessions and at the beginning of each reading); and
- The CFA Program curriculum, which contains the readings and end-of-reading questions, that candidates receive upon exam registration.

Therefore, the key to your success on the CFA examinations is studying and understanding the CBOK. The following sections provide background on the CBOK, the organization of the curriculum, and tips for developing an effective study program.

CURRICULUM DEVELOPMENT PROCESS

The CFA Program is grounded in the practice of the investment profession. Beginning with the Global Body of Investment Knowledge (GBIK), CFA Institute performs a continuous practice analysis with investment professionals around the world to determine the knowledge, skills, and abilities (competencies) that are relevant to the profession. Regional expert panels and targeted surveys are conducted annually to verify and reinforce the continuous feedback from the GBIK collaborative website. The practice analysis process ultimately defines the CBOK. The CBOK reflects the competencies that are generally accepted and applied by investment professionals. These competencies are used in practice in a generalist context and are expected to be demonstrated by a recently qualified CFA charterholder.

The Education Advisory Committee, consisting of practicing charterholders, in conjunction with CFA Institute staff, designs the CFA Program curriculum in order to deliver the CBOK to candidates. The examinations, also written by charterholders, are designed to allow you to demonstrate your mastery of the CBOK as set forth in the CFA Program curriculum. As you structure your personal study program, you should emphasize mastery of the CBOK and the practical application of that knowledge. For more information on the practice analysis, CBOK, and development of the CFA Program curriculum, please visit www.cfainstitute.org.

ORGANIZATION OF THE CURRICULUM

The Level II CFA Program curriculum is organized into 10 topic areas. Each topic area begins with a brief statement of the material and the depth of knowledge expected.

Each topic area is then divided into one or more study sessions. These study sessions—18 sessions in the Level II curriculum—should form the basic structure of your reading and preparation.

Each study session includes a statement of its structure and objective and is further divided into specific reading assignments. An outline illustrating the organization of these 18 study sessions can be found at the front of each volume of the curriculum.

The readings and end-of-reading questions are the basis for all examination questions and are selected or developed specifically to teach the knowledge, skills, and abilities reflected in the CBOK. These readings are drawn from content commissioned by CFA Institute, textbook chapters, professional journal articles, research analyst reports, and cases. All readings include problems and solutions to help you understand and master the topic areas.

Reading-specific Learning Outcome Statements (LOS) are listed at the beginning of each reading. These LOS indicate what you should be able to accomplish after studying the reading. The LOS, the reading, and the end-of-reading questions are dependent on each other, with the reading and questions providing context for understanding the scope of the LOS.

You should use the LOS to guide and focus your study because each examination question is based on the assigned readings and one or more LOS. The readings provide context for the LOS and enable you to apply a principle or concept in a variety of scenarios. The candidate is responsible for the entirety of the required material in a study session, which includes the assigned readings as well as the end-of-reading questions and problems.

We encourage you to review the information about the LOS on our website (www. cfainstitute.org/programs/cfaprogram/courseofstudy/Pages/study_sessions.aspx), including the descriptions of LOS "command words" (www.cfainstitute.org/programs/ Documents/cfa_and_cipm_los_command_words.pdf).

FEATURES OF THE CURRICULUM

**OPTIONAL
SEGMENT**

Required vs. Optional Segments   You should read all of an assigned reading. In some cases, though, we have reprinted an entire chapter or article and marked certain parts of the reading as "optional." The CFA examination is based only on the required segments, and the optional segments are included only when it is determined that they might help you to better understand the required segments (by seeing the required material in its full context). When an optional segment begins, you will see an icon and a dashed vertical bar in the outside margin that will continue until the optional segment ends, accompanied by another icon. *Unless the material is specifically marked as optional, you should assume it is required.* You should rely on the required segments and the reading-specific LOS in preparing for the examination.

END OPTIONAL SEGMENT

End-of-Reading Problems/Solutions   *All problems in the readings as well as their solutions (which are provided directly following the problems) are part of the curriculum and are required material for the exam.* When appropriate, we have included problems within and after the readings to demonstrate practical application and reinforce your understanding of the concepts presented. The problems are designed to help you learn these concepts and may serve as a basis for exam questions. Many of these questions are adapted from past CFA examinations.

Glossary and Index   For your convenience, we have printed a comprehensive glossary in each volume. Throughout the curriculum, a **bolded** word in a reading denotes a term defined in the glossary. The curriculum eBook is searchable, but we also publish an index that can be found on the CFA Institute website with the Level II study sessions.

Source Material   The authorship, publisher, and copyright owners are given for each reading for your reference. We recommend that you use the CFA Institute curriculum rather than the original source materials because the curriculum may include only selected pages from outside readings, updated sections within the readings, and problems and solutions tailored to the CFA Program.

LOS Self-Check   We have inserted checkboxes next to each LOS that you can use to track your progress in mastering the concepts in each reading.

DESIGNING YOUR PERSONAL STUDY PROGRAM

Create a Schedule   An orderly, systematic approach to exam preparation is critical. You should dedicate a consistent block of time every week to reading and studying. Complete all reading assignments and the associated problems and solutions in each study session. Review the LOS both before and after you study each reading to ensure that you have mastered the applicable content and can demonstrate the knowledge, skill, or ability described by the LOS and the assigned reading. Use the LOS self-check to track your progress and highlight areas of weakness for later review.

As you prepare for your exam, we will e-mail you important exam updates, testing policies, and study tips. Be sure to read these carefully. Curriculum errata are periodically updated and posted on the study session page at www.cfainstitute.org. You can also sign up for an RSS feed to alert you to the latest errata update.

Successful candidates report an average of more than 300 hours preparing for each exam. Your preparation time will vary based on your prior education and experience. For each level of the curriculum, there are 18 study sessions. So, a good plan is to devote 15–20 hours per week for 18 weeks to studying the material. Use the final four to six weeks before the exam to review what you have learned and practice with topic and mock exams. This recommendation, however, may underestimate the hours needed for appropriate examination preparation depending on your individual circumstances, relevant experience, and academic background. You will undoubtedly adjust your study time to conform to your own strengths and weaknesses and to your educational and professional background.

You will probably spend more time on some study sessions than on others, but on average you should plan on devoting 15–20 hours per study session. You should allow ample time for both in-depth study of all topic areas and additional concentration on those topic areas for which you feel the least prepared.

An interactive study planner is available in the candidate resources area of our website to help you plan your study time. The interactive study planner recommends completion dates for each topic of the curriculum. Dates are determined based on study time available, exam topic weights, and curriculum weights. As you progress through the curriculum, the interactive study planner dynamically adjusts your study plan when you are running off schedule to help you stay on track for completion prior to the examination.

CFA Institute Topic Exams   The CFA Institute topic exams are intended to assess your mastery of individual topic areas as you progress through your studies. After each test, you will receive immediate feedback noting the correct responses and indicating the relevant assigned reading so you can identify areas of weakness for further study. For more information on the topic tests, please visit www.cfainstitute.org.

CFA Institute Mock Exams   The three-hour mock exams simulate the morning and afternoon sessions of the actual CFA examination, and are intended to be taken after you complete your study of the full curriculum so you can test your understanding of the curriculum and your readiness for the exam. You will receive feedback at the end of the mock exam, noting the correct responses and indicating the relevant assigned readings so you can assess areas of weakness for further study during your review period. We recommend that you take mock exams during the final stages of your preparation for the actual CFA examination. For more information on the mock examinations, please visit www.cfainstitute.org.

Preparatory Providers   After you enroll in the CFA Program, you may receive numerous solicitations for preparatory courses and review materials. When considering a prep course, make sure the provider is in compliance with the CFA Institute Prep Provider Guidelines Program (www.cfainstitute.org/utility/examprep/Pages/index.aspx). Just remember, there are no shortcuts to success on the CFA examinations; reading and studying the CFA curriculum is the key to success on the examination. The CFA examinations reference only the CFA Institute assigned curriculum—no preparatory course or review course materials are consulted or referenced.

SUMMARY

Every question on the CFA examination is based on the content contained in the required readings and on one or more LOS. Frequently, an examination question is based on a specific example highlighted within a reading or on a specific end-of-reading question and/or problem and its solution. To make effective use of the CFA Program curriculum, please remember these key points:

1   All pages of the curriculum are required reading for the examination except for occasional sections marked as optional. You may read optional pages as background, but you will not be tested on them.

2   All questions, problems, and their solutions—found at the end of readings—are part of the curriculum and are required study material for the examination.

3   You should make appropriate use of the topic and mock examinations and other resources available at www.cfainstitute.org.

4 Use the interactive study planner to create a schedule and commit sufficient study time to cover the 18 study sessions, review the materials, and take topic and mock examinations.

5 Some of the concepts in the study sessions may be superseded by updated rulings and/or pronouncements issued after a reading was published. Candidates are expected to be familiar with the overall analytical framework contained in the assigned readings. Candidates are not responsible for changes that occur after the material was written.

FEEDBACK

At CFA Institute, we are committed to delivering a comprehensive and rigorous curriculum for the development of competent, ethically grounded investment professionals. We rely on candidate and member feedback as we work to incorporate content, design, and packaging improvements. You can be assured that we will continue to listen to your suggestions. Please send any comments or feedback to info@cfainstitute.org. Ongoing improvements in the curriculum will help you prepare for success on the upcoming examinations and for a lifetime of learning as a serious investment professional.

Alternative Investments

Study Session 13   Alternative Investments

TOPIC LEVEL LEARNING OUTCOME

The candidate should be able to analyze and evaluate real estate and private equity using appropriate valuation concepts and techniques.

13

Alternative Investments

This study session discusses the following categories of alternative investments: real estate, private equity, and commodities. Real estate investments, both private investment and investment through publicly traded securities, are described, and methods for analysis and evaluation are presented. Private equity, including venture capital and leveraged buyouts, is examined from the perspectives of a private equity firm evaluating equity investments for its portfolio and an investor evaluating participation in a private equity fund. The study session concludes with an overview of investing in commodities.

READING ASSIGNMENTS

READING

39

Private Real Estate Investments

by Jeffrey D. Fisher and Bryan D. MacGregor, PhD, MRICS, MRPTI

Jeffrey D. Fisher (USA). Bryan D. MacGregor, PhD, MRICS, MRTPI, is at the University of Aberdeen, Scotland (United Kingdom).

LEARNING OUTCOMES

Mastery	The candidate should be able to:
☐	a. classify and describe basic forms of real estate investments;
☐	b. describe the characteristics, the classification, and basic segments of real estate;
☐	c. explain the role in a portfolio, economic value determinants, investment characteristics, and principal risks of private real estate;
☐	d. describe commercial property types, including their distinctive investment characteristics;
☐	e. compare the income, cost, and sales comparison approaches to valuing real estate properties;
☐	f. estimate and interpret the inputs (for example, net operating income, capitalization rate, and discount rate) to the direct capitalization and discounted cash flow valuation methods;
☐	g. calculate the value of a property using the direct capitalization and discounted cash flow valuation methods;
☐	h. compare the direct capitalization and discounted cash flow valuation methods;
☐	i. calculate the value of a property using the cost and sales comparison approaches;
☐	j. describe due diligence in private equity real estate investment;
☐	k. discuss private equity real estate investment indices, including their construction and potential biases;
☐	l. explain the role in a portfolio, the major economic value determinants, investment characteristics, principal risks, and due diligence of private real estate debt investment;
☐	m. calculate and interpret financial ratios used to analyze and evaluate private real estate investments.

1   INTRODUCTION

Real estate investments comprise a significant part of the portfolios of many investors, so understanding how to analyze real estate investments and evaluate the role of real estate investments in a portfolio is important. Real estate investments can take a variety of forms, from private equity investment in (ownership of) real estate properties (real estate properties, hereafter, may simply be referred to as real estate) to publicly traded debt investment, such as mortgage-backed securities. While this reading discusses the basic forms of real estate investments and provides an overview of the real estate market, its focus is private equity investment in commercial (or income-producing) real estate.

Private equity investment in real estate is sometimes referred to as direct ownership, in contrast to indirect ownership of real estate through publicly traded equity securities, such as real estate investment trusts (REITs). Similarly, lending in the private market, such as mortgage lending by banks or insurance companies, is sometimes referred to as direct lending. **Mortgages** are loans with real estate serving as collateral for the loan. Publicly traded debt investment, such as mortgage-backed securities (MBSs), are sometimes referred to as indirect lending. Each form of real estate investment has characteristics that an investor should be aware of when considering and making a real estate investment. Also, real estate has characteristics that differentiate it from other asset classes.

Private real estate investments—equity and debt—are often included in the portfolios of investors with long-term investment horizons and with the ability to tolerate relatively lower liquidity. Examples of such investors are endowments, pension funds, and life insurance companies. Other real estate investors may have short investment horizons, such as a real estate developer who plans to sell a real estate property to a long-term investor once the development of the property is complete. Publicly traded, pooled-investment forms of real estate investments, such as REITs, may be suitable for investors with short investment horizons and higher liquidity needs.

Valuation of commercial real estate properties constitutes a significant portion of this reading. Regardless of the form of real estate investment, the value of the underlying real estate is critical to its value. The concepts and valuation techniques described in this reading are generally applicable to global real estate markets. Valuation of the underlying real estate is of importance to private real estate equity and debt investors because the value of each type of investment is inextricably tied to the value of the underlying real estate. Also, because real estate properties do not transact frequently and are unique, we rely on estimates of value or appraisals rather than transaction prices to assess changes in value over time. However, transaction prices of similar properties can be useful in estimating value. In creating real estate indices that serve as benchmarks for performance evaluation, appraised values—rather than transaction prices—are often used. In recent years, several indices based on actual transactions have been developed. Both types of indices are discussed in this reading.

The reading is organized as follows: Section 2 describes basic forms of real estate investment, covering equity and debt investments and public and private investments. Section 3 discusses characteristics of real estate and classifications of real estate properties. Section 4 focuses on private equity investment in real estate. It discusses benefits of and risks associated with investing in real estate. The main types of commercial real estate markets and characteristics of each are covered. Section 5 introduces the appraisal (valuation) process and the main approaches used by appraisers to estimate value. Section 6 discusses the income approach, and Section 7 discusses the cost and sales comparison approaches. Section 8 discusses reconciling the results from these three approaches. Section 9 discusses the due diligence process typically followed when acquiring real estate investments. Section 10 presents a brief international perspective. Section 11 considers real estate market indices. Section 12 discusses some aspects of private market real estate debt. A summary and practice problems complete the reading.

REAL ESTATE INVESTMENT: BASIC FORMS

2

Investment in real estate has been defined from a capital market perspective in the context of quadrants, or four main areas through which capital can be invested. The quadrants are a result of two dimensions of investment. The first dimension is whether the investment is made in the private or public market. The private market often involves investing directly in an asset (for example, purchasing a property) or getting a claim on an asset (for example, through providing a mortgage to the purchaser). The investment can made indirectly through a number of different investment vehicles, such as a partnership or commingled real estate fund (CREF). In either case, the transactions occur in the private market. The public market does not involve such direct investment; rather, it involves investing in a security with claims on the underlying position(s)—for example, through investments in a real estate investment trust (REIT), a real estate operating company (REOC), or a mortgage-backed security.

The second dimension, as illustrated in the examples above, is whether the investment is structured as equity or debt. An "equity" investor has an ownership interest: Such an investor may be the owner of the real estate property or may invest in securities of a company or a REIT that owns the real estate property. The owner of the real estate property controls such decisions as whether to obtain a mortgage loan on the real estate, who should handle property management, and when to sell the real estate. In the case of a REIT, that control is delegated to the managers of the REIT by the shareholders. A "debt" investor is in a position of lender: Such an investor may loan funds to the "entity" acquiring the real estate property or may invest in securities based on real estate lending. Typically, the real estate property is used as collateral for a mortgage loan. If there is a loan on the real estate (mortgage), then the mortgage lender has a priority claim on the real estate. The value of the equity investor's interest in the real estate is equal to the value of the real estate less the amount owed to the mortgage lender.

Combining the two dimensions, we have four quadrants: private equity, public equity, private debt, and public debt, as illustrated in Exhibit 1.

Exhibit 1	Examples of the Basic Forms of Real Estate Investment	
	Equity	**Debt**
Private	Direct investments in real estate. This can be through sole ownership, joint ventures, real estate limited partnerships, or other forms of commingled funds.	Mortgages
Publicly traded	Shares of real estate operating companies and shares of REITs	Mortgage-backed securities (residential and commercial)

Each of the basic forms of real estate investment has its own risks, expected returns, regulations, legal structures, and market structures. Private real estate investment, compared with publicly traded real estate investment, typically involves larger investments because of the indivisibility of real estate property and is more illiquid. Publicly traded real estate investment allows the real estate property to remain undivided but the ownership or claim on the property to be divided. This leads to more liquidity and allows investors to diversify by purchasing ownership interests in more properties than if an entire property had to be owned by a single investor and/or to diversify by having claims against more properties than if an entire mortgage had to be funded and retained by a single lender.

Real estate requires management. Private equity investment (ownership) in real estate properties requires property management expertise on the part of the owner or the hiring of property managers. Real estate owned by REOCs and REITs is professionally managed and requires no real estate management expertise on the part of an investor in shares of the REOCs and REITs.

Equity investors generally expect a higher rate of return than lenders (debt investors) because they take on more risk. The lenders' claims on the cash flows and proceeds from sale must be satisfied before the equity investors can receive anything. As the amount of debt on a property, or financial leverage, increases, risk increases for both debt and equity and an investor's—whether debt or equity—return expectations will increase. Of course, the risk is that the higher return will not materialize, and the risk is even higher for an equity investor.

Debt investors in real estate, whether through private or public markets, expect to receive their return from promised cash flows and typically do not participate in any appreciation in value of the underlying real estate. Thus, debt investments in real estate are similar to other fixed-income investments, such as bonds. The returns to equity real estate investors have two components: an income stream resulting from such activities as renting the property and a capital appreciation component resulting from changes in the value of the underlying real estate. If the returns to equity real estate investors are less than perfectly positively correlated with the returns to stocks and/or bonds, then adding equity real estate investments to a traditional portfolio will potentially have diversification benefits.

Real estate markets in each of the four quadrants in Exhibit 1 have evolved and matured to create relatively efficient market structures for accessing all types of capital for real estate (i.e., public and private debt and equity). Such structures are critical for the success of the asset class for both lenders and equity investors. The categorization of real estate investment into the four quadrants helps investors identify the form(s) that best fit(s) their objectives. For example, some investors may prefer to own and manage real estate. Other investors may prefer the greater liquidity and professional management associated with purchasing publicly traded REITs. Other investors may prefer mortgage lending because it involves less risk than equity investment or unsecured lending; the mortgage lender has a priority claim on the real estate used as collateral for the mortgage. Still other investors may want to invest in each quadrant or allocate more capital to one quadrant or another over time as they perceive shifts in the relative value of each. Each quadrant offers differences in risk and expected return, including the impact of taxes on the return. So investors should explore the risk and return characteristics of each quadrant as part of their investment decisions. The balance of this reading focuses on private investment in real estate—particularly, equity investment.

EXAMPLE 1

Form of Investment

An investor is interested in adding real estate to her portfolio for the first time. She has no previous real estate experience but thinks adding real estate will provide some diversification benefits. She is concerned about liquidity because she may need the money in a year or so. Which form of investment is *most likely* appropriate for her?

A Shares of REITs

B Mortgage-backed securities

C Direct ownership of commercial real estate property

Solution:

A is correct. She is probably better-off investing in shares of publicly traded REITs, which provide liquidity, have professional management, and require a lower investment than direct ownership of real estate. Using REITs, she may be able to put together a diversified real estate investment portfolio. Although REITs are more correlated with stocks than direct ownership of real estate, direct ownership is much less liquid and a lot of properties are needed to have a diversified real estate portfolio. Also, adding shares of REITs to her current portfolio should provide more diversification benefits than adding debt in the form of mortgage-backed securities and will allow her to benefit from any appreciation of the real estate. Debt investments in real estate, such as MBSs, are similar to other fixed-income investments, such as bonds. The difference is that their income streams are secured on real estate assets, which means that the risks are default risks linked to the performance of the real estate assets and the ability of mortgagees to pay interest. In contrast, adding equity real estate investments to a traditional portfolio will potentially have diversification benefits.

REAL ESTATE: CHARACTERISTICS AND CLASSIFICATIONS

3

Regardless of the form of investment, the value of the underlying real estate property is critical to the performance of the investment. If the property increases in value, the equity investor will benefit from the appreciation and the debt investor is more likely to receive the promised cash flows. If the property declines in value, however, the equity investor and even the debt investor may experience a loss.

3.1 Characteristics

Real estate has characteristics that distinguish it from the other main investment asset classes and that complicate the measurement and assessment of performance. These include the following:

■ *Heterogeneity and fixed location*: Whereas all bonds of a particular issue and stocks of a particular type in a specific company are identical, no two properties are the same. Even identically constructed buildings with the same tenants and leases will be at different locations. Buildings differ in use, size, location, age, type of construction, quality, and tenant and leasing arrangements. These factors are important in trying to establish value and also in the amount of specific risk in a real estate investment.

- *High unit value*: The unit value of a real estate property is much larger than that of a bond or stock because of its indivisibility. The amount required to make a private equity investment in real estate limits the pool of potential private equity investors and the ability to construct a diversified real estate portfolio. This factor is important in the development of publicly traded securities, such as REITs, which allow partial ownership of an indivisible asset.

- *Management intensive*: An investor in bonds or stocks is not expected to be actively involved in managing the company, but a private real estate equity investor or direct owner of real estate has responsibility for management of the real estate, including maintaining the properties, negotiating leases, and collecting rents. This active management, whether done by the owner or by hired property managers, creates additional costs that must be taken into account.

- *High transaction costs*: Buying and selling of real estate is also costly and time consuming because others, such as appraisers, lawyers, and construction professionals, are likely to be involved in the process until a transaction is completed.

- *Depreciation*: Buildings depreciate as a result of use and the passage of time. A building's value may also change as the desirability of its location and its design changes from the perspective of end users.

- *Need for debt capital*: Because of the large amounts required to purchase and develop real estate properties, the ability to access funds and the cost of funds in the credit markets are important. As a result, real estate values are sensitive to the cost and availability of debt capital. When debt capital is scarce or interest rates are high, the value of real estate tends to be lower than when debt capital is readily available or interest rates are low.

- *Illiquidity*: As a result of several of the above factors, real estate properties are relatively illiquid. They may take a significant amount of time to market and to sell at a price that is close to the owner's perceived fair market value.

- *Price determination*: As a result of the heterogeneity of real estate properties and the low volume of transactions, estimates of value or appraisals rather than transaction prices are usually necessary to assess changes in value or expected selling price over time. However, the transaction prices of similar properties are often considered in estimating the value of or appraising a property. The limited number of participants in the market for a property, combined with the importance of local knowledge, makes it harder to know the market value of a property. In a less efficient market, those who have superior information and skill at evaluating properties may have an advantage. This is quite different from stocks in publicly traded companies, where many buyers and sellers value and transact in the shares in an active market.

The above factors fundamentally affect the nature of real estate investment. To overcome some of these problems, markets in securitized real estate, most notably through REITs, have expanded. REITs are a type of publicly traded equity investment in real estate. The REIT provides or hires professional property managers. Investing in shares of a REIT typically allows exposure to a diversified portfolio of real estate. The shares are typically liquid, and active trading results in prices that are more likely to reflect market value. A separate reading discusses REITs in greater detail.

Investment Characteristics

An investor states that he likes investing in real estate because the market is less efficient. Why might an investor prefer to invest in a less efficient market rather than a more efficient market?

Solution:

In a less efficient market, an investor with superior knowledge and information and/or a better understanding of the appropriate price to pay for properties (superior valuation skills) may earn a higher return, provided that market prices adjust to intrinsic values, by making more informed investment decisions.

3.2 Classifications

There are many different types of real estate properties. One simple classification distinguishes between residential and non-residential properties. Another potential classification is single-family residential, commercial, farmland, and timberland.

Residential properties include *single-family houses* and *multi-family properties*, such as apartments. In general, residential properties are properties that provide housing for individuals or families. Single-family properties may be owner-occupied or rental properties, whereas multi-family properties are rental properties even if the owner or manager occupies one of the units. Multi-family housing is usually differentiated by location (urban or suburban) and shape of structure (high-rise, low-rise, or garden apartments). Residential real estate properties, particularly multi-family properties, purchased with the intent to let, lease, or rent (in other words, produce income) are typically included in the category of **commercial real estate properties** (sometimes called income-producing real estate properties).

Non-residential properties include commercial properties other than multi-family properties, farmland, and timberland. Commercial real estate is by far the largest class of real estate for investment and is the focus of this reading. Commercial real estate properties are typically classified by end use. In addition to multi-family properties, commercial real estate properties include office, industrial and warehouse, retail, and hospitality properties. However, the same *building* can serve more than one end use. For example, it can contain both office and retail space. In fact, the same building can contain residential as well as non-residential uses of space. A property that has a combination of end users is usually referred to as a *mixed-use development*. Thus, the classifications should be viewed mainly as a convenient way of categorizing the use of space for the purpose of analyzing the determinants of supply and demand and economic performance for each type of space.

- *Office* properties range from major multi-tenant office buildings found in the central business districts of most large cities to single-tenant office buildings. They are often built to suit or considering the needs of a specific tenant or tenants. An example of a property developed and built considering the needs of prospective tenants would be a medical office building near a hospital.

- *Industrial and warehouse* properties include property used for light or heavy manufacturing as well as associated warehouse space. This category includes special purpose buildings designed specifically for industrial use that would be difficult to convert to another use, buildings used by wholesale distributors, and combinations of warehouse/showroom and office facilities. Older buildings that originally had one use may be converted to another use. For example, office space may be converted to warehouse or light industrial space and warehouse or light industrial space may be converted to residential or office space. Frequently, the conversion is based on the desirability of the area for the new use.

▪ *Retail* properties vary from large shopping centers with several stores, including large department stores, as tenants to small stores occupied by individual tenants. As indicated earlier, it is also common to find retail space combined with office space, particularly on the ground floor of office buildings in major cities, or residential space.

▪ *Hospitality* properties vary considerably in size and amenities available. Motels and smaller hotels are used primarily as a place for business travelers and families to spend a night. These properties may have limited amenities and are often located very close to a major highway. Hotels designed for tourists who plan to stay longer usually have a restaurant, a swimming pool, and other amenities. They are also typically located near other attractions that tourists visit. Hotels at "destination resorts" provide the greatest amount of amenities. These resorts are away from major cities, where the guests usually stay for several days or even several weeks. Facilities at these resort hotels can be quite luxurious, with several restaurants, swimming pools, nearby golf courses, and so on. Hotels that cater to convention business may be either in a popular destination resort or located near the center of a major city.

▪ *Other types* of commercial real estate that can be owned by investors include parking facilities, restaurants, and recreational uses, such as country clubs, marinas, sports complexes, and so on. Retail space that complements the recreational activity (such as gift and golf shops) is often associated with, or part of, these recreational real estate properties. Dining facilities and possibly hotel or residential facilities may also be present. A property might also be intended for use by a special institution, such as a hospital, a government agency, or a university. The physical structure of a building intended for a specific use may be similar to the physical structure of buildings intended for other uses. For example, government office space is similar to other office space. Some buildings intended for one use may not easily be adapted for other uses. For example, buildings used by universities and hospitals may not easily be adapted to other uses.

Some commercial property types are more management intensive than others. Of the main commercial property types, hotels require the most day-to-day management and are more like operating a business than multi-family, office, or retail space. Shopping centers (shopping malls) are also relatively management intensive because it is important for the owner to maintain the right tenant mix and promote the mall. Many of the "other" property types, such as recreational facilities, can also require significant management. Usually, investors consider properties that are more management intensive as riskier because of the operational risks. Therefore, investors typically require a higher rate of return on these management-intensive properties.

Farmland and timberland are unique in that each can be used to produce a saleable commodity. Farmland can be used to produce crops or as pastureland for livestock, and timberland can be used to produce timber (wood) for use in the forest products industry. While crops and livestock are produced annually, timber has a much longer growing cycle before the product is saleable. Also, the harvesting of timber can be deferred if market conditions are perceived to be unfavorable. Sales of the commodities or leasing the land to another entity generate income. Harvest quantities and commodity prices are the primary determinants of revenue. These are affected by many factors outside of the control of the producer and include weather and population demographics. In addition to income-generating potential, both farmland and timberland have potential for capital appreciation.

Commercial Real Estate Segments

Commercial real estate properties are *most likely* to include:

A   residential, industrial, hospitality, retail, and office.

B   multi-family, industrial, warehouse, retail, and office.

C   multi-family, industrial, hospitality, retail, and timberland.

Solution:

B is correct. Commercial real estate properties include multi-family, industrial, warehouse, retail, and office as well as hospitality and other. Residential properties include single-family, owner-occupied homes as well as income-producing (commercial) residential properties. Timberland is a unique category of real estate.

PRIVATE MARKET REAL ESTATE EQUITY INVESTMENTS

4

There are many different types of equity real estate investors, ranging from individual investors to large pension funds, sovereign wealth funds, and publicly traded real estate companies. Hereafter, for simplicity, the term *investor* refers to an equity investor in real estate. Although there may be some differences in the motivations for each type of investor, they all hope to achieve one or more of the following benefits of equity real estate investment:

- *Current income*: Investors may expect to earn current income on the property through letting, leasing, or renting the property. Investors expect that market demand for space in the property will be sufficient to produce net income after collecting rents and paying operating expenses. This income constitutes part of an investor's return. The amount available to the investor will be affected by taxes and financing costs.

- *Price appreciation (capital appreciation)*: Investors often expect prices to rise over time. Any price increase also contributes to an investor's total return. Investors may anticipate selling properties after holding them for a period of time and realizing the capital appreciation.

- *Inflation hedge*: Investors may expect both rents and real estate prices to rise in an inflationary environment. If rents and prices do in fact increase with inflation, then equity real estate investments provide investors with an inflationary hedge. This means that the real rate of return, as opposed to the nominal rate of return, may be less volatile for equity real estate investments.

- *Diversification*: Investors may anticipate diversification benefits. Real estate performance has not typically been highly correlated with the performance of other asset classes, such as stocks, bonds, or money market funds, so adding real estate to a portfolio may lower the risk of the portfolio (that is, the volatility of returns) relative to the expected return.

Exhibit 2 shows correlations of returns, for the period 1978–2009, between several asset classes in the United States based on various reported indices. The indices used are the National Council of Real Estate Investment Fiduciaries (NCREIF) Property Index for private real estate equity investments, the S&P 500 Index for stocks, the

Barclays Capital Government Bond for bonds, the National Association of Real Estate Investment Trusts (NAREIT) Equity REIT Index for publicly traded real estate investments, 90-day T-bills, and the all items US Consumer Price Index for All Urban Consumers (CPI-U).

Note that the correlation between the NCREIF index and the S&P 500 is relatively low and the correlation between the NCREIF index and bonds is negative. This indicates the potential for diversification benefits of adding private equity real estate investment to a stock and bond portfolio. Also note that publicly traded REITs have a higher correlation with stocks and bonds than private real estate, which suggests that public and private real estate do not necessarily provide the same diversification benefits. When real estate is publicly traded, it tends to behave more like the rest of the stock market than the real estate market. However, some argue that because the NCREIF index is appraisal based and lags changes in the transactions market, its correlation with stock indices that are based on transactions is dampened. This issue is discussed in more detail later in the reading. As a final note on the correlations, note that the NCREIF index had a higher correlation with the CPI-U than the other alternatives with the exception of T-bills. This suggests that private equity real estate investments may provide some inflation protection.

Although the correlations discussed above are based on US data, evidence suggests that real estate provides similar diversification benefits in other countries.

Exhibit 2	Correlation among Returns on Various Asset Classes (1978–2009)					
	CPI-U	Bonds[a]	S&P 500	T-Bills	NCREIF[b]	REITs[c]
CPI-U	1					
Bonds	−0.2423	1				
S&P 500	0.0114	0.0570	1			
T-bills	0.4885	0.1586	0.0953	1		
NCREIF	0.3214	−0.0978	0.1363	0.3911	1	
REITs	0.1135	0.1258	0.5946	0.0602	0.2527	1

[a] Barclays Capital Government Bond
[b] National Council of Real Estate Investment Fiduciaries Property Index (NPI)
[c] National Association of Real Estate Investment Trusts Equity REIT Index

▪ *Tax Benefits*: A final reason for investing in real estate, which may be more important to some investors in certain countries than others, is the preferential tax benefits that may result. Private real estate investments may receive a favorable tax treatment compared with other investments. In other words, the same before-tax return may result in a higher after-tax return on real estate investments compared with the after-tax return on other possible investments. The preferential tax treatment in the United States comes from the fact that real estate can be depreciated for tax purposes over a shorter period than the period over which the property actually deteriorates. Although some real estate investors, such as pension funds, do not normally pay taxes, they compete with taxable investors who might be willing to pay more for the same property. Publicly traded REITs also have some tax benefits in some countries. For example, in the United States, there is no corporate income tax paid by the REIT. That is, by qualifying for REIT status, the corporation is exempt from corporate taxation as long as it follows certain guidelines required to maintain REIT status.

Motivations for Investing in Real Estate

Why would an investor want to include real estate equity investments in a port-folio that already has a diversified mixture of stocks and bonds?

Solution:

Real estate equity offers diversification benefits because it is less than perfectly correlated with stocks and bonds; this is particularly true of direct ownership (private equity investment). In other words, there are times when stocks and bonds may perform poorly but private equity real estate investments perform well and vice versa. Thus, adding real estate equity investments to a portfolio may reduce the volatility of the portfolio.

4.1 Risk Factors

Investors want to have an expected return that compensates them for incurring risk. The higher the risk, the higher should be the expected return. In this section, we consider risk factors associated with investing in commercial real estate. Most of the risk factors listed affect the value of the real estate property and, therefore, the investment—equity or debt—in the property. Leverage affects returns on investments in real estate but not the value of the underlying real estate property. Following are characteristic sources of risk or risk factors of real estate investment.

■ *Business conditions*: Fundamentally, the real estate business involves renting space to users. The demand for space depends on a myriad of international, national, regional, and local economic conditions. GDP, employment, house-hold income, interest rates, and inflation are particularly relevant to real estate. Changes in economic conditions will affect real estate investments because both current income and real estate values may be affected.

■ *Long lead time for new development*: New development projects typically require a considerable amount of time from the point the project is first con-ceived until all the approvals are obtained, the development is complete, and it is leased up. During this time, market conditions can change considerably from what was initially anticipated. If the market has weakened, rents can be lower and vacancy higher than originally expected, resulting in lower returns to the developer. Alternatively, the demand can be greater than was anticipated, leading to a shortage of space to meet current demand. These dynamics tend to result in wide price swings for real estate over the development period.

■ *Cost and availability of capital*: Real estate must compete with other assets for debt and equity capital. The willingness of investors to invest in real estate depends on the availability of debt capital and the cost of that capital as well as the expected return on other investments, such as stocks and bonds, which affects the availability of equity capital. A shortage of debt capital and high interest rates can significantly reduce the demand for real estate and lower prices. Alternatively, an environment of low interest rates and easy access to debt capital can increase the demand for real estate investments. These capital market forces can cause prices to increase or decrease regardless of any changes in the underlying demand for real estate from tenants.

■ *Unexpected inflation*: Inflation risk depends on how the income and price of an asset is affected by unexpected inflation. Fixed-income securities are usually negatively affected by inflation because the purchasing power of the income decreases with inflation and the face value is fixed at maturity. Real estate may offer some inflation protection if the leases provide for rent increases due to inflation or the ability to pass any increases in expenses due to inflation on to tenants. Construction costs for real estate also tend to increase with inflation, which puts upward pressure on real estate values. Thus, real estate equity investments may not have much inflation risk depending on how net operating income (NOI) and values respond to inflation being higher than expected. In a weak market with high vacancy rates and low rents, when new construction is not feasible, values may not increase with inflation.

- *Demographics*: Linked to the above factors are a variety of demographic factors, such as the size and age distribution of the population in the local market, the distribution of socio-economic groups, and rates of new household formation. These demographic factors affect the demand for real estate.

- *Lack of liquidity*: Liquidity is the ability to convert an asset to cash quickly without a significant price discount or loss of principal. Real estate is considered to have low liquidity (high liquidity risk) because of the large value of an individual investment and the time and cost it takes to sell a property at its current value. Buyers are unlikely to make large investments without conducting adequate due diligence, which takes both time and money. Therefore, buyers are not likely to agree to a quick purchase without a significant discount to the price. Illiquidity means both a longer time to realize cash and also a risk that the market may move against the investor.

- *Environmental*: Real estate values can be affected by environmental conditions, including contaminants related to a prior owner or an adjacent property owner. Such problems can significantly reduce the value because of the costs incurred to correct them.

- *Availability of information*: Of increasing importance to investors, especially when investing globally, is having adequate information to make informed investment decisions. A lack of information to do the property analysis adds to the risk of the investment. The amount of data available on real estate space and capital markets has improved considerably. While some countries have much more information available to investors than others, in general, the availability of information has been increasing on a global basis because real estate investment has become more global and investors want to evaluate investment alternatives on a comparable basis. Real estate indices have become available in many countries around the world. These indices allow investors to benchmark the performance of their properties against that of peers and also provide a better understanding of the risk and return for real estate compared with other asset classes. Indices are discussed in more detail in Section 11.

- *Management*: Management involves the cost of monitoring an investment. Investment management can be categorized into two levels: asset management and property management. Asset management involves monitoring the investment's financial performance and making changes as needed. Property management is exclusive to real estate investments. It involves the overall day-to-day operation of the property and the physical maintenance of the property, including the buildings. Management risk reflects the ability of the property and asset managers to make the right decisions regarding the operation of the property, such as negotiating leases, maintaining the property, marketing the property, and doing renovations when necessary.

- *Leverage*: Leverage affects returns on investments in real estate but not the value of the underlying real estate property. Leverage is the use of borrowed funds to finance some of the purchase price of an investment. The ratio of borrowed funds to total purchase price is known as the loan-to-value (LTV) ratio. Higher LTV ratios mean greater amounts of leverage. Real estate transactions can be more highly leveraged than most other types of investments. But increasing leverage also increases risk because the lender has the first claim on the cash flow and on the value of the property if there is default on the loan. A small change in NOI can result in a relatively large change in the amount of cash flow available to the equity investor after making the mortgage payment.

■ *Other risk factors*: Many other risk factors exist, such as unobserved physical defects in the property, natural disasters (for example, earthquakes and hurricanes), and acts of terrorism. Unfortunately, the biggest risk may be one that was unidentified as a risk at the time of purchasing the property. Unidentified risks can be devastating to investors.

Risks that are identified can be planned for to some extent. In some cases, a risk can be converted to a known dollar amount through insurance. In other cases, risk can be reduced through diversification or shifted to another party through contractual arrangements. For example, the risk of expenses increasing can be shifted to tenants by including expense reimbursement clauses in their leases. The risk that remains must be evaluated and reflected in contractual terms (for example, rental prices) such that the expected return is equal to or greater than the required return necessary to make the investment.

EXAMPLE 5

Commercial Real Estate Risk

An investor is concerned about interest rates rising and decides that she will pay all cash and not borrow any money to avoid incurring any risk due to interest rate changes. This strategy is *most likely* to:

A reduce the risk due to leverage.

B eliminate the risk due to inflation.

C eliminate the risk due to interest rate changes.

Solution:

A is correct. If less money is borrowed, there is less risk due to the use of financial leverage. There is still risk related to changes in interest rates. If interest rates rise, the value of real estate will likely be affected even if the investor did not borrow any money. Higher interest rates mean investors require a higher rate of return on all assets. The resale price of the property will likely depend on the cost of debt to the next buyer, who may be more likely to obtain debt financing. Furthermore, the investor may be better off getting a loan at a fixed interest rate before rates rise. There is still risk of inflation, although real estate tends to have a low amount of inflation risk. But borrowing less money doesn't necessarily mean the property is less affected by inflation.

4.2 Real Estate Risk and Return Relative to Stocks and Bonds

The characteristics of real estate and the risk factors described above ultimately affect the risk and return of equity real estate investments. The structure of leases between the owner and tenants also affects risk and return. More will be discussed about the nature of real estate leases later in this reading, but in general, leases can be thought of as giving equity real estate investment a bond-like characteristic because the tenant has a legal agreement to make periodic payments to the owner. At the end of the lease term, however, there will be uncertainty as to whether the tenant will renew the lease and what the rental rate will be at that time. These issues will depend on the availability of competing space and also on factors that affect the profitability of the companies leasing the space and the strength of the overall economy in much the same way that stock prices are affected by the same factors. These factors give a stock market characteristic to the risk of real estate. On balance, because of these two influences (bond-like and stock-like characteristics), real estate, as an asset class, tends to have a risk and return (based on historical data) profile that falls between the risk and return profiles of stocks and bonds. By this, we mean the risk and return characteristics of a portfolio of real estate versus a portfolio of stocks and a portfolio of bonds. An individual real estate investment could certainly have risk that is greater or less than that of an individual stock or bond. Exhibit 3 illustrates the basic risk–return relationships of stocks, bonds, and private equity real estate. In Exhibit 3, risk is measured by the standard deviation of expected returns.

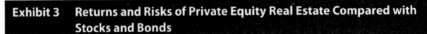

Exhibit 3   Returns and Risks of Private Equity Real Estate Compared with Stocks and Bonds

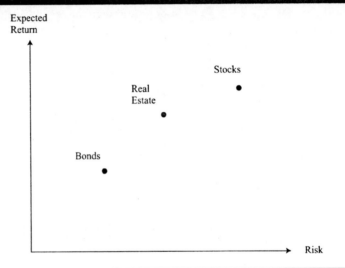

EXAMPLE 6

Investment Risk

Which is a riskier investment, private equity real estate or bonds? Explain why.

Solution:

Empirical evidence suggests that private equity real estate is riskier than bonds. Although real estate leases offer income streams somewhat like bonds, the income expected when leases renew can be quite uncertain and depend on market conditions at that time, which is unlike the more certain face value of a bond at maturity.

4.3 Commercial Real Estate

In this section, the main economic factors that influence demand for each commercial real estate property type and typical lease terms are discussed. It is important to discuss lease terms because they affect a property's value. The main property types included in institutional investors' portfolios are office, industrial and warehouse, retail, and multi-family (apartments). These property types are often considered the *core* property types used to create a portfolio that is relatively low risk, assuming the properties are in good locations and well leased (fiscally sound and responsible tenants, low vacancies, and good rental terms). Another type of property that might be held by an institutional investor is hospitality properties (for example, hotels). Hotels are usually considered riskier because there are no leases and their performance may be highly correlated with the business cycle—especially if there is a restaurant and the hotel depends on convention business.

For each property type, location is a critical factor in determining value. Properties with the highest value per unit of space are in the best locations and have modern features and functionality. Moderately valued properties are typically in adequate but not prime locations and/or have slightly outdated features. Properties with the lowest values per unit of space are in poor locations and have outdated features.

4.3.1 *Office*

The demand for office properties depends heavily on employment growth—especially in those industries that use large amounts of office space, such as finance and insurance. The typical amount of space used per employee is also important because it tends to increase when the economy is strong and decline when the economy is weak. There also has been a tendency for the average amount of space per employee to decrease over time as technology has allowed more employees to spend more time working away from the office and less permanent space is needed.

The average length of an office building lease varies globally. For example, leases on office space average 3–5 years in the United States and around 10 years in the United Kingdom. However, lease lengths may vary based on a number of factors, including the desirability of the property and the financial strength of the tenant as well as other terms in the lease, such as provisions for future rent changes and whether there are options to extend the lease.

An important consideration in office leases is whether the owner or tenant incurs the risk of operating expenses, such as utilities, increasing in the future. A "net lease" requires the tenant to be responsible for paying operating expenses, whereas a "gross lease" requires the owner to pay the operating expenses. The rent for a net lease is lower than that for an equivalent gross lease because the tenant must bear the operating expenses as well as the risk of expenses being higher than expected.

Not all office leases are structured as net or gross leases. For example, a lease may be structured so that in the first year of the lease, the owner is responsible for paying the operating expenses and for every year of the lease after that, the owner pays for expenses up to the amount paid in the first year. Any increase in expenses above that amount is "passed through" to the tenant as an "expense reimbursement." That is, the tenant bears the risk of any increase in expenses, although the owner benefits from any decline in expenses. In a multi-tenant building, the expenses may be prorated among the tenants on the basis of the amount of space they are leasing. While having a small number of tenants can simplify managing a property, it increases risk. If one tenant gets into financial difficulties or decides not to renew a lease, it can have a significant effect on cash flows.

There are differences in how leases are structured over time and in different countries. It is important to have an understanding of how leases are typically structured in a market and to stay informed about changes in the typical structure. Lease terms will affect the return and risk to the investor. For example, in the United Kingdom, until the early 1990s, lease terms averaged about 20 years in length, but they have now fallen by nearly half. Rents are typically fixed for five years and then set at the higher of the then market rent or contract rent upon review; these are known as upward-only rent reviews. Leases are typically on a full repairing and insuring (FRI) basis; the tenant is responsible for most costs. Therefore, detailed cost (expense) analysis is much less important in deriving net operating income—a critical measure in estimating the value of a commercial property—in the United Kingdom than in markets where operating costs are typically the responsibility of the owner.

EXAMPLE 7

Net and Gross Leases

What is the net rent equivalent for an office building where the gross rent is $20 per square foot and operating expenses are $8 per square foot?

Solution:

On a gross lease, the owner pays the operating expense, whereas on a net lease the tenant pays. So we might expect the rent on a net lease to be $20 − $8 or $12 per square foot. Because the risk of change in operating expenses is borne by the tenant rather than the owner, the rent might even be lower than $12.

4.3.2 Industrial and Warehouse

The demand for industrial and warehouse space is heavily dependent on the overall strength of the economy and economic growth. The demand for warehouse space is also dependent on import and export activity in the economy. Industrial leases are often net leases, although gross leases or leases with expense reimbursements, as described above for office properties, also occur.

4.3.3 Retail

The demand for retail space depends heavily on trends in consumer spending. Consumer spending, in turn, depends on the health of the economy, job growth, population growth, and savings rates.

Retail lease terms, including length of leases and rental rates, vary not only on the basis of the quality of the property but also by the size and the importance of the tenant. For example, in the United States, the length of leases for the smaller tenants in a shopping center are typically three to five years and are longer for larger "anchor" tenants, such as a department store. Anchor tenants may be given rental terms designed to attract them to the property. The quality of anchor tenants is a factor in attracting other tenants.

A unique aspect of many retail leases is the requirement that the tenants pay additional rent once their sales reach a certain level. This type of lease is referred to as a "percentage lease." The lease will typically specify a "minimum rent" that must be paid regardless of the tenant's sales and the basis for calculating percentage rent once the tenant's sales reach a certain level or breakpoint. For example, the lease may specify a minimum rent of $30 per square foot plus 10 percent of sales over $300 per square foot. Note that at the breakpoint of $300 per square foot in sales, we obtain the same rent per square foot based on either the minimum rent of $30 or 10 percent of $300. This is a typical way of structuring the breakpoint, and the sales level of $300 would be referred to as a "natural breakpoint."

EXAMPLE 8

Retail Rents

A retail lease specifies that the minimum rent is $40 per square foot plus 5 percent of sales revenue over $800 per square foot. What would the rent be if the tenant's sales are $1,000 per square foot?

Solution:

The rent per square foot will be $40 plus 5% × ($1,000 − $800) or $40 + $10 = $50. We get the same answer by multiplying 5% × $1,000 (= $50) because $800 is the "natural breakpoint," meaning that 5 percent of $800 results in the minimum rent of $40. A lease may not have the breakpoint set at this natural level, in which case it is important that the lease clearly defines how to calculate the rent.

4.3.4 *Multi-Family*

The demand for multi-family space depends on population growth, especially for the age segment most likely to rent apartments. In other words, population demographics are important. The relevant age segment can be very broad or very narrow depending on the propensity to rent in the culture. Homeownership rates vary from country to country. The relevant age segment for renters can also vary by type of property being rented out or by locale. For example, in the United States, the typical renter has historically been between 25 and 35 years old. However, the average age of a renter of property in an area attractive to retirees may be higher.

Demand also depends on how the cost of renting compares with the cost of owning—that is, the ratio of home prices to rents. As home prices rise and become less affordable, more people will rent. Similarly, as home prices fall, there may be a shift from renting to owning. Higher interest rates will also make homeownership more expensive because for owners that partially finance the purchase with debt, the financing cost will be higher and for other homeowners, the opportunity cost of having funds tied up in a home will increase. This increase in the cost of ownership may cause a shift toward renting. If interest rates decrease, there may be a shift toward homeownership.

Multi-family properties typically have leases that range from six months to two years, with one year being most typical. The tenant may or may not be responsible for paying expenses, such as utilities, depending on whether there are separate meters for each unit. The owner is typically responsible for the upkeep of common property, insurance, and repair and maintenance of the property. The tenant is typically responsible for cleaning the space rented and for insurance on personal property.

EXAMPLE 9

Economic Value Determinants

1 The primary economic driver of the demand for office space is *most likely*:
   A job growth.
   B population growth.
   C growth in savings rates.

2 The demand for which of the following types of real estate is likely *most* affected by population demographics?
   A Office

    B Multi-family

    C Industrial and warehouse

Solution to 1:

A is correct. Job growth is the main economic driver of office demand, especially jobs in industries that are heavy users of office space, such as finance and insurance. As jobs increase, companies need to provide office space for the new employees. Population growth may indirectly affect the demand for office space because it affects demand and job growth. Growth in savings rates affects consumer spending and the demand for retail space.

Solution to 2:

B is correct. Population demographics are a primary determinant of the demand for multi-family space.

---

5 OVERVIEW OF THE VALUATION OF COMMERCIAL REAL ESTATE

Regardless of the form of real estate investment, the value of the underlying real estate is critical because the value of any real estate investment is inextricably tied to the value of the underlying real estate. Commercial real estate properties do not transact frequently, and each property is unique. Therefore, estimates of value or appraisals, rather than transaction prices, are used to assess changes in value or expected selling price over time. Appraisals are typically done by individuals with recognized expertise in this area. These can be independent experts hired to do the appraisals or in-house experts.

5.1 Appraisals

Appraisals (estimates of value) are critical for such infrequently traded and unique assets as real estate properties. For publicly traded assets, such as stocks and bonds, we have frequent transaction prices that reflect the value that investors are currently placing on these assets. In contrast, commercial real estate, such as an apartment or office building, does not trade frequently. For example, a particular building might sell once in a 10-year period. Thus, we cannot rely on transactions activity for a particular property to indicate how its value is changing over time.

There are companies, such as real estate investment trusts, that invest primarily in real estate and have publicly traded shares. REITs are available in many countries around the world. REIT prices can be observed as with any publicly traded share. REITs are businesses that buy and sell real estate; often do development; decide how properties are to be financed, when to refinance, and when to renovate properties; and make many other ongoing management decisions that determine the success of the REIT. Therefore, the prices of REIT shares reflect both the performance of the management of the company that owns the real estate and the value of the underlying properties.

Thus, although it is useful to know how the values of REIT shares are changing over time as an indicator of changing conditions in the real estate market, it does not substitute for the need to estimate the value of individual properties. In fact, knowing the appraised value of properties held by REITs is helpful in estimating the value of the REIT, although, as suggested above, many other factors can affect REIT share prices over time.

Appraisals can be used to evaluate the performance of the investment or to determine an estimate of price or value if a transaction is anticipated. Even if there has been a recent transaction of the property, because it is only one transaction between a particular buyer and seller, the transaction price at which the property sold may not reflect the value a typical investor might place on the property at that time.[1] There may be circumstances under which a buyer may be willing to pay more than a typical buyer would pay or a seller may be willing to accept less than a typical seller would accept. Thus, even when there is a transaction, an appraisal is often used as a basis for estimating the value of the property rather than just assuming that the agreed upon transaction price equals the value. For example, an appraisal is likely to be required if the purchaser of the property wants to finance a portion of the purchase with debt. The lender will typically require an independent appraisal of the property to estimate the value of the collateral for the loan. Even if the purchaser is not borrowing to finance a portion of the purchase, the purchaser may have an appraisal done to help establish a reasonable offer price for the property. Similarly, the seller may have an appraisal done to help establish the asking price for the property.

Properties are also appraised for other reasons. Another important use of appraisals is for performance measurement—that is, to measure the performance of real estate that is managed for a client. For example, a pension fund may have decided to invest in real estate in addition to stocks and bonds to diversify its portfolio. It may have invested directly in the real estate or through an investment manager that acquires and manages the real estate portfolio. In either case, the pension fund wants to know how its real estate investments are performing. This performance can be evaluated relative to the performance of stocks and bonds and against a benchmark that measures the performance of the relevant real estate asset class. The benchmark is used in the same way that a stock index might be used as a benchmark for measuring the performance of a stock portfolio.

Measuring the performance of a real estate portfolio requires estimating property values on a periodic basis, such as annually. Although more frequent measures may be desirable, it may not be practical because appraising property values is a time-consuming and costly process. It may involve an independent appraisal by a firm that specializes in appraising investment properties, or it may be done by an appraiser who works for the investment management firm. In either case, the appraiser is tasked with estimating the value of the property.

5.1.1 *Value*

The focus of an appraisal is usually on what is referred to as the *market value* of the property. The market value can be thought of as the most probable sale price. It is what a *typical* investor is willing to pay for the property. There are other definitions of value that differ from market value. For example, *investment value* (sometimes called worth) is the value to a *particular* investor. It could be higher or lower than market value depending on the particular investor's motivations and how well the property fits into the investor's portfolio, the investor's risk tolerance, the investor's tax circumstances, and so on. For example, an investor who is seeking to have a globally well-diversified portfolio of real estate that does not already have any investments in New York City and Shanghai may place a higher value on acquiring a property in either of those locations than an investor who already has New York City and Shanghai properties in his or her portfolio.

---

1 The term special purchaser is used in some countries, such as the United Kingdom, to refer to purchasers who are not typical.

There are other types of value that are relevant in practice, such as *value in use*, which is the value to a particular user—for example, the value of a manufacturing plant to the company using the building as part of its business. For property tax purposes, the relevant value is the assessed value of the property, which may differ from market value because of the way the assessor defines the value. In most cases, the focus of an appraisal is on market value.

Potential sellers and buyers care about market value because it is useful to know when negotiating price. The market value may differ from the value that the potential buyer or seller originally placed on the property and from the price that is ultimately agreed upon.[2] A seller in distressed circumstances may be willing to accept less than market value because of liquidity needs, and a particular buyer (investor) may be willing to pay more than market value because the worth (investment value) to that buyer exceeds the value to a typical investor.

Lenders usually care about market value because if a borrower defaults on a mortgage loan, the market value less transaction costs is the maximum that the lender can expect to receive from the sale of the property. But there are some exceptions. In some cases, the lender may ask for a more conservative value, which can be referred to as a *mortgage lending value*. For example, in Germany the mortgage lending value is the value of the property which, based on experience, may throughout the life of the loan be expected to be generated in the event of sale, irrespective of temporary (e.g., economically induced) fluctuations in value on the relevant property market and excluding speculative elements. In determining the mortgage lending value, the future saleability of the property is to be taken as a basis within the scope of a "prudent valuation," taking into consideration the long-term, permanent features of the property, the normal regional market situation, and the present and possible alternative uses. Some have argued that over the decades in which it has been applied, the mortgage lending value has helped mortgage lending in Germany to have a stabilizing effect on the German real estate market by evening out current, possibly exaggerated market expectations. The mortgage lending value contrasts with the notion of "mark-to-market" or "fair value" accounting, which would value an asset at its market value at the time the loan is made.

EXAMPLE 10

Market Value

A property that was developed two years ago at a cost of ¥60.0 million, including land, is put on the market for that price. It sells quickly for ¥50.0 million. After the closing, the purchaser admits he would have paid up to ¥65.0 million for the property because he owned vacant land next to the property purchased. A very similar property (approximately the same size, age, etc.) recently sold for ¥55.0 million.

1 The purchaser is *most likely* a:

   A typical investor.

   B particular investor.

   C short-term investor.

2 The market value of the property is *closest* to:

   A ¥50.0 million.

---

2 For further discussion of the various definitions of value, refer to such publications as the "Uniform Standards of Professional Appraisal Practice," the Royal Institution of Chartered Surveyors (RICS) *Red Book*, and "The International Valuation Standards."

B ¥55.0 million.

C ¥65.0 million.

3 The investment value of the property to the buyer is *closest* to:

A ¥50.0 million.

B ¥60.0 million.

C ¥65.0 million.

Solution to 1:

B is correct. This investor may be willing to pay more than the typical investor because of his particular circumstances.

Solution to 2:

B is correct. The purchaser paid ¥50.0 million rather than the ¥65.0 million he was willing to pay for the property. However, we have to be careful about using a transaction price as an indication of market value because the market may have been thin and the seller may have been distressed and willing to accept less than the property would have sold for if it had been kept on the market for a longer period of time. The quick sale suggests that the price may have been lower than what a typical investor may be willing to pay. There was a comparable property that sold for ¥55.0 million. Combining these facts and based only on this information, it is reasonable to assume that the market value is closest to ¥55.0 million. Note that what it cost to develop the property two years ago is not particularly relevant. Markets may have deteriorated since that time, and new construction may not be feasible.

Solution to 3:

C is correct. The investment value of the property is ¥65.0 million. The purchaser was willing to pay up to ¥65.0 million, suggesting that his investment value was higher than the amount paid. He paid only as much as he had to, based on negotiations with the seller.

5.2 Introduction to Valuation Approaches

In general, there are three different approaches that appraisers use to estimate value: the **income approach**, the **cost approach**, and the **sales comparison approach**. The income approach considers what price an investor would pay based on an expected rate of return that is commensurate with the risk of the investment. The value estimated with this approach is essentially the present value of the expected future income from the property, including proceeds from resale at the end of a typical investment holding period. The concept is that value depends on the expected rate of return that investors would require to invest in the property.

The cost approach considers what it would cost to buy the land and construct a new property on the site that has the same utility or functionality as the property being appraised (referred to as the *subject property*). Adjustments are made if the subject property is older or not of a modern design, if it is not feasible to construct a new property in the current market, or if the location of the property is not ideal for its current use. The concept is that you should not pay more for a property than the cost of buying vacant land and developing a comparable property.

The sales comparison approach considers what similar or *comparable properties* (comparables) transacted for in the current market. Adjustments are made to reflect comparables' differences from the subject property, such as size, age, location, and condition of the property and to adjust for differences in market conditions at the times of sale. The concept is that you would not pay more than others are paying for similar properties.

These approaches are unlikely to result in the same value because they rely on different assumptions and availability of data to estimate the value. The idea is to try to triangulate on the market value by approaching the estimate three different ways. The appraiser may have more confidence in one or more of the approaches depending on the availability of data for each approach. Part of the appraisal process is to try to *reconcile* the differences in the estimates of value from each approach and come up with a final estimate of value for the subject property.

5.2.1 Highest and Best Use

Before we elaborate on the three approaches to estimating value, it is helpful to understand an important concept known as *highest and best use*. The highest and best use of a vacant site is the use that would result in the highest value for the land. This concept is best illustrated with an example. Suppose you are trying to determine the highest and best use of a vacant site. Three alternative uses—apartment, office, and retail—have been identified as consistent with zoning regulations and are financially feasible at the right land value. The physical characteristics of the site make construction of buildings consistent with each of these uses possible. Exhibit 4 summarizes relevant details for each potential use:

Exhibit 4 Highest and Best Use			
	Apartment	**Office**	**Retail**
Value after construction	$2,500,000	$5,000,000	$4,000,000
Cost to construct building	(2,000,000)	(4,800,000)	(3,000,000)
Implied land value	$500,000	$200,000	$1,000,000

The value after construction is what the property would sell for once it is constructed and leased. The cost to construct the building includes an amount for profit to the developer. The profit compensates the developer for handling the construction phase and getting the property leased. Subtracting the cost to construct from the value after construction gives the amount that could be paid for the land. In this case, the retail use results in the highest price that can be paid for the land. So retail is the highest and best use of the site, and the land value would be $1 million.

The idea is that the price would be bid up to that amount by investors or developers who are competing for the site, including several bidders planning to develop retail. Note that the highest and best use is not the use with the highest total value, which in this example is office. Even though office has a higher value if it is built, the higher construction costs result in a lower amount that can be paid for the land. A developer cannot pay $1 million for the land and build the office building. If they did, they would have a $5.8 million total investment in the land and construction cost but the value would be only $5 million. So that would result in an $800,000 loss in value because an office building is not the highest and best use of the site.

The theory is that the land value is based on its highest and best use *as if vacant* even if there is an existing building on the site. If there is an existing building on the site that is not the highest and best use of the site, then the value of the building—not the land—will be lower. For example, suppose that a site with an old warehouse on it would sell for $1.5 million as a warehouse (land and building). If vacant, the land is worth $1 million. Thus, the value of the existing building (warehouse) is $500,000

(= $1,500,000 – $1,000,000). As long as the value under the existing use is more than the land value, the building should remain on the site. If the value under the existing use falls below the land value, any building(s) on the site will likely be demolished so the building that represents the highest and best use of the site can be constructed. For example, if the value as a warehouse is only $800,000, it implies a building value of negative $200,000. The building should be demolished, assuming the demolition costs are less than $200,000.

EXAMPLE 11

Highest and Best Use

Two uses have been identified for a property. One is an office building that would have a value after construction of $20 million. Development costs would be $16 million, which includes a profit to the developer. The second use is an apartment building that would have a value after construction of $25 million. Development costs, including a profit to the developer, would be $22 million. What is the highest and best use of the site and the implied land value?

Solution:

	Office	Apartment
Value on completion	$20,000,000	$25,000,000
Cost to construct building	(16,000,000)	(22,000,000)
Implied land value	$4,000,000	$3,000,000

An investor/developer could pay up to $4 million for the land to develop an office building but only $3 million for the land to develop an apartment building. The highest and best use of the site is an office building with a land value of $4 million. Of course, this answer assumes a competitive market with several potential developers who would bid for the land to develop an office building.

We will now discuss each of the approaches to estimating value in more detail and provide examples of each.

THE INCOME APPROACH TO VALUATION

6

The **direct capitalization method** and **discounted cash flow method** (DCF) are two income approaches used to appraise a commercial (income-producing) property. The direct capitalization method estimates the value of an income-producing property based on the level and quality of its net operating income. The DCF method discounts future projected cash flows to arrive at a present value of the property. Net operating income, a measure of income and a *proxy for cash flow*, is a focus of both approaches.

6.1 General Approach and Net Operating Income

The income approach focuses on net operating income[3] generated from a property. There are two income approaches, each of which considers growth. The first, the direct capitalization method, capitalizes the current NOI using a growth implicit **capitalization rate**. When the capitalization rate is applied to the forecasted first-year NOI for the property, the implicit assumption is that the first-year NOI is representative of what the typical first-year NOI would be for similar properties. The second, the DCF method, applies an explicit growth rate to construct an NOI stream from which a present value can be derived. As we will see, there is some overlap because, even for the second method, we generally estimate a terminal value by capitalizing NOI at some future date.

Income can be projected either for the entire economic life of the property or for a typical holding period with the assumption that the property will be sold at the end of the holding period. We will see that there are many different ways of applying the income approach depending on how complex the income is for the property being valued. But no matter how the approach is applied, the concept is that the value is based on discounting the cash flows, typically represented by NOI in real estate contexts. The discount rate should reflect the risk characteristics of the property. It can be derived from market comparisons or from specific analysis; we will examine both cases.

When the property has a lot of different leases with different expiration dates and complex lease provisions, the income approach is often done with spreadsheets or software.[4] At the other extreme, when simplifying assumptions can be made about the pattern of future income, simple formulas often can be used to estimate the value.

To value a property using an income approach, we need to calculate the **net operating income** for the property. NOI is a measure of the income from the property after deducting operating expenses for such items as property taxes, insurance, maintenance, utilities, repairs, and insurance but before deducting any costs associated with financing and before deducting federal income taxes. This is not to suggest that financing costs and federal income taxes are not important to an investor's cash flows. It simply means that NOI is a before-tax unleveraged measure of income.[5]

There may be situations where the lease on a property requires the tenants to be responsible for some or all of the expenses so that they would not be deducted when calculating NOI. Or they might be deducted, but then the additional income received from the tenants due to reimbursement of these expenses would be included when calculating the NOI. Of course, when the tenant must pay the expenses, we might expect the rent to be lower. It is necessary to consider specific lease terms when estimating NOI. As mentioned before, typical lease terms vary from country to country.

A general calculation of NOI is shown in Exhibit 5.

Exhibit 5   Calculating NOI

Rental income at full occupancy

+ Other income (such as parking)

---

[3] NOI in this real estate property context is similar to earnings before interest, taxes, depreciation, and amortization (EBITDA) in a financial reporting context.

[4] One example is a software package called ARGUS Valuation DCF, which was initially used primarily in the United States. There are now versions in many other languages, including Japanese, Chinese, German, and Spanish. See www.argussoftware.com for further information.

[5] Cash flows may also be affected by capital expenditures for such items as a roof replacement. Sometimes such items are accounted for by including a "reserve allowance" as one of the expenses. The reserve allowance spreads the cost of the capital expenditure over time. At other times, the expenditure may be deducted from NOI in the year it is expected to occur.

Exhibit 5   (Continued)

= *Potential gross income (PGI)*

  – Vacancy and collection loss

= *Effective gross income (EGI)*

  – Operating expenses (OE)

= *Net operating income (NOI)*

EXAMPLE 12

Net Operating Income

A 50-unit apartment building rents for $1,000 per unit per month. It currently
has 45 units rented. Operating expenses, including property taxes, insurance,
maintenance, and advertising, are typically 40 percent of effective gross income.
The property manager is paid 10 percent of effective gross income. Other income
from parking and laundry is expected to average $500 per rented unit per year.
Calculate the NOI.

Solution:

Rental income at full occupancy	50 × $1,000 × 12 =	$600,000
Other income	50 × $500 =	+25,000
Potential gross income		$625,000
Vacancy loss	5/50 or 10% × $625,000 =	−62,500
Effective gross income		$562,500
Property management	10% of $562,500 =	−56,250
Other operating expenses	40% of $562,500 =	−225,000
Net operating income		$281,250

6.2 The Direct Capitalization Method

The direct capitalization method capitalizes the current NOI at a rate known as the
capitalization rate, or cap rate for short. If we think about the inverse of the cap rate
as a multiplier, the approach is analogous to an income multiplier. The direct capitalization method differs from the DCF method, in which future operating income
(a proxy for cash flow) is discounted at a discount rate to produce a present value.

6.2.1 *The Capitalization Rate and the Discount Rate*

The cap and discount rates are closely linked but are not the same. Briefly, the discount
rate is the return required from an investment and comprises the risk-free rate plus
a risk premium specific to the investment. The cap rate is lower than the discount
rate because it is calculated using the current NOI. So, the cap rate is like a current
yield for the property whereas the discount rate is applied to current and future NOI,
which may be expected to grow. In general, when income and value are growing at a
constant compound growth rate, we have:

Cap rate = Discount rate – Growth rate   (1)

The growth rate is implicit in the cap rate, but we have to make it explicit for a DCF valuation.

6.2.2 Defining the Capitalization Rate

The capitalization rate is a very important measure for valuing income-producing real estate property. The cap rate is defined as follows:

Cap rate = NOI/Value   **(2)**

where the NOI is usually based on what is expected during the current or first year of ownership of the property. Sometimes the term *going-in cap rate* is used to clarify that it is based on the first year of ownership when the investor is *going into* the deal. (Later, we will see that the *terminal cap rate* is based on expected income for the year after the anticipated sale of the property.)

The value used in the above cap rate formula is an estimate of what the property is worth at the time of purchase. If we rearrange the above equation and solve for value we see that:

Value = NOI/Cap rate   **(3)**

So, if we know the appropriate cap rate, we can estimate the value of the property by dividing its first-year NOI by the cap rate.

Where does the cap rate come from? That will be an important part of our discussion. A simple answer is that it is based on observing what other similar or comparable properties are selling for. Assuming that the sale price for a comparable property is a good indication of the value of the subject property, we have:

Cap rate = NOI/Sale price of comparable   **(4)**

We would not want to rely on the price for just one sale to indicate what the cap rate is. We want to observe several sales of similar properties before drawing conclusions about what cap rates investors are willing to accept for a property. As we will discuss later, there are also reasons why we would expect the cap rate to differ for different properties, such as what the future income potential is for the property—that is, how it is expected to change after the first year. This is important because the cap rate is only explicitly based on the first-year income. But the cap rate that investors are willing to accept depends on how they expect the income to change in the future and the risk of that income. These expectations are said to be implicit in the cap rate.

The cap rate is like a snapshot at a point in time of the relationship between NOI and value. It is somewhat analogous to the price–earnings multiple for a stock except that it is the reciprocal.[6] The reciprocal of the cap rate is price divided by NOI. Just as stocks with greater earnings growth potential tend to have higher price–earnings multiples, properties with greater income growth potential have higher ratios of price to current NOI and thus lower cap rates.

It is often necessary to make adjustments based on specific lease terms and characteristics of a market. For example, a similar approach is common in the United Kingdom, where the term fully let property is used to refer to a property that is leased at market rent because either it has a new tenant or the rent has just been reviewed. In such cases, the appraisal is undertaken by applying a capitalization rate to this rent rather than to NOI because leases usually require the tenant to pay all costs. The cap rate derived by dividing rent by the recent sales prices of comparables is often called the all risks yield (ARY). Note that the term "yield" in this case is used like a "current yield" based on first-year NOI. It is a cap rate and will differ from the total return that an investor might expect to get from future growth in NOI and value. If it is assumed,

---

6 In the United Kingdom, the reciprocal of the cap rate is called the "years purchase" (YP). It is the number of years that it would take for income at the current level to be equal to the original purchase price.

however, that the rent will be level in the foreseeable future (like a perpetuity), then the cap rate will be the same as the return and the all risks yield will be an internal rate of return (IRR) or yield to maturity.

In simple terms, the valuation is:

Market value = Rent/ARY (5)

Again, this valuation is essentially the same as dividing NOI by the cap rate as discussed earlier except the occupant is assumed to be responsible for all expenses so the rent is divided by the ARY.[7] ARY is a cap rate and will differ from the required total return (the discount rate) an investor might expect to get by future growth in NOI and value. If rents are expected to increase after every rent review, then the investor's expected return will be higher than the cap rate. If rents are expected to increase at a constant compound rate, then the investor's expected return (discount rate) will equal the cap rate plus the growth rate.

EXAMPLE 13

Capitalizing NOI

A property has just been let at an NOI of £250,000 for the first year, and the capitalization rate on comparable properties is 5 percent. What is the value of the property?

Solution:

Value = NOI/Cap rate = £250,000/0.05 = £5,000,000

Suppose the rent review for the property in Example 13 occurs every year and rents are expected to increase 2 percent each year. An approximation of the IRR would simply be the cap rate plus the growth rate; in this case, a 5 percent cap rate plus 2 percent rent growth results in a 7 percent IRR. Of course, if the rent review were less frequent, as in the United Kingdom where it is typically every five years, then we could not simply add the growth rate to the cap rate to get the IRR. But it would still be higher than the cap rate if rents were expected to increase.

6.2.3 Stabilized NOI

When the cap rate is applied to the forecasted first-year NOI for the property, the implicit assumption is that the first-year NOI is representative of what the typical first-year NOI would be for similar properties. In some cases, the appraiser might project an NOI to be used to estimate value that is different from what might actually be expected for the first year of ownership for the property if what is actually expected is not typical.

An example of this might be when a property is undergoing a renovation and there is a temporarily higher-than-typical amount of vacancy until the renovation is complete. The purpose of the appraisal might be to estimate what the property will be worth once the renovation is complete. A cap rate will be used from properties that are not being renovated because they are more typical. Thus, the appraiser projects what is referred to as a **stabilized NOI**, which is what the NOI would be if the property were not being renovated—in other words, what the NOI will be once the renovation is complete. This NOI is used to estimate the value. Of course, if the

---

7 In practice, management costs should also be considered, although operating costs falling on the landlord are typically much lower than in the United States.

property is being purchased before the renovation is complete, a slightly lower price will be paid because the purchaser has to wait for the renovation to be complete to get the higher NOI. Applying the cap rate to the lower NOI that is occurring during the renovation will understate the value of the property because it implicitly assumes that the lower NOI is expected to continue.[8]

EXAMPLE 14

Value of a Property to be Renovated

A property is being purchased that requires some renovation to be competitive with otherwise comparable properties. Renovations satisfactory to the purchaser will be completed by the seller at the seller's expense. If it were already renovated, it would have NOI of ¥9 million next year, which would be expected to increase by 3 percent per year thereafter. Investors would normally require a 12 percent IRR (discount rate) to purchase the property after it is renovated. Because of the renovation, the NOI will only be ¥4 million next year. But after that, the NOI is expected to be the same as it would be if it had already been renovated at the time of purchase. What is the value of or the price a typical investor is willing to pay for the property?

Solution:

If the property was already renovated (and the NOI stabilized), the value would be:

Value if renovated = ¥9,000,000/(0.12 − 0.03) = ¥100,000,000

But because of the renovation, there is a loss in income of ¥5 million during the first year. If for simplicity we assume that this would have been received at the end of the year, then the present value of the lost income at a 12 percent discount rate is as follows:

Loss in value = ¥5,000,000/(1.12) = ¥4,464,286

Thus, the value of the property is as follows:

Value if renovated	¥100,000,000
Less loss in value	− ¥4,464,286
= Value	¥95,535,714

An alternative approach is to get the present value of the first year's income and the value in a year when renovated.

{¥4,000,000 + [¥9,000,000(1.03)]/(0.12− 0.03)]}/(1.12) = ¥95,535,714

6.2.4 Other Forms of the Income Approach

Direct capitalization usually uses NOI and a cap rate. However, there are some alternatives to the use of NOI and a cap rate. For example, a *gross income multiplier* might be used in some situations. The gross income multiplier is the ratio of the sale price to the gross income expected from the property in the first year after sale. It may be obtained from comparable sales in a similar way to what was illustrated for cap rates. The problem with using a gross income multiplier is that it does not explicitly consider vacancy rates and operating expenses. Thus, it implicitly assumes that the ratio

---

[8] Some readers may correctly think that, rather than use a stabilized NOI, a lower cap rate could be used to reflect the fact that the NOI will be higher in the future. The problem is that it is not easy to know how much lower the cap rate should be if there are no sales of comparable properties intended for renovation.

of vacancy and expenses to gross income is similar for the comparable and subject properties. But if, for example, expenses were expected to be lower on one property versus another because it was more energy efficient, an investor would pay more for the same rent. Thus, its gross income multiplier should be higher. Use of a gross rent multiplier is also considered a form of direct capitalization but is generally not considered as reliable as using a capitalization rate.

6.3 The Discounted Cash Flow (DCF) Method

The direct capitalization method typically estimates value by capitalizing the first-year NOI at a cap rate derived from market evidence.[9]

6.3.1 The Relationship between Discount Rate and Cap Rate

If the income and value for a property are expected to change over time at the same compound rate—for example, 3 percent per year—then the relationship between the cap rate and discount rate is the same as in Equation 1:

Cap rate = Discount rate – Growth rate

To see the intuition behind this, let us solve for the discount rate, which is the return that is required to invest in the property.

Discount rate = Cap rate + Growth rate

Recall that the cap rate is based on first-year NOI. The growth rate captures how NOI will change in the future along with the property value. Thus, we can say that the investor's return (discount rate) comes from the return on first-year income (cap rate) plus the growth in income and value over time (growth rate). Although income and value may not always change at the same compound rate each year, this formula gives us insight into the relationship between the discount rate and the cap rate. Essentially, the difference between the discount and cap rates has to do with growth in income and value.

Intuitively, given that both methods start from the same NOI in the first year, you would pay more for an income stream that will grow than for one that will be constant. So, the price is higher and the cap rate is lower when the NOI is growing. This is what is meant by the growth being *implicit* in the cap rate. If the growth rate is constant, we can extend Equation 3 using Equation 1 to give:

$$V = NOI/(r - g) \tag{6}$$

where:

r = the discount rate (required return)
g = the growth rate for income (given constant growth in income, value will grow at the same rate)

This equation is analogous to the dividend growth model applied to stocks. If NOI is not expected to grow at a constant rate, then NOIs are projected into the future and each period's NOI is discounted to arrive at a value of the property. Rather than project NOIs into infinity, typically, NOIs are projected for a specified holding period and a terminal value (estimated sale price) at the end of the holding period is estimated.

---

9 The DCF method (sometimes referred to as a yield capitalization method) involves projecting income beyond the first year and discounting that income at a discount rate (yield rate). The terms *yield rate* and *discount rate* are being used synonymously in this discussion, as are the terms *yield capitalization* and *discounted cash flow* analysis.

EXAMPLE 15

Growth Explicit Appraisal

NOI is expected to be $100,000 the first year, and after that, NOI is expected to increase at 2 percent per year for the foreseeable future. The property value is also expected to increase by 2 percent per year. Investors expect to get a 12 percent IRR given the level of risk, and therefore, the value is estimated using a 12 percent discount rate. What is the value of the property today (beginning of first year)?

Solution:

$$V = NOI/(r - g)$$
$$= \$100{,}000/(0.12 - 0.02)$$
$$= \$100{,}000/0.10$$
$$= \$1{,}000{,}000$$

6.3.2 *The Terminal Capitalization Rate*

When a DCF methodology is used to value a property, generally, one of the important inputs is the estimated sale price of the property at the end of a typical holding period. This input is often referred to as the estimated terminal value. Estimating the terminal value of a property can be quite challenging in practice, especially given that the purpose of the analysis is to estimate the value of the property today. But if we do not know the value of the property today, how can we know what it will be worth in the future when sold to another investor? This means we must also use some method for estimating what the property will be worth when sold in the future.

In theory, this value is based on the present value of income to be received by the *next* investor. But we usually do not try to project NOI for another holding period beyond the initial one. Rather, we rely on the direct capitalization method using the NOI of the first year of ownership for the next investor and a cap rate. The cap rate used to estimate the resale price or terminal value is referred to as a *terminal cap rate* or *residual cap rate*. It is a cap rate that is selected at the time of valuation to be applied to the NOI earned in the first year after the property is expected to be sold to a new buyer.

Selecting a terminal cap rate is challenging. Recall that the cap rate equals the discount rate less the growth rate when income and value are growing constantly at the same rate. Whether constant growth is realistic or not, we know that the cap rate will be higher (lower) if the discount rate is higher (lower). Similarly, the cap rate will be lower if the growth rate is expected to be higher, and vice versa. These relationships also apply to the terminal cap rate as well as the going-in cap rate.

The terminal cap rate could be the same, higher, or lower than the going-in cap rate depending on expected discount and growth rates at the time of sale. If interest rates are expected to be higher in the future, pushing up discount rates, then terminal cap rates might be higher. The growth rate is often assumed to be a little lower because the property is older at the time of sale and may not be as competitive. This situation would result in a slightly higher terminal cap rate. Uncertainty about what the NOI will be in the future may also result in selecting a higher terminal cap rate. The point is that the terminal cap rate is not necessarily the same as the going-in cap rate at the time of the appraisal.

Appraisal with a Terminal Value

Net operating income (NOI) is expected to be level at $100,000 per year for the next five years because of existing leases. Starting in Year 6, the NOI is expected to increase to $120,000 because of lease rollovers and increase at 2 percent per year thereafter. The property value is also expected to increase at 2 percent per year after Year 5. Investors require a 12 percent return and expect to hold the property for five years. What is the current value of the property?

Solution:

Exhibit 6 shows the projected NOI for this example. Because NOI and property value are expected to grow at the same constant rate after Year 5, we can calculate the cap rate at that time based on the discount rate less the growth rate. That gives us a terminal cap rate that can be used to estimate the value that the property could be sold for at the end of Year 5 (based on the income a buyer would get after that). We can then discount this value along with the income for Years 1–5 to get the present value.

Exhibit 6　Projected Income

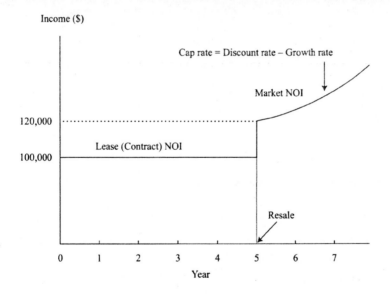

Step 1　Estimate resale price after five years.

Resale (residual) or "terminal" cap rate = 12% – 2% = 10%

Apply this to NOI in Year 6:

Resale = $120,000/0.10 = $1,200,000

Note: The value that can be obtained by selling the property at some point in the future is often referred to as the "*reversion.*"

(continued)

| **Exhibit 6** | **(Continued)** |

Step 2   Discount the level NOI for the first five years and the resale price.[10]

PMT = $100,000

FV = $1,200,000

$n = 5$

$i = 12\%$

Solving for PV, the current value of the property is estimated to be $1,041,390.

Note that the implied going-in cap rate is $100,000/$1,041,390 = 9.60%.

In Example 16, the going-in cap rate is lower than the terminal cap rate. An investor is willing to pay a higher price for the current NOI because he or she knows that it will increase when the lease is renewed at market rents in five years. The expected rent jump on lease renewal is implicit in the cap rate.

As noted earlier, we often expect the terminal cap rate to be higher than the going-in cap rate because it is being applied to income that is more uncertain. Also, the property is older and may have less growth potential. Finding a lower implied going-in cap rate in this example is consistent with this. However, there are times when we would expect the terminal cap rate to be lower than the going-in cap rate—for example, if we thought that interest rates and thus discount rates would be lower when the property is sold in the future or we expected that markets would be a lot stronger in the future with expectations for higher rental growth than in the current market.

EXAMPLE 17

Appraisal with Level NOI

Suppose the NOI from a property is expected to be level at $600,000 per year for a long period of time such that, for all practical purposes, it can be assumed to be a perpetuity. What is the value of the property assuming investors want a 12 percent rate of return?

Solution:

In this case, the growth rate is zero, so we have:

Value = NOI/Discount rate
Value = $600,000/0.12 = $5,000,000

Note that in this case the cap rate will be the same as the discount rate. This is true when there is no expected change in income and value over time.

---

[10] The solution is shown as if it were obtained with either a financial calculator or Microsoft Excel functions.

6.3.3 *Adapting to Different Lease Structures*

Lease structures vary across locales and can have an effect on the way value is typically estimated in a specific locale. For example, in the United Kingdom, lease structures have influenced the development of specific approaches to appraisal. In the United Kingdom, the term valuation is typically used rather than the term appraisal. A valuation, like an appraisal, is usually an assessment of "the most likely selling price" of a property or its market value (MV). While the cost approach (discussed in Section 7.1) is used in particular circumstances and the sales comparison approach dominates the single-family home market, the most common approach to valuing commercial property combines elements of direct capitalization (often with implicit discounted cash flow analysis) and explicit discounted cash flow analysis. This combination has been developed in response to the typical structure of UK leases.

In Section 6.2.2, we discussed the use of a cap rate called the all risks yield to value a fully let property (a property fully leased at current market rents with the tenant[s] paying all operating expenses) in the United Kingdom. If the appraisal date falls between the initial letting (or the last rent review) and the next rent review, adjustments have to be made because the contract rent (referred to as passing rent) is not equal to the current market rent (referred to as the open market rent). If the current market rent is greater than the contract rent, then the rent is likely to be adjusted upward at the time of the rent review and the property has what is referred to in the United Kingdom as a "*reversionary potential*" because of the higher rent at the next rent review.[11] This expected increase in rent has to be included in the appraisal.

There are several ways of dealing with this expected change in rent, but each should result in a similar valuation. One way, which is referred to as the "term and reversion approach" in the United Kingdom, simply splits the income into two components. The *term rent* is the fixed passing (current contract) rent from the date of appraisal to the next rent review, and the *reversion* is the estimated rental value (ERV). The values of the two components of the income stream are appraised separately by the application of different capitalization rates.

The capitalization rate used for the reversion is derived from sales of comparable fully let properties, on the basis that the reversion is equivalent to a fully let property, because both have potential for income growth every five years due to rent review.[12] However, the capitalized reversionary income is a future value, so it has to be discounted from the time of the rent review to the present. By convention, the rate used to discount this future reversionary value to the present is the same as the capitalization rate used to calculate the reversionary value, although they do not have to be the same.

The discount rate applied to the term rent is typically lower than that for the reversion because the term rent is regarded as less risky because it is secured by existing leases and tenants are less likely to default when they have leases with below-market-rate rents. Example 18 illustrates estimating the value of a property with term rent and reversion.

---

11 The term *reversion* is used in the United States to refer to the proceeds from the sale of a property that may or may not be at the end of a lease. Reversion and reversionary potential are similar in that they both refer to expected future benefits.

12 This assumes capitalization rates will not change significantly between the time of the appraisal and the time of the rent review.

EXAMPLE 18

A Term and Reversion Valuation

A property was let for a five-year term three years ago at £400,000 per year. Rent reviews occur every five years. The estimated rental value (ERV) in the current market is £450,000, and the all risks yield (cap rate) on comparable fully let properties is 5 percent. A lower rate of 4 percent is considered appropriate to discount the term rent because it is less risky than market rent (ERV). Exhibit 7 shows the assumed cash flows for this example. Estimate the value of the property.

Exhibit 7   Assumed Cash Flows

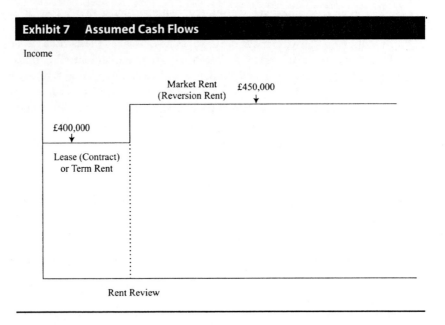

Solution:

The first step is to find the present value of the term rent of £400,000 per year for two years. At a 4 percent discount rate, the present value of £400,000 per year for two years is £754,438. The second step is to estimate the present value of the £450,000 ERV at the time of the rent review. At a 5 percent capitalization rate, this value is £9,000,000 (= £450,000/0.05). This value is at the time of rent review and must be discounted back for two years to the present. Using a discount rate that is the same as the capitalization rate of 5 percent results in a present value of £8,163,265. Adding this to the value of the term rent of £754,438 results in a total value of £8,917,703. In summary:

Term rent		£400,000	
PV 2 years at 4%		× 1.8860947	
Value of term rent			= £754,438
Reversion to ERV	£450,000		
PV perpetuity at 5%	÷ 0.05		
Value at rent review		= £9,000,000	
PV 2 years at 5%		× 0.9070295	

Value of reversion	= £8,163,265
Total capital value	£8,917,703

Note that despite the differences in terminology, this example is similar to Example 16, in which there was level income for five years and an assumed resale at the end of the fifth year. Recall that the value associated with resale of the property in the future is often referred to as the reversion value. It is the same concept as in this example. The value of the property is equal to the value of the income received for a period of time plus the expected value from sale in the future (at the end of the period) regardless of whether the property is actually sold or not. In Example 18, the property could be sold at the time of rent review for £9 million. So the total value is equal to the present value of the income until the rent review plus the present value of what the property could be sold for at rent review.

A variation of the above method that is sometimes used in the United Kingdom is referred to as the "layer method." The only difference is that it deals with the higher income expected from the rent review in a different way mathematically. It assumes that one source of income is the current contract rent as if it would continue indefinitely (perpetuity) and then adds to the value of this income the value from the incremental rent expected to be received after the rent review. A cap rate close to or equal to the all risks yield is normally applied to the contract rent because it is regarded as secure income—rent reviews are upward only in the United Kingdom and rental growth should ensure that the rent from the new lease will be at least as high as the current rent. The additional income expected after the rent review is often capitalized at a higher rate than the all risks yield because it is regarded as more risky although it could increase even more after subsequent rent reviews, and as we have seen, a higher growth rate for income results in a lower cap rate. Example 19 illustrates the use of the layer method.

EXAMPLE 19

The Layer Method

Consider the same property as in Example 18. The cash flow is shown in Exhibit 8. The current contract (term) rent is to be discounted at 5 percent, and the incremental rent is to be discounted at 6 percent. Estimate the value of the property using the layer method.

Exhibit 8	Assumed Cash Flows

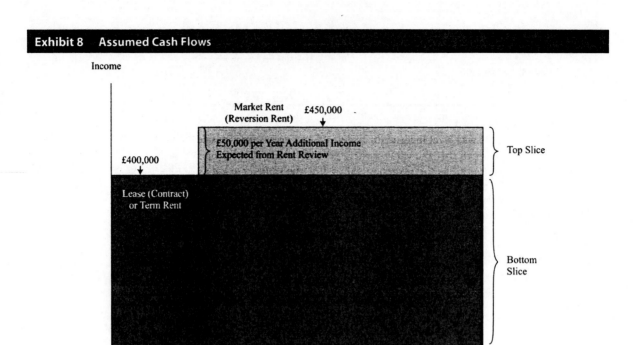

Solution:

Using the layer method, the valuation is as follows:

Term rent	£400,000	
PV in perpetuity at 5%	÷ 0.05	
Value of bottom slice		= £8,000,000
Reversion to ERV	£450,000	
Less bottom slice	– £400,000	
Top slice rent =	£50,000	
PV perpetuity at 6%	× 16.6666667	
PV 2 years at 6%	× 0.8899964	
Value of top slice		= £741,664
Total capital value		£8,741,664

This method produces a slightly different answer from that shown in Example 18. In theory, the cap rates could have been adjusted to produce the same answer as in Example 18; in practice, adjustments involve both market convention and subjectivity.

6.3.4 *The Equivalent Yield*

In Examples 18 and 19, different cap rates were applied to the two different sources of income (current contract rent versus market rent to be received at rent review). There is a single discount rate that could be applied mathematically to both income streams that would result in the same value. This rate is referred to as the "equivalent yield." Again, we must be careful about terminology because this rate will not be an IRR unless one assumes there will not be any increase in rent after the first rent review. Otherwise, the equivalent yield is simply an average of the two separate cap rates—although not a simple average because of the mathematics of discounting. A concept proposed by Investment Property Databank (IPD) in the United Kingdom is to show the "effective yield" for a property being valued, where the effective yield is an IRR calculation based on reasonable assumptions for future rent reviews beyond the first one. The concept of an effective yield would be the same as the discount rate that would be used to value a property using discounted cash flow analysis, and an effective yield can be calculated regardless of how the value was estimated. That is, based on the value being estimated by the appraiser, what would the investor expect to earn as an IRR based on projected future cash flows either to perpetuity or with a resale at the end of a holding period? In theory, the holding period would not matter because the resale price represents the present value of income beyond the holding period. So having a holding period assumption is more for convenience and being realistic about how far into the future cash flows can be estimated.

6.4 Advanced DCF: Lease-by-Lease Analysis

The use of a DCF approach for real estate income-producing properties, especially when there are lots of tenants and more complex leases, is intuitively appealing. The general steps to a DCF analysis are as follows:

- Project income from existing leases
- Make assumptions about lease renewals
- Make assumptions about operating expenses
- Make assumptions about capital expenditures
- Make assumptions about absorption of any vacant space
- Estimate resale value (reversion)
- Select discount rate to find PV of cash flows

6.4.1 *Project Income from Existing Leases*

This step involves capturing the start and end dates for each lease and the various determinants of rent under the lease, such as the base rent, projected increases in the base rent (steps), and adjustments that may occur because the lease is linked to an index (such as a CPI adjustment). The projected income from existing leases would include income from expense reimbursements on leases that provide for the tenant being billed for some portion of the operating expenses because either it is a net lease or it is a gross lease but has a provision for pass-through of expenses to the tenant if they exceed a certain amount.

6.4.2 *Make Assumptions about Lease Renewals*

Assumptions also have to be made about what will happen when a lease comes up for renewal—often referred to as market leasing assumptions. That is, does the appraiser think it will be renewed or not? These assumptions are usually not as simple as saying it will be renewed or will not be renewed but involve estimating a probability that the lease will be renewed, which is referred to as the renewal probability. For example, for a particular tenant or group of tenants, it might be assumed that there is a 70 percent chance that the lease will be renewed and a 30 percent chance that it will not be renewed. Estimating this probability obviously involves some judgment, but the estimate will be based on historical experience with different types of tenants as well as consideration of economic conditions likely to exist at the time of the lease renewal.

The assumption about lease renewal probabilities affects cash flows in several ways. First, the assumption about the rent that would be received from an existing tenant that renews a lease may be lower than that expected from a new tenant found to lease the space if the existing tenant does not renew. This is because the owner may be willing to accept a lower rent from an existing tenant that is already in place and has been paying rent on time, and the space will not be vacant until a new tenant is found. Second, a new tenant is more likely to ask the owner to spend money to fix up the tenant's space—so-called tenant improvements (TIs). Third, finding a new tenant is likely to involve paying leasing commissions to a broker, whereas the commissions might be avoided or be less if an existing tenant renews.

In conjunction with making assumptions about the lease renewal probability, the analyst would also indicate how many months it will take to lease the space if the lease is not renewed. This is usually done by specifying the number of months vacant if a lease is not renewed. Combining assumptions about the renewal probability, the number of months vacant, and the length for a new lease is one way to estimate a vacancy rate for the property. For example, a 60 percent renewal probability with 10 months vacant if not renewed suggests that there is a 40 percent chance the lease will not be renewed, so on average there would be 40% × 10 months or 4 months vacancy when the lease comes up for renewal. If the typical lease is 3 years or 36 months, then this suggests a vacancy rate due to this lease of 4 months every 40 months (36 + 4) or a 10 percent vacancy rate.

6.4.3 *Make Assumptions about Operating Expenses*

Operating expenses involve items that must be paid by the owner, such as property taxes, insurance, maintenance, management, marketing, and utilities. Even if the tenant is responsible for paying some or all of the expenses, they often must first be paid by the owner, and then the owner is reimbursed by the tenant. So they would be included as an expense, and there would be additional reimbursement income from the tenant for those expenses that are the tenant's responsibility.

Operating expenses are often categorized as fixed, variable, or a hybrid of the two. By variable expenses, we mean that they depend on the level of occupancy, whereas fixed expenses do not depend on the level of occupancy. Fixed expenses can still change over time—for example, they may increase with inflation. Most expenses change over time because of inflation. But some expenses also depend on the occupancy of the property, such as the management fee, which is often a percentage of income collected from tenants. Insurance and property taxes are more likely to be fixed and not vary with occupancy. Utilities may be a hybrid. With more tenants, there will be higher utility expenses, but there is usually some fixed amount of utility expense even for a building that is almost empty; common areas (lobbies, hallways, and so on) must be heated/air conditioned and adequately lit. The temperature of unoccupied spaces may be kept within a certain range to prevent damage. Thus, utilities might be considered to be partially fixed and partially variable.

EXAMPLE 20

Utility Expenses

Utilities are assumed to be 25 percent fixed and 75 percent variable. If a 200,000 square foot building was fully occupied, the utility expense would be $4 per square foot. Assuming that all utility expenses are allocated to occupied space, what is the utility expense per occupied square foot if the building is 80 percent occupied?

Solution:

The fixed portion is ($4 × 0.25 × 200,000)/(0.80 × 200,000) = $1.25 per occupied square foot.

The variable portion is $4 × 0.75 = $3.00 per occupied square foot.

The total utility expense is $4.25 per occupied square foot.

6.4.4 *Make Assumptions about Capital Expenditures*

In addition to the operating expenses discussed above, there may be additional expenditures that have to be paid for items that are not ordinary annual expenses, such as a new heating and air conditioning system or replacing a roof. These items are referred to as capital expenditures (or capex), and they affect cash flows. Funds used to fix up a tenant's space for a new lease are also considered capital expenditures, as are funds spent to renovate the building. These capital expenditures are deducted from the NOI to calculate cash flow that would be discounted when doing a DCF analysis. Note that these expenditures will differ in most years, and in some years there may not be any. They are lumpy by nature. In some cases, analysts estimate on average what the annual amount of capital expenditures will be and have a deduction each year for capital expenditures rather than project exactly in which year(s) they might spend the money. In such cases, capex should still be a deduction from NOI, although some analysts include it along with other operating expenses and call it a "replacement reserve." Regardless of how the capex is handled, the present value of the cash flows should be essentially the same.

6.4.5 *Make Assumptions about Absorption of Any Vacant Space*

The property being valued may also have some space that is currently vacant and needs to be leased up. Accounting for currently vacant space involves making an assumption as to when the space is likely to be leased, which could involve several leases starting at different points in time in the future. Until the space is leased, it will be reflected in the vacancy rate for the property, as will space that is vacant as a result of the lease renewal assumptions discussed above.

6.4.6 *Estimate Resale Value (Reversion)*

When doing a DCF analysis, the usual practice is to make an assumption as to how long the property will be held by the initial investor. For example, it might be assumed that the property will be held for 10 years and then sold to a second investor. An alternative would be to project cash flows for the entire economic life of the property, although there would still normally be value to the land after the building is ready for demolition.

Obviously, it is harder to project cash flows the further we go in the future, so for practical purposes, a holding period of about 10 years is typically used. This allows us to capture the details of existing leases and what will happen when most if not all of them renew if the lease term of the longest lease is 10 years or less. Having a holding period that goes beyond when existing leases expire can make it easier to estimate the resale price at the end of the holding period because all leases will be at market rents and have normal rent growth thereafter. In contrast, if there were unexpired leases that had unusually low (or high) contract rent, they could bias the estimate of the resale price if not properly accounted for when estimating the resale price.

The way the resale price is often estimated is to use the concept of a terminal cap rate that was discussed earlier. The idea is that, although we want to capture the details of the leases for the next 10 years or so of the holding period, to get the resale price we will revert to a more simple direct capitalization approach. If the holding period is 10 years, the expected NOI in Year 11 would be used to estimate the resale price because this is the first year of NOI for the next buyer.

Recall our earlier discussion of the terminal cap rate and the relationship between the cap rate, the discount rate, and expected future growth in NOI and value. The terminal cap rate will capture how income and value is projected to change for a new investor. We could say that the resale price will be the present value of cash flows expected after that. So even though we select a holding period when the property will be sold, we are still implicitly considering all future cash flows for the property. We only try to capture the detail on a year-by-year basis up until the end of the holding period plus one year.

Note that, in theory, the length of the holding period does not matter because the resale price reflects the present value of cash flows expected after the holding period. So the choice of a holding period is somewhat arbitrary, and it is more important to pick one that goes beyond the term of existing leases for the reasons discussed above. To elaborate, if there was a major lease that had significantly below-market rent under the contract terms of the lease, its income would be expected to increase when the lease ends, which should result in higher income from that point forward. The analyst would want to capture this in his or her analysis. But if the income used to estimate the resale price is before the lease expires, applying a cap rate to that income may underestimate the resale price because it would not capture the growth in income and value when this lease renews.

6.4.7 *Select Discount Rate to Find PV of Cash Flows*

Ultimately, the purpose of a DCF analysis is to discount the projected future cash flows, including the resale price, to get a present value. This requires selection of an appropriate discount rate to capture the riskiness of the cash flows. Knowing what the discount rate should be can be a challenge because it is not directly observable. That is, analysts do not know what the investor projected as cash flows in the future and what return was expected at the time a property was purchased—although analysts could ask the buyer, which is one of the ways, analysts try to determine what discount rate to use. That is, analysts can survey buyers of properties in the market to find out what return they expected when they purchased the property. Some companies and organizations publish the results of investor surveys.

The discount rate should be higher than what the mortgage rate would be for a loan on the property—regardless of whether the investor plans to actually get a loan. This is because investing in the property is usually considered riskier than making a loan on the property. The lender gets repaid before the investor receives any cash flow, and thus the lender bears less risk than the investor. So the discount rate should have a risk premium beyond that reflected in the mortgage rate.

Some argue that more than one discount rate is applicable because some cash flows expected from a property are riskier than others. For example, a lower discount rate might be used to find the present value of the income from existing leases, but a higher discount rate might be used for the income from lease renewals and resale. That said, even if a single discount rate is used, it can be thought of as an average of the different rates that might be applied to different components of the cash flow. So, the important thing is to use a discount rate that reflects, on average, how risky the investment is compared with alternatives.

EXAMPLE 21

Direct Capitalization and Discounted Cash Flow

What is the main difference between direct capitalization and discounted cash flow (DCF) analysis?

Solution:

Direct capitalization applies a capitalization rate or an income multiplier to the forecasted first-year NOI. Thus, expected increases (growth) in NOI in the future must be implicit in the multiplier or cap rate. In contrast, when doing a DCF, the future cash flows are projected each year until sale of the property. Then each year's cash flow and the expected resale proceeds are discounted using a discount rate. Thus, the future income pattern, including the effect of growth, is explicit in a DCF. Furthermore, DCF often considers other cash flows that might occur in the future that are not reflected in NOI, such as capital expenditures.

6.5 Advantages and Disadvantages of the Income Approach

We have seen that there are many ways of applying the income approach, ranging from a relatively simple use of a cap rate with direct capitalization to more advanced DCF analysis that involves projecting cash flows over a holding period and capturing the details of the leases for each year of the holding period.

The *advantage* of the more complex DCF approach is that it captures the cash flows that investors actually care about. And this approach does not depend on current transactions from comparable sales as long as we feel that we can select an appropriate discount rate.

The *disadvantage* is the amount of detailed information that is needed and the need to forecast what will happen in the future even if it is just forecasting a growth rate for the NOI and not doing a detailed lease-by-lease analysis. Selecting an appropriate discount rate is critical, as is selecting an appropriate terminal cap rate. Small variations in assumptions can have a significant impact on the value.

Because it can be tedious to capture all the details of existing leases, specialized software is often used to do DCF analysis.

6.6 Common Errors

Discounted cash flow analysis requires a lot of assumptions, and analysts may knowingly or otherwise make assumptions that are not consistent with reality. The following are some of the more common erroneous assumptions:

- The discount rate does not reflect the risk.
- Income growth is greater than expense growth.
- The terminal cap rate is not logical compared with the implied going-in cap rate.
- The terminal cap rate is applied to an income that is not typical.
- The cyclical nature of real estate markets is not recognized.

EXAMPLE 22

Disadvantages of and Errors in Discounted Cash Flow Analysis

A property is being valued using an 8 percent discount rate. A terminal capitalization rate of 5.5 percent was used to estimate the resale price. After solving for value, the appraiser calculates the implied going-in capitalization rate to be 6 percent. Market rents and property values have been increasing about 1 percent per year, and that is expected to continue in the foreseeable future. Current mortgage rates for a loan on the property would be 7.5 percent. Do the assumed discount and terminal capitalization rates seem reasonable?

Solution:

There are several "red flags" or warning signs. First, the discount rate is only 50 basis points above the mortgage rate. Whether this is a sufficient risk premium for an equity investor is questionable. Second, the terminal capitalization rate is less than the going-in capitalization rate, which suggests either interest rates will fall in the future or NOI and property values will increase at an even faster rate in the future. Usually, terminal capitalization rates are the same as or slightly higher than going-in capitalization rates to reflect the fact that the property will be older when sold, and older properties usually have less NOI growth. Finally, the difference between the discount rate of 8 percent and the going-in capitalization rate of 6 percent implies 2 percent per year growth. Yet NOI and property values are expected to increase only about 1 percent per year. Overall, it appears that the appraiser may be overvaluing the property.

7   THE COST AND SALES COMPARISON APPROACHES TO VALUATION

We now turn to two other approaches to valuation: the cost approach and the sales comparison approach. The cost approach is typically used for unusual properties or those with specialized use for which market comparables are difficult to obtain. The sales comparison approach is most commonly used for single-family homes, where income is not relevant and sales data for reasonable comparables is available.

7.1 The Cost Approach

The cost approach involves estimating the value of the building(s) based on adjusted replacement cost. The estimated value of the land (usually from a sales comparison approach) is added to the estimated value of the building to arrive at the estimated total value of the property. To determine the value of the building, the **replacement cost**, assuming it was built today using current construction costs and standards, is first estimated.[13] The replacement cost is adjusted for different types of depreciation (loss in value) to arrive at a **depreciated replacement cost**.[14]

The first type of depreciation is for **physical deterioration**, which is generally related to the age of the property because components of the property wear out over time. There are two types of physical deterioration: curable and incurable. Curable means that fixing the problem will add value that is at least as great as the cost of the cure. For example, replacing a roof might increase the value of the property by at least as much as the cost of doing so and, therefore, is curable. Fixing a structural problem with the foundation of the building may cost more to cure than the amount that it would increase the value of the property if cured and would be considered incurable deterioration.

---

13 There is sometimes a distinction made between "replacement cost" and "reproduction cost," where reproduction cost refers to the cost of creating an exact replica of the building using the original building materials. In contrast, replacement cost refers to creating a building that provides the same utility to users but is constructed with modern building materials. Reproduction cost may be higher than replacement cost because it is not economical to construct the building using the original materials. Thus, replacement cost is more relevant as a starting point to estimate value using the cost approach.

14 It should be noted that the depreciation being estimated for the cost approach may have little relationship to the amount of depreciation that would be used on financial statements using a historical cost approach to accounting.

The replacement cost estimate for the property assumes it is a new building that has no obsolescence. That is, it is the value assuming nothing needs cured. Thus, the cost of fixing any curable items would have to be deducted from the replacement cost. A prospective purchaser would not pay as much for a property that had items that need to be fixed and would likely deduct the cost of fixing them from the purchase price.

After deducting the cost of fixing curable items from the replacement cost of the property, a deduction still has to be made for incurable depreciation. A buyer would pay less for a building that is older and has wear and tear. Because incurable depreciation by definition would not be feasible to fix because it does not increase value as much as the cost to fix, we would not deduct the cost of fixing it from the replacement cost. Rather, appraisers try to estimate how a property's age is likely to affect its value. A simple way that is often used to estimate this depreciation is to base it on the effective age of the property relative to its economic life. The effective age can differ from the actual age if it has more or less than the normal amount of wear and tear. For example, if the property has an effective age of 10 years and its economic life is usually 50 years, then the physical depreciation is assumed to be 10/50 or 20 percent. This ratio is applied to the value calculated above, which is after subtracting the curable depreciation from the replacement cost so as to not double count. That is, we have already accounted for the loss in value due to curable depreciation.

The second type of depreciation is referred to as **functional obsolescence**. It is a loss in value due to a design that is different from that of a new building constructed with an appropriate design for the intended use of the property. This could result from changes in design standards since the building was constructed or because the building had a poor design to start, even if it were a relatively new building. Functional obsolescence usually results in the building generating less NOI than it otherwise would because the building may be less efficient and have a higher operating expense or may not command as much rent as a building with the proper design. The amount of functional obsolescence is often estimated by the present value of the income loss due to the obsolescence. For example, suppose an office has a poorly designed elevator system such that there tends to be unusually long waiting times for tenants and visitors to use them. This situation affects the types of tenants that are willing to rent space in the building, and the rent is less than it would be if the elevators had greater capacity. The appraiser determines that this design flaw likely reduces NOI by about $25,000 per year. An 8 percent cap rate is considered appropriate to estimate the value of the property. This cap rate can be applied to the $25,000 loss in NOI due to the poor elevator design to arrive at a $312,500 loss in value due to functional obsolescence. This amount is deducted from the replacement cost.

Finally, there is depreciation that is external to the property. This *external obsolescence* is due to either the location of the property or economic conditions. **Locational obsolescence** results when the location is not optimal for the property. It usually occurs because something happens after the building was constructed that changes the desirability of the location for the existing use; the existing use may no longer be the highest and best use of the site.

For example, a luxury apartment building is on a site where the highest and best use when it was first developed was to construct the luxury apartment. But perhaps after the apartment was constructed, a manufacturing plant that was allowed by the zoning was built on a nearby site, and this made the location much less desirable for a luxury apartment building. That is, a luxury apartment building is no longer the highest and best use of the site. Perhaps now the highest and best use is an apartment building that would have lower rents and appeal to people working at the manufacturing plant.

After the manufacturing plant was built, rents had to be lowered on the apartment building currently on the site. Thus, its value is lower than it would be on a site where the highest and best use is still a luxury apartment building. Suppose the decline in the value of the apartment building (land and building) is $200,000. This amount is the total loss in value due to the manufacturing plant. But some of this loss in value would show up in the land value being lower, which would be reflected in comparable land sales taking place after the manufacturing plant was built being lower than before it was built and lower at better locations. For example, a vacant site near the manufacturing plant would have sold for $100,000 before the manufacturing plant was built but would now sell for $75,000 to be used for low-income housing. Thus, some of the loss in value of the property would already be reflected in the lower land value, and this portion does not have to be deducted from the replacement cost of the building.

The land value for the existing luxury office building near the manufacturing plant would be $75,000 based on its use for lower-income apartments if vacant. Because the land value reflects a $25,000 loss in value, the amount of locational obsolescence attributed to the building would be the $200,000 total decline in value less the $25,000 attributed to the land or $175,000. Thus, $175,000 is deducted from the replacement cost of the building in the cost approach.

Economic obsolescence results when new construction is not feasible under current economic conditions. This usually occurs when rent levels are not sufficiently high to generate a value for a newly constructed property that is at least equal to the development costs (including a profit to the developer). Thus, the replacement cost of the new property exceeds what it would really be worth if it were developed. In this situation, even a new building would have a loss in value.

In Exhibit 9, the cost approach is illustrated for a small office building. The building has a replacement cost of $16 million plus a developer's profit of $750,000. This is what it would cost to build a brand new building that has the same utility as the property being valued. The land value of $4 million is based on comparable sales of other parcels of land. The subject property is not new and has some deferred maintenance that is curable; spending money to fix these items (such as replacing the roof) will add at least as much value as the cost of curing the problem. The cost to cure the building amounts to $1 million. It has to be deducted from replacement cost because the subject property needs these repairs whereas the replacement cost assumes everything is new.

An older building will also have additional physical deterioration (wear and tear) due to age that is not curable but must be accounted for. As discussed previously, a common way of doing this is to use the ratio of the effective age of the property to its economic life. Effective age could be higher or lower than the actual age, depending on how well maintained the property is or whether it has unusually large or small deterioration. In this case, the effective age is 10 years and the economic life is 50 years, which means it is 10/50 or 20 percent worn out. This ratio is applied to the amount we arrived at after deducting the curable depreciation from the replacement cost.[15] This results in a deduction of $3,150,000 [= (16,750,000 − 1,000,000)0.20] for wear and tear that is not curable.

Next, functional obsolescence, which has to do with design problems, is considered. In this case, the property is deemed to have a poor floor plan compared with a modern building. It also has higher-than-average energy consumption. Keep in mind that we are estimating the value of the property "as is" with its existing design flaws. The deduction for this functional obsolescence is estimated at $1.75 million.

Locational obsolescence also has to be considered. The construction of roads in an adjacent park reduced the amenity value compared with a typical office building in this market. In other words, the location is not the most desirable location for this office building. This lowers the market rent for the property, which is estimated to lower the value by $1 million. Finally, there is some economic obsolescence, which

---

15 To not deduct the curable items before applying the 20 percent to account for incurable items would be double-counting. If the curable items were fixed, they would be brand new. We are trying to capture the additional depreciation on the portions of the building that cannot be cured.

is due to recent construction of competing properties that has resulted in a higher vacancy rate than would be typical for a new building. It results in a loss in value of $1 million. Subtracting all of the depreciation discussed above results in a depreciated building value of $8.85 million. Finally, adding the land value of $4 million results in a value estimate of $12.85 million.

Exhibit 9	**The Cost Approach**				
Market value of the land (from comparables)					$4,000,000
Replacement cost, including constructor's profit					
	Building costs (psf)	$200			
	Total area (sf)	80,000			
				$16,000,000	
Developer's profit			$750,000		
				$16,750,000	
Reduction for curable deterioration			$1,000,000		
				$15,750,000	
Reduction for incurable deterioration					
	Total economic life	50			
	Remaining economic life	40			
	Effective age	10			
	Ratio of effective to total	20%			
Reduction for incurable deterioration			$3,150,000		
				$12,600,000	
Reduction for functional obsolescence (poor floor plan and substandard energy efficiency)			$1,750,000		
				$10,850,000	
Reduction for locational obsolescence (recent construction of roads in park land thus reducing amenity)			$1,000,000		
				$9,850,000	
Reduction for economic obsolescence (recent construction of competing properties thus increasing supply and vacancy rates)			$1,000,000		
Building value				$8,850,000	
Final appraised value (building and land)					**$12,850,000**

The Cost Approach

A 12-year-old industrial property is being valued using the cost approach. The appraiser feels that it has an effective age of 15 years based on its current condition. For example, there are cracks in the foundation that are not feasible to repair (incurable physical depreciation). That is, it would cost more to try to repair these problems than the value that would be created in the property. The appraiser believes that it has a 60-year remaining economic life (75-year total economic life).

The building was constructed using a greater ceiling height than users require in the current market (super-adequacy). It would cost $27 million to reproduce (reproduction cost) the building with the same ceiling height but $25 million to construct a replacement property (replacement cost) with the same utility but a normal ceiling height.

The higher ceiling results in increased heating and air-conditioning costs of $50,000 per year. A cap rate that would be used to value the property would be 10 percent.

The building was designed to include a cafeteria that is no longer functional (functional obsolescence). This area can be converted to usable space at a conversion cost of $25,000, and it is believed that the value of the property would increase by at least this amount (curable functional obsolescence).

The roof needs to be replaced at a cost of $250,000, and other necessary repairs amount to $50,000. The costs of these repairs will increase the value of the building by at least their $300,000 cost (curable physical depreciation).

The road providing access to the property is a two-lane road, whereas newer industrial properties are accessible by four-lane roads. This has a negative impact on rents (locational obsolescence), which is estimated to reduce NOI by $100,000 per year.

Based on comparable sales of vacant land, the land is estimated to be worth $5 million. Estimate the value using the cost approach.

Solution:

Preliminary Calculations:

Replacement cost (built to current standards)					$25,000,000
Physical depreciation					
Roof		$250,000			
Other		50,000			
Total curable physical depreciation		$300,000			$300,000
Replacement cost after curable physical depreciation					$24,700,000
Ratio of effective age to total economic life		= 15/75 = 20%			
Incurable physical depreciation	20.00%	x	$24,700,000	=	$4,940,000
Curable functional obsolescence					
Conversion of cafeteria					$25,000
Incurable functional obsolescence					
Extra HVAC costs	$50,000	/	10.00%	=	$500,000
Locational obsolescence	$100,000	/	10.00%	=	$1,000,000

Cost Approach Summary:

Replacement Cost		$25,000,000
Physical deterioration:		
Curable	$300,000	
Incurable	$4,940,000	
Functional obsolescence		
Curable	$25,000	
Incurable	$500,000	
Locational obsolescence	$1,000,000	
Total depreciation	$6,765,000	$6,765,000
Depreciated cost		$18,235,000
Plus: Land value		5,000,000
Estimated value from cost approach		$23,235,000

7.2 The Sales Comparison Approach

The sales comparison approach implicitly assumes that the value of a property depends on what other comparable properties are selling for in the current market. Ideally, the comparables would be exactly the same as the subject property in terms of size, age, location, quality of construction, amenities, view, and so on, and would be sold on the same date as the date of the appraised value. Obviously, this is impossible, so adjustments have to be made to each of the comparables for differences from the "subject" property due to these factors. The idea is to determine what the comparables would have sold for if they were like the subject property.

Exhibit 10 shows the sales comparison approach applied to a subject property. There have been sales of five comparable properties within the last year. They are similar to the subject property, but there are always some differences that need to be accounted for. The idea is to determine how much each of the comparables would have sold for if they were exactly the same as the subject property. Calculating the price per square foot (or square meter) is often a good way to account for differences in size, although other measures of size may be appropriate in some cases, such as cubic feet (or cubic meters) for a warehouse or number of units in an apartment building.

Next, the price per square foot is adjusted for each of the comparables. For example, Comparable 1 is in good condition. The subject property is in only average condition. Thus, we lower the price per square foot of the comparable to determine what it would have sold for if it were in only average condition like the subject property. Each comparable is adjusted to what it would sell for if its location, condition, age, and time of sale were the same as the subject property. Notice that after these adjustments, the range in price per square foot is tighter across the five comparables.

In this example, we average the price per square foot for each of the comparables, although in many cases more weight may be given to comparables that the appraiser feels are more similar to the subject property or where they feel more confident in the adjustments. We multiply this price per square foot by the square feet of the subject property to arrive at our estimate of value using the sales comparison approach.

| Exhibit 10 | The Sales Comparison Approach |

Variable	Subject Property	Comparables				
		1	**2**	**3**	**4**	**5**
Size (square feet)	15,000	25,000	20,000	10,000	16,000	12,500
Age (years)	10	1	5	10	15	20
Condition	Average	Good	Good	Good	Average	Poor
Location	Prime	Prime	Secondary	Secondary	Secondary	Prime
Date of sale (months ago)		3	9	6	7	12
Sale price		$5,500,000	$3,000,000	$1,300,000	$1,750,000	$1,300,000
Sale price psf		$220	$150	$130	$109	$104
Adjustments						
Age (years)		−22.5%	−12.5%	0.0%	12.5%	25.0%
Condition		−10.0%	−10.0%	−10.0%	0.0%	10.0%
Location		0.0%	20.0%	20.0%	20.0%	0.0%
Date of sale (months ago)		1.5%	4.5%	3.0%	3.5%	6.0%
Adjusted price psf		$151.80	$153.00	$146.90	$148.24	$146.64
Average price psf	$149.30					
Appraised value	**$2,239,500**					

The following indicates how the adjustments were made to the comparables to reflect the characteristics of the subject property. The adjustments to Comparable 1 are discussed to help clarify the process.

1 Depreciated at 2.5 percent per annum. Because the subject property is nine years older, a depreciation adjustment of −22.5% (= 9 × 2.5%) reduces the value of Comparable 1.

2 Condition adjustment after average depreciation is taken into account: Good, none; Average, 10%; Poor, 20%. Because Comparable 1 is in good condition and the subject property is in only average condition, a condition adjustment of −10 percent reduces the value of Comparable 1.

3 Location adjustment: Prime, none; Secondary, 20%. Comparable 1 and the subject property are both in prime locations, so no location adjustment is made.

4 Market has been rising by 0.5 percent per month. Thus, an adjustment of 1.5 percent is made to the sale price of Comparable 1 because the sale occurred three months ago.

EXAMPLE 24

The Sales Comparison Approach

Referring to Exhibit 10, suppose there is a sixth comparable that sold one month ago for $2.686 million. It is 15,000 square feet, eight years old, in good condition, and in a prime location. What is the adjusted price per square foot based on this comparable?

Solution:

The sale price per square foot is $2,686,000/15,000 = $179. This price must be adjusted downward by 5 percent because it is two years newer than the subject, down by 10 percent because the condition is better than that of the subject property, and up by 1/2 percent because prices have increased since this comparable sold. This results in an adjusted price per square foot of $153.05.

7.3 Advantages and Disadvantages of the Cost and Sales Comparison Approaches

The cost approach to valuation is sometimes said to set an upper limit on the value. It is assumed that an investor would never pay more than the cost to buy land and develop a comparable building. This assumption may be somewhat of an overstatement because it can take time and effort to develop another building and find tenants. Furthermore, there may not be the demand for another building of the same type in the market. That said, one would question a value that is much higher than implied by the cost approach. The main disadvantage of the cost approach is that it can be difficult to estimate the depreciation for a property that is older and/or has much obsolescence. So the cost approach will be most reliable for newer properties that have a relatively modern design in a stable market.

The sales comparison approach relies on a reasonable number of comparable sales to be able to gauge what investors are expected to be willing to pay for the subject property. When the market is active, the sales comparison approach can be quite reliable. But when the market is weak, there tends to be fewer transactions, which makes it difficult to find comparable properties at a location reasonably close to the subject property. Even in an active market, there may be limited comparable sales for some properties, such as regional malls or special purpose properties.

Finally, the sales comparison approach assumes the investors who are buying properties are behaving rationally. That is, it assumes that the prices paid by investors in the current market are representative of market values. However, as mentioned in Section 5.1.1, the investment value to a particular investor may result in that investor being willing to pay a price in excess of market value. Also, there are times when investors in general are overly exuberant and there is a "bubble" in prices being paid for properties. This raises the question of whether these prices still represent "market value" because it seems likely that prices will eventually fall back to a more normal level. It is often argued that the appraiser's job is to measure what investors are willing to pay whether they think it is rational or not because market value is a most probable selling price.

RECONCILIATION   8

We have discussed three different approaches to valuation: the income, cost, and sales comparison approaches. It would be highly unusual to get the same answer from all three approaches. They rely on different sources of data and different assumptions, and although in theory they should produce the same answer, in practice, this would be unlikely because of imperfections in the data and inefficiencies in the market. Thus, the appraiser needs to *reconcile* the differences and arrive at a final conclusion about the value.

Some approaches may be more applicable than others, depending on the property types and market conditions. The purpose of reconciliation is to decide which approach or approaches you have the most confidence in and come up with a final estimate of value. In an active market with lots of transactions, the appraiser may have more confidence in the sales comparison approach. This may be the case for apartment buildings in many markets. When there are fewer transactions, as might be the case during weak markets or for property types that do not transact as frequently, the appraiser may have more confidence in the income approach. For example, there may be only one large regional mall in a smaller town, so there are no comparable sales of regional malls to rely on. But the appraiser may have all the details of the existing leases and be pretty confident in what investors want as a rate of return for regional malls around the country because they have similar kinds of tenants.

EXAMPLE 25

Choosing among the Three Approaches

Suppose it is a weak market with hardly any transactions taking place and no new construction during the past year. Investors indicate that they will purchase properties if they can get an adequate return for the risk. What does this suggest about the reliability of the three approaches?

Solution:

The sales comparison approach relies on having transactions to use as comparables. Therefore, in a weak market with few transactions, it is difficult to apply this approach. The replacement cost of a building could be calculated, but if new construction is not feasible, then there is economic depreciation that can be hard to estimate. There is a loss in value because market rents are not high enough to provide an adequate return on new construction. Assuming the property being appraised is generating income, a value can always be calculated using the income approach as long as the appraiser can determine an appropriate discount rate that reflects what the typical investor would require to invest in the property. Thus, in this kind of market, the income approach is likely to be the most reliable.

---

9   DUE DILIGENCE

The property value is usually estimated as part of the process of a property transaction, whether done by a hired appraiser[16] or by the investor. In addition, investors—both private debt and equity investors—will normally go through a process of "due diligence" to verify other facts and conditions that might affect the value of the property and that might not have been identified by the appraiser. The following is an example of items that are usually part of this process:

- Review the leases for the major tenants and review the history of rental payments and any defaults or late payments.

- Get copies of bills for operating expenses, such as utility expenses.

---

16 Terminology may vary among locales. For example, an appraiser is called a "valuer" in the United Kingdom and other parts of Europe.

- Look at cash flow statements of the previous owner for operating expenses and revenues.

- Have an environmental inspection to be sure there are no issues, such as a contaminant material on the site.

- Have a physical/engineering inspection to be sure there are no structural issues with the property and to check the condition of the building systems, structures, foundation, and adequacy of utilities.

- Have an attorney or appropriate party review the ownership history to be sure there are no issues related to the seller's ability to transfer free and clear title that is not subject to any previously unidentified liens.

- Review service and maintenance agreements to determine whether there are recurring problems.

- Have a property survey to determine whether the physical improvements are in the boundary lines of the site and to find out if there are any easements that would affect the value.

- Verify that the property is compliant with zoning, environmental regulations, parking ratios, and so on.

- Verify that property taxes, insurance, special assessments, and so on, have been paid.

When an investor decides to acquire commercial real estate, they will often sign a contract or "letter of intent" that states the investor's intent to acquire the property at a specified price but subject to due diligence. If problems are found during the due diligence period, the investor is likely to try to renegotiate the price or back out of the deal, which he or she can do because either the contract contains a conditional clause or a letter of intent was used. A contract that contains a conditional clause or a letter of intent is not a binding contract. The prospective buyer may have to forfeit a deposit depending on the terms of the conditional contract or the letter of intent. In some countries, it may not be customary to use a conditional contract or a letter of intent as a first step. In such countries, some due diligence should be done before entering into a contract that will be binding. Conducting due diligence can be costly but lowers the risk of acquiring a property or lending funds on a property with unexpected legal or physical problems.

EXAMPLE 26

Due Diligence

What is the primary purpose of due diligence?

Solution:

Due diligence is done to identify legal, environmental, physical, and other unanticipated problems that have not been disclosed by the seller that could be quite costly to remediate or that could negatively affect value. If identified, an issue or issues could result in negotiating a lower price or allow the investor to walk away from the transaction.

10   VALUATION IN AN INTERNATIONAL CONTEXT

As mentioned earlier in the reading, different lease structures and conventions can result in slightly different approaches to valuation in different countries, but the underlying principles are very similar and tending to converge with increasing amounts of cross-border investment in real estate and the need for standardized ways of analyzing properties. This is especially evident in the increasing use of DCF analysis—especially for properties that are institutionally owned.

We have discussed the different approaches and techniques that are used to value properties, such as the sales comparison, cost, and income approaches. And we have discussed several ways of applying the income approach because variations in its application tend to occur depending on the lease structure of the property and tradition in the country. Differences across countries will mainly be based on which approaches are emphasized and which of the ways of applying the approach is used.

As an example, Germany has a tradition of valuing the land and building separately even when using the income approach. The land is valued using a sales comparison approach because the government has good data on land sales. So when using the income approach, it is simply assumed that the land is being leased. That is, the land is assumed to be owned by an entity other than the entity that owns the building. Thus, an assumed land lease payment is deducted from the NOI. The resulting cash flow represents income to the building and can be discounted or a cap rate can be applied to it in the same way we have illustrated in this reading. The resulting value will be for the building, and this value can then be added to the value of the land from the sales comparison approach to get the total value. This same approach is used in the United States when the land is actually being leased from a third party. The point is that this is just a slight variation in applying the concepts and techniques illustrated in this reading.

We now set out some general international comparisons. In different international markets, professionals operate in different regulatory environments, have different training, may use specific definitions of the key concepts, may apply different interpretations of common concepts, use variations of basic methods, and have differing availability of key data. These issues affect the local practices of appraisal to different extents in different countries.

Although there has been a progressive extension of international standards and common approaches,[17] it is always useful to be aware of local approaches.[18] However, it is important to bear in mind that the general concepts are the same and that value should have the same bases in any market, that is, it is derived from an income stream that has a risk associated with it. Any appraisal method, however much it may appear otherwise, is simply a way to establish an appropriate value for that income.

Some key differences among countries are summarized in Exhibit 11.

---

[17] The quest for international standards in valuation has a long history. The RICS in the United Kingdom has for many years produced its valuation standards rules and guidance in the form of the *Red Book* and has been expanding internationally as the main international professional body for appraisers. In Europe, since the early 1980s, the European Group of Valuers' Associations has produced its *Blue Book* of valuation standards. The International Valuation Standards Council (ISVC) produces the "International Valuation Standards."

[18] For those interested in the differences within Europe, the European Mortgage Federation in 2009 produced a study titled "EMF Study on the Valuation of Property for Lending Purposes." It analyzes 16 separate European markets according to a number of criteria, including the regulatory framework, methods, and the training of valuers.

Exhibit 11   Summary of International Valuation Methodologies[19]

Country	Valuation Framework	Valuation Approaches	Lease Structure and Rent Reviews	Landlord vs. Tenant Expense Responsibility	Globalization
China	People's Republic of China and Regulations for Urban Land Valuation	Sales Comparison, Cost, and Income Approaches	2- to 3-year terms Upon expiry	Landlord: structure Tenant: interior, maintenance, insurance	DCF methodology gaining popularity
France	La Charte de l'Expertise en Évaluation Immobilière, [Le COB]	Sales Comparison and Cost Approaches, Comparative Implicit Capitalization	3-, 6-, 9-year terms Upon expiry, rental changes tie to INSEE Index	Landlord: structure Tenant: interior, maintenance, insurance	DCF gaining popularity with international investments/ valuations
Germany	WertV, WertR BelWertV	Sales Comparison, Cost, and Income Approaches	5-, 10-year terms Upon expiry, rental changes tie to cost of living index	Landlord: structure 'Dach und Fach' Tenant: interior	DCF gaining popularity with international investments/ valuations
Japan	Ministry of Land, Infrastructure, Transport and Tourism	Sales Comparison, Cost, and Income Approaches	3-, 5-year terms 6 months prior to lease expiration	Landlord: repair Tenant: inside maintenance, insurance	DCF used as an analysis tool and widely used in international investments/ valuations
United Kingdom	Royal Institution of Chartered Surveyors (RICS) Red Book	Sales Comparison and Cost Approaches, Implicit Capitalization	Recently changed from 25 years to 10, 15 years 5-year upward only	Landlord: minimal Tenant: all repairs, insurance	DCF used as an analysis tool and widely used in international investments/ valuations
United States	Universal Standards of Professional Appraisal Practice (USPAP)	Sales Comparison and Cost Approaches, Implicit Capitalization, DCF	3-, 5-year terms 10+ years Upon expiry	Depends on lease structure	DCF used extensively by institutional investors

INDICES

11

An investor will find a variety of real estate indices to choose from and may find one that seems representative of the market of interest to them. However, the investor should be aware of how the index is constructed and the inherent limitations resulting

---

19 An excellent reference on differences in appraisal practices across countries can be found in *Real Estate Valuation in Global Markets*, 2nd edition, edited by Howard Gelbtuch, MAI, and published by the Appraisal Institute in 2011.

from the construction method. Investors should also be aware that the apparent low correlation of real estate with other asset classes may be due to limitations in real estate index construction.

11.1 Appraisal-Based Indices

Many indices rely on appraisals to estimate how the value of a portfolio of properties or the real estate market in general is changing over time. Real estate indices often rely on appraisals to estimate values because there usually are not sufficient transactions of the same property to rely on transactions to indicate value. Even though there may be real estate transactions occurring, it is not the same property; differences in sale prices (transaction prices) can be due to changes in the market or differences in the characteristics of the property (size, age, location, and so on). Appraisal-based indices combine valuation information from individual properties and provide a measure of market movements.

A well-known index that measures the change in values of real estate held by institutional investors in the United States is the NCREIF Property Index (NPI).[20] Members of NCREIF, who are investment managers and pension fund plan sponsors, contribute information on the appraised value along with the NOI, capital expenditures, and other information, such as occupancy, to NCREIF every quarter. This information is then used to create an index that measures the performance of these properties quarterly. The return for all the properties is calculated as follows:[21]

$$\text{Return} = \frac{\text{NOI} - \text{Capital expenditures} + (\text{Ending market value} - \text{Beginning market value})}{\text{Beginning market value}} \quad (7)$$

In Equation 7, the beginning and ending market values are based on the appraisals of the properties.

The return calculated with this formula is commonly known as the holding period return and is equivalent to a single-period IRR (the IRR if the property were purchased at the beginning of the quarter at its beginning market value and sold at the end of the quarter at its ending market value). A similar equation is used to calculate the returns on stocks and bonds, but in those cases an actual transaction price is typically used. Because this is not possible for real estate, the appraised value is used.

The above return is first calculated for each individual property and then value weighted to get the return for all properties in the index. An alternative would be to equal weight each property, but value weighing gives the return for the portfolio of properties because properties with more value do affect the portfolio more than properties with less value (and less income).

We saw earlier that taking the NOI and dividing by the beginning market value gives the cap rate for the property, which is also referred to as the income return for the property or for the index when it is for all properties. The remaining component in the equation ([Ending market value − Beginning market value − Capital expenditures]/Beginning market value) is referred to as the capital return. It is the change in value net of capital expenditures. To have a positive capital return, the value must increase by more than any funds invested in the property for capital expenditures. That is, replacing the roof may increase the market value but results in a positive rate of return only if the value increases by more than what was spent to replace the roof.

---

20 See www.ncreif.org for further information. NCREIF provides a variety of indices based on different factors, such as property type and location.
21 The actual formula used by NCREIF differs slightly to capture the fact that the NOI and capital expenditures may occur throughout the quarter and not just at the very end. But the differences between the NPI calculation and the simplified formula shown in Equation 7 are not significant.

It should also be noted that the income return is not the same as cash flow because cash flow is calculated after capital expenditures. That is, the amount of cash flow available each quarter is NOI – Capital expenditures. Thus, we can also think of the total return in the above formula as measuring the cash flow (NOI – Capital expenditures) plus the change in value (Ending market value – Beginning market value).

Having an index like the one described above is important because it allows us to compare the performance of real estate with other asset classes, such as stocks and bonds. The quarterly returns are also important for measuring risk, which is often measured as the volatility or standard deviation of the quarterly returns. The index is also a benchmark to which the returns for individual funds can be compared. For example, an investment manager may have a fund of properties that a pension fund or wealthy investor has invested in, and the pension fund or investor may want to know if that investment manager has done better or worse than a benchmark that reflects how the broader market has performed.

Appraisal-based indices, such as the NCREIF Property Index, are also available in many other countries. Many of them are available from Investment Property Databank (IPD), which produces indices for 23 countries.[22] The IPD indices are calculated in a similar manner to the NPI.[23]

EXAMPLE 27

Appraisal-Based Indices

Why are appraisals often used to create real estate performance indices?

Solution:

Because properties do not transact very frequently, it is more difficult to create transaction-based indices as is done for publicly traded securities. Appraisal-based indices can be constructed even when there are no transactions by relying on quarterly or annual appraisals of the property. Of course when there are no transactions, it is also difficult for appraisers to estimate value.

11.2 Transaction-Based Indices

In recent years, indices have been created that are based on actual transactions rather than appraised values. These indices have been made possible by companies that collect information on enough transactions to create an index based only on transactions. In fact, both NCREIF and IPD have transaction information that can be used for this purpose. When creating a transaction-based index, the fact that the same property does not sell very frequently is still an issue. So, to develop an index that measures changes in value quarterly as discussed above for the appraisal index, the fact that there are different properties selling every quarter needs to be controlled for. Some econometric technique, usually involving a regression analysis, is used to address the issue and to create the index. There are two main ways this is done. One is to create what is referred to as a repeat sales index, and the other is to create what is referred to as a hedonic index.

---

[22] Australia, Austria, Belgium, Canada, Denmark, Finland, France, Germany, Ireland, Italy, Japan, South Korea, the Netherlands, New Zealand, Norway, Poland, Portugal, South Africa, Spain, Sweden, Switzerland, the United Kingdom, and the United States.

[23] See www.ipd.com for further information.

A repeat sales index, as the name implies, relies on repeat sales of the same property. A particular property may sell only twice during the entire period of the index. But if there are at least some properties that have sold each quarter, the repeat sales regression methodology can use this information to create an index. Of course, the more sales, the more reliable is the index. In general, the idea of this type of index is that, because it is the same property that sold twice, the change in value between the two sale dates indicates how market conditions have changed over time. The regression methodology allocates this change in value to each time period—that is, each quarter based on the information from sales that occurred that quarter. The details of how the regression works is beyond the scope of this reading. An example of a repeat sales index for commercial real estate in the United States is the Moody's REAL index.[24]

A hedonic index does not require repeat sales of the same property. It requires only one sale. The way it controls for the fact that different properties are selling each quarter is to include variables in the regression that control for differences in the characteristics of the property, such as size, age, quality of construction, and location. These independent variables in the regression reflect how differences in characteristics cause values to differ so that they can be separated from the differences in value due to changes in market conditions from quarter to quarter. Again, the details of this regression are beyond the scope of this reading. The point is that there are ways of constructing indices that are based only on transactions. But they require a lot of data and are usually most reliable at the national level for the major property types, but sometimes they are reliable at the regional level of a country if sufficient transactions are available.

EXAMPLE 28

Transaction-Based Indices

Describe two main ways of creating transaction-based indices.

Solution:

The two main ways are (1) a repeat sales index and (2) a hedonic index. A repeat sales index requires repeat sales of the same property; because it is the same property, controls for differences in property characteristics, such as its size and location, are not required. A hedonic index requires only one sale of a property and thus can usually include more properties than a repeat sales index, but it must control for "hedonic" characteristics of the property, such as its size and location.

11.3 Advantages and Disadvantages of Appraisal-Based and Transaction-Based Indices

All indices, whether appraisal- or transaction-based, have advantages and disadvantages. Appraisal-based indices are often criticized for having appraisal lag, which results from appraised values tending to lag when there are sudden shifts in the market. In an upward market, transaction prices usually start to rise first, and then as these higher prices are reflected in comparable sales and investor surveys, they are captured in appraised values. Thus, appraisal-based indices may not capture the price increase until a quarter or more after it was reflected in transactions. The same lag would also occur in a down market, with appraised values not falling as soon as transaction prices.

---

24 See www.realindices.com for further information.

Another cause of appraisal lag is that all properties in an appraisal-based index may not be appraised every quarter. A manager may assume the value has stayed the same for several quarters until he or she goes through the appraisal process to estimate a new value. This causes a lag in the index. That being said, if the investment managers are all using appraised values to measure returns and if the index is based on appraised values, then it is an "apples to apples" comparison.

If the purpose of the index is for comparison with other asset classes that are publicly traded, however, appraisal lag is more of an issue. Appraisal lag tends to "smooth" the index, meaning that it has less volatility. It behaves somewhat like a moving average of what an index would look like if it were based on values obtained from transactions rather than appraisals. Thus, appraisal-based indices may underestimate the volatility of real estate returns. Because of the lag in appraisal-based real estate indices, they will also tend to have a lower correlation with other asset classes. This is problematic if the index is used in asset allocation models to determine how much of a portfolio should be allocated to real estate versus other asset classes. The allocation to real estate would likely be overestimated.

There are two general ways of adjusting for the appraisal lag. The first is to "unsmooth" the appraisal-based index. Several techniques have been developed to do this, although they are beyond the scope of this reading. In general, these techniques attempt to adjust for the appraisal lag; the resulting unsmoothed index will have more volatility and more correlation with other asset classes. The second way of adjusting for the appraisal lag is to use a transaction-based index when comparing real estate with other asset classes.

Transaction-based indices tend to lead appraisal-based indices for the reasons discussed above but can be noisy (that is, they include random elements in the observations) because of the need to use statistical techniques to estimate the index. So, there may be upward or downward movements from quarter to quarter that are somewhat random even though in general (viewed over a year or more) the index is capturing the correct movements in the market. The challenge for those creating these indices is to try to keep the noise to a minimum through use of appropriate statistical techniques and collecting as much data as possible.

EXAMPLE 29

Comparing Appraisal-Based and Transaction-Based Indices

What are the main differences between the performance of appraisal-based and transaction-based indices?

Solution:

An appraisal-based index will tend to have less volatility and lag a transaction-based index, resulting in a lower correlation with other asset classes being reported for an appraisal-based index.

PRIVATE MARKET REAL ESTATE DEBT   12

Thus far, our focus has been on analyzing a property without considering whether there would be debt financing on the property or it would be purchased on an all-cash basis. This is because the way a property is financed should not affect the property's value. This does not mean that the overall level of interest rates and availability of debt in the market do not affect values. It means that, for a given property, the investor paying all cash should be paying the same price as one who decides to use some debt financing. Of course, investors who do use debt financing will normally expect to earn a higher rate of return on their equity investment. This is because they expect to earn a greater return on the property than what they will be paying the lender. Thus, there will be positive financial leverage. By borrowing money, the investor is taking on more risk in anticipation of a higher return on equity invested. The risk is higher because with debt there will be more uncertainty as to what return the investor will actually earn on equity because the investor gets what is left over after paying the lender. A small drop in property value can result in a large decrease in the investor's return if a high amount of debt was used to finance the property. When a property is valued without explicitly considering financing, the discount rate can be thought of as a weighted average of the rate of return an equity investor would want and the interest rate on the debt.

The maximum amount of debt that an investor can obtain on commercial real estate is usually limited by either the ratio of the loan to the appraised value of the property (loan to value or LTV) or the debt service coverage ratio (DSCR), depending on which measure results in the lowest loan amount. The debt service coverage ratio is the ratio of the first-year NOI to the loan payment (referred to as debt service for commercial real estate). That is,

$$\text{DSCR} = \text{NOI/Debt service} \tag{8}$$

The debt service includes both interest and principal payments on the mortgage. The principal payments are the portion of the loan payment that amortizes the loan over the loan term. An "interest-only" loan would be one that has no principal payments, so the loan balance would remain constant over time. Interest-only loans typically either revert to amortizing loans at some point or have a specified maturity date. For example, an interest-only loan might be made that requires the entire balance of the loan to be repaid after 7–10 years (referred to as a "balloon payment"). Lenders typically require a DSCR of 1.2 or greater to provide a margin of safety that the NOI from the property can cover the debt service.

EXAMPLE 30

Loans on Real Estate

A property has been appraised for $5 million and is expected to have NOI of $400,000 in the first year. The lender is willing to make an interest-only loan at an 8 percent interest rate as long as the loan-to-value ratio does not exceed 80 percent and the DSCR is at least 1.25. The balance of the loan will be due after seven years. How much of a loan can be obtained?

Solution:

Based on the loan-to-value ratio, the loan would be 80 percent of $5 million or $4 million. With a DSCR of 1.25, the maximum debt service would be $400,000/1.25 = $320,000. This amount is the mortgage payment that would result in a 1.25 DSCR for an interest-only loan.

If the loan is interest only, then we can obtain the loan amount by simply dividing the mortgage payment by the interest rate. Therefore, the loan amount would be $320,000/0.08 = $4,000,000.

In this case, we obtain the same loan amount based on either the LTV or DSCR requirements of the lender. If one ratio had resulted in a lower loan amount, that would normally be the maximum that could be borrowed.

When financing is used on a property, equity investors often look at their first-year return on equity or "equity dividend rate" as a measure of how much cash flow they are getting as a percentage of their equity investment. This is sometimes referred to as a "cash-on-cash" return because it measures how much cash they are receiving as a percentage of the cash equity they put into the investment.

EXAMPLE 31

Equity Dividend Rate

Using the information in Example 30, what is the equity dividend rate or cash-on-cash return assuming the property is purchased at its appraised value?

Solution:

The first-year cash flow is the NOI less the mortgage payment.

NOI	$400,000
DS	$320,000
Cash flow	$80,000

The amount of equity is the purchase price less the loan amount.

Price	$5,000,000
Mortgage	$4,000,000
Equity	$1,000,000

The equity yield rate is the Cash flow/Equity = $80,000/$1,000,000 = 8%. Keep in mind that this is not an IRR that would be earned over a holding period until the property is sold. The equity investor does not share any of the price appreciation in the value of the property with the lender.

For loans called "participation" loans, the lender might receive some of the price appreciation, but it would be in exchange for a lower interest rate on the loan.

EXAMPLE 32

Leveraged IRR

Refer to the previous examples 30 and 31. Suppose the property is sold for $6 million after five years. What IRR will the equity investor receive on his or her investment?

Solution:

The cash flow received by the equity investor from the sale will be the sale price less the mortgage balance, or $6 million − $4 million = $2 million. Using a financial calculator,

PV = −$1,000,000 (using a calculator, this is input as a negative
    to indicate the negative cash flow at the beginning of the
    investment)
PMT = $80,000
    $n = 5$
FV = $2,000,000
Solve for i = 21.14%

This is an IRR based on the equity invested in the property.

EXAMPLE 33

Unleveraged IRR

Refer to the previous examples 30, 31, and 32. What would the IRR be if the property were purchased on an all-cash basis (no loan)?

Solution:

Now the equity investor will receive all the cash flow from sale ($6 million) and the NOI ($400,000). The initial investment will be $5 million. Using a financial calculator,

PV = −$5,000,000
PMT = $400,000
    $n = 5$
FV = $6,000,000
Solve for i = 11.20%

This is an IRR based on an unleveraged (all-cash) investment in the property. The difference between this IRR (11.20 percent) and the IRR the equity investor receives with a loan calculated in Example 32 of 21.14 percent reflects positive financial leverage. The property earns 11.20 percent before adding a loan, and the loan is at 8 percent, so the investor is benefiting from the spread between 11.20 percent and 8 percent.

SUMMARY

Real estate property is an asset class that plays a significant role in many investment portfolios. Because of the unique characteristics of real estate property, it tends to behave differently from other asset classes, such as stocks, bonds, and commodities, and thus has different risks and diversification benefits. Private real estate investments are especially unique because the investments are not publicly traded and require different analytic techniques from publicly traded assets. Because of the lack of transactions, the appraisal process is required to value real estate property. Many of the indices and benchmarks used for private real estate also rely on appraisals, and because of this characteristic, they behave differently from indices for publicly traded assets, such as the S&P 500.

The factors that affect the performance of private real estate investments tend to be similar across countries, and the methods for valuing real estate property tend to be similar. Cross-border investment is facilitated by the development of standardized ways of analyzing real estate and by responses to the demand for transparency and sufficient data to do the necessary due diligence. As the availability of real estate data improves along with the technology to analyze the data, real estate markets are likely to become more efficient.

Key points of the reading include the following:

- Real estate investments make up a significant portion of the portfolios of many investors.

- Real estate investments can occur in four basic forms: private equity (direct ownership), publicly traded equity (indirect ownership claim), private debt (direct mortgage lending), and publicly traded debt (securitized mortgages).

- Each of the basic forms of real estate investment has its own risks, expected returns, regulations, legal structures, and market structures.

- There are many motivations for investing in real estate income property. The key ones are current income, price appreciation, inflation hedge, diversification, and tax benefits.

- Equity investors generally expect a higher rate of return than lenders (debt investors) because they take on more risk. The returns to equity real estate investors have two components: an income stream and a capital appreciation. Adding equity real estate investments to a traditional portfolio will potentially have diversification benefits because of the less-than-perfect correlation of equity real estate returns with returns to stocks and bonds. If the income stream can be adjusted for inflation and real estate prices increase with inflation, then equity real estate investments may provide an inflation hedge.

- Debt investors in real estate expect to receive their return from promised cash flows and typically do not participate in any appreciation in value of the underlying real estate. Thus, debt investments in real estate are similar to other fixed-income investments, such as bonds.

- Regardless of the form of real estate investment, the value of the underlying real estate property can affect the performance of the investment. Location is a critical factor in determining the value of a real estate property.

- Real estate property has some unique characteristics compared with other investment asset classes. These characteristics include heterogeneity and fixed location, high unit value, management intensiveness, high transaction costs, depreciation, sensitivity to the credit market, illiquidity, and difficulty of value and price determination.

- There are many different types of real estate properties in which to invest. The main commercial (income-producing) real estate property types are office, industrial and warehouse, retail, and multi-family. There are other types of commercial properties, which are typically classified by their specific use.

- There are risk factors common to commercial property, but each property type is likely to have a different susceptibility to these factors. The key risk factors that can affect commercial real estate include business conditions, lead time for new development, cost and availability of capital, unexpected inflation, demographics, lack of liquidity, environmental issues, availability of information, management expertise, and leverage.

■ Location, lease structures, and economic factors, such as employment growth, economic growth, consumer spending, and population growth, affect the value of each property type.

■ An understanding of the lease structure is important when analyzing a real estate investment.

■ Appraisals estimate the value of real estate income property. Definitions of value include market value, investment value, value in use, and mortgage lending value.

■ Generally, three different approaches are used by appraisers to estimate value: income, cost, and sales comparison.

■ The income approach includes direct capitalization and discounted cash flow methods. Both methods focus on net operating income as an input to the value of a property.

■ The cost approach estimates the value of a property based on adjusted replacement cost. This approach is typically used for unusual properties for which market comparables are difficult to obtain.

■ The sales comparison approach estimates the value of a property based on what comparable properties are selling for in the current market.

■ Due diligence investigates factors that might affect the value of a property. These factors include leases and lease history; operating expenses; environmental issues; structural integrity; lien, ownership, and property tax history; and compliance with relevant laws and regulations.

■ Appraisal-based and transaction-based indices are used to track the performance of private real estate. Appraisal-based indices tend to lag transaction-based indices and appear to have lower volatility and lower correlation with other asset classes than transaction-based indices.

■ When debt financing is used to purchase a property, additional ratios and returns calculated and interpreted by debt and/or equity investors include the loan-to-value ratio, the debt service coverage ratio, the equity dividend rate (cash-on-cash return), and leveraged and unleveraged internal rates of return.

PRACTICE PROBLEMS

The following information relates to Questions 1–12

Amanda Rodriguez is an alternative investments analyst for a US investment management firm, Delphinus Brothers. Delphinus' Chief Investment Officer, Michael Tang, has informed Rodriguez that he wants to reduce the amount invested in traditional asset classes and gain exposure to the real estate sector by acquiring commercial property in the United States. Rodriguez is to analyze potential commercial real estate investments for Delphinus Brothers. Selected data on three commercial real estate properties is presented in Exhibit 1.

Exhibit 1	Selected Property Data		
	Property #1	**Property #2**	**Property #3**
Property Type	**Downtown Office Building**	**Grocery-Anchored Retail Center**	**Multi-Family Building**
Location	New York, NY	Miami, FL	Boston, MA
Occupancy	90.00%	93.00%	95.00%
Square Feet or Number of Units	100,000 sf	205,000 sf	300 units
Gross Potential Rent	$4,250,000	$1,800,000	$3,100,000
Expense Reimbursement Revenue	$330,000	$426,248	$0
Other Income (includes % Rent)	$550,000	$15,000	$45,000
Potential Gross Income	$5,130,000	$2,241,248	$3,145,000
Vacancy Loss	($513,000)	($156,887)	($157,250)
Effective Gross Income	$5,079,000	$2,084,361	$2,987,750
Property Management Fees	($203,160)	($83,374)	($119,510)
Other Operating Expenses	($2,100,000)	($342,874)	($1,175,000)
Net Operating Income (NOI)	$2,775,840	$1,658,113	$1,693,240

Rodriguez reviews the three properties with Tang, who indicates that he would like her to focus on Property #1 because of his prediction of robust job growth in New York City over the next ten years. To complete her analysis, Rodriquez assembles additional data on Property #1, which is presented in Exhibits 2, 3 and 4.

As part of the review, Tang asks Rodriguez to evaluate financing alternatives to determine if it would be better to use debt financing or to make an all cash purchase. Tang directs Rodriguez to inquire about terms with Richmond Life Insurance Company, a publicly traded company, which is an active lender on commercial real estate property. Rodriguez obtains the following information from Richmond Life for a loan on Property #1: loan term of 5 years, interest rate of 5.75% interest-only, maximum loan to value of 75%, and minimum debt service coverage ratio of 1.5x.

Exhibit 2	6-Year Net Operating Income (NOI) and DCF Assumptions for Property #1					
	Year 1	**Year 2**	**Year 3**	**Year 4**	**Year 5**	**Year 6**
NOI	$2,775,840	$2,859,119	$2,944,889	$3,033,235	$3,124,232	$3,217,959

DCF Assumptions	
Investment Hold Period	5 years
Going-in Cap Rate	5.25%
Terminal Cap Rate	6.00%
Discount Rate	7.25%
Income/Value Growth Rate	Constant

Exhibit 3	Sales Comparison Data for Property #1			
Variable	**Property 1**	**Sales Comp A**	**Sales Comp B**	**Sales Comp C**
Age (years)	10	5	12	25
Condition	Good	Excellent	Good	Average
Location	Prime	Secondary	Secondary	Prime
Sale price psf		$415 psf	$395 psf	$400 psf
Adjustments				
Age (years)		−10%	2%	10%
Condition		−10%	0%	10%
Location		15%	15%	0%
Total Adjustments		**−5%**	**17%**	**20%**

Exhibit 4	Other Selected Data for Property #1
Land Value	$7,000,000
Replacement Cost	$59,000,000
Total Depreciation	$5,000,000

After reviewing her research materials, Rodriguez formulates the following two conclusions:

Conclusion 1   Benefits of private equity real estate investments include owners' ability to attain diversification benefits, to earn current income, and to achieve tax benefits.

Conclusion 2   Risk factors of private equity real estate investments include business conditions, demographics, the cost of debt and equity capital, and financial leverage.

1   Which of the following is *most likely* accurate regarding Property #2 described in Exhibit 1?

  A   Operating expense risk is borne by the owner.

  B   The lease term for the largest tenant is greater than three years.

  C   There is a significant amount of percentage rent linked to sales levels.

2   Based upon Exhibits 2, 3 and 4, which of the following statements is *most* accurate regarding the valuation of Property #1?

  A   The cost approach valuation is $71,000,000.

  B   The adjusted price psf for Sales Comp B is $423 psf.

  C   The terminal value at the end of year 5 in the income approach is $53,632,650.

3   Based on Exhibit 2, the growth rate of Property #1 is *closest* to:

  A   0.75%

  B   1.25%.

  C   2.00%.

4   Based on Exhibit 2, the value of Property #1 utilizing the discounted cash flow method is *closest* to:

  A $48,650,100.

  B $49,750,900.

  C $55,150,300.

5   Based on Exhibit 2, relative to the estimated value of Property #1 under the discounted cash flow method, the estimated value of Property #1 using the direct capitalization method is:

  A   equal.

  B   lower.

  C   higher.

6   Based upon Exhibits 1 and 3, the estimated value of Property #1 using the sales comparison approach (assigning equal weight to each comparable) is *closest* to:

  A   40,050,000.

  B   40,300,000.

  C   44,500,000.

7   In the event that Delphinus purchases Property #2, the due diligence process would *most likely* require a review of:

  A   all tenant leases.

  B   tenant sales data.

  C   the grocery anchor lease.

8   Compared to an all-cash purchase, a mortgage on Property #1 through Richmond Life would *most likely* result in Delphinus earning:

  A   a lower return on equity.

  B   a higher return on equity.

  C   the same return on equity.

9 Assuming an appraised value of $48,000,000, Richmond Life Insurance Company's maximum loan amount on Property #1 would be *closest* to:

    A $32,000,000.

    B $36,000,000.

    C $45,000,000.

10 Rodriguez's Conclusion 1 is:

    A correct.

    B incorrect, because tax benefits do not apply to tax-exempt entities.

    C incorrect, because private real estate is highly correlated to stocks.

11 Rodriguez's Conclusion 2 is:

    A correct.

    B incorrect, because inflation is not a risk factor.

    C incorrect, because the cost of equity capital is not a risk factor.

12 Richmond Life Insurance Company's potential investment would be *most likely* described as:

    A private real estate debt.

    B private real estate equity.

    C publicly traded real estate debt.

The following information relates to Questions 13–28

First Life Insurance Company, Ltd., a life insurance company located in the United Kingdom, maintains a stock and bond portfolio and also invests in all four quadrants of the real estate market; private equity, public equity, private debt, and public debt. Each of the four real estate quadrants has a manager assigned to it. First Life intends to increase its allocation to real estate. The Chief Investment Officer (CIO) has scheduled a meeting with the four real estate managers to discuss the allocation to real estate and to each real estate quadrant. Leslie Green, who manages the private equity quadrant, believes her quadrant offers the greatest potential and has identified three investment properties to consider for acquisition. Selected information for the three properties is presented in Exhibit 1.

Exhibit 1	Selected Information on Potential Private Equity Real Estate Investments		
	Property		
	A	**B**	**C**
Property description	**Single Tenant Office**	**Shopping Center**	**Warehouse**
Size (square meters)	3,000	5,000	9,000
Lease type	Net	Gross	Net
Expected loan to value ratio	70%	75%	80%
Total economic life	50 years	30 years	50 years
Remaining economic life	30 years	23 years	20 years

Exhibit 1 (Continued)			
	Property		
	A	**B**	**C**
Property description	**Single Tenant Office**	**Shopping Center**	**Warehouse**
Rental income (at full occupancy)	£575,000	£610,000	£590,000
Other income	£27,000	£183,000	£29,500
Vacancy and collection loss	£0	£61,000	£59,000
Property management fee	£21,500	£35,000	£22,000
Other operating expenses	£0	£234,000	£0
Discount rate	11.5%	9.25%	11.25%
Growth rate	2.0%	See Assumption 2	3.0%
Terminal cap rate		11.00%	
Market value of land	£1,500,000	£1,750,000	£4,000,000
Replacement costs			
▪ Building costs	£8,725,000	£4,500,000	£12,500,000
▪ Developer's profit	£410,000	£210,000	£585,000
Deterioration – curable and incurable	£4,104,000	£1,329,000	£8,021,000
Obsolescence			
▪ Functional	£250,000	£50,000	£750,000
▪ Locational	£500,000	£200,000	£1,000,000
▪ Economic	£500,000	£100,000	£1,000,000
Comparable adjusted price per square meter			
▪ Comparable Property 1	£1,750	£950	£730
▪ Comparable Property 2	£1,825	£1,090	£680
▪ Comparable Property 3	£1,675	£875	£725

To prepare for the upcoming meeting, Green has asked her research analyst, Ian Cook, for a valuation of each of these properties under the income, cost and sales comparison approaches using the information provided in Exhibit 1, and the following two assumptions:

Assumption 1   The holding period for each property is expected to be five years.

Assumption 2   Property B is expected to have the same net operating income for the holding period due to existing leases, and a one-time 20% increase in year 6 due to lease rollovers. No further growth is assumed thereafter.

In reviewing Exhibit 1, Green notes the disproportionate estimated obsolescence charges for Property C relative to the other properties and asks Cook to verify the reasonableness of these estimates. Green also reminds Cook that they will need to conduct proper due diligence. In that regard, Green indicates that she is concerned whether a covered parking lot that was added to Property A encroaches (is partially located) on adjoining properties. Green would like for Cook to identify an expert and present documentation to address her concerns regarding the parking lot.

In addition to discussing the new allocation, the CIO informs Green that she wants to discuss the appropriate real estate index for the private equity real estate quadrant at the upcoming meeting. The CIO believes that the current index may result in over-allocating resources to the private equity real estate quadrant.

13 The *most* effective justification that Green could present for directing the increased allocation to her quadrant would be that, relative to the other quadrants, her quadrant of real estate investments:

   A provides greater liquidity.

   B requires less professional management.

   C enables greater decision-making control.

14 Relative to the expected correlation between First Life's portfolio of public REIT holdings and its stock and bond portfolio, the expected correlation between First Life's private equity real estate portfolio and its stock and bond portfolio is *most likely* to be:

   A lower.

   B higher.

   C the same.

15 Which of the properties in Exhibit 1 exposes the owner to the greatest risk related to operating expenses?

   A Property A

   B Property B

   C Property C

16 Which property in Exhibit 1 is *most likely* to be affected by import and export activity?

   A Property A

   B Property B

   C Property C

17 Which property in Exhibit 1 would *most likely* require the greatest amount of active management?

   A Property A

   B Property B

   C Property C

18 Which property in Exhibit 1 is *most likely* to have a percentage lease?

   A Property A

   B Property B

   C Property C

19 The disproportionate charges for Property C noted by Green are *least likely* to explicitly factor into the estimate of property value using the:

   A cost approach.

   B income approach.

   C sales comparison approach.

20 Based upon Exhibit 1, which of the following statements regarding Property A is *most* accurate?

   A The going-in capitalization rate is 13.5%.

   B It appears the riskiest of the three properties.

   C The net operating income in the first year is £298,000.

21 Based upon Exhibit 1, the value of Property C using the direct capitalization method is *closest* to:

A £3,778,900.

B £4,786,700.

C £6,527,300.

22 Based upon Exhibit 1 and Assumptions 1 and 2, the value of Property B using the discounted cash flow method, assuming a five-year holding period, is *closest* to:

A £4,708,700.

B £5,035,600.

C £5,050,900.

23 Which method under the income approach is *least likely* to provide a realistic valuation for Property B?

A Layer method

B Direct capitalization method

C Discounted cash flow method

24 Based upon Exhibit 1, the value of Property A using the cost approach is *closest* to:

A £5,281,000.

B £6,531,000.

C £9,385,000.

25 Based upon Exhibit 1, the value of Property B using the sales comparison approach is *closest* to:

A £4,781,000.

B £4,858,000.

C £6,110,000.

26 Which due diligence item would be *most* useful in addressing Green's concerns regarding Property A?

A Property survey

B Engineering inspection

C Environmental inspection

27 The real estate index currently being used by First Life to evaluate private equity real estate investments is *most likely:*

A an appraisal-based index.

B a transaction-based index.

C the NCREIF property index.

28 Based upon Exhibit 1, the property expected to be most highly leveraged is:

A Property A

B Property B

C Property C

SOLUTIONS

1   B is correct. The lease term for the anchor tenant is typically longer than the usual 3 to 5 year term for smaller tenants. The data in Exhibit 1 suggest that the operating expenses are passed on to the tenant; the sum of Property Management Fees and Other Operating Expenses equal the Expense Reimbursement Revenue. Also, Other Income is only $15,000 suggesting that there is a minimal amount of percentage rent linked to sales thresholds.

2   C is correct. The terminal value using the income approach is $53,632,650 (= Year 6 NOI/terminal cap rate = $3,217,959 / 0.06). The value of the property using the cost approach is $61,000,000 (= Land Value + Building Replacement Cost − Total Depreciation = $7,000,000 + $59,000,000 − $5,000,000). The adjusted sales price per square foot for Sales Comp B is $462 psf (= $395 × 1.17).

3   C is correct. There is a constant growth rate in income and value; growth rate = discount rate (7.25%) − going-in cap rate (5.25%) = 2.00%.

4   B is correct. The value of Property 1 using the discounted cash flow method is $49,750,931, or $49,750,900 rounded, calculated as follows:

		Discount period	Discounted value*
Year 1 NOI	$2,775,840	1	$2,588,196
Year 2 NOI	$2,859,119	2	$2,485,637
Year 3 NOI	$2,944,889	3	$2,387,135
Year 4 NOI	$3,033,235	4	$2,292,540
Year 5 NOI	$3,124,232	5	$2,201,693
Terminal Value**	$53,632,650	5	$37,795,731
Property #1 DCF value			$49,750,932

* Discount rate = 7.25%
** The terminal value = Year 6 NOI/terminal cap rate = $3,217,959/0.06 = $53,632,650

5   C is correct. The direct capitalization method estimate of value for Property #1 is $52,873,143 (= Year 1 NOI/Going-in Cap Rate = $2,775,840/0.0525), which is greater than the estimated DCF value of $49,750,932.

Value of Property #1 under the discounted cash flow method:

		Discount period	Discounted value*
Year 1 NOI	$2,775,840	1	$2,588,196
Year 2 NOI	$2,859,119	2	$2,485,637
Year 3 NOI	$2,944,889	3	$2,387,135
Year 4 NOI	$3,033,235	4	$2,292,540
Year 5 NOI	$3,124,232	5	$2,201,693
Terminal Value**	$53,632,650	5	$37,795,731
Property #1 DCF value			$49,750,932

* Discount rate = 7.25%
** The terminal value = Year 6 NOI/terminal cap rate = $3,217,959/0.06 = $53,632,650

6 C is correct. The estimate of the value of Property #1 using the sales comparison approach is:

	Unadjusted psf	**Adjusted psf**
Sales Comp 1	$415	$394 (= $415 × 0.95)
Sales Comp 2	$395	$462 (= $395 × 1.17)
Sales Comp 3	$400	$480 (= $400 × 1.20)
Average*	$403	$445

Estimated Value of Property #1 = $44,500,000 (= $445 psf × 100,000 sf)

7 C is correct. The due diligence process includes a review of leases for major tenants which would include the grocery anchor tenant. Typically, only major tenant leases will be reviewed in the due diligence process, and smaller tenant leases will likely not be reviewed. Also, the fact that Other Income is only $15,000 suggests that percentage rent linked to sales levels is minimal and has not been underwritten in the valuation and acquisition process.

8 B is correct. Delphinus will expect to earn a higher return on equity with the use of a mortgage to finance a portion of the purchase. The quoted mortgage interest rate of 5.75% is less than the discount rate of 7.25%.

9 A is correct. The maximum amount of debt that an investor can obtain on commercial real estate is usually limited by either the ratio of the loan to the appraised value of the property (loan to value or LTV) or the debt service coverage ratio (DSCR) depending on which measure results in the lowest loan amount. The maximum LTV is 75% of the appraised value of $48,000,000 or $36,000,000. The loan amount based on the minimum DSCR would be $32,183,652 determined as follows:

Maximum debt service = Year 1 NOI/DSCR = $2,775,840/1.5 = $1,850,560

Loan amount (interest only loan) = maximum debt service/mortgage rate = $1,850,560/0.0575 = $32,183,652 (rounded to $32,000,000).

10 A is correct. Benefits of private equity real estate investments include owners' ability to attain diversification benefits, to earn current income, and to achieve tax benefits.

11 A is correct. Business conditions, demographics, the cost of debt and equity capital, and financial leverage are characteristic sources of risk for real estate investments.

12 A is correct. Richmond Life's investment would be a mortgage which falls under private debt on the four quadrants.

13 C is correct. Private equity investments in real estate enable greater decision-making control relative to real estate investments in the other three quadrants. A private real estate equity investor or direct owner of real estate has responsibility for management of the real estate, including maintaining the properties, negotiating leases and collecting rents. These responsibilities increase the investor's control in the decision-making process. Investors in publicly traded REITs or real estate debt instruments would not typically have significant influence over these decisions.

14 A is correct. Evidence suggests that private equity real estate investments have a lower correlation with stocks and bonds than publicly traded REITs. When real estate is publicly traded it tends to behave more like the rest of the stock market than the real estate market.

15 B is correct. Property B is a gross lease, which requires the owner to pay the operating expenses. Accordingly, the owner, First Life, incurs the risk of Property B's operating expenses, such as utilities, increasing in the future.

16 C is correct. Property C is a warehouse, and is most likely affected by import and export activity in the economy. Property A (office) and Property B (retail) would typically be less dependent on import and export activity when compared to a warehouse property.

17 B is correct. Property B is a shopping center and would most likely require more active management than a single tenant office (Property A) or a warehouse (Property C); the owner would need to maintain the right tenant mix and promote the facility.

18 B is correct. Property B is a shopping center, a type of retail property. A percentage lease is a unique aspect of many retail leases, which requires the tenant to pay additional rent once their sales reach a certain level. The lease will typically specify a "minimum rent" that must be paid regardless of the tenant's sales. Percentage rent may be paid by the tenant once the tenant's sales reach a certain level or breakpoint.

19 B is correct. Obsolescence charges reduce the value of a property using the cost approach and are factored into the sales comparison approach by adjustments, including condition and location, to the price per square foot. The cash flows to the property should reflect obsolescence; less rent is received if the property is not of an appropriate design for the intended use, is in a poor location, or if economic conditions are poor. Therefore, obsolescence is implicitly, not explicitly, factored into the estimate of property value using the income approach.

20 B is correct. Property A has been assigned the highest discount rate (11.5%) and thus is considered to be the riskiest investment of the three alternatives. This may be because of the reliance on a single tenant. The going-in capitalization rate is 9.5% (cap rate = discount rate − growth rate). The net operating income (NOI) is £580,500 (= rental income + other income − property management fee = £575,000 + £27,000 − £21,500).

21 C is correct. Under the direct capitalization method, the value of the property = $NOI/(r − g)$.

Calculate net operating income (NOI):

> NOI = rental income + other income − vacancy and collection loss − property management costs
>
> NOI = £590,000 + £29,500 − £59,000 − £22,000 = £538,500

Then, value the property using the cap rate:

> Value of property = £538,500/(11.25% − 3.0%) = £6,527,273, rounded to £6,527,300.

22 B is correct. The value of Property B using the discounted cash flow method is £5,035,600.

The value using the discounted cash flow method is based on the present value of the net operating income (NOI) and the estimated property resale price.

Calculate NOI (constant during five-year holding period from Assumption 2)

NOI = rental income (at full occupancy) + other income − vacancy and collection loss − property management fee − other operating expenses

NOI = £610,000 + £183,000 − £61,000 − £35,000 − £234,000 = £463,000

Estimate property value at end of five years:

NOI starting in year 6 is 20% higher due to lease rollovers (from Assumption 2)

NOI starting in year 6 = £463,000 × 1.20 = £555,600

Terminal cap rate (given) = 11%

Applying the terminal cap rate yields a property value of £5,050,909 (= £555,600/0.11)

Find the present value of the expected annual NOI and the estimated property resale value using the given discount rate of 9.25%:

$$N = 5$$
$$FV = £5,050,909$$
$$PMT = £463,000$$
$$I = 9.25$$

Solving for PV, the current value of the property is estimated to be £5,034,643, or £5,034,600 rounded.

23 B is correct. The net operating income for Property B is expected to be level for the next 5 years, due to existing leases, and grow 20% in year 6. A direct capitalization method would not be appropriate due to the multiple growth rates. A discounted cash flow method that assigns a terminal value, or a layer method, should be used.

24 A is correct. The value of Property A using the cost method is equal to the replacement cost, adjusted for the different types of depreciation (loss in value):

Value of Property A = land value + (replacement building cost + developer's profit) − deterioration − functional obsolescence − locational obsolescence − economic obsolescence = £1,500,000 + (£8,725,000 + £410,000) − £4,104,000 − £250,000 − £500,000 − £500,000 = £5,281,000

25 B is correct. The value of a property using the sales comparison approach equals the adjusted price per square meter using comparable properties times property size. The value of Property B using the sales comparison approach is:

Average adjusted price per square meter of comparable properties 1, 2, and 3 for Property B = (£950 + £1,090 + £875)/3 = £971.67

Applying the £971.67 average adjusted price per square meter to Property B gives a value of £4,858,300 (= £971.67 × 5,000 square meters = £4,858,350, or £4,858,000 rounded).

26 A is correct. A property survey can determine whether the physical improvements, such as the covered parking lot, are in the boundary lines of the site and if there are any easements that would affect the value of the property.

27 A is correct. An appraisal-based index is most likely to result in the over-allocation mentioned by the CIO due to the appraisal lag. The appraisal lag tends to "smooth" the index meaning that it has less volatility. It behaves somewhat like a moving average of what an index would look like if based on values obtained from transactions rather than appraisals. Thus, appraisal-based indices may underestimate the volatility of real estate returns. Because of the lag in the index, appraisal-based real estate indices will also tend to have a lower correlation with other asset classes. This is problematic if the index is used in asset allocation models; the amount allocated to the asset class that appears to have lower correlation with other asset classes and less volatility will be greater than it should be.

28 C is correct. Property C has an expected loan to value ratio of 80%, which is higher than the loan to value ratio for Property A (70%) or Property B (75%).

Publicly Traded Real Estate Securities

by Anthony Paolone, CFA, Ian Rossa O'Reilly, CFA, and David Kruth, CFA

Anthony Paolone, CFA (USA). Ian Rossa O'Reilly, CFA (Canada). David Kruth, CFA (USA).

LEARNING OUTCOMES

Mastery	The candidate should be able to:
☐	a. describe types of publicly traded real estate securities;
☐	b. explain advantages and disadvantages of investing in real estate through publicly traded securities;
☐	c. explain economic value determinants, investment characteristics, principal risks, and due diligence considerations for real estate investment trust (REIT) shares;
☐	d. describe types of REITs;
☐	e. justify the use of net asset value per share (NAVPS) in REIT valuation and estimate NAVPS based on forecasted cash net operating income;
☐	f. describe the use of funds from operations (FFO) and adjusted funds from operations (AFFO) in REIT valuation;
☐	g. compare the net asset value, relative value (price-to-FFO and price-to-AFFO), and discounted cash flow approaches to REIT valuation;
☐	h. calculate the value of a REIT share using net asset value, price-to-FFO and price-to-AFFO, and discounted cash flow approaches.

INTRODUCTION

1

This reading provides an overview of the publicly traded real estate securities, focusing on equity real estate investment trusts (REITs) and their valuation.

Real estate investments may play several roles in a portfolio. Investment in commercial real estate property—also called income-producing, rental, or investment property—may be either in the form of direct ownership investment or indirect investment by means of equity securities. They can provide an above-average current yield compared with other equity investments and may provide a degree of protection against inflation, especially when rental rates are inflation-indexed, rise periodically by pre-determined amounts, or are easily adjusted. Real estate investment can be an effective means of diversification in many investment portfolios.

REITs are the most widely held type of real estate equity security. The valuation of REITs is similar in some respects to the valuation of other kinds of equity securities, but also takes into account unique aspects of real estate and sometimes uses specialized measures. This reading introduces and describes REIT valuation.

The reading is organized as follows: Section 2 provides an overview of publicly traded real estate securities. Section 3 describes publicly traded equity REITs in detail, including their structure, investment characteristics, and analysis and due diligence considerations. Section 4 presents real estate operating companies (REOCs). Sections 5, 6, and 7 present net asset value, relative valuation, and discounted cash flow valuation for REIT shares, respectively. After a mini case study in Section 8, Section 9 summarizes the reading.

2   TYPES OF PUBLICLY TRADED REAL ESTATE SECURITIES

Publicly traded real estate securities fall into two principal categories: equity (i.e., ownership) investments in properties and debt investments (i.e., primarily mortgages secured by properties). Globally, the principal types of publicly traded real estate securities are real estate investment trusts, real estate operating companies, and mortgage-backed securities.

■ **Real estate investment trusts (REITs)** are tax-advantaged entities (companies or trusts) that typically own, operate, and—to a limited extent—develop income-producing real estate property (hereafter, "real estate property" may simply be referred to as "real estate"). Such REITs are called equity REITs. Mortgage REITs make loans secured by real estate. REITs' tax-advantage is a result of being allowed to deduct dividends paid; this deduction effectively makes REITs exempt from corporate income tax.

■ **Real estate operating companies** (REOCs) are ordinary taxable real estate ownership companies. Businesses are organized as REOCs, as opposed to REITs, when they are located in countries that do not have a tax-advantaged REIT regime in place or when they engage to a large extent in the development of real estate properties, often with the intent to sell. The primary cash inflows are from sales of developed or improved properties rather than from recurring lease or rental income.

■ **Mortgage-backed securities** (MBS) are asset-backed securitized debt obligations that represent rights to receive cash flows from portfolios of mortgage loans—mortgage loans on commercial properties in the case of commercial mortgage-backed securities (CMBS) and mortgage loans on residential properties in the case of residential mortgage-backed securities (RMBS). The market capitalization of publicly traded real estate equity securities is greatly exceeded by the market value of real estate debt securities, in particular mortgage-backed securities. Real estate debt securities are discussed further in fixed-income readings in the CFA program curriculum.

In addition to publicly traded real estate securities, there are privately held real estate securities that include private REITs and REOCs, privately held mortgages, private debt issues, and bank debt. Exhibit 1 shows how real estate securities may be classified in four quadrants.

Exhibit 1	Types of Real Estate Securities	
	Public	**Private**
Equity	Equity REITs, REOCs	Private REITs, Private REOCs
Debt	Mortgage REITs, CMBS, RMBS	Mortgages, Private debt, Bank debt

As of the end of September 2011, the market value of publicly traded real estate investment trusts and real estate operating companies globally was approximately US$800 billion, whereas the total face value of residential and commercial mortgage-related securities was approximately US$9 trillion. Details about relative sizes by geographic areas and/or security types are shown in Exhibit 2.

Exhibit 2	Relative Size and Composition of Publicly Traded Real Estate Equity Securities Markets As of 30 September 2011

Panel A: Percentage of market value of publicly traded real estate equity securities (REITs and REOCs) in developed markets

By Region		By Country	
North America	50	United States	44.4
Asia	35	Hong Kong	11.7
Europe	15	Japan	10.2
		Australia	8.4
		United Kingdom	5.5
		Canada	5.3
		Singapore	4.2
		France	3.9
		Switzerland	1.4
		Netherlands	1.3
		Sweden	1.1
		Others	2.6

Panel B: Percentage of market value of publicly traded equity real estate equity securities in developed markets by type of structure

	Global	North America	Europe	Asia
REITs	74	97	68	43
Non-REITs, REOCs	26	3	32	57

Source: Based on data from FTSE EPRA/NAREIT

Publicly traded real estate securities typically retain some of the characteristics of direct ownership of income-producing real estate. Income-producing real estate usually provides relatively predictable, recurring, contractual rental income under the terms of lease agreements. It also tends to generate capital appreciation over the long term (provided there are no major distortions to rental markets from over-building) because the replacement cost of buildings and prices for land tend to increase. Capital appreciation can result from general price inflation, the scarcity of well-located property, local population increases, and/or growth in economic activity. It should be noted, however, that changes in discount rates (the required rate of return of property investors) can also have significant effects on the value of income-producing real estate.

As an investment asset class, income-producing real estate offers the advantages of stability of income based on its contractual revenue from leases and a measure of long-term inflation protection because, over the long term, rents tend to rise with inflation. In the United States over the past 30 years (1980–2010), the FTSE NAREIT All Equity REITs Index achieved a compounded annual total return of 11.9 percent compared with 10.7 percent for the S&P 500 Index and 8.9 percent for the Barclays Capital Aggregate Bond Index. The US Consumer Price Index increased an average of 3.2 percent annually over the period.

The relative stability of income from income-producing real estate also permits substantial financial leverage to be used, typically in the form of mortgage debt (i.e., debt secured by a lien on real property as collateral). Use of financial leverage can enhance rates of return on equity capital when, on an after-tax basis, the rate of return on assets exceeds the interest rate on the mortgage. The ability, however, to use above-average financial leverage brings greater risk.

3   PUBLICLY TRADED EQUITY REITS

Most REITs are **equity REITs** that invest in ownership positions in income-producing real estate. Equity REITs seek to grow cash flows from their owned real estate, to expand ownership through investing in additional properties, and to selectively develop, improve, or redevelop properties.

Publicly traded equity REITs are the focus of this reading.[1] Other REIT types include mortgage REITs and hybrid REITs. **Mortgage REITs** are REITs that invest the bulk (typically 75 percent or more) of their assets in interest-bearing mortgages, mortgage securities, or short-term loans secured by real estate. The total market value of mortgage REITs is relatively small in comparison with equity REITs. **Hybrid REITs** are REITs that own and operate income-producing real estate, as do equity REITs, but invest in mortgages as well. There are relatively few hybrid REITs.

3.1 Market Background

For many decades, real estate equities have represented significant parts of European (notably the United Kingdom) stock markets, whereas real estate development and ownership has featured prominently in the diversified activities of a large number of Asian companies, notably in Hong Kong and Singapore. Real estate equities, although introduced earlier in the US market, did not gain a large representation in US equity markets until after the severe commercial property collapse of the early 1990s. That collapse left many properties either in financially troubled developer/investor hands or in foreclosure. Many such properties were securitized successfully as REITs, exploiting the conservative operating policies mandated by the REIT structure (especially the reliance on contractual rental income) and the conservative financial policies demanded by REIT investors, as discussed in Section 3.3.

---

1 Besides publicly traded REITs, private REITs exist. **Private REITs** are similar to equity REITs in their business model but do not trade on active exchanges. Private REITs are generally sponsored by real estate organizations and have limited liquidity. They are bought by institutional investors or are marketed to small investors by financial planners.

HISTORICAL DEVELOPMENT OF REITS

US REITs, which have provided a model for REIT legislation worldwide, can trace their origins to business trusts formed in Boston, Massachusetts, in the mid-nineteenth century, when the wealth created by the industrial revolution led to increasing demand for real estate investments. State laws at the time prevented a corporation from owning real estate other than that required for its business. The so-called "Massachusetts trust" was the first US legal entity created to specifically permit investment in real estate. It provided for the transfer of shares, limited liability for passive investors, elimination of federal taxation at the trust level, and the retention of specialized management. The structure became less desirable because of changes in tax laws in the first half of the twentieth century, but was revived by the US Congress in 1960. By the early 1970s, a substantial portion of US REITs' assets was concentrated in high risk construction and development loans. Banks, thrifts, and insurance companies could not directly engage in such high-yield lending because of regulations and statutory restrictions, but they did so indirectly by sponsoring publicly funded REITs that bore their names. But poor lending practices, high leverage, and conflicts of interest between banks and their REIT subsidiaries, as well as the effects of an economic recession, a real estate downturn, and changes in tax laws combined to generate numerous developer bankruptcies and a major decline in the number of REITs and their assets. Record high interest rates caused a severe contraction in the real estate industry in the early 1980s. It was not until the early 1990s, after another even more severe commercial property collapse, that REITs became the securitization vehicle of choice in moving property ownership from distressed owners into the better capitalized hands of long-term, income-oriented investors.

From 1990 to 1995, the equity market capitalization of US REITs rose from US$8.5 billion to US$56 billion and the number of REITs almost doubled to 223. As of early 2011, the US REIT industry consists of about 150 REITs with an equity capitalization of approximately US$350 billion.

REITs are important in a number of markets outside the United States. Beginning in the early 1990s, Canada had a significant increase in equity REITs. As of 2011, there are approximately 30 REITs in Canada with a market capitalization of C$38 billion. The REIT structure was introduced in Australia in 1971; as of 2011, there are 70 A-REITs with a market capitalization of over A$100 billion. REITs have been introduced in Japan (J-REITs in 2001), Singapore (S-REITs in 2002), Hong Kong (2005), the United Kingdom (2006), and Germany (G-REITs in 2007). In Brazil, REITs (called Fundos de Investimento Imobiliaro, or FIIs) have existed since 1993 but were first accorded exemption from income taxation in 2006 if owned by individual investors and listed on the stock exchange. The first REIT in the United Arab Emirates was formed in Dubai in 2010. As of early 2011, there are about 30 countries with legislation authorizing REITs.

REIT-type legislation is currently being studied in China, India, and Pakistan. In China, the planned large-scale introduction of REITs has been delayed by the financial crisis of 2007–2009 and government controls on the real estate industry. As a result of their strong growth since the early 1990s, REITs now represent the majority of the available publicly traded real estate equity securities in the world by number and market value.

As shown in Exhibit 3, REIT ownership in the United States—the largest market for REITs in the world—is widely diversified by type of investor.

Exhibit 3	Estimated Ownership of US REITs by Type of Investor
Type of Investor	**Percent**
Index funds	25
Individual investors	15
REIT sector dedicated funds	15

(continued)

Exhibit 3 (Continued)	

Type of Investor	Percent
Pension funds	10
Insiders (managements, boards)	5
Other institutional investors (e.g., stock funds, income funds, hedge funds)	30

Source: J.P. Morgan estimates.

3.2 REIT Structure

REITs can have simple structures in which they hold and operate their properties directly; however, REITs are generally structured to facilitate the tax-efficient acquisition of properties. Umbrella partnership REITs (UPREITs) and DOWNREITs are examples of structures in which partnerships hold REIT properties; the structures have the purpose of avoiding recognition of taxable income if appreciated property is transferred to the REIT. In the United States, most REITs are structured as **UPREITs**, under which the REIT has a controlling interest in and serves as the general partner (with responsibility for operations) of a partnership that owns and operates all or most of the properties.[2] A **DOWNREIT** structure is a variation of the UPREIT under which the REIT owns more than one partnership and may own properties at both the REIT level and the partnership level. A DOWNREIT can form partnerships for each property acquisition it undertakes.

REITs are subject to the same regulatory, financial reporting, disclosure, and governance requirements as other public companies.

3.3 Investment Characteristics

REITs are typically exempt from income taxation at the corporate (or trust) level if a specified majority of their income and assets relate to income-producing property (75 percent or more, depending on the country) and all or virtually all their potentially taxable income is distributed to shareholders (or unit holders). REITs are a tax-efficient conduit for cash flows from rental income. In the United States, REIT distributions to shareholders are classified for tax purposes into ordinary income (taxed at investors' top marginal tax rates); return of capital (the portion of distributions in excess of a REIT's earnings, treated as a return of capital and deducted from the investor's share cost basis for tax purposes); and capital gains (qualifying for lower capital gains tax rates).

The investment characteristics of both public and private REITs generally include the following:

- Exemption from income taxes at the corporate/trust level: REITs are typically required to distribute most of their potentially taxable income to gain exemption from corporate taxation.

- High income distributions: As a result of the distribution requirement, dividend yields are typically significantly higher than the yields on most other publicly traded equities. Exhibit 4 shows representative historic yields for REITs, stocks, and bonds in the United States.

---

2 An UPREIT offers partnership-limited units (convertible into REIT units) to property sellers who do not pay capital gains taxes on their sale of property until they convert their limited-partnership units into REIT shares. Advantages to a property seller, in addition to tax deferral, include diversification, greater liquidity, and professional management.

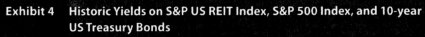

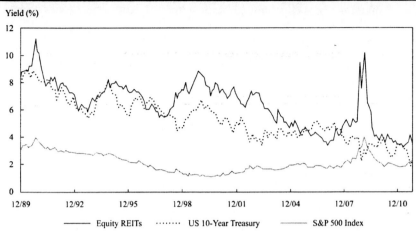

Exhibit 4   Historic Yields on S&P US REIT Index, S&P 500 Index, and 10-year US Treasury Bonds

- Relatively low volatility of reported income: As a result of REIT regulations that require income to be predominantly from rents and interest, REITs typically use conservative, rental-property-focused business models. The contractual nature of rental income (with the exception of hotel REITs) results in relatively stable revenue streams.

- More frequent secondary equity offerings compared with industrial companies: As a result of the distribution requirement, REITs may not be able to retain earnings to finance growth and may need to issue equity to finance property acquisitions. REIT investors should be ready to evaluate the merits of these acquisitions and related financings.

As a result of these features, REITs are relatively stable savings, retirement, and income-producing investments. Compared with direct investments in income-producing property, REITs offer much greater ease of ownership in both small and large amounts, greater liquidity, and opportunities for broader diversification.

3.3.1 *Advantages of Publicly Traded Equity Real Estate Securities*

Compared with owning private real estate assets, publicly traded equity real estate securities, whether equity REITs or REOCs, offer the following advantages:

- *Greater liquidity*: The ability to trade shares on stock exchanges provides greater liquidity than is available in buying and selling real estate in property markets. Thus, such securities permit greater flexibility in timing the realization of cash values and gains/losses. By comparison, direct investments in real estate and in real estate partnerships are generally less immediately liquid and have greater transaction costs even where property markets are quite active and highly sophisticated. These contrasts result from the fact that property transactions are large in relation to average stock market transactions, involve unique properties, and require considerably more time to complete because of the need to negotiate the terms of the transaction and to conduct due diligence (which may include financial, legal, and environmental considerations).

- *Lower investment requirements*: Shares that represent fractional interests in REITs or REOCs can be bought with a much lower investment than a single commercial property.

■ *Limited liability*: Similar to shareholders of other public companies, REIT investors have no liability for the debts and obligations of the REITs in which they invest beyond their original capital investment. Other types of real estate investments, such as limited partnership interests, also can offer limited liability; however, some types of real estate investment (e.g., general partnership interests) can expose the investor to potential liability exceeding his or her original investment.

■ *Access to superior quality and range of properties*: Certain institutional-quality properties are difficult to acquire because most owners (pension funds, private corporations, and REITs) hold them for the long term. Such properties include super-regional shopping malls, large, prominent ("trophy") office buildings, and to a limited extent, landmark luxury hotels. These properties can command superior demand and pricing compared with other properties, given their extremely attractive location, architecture, and/or quality of construction. Investors can gain access to such properties by purchasing the shares of REITs that own them.

■ *Active professional management*: Direct real estate ownership demands real estate expertise or asset/property management skills. Investors in publicly traded real estate equity securities do not require such expertise or skills; investors in REITs and REOCs benefit from having their property interests actively managed on their behalf by professional managers and from having their business interests overseen and guided by boards of directors. The REITs' standards of operating and financial efficiency benefit from the scrutiny and influence of public investors, which encourages best practices on the part of management and boards. Despite the constraint of low-income retention rates, capable managements can still add value by careful specialization by property type and region; by efficient operations focusing on maximizing rental rates and occupancies and minimizing operating costs; by property enhancements, refinancing, sales, and reinvestments; and/or by selected new development activity and property acquisitions financed on attractive terms with debt and/or equity.

■ *Diversification*: By investing in REITs, investors can diversify their real estate portfolios by geography and property type. Such diversification is hard to achieve in direct property investing because of the typically large size and value of each property.

In addition, REITs tend to offer additional advantages compared with publicly traded REOCs:

■ *Taxation*: REITs are typically exempt from the double taxation of income that comes from taxes being due at the corporate level and again when dividends or distributions are made to shareholders, as is the case in some jurisdictions such as the United States. In most jurisdictions, there are no taxes payable by a REIT if it: (1) meets certain requirements for types of assets held, typically rental property (75 percent of total assets in real estate for US REITs), (2) derives the bulk of its income from rents or mortgage interest on real estate (75 percent for US REITs), (3) has limited non-rental property assets, and (4) pays out in dividends/distributions nearly all of its taxable income (at least 90 percent in the United States). The dividends/distributions that REIT shareholders receive are typically divided into ordinary taxable income, capital gains, and return of capital, and are taxed at their respective rates in the first two cases. REIT shareholders do not have to pay current income tax on the portion of distributions that exceeds the REIT's taxable income (calculated after depreciation charges) because that portion of distributions is treated as a return of capital, which is deducted from the shareholders' cost basis for his/her shares. When the shares are eventually sold, the excess of the amount received over the cost basis of the shares is taxed as capital gains. This treatment of portions of their distributions as return of capital is generally favorable for investors from a tax perspective.

■ *Earnings predictability*: The contractual nature of REITs' rental income tends to give them a greater degree of earnings predictability than that of most industrial and natural resource companies.

■ *High income payout ratios and yields*: The typically high income payout ratios of REITs make them among the most stable and highest yielding of publicly traded equities.

REOCs have the following advantage compared with REITs:

■ *Operating flexibility*: REOCs are free to invest in any kind of real estate or related activity subject only to the limitations that may be imposed by their articles of incorporation and/or the market. This flexibility gives management the opportunity to allocate more resources to development activity, which has the potential of delivering high returns. Compared with REITs, REOCs can retain more of their income for re-investment when they believe attractive opportunities exist to create value for investors. REOCs are free to use a wider range of capital structures and degrees of financial leverage in their activities.

In contrast with REOCs, REITs are constrained in their investments, operations, and distributions; these constraints may prevent REITs from maximizing their returns.

EXAMPLE 1

Advantages of Publicly Traded Real Estate Investments

1 Which of the following assets requires the *most* expertise in real estate on the part of the investor?

   A A REOC share

   B An equity REIT share

   C A direct investment in a single property

2 Which of the following has the *most* operating and financial flexibility?

   A A REOC

   B An equity REIT

   C A direct investment in a single property

Solution to 1:

C is correct. Direct investment in a single property requires a high level of real estate expertise. Investment in publicly traded equity investments (in REITs or REOCs) requires much less expertise because investors benefit from having their property interests actively managed on their behalf by professional managers and from having their business interests overseen and guided by boards of directors, as in the case of all public corporations.

Solution to 2:

A is correct. REOCs are free to invest in any kind of real estate or related activity without limitation. This freedom gives management the opportunity to create more value in development activity and in trading real estate and to retain as much of their income as they believe is appropriate. A wider range of capital structures and degrees of financial leverage may be used in the process. In contrast with REOCs, REITs face restrictions on the amount of income and assets accounted for by activities other than collecting rent and interest payments. Direct investment is less liquid and divisible than REOC and REIT shares, which limits the operational flexibility of such investment.

3.3.2 *Disadvantages of Publicly Traded Equity Real Estate Securities*

Potential disadvantages of publicly traded real estate securities include those related to the following:

■ *Taxation*: Although REITs are typically tax-advantaged compared with generic common share investment, direct property investment has tax advantages compared with both REIT and REOC investing. Unlike direct property ownership and partnership investments in some countries, REITs and REOCs generally cannot pass on tax losses to their investors as deductions from their taxable income. Also, in jurisdictions permitting deferral of tax when a property investment is exchanged or sold and replaced by similar property within a short period of time (e.g., the 180-day "Section 1031 Like-Kind Exchange" rule in the United States), REIT shares do not qualify for such tax-deferred exchanges.

■ *Control*: Minority shareholders in a publicly traded REIT have less control over property-level investment decisions than do direct property owners.

■ *Costs*: The maintenance of a publicly traded REIT structure is costly and may not be recouped by offsetting benefits if the REIT lacks sufficient economies of scale or the value added by management is small.

■ *Stock market determined pricing and returns*: The stock market value of a REIT is more volatile than the appraised **net asset value** of a REIT, suggesting risk is lower for direct property investors. But net asset values based on appraised values rather than actual transaction prices tend to underestimate volatility.[3] Appraised values tend to be backward-looking by nature (because of typically being based on the sales price of comparable property transactions that have already closed) and may not react to changes in market trends. Additionally, there is a psychological tendency to smooth valuations by ignoring outlier transactions.

■ *Structural conflicts and related costs*: The use of UPREIT and DOWNREIT structures can create conflicts of interest between the partnership and REIT shareholders when it comes to making decisions on the disposition of properties or increasing company debt levels and may involve additional administrative costs. For example, the disposition of a particular property or the use of more mortgage debt financing might have tax implications for the limited partners who sold the property to the operating partnership and tax considerations could cause their interests to vary from the best interests of the REIT as a whole.

■ *Relatively moderate income growth potential*: The relatively low rate of income retention by REITs implies a low rate of reinvestment for future growth. This low rate of reinvestment tends to reduce income growth potential. Relatedly, the stock market's tendency to focus on earnings growth can cause REIT shares to underperform in periods during which the market highly values fast-growing companies; such periods tend to coincide with time of high consumer, business, and investor confidence.

---

3 Appraised values are based on a range of considerations including recent market prices for comparable property sales (assuming willing buyers and willing sellers were involved), discounted cash flow analysis, and **depreciated replacement cost**. Property appraisal is discussed in the reading on private real estate investment.

- *Potential for forced equity issuance at disadvantageous prices*: REITs typically use financial leverage and are regularly in the debt markets to refinance their maturing debt. If a REIT's management of its overall financial leverage and the timing and type of its debt maturities is flawed, these issues can combine with a lack of substantial retained cash flow to force equity issuance at dilutive prices, especially during periods of weak credit availability (e.g., 2008–2009). Note that timely debt and equity financing and share repurchase activity if market prices fall below intrinsic values, using the retained portion of operating cash flows or the proceeds of debt issuance or property sales, can yield benefits to remaining REIT shareholders.

EXAMPLE 2

Publicly Traded Real Estate Investments

1 Which of the following types of real estate investment is *most* appropriate for an investor seeking to maximize control?
   A   REIT
   B   REOC
   C   Direct investment in income-producing property
2 Which of the following best represents an advantage of REITs over a direct investment in an income-producing property?
   A   Diversification
   B   Operating flexibility
   C   Income growth potential

Solution to 1:

C is correct. Control is most characteristic of a direct investment in and ownership of income-producing property.

Solution to 2:

A is correct. REITs provide diversification of property holdings. B is incorrect because REITs do face restrictions on the amount of income and assets accounted for by activities other than collecting rent and interest payments; these restrictions can prevent a REIT from maximizing its returns. C is incorrect because the relatively low rates of income retention that are required to maintain a REIT's tax-free status can detract from income growth potential.

EXAMPLE 3

Investment Objectives

Two real estate investors are each choosing from among the following investment types: REOC, equity REIT, or a direct investment in an income-producing property. Investor A's primary objective is liquidity, and Investor B's primary objective is maximum growth/capital gain potential. State and explain which real estate investment type best suits:

1 Investor A.
2 Investor B.

Solution to 1:

For Investor A, with a liquidity objective, REOC and REIT investments are most appropriate because REOCs and REITs are traded on stock exchanges and are more liquid. Direct investments in income-producing property are generally less liquid.

Solution to 2:

For Investor B, with a maximum growth objective, REOCs and direct property investment are most appropriate because REOCs and direct investors are free to invest in any kind of real estate or related activity without limitation and to reinvest as much of their income as they believe is appropriate for their objectives. This freedom gives them the opportunity to create more value in development activity and in trading real estate. REITs' constraints prevent them from retaining earnings to reinvest, so their growth opportunities are more limited.

3.4 Considerations in Analysis and Due Diligence

For equity REITs as a group, key specific investment characteristics, opportunities, and risks should be assessed when conducting due diligence of their shares for investment purposes.

- *Remaining lease terms.* Short remaining lease terms provide mark-to-market opportunities on rents. They are a positive consideration in an expansionary economy and/or rental rate environment and a negative one in a declining economy and/or rental market. Hotels and multi-family residential properties have the shortest lease terms, whereas shopping centers, offices, and industrial buildings typically have the longest lease terms.

- *Inflation protection.* Leases that have pre-set periodic increases in rent throughout the lease term (or that have minimum or base rents linked to the local inflation rate) provide a degree of inflation protection for investors.

- *Market rent analysis.* Current market rents should be compared with rents paid by existing tenants. Low in-place rents provide upside potential to cash flows upon lease re-negotiation and high in-place rents represent additional risk to maintaining current cash flows.

- *Costs of re-leasing space.* Costs to lease space when a lease matures typically include brokerage commissions, allowances for tenants' improvements to their space, free rent, and downtime between leases. Such costs can be burdensome for landlords.

- *Tenant concentration.* Tenants that rent significant amounts of space and the percentage of rents paid by these significant tenants should be noted. Assessing the financial strength of significant tenants and the risk they pose to the REIT are important parts of necessary due diligence.

- *Availability of new competitive supply.* The potential for new competitive supply to the REIT's existing properties should be analyzed by examining new buildings under construction or planned by other developers and by assessing the likelihood of more projects gaining approval.

- *Balance sheet/leverage analysis.* A detailed review of the REIT's balance sheet, including leverage levels, cost of debt, and debt maturity profile should be completed.

- *Management.* Due diligence should include a review of senior management's background, skill sets, track records, years of experience, and length of time with the REIT.

The next section describes subtypes of equity REITs and any due diligence considerations that apply specifically to the subtypes.

3.5 Equity REITs: Property Subtypes

Equity REITs, the predominant form of REITs, are actively managed enterprises seeking to maximize the returns from their property portfolios by applying management skills in operations and finance. For this reason, most REITs focus on a particular property type, striving to excel in operating efficiency and growth while still being mindful of risk-reducing strategies, including diversification by geography and by the number and quality of properties and tenants. The analysis of equity REITs is conducted along the same lines as that of publicly traded equities in general: commencing with industry analysis, followed by company analysis, and then equity valuation. Certain specific economic value determinants, investment characteristics, risks, and areas for analysis and due diligence, apply to each property subtype of REITs shown in Exhibit 5.

Exhibit 5	Global REITs by Property Type Held
Property Type	**Percentage of Total**
Shopping center/Retail	23.3
Office	14.5
Residential	11.3
Healthcare	6.8
Hotel/Resort	2.7
Industrial	4.2
Industrial/Office	1.0
Self-storage	2.6
Diversified	33.6

The following sections discuss these property types in more detail.

3.5.1 *Shopping Center/Retail REITs*

Shopping center or **retail REITs** invest in such retail properties as regional shopping malls, community/neighborhood shopping centers, and to a lesser degree, premium retail space in leading cities.

Regional shopping malls are large spaces, often enclosed, in which retailing tends to be in higher-priced discretionary goods (e.g., fashionable clothing). Tenants' leases in regional malls usually have terms of 3–10 years and typically require tenants—except for the largest "anchor" retailers—to pay the greater of a fixed-minimum rental rate and a percentage of their sales. "Anchor" retailers, however, have very long-term, fixed-rent leases or own their premises. As part of their total rent under typical **net leases**, tenants pay a **net rent**, all of which goes to the landlord, plus a share of the common area costs of the mall based on their proportionate share of the space leased. Despite the link between tenants' sales and rent, revenue streams are relatively stable because of high levels of minimum rent that often represent well over 90 percent of revenue.

Community shopping centers—consisting of stores linked by open-air walkways or, in the case of so-called "power centers" or "big-box centers," linked by parking lots— generally provide such basic necessity goods and services as food and groceries, home furnishings, hardware, discount merchandise, fast food, and banking, with similar lease maturities but non-participatory rents that are usually subject to periodic increases.

For shopping center REITs, analysts often analyze such factors as rental rates and sales per square foot/meter for the rental property portfolio, dividing them into same portfolio and new space addition components.

3.5.2 Office REITs

Office REITs invest in and manage multi-tenanted office properties in central business districts of cities and suburban markets. Lease terms are typically long (5–25 years) with contractual base rents that are fixed and adjust upward (typically every 5–10 years). In addition to base rents, tenants pay their proportionate share of operating expenses, common area costs, and property taxes. Rental income tends to be stable year-to-year, but over the longer term (5–10 years) it can be affected by changes in office market vacancy and rental rates that characterize the office industry cycle. This cycle arises because of long office tower construction and interior finishing periods (three or more years) and the willingness of developers to build large buildings in which only a portion of the space has been preleased. These factors result in the commencement of construction of new space during periods of strong economic growth and the completion of new space potentially during economic downturns when tenant demand is low.

Analysts of office REITs pay particular attention to new space under construction in a REIT's local market, to site locations and access to public transportation and highways, and to business conditions for a REIT's principal tenants. Analysts also focus on the quality of a REIT's office space, focusing on such factor as location, convenience, utilitarian and architectural appeal, and the age and durability of the building.

3.5.3 Industrial REITs

Industrial REITs hold portfolios of single-tenant or multi-tenant industrial properties that are used as warehouses, distribution centers, light manufacturing facilities, and small office or "flex" space for sales, administrative, or related functions.

Industrial property and industrial REITs are less cyclical than some other property/REIT types including hotel, health care, and storage. The long-term net leases (5–25 years) that pertain to industrial space, the short time required to build industrial buildings (usually well under a year), and the tendency to build and prelease and/or build space to suit particular tenants dampen any rapid change of rental income and values.

Analysts pay particular attention to trends in tenants' requirements and the impact these can have on the obsolescence of existing space and the need for new types of space. Strategic property locations—such as near a port, airport, or highway—are important positive considerations. Shifts in the composition of national and local industrial bases and trade play important roles in this regard and can sometimes be difficult to detect and forecast. Trends in new supply and demand in the local market are closely scrutinized.

3.5.4 Multi-family/Residential REITs

Multi-family/residential REITs invest in and manage rental apartments for lease to individual tenants, typically using one-year leases. Rental apartment demand tends to be relatively stable, but fluctuations in rental income can occur as a result of competition from condominium construction, tenant (move-in) inducements, regional economic strengths and weaknesses, the effects of inflation on such operating costs as energy and other utility costs, and taxes and maintenance costs (because apartment leases often tend to be **gross leases** under which many or all of such costs are paid for by the landlord).

Analysts pay particular attention to local demographics and income trends, age and competitive appeal, cost and availability of homeownership in local markets, and the degree of government control of local residential rents. Fuel and energy costs receive particular attention because properties are usually leased under gross leases that require landlords to pay for part or all of the building operating costs.

3.5.5 Storage REITs

Storage REITs own and operate self-storage properties, sometimes referred to as mini-warehouse facilities. Space in these facilities is rented under gross leases (i.e., no additional payments are due for operating costs or property taxes), usually on a monthly basis by individuals for storing personal items and by small businesses. Ease of entry into this growing field has led to periods of overbuilding.

Analysts pay special attention to the rate of construction of new competitive facilities, trends in housing sales activity that can affect the demand for temporary storage, local demographic trends, new business start-up activity, and seasonal trends in demand for storage facilities that can be significant in some markets.

3.5.6 Health Care REITs

Health care REITs invest in skilled nursing facilities (nursing homes), assisted living and independent residential facilities for retired persons, hospitals, medical office buildings, and rehabilitation centers. In many countries, REITs are not permitted to operate these facilities themselves if they wish to maintain their REIT status and must lease them to health care providers; these leases are usually net leases. REITs may jeopardize their tax status (no tax at trust level) if they are found to be operating a business in violation of their passive investment restriction. Although largely resistant to the effects of economic recessions, health care REITs are exposed to the effects of population demographics, government funding programs for health care, construction cycles, the financial condition of health care facilities operators/lessees, and any costs arising from litigation by residents.

Analysts scrutinize operating trends in facilities, in government funding, in litigation settlements, and insurance costs. Amounts of competitors' new facilities under construction in relation to prospective demand and prospects for acquisitions are also key points of focus.

3.5.7 Hotel REITs

Hotel REITs own hotel properties but, similar to health care REITs, in many countries they must refrain from operating their properties themselves to maintain their tax-advantaged REIT status. Hotel REITs typically lease all their properties to taxable REIT subsidiaries (or to third-party lessees) who operate them ensuring the hotel REIT parent receives passive rental income. This rental income typically accounts for the major portion of a hotel's net operating cash flow. Management of the hotel is usually turned over to hotel management companies, many of which own widely recognized hotel brands. The net effect of this structure is that although the hotel REIT is tax exempt to the extent that it meets its income distribution and other REIT requirements, a minor portion of net operating cash flow from hotel properties may be subject to income taxation. The hotel sector is cyclical because it is not protected by long-term leases and is thus exposed to business-cycle driven short-term changes in regional, national, and international business and leisure travel. Exposure to travel disruptions also increases revenue volatility.

Analysts examine trends in occupancies, average room rates, and operating profit margins by hotel type and geographic location; statistics are compared with industry averages published by government and private-sector hotel industry statistics providers. Revenue per available room (RevPAR), the product of average room rate by average occupancy, is a widely monitored barometer of the hotel business. Attention is also paid to trends in hotel room forward bookings by category (individual, corporate, group, and convention), in food and beverage and banqueting sales, and in margins. Expenditures on maintaining and improving property, plant, and equipment are scrutinized, and the rates of new room construction and completion in local markets are watched very closely in view of the cyclicality of demand and the long duration of hotel construction (typically 1.5 to 3 years). Because income is so variable in this sector, analysts need to be wary of hotel REITs that use high financial leverage.

3.5.8 Diversified REITs

Diversified REITs own and operate in more than one type of property and are more common in Europe and Asia than in the United States. Some investors favor the reduced risk and wider opportunities that come from diversification. An analysis of management's experience with each property type and degree of local market presence are obviously important in reviewing diversified REITs.

3.6 Economic Drivers

Exhibit 6 shows major economic factors affecting REITs and their relative importance for different types of equity REITs. The measures of relative importance should be viewed as an approximate guide only because the relative importance can vary especially for extreme changes in the economic factors. Over the course of a full business cycle, however, the measures of relative importance shown tend to apply.

Risks tend to be greatest for those REITs in property-type sectors where tenant/occupant demand for space can fluctuate most widely in the short-term (notably hotels) and in which dislocations between supply and demand are most likely to occur (notably office, hotel, and health care). However, the quality and locations of properties held by a REIT, their leasing, and financing status are also extremely important factors in determining a REIT's risk profile.

Exhibit 6	Importance of Factors Affecting Economic Value for Various Property Types				
	National GDP Growth	Job Creation	Retail Sales Growth	Population Growth	New Space Supply vs. Demand
Retail	1	3	2	4	4
Office	1	2	5	4	3
Industrial	1	5	2	3	4
Multi-family	1	2	5	2	4
Storage	1	3	5	2	4
Health care	1	4	5	2	3
Hotels	1	2	5	4	3

Note: 1 = most important, 5 = least important
Source: Based on data from the authors' research

Growth in the economy or national GDP is generally the most important single economic factor affecting the outlook for all types of property and REITs. Retail sales growth is reflected in the sales growth of shopping center tenants and influences directly (through rental rates based on a percentage of sales) and indirectly (through tenants' ability to pay more rent and landlords' efforts to take advantage of this increase) the rental rates and occupancies in shopping centers.

Job creation tends to be reflected in increased demand for office space to accommodate white collar workers and in requirements for more retail space to cater to related increases in spending. Job creation also tends to be reflected in (1) increased demand for multi-family accommodation as newly employed people gain the financial means to rent their own accommodation, (2) greater hotel room demand as leisure and business travel increase in response to an expanded workforce, and (3) increased use of storage space as personal and small business needs for space rise.

Office, hotel, and health care properties and the REITs that invest in those property types are more prone to supply–demand dislocations because of (1) the long time taken to construct new space (space on which construction commences in a booming economy may be completed two or three years later, potentially during a recession) and (2) the large size of many facilities, which can contribute to excess supply on completion. Population growth tends to be reflected in increased demand for multi-family accommodations, storage, and health care facilities.

EXAMPLE 4

REITs and Due Diligence

1   Which of the following statistics is similarly relevant for a shopping center, office, or hotel REIT?

   A   Occupancy

   B   Forward bookings

   C   Sales per square foot

2   Which of the following types of REITs is *least* directly sensitive to population growth?

   A   Office

   B   Health care

   C   Multi-family residential

3   In addition to the analysis of occupancy, rental rate, lease expiry, and financing statistics, analysts of office REITs are *most likely* to pay particular attention to trends in:

   A   job creation.

   B   population growth.

   C   retail sales growth.

4   Which of the following types of REITs would be expected to experience the *greatest* cash flow volatility?

   A   Hotel

   B   Industrial

   C   Shopping center

Solution to 1:

A is correct. Occupancy is a critical variable for all three types of REITs. Forward bookings would be relevant for only hotel REITs; sales per square foot for shopping center REITs.

Solution to 2:

A is correct. Population growth ranks as a less significant factor for office REITs and a more significant factor for health care and multi-family residential REITs. Different economic factors affect different property types to a varying degree, given their lease structures and competitive environment.

Solution to 3:

A is correct. Job creation is most significant for office REITs. Population growth is more significant for multi-family, storage, and health care REITs than for office REITs, as shown in Exhibit 6, whereas retail sales growth is more significant for shopping center/retail and industrial REITs than for office REITs.

Solution to 4:

A is correct. Hotel room demand fluctuates with economic activity; there are no long-term leases on hotel rooms to protect hotel REITs' revenue streams from changes in demand. Industrial and shopping center REITs benefit from long-term leases on their properties and from the relatively mild dislocations between supply and demand caused by the construction of new space in these sub-sectors.

4 REAL ESTATE OPERATING COMPANIES

Publicly traded real estate equities exist in forms other than REITs. **Real estate operating companies** (REOCs) are ordinary taxable corporations that operate in the real estate industry in countries that do not have a tax-advantaged REIT regime in place or are engaged in real estate activities of a kind and to an extent that do not fit within their country's REIT framework. Such ineligible activity generally takes the form of development or land investment in which the cash flows are not recurring income from lease revenues. Examples of such REOCs are

- Hongkong Land, a leading office investor and residential developer listed in Singapore (registered in Bermuda, part of Singapore Straits Times Index; this company left Hong Kong prior to the 1997 transfer to China),
- Brookfield Office Properties, an international office investor and property manager listed in Toronto and New York with a low income payout ratio, and
- China Vanke, China's largest residential property developer.

REOCs offer essentially the same advantages and disadvantages as REITs with respect to investing in real estate directly, but with some differences.

REITs and REOCs face similar operating and financial risks as private real estate investments, including leasing, operating, financing, and market risks as well as exposure to general economic risk. Despite certain advantages of REOCs, such as operating flexibility, the equity markets of most countries show a preference for the tax advantages, high-income distributions, and rigorous operating and financial mandates that come with REIT status. Consequently, in many markets there is a tendency for REOCs to experience less access to equity capital and lower market valuations (and higher cost of equity) than REITs. REOCs are usually able to elect to convert to

REIT status if they meet the general requirements of REITs but, depending on their countries of domicile, must consider potential local tax consequences for themselves and their shareholders that may be triggered by the change.[4]

REOCs

1   Which of the following statements is *most* accurate?

    A   REOCs are subject to the same tax rules as trusts.

    B   REOCs are subject to the same tax rules as ordinary corporations.

    C   REITs usually cannot elect to convert to REOCs without changing their income payout rates and sources of income.

2   Which of the following statements is *most* accurate? REOCs:

    A   can invest in any type of real estate without losing their tax status.

    B   are a more prevalent and popular investment asset class than REITs globally.

    C   do not pay any income taxes if they pay out all their taxable income to their shareholders.

Solution to 1:

B is correct. REOCs are taxed in the same way as ordinary corporations. A is not correct because REOCs are taxed as corporations; C is not correct because REITs do not need to change their income payout rates or sources of income to become REOCs.

Solution to 2:

A is correct. REOCs, unlike REITs, can generally invest in any type of real estate without losing their tax status. C is incorrect because REOCs do not enjoy such a tax advantage. B is incorrect because, as shown in Exhibit 2, REOCs globally represent less invested capital than REITs.

VALUATION: NET ASSET VALUE APPROACH

5

Approaches analysts take to valuing equity include those based on asset value estimates, price multiple comparisons, and discounted cash flow. These general approaches are used to value shares of REITs and REOCs and will be addressed in Sections 5, 6, and 7, respectively.

Two possible measures of value that analysts might use are book value per share (BVPS) and net asset value per share (NAVPS) based on reported accounting values and market values for assets, respectively. NAVPS is the relevant valuation measure for valuing REITs and REOCs.

NAVPS is often used as a fundamental benchmark for the value of a REIT or REOC. Discounts in the REIT share price from NAVPS are interpreted as indications of potential undervaluation, and premiums in the REIT share price to NAVPS, in the

---

4 Because their leverage is high and they can use accelerated depreciation, REOCs' cash tax liabilities are frequently relatively low.

absence of indications of positive future events, such as a successful property development completion or expected high value creation by a management team, suggest potential overvaluation. By way of qualification, however, these assessments must be made in the context of the stock market's tendency to be forward looking in its valuations and at times to have different investment criteria from property markets.

The net asset value may be viewed as the largest component of the intrinsic value of a REIT or REOC, the balance being investors' assessments of the value of any non-asset-based income streams (e.g., fee or management income), the value added by management of the REIT or REOC, and the value of any contingent liabilities.[5]

Section 5.1 explains why BVPS can diverge from NAVPS; analysts need to understand in detail the accounting for REITs' investment properties in order to evaluate the relevance of accounting information. Section 5.2 then illustrates the estimation of NAVPS.

5.1 Accounting for Investment Properties

The value of the investment property portfolio of a REIT or REOC is a very important element in the valuation of its shares. Analysts should take care to understand the basis on which a REIT's investment properties are valued. If accounting is on a fair value basis, accounting values may be relevant for asset-based valuation. If historical cost values are used, however, accounting values are generally not relevant.

Investment property is defined under International Financial Reporting Standards (IFRS) as property that is owned (or, in some cases, leased under a finance lease) for the purpose of earning rentals or capital appreciation or both. Buildings owned by a company and leased to tenants are investment properties. In contrast, other long-lived tangible assets (i.e., property considered to be property, plant, and equipment) are owner-occupied properties used for producing the company's goods and services or for housing the company's administrative activities. Investment properties do not include long-lived tangible assets held for sale in the ordinary course of business. For example, the houses and property owned by a housing construction company are considered to be its inventory.

Under IFRS, companies are allowed to value investment properties using either a cost model or a fair value model. The cost model is identical to the cost model used for property, plant, and equipment. Under the fair value model, all changes in the fair value of the asset affect net income. To use the fair value model, a company must be able to reliably determine the property's fair value on a continuing basis. In general, a company must apply its chosen model (cost or fair value) to all of its investment property. If a company chooses the fair value model for its investment property, it must continue to use the fair value model until it disposes of the property or changes its use such that it is no longer considered investment property (e.g., it becomes owner-occupied property or part of inventory). The company must continue to use the fair value model for that property even if transactions on comparable properties, used to estimate fair value, become less frequent.

Investment property appears as a separate line item on the balance sheet. Companies are required to disclose whether they use the fair value model or the cost model for their investment property. If the company uses the fair value model, it must make additional disclosures about how it determines fair value and must provide reconciliation between the beginning and ending carrying amounts of investment property. If

---

5 The intrinsic value of an investment, as discussed in other parts of the CFA curriculum, is the value ascribed to an investment on the basis of a hypothetically complete understanding of its characteristics. It is generally estimated on a going-concern basis.

the company uses the cost model, it must make additional disclosures—for example, the depreciation method and useful lives must be disclosed. In addition, if the company uses the cost model, it must also disclose the fair value of investment property.

In contrast to IFRS, under US generally accepted accounting principles (US GAAP), there is no specific definition of investment property. Most operating companies and real estate companies in the United States that hold investment-type property use the historical cost accounting model. This model does not accurately represent the economic values of assets and liabilities or the current economic return or income to a business in environments of significant price and cost changes. This issue is especially evident in companies whose businesses involve the purchase and long-term retention of assets, notably real estate, because under historical cost accounting, assets including buildings are generally carried at depreciated historical cost. These figures can be written down when they undergo a permanent impairment in economic value, but they can only be written up under exceptional circumstances, such as mergers, acquisitions, or reorganizations. The historical cost accounting practices that prevail in regard to investment property assets in the United States, the largest market for REITs in the world, tend to distort the measure of economic income and asset value by understating carrying values on long-held property assets and overstating depreciation on assets that are often appreciating in value because of general price inflation or other property-specific reasons.

5.2 Net Asset Value Per Share: Calculation

As a result of shortcomings in accounting reported values, investment analysts and investors use estimates of **net asset value per share**. NAVPS is the difference between a real estate company's assets and its liabilities, *all taken at current market values instead of accounting book values*, divided by the number of shares outstanding. NAVPS is a superior measure of the net worth of a company compared with book value per share.

In valuing a REIT's or REOC's real estate portfolio, analysts will look for the results of existing appraisals if they are available (such as those provided by companies reporting under IFRS). If they are not available or if they disagree with the assumptions or methodology of the appraisals, analysts will often capitalize the rental streams—represented by net operating income (NOI)—produced by a REIT's or REOC's properties, using a market required rate of return. The market required rate of return, usually referred to as the **capitalization rate** or "**cap rate**," is the rate used in the marketplace in recent transactions to capitalize similar-risk future income streams into a present value. It is calculated as the NOI of a comparable property or portfolio of comparable properties divided by the total value of the comparable(s) as represented by transaction prices. Analysts will often seek to corroborate the property valuations obtained with price per square foot information on transactions involving similar types of properties, as well as replacement cost information (adjusted for depreciation and the age and condition of the buildings). These estimated asset values will be substituted for the book values of the properties on the balance sheet and adjustments made to any related accounting assets, such as capitalized leases, to avoid double counting.

Generally, goodwill, deferred financing expenses, and deferred tax assets will be excluded to arrive at a "hard" economic value for total assets. Liabilities will be similarly adjusted to replace the face value of debt with market values if these are significantly different (e.g., as a result of changes in interest rates) and any such "soft" liabilities as deferred tax liabilities will be removed. The revised net worth of the company divided by the number of shares outstanding is the NAV. Although this figure is calculated before provision for any income or capital gains taxes that might be payable on liquidation, the inability to predict how the company or its assets might be sold and the prospect that it might be kept intact in an acquisition cause investors to look to the pre-tax asset value as their primary net worth benchmark. If a company has held its assets for many years and has a very low remaining depreciable value for its assets for tax purposes, this can color investors' perspectives on valuation. Quantifying the effects of a low adjusted cost base, however, is impeded by lack of knowledge of the tax circumstances and strategies of a would-be acquirer.

Exhibit 7 provides an example of the calculations involved in estimating NAV based on capitalizing rental streams. Because the book values of assets are based on historical costs, the analyst estimates NAVPS. First, by capitalizing NOI with certain adjustments, the analyst obtains an estimate of the value of rental properties, then the value of other tangible assets is added and the total netted of liabilities. This net amount, NAV, is then divided by the number of shares outstanding to obtain NAVPS.

The second line in Exhibit 7 shows the adjustment to remove **non-cash rents**; these are the result of the accounting practice of "straight lining" the rental revenue from long-term leases. (The amount of this deduction is the difference between the average contractual rent over the leases' terms and the cash rent actually paid.) NOI is also increased to reflect a full year's rent for properties acquired during the course of the year, resulting in pro forma "cash NOI" for the previous 12 months of $267,299,000. This figure is then increased to include expected growth for the next 12 months at 1.5 percent, resulting in expected next 12-months cash NOI of $271,308,000.

An appropriate capitalization rate is then estimated based on recent transactions for comparable properties in the property market. An estimated value for the REIT's operating real estate is obtained by dividing expected next 12-months cash NOI by the decimalized capitalization rate (in this case, 0.07). The book values of the REIT's other tangible assets including cash, accounts receivable, land for future development, and prepaid expenses are added to obtain estimated gross asset value. (Land is sometimes taken at market value if this can be determined reliably; but because land is often difficult to value and of low liquidity, analysts tend to use book values.) From this figure, debt and other liabilities (but not deferred taxes because this item is an accounting provision rather than an economic liability) are subtracted to obtain net asset value. Division by the number of shares outstanding produces NAVPS.

Exhibit 7	Analyst Adjustments to REIT financials to obtain NAVPS
Office Equity REIT Inc.	
Net Asset Value Per Share Estimate	
(In Thousands, Except Per Share Data)	
Last 12-months real estate NOI	$270,432
Less: Non-cash rents	7,667
Plus: Adjustment for full impact of acquisitions (1)	4,534
Pro forma cash NOI for last 12 months	$267,299
Plus: Next 12 months growth in NOI (2)	$4,009
Estimated next 12 months cash NOI	$271,308
Assumed cap rate (3)	7.00%
Estimated value of operating real estate	$3,875,829
Plus: Cash and equivalents	$65,554
Plus: Land held for future development	34,566
Plus: Accounts receivable	45,667
Plus: Prepaid/Other assets (4)	23,456
Estimated gross asset value	$4,045,072
Less: Total debt	$1,010,988

Exhibit 7	(Continued)

Office Equity REIT Inc.
Net Asset Value Per Share Estimate
(In Thousands, Except Per Share Data)

Less: Other liabilities	119,886
Net asset value	$2,914,198
Shares outstanding	55,689

1 50 percent of the expected return on acquisitions was made in the middle of 2010.

2 Growth is estimated at 1.5 percent.

3 Cap rate is based on recent comparable transactions in the property market.

4 This figure does not include intangible assets.

NAVPS is calculated to be $2,914,198 divided by 55,689 shares, which equals $52.33 per share.

5.3 Net Asset Value Per Share: Application

REITs have a relatively active private investment market for their business assets; namely, the direct investment property market. This market facilitates the estimation of a REIT's or REOC's net asset value: an estimate of the value of their underlying real estate if it were sold in the private market, debt obligations were satisfied, and the remaining capital—the net asset value—was distributed to shareholders. This approach is unique to REITs and REOCs because commercial real estate assets transact relatively frequently in the private market, and as a result an investor can make observations about how such properties trade on the basis of the capitalization rate (the rate obtained by dividing net operating income by total value) or on the basis of price per square foot, and apply these valuations to the assets of a public company. In fact, in the United States, it is estimated that only 10–15 percent of commercial real estate is held by publicly traded REITs, thus making the private market far larger than the public market, although less active. To draw a parallel, using a NAV approach to value REITs is much like using the sum-of-the-parts approach to valuing a company with multiple business lines.

The NAV approach to valuation is most often used by sector-focused real estate investors that view REITs and REOCs primarily as liquid forms of commercial real estate ownership. Value-oriented investors also tend to focus on NAV when stocks are trading at significant discounts to the underlying value of the assets. In addition, NAV analysis becomes particularly important when there is significant leveraged buyout (LBO) activity in the broader market. At such times, LBO sponsors attempt to buy REITs trading at large discounts to NAV to realize their underlying real estate value. Conversely, when REIT stocks trade at large premiums to NAV, IPO activity and stock issuance activity increases because the public markets are essentially ascribing more value to the real estate than the private markets are. Over time, REITs and REOCs in the United States and globally have at times traded at premiums-to-NAV of more than 25 percent and at other times at discounts from NAV exceeding 25 percent. Thus, if the NAV of a REIT were $20/share, the stock might trade as low as $15/share or as high as $25/share, depending on a range of factors.

5.3.1 *Important Considerations in a NAV-Based Approach to Valuing REITs*

Although NAV estimates provide investors with a specific value, there are a number of important considerations that should be taken into account when using this approach to value REITs and REOCs. First, investors must understand the implications of using a private market valuation tool on a publicly traded security. In this context, it is useful to examine how NAVs are calculated.

The methods most commonly used to calculate NAV are (1) using a capitalization rate or "cap rate" approach to valuing the NOI of a property or portfolio of properties; (2) applying value per square foot (or unit) to a property or portfolio of properties; and/or (3) using appraised values disclosed in the company's financial statements (permitted under IFRS but not hitherto or currently under US GAAP).[6] An analyst may adjust these appraised values reported by the company if he or she does not agree with the underlying assumptions and if there is sufficient information to do so. In the first two instances, the cap rates and values per square foot are derived from observing transactions that have occurred in the marketplace. In contrast, most sophisticated direct purchasers of commercial real estate arrive at a purchase price after doing detailed forecasting of the cash flows they expect to achieve from owning and operating a specific property over their investment time horizon. These cash flows are then discounted to a present value or purchase price. Whatever that present value or purchase price is, an analyst can estimate value by dividing an estimate of NOI by the cap rate, essentially the required rate of current return for income streams of that risk. In addition, an analyst can take the present value or purchase price and divide by the property's rentable area for a value per square foot. The point is that cap rates and values per square foot result from a more detailed analysis and discounted cash flow process. The discount rate used by a private owner/operator of commercial real estate could be different from the discount rate used by investors purchasing shares of REITs.

NAV reflects the value of a REIT's assets to a private market buyer, which may or may not be the same as the value that public equity investors ascribe to the business. This fact is one of the reasons for the wide historical premium/discount range stocks trade at relative to NAV estimates. Another reason is that the stock market tends to focus more on the outlook for short-term future changes in income and asset value than the property market, which is more focused on long term valuation. As alluded to earlier, it is possible that REITs and REOCs can trade at some premium or discount to NAV until the premium/discount becomes wide enough for market forces to close the arbitrage gap.

Another factor to consider when using a NAV approach to REIT/REOC valuation is that NAV implicitly treats a company as an individual asset or static pool of assets. In reality, such treatment is not consistent with a going concern assumption. Management teams have different track records and abilities to produce value over time, assets can be purchased and sold, and capital market decisions can add or subtract value. An investor must thus consider how much value a management team can add to (or subtract from) current NAV. For instance, an investor may be willing to purchase REIT A trading at a 10 percent premium to NAV versus REIT B trading at a small discount to NAV because the management team of REIT A has a stronger track record and better opportunities to grow the NAV compared with REIT B, therefore justifying the premium at which REIT A trades relative to REIT B.

NAV estimates can also become quite subjective when property markets become illiquid and few transactions are observable, or when REITs and REOCs own hundreds of properties, making it difficult for an investor to estimate exactly how much the portfolio would be worth if the assets were sold individually. There may also be a

---

6 At the time of this writing, US GAAP requires property assets to be carried in financial statements at depreciated cost.

large-portfolio premium in good economic environments when prospective strategic purchasers may be willing to pay a premium to acquire a large amount of desired property at once, or a large-portfolio discount when there are few buyers for the kind of property in question. In addition, such assets as undeveloped land, very large properties with few comparable assets, properties with specific uses, service businesses, and joint ventures complicate the process of estimating NAV with accuracy and confidence.

5.3.2 Further Observations on NAV

Among institutional investors, the most common view is that if REIT management is performing well in the sense of creating value, REITs and REOCs should trade at premiums to underlying NAVPS. The rationale is based on the following:

1 Investors in the stocks have liquidity on a day-to-day basis, whereas a private investor in real estate does not, thus warranting a lower required return rate (higher value) in the public market than the private market for the same assets.

2 The competitive nature of the public markets and size of the organizations should attract above-average management teams, which should produce better real estate operating performance and lead to better investment decisions than the average private real estate concern.

In conclusion, although NAV is by its nature an absolute valuation metric, in practice it is often more useful as a relative valuation tool. If all REITs are trading above NAV or below NAV, selecting individual REITs could become a relative exercise—that is, purchasing the REIT stock trading at the smallest premium to NAV when REITs are trading above NAV, or selling the REIT trading at the smallest discount to NAV when REITs are all trading at a discount to NAV. In practice, NAV is also used as a relative metric by investors looking at implied cap rates. To calculate the implied cap rate of a REIT or REOC, the current price is used in an NAV model to work backward and solve for the cap rate. By doing so, an investor looking at two similar portfolios of real estate could ascertain if the market is valuing these portfolios differently based on the implied cap rates.

VALUATION: RELATIVE VALUE (PRICE MULTIPLE) APPROACH

6

Conventional equity valuation approaches, including "market-based" or relative value approaches, are used with some adaptations to value REITs and REOCs. Such multiples as price-to-funds from operations (P/FFO), price-to-adjusted funds from operations (P/AFFO), and enterprise value-to-earnings before interest, taxes, depreciation, and amortization (EV/EBITDA) are used for valuing shares of REITs and REOCs in much the same way as for valuing shares in other industries. Funds from operations and adjusted funds from operations are defined and discussed in detail in Section 6.2.

6.1 Relative Value Approach to Valuing REIT Stocks

The relative value measures most frequently used in valuing REIT shares are P/FFO and P/AFFO. The ratio EV/EBITDA is used to a lesser extent. Like the P/E and P/CF multiples used for valuing equities in industrial sectors, P/FFO and P/AFFO multiples allow investors to quickly ascertain the value of a given REIT's shares compared with other REIT shares, or to compare the current valuation level of a REIT's shares with historical levels.[7] Within the REIT sector, P/FFO and P/AFFO multiples are also often compared with the average multiple of companies owning similar properties; for example, comparing the P/FFO multiple of a REIT that owns office properties with the average P/FFO multiple for all REITs owning office properties. These multiples are typically calculated using current stock prices and year-ahead estimated FFO or AFFO.

There are three main drivers behind the P/FFO, P/AFFO, and EV/EBITDA multiples of most REITs and REOCs:

1 *Expectation for growth in FFO/AFFO*: The higher the expected growth, the higher the multiple or relative valuation. Growth can be driven by business model (e.g., REITs and REOCs successful in real estate development often generate above-average FFO/AFFO growth over time), geography (e.g., having a concentration of properties in primary, supply-constrained markets, such as New York City or London, can give landlords more pricing power and higher cash flow growth than can be obtained in secondary markets), and other factors (e.g., management skill or lease structure).

2 *Risk associated with the underlying real estate*: For example, owning apartments is viewed as having less cash flow variability than owning hotels. As such, apartment-focused REITs have tended to trade at relatively high multiples compared with hotel REITs.

3 *Risks associated with company's capital structures and access to capital*: As financial leverage increases, equities' FFO and AFFO multiples decrease because required return increases as risk increases.

Financial disclosure and transparency can also have material effects on multiples. As discussed in Section 6.2, FFO has some shortcomings; but because it is the most standardized measure of a REIT or REOC's earning power, P/FFO is the most frequently used multiple in analyzing the sector. It is, in essence, the REIT sector equivalent of P/E. Investors can derive a quick "cash flow" multiple by looking at P/AFFO because AFFO makes a variety of adjustments to FFO that result in an approximation of cash earnings.

6.2 Funds from Operations and Adjusted Funds from Operations

REIT analysts and investors make extensive use of two cash flow measures that are particularly relevant to real estate.[8] The objective of both is to improve on net earnings as a measure of profit. **Funds from operations** (FFO) is a widely accepted and reported supplemental measure of the operating income of a REIT or real estate operating company. FFO is defined as accounting net earnings excluding (1) depreciation charges (depreciation expense) on real estate, (2) deferred tax charges (the deferred portion of tax expenses), and (3) gains or losses from sales of property and debt restructuring.

Why is depreciation excluded? Investors believe that real estate maintains its value to a greater extent than other business assets, often appreciating in value over the long-term, and that depreciation deductions under IFRS and US GAAP do not represent economic reality. A taxable REOC that uses a moderate degree of leverage and regularly chooses to reinvest most of its income in its business usually will be able to defer a large part of its annual tax liability; that is, its cash income taxes will be low as a result of the accelerated depreciation rates for tax purposes permitted in most countries. Analysts tend to exclude the deferred tax liability and the related

---

7 Comparisons with the overall market are not generally made.

8 Note that "cash flow" is used in an approximate sense. FFO is closer to a cash number than net earnings, but it is not exactly a cash number.

periodic deferred tax charges because they regard them as economically questionable. The deferred tax liability may not be paid for many years, if at all, or may change in amount depending on future tax rates, laws, and corporate tax planning. Gains and losses from sales of property and debt restructuring are excluded on the grounds that they do not represent sustainable, normal income. Accordingly, depreciation and deferred tax charges are added back to net earnings, and gains and losses from sales of property and debt restructuring are excluded in computing FFO.

Adjusted funds from operations (AFFO), also known as **funds available for distribution** (FAD) or **cash available for distribution** (CAD), is a refinement of FFO that is designed to be a more accurate measure of current economic income. AFFO is most often defined as FFO adjusted to remove any non-cash rent and to subtract maintenance-type capital expenditures and leasing costs (including leasing agents' commissions and tenants' improvement allowances). So-called **straight-line rent** is the average contractual rent over a lease term and this figure is recognized as revenue under IFRS and US GAAP. The difference between this figure and the cash rent paid during the period is the amount of the non-cash rent or **straight-line rent adjustment**. Because most long-term leases contain escalating rental rates, this difference in rental revenue recognition can be significant. Also, deductions from FFO for capital expenditures related to maintenance and for leasing the space in properties reflect costs that need to be incurred to maintain the value of properties. The purpose of the adjustments to net earnings made in computing FFO and AFFO is to obtain a more tangible, cash-focused measure of sustainable economic income that reduces reliance on non-cash accounting estimates and excludes non-economic, non-cash charges.

AFFO is superior to FFO as a measure of economic income because it takes into account the capital expenditures necessary to maintain the economic income of a property portfolio. It is open, however, to more variation and error in estimation than FFO. The precise annual provision required to maintain and lease the space in a property is difficult to predict, and the actual expense in any single year may be significantly more or less than the norm because of the timing of capital expenditure programs and the uneven expiration schedule of leases. Consequently, estimates of FFO are more frequently cited measures, although analysts and investors will tend to base their investment judgments to a significant degree on their AFFO estimates. Although many REITs and REOCs compute and refer to AFFO in their disclosures, their methods of computation and their assumptions vary. Firms that compile statistics and estimates of publicly traded enterprises for publications, such as Bloomberg and Thomson Reuters, tend not to gather AFFO estimates because of the absence of a universally accepted methodology for computing AFFO and inconsistent corporate reporting of actual AFFO figures, which hinders corroboration of analysts' estimates.

Net operating income was previously mentioned in relation to checking NAV estimates. It is an important income measure that analysts use as a starting point in making their adjustments to income and book value of assets. **Net operating income** (NOI) is defined as gross rental revenue minus operating costs (which include estimated vacancy and collection losses, insurance costs, taxes, utilities, and repairs and maintenance expenses) but before deducting depreciation, corporate overhead, and interest expense. After deduction from NOI of general and administrative (G&A) expenses, the figure obtained is earnings before interest, depreciation, and amortization (EBITDA). Subtracting interest expense from EBITDA results in FFO, and the further deduction of non-cash rent, maintenance type capital expenditures, and leasing commissions gives AFFO. Exhibit 8 illustrates the most straightforward, convenient way of calculating FFO and AFFO for hypothetical Office Equity REIT Inc.

Exhibit 8	Calculation of FFO and AFFO Office Equity REIT Inc (in thousands, except per share data)

Panel A: Calculation of funds from operations

Net income available to common	$160,638
Add: Depreciation and amortization	$101,100
Funds from operations	$261,738
FFO per share (55,689 shares outstanding)	**$4.70**

Panel B: Calculation of adjusted funds from operations

Funds from operations	$261,738
Less: Non-cash (straight-line) rent adjustment	$21,103
Less: Recurring maintenance-type capital expenditures and leasing commissions	$55,765
Adjusted funds from operations	$184,870
AFFO per share (55,689 shares outstanding)	**$3.32**

EXAMPLE 6

Analyst Adjustments (I)

1   Which of the following is the *best* measure of a REIT's current economic return to shareholders?

  A   NOI

  B   FFO

  C   AFFO

2   An analyst gathers the following information for a REIT:

NOI	$115 million
Book value of properties	$1,005 million
Market value of debt outstanding	$505 million
Market cap rate	7%
Shares outstanding	100 million
Book value per share	$5.00

The REITs NAV per share is *closest* to:

  A $10.05.

  B $11.38.

  C $16.42.

3   All else equal, estimated NAV per share will decrease with an increase in/to the:

  A   capitalization rate.

  B   estimated growth rate.

  C   deferred tax liabilities.

Solution to 1:

C is correct. AFFO is calculated from FFO by deducting non-cash rent, capital expenditures for maintenance, and leasing costs.

B is incorrect because it does not account for non-cash rent, capital expenditures for maintenance, and leasing costs. A is incorrect because it does not account for interest expense, general and administrative expense, non-cash rent, capital expenditures for maintenance, and leasing costs, which are appropriate deductions in calculating current economic return.

Solution to 2:

B is correct. The NAVPS estimates real estate values by capitalizing NOI. Valuing $115 million of NOI with a capitalization rate of 7 percent yields a value for the properties of $1,642,857,000. After deducting $505 million of debt at market value, NAV is $1,137,857,000; NAVPS equals NAV divided by 100 million shares outstanding, or $11.38.

A is incorrect because it is the book value of the assets (not the net assets) per share: $1,005 million divided by 100 million shares = $10.05 per share. It does not take into account the market value of the assets and does not deduct debt. C is incorrect because it is the market value of the real estate; that is, NOI capitalized at 7 percent, divided by 100 million shares: $1,642,857,000/100,000,000 = $16.42. This calculation excludes other assets and liabilities of the entity.

Solution to 3:

A is correct. The capitalization rate is used to calculate the estimated value of operating real estate because it is the NOI as a percentage of the value of operating real estate: NOI/Capitalization rate = Estimated value. As the capitalization rate increases, the estimated value of operating real estate and thus the NAV will decrease.

B is incorrect because an increase in the estimated growth rate would increase the estimated NOI, and the estimated value of operating income. C is incorrect because deferred liabilities are not counted as "hard" liabilities and subtracted from the NAV.

EXAMPLE 7

Analyst Adjustments (II)

1 An increase in the capitalization rate will *most likely* decrease a REIT's:

A cost of debt.

B estimated NOI.

C estimated NAV.

2 An analyst gathers the following information for a REIT:

Non-cash (straight-line) rent	£207,430
Depreciation	£611,900
Recurring maintenance-type capital expenditures and leasing commissions	£550,750
Adjusted funds from operations	£3,320,000
AFFO per share	£3.32

The REIT's funds from operations (FFO) per share is *closest* to:

    A £3.93.

    B £4.08.

    C £4.48.

3 Which of the following estimates is *least likely* to be compiled by firms that publish REIT analysts' estimates?

    A FFO

    B AFFO

    C Revenues

Solution to 1:

C is correct. The capitalization rate is used to estimate the market value of real estate, which is then used to calculate NAV.

A is incorrect because a higher capitalization rate does not decrease the REIT's cost of debt. B is incorrect because the estimated NOI is based on income growth, not the capitalization rate.

Solution to 2:

B is correct. FFO = AFFO + Non-cash (straight-line) rent + Recurring maintenance-type capital expenditures and leasing commissions = 3,320,000 + 550,750 + 207,430 = £4,078,180. The number of shares outstanding = 3,320,000/3.32 = 1,000,000. FFO/share = 4,078,180/1,000,000 ≈ £4.08.

A is incorrect because it adds depreciation to AFFO (3,320,000 + 611,900 = £3,931,900. 3,931,900/1,000,000 ≈ £3.93 per share.) Depreciation is added to NOI (not AFFO) to find FFO. C is incorrect because it also adds depreciation to AFFO + Non-cash (straight-line) rent + Recurring maintenance-type capital expenditures and leasing commissions. That is incorrect because depreciation is not part of the difference between FFO and AFFO.

Solution to 3:

B is correct. Firms that compile statistics and estimates of REITs tend not to gather AFFO estimates because of the absence of a universally accepted methodology for computing AFFO and inconsistent corporate reporting of actual AFFO figures.

6.3 P/FFO and P/AFFO Multiples: Advantages and Drawbacks

The US REIT industry began to expand rapidly in the 1990s. Exhibit 9 presents some evidence on the US REIT market for 1995–2011 (essentially, two complete commercial real estate cycles). REITs' trading multiples were lowest in late 1999 and early 2000, at about 7 to 8 times (denoted 8x) for P/FFO and about 9 to 10x for P/AFFO. Multiples for REITs and REOCs were at their highest in early 2007, when P/FFO multiples approached 20x and P/AFFO multiples were about 24x.

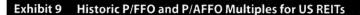

Exhibit 9   Historic P/FFO and P/AFFO Multiples for US REITs

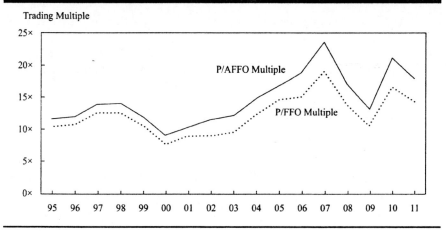

The key benefits of using P/FFO and P/AFFO multiples in the valuation of REITs and REOCs are as follows:

1 Multiples of earnings measures of this kind are widely accepted in evaluating shares across global stock markets and industries.

2 In light of this acceptance, portfolio managers can put the valuation of REITs and REOCs into context with other investment alternatives.

3 FFO estimates are readily available through market data providers, such as Bloomberg and Thomson Reuters, which facilitates calculating P/FFO multiples.

4 Multiples can be used in conjunction with such items as expected growth and leverage levels to deepen the relative analysis among REITs and REOCs.[9]

There are also drawbacks. Multiples are not a perfect basis for valuation because of the following:

1 Applying a multiple to FFO or AFFO may not capture the intrinsic value of all real estate assets held by the REIT or REOC; for example, land parcels and empty buildings may not currently produce income and hence do not contribute to FFO but have value.

2 P/FFO does not adjust for the impact of recurring capital expenditures needed to keep properties operating smoothly; and although P/AFFO should do so, wide variations in estimates and assumptions are incorporated into the calculation of AFFO.

3 In recent years, an increased level of such one-time items as gains and accounting charges, as well as new revenue recognition rules, have affected the income statement, thus making P/FFO and P/AFFO more difficult to compute and complicating comparisons between companies.

---

9 Neither FFO nor AFFO take into account differences in leverage; leverage ratios can be used to adjust for differences in leverage among REITs when comparing valuations based on FFO and AFFO multiples.

7   VALUATION: DISCOUNTED CASH FLOW APPROACH

REITs and REOCs generally return a significant portion of their income to their investors and tend to be high-dividend paying shares. Thus, dividend discount models for valuation are applicable. Discounted cash flow approaches are applied in the same manner as they are for companies in other industries. Most typically, investors use two- or three-step dividend discount models with near-term, intermediate-term, and/or long-term growth assumptions. In discounted cash flow models, investors will often use intermediate-term cash flow projections and a terminal value based on historical cash flow multiples.

7.1 Considerations in Forecasting Longer-Term Growth Rates

In looking at the specific drivers of growth for REITs and REOCs, four key considerations are generally taken into account when forecasting longer-term growth rates in these models.

1 *Internal growth potential* that stem from rent increases over time. In general, companies with portfolios of real estate located in supply-constrained markets with robust demand have a better ability to raise rents and increase cash flow. The opposite is true for portfolios in more supply-saturated markets or markets with tepid tenant demand conditions and prospects. Over the long term, well-managed property portfolios in good markets tend to generate cash flow growth at a level slightly above inflation.

2 *Investment activities*, such as acquisitions, new development, re-development, or dispositions of assets, have an impact on long-term growth. Successful development-oriented companies have shown better growth over time because returns on invested capital are generally higher on development than on acquisitions. Somewhat counter-intuitively, dispositions of weaker assets with below-average growth prospects are often dilutive to earnings because the cap rates at which such properties are sold are higher than the yields at which proceeds are re-invested, which reflects lower risk premiums. Thus, a REIT or REOC that undergoes a repositioning of a material portion of its portfolio into higher-quality properties could face cash flow growth pressure in the near term.

3 *Capital structure* can have an impact on growth, particularly in the short term as companies raise or lower their leverage. This is because of the positive leverage spread enjoyed by most REITs and REOCs; that is, going-in cap rates on property investments exceed the cost of debt. These benefits, however, can be reversed by adverse changes in the capital markets or missteps by management on acquisitions or operations. In general, REIT investors tend to be conservative and oriented toward stable, recurring income and to be averse to high leverage in REITs.

4 *Retaining and reinvesting a portion of free cash flow* can make a contribution to the growth rate. Although REITs often pay out the majority of cash flow to investors in the form of dividends, the high rates of depreciation allowed under most countries' tax laws allow companies, including REITs, to retain enough cash flow without incurring current income taxes to add 1 to 3 percentage points to annual growth.

7.2 Some Perspective on Long-Term Growth Rates

If the previously mentioned components of growth are added together, an analyst can derive a long-run growth rate. For successfully managed REITs and REOCs with good portfolios, the resulting growth rate should be in the high-single-digit percentage range. Given core cash flow growth of about 3–4 percent, 1–2 percent growth from investment activity over time, 2–3 percent growth from the financial leverage that magnifies the two growth drivers, and another 0–1 percent from reinvesting free cash flow, the long-run growth rate estimate ranges from 6 to 10 percent and the averages of the components would add up to an 8 percent long-run growth rate. The long-run growth for the average US REIT from the mid-1990s through 2010, however, was barely more than 0 percent per year, with only the top companies achieving 4–7 percent average annual cash flow growth. So, although in theory REITs and REOCs should show higher growth rates, in reality the impact of the business cycle, operational and investment missteps, and a highly dilutive process of balance sheet strengthening through equity issuance after the credit crisis of 2008 and 2009 all have had a negative effect on growth.

The other key component in discounted cash flow models and dividend discount models is required returns. Although a detailed discussion about deriving required returns is beyond the scope of this reading, most rates used in practice have ranged widely from 7 percent to 13 percent. The conventional argument is that the risk premium—and thus the discount rate—associated with REITs and REOCs should be lower than the average stock in the broader market because the underlying business of owning income-producing real estate should be less volatile because of contractual revenue streams from leases. A long-term look at the betas of REIT shares suggests values tend to be less than 1.0, which supports this view.

Considering the points just outlined, the key drawback to using dividend discount models and discounted cash flow models for valuing REITs and REOCs is the high sensitivity of these valuation models to the key inputs of growth and discount rates.

EXAMPLE 8

Valuation (I)

1 When using a relative P/AFFO or P/FFO multiple approach in the valuation of a REIT or REOC, which of the following considerations is the *most* important to take into account?

    A The discount rate

    B The NOI capitalization rate

    C Relative AFFO or FFO growth rates and different leverage levels

2 Which of the following is the *most* significant contributor to P/FFO and P/AFFO valuation multiples for REITs and REOCs?

    A The average age of the management team

    B The exchange on which the REIT stock is listed

    C The geographic location of properties in a REIT's portfolio

3 Which of the following is *not* a challenge in accurately estimating net asset value (NAV)?

    A Estimating the value of goodwill and intangible assets

    B Identifying the capitalization rates on comparable properties trading in the property market

   C Ascribing an accurate value to a REIT's land holdings, projects under development, and joint ventures

4 Which of the following is *least likely* to cause persistent differences between estimated NAVs and stock prices?

   A A surplus of takeover arbitrage capital in the markets

   B Different discount rates being applied to privately held assets versus a liquid security

   C A strong history of growth that prompts stock investors to pay a premium to the real estate value for a good management team

5 Which of the following are important in using a discounted cash flow model to value REITs?

   A The capitalization rate

   B The net asset value discount

   C The payout ratio and the amount of financial leverage used by the REIT

Solution to 1:

C is correct. The main drivers of a relative multiple approach to valuation are risks associated with capital structure (leverage) and underlying real estate as well as expectations for growth (relative AFFO or FFO growth rates), so both should be considered.

A and B are incorrect because they relate to the dividend discount model and NAV approaches to valuation, respectively.

Solution to 2:

C is correct. Geography determines expectations for growth and risks, two main drivers of a relative multiple approach to valuation.

A is incorrect because although management skill may contribute to expected growth, management age does not. B is incorrect because the REIT's listing exchange is largely irrelevant to its investment value.

Solution to 3:

A is correct. These "soft" assets are ascribed no value by analysts in a net asset value calculation.

B is incorrect because estimating cap rates is a challenge in that they can be somewhat subjective when the properties sold differ significantly and/or few transactions are observable. C is incorrect because such assets as undeveloped land, buildings under construction, large properties with few comparable assets, service businesses, and joint ventures complicate the process of estimating NAV with accuracy and confidence.

Solution to 4:

A is correct. A surplus of takeover arbitrage capital in the markets is likely to close the gap between share prices and net asset values by generating takeovers.

B is incorrect because different discount rates may be used to reflect differences in liquidity, which persist until both securities are either publicly or privately traded. C is incorrect because the management's reputation and its effect on security value persist as long as the management remains.

Solution to 5:

C is correct. The payout ratio or level of retained cash flow affects long-term growth rates and the REIT's financial leverage is a determinant of its overall risk exposure and thus discount rate. Both growth and discount rates are key components of the discounted cash flow model.

A and B are incorrect because they both relate to the net asset value approach to REIT valuation.

REIT VALUATION: MINI CASE STUDY

8

In this section, we undertake the valuation of a REIT by using the previously outlined approaches for valuation. The REIT in our example is Capitol Shopping Center REIT Inc (CRE), a fictitious company that owns and operates retail shopping centers primarily in the Washington DC metropolitan area. The following are CRE's income statements, balance sheets, and cash flow statements for 2009 and 2010.

Exhibit 10	Capitol Shopping Center REIT Inc. (in thousands, except per share data)

Panel A: Income statements

	Three Months Ending 31 December		Year Ending 31 December	
	2010	2009	2010	2009
Rental revenue	$133,700	$130,300	$517,546	$501,600
Other property income	3,600	2,100	14,850	13,450
Total property revenue	$137,300	$132,400	$532,396	$515,050
Rental expenses	$29,813	$28,725	$112,571	$109,775
Property taxes	15,050	14,850	57,418	55,375
Total property expenses	$44,863	$43,575	$169,989	$165,150
Property net operating income	$92,437	$88,825	$362,407	$349,900
Other income	$450	$385	$1,840	$1,675
General & Administrative expenses	$6,150	$7,280	$23,860	$26,415
EBITDA	$86,737	$81,930	$340,387	$325,160
Depreciation & amortization	$28,460	$27,316	$115,110	$111,020
Net interest expense	$25,867	$25,015	$100,823	$99,173
Net income available to common	$32,410	$29,599	$124,454	$114,967
Weighted average common shares	61,100	60,100	60,600	60,100
Earnings per share	$0.53	$0.49	$2.05	$1.91

Panel B: Balance sheets

	Year Ending 31 December	
	2010	2009
Assets		
Real estate, at cost		
Operating real estate	$3,627,576	$3,496,370
Land held for future development	$133,785	$133,785

(continued)

Exhibit 10   (Continued)

Panel B: Balance sheets

	Year Ending 31 December	
	2010	**2009**
	$3,761,361	$3,630,155
Less accumulated depreciation	($938,097)	($822,987)
Net real estate	$2,823,264	$2,807,168
Cash and equivalents	$85,736	$23,856
Accounts receivable, net	$72,191	$73,699
Deferred rent receivable, net	$38,165	$33,053
Prepaid expenses and other assets	$106,913	$101,604
Total Assets	$3,126,269	$3,039,380
Liabilities and Shareholders' Equity		
Liabilities		
Mortgages payable	$701,884	$647,253
Notes payable	$1,090,745	$1,090,745
Accounts payable and other liabilities	$219,498	$200,439
Total liabilities	$2,012,127	$1,938,437
Common shares and equity	$1,114,142	$1,100,943
Total Liabilities and Shareholders' Equity	$3,126,269	$3,039,380

Panel C: Cash Flow Statements

	Year Ending 31 December	
	2010	**2009**
Operating Activities		
Net income	$124,454	$114,967
Depreciation and amortization	$115,110	$111,020
Change in accounts receivable	$1,508	$452
Change in deferred rents	($5,112)	($4,981)
Change in prepaid expenses and other assets	($5,309)	$1,237
Change in accounts payable and other liabilities	$19,059	($11,584)
Net cash provided by operating activities	$249,710	$211,111
Investing Activities		
Acquisition of real estate	($111,200)	($22,846)
Capital expenditures on operating real estate	($20,006)	($18,965)
Net cash used in investing activities	($131,206)	($41,811)
Financing Activities		
Issuance of mortgages	$54,631	$14,213
Issuance of common shares	$58,425	$0
Dividends paid to common shareholders	($169,680)	($165,275)
Net cash used in financing activities	($56,624)	($151,062)
Increase (decrease) in cash and equivalents	$61,880	$18,238

Exhibit 10   (Continued)

Panel C: Cash Flow Statements

	Year Ending 31 December	
	2010	**2009**
Cash and cash equivalents, beginning of year	$23,856	$5,618
Cash and cash equivalents, end of year	$85,736	$23,856

CRE also publishes a supplemental investor packet that provides further disclosures used by the investment community to analyze the company. The following shows its adjustments to arrive at FFO and AFFO, and its calculation of dividend payouts based on dividends paid.

Exhibit 11   Capitol Shopping Center REIT Inc. FFO, AFFO, and Dividend Payouts (in thousands, except per share data)

	Three Months Ending 31 December		Year Ending 31 December	
	2010	**2009**	**2010**	**2009**
Funds from operations				
Net income available to common	$32,410	$29,599	$124,454	$114,967
Depreciation & amortization	$28,460	$27,316	$115,110	$111,020
Funds from operations	$60,870	$56,915	$239,564	$225,987
FFO/Share	$1.00	$0.95	$3.95	$3.76
Adjusted funds from operations				
Funds from operations	$60,870	$56,915	$239,564	$225,987
Less Non-cash rents (1)	($1,469)	($1,325)	($5,112)	($4,981)
Less Recurring capital expenditures (2)	($5,638)	($5,101)	($20,006)	($18,965)
Adjusted funds from operations	$53,763	$50,489	$214,446	$202,041
AFFO/Share	$0.88	$0.84	$3.54	$3.36
Dividends/Share	$0.70	$0.69	$2.80	$2.75
Dividend Payout Ratios				
On FFO	70.0%	72.6%	70.9%	73.1%
On AFFO	79.6%	82.1%	79.1%	81.8%
Weighted average common shares	61,100	60,100	60,600	60,100

1   Non-cash rents include the impact of straight-lining contractual rent increases in leases, per accounting rules. The change in deferred rents can often provide the impact of this accounting on rental revenues.

2   Recurring capital expenditures include those costs needed to maintain the revenue-producing ability of existing assets, such as leasing commissions to keep or attract new tenants, maintenance items such as roofs and parking lot repairs, and basic build-outs of space as an inducement to attract tenants.

The historical stock price and company's financial statements, including disclosures, are used to complete a simple analysis of the balance sheet, as follows.

Exhibit 12	Capitol Shopping Center REIT Inc. Balance Sheet Analysis (in thousands, except per-share data)	
	Year Ending 31 December	
	2010	**2009**
Ending debt	$1,792,629	$1,737,998
Ending stock price	$72.36	$61.50
Ending shares	61,100	60,100
Ending market capitalization	$4,421,196	$3,696,150
Debt/Total market capitalization	*40.5%*	*47.0%*
Peer group debt/Total market capitalization	47.1%	56.7%
All REITs debt/Total market capitalization	42.8%	49.6%
EBITDA	$340,387	$325,160
Interest expense	$100,823	$99,173
Interest coverage	*3.38x*	*3.28x*
Peer group interest coverage	2.35x	2.16x
All REITs interest coverage	2.58x	2.27x
Ending net debt	$1,706,893	$1,714,142
EBITDA	$340,387	$325,160
Net debt-to-EBITDA	*5.01x*	*5.27x*
Peer group net debt-to-EBITDA	7.10x	8.60x
All REITs net debt-to-EBITDA	6.70x	7.80x
Ending net debt	$1,706,893	$1,714,142
Ending gross real estate	$3,761,361	$3,630,155
Net debt/Gross real estate (Book)	*45.4%*	*47.2%*
Peer group net debt/Gross real estate (Book)	52.8%	55.1%
All REITs net debt/Gross real estate (Book)	49.6%	52.6%

The exhibits provide a recent historical picture of CRE's financial performance and balance sheet. Some key points about the company's properties operations, dividend policy, recent business activity, and historical trading attributes follow.

- CRE owns properties that are generally considered defensive in the commercial real estate sector. This is because many of its properties are tenanted by basic necessity goods retailers such as grocery stores, drug stores, dry cleaners, etc.

- CRE's location in the Washington, DC metropolitan area is generally viewed as favorable for two key reasons: (1) Washington, DC is the capital of the United States, and the government is the largest driver of employment, which has historically provided more stability compared with the private sector; and (2) the city is a fairly dense area with strict zoning restrictions and new construction of shopping centers is difficult, which limits competing new supply.

- CRE has been able to increase its rents and net operating income by 2–3 percent each year, on average, in the past decade.

- The past two reported years (2009 and 2010) were difficult for the broader commercial real estate markets. CRE was able to achieve positive growth while many of its REIT peers saw FFO and AFFO decline. As forecasts call for improving fundamental property-level conditions, CRE's portfolio may not have as much "upside" because it did not experience the decline in occupancy and rents that other REITs did.

- In the middle of 2010, the company purchased a portfolio of three shopping centers from a local developer for a total price of $111.2 million. The return on these assets in the first year is an estimated 6.75 percent. The company was able to achieve a better going-in cap rate on this acquisition than the market averages of 6.0–6.25 percent because of its strong relationships and reputation with tenants, commercial property brokers, and competitors as well as its ability to act quickly because of its strong balance sheet. In addition, the property is not fully leased, leaving potential to increase net operating income if CRE can attract additional tenants. CRE funded the purchase with a $54.6 million mortgage at a 6 percent interest rate and cash from a common stock offering of 1 million shares and from cash on hand.

- The company intends to make additional acquisitions in the future as part of its growth plan. It intends to use a combination of debt, common equity, and internally generated cash to make these purchases. It typically requires the properties it acquires to generate an unleveraged internal rate of return of 9.5 percent in the form of current yield and capital appreciation over time.

- CRE's balance sheet strategy is to operate at less than 50 percent debt/market capitalization, with a preference for leverage to be closer to 40 percent. At year-end 2010, CRE's debt/market capitalization was 40.5 percent and its interest coverage was 3.38x. The company's current in-place average debt cost is 5.7 percent. By comparison, CRE's peers operate at an average leverage level of 47.1 percent and have an interest coverage ratio of 2.35x.

- CRE's board has chosen a dividend policy that provides an approximate 80 percent payout of cash flow, or AFFO. This level allows the company to pay an attractive dividend to shareholders, retain some cash flow, provide a cushion in the event of a downturn, and remain in compliance with REIT payout requirements in the United States. It is easily able to meet these REIT payout requirements because the requirements are based on taxable net income, which is calculated after deducting depreciation. In fact, CRE's dividend level has run well in excess of taxable net income, according to comments made by its management.

- Over the last decade, CRE has traded between 9 and 19x FFO, while its peers have traded between 8 and 18x, and all REITs have traded between 7 and 20x. On an AFFO basis, CRE's historical multiple has been 10–21x, with its peers trading between 9–19x, and all REITs being in the 9–24x range.

- Currently, shopping center REITs are estimated to be trading at 7.6 percent above analyst estimates of net asset value (NAV). The overall REIT sector is estimated to be trading at a 14.8 percent premium to estimate NAV.

- CRE's historical beta to the broader equity market is 0.80. The current risk-free rate of return is 4.0 percent, and the market risk premium is estimated at 5.0 percent.

Investors and analysts that cover CRE have published estimates for its FFO/share, AFFO/share, and dividends/share for the next three years. Putting the average, or "consensus," of these estimates together with the company's reported results reveals the following FFO/AFFO and dividend snapshot.

Exhibit 13   Capitol Shopping Center REIT Inc. Historical and Forecast Earnings and Dividends (all amounts are per-share)

| | Year Ending 31 December | | | | |
	2009A	**2010A**	**2011E**	**2012E**	**2013E**
CRE's FFO/Share	$3.76	$3.95	$4.23	$4.59	$4.80
Growth	—	5.1%	7.1%	8.5%	4.6%
Peer group FFO/Share growth	—	3.4%	6.8%	8.2%	4.2%
All REITs FFO/Share growth	—	1.2%	7.9%	9.8%	10.2%
CRE's AFFO/Share	$3.36	$3.54	$3.76	$4.09	$4.31
Growth	—	5.4%	6.2%	8.8%	5.4%
Peer group AFFO/Share growth	—	−1.0%	6.2%	9.1%	4.8%
All REITs AFFO/Share growth	—	−3.0%	8.1%	9.7%	10.8%
CRE's dividends/Share	$2.75	$2.80	$2.98	$3.25	$3.40
Growth	—	1.8%	6.4%	9.1%	4.6%
Peer group dividends/Share growth	—	−2.0%	5.6%	7.9%	5.1%
All REITs dividends/Share growth	—	−5.0%	7.8%	8.9%	6.0%
CRE's dividend payout on AFFO	81.8%	79.1%	79.3%	79.5%	78.9%

Taking the recent stock price of $69.85/share and focusing on the next two years (as most analysts looking at multiples do), comparative FFO/AFFO multiples for CRE can be determined. A look at the multiples of its direct peers and the entire REIT industry trade is also included.

Exhibit 14   Comparative Multiple Analysis

| | P/FFO | | P/AFFO | |
	2011E	**2012E**	**2011E**	**2012E**
Capitol Shopping Center REIT, Inc (CRE) (1)	16.5x	15.2x	18.6x	17.1x
Shopping center oriented REITs	14.5x	13.3x	16.1x	14.5x
All REITs	14.2x	12.8x	16.5x	14.6x
CRE's Premium/(Discount) To...				
Shopping center REITs	13.8%	14.3%	15.5%	17.9%
All REITs	16.2%	18.8%	12.7%	17.1%

1 Based on a current stock price of $69.85.

8.1 Checking the Valuation: Analysis Based on Relative Valuation

In analyzing CRE's FFO/AFFO multiples, we find that at the current stock price of $69.85, CRE trades at a premium valuation level compared with its direct peers (other shopping center REITs) as well as the overall REIT industry. When considering whether this level is warranted or not, the following items should be considered:

1   Is CRE's expected FFO and AFFO growth likely to be better or worse than those of its peers and the overall REIT industry in the next two years?

2   What is the historical FFO/AFFO multiple range for CRE, shopping center REITs, and the overall REIT industry?

3   Are there any company-specific considerations that justify a higher or lower relative multiple?

For the first consideration, we estimate that CRE's FFO and AFFO growth in 2011 should be approximately 6–7 percent and move up to 8–9 percent in 2012. As shown in Exhibit 13, this estimate is roughly in-line with that of its shopping center–focused peers but is lower than the growth expected from all REITs, which should average about 8 percent in 2011 and move up to nearly 10 percent in 2012. On its own, this estimate would suggest that CRE is expensive relative to its peers because its FFO and AFFO multiples are at premiums but its growth is largely in-line with its peers. CRE also appears expensive relative to all REITs because expected FFO and AFFO growth is lower than what is expected from REITs as a whole, yet CRE's multiples are higher than the REIT group average.

Regarding the second consideration, the company's FFO multiple has ranged from 9–19x over the last 10 years, compared with 8–18x for its peers and 7–20x for the overall REIT industry. Regarding historical AFFO trading multiples, CRE's range in the last 10 years has been 10–21x, with its shopping center REIT peers in the 9–19x range and the overall REIT industry in the 9–24x range. Based on these figures, it appears CRE has historically traded at some premium to its peers, but the current premium is larger than usual. Similarly, CRE appears to be trading at a larger premium to the overall REIT group than it has historically. In addition, it is noteworthy that for CRE's stock and the REIT sector, P/FFO and P/AFFO valuations are at the upper end of the historical range, suggesting that REITs in general are not cheap based on historical multiples.

Addressing the third consideration, it is notable that the company's geographic exposure is considered lower risk. In addition, the company has demonstrated positive AFFO growth during times when its peers saw declining AFFO, such as in 2010. It was also able to increase its dividend when other REITs made dividend cuts. An analyst might also note that CRE's leverage of 40.5 percent on the basis of debt to total market cap and interest coverage level of 3.38x is more conservative than its peers, as are virtually all of its other balance sheet leverage metrics. These points suggest that some premium valuation is warranted because of lower financial risk.

In total, the above analysis points to CRE being overvalued when using a relative multiple approach to valuation, or P/FFO and P/AFFO multiples. To derive a specific current value estimate for CRE, an investor might ascribe overall REIT group P/FFO and P/AFFO multiples to CRE in the near-term because of the company's expected growth being lower than the average REIT, offset by the company's historical premium for its geography and track record. In doing so, an investor would arrive at a share value of $60.07 using P/FFO of 14.2x for 2011 for the overall REIT group multiplied by CRE's expected FFO in 2011 of $4.23/share. Using the same methodology for AFFO equates to a $62.04 share value. These values imply that the share would need to decline by 11–14 percent to become more attractive to an investor using P/FFO and P/AFFO multiples.

8.2 Further Analysis Based on Net Asset Value Per Share

We now use NAVPS to value the shares of Capitol Shopping Center REIT Inc. To find the value, we use the previously detailed financial statements and commentary about where assets trade that are similar to those owned by CRE. By finding this information, we can estimate a value for the company if its properties were sold, debt was paid off, and capital was returned to shareholders. Our calculation to arrive at NAVPS is shown in Exhibit 15.

Exhibit 15	Capitol Shopping Center REIT Inc. Net Asset Value (NAV) Estimate (in thousands, except per-share data)
Last 12-Months real estate NOI	$362,407
Less: Non-cash rents	(5,112)
Plus: Adjustment for full impact of acquisitions (1)	3,753
Pro forma cash NOI for last 12 months	$361,048
Plus: Next 12-months growth (2)	$9,026
Estimated next 12-months cash NOI	$370,074
Assumed cap rate (3)	6.125%
Estimated value of operating real estate	$6,042,024
Plus: Cash and equivalents	$85,736
Plus: Land held for future development	133,785
Plus: Accounts receivable	72,191
Plus: Prepaid/Other assets (4)	53,457
Estimated gross asset value	$6,387,193
Less: Total debt	$1,792,629
Less: Other liabilities	219,498
Net asset value	$4,375,066
Shares outstanding	61,100
NAV/Share	**$71.61**

1 Calculated as half of the 6.75% return on the company's $111.2 million investment made in the middle of 2010.

2 Assuming the 2.5% midpoint of the company's historical 2-3% growth.

3 At the midpoint of recent transactions in the market of 6-6.25%.

4 We cut this to half of book to account for any non-tangible assets that could be included in the accounting figure.

Note: Due to rounding to nearest thousand, figures may not sum precisely.

As shown in Exhibit 15, CRE's NAV is estimated at $71.61/share. This NAV is higher than the current stock price of $69.85, implying that CRE is trading at a 2.5 percent *discount* to NAV. Although this value alone does not show that the shares are significantly undervalued compared with its real estate, an investor should also consider that (1) CRE's direct peers are trading at NAV *premiums* of 7–8 percent, (2) the overall REIT industry is trading at an average NAV premium of almost 15 percent, and (3) Capitol Shopping Center REIT's management team has been able to earn more from its properties and grow its cash flow faster than its competitors in the marketplace. Considering these factors, an investor could conclude that CRE should at least trade at a NAV premium in line with its direct peers, implying a value of about $77 for the shares. If it trades at a NAV premium in line with the overall REIT group, the share value is $82.

Whether the analyst takes a pure NAV valuation approach to valuing shares of CRE or uses NAV as a relative metric, the conclusion is that the shares of Capitol Shopping Center REIT are undervalued using this valuation method.

8.3 Further Analysis Based on a Dividend Discount Model Approach to Valuation

The final approach we take to valuing shares of Capitol Shopping Center REIT is to use a two-step dividend discount model (DDM). In the first step, we use the published estimates for the company's dividend in 2011, 2012, and 2013. In the second step, we assume a long-run dividend growth rate of 5 percent, essentially using Gordon's constant growth model. We arrive at this growth rate after considering the company's historical NOI growth of 2–3 percent, roughly 40–50 percent financial leverage, and future acquisitions that help drive growth. In addition, we assume CRE's board maintains an 80 percent dividend payout ratio. To arrive at a discount rate, we observe that CRE's historical beta to the broader equity market is 0.80, the assumed risk-free rate is 4 percent, and the assumed equity risk premium is 5 percent. Using the capital asset pricing model (CAPM), we calculate a cost of equity capital of 4% + 0.8(5%) = 8 percent for the stock. The next table combines our assumptions to derive a net present value of the projected dividends.

Exhibits 16 and 17 provide a summary of the dividends we use for steps one and two in the model.

Exhibit 16   Capitol Shopping Center REIT Inc. Dividends for Use in a Two-Step DDM (all amounts are per-share)

| | Year Ending 31 December | | | |
| | Step One | | Step Two | |
	2011E	2012E	2013E	In Perpetuity
AFFO/Share	$3.76	$4.09	$4.31	...
Growth	—	8.8%	5.4%	5.0%
Dividends/Share	$2.98	$3.25	$3.40	...
Growth	—	9.1%	4.6%	5.0%
Dividend payout on AFFO	79.3%	79.5%	78.9%	80.0%

Exhibit 17   Capitol Shopping Center REIT Inc. Valuation Using Two-Step DDM (all amounts are per-share)

| | Year Ending 31 December | | | |
| | Step One | | | Step Two |
	2011E	2012E	2013E	2014E
Dividends/Share	$2.98	$3.25	$3.40	$3.57
Value of stock at end of 2013 (1)	—	—	$119.00	
Cash flow to investors	$2.98	$3.25	$122.40	

(continued)

Exhibit 17	(Continued)			
		Year Ending 31 December		
		Step One		**Step Two**
	2011E	**2012E**	**2013E**	**2014E**

Net Present Value of Cash Flow (Dividends) = $102.71

1 Calculated as $3.57/(0.08 − 0.05).

Using a two-step dividend discount model approach to valuation, we calculate a share value of $102.71 for Capitol Shopping Center REIT Inc. This value is about 47 percent higher than the current price of $69.85 and suggests that the shares are currently undervalued. Compared with the relative valuation approaches, this approach indicates that CRE is undervalued, not overvalued. This result is consistent with the NAV approach, which also indicated that CRE is undervalued. The discrepancy between estimated value and price is largest using the dividend discount model. This result is not particularly surprising in light of the sensitivity of results when using this valuation approach to small differences in valuation assumptions that we referred to earlier.

8.4 Selection of Valuation Methods

As this discussion demonstrates, different valuation methods can yield different results. Under such circumstances, an analyst should re-examine the assumptions made to investigate why the approaches are generating such different results. The method(s) selected by an analyst may depend on which one(s) the analyst believes use(s) the most reliable assumptions, which one(s) the analyst believes will be used by other investors, or which one(s) best reflect the analyst's own investment philosophy or view of value. The analyst may choose to take a single valuation approach, a mid-point in the range of values obtained by using several approaches, or elect to use a weighted average of the values obtained based on the analyst's view of the relative reliability of the models used to arrive at the values.

EXAMPLE 9

Valuation (II)

1 If the outlook for economic growth turns negative and property market transaction volumes decline, it is *least likely* that CRE's:

   A P/FFO and P/AFFO would be lower.

   B relative P/FFO and P/ AFFO multiples would be higher.

   C NAV becomes the most useful valuation method.

2 If other REITs have no land on their balance sheets, how is CRE's "Land held for future development" *best* factored into a relative P/FFO or P/ AFFO multiple valuation?

   A There should be no impact on multiples as a result of land value.

   B CRE would warrant lower multiples to account for land value.

   C CRE would warrant higher multiples to account for land value.

3 An analyst speaks with private market real estate investors and learns that because interest rates have just increased 200 bps, buyers will require future property acquisitions to have going-in cap rates that are 100–200 bps higher than those on recent property market transactions. The analyst's estimate of NAV for CRE *most likely*:

   A increases as cap rates are higher.

   B decreases as cap rates are higher.

   C remain the same unless CRE has debt maturing in the near term.

4 An analyst determines that CRE purchased its "Land held for future development" 15 years ago, and that on average land values at that time were one-third of what they are today. Which of the following *best* adjusts NAV to reflect this consideration?

   A The cap rate on operating assets should be changed.

   B Land value, and thus NAV, should be adjusted higher to reflect today's valuations.

   C NAV is still mainly a representation of book values, thus there should be no adjustments.

5 Zoning in CRE's real estate markets is changed to allow more new space in the future, dampening CRE's long-term FFO growth by about 0.5 percent. The effect on CRE's valuation using a dividend discount model is *most likely* that the present value of the dividend stream:

   A decreases because of lower growth.

   B remains the same.

   C increases because of the new supply.

Solution to 1:

C is correct. NAV becomes more subjective in a negative and less liquid market with fewer observable transactions, and thus this basis of valuation becomes less useful and reliable.

A and B are incorrect because P/FFO and P/AFFO are likely to fall in a negative economic environment, but investors may be willing to pay a relative premium for CRE's stock based on its superior stability in economically challenging times.

Solution to 2:

C is correct. Although it may not produce income that contributes to FFO or AFFO, the land has value and represents a source of greater internal growth potential. For that reason, A and B are incorrect.

Solution to 3:

B is correct. Estimated real estate value decreases as the cap rate increases. Because NAV is derived directly from estimated real estate value, it also decreases. For this reason, A is incorrect. C is incorrect because an increase in cap rates decreases asset values. The fact that CRE has debt maturing in the near term is not a key factor influencing NAV.

Solution to 4:

B is correct. An analyst tries to attribute market values to real property owned.

A is incorrect because the cap rate used by analysts in calculating NAVs represents the return on only the income-producing asset portfolio and does not relate to land holdings that are not currently producing any income. C is incorrect because NAV is not a representation of book values, which rely on accounting methodology rather than market values.

Solution to 5:

A is correct. Lower growth affects the projected dividend stream, decreasing its present value. For that reason, B and C are incorrect.

EXAMPLE 10

Valuation (III)

1 An analyst gathers the following information for two REITs:

	Price/NAV	Capitalization rate used in NAV
REIT A	100%	6%
REIT B	99%	8%

If the REITs have similar property portfolio values, interest expense, and corporate overhead, which REIT *most likely* has the higher Price/FFO?

A   REIT A

B   REIT B

C   They will have similar P/FFOs because their ratios of price to NAV are almost identical.

2 An analyst gathers the following information for two REITs:

	P/NAV	P/AFFO	AFFO Payout Ratio	Est. annual AFFO growth
REIT A	98%	12.8 X	50%	4.0%
REIT B	101%	13.0 X	90%	3.5%

All else being equal, if both REITs have a 10 percent rate of return on retained and reinvested cash flows, which of the REITs is *most* attractively priced?

A   REIT A

B   REIT B

C   Neither REIT is more attractively priced than the other

Solution to 1:

A is correct. A lower capitalization rate (i.e., a lower NOI with such other parameters as interest costs and corporate expenses being the same) implies a lower FFO and hence a higher P/FFO ratio if P/NAV ratios are similar, as is the case here.

B is incorrect because A has a lower capitalization rate, implying a lower FFO and hence a higher P/FFO ratio if P/NAV ratios are similar, as is the case here. C is incorrect because it neglects the effect of the lower capitalization rate of REIT A.

Solution to 2:

B is correct. REIT B is cheaper because it is able to generate almost the same growth in AFFO as REIT A while retaining only 10 percent of AFFO compared with a 50 percent retention rate in the case of REIT A. Because both REITS are achieving a 10 percent return on retained AFFO, it suggests that REIT B has much more growth in returns coming from its existing portfolio of properties. Given very similar P/AFFO multiples for the two REITs, REIT B is more attractively priced. Also for these reasons, A and C are incorrect.

SUMMARY

This reading has presented publicly traded real estate securities, including their structure, economic drivers, investment characteristics, and valuation. Among the important points made by the reading are the following:

- The principal types of publicly traded real estate securities available globally are real estate investment trusts, real estate operating companies, and residential and commercial mortgage-backed securities.

- Publicly traded equity real estate securities offer investors participation in the returns from investment real estate with the advantages of superior liquidity in small and large amounts; greater potential for diversification by property, geography, and property type; access to a superior quality and range of properties; the benefit of management services; limited liability; the ability to use shares as tax-advantaged currency in making acquisitions; protection accorded by corporate governance, disclosure, and other securities regulations; and, in the case of REITs, exemption from income taxation within the REIT if prescribed requirements are met.

- Disadvantages include the costs of maintaining a publicly traded corporate structure, pricing determined by the stock market and returns that can be volatile, potential for structural conflicts of interest, and tax differences compared with direct ownership of property that can be disadvantageous under some circumstances.

- Compared with other publicly traded shares, REITs offer higher than average yields and greater stability of income and returns. They are amenable to a net asset value approach to valuation because of the existence of active private markets for their real estate assets. Compared with REOCs, REITs offer higher yields and income tax exemption but have less operating flexibility to invest in a broad range of real estate activities as well as less potential for growth from reinvesting their operating cash flows because of their high income-to-payout ratios.

- In assessing the investment merits of REITs, investors analyze the effects of trends in general economic activity, retail sales, job creation, population growth, and new supply and demand for specific types of space. They also pay particular attention to occupancies, leasing activity, rental rates, remaining lease terms, in-place rents compared with market rents, costs to maintain space and re-lease space, tenants' financial health and tenant concentration in the portfolio, financial leverage, debt maturities and costs, and the quality of management.

- Analysts make adjustments to the historic cost-based financial statements of REITs and REOCs to obtain better measures of current income and net worth. The three principal figures they calculate and use are (1) funds from operations or accounting net earnings excluding depreciation, deferred tax charges, and gains or losses on sales of property and debt restructuring; (2) adjusted funds from operations, or funds from operations adjusted to remove straight-line rent and to provide for maintenance-type capital expenditures and leasing costs, including leasing agents' commissions and tenants' improvement allowances; and (3) net asset value or the difference between a real estate companies' assets and liabilities ranking prior to shareholders' equity, all valued at market values instead of accounting book values.

- REITs and REOCs are valued using a net asset value per share, price-to-FFO, price-to-AFFO, price-to-NAV, or a discounted cash flow approach, or combinations of these approaches. Three important factors influencing the P/FFO and P/AFFO of REITs and REOCs are expectations for growth in FFO/AFFO, risks associated with the underlying real estate, and risks associated with companies' capital structure and access to capital. The P/NAV approach to valuation can be used as either an absolute basis of valuation or a relative valuation approach. NAV reflects, however, the estimated value of a REIT's assets to a private market buyer, which may or may not be the same as the value that public equity investors ascribe to the business; this fact is one of the reasons for the wide historical premium/discount range at which REITs trade relative to NAV estimates.

- REITs and REOCs generally return a significant portion of their income to their investors and as a result tend to pay high dividends. Thus, dividend discount or discounted cash flow models for valuation are also applicable. These valuation approaches are applied in the same manner as they are for shares in other industries. Most typically, investors utilize two- or three-step dividend discount models with near-term, intermediate-term, and/or long-term growth assumptions. In discounted cash flow models, investors will often use intermediate-term cash flow projections and a terminal value based on historical cash flow multiples.

PRACTICE PROBLEMS

The following information relates to Questions 1–6

Hui Lin, CFA is an investment manager looking to diversify his portfolio by adding equity real estate investments. Lin and his investment analyst, Maria Nowak, are discussing whether they should invest in publicly traded real estate investment trusts (REITs) or public real estate operating companies (REOCs). Nowak expresses a strong preference for investing in public REITs in taxable accounts.

Lin schedules a meeting to discuss this matter, and for the meeting, Lin asks Nowak to gather data on three specific REITs and come prepared to explain her preference for public REITs over public REOCs. At the meeting, Lin asks Nowak:

"Why do you prefer to invest in public REITs over public REOCs for taxable accounts?"

Nowak provides Lin with an explanation for her preference of public REITs and provides Lin with data on the three REITs shown in Exhibits 1 and 2.

The meeting concludes with Lin directing Nowak to identify the key investment characteristics along with the principal risks of each REIT and to investigate the valuation of the three REITs. Specifically, Lin asks Nowak to value each REIT using four different methodologies:

Method 1   Net asset value

Method 2   Discounted cash flow valuation using a two-step dividend model

Method 3   Relative valuation using property subsector average P/FFO multiple

Method 4   Relative valuation using property subsector average P/AFFO multiple

Exhibit 1   Select REIT Financial Information

	REIT A	REIT B	REIT C
Property subsector	**Office**	**Storage**	**Health Care**
Estimated 12 months cash net operating income (NOI)	$350,000	$267,000	$425,000
Funds from operations (FFO)	$316,965	$290,612	$368,007
Cash and equivalents	$308,700	$230,850	$341,000
Accounts receivable	$205,800	$282,150	$279,000
Debt and other liabilities	$2,014,000	$2,013,500	$2,010,000
Non-cash rents	$25,991	$24,702	$29,808
Recurring maintenance-type capital expenditures	$63,769	$60,852	$80,961
Shares outstanding	56,100	67,900	72,300

Exhibit 2 REIT Dividend Forecasts and Average Price Multiples			
	REIT A	**REIT B**	**REIT C**
Expected annual dividend next year	$3.80	$2.25	$4.00
Dividend growth rate in years 2 and 3	4.0%	5.0%	4.5%
Dividend growth rate (after year 3 into perpetuity)	3.5%	4.5%	4.0%
Assumed cap rate	7.0%	6.25%	6.5%
Property subsector average P/FFO multiple	14.4x	13.5x	15.1x
Property subsector average P/AFFO multiple	18.3x	17.1x	18.9x

Note: Nowak estimates an 8% cost of equity capital for all REITs and a risk-free rate of 4.0%.

1 Nowak's *most likely* response to Lin's question is that the type of real estate security she prefers:

A offers a high degree of operating flexibility.

B provides dividend income that is exempt from double taxation.

C has below-average correlations with overall stock market returns.

2 Based upon Exhibits 1 and 2, the value per share for REIT A using valuation Method 1 is *closest* to:

A $51.26.

B $62.40.

C $98.30.

3 Based upon Exhibits 1 and 2, the value per share of REIT B using valuation Method 3 is *closest* to:

A $40.77.

B $57.78.

C $73.19.

4 Based on Exhibit 2, the value per share of REIT C using valuation Method 2 is *closest* to:

A $55.83.

B $97.57.

C $100.91.

5 Based upon Exhibits 1 and 2, the value per share of REIT A using valuation Method 4 is *closest* to:

A $58.32.

B $74.12.

C $103.40.

6 The risk factor *most likely* to adversely impact an investment in REIT B is:

A new competitive facilities.

B tenants' sales per square foot.

C obsolescence of existing space.

The following information relates to Questions 7–12

Tim Wang is a financial advisor specializing in commercial real estate investing. He is meeting with Mark Caudill, a new client who is looking to diversify his investment portfolio by adding real estate investments. Caudill has heard about various investment vehicles related to real estate from his friends and is seeking a more in-depth understanding of these investments from Wang.

Wang begins the meeting by advising Caudill of the many options that are available when investing in real estate, including:

Option 1   Direct ownership in real estate

Option 2   Publicly traded real estate investment trusts (REITs)

Option 3   Publicly traded real estate operating companies (REOCs)

Option 4   Publicly-traded residential mortgage-backed securities (RMBSs)

Wang next asks Caudill about his investment preferences. Caudill responds by telling Wang that he prefers to invest in equity securities that are highly liquid, provide high income, and are not subject to double taxation.

Caudill asks Wang how the economic performance of REITs and REOCs is evaluated, and how their shares are valued. Wang advises Caudill there are multiple measures of economic performance for REITs and REOCs, including:

Measure 1   Net operating income (NOI)

Measure 2   Funds from operations (FFO)

Measure 3   Adjusted funds from operations (AFFO)

In response, Caudill asks Wang:

> "Which of the three measures is the best measure of a REIT's current economic return to shareholders?"

To help Caudill's understanding of valuation, Wang presents Caudill with data on Baldwin, a health care REIT that primarily invests in independent and assisted senior housing communities in large cities across the United States. Select financial data on Baldwin for the past two years are provided in Exhibit 1.

Before the meeting, Wang had put together some valuation assumptions for Baldwin in anticipation of discussing valuation with Caudill. Wang explains the process of valuing a REIT share using discounted cash flow analysis, and proceeds to estimate the value of Baldwin on a per share basis using a two-step dividend discount model using the data provided in Exhibit 2.

Exhibit 1 Baldwin REIT Summarized Income Statement (in thousands of dollars, except per share data)		
	Year Ending December 31	
	2011	**2010**
Rental income	339,009	296,777
Other property income	6,112	4,033
Total income	345,121	300,810
Rental expenses		
Property operating expenses	19,195	14,273
Property taxes	3,610	3,327

(continued)

Exhibit 1	(Continued)	
	Year Ending December 31	
	2011	**2010**
Total property expenses	22,805	17,600
Net operating income	322,316	283,210
Other income (gains on sale of properties)	2,162	1,003
General and administrative expenses	21,865	19,899
Depreciation and amortization	90,409	78,583
Net interest expenses	70,017	56,404
Net income	142,187	129,327
Weighted average shares outstanding	121,944	121,863
Earnings per share	1.17	1.06
Dividend per share	0.93	0.85
Price/FFO, based upon year-end stock price	11.5x	12.7x

Exhibit 2	Baldwin Valuation Projections and Assumptions
Current risk-free rate	4.0%
Baldwin beta	0.90
Market risk premium	5.0%
Appropriate discount rate (CAPM)	8.5%
Expected dividend per share, 1 year from today	$1.00
Expected dividend per share, 2 years from today	$1.06
Long-term growth rate in dividends, starting in year 3	5.0%

7 Based on Caudill's investment preferences, the type of real estate investment Wang is *most likely* to recommend to Caudill is:

 A Option 2.

 B Option 3.

 C Option 4.

8 Relative to Option 2 and Option 3, an advantage of investing in Option 1 is:

 A greater liquidity.

 B lower investment requirements.

 C greater control over property level investment decisions.

9 The Baldwin REIT is *least likely* to experience long-run negative effects from a/ an:

 A economic recession.

 B unfavorable change in population demographics.

 C major reduction in government funding of health care.

10 The *most appropriate* response to Caudill's question is:

   A Measure 1

   B Measure 2

   C Measure 3

11 Based on Exhibit 1, the 2011 year-end share price of Baldwin was *closest* to:

   A $13.23.

   B $21.73.

   C $30.36.

12 Based upon Exhibit 2, the intrinsic value of the Baldwin REIT on a per share basis using the two-step dividend discount model is *closest* to:

   A $26.72.

   B $27.59.

   C $28.83.

SOLUTIONS

1   B is correct. REITs are tax-advantaged entities whereas REOC securities are not typically tax-advantaged entities. More specifically, REITs are typically exempted from the double taxation of income that comes from taxes being due at the corporate level and again when dividends or distributions are made to shareholders in some jurisdictions such at the United States.

2   B is correct. The NAV is $62.40.

Estimated Cash NOI	350,000
Assumed cap rate	0.07
Estimated value of operating real estate (350,000/.07)	5,000,000
Plus: cash + accounts receivable	514,500
Less: Debt and other liabilities	2,014,000
Net Asset Value	3,500,500
Shares outstanding	56,100
NAV/share	$62.40

3   B is correct. The value per share is $57.78, calculated as:

Funds from operations (FFO) = $290,612

Shares outstanding = 67,900 shares

FFO/share = $290,612/67,900 shares = $4.28

Applying the property subsector average P/FFO multiple of 13.5x yields a value per share of:

$4.28 × 13.5 = $57.78.

4   C is correct. The value per share for REIT C is $100.91.

	Step One			Step Two
	Year 1	Year 2	Year 3	Year 4
Dividends per share:	$4.00	$4.18	$4.37	$4.54
Value of stock at end of 2013[a]:			$113.57	
			$117.94	
Discount rate: 8.00%				
Net present value of all dividends[b]: $100.91				

[a] Calculated as $4.54 / (0.08 − 0.04) = $113.57
[b] Calculated as: $4.00 / (1.08) + $4.18 / (1.08)^2 + $117.94 / (1.08)^3 = $100.91

5   B is correct. The value per share is $74.11, calculated as:

Funds from operations (FFO) = $316,965

Less: Non-cash rents: $25,991

Less: Recurring maintenance-type capital expenditures: $63,769

Equals: AFFO: $227,205

Shares outstanding = 56,100 shares

AFFO/share = $227,205/56,100 shares = $4.05.

Applying the property subsector average P/AFFO multiple of 18.3x yields a value per share of:

$4.05 × 18.3 = $74.12.

6 A is correct. As a storage REIT, this investment faces competitive pressures because of the ease of entry into the field of self-storage properties can lead to ～ periods of overbuilding.

7 A is correct. Option 2, publicly traded REITs, best satisfy Caudill's investment preferences. REITs are equity investments that, in general, are income tax exempt at the corporate/trust level, so there is no double income taxation. To qualify for the income tax exemption, REITs are legally obligated to pay out a high percentage of income to their shareholders, and this typically results in relatively high income for investors. Lastly, public REITs are generally liquid as they are traded in stock exchanges.

8 C is correct. Direct property ownership offers greater control over property level investment decisions in comparison to the level of control exhibited by shareholders in REITs and REOCs.

9 A is correct. Baldwin, a health care REIT, is largely resistant to economic recessions but is exposed to changes in population demographics and changes in government funding for health care.

10 C is correct. Measure 3, adjusted funds from operations (AFFO), is a refinement of FFO that is designed to be a more accurate measure of current economic income. In essence, FFO is adjusted to remove any non-cash rent and to include a provision for maintenance-type capital expenditures and leasing costs. Maintenance expenses are required for a business to continue as a going concern.

11 B is correct. Baldwin's FFO per share in 2011 was $1.89, and the resulting share price was $21.73. First, calculate FFO per share in 2011, and then apply the year-end P/FFO multiple of 11.5x.

FFO = accounting net earnings, excluding: (a) depreciation charges on real estate, (b) deferred tax charges, and (c) gains or losses from sales of property and debt restructuring.

2011 accounting net income: $142,187

2011 depreciation charges: $90,409

2011 deferred tax charges: N/A

2011 gains on sale of properties (other income): $2,162

2011 shares outstanding = 121,944

2011 year-end price/FFO = 11.5x

2011 Baldwin's FFO per share = ($142,187 + $90,409 − $2,162)/121,944 shares = $1.89. At the given 2011 year-end price/FFO multiple of 11.5x, this results in a share price for Baldwin of $1.89 × 11.5 = $21.73.

12 C is correct. The estimated value per share for the Baldwin REIT using a two-step dividend discount model is $28.83, calculated as:

	Step One		Step Two
	Year 1	Year 2	Year 3
Dividends per share:	$1.00	$1.06	$1.11
Value of stock at end of Year 2[1]:		$31.80	
		$32.86	
Discount rate: 8.50%			
Net present value of all dividends[2]: $28.83			

[1] Calculated as $1.11/(0.085 − 0.05) = $31.80
[2] Calculated as: $1.00/(1.085) + $32.86/(1.085)^2 = $28.83

Private Equity Valuation

by Yves Courtois, CFA, and Tim Jenkinson, PhD

Yves Courtois, CMT, CFA, is at KPMG (Luxembourg). Tim Jenkinson, PhD, is at Said Business School, Oxford University (United Kingdom).

LEARNING OUTCOMES

Mastery	The candidate should be able to:
☐	a. explain sources of value creation in private equity;
☐	b. explain how private equity firms align their interests with those of the managers of portfolio companies;
☐	c. distinguish between the characteristics of buyout and venture capital investments;
☐	d. describe valuation issues in buyout and venture capital transactions;
☐	e. explain alternative exit routes in private equity and their impact on value;
☐	f. explain private equity fund structures, terms, valuation, and due diligence in the context of an analysis of private equity fund returns;
☐	g. explain risks and costs of investing in private equity;
☐	h. interpret and compare financial performance of private equity funds from the perspective of an investor;
☐	i. calculate management fees, carried interest, net asset value, distributed to paid in (DPI), residual value to paid in (RVPI), and total value to paid in (TVPI) of a private equity fund;
	A Note on Valuation of Venture Capital Deals: (Appendix 41)
☐	j. calculate pre-money valuation, post-money valuation, ownership fraction, and price per share applying the venture capital method 1) with single and multiple financing rounds and 2) in terms of IRR;
☐	k. demonstrate alternative methods to account for risk in venture capital.

1   INTRODUCTION

Private equity is playing an increasing role in the global economy. In the last decade, private equity has grown from a small, niche activity to a critical component of the financial system. One manifestation of this has been the huge amount of money that investors have committed to private equity, estimated at around $1.5 trillion globally between 1998 and 2006. And this is just the equity portion of total financing. As will be explained later, many private equity deals employ significant amounts of debt, and so the value of the transactions involving private equity funds is often 2 or 3 times the actual equity raised. Until recently, few people even knew the names of the main private equity players. But now such organizations as Blackstone, Carlyle, KKR, Texas Pacific Group, and Permira are recognized as major forces in the global financial system. Fund sizes have grown—to over $20 billion at their largest—as have the size and complexity of the transactions that private equity funds are able to undertake, such as the $45 billion acquisition of the US energy company TXU. In 2006, it was estimated that private equity funds were involved in approximately one-quarter of all merger and acquisition activities.

There can be two perspectives on private equity valuation. In Section 2, we primarily take the perspective of the private equity firm that is evaluating potential investments. When a private equity firm is performing valuations of potential acquisitions, this effort is particularly complex because in most cases, except for public-to-private transactions, there will be no market prices to refer to. Private equity firms can face considerable challenges in valuing these companies, and this reading discusses the main ways in which valuation is approached. In Section 3, we take the perspective of an outside investor who is looking at the costs and risks of investing in a fund sponsored by the private equity firm.

Definitions of private equity differ, but in this reading we include the entire asset class of equity investments that are not quoted on stock markets. The private equity class stretches from venture capital (VC)—working with early stage companies that in many cases have no revenues but have potentially good ideas or technology—all the way through to large buyouts (leveraged buyout, or LBO) in which the private equity firm buys the entire company. In some cases, these companies might themselves be quoted on the stock market, and the private equity fund performs a public-to-private transaction thereby removing the entire company from the stock market. But in the majority of cases, buyout transactions will involve privately owned companies and, very often, a particular division of an existing company. There are many other forms of later-stage financing, such as providing capital to back the expansion of existing businesses, but for this reading we will refer simply to *venture capital* and *buyouts* as the two main forms of private equity.

Many classifications of private equity are available. Exhibit 1 provides a set of classifications proposed by the European Venture Capital Association (EVCA).

Exhibit 1	Classification of Private Equity in Terms of Stage and Type of Financing of Portfolio Companies	
Broad Category	**Subcategory**	**Brief Description**
Venture capital	Seed stage	Financing provided to research business ideas, develop prototype products, or conduct market research.
	Start-up stage	Financing to recently created companies with well articulated business and marketing plans.
	Expansion stage	Financing to companies that have started their selling effort and may be already breaking even. Financing may serve to expand production capacity, product development, or provide working capital.
	Replacement capital	Financing provided to purchase shares from other existing venture capital investors or to reduce financial leverage.
Buyout	Acquisition capital	Financing in the form of debt, equity, or quasi-equity provided to a company to acquire another company.
	Leverage buyout	Financing provided by a LBO firm to acquire a company.
	Management buyout	Financing provided to the management to acquire a company, specific product line, or division (carve-out).
Special situations	Mezzanine finance	Financing generally provided in the form of subordinated debt and an equity kicker (warrants, equity, etc.) frequently in the context of LBO transactions.
	Distressed securities	Financing of companies in need of restructuring or facing financial distress.
	One-time opportunities	Financing in relation to changing industry trends and new government regulations.
	Others	Other forms of private equity financing are also possible (i.e., activist investing, etc.).

Source: www.evca.com.

These classifications are not exhaustive. Private equity funds may also be classified depending on their geographical (national, regional, or global) and/or sector focus (e.g., diversified industrials, telecommunications, biotechnologies, healthcare, industrials, etc.).

How is the invested money split between venture capital and buyout deals? In broad terms, around four-fifths of the money has been flowing into buyouts in recent years in both the United States and Europe. In part this is because of the sheer scale of buyouts in which an individual deal can absorb several billion dollars of capital. In contrast, venture capital deals tend to drip feed money into companies as they develop. But investors also have been increasingly focusing on buyout funds, in which, in recent years at least, the average returns earned have tended to be higher.

Where does the money come from and how are the private equity funds organized? Most of the money comes from institutional investors, such as pension funds, endowments, and insurance companies, although many high-net-worth individuals also invest directly or through fund-of-funds intermediaries who provide their investors with a more diversified portfolio of investments. At present, the proportion of assets allocated by investors to private equity is considerably higher in the United States than in Europe, although surveys of European investors find that the fund managers plan to increase their allocation to private equity. So the flow of money into private equity is likely to continue and indeed grow, depending, of course, on market conditions.

One distinctive characteristic of private equity investment is a buy-to-sell orientation. Private equity fund investors typically expect their money returned, with a handsome profit, within 10 years of committing their funds. The economic incentives of the funds are aligned with this goal, as is explained later. In the next section we discuss this buy-to-sell approach and how funds are typically organized.

2   INTRODUCTION TO VALUATION TECHNIQUES IN PRIVATE EQUITY TRANSACTIONS

This reading is not intended to be a comprehensive review of valuation techniques applicable to private equity transactions. Instead, we highlight some essential considerations specific to private equity. As you might expect, private equity firms are a rich laboratory for applying the principles of asset and equity valuation. The case study on venture capital valuation that follows this reading demonstrates how a specific valuation technique can be applied.

First and foremost, we must distinguish between the price paid for a private equity stake and the valuation of such private equity stake. The price paid for a private equity stake is the outcome of a negotiation process between two or more parties with each possibly assigning a different value to that same private equity stake. Unlike shares of public companies that are traded regularly on a regulated market, buyers and sellers of private equity interests generally employ more efforts to uncover their value. Private equity valuation is thus time bound and dependent on the respective motives and interests of buyers and sellers.

The selection of the appropriate valuation methodologies depends largely on the stage of development of a private equity portfolio company. Exhibit 2 provides an overview of some of the main methodologies employed in private equity valuation and an indication of the stage of company development for which they may apply.

Exhibit 2	Overview of Selected Valuation Methodologies and Their Possible Application in Private Equity	
Valuation Technique	**Brief Description**	**Application**
Income approach: Discounted cash flows (DCF)	Value is obtained by discounting expected future cash flows at an appropriate cost of capital.	Generally applies across the broad spectrum of company stages. Given the emphasis on expected cash flows, this methodology provides the most relevant results when applied to companies with a sufficient operating history. Therefore, most applicable to companies operating from the expansion up to the maturity phase.
Relative value: Earnings multiples	Application of an earnings multiple to the earnings of a portfolio company. The earnings multiple is frequently obtained from the average of a group of public companies operating in a similar business and of comparable size. Commonly used multiples include: Price/Earnings (P/E), Enterprise Value/EBITDA, Enterprise Value/Sales.	Generally applies to companies with a significant operating history and predictable stream of cash flows. May also apply with caution to companies operating at the expansion stage. Rarely applies to early stage or start-up companies.

Exhibit 2	(Continued)	
Valuation Technique	**Brief Description**	**Application**
Real option	The right to undertake a business decision (call or put option). Requires judgmental assumptions about key option parameters.	Generally applies to situations in which the management or shareholders have significant flexibility in making radically different strategic decisions (i.e., option to undertake or abandon a high risk, high return project). Therefore, generally applies to some companies operating at the seed or start-up phase.
Replacement cost	Estimated cost to recreate the business as it stands as of the valuation date.	Generally applies to early (seed and start-up) stage companies or companies operating at the development stage and generating negative cash flows. Rarely applies to mature companies as it is difficult to estimate the cost to recreate a company with a long operating history. For example, it would be difficult to estimate the cost to recreate a long established brand like Coca-Cola, whereas the replacement cost methodology may be used to estimate the brand value for a recently launched beverage (R&D expenses, marketing costs, etc.).

One other methodology, the venture capital method, is discussed more fully as part of the case study that follows this reading.

Note that in a vibrant and booming private equity market, there is a natural tendency among participants to focus primarily on the earnings approach to determine value. This approach is perceived as providing a benchmark value corresponding best to the state of the current private equity market. Because of the lack of liquidity of private equity investments, the concurrent use of other valuation metrics is strongly recommended.

Thus, valuation does not involve simply performing a net present value calculation on a static set of future profit projections. The forecasts of the existing management or vendors are, of course, a natural place to start, but one of the key ways private equity firms add value is by challenging the way businesses are run. The business would have additional value if the private equity firm improves the business's financing, operations, management, and marketing.

In most transactions, private equity investors are faced with a set of investment decisions that are based on an assessment of prospective returns and associated probabilities. Private equity firms are confronted generally with a large flow of information arising from detailed due diligence investigations and from complex financial models. It is essential to understand the extent of the upside and downside potential of internal and external factors affecting the business and their resulting effect on net income and free cash flows. Any possible scenario must pass the judgmental test of how realistic it is. The defined scenarios should be based not only on the analysis of past events, but on what future events may realistically happen, given knowledge of the present. The interplay between exogenous factors (such as favorable and unfavorable macroeconomic conditions, interest rates, and exchange rates) and value drivers for the business (such as sales margins and required investments) should also be considered carefully. For example, what will be the sales growth if competition increases or if competing new technologies are introduced?

When building the financial forecasts, all variables in the financial projections should be linked to key fundamental factors influencing the business with assigned subjective probabilities. The use of Monte Carlo simulation, often using a spreadsheet add-in such as Crystal Ball™ or @RISK, further enhances the quality of the analysis and may be instrumental in identifying significant financial upsides and downsides to the business. In a Monte Carlo simulation, the analyst must model the fundamental value drivers of the portfolio company, which are in turn linked to a valuation model. Base case, worst case, and best case scenarios (sometimes called a triangular approach) and associated probabilities should be discussed with line managers for each value driver with the objective being to ensure that the simulation is as close as possible to the realities of the business and encompasses the range of possible outcomes.

Other key considerations when evaluating a private equity transaction include the value of control, the impact of illiquidity, and the extent of any country risk. Estimating the discount for illiquidity and marketability and a premium for control are among the most subjective decisions in private equity valuation. The control premium is an incremental value associated with a bloc of shares that will be instrumental in gaining control of a company. In most buyouts, the entire equity capital is acquired by the private equity purchasers. But in venture capital deals, investors often acquire minority positions. In this case the control premium (if any) largely depends on the relative strength and alignment of interest of shareholders willing to gain control. For example, in a situation with only a limited number of investors able to acquire control, the control premium is likely to be much more significant relative to a situation with a dominant controlling shareholder invested along with a large number of much smaller shareholders.

The distinction between marketability and liquidity is more subtle. The cost of illiquidity may be defined as the cost of finding prospective buyers and represents the speed of conversion of the assets to cash, whereas the cost of marketability is closely related to the right to sell the assets. In practice, the marketability and liquidity discounts are frequently lumped together.

The cost for illiquidity and premium for control may be closely related because illiquidity may be more acute when there is a fierce battle for control. But there are many dimensions to illiquidity. The size of the illiquidity discount may be influenced by such factors as the shareholding structure, the level of profitability and its expected sustainability, the possibility of an initial public offering (IPO) in the near future, and the size of the private company. Because determining the relative importance of each factor may be difficult, the illiquidity discount is frequently assessed overall on a judgmental basis. In practice, the discount for illiquidity and premium for control are both adjustments to the preliminary value estimate instead of being factored into the cost of capital.

When valuing private equity portfolio companies in emerging markets, country risk may also represent a significant additional source of risk frequently added to a modified version of the standard CAPM. Estimating the appropriate country risk premium represents another significant challenge in emerging markets private equity valuation. These technical hurdles relate not only to private equity investments in emerging markets but also increasingly to global private equity transactions conducted "en-bloc" in multiple countries. More than 15 approaches exist for the estimation of the country risk premium.[1]

Valuation in private equity transactions is, therefore, very challenging. Whereas traditional valuation methodologies, such as discounted cash flow analysis, adjusted present value, and techniques based on comparisons from the public market of precedent transactions, are used frequently by investment and valuation professionals, they are applied to private equity situations with care, taking into consideration stress

---

1 The modified country spread model, also called the modified Goldman model, is frequently used in practice. The Erb, Harvey, and Viskanta model, also called the country risk rating model, is gaining increasing popularity among valuation practitioners, partly because of its ease of use and theoretical appeal. For a comprehensive analysis of this topic, see *Estimating Cost of Capital in Emerging Markets*, Yves Courtois, CFA Institute webcasts, www.cfainstitute.org.

tests and a range of possible future scenarios for the business. Given the challenges of private equity valuation, value estimates based on a combination of several valuation methodologies will provide the strongest support for the estimated value. Private equity valuation is a process that starts as a support for decision making at the transaction phase but should also serve as a monitoring tool to capture new opportunities, or protect from losses, with the objective to continuously create value until the investment is exited. It also serves as a performance reporting tool to investors while the company remains in the fund portfolio. These ongoing valuation and reporting issues are discussed in Section 3.

2.1 How Is Value Created in Private Equity?

The question of how private equity funds actually create value has been much debated inside and outside the private equity industry. The survival of the private equity governance model depends on some economic advantages it may have over the public equity governance model. These potential advantages, described more fully below, include 1) the ability to re-engineer the private firm to generate superior returns, 2) the ability to access credit markets on favorable terms, and 3) a better alignment of interests between private equity firm owners and the managers of the firms they control.

Do private equity houses have superior ability to re-engineer companies and, therefore, generate superior returns? Some of the largest private equity organizations, such as Kohlberg Kravis Roberts (KKR), The Carlyle Group, Texas Pacific Group (TPG), or Blackstone Group, have developed in-house high-end consulting capabilities supported frequently by seasoned industry veterans (former CEOs, CFOs, senior advisers), and have a proven ability to execute deals on a global basis. Irrespective of their size, some of the very best private equity firms have developed effective re-engineering capabilities to add value to their investments. But it is hard to believe that this factor, all else being equal, is the main driver of value added in private equity. Assuming that private equity houses have a superior ability to re-engineer companies, this would mean that public companies have inherently less ability to conduct re-engineering or organizational changes relative to corporations held by private equity organizations. Many public companies, like General Electric or Toyota, have established a long track record of creating value. Thus, only a part of value added created by private equity houses may be explained by superior reorganization and re-engineering capabilities. The answer must also come from other factors.

Is financial leverage the main driver of private equity returns in buyouts? Ample availability of credit at favorable terms (such as low credit spreads and few covenants) led in 2006 and the first half of 2007 to a significant increase in leverage available to buyout transactions. Borrowing 6 to 8 times EBITDA (earnings before interest, taxes, depreciation, and amortization) has been frequent for large transactions conducted during this period. Note that in private equity, leverage is typically measured as a multiple of EBITDA instead of equity. Relative to comparable publicly quoted companies, there is a much greater use of debt in a typical buyout transaction.

When considering the impact of leverage on value, we should naturally turn to one of the foundations of modern finance: the Modigliani–Miller theorem.[2] This theorem, in its basic form, states that, in the absence of taxes, asymmetric information, bankruptcy costs, and assuming efficient markets, the value of a firm is not affected by how the firm is financed. In other words, it should not matter if the firm is financed by equity or debt. The relaxing of the "no taxes assumption" raises interesting questions in leveraged buyouts as the tax shield on the acquisition debt creates value as a

---

2 F. Modigliani and M. Miller, "The Cost of Capital, Corporation Finance and the Theory of Investment." *American Economic Review* (June 1958).

result of tax deductibility of interest. One would also expect that the financial leverage of a firm would be set at a level where bankruptcy costs do not outweigh these tax benefits. Unlike public companies, private equity firms may have a better ability to raise higher levels of debt as a result of a better control over management but also as a result of their reputation for having raised, and repaid, such high levels of debt in previous transactions.

Such debt financing is raised initially from the syndicated loan market, but then is frequently repackaged via sophisticated structured products, such as collateralized loan obligations (CLOs), which consist of a portfolio of leveraged loans. In some cases the private equity funds issue high-yield bonds as a way of financing the portfolio company, and these often are sold to funds that create collateralized debt obligations (CDOs). This raises the question of whether a massive transfer of risks to the credit markets is taking place in private equity. If the answer to this last question is positive, then one would expect that it will self-correct during the next economic downturn. Note that at the time of this writing (early 2008), the CDO and CLO markets were undergoing a significant slowdown as a result of the credit market turmoil that started in the summer of 2007, triggered by the subprime mortgage crisis. The CDO and CLO markets are (at this time) inactive. As a result, the LBO market for very large transactions ("mega buyouts") was affected by a lack of financing. Additional leverage is also gained by means of equity-like instruments at the acquisition vehicle level, which are frequently located in a favorable jurisdiction such as Luxembourg, the Channel Islands, Cayman Islands, or the British Virgin Islands. Note that acquisitions by large buyout private equity firms are generally held by a top holding company in a favorable tax jurisdiction. The top holding company's share capital and equity-like instruments are held in turn by investment funds run by a general partner who is controlled by the private equity buyout firm. These instruments are treated as debt for tax purposes within the limits of thin capitalization rules in certain jurisdictions. In Luxembourg, such equity-like instruments are called convertible preferred equity certificates, or CPECs.

The effect of leverage may also be analyzed through Jensen's free cash flow hypothesis.[3] According to Jensen, low growth companies generating high free cash flows tend to invest in projects destroying value (i.e., with a negative net present value) instead of distributing excess cash to shareholders. This argument is a possible explanation[4] as to why a LBO transaction may generate value as excess cash is used to repay the senior debt tranche, effectively removing the management's discretionary use of cash. Part of the value added in private equity may thus be explained by the level of financial leverage.

What other factors may then significantly explain the returns earned by private equity funds? One important factor is the alignment of economic interests between private equity owners and the managers of the companies they control, which can crystallize management efforts to achieve ambitious milestones set by the private equity owners. Results-driven management pay packages, along with various contractual clauses, ensure that managers receive proper incentives to reach their targets, and that they will not be left behind after the private equity house exits their investment. Examples of such contract terms include tag-along, drag-along rights, which are contractual provisions in share purchase agreements that ensure any potential future acquirer of the company may not acquire control without extending an acquisition offer to all shareholders, including the management of the company.

---

3 Jensen, M., "Agency Costs of Free Cash Flow, Corporate Finance and Takeovers," *American Economic Review*, vol. 76 no. 2 (1986).
4 Jensen, M., "Eclipse of the Public Corporation," *Harvard Business Review*, 67 (1989).

Empirical evidence also shows that managers from public companies subsequently acquired by private equity groups tend to acknowledge an increased level of directness and intensity of input enabling them to conduct higher value-added projects over a longer time frame after the buyout, as opposed to the "short-termism" prevailing during their public market period. This short-termism is mostly driven by shareholders' expectations, the analyst community, and the broad market participants who place a significant emphasis on management to meet quarterly earnings targets. As private equity firms have a longer time horizon in managing their equity investments, they are able to attract talented managers having the ability to implement sometimes profound restructuring plans in isolation of short-term market consequences. Note however, that private equity firms are not the sole catalysts of change at large companies. Some large organizations, for example General Electric, have a proven ability to stir entrepreneurship at all levels within the company and generate substantial value over a long time horizon.

Effective structuring of investments terms (called the "term sheet") results in a balance of rights and obligations between the private equity firm and the management team. In addition to the clauses discussed above, the following contractual clauses are important illustrations of how private equity firms ensure that the management team is focused on achieving the business plan and that if the objectives are not met, the control and equity allocation held by the private equity firm will increase:

- *Corporate board seats*: ensures private equity control in case of major corporate events such as company sale, takeover, restructuring, IPO, bankruptcy, or liquidation.

- *Noncompete clause*: generally imposed on founders and prevents them from restarting the same activity during a predefined period of time.

- *Preferred dividends and liquidation preference*: private equity firms generally come first when distributions take place, and may be guaranteed a minimum multiple of their original investment before other shareholders receive their returns.

- *Reserved matters*: some domains of strategic importance (such as changes in the business plan, acquisitions, or divestitures) are subject to approval or veto by the private equity firm.

- *Earn-outs (mostly in venture capital)*: mechanism linking the acquisition price paid by the private equity firm to the company's future financial performance over a predetermined time horizon, generally not exceeding 2 to 3 years.

Effective contractual structuring of the investment can thus be a significant source of return to private equity firms. In particular, it may allow venture capital firms, which invest in companies with considerable uncertainties over their future, to significantly increase their level of control over time and even seize control in case the company fails to achieve the agreed goals.

2.2 Using Market Data in Valuation

In most private equity transactions—with the exception of public-to-privates—there is no direct market evidence on the valuation of the company being acquired. But virtually all valuation techniques employ evidence from the market at differing stages in the calculation, rather than relying entirely on accounting data and management forecasts.

The two most important ways in which market data are used to infer the value of the entity being acquired are by analyzing comparison companies that are quoted on public markets and valuations implied by recent transactions involving similar entities. Typically, these techniques focus on the trading or acquisition multiples that exist in the public markets or in recent transactions. For instance, suppose a valuation is sought in the food sector for a retail chain, which is currently a privately owned company. The comparison company approach would look at the trading multiples—such as enterprise value to EBITDA—of comparable public companies, and use this multiple to value the target. Similarly, if there are recent M&A transactions in the food retail sector, the transactions multiples paid could be used to inform the current market value of the target. Of course, it is very important to make sure that the comparisons are appropriate, and this is not always possible, especially for certain businesses that operate in niche sectors or that are pioneering in terms of their products or services.

The use of market data is also important in the DCF approaches, in particular in estimating an appropriate discount rate. Cost of capital for private companies is estimated generally using the same weighted average cost of capital (WACC) formula[5] used for public companies. A serious challenge, however, in assessing the cost of equity in private equity settings is the lack of public historical data on share prices and returns. Therefore, beta (β), which represents the relative exposure of company shares to the market, must be estimated by means of a proxy. This is performed typically by estimating the beta for comparable companies, and then adjusting for financial and operating leverage. When conducting this benchmark exercise, several issues that may depend on analyst judgment should be considered: To what extent are the selected comparable public firms genuinely comparable to the target firm? Should outlying companies be excluded? What is the target debt-to-equity ratio of the target firm vs. industry average? What group of comparable public companies should be selected if the target firm operates in several business segments?

Finally, in DCF valuation techniques, forecasts of future financial performance usually are only available for a few years ahead. Therefore, it is almost always necessary to estimate the terminal value of the company beyond this forecasting horizon. In order to do this, it is possible to apply a perpetual growth rate assumption, although small changes in the assumed growth rate, which are very difficult to predict, can have a significant impact on the resulting valuation. An alternative is to use an assumption about the trading multiple that exists (or is predicted to exist) in public markets, and apply this to the last years' forecast values. For instance, if over the economic cycle the average enterprise value to EBITDA ratio for the publicly quoted companies in an industry is 10, then this might be applied to the final forecast value for EBITDA for the private target as a way of estimating the terminal value.

2.3 Contrasting Valuation in Venture Capital and Buyout Settings

Buyout and venture capital funds are the two main categories of private equity investments both in terms of number of funds and invested amounts. Whereas a venture capital firm may have a specialized industry focus—looking for the next rising star in technology, in life sciences, or another industry—LBO firms generally invest in a portfolio of firms with more predictable cash flow patterns. Venture capital firms (investing in new firms and new technologies) seek revenue growth, whereas buyout firms (investing in larger, established firms) focus more on EBIT or EBITDA growth. The approach to company valuation is thus fundamentally different, and Exhibit 3 presents some of the key distinctions.

---

5 WACC = $[E/(E + D)] \times$ (Cost of equity) + $[D/(E + D)] \times$ (Cost of debt) $(1 - \text{Tax rate})$, where E is the market value of equity and D is the market value of debt.

Exhibit 3 Characteristics of Buyout and Venture Capital Investments	
Buyout Investments:	**Venture Capital Investments:**
■ Steady and predictable cash flows	■ Low cash flow predictability, cash flow projections may not be realistic
■ Excellent market position (can be a niche player)	■ Lack of market history, new market and possibly unproven future market (early stage venture)
■ Significant asset base (may serve as basis for collateral lending)	■ Weak asset base
■ Strong and experienced management team	■ Newly formed management team with strong individual track record as entrepreneurs
■ Extensive use of leverage consisting of a large proportion of senior debt and significant layer of junior and/or mezzanine debt	■ Primarily equity funded. Use of leverage is rare and very limited
■ Risk is measurable (mature businesses, long operating history)	■ Assessment of risk is difficult because of new technologies, new markets, lack of operating history
■ Predictable exit (secondary buyout, sale to a strategic buyer, IPO)	■ Exit difficult to anticipate (IPO, trade sale, secondary venture sale)
■ Established products	■ Technological breakthrough but route to market yet to be proven
■ Potential for restructuring and cost reduction	■ Significant cash burn rate required to ensure company development and commercial viability
■ Low working capital requirement	■ Expanding capital requirement if in the growth phase
■ Buyout firm typically conducts full blown due diligence approach before investing in the target firm (financial, strategic, commercial, legal, tax, environmental)	■ Venture capital firm tends to conduct primarily a technology and commercial due diligence before investing; financial due diligence is limited as portfolio companies have no or very little operating history
■ Buyout firm monitors cash flow management, strategic, and business planning	■ Venture capital firm monitors achievement of milestones defined in business plan and growth management
■ Returns of investment portfolios are generally characterized by lower variance across returns from underlying investments; bankruptcies are rare events	■ Returns of investment portfolios are generally characterized by very high returns from a limited number of highly successful investments and a significant number of write-offs from low performing investments or failures
■ Large buyout firms are generally significant players in capital markets	■ Venture capital firms tend to be much less active in capital markets
■ Most transactions are auctions, involving multiple potential acquirers	■ Many transactions are "proprietary," being the result of relationships between venture capitalists and entrepreneurs
■ Strong performing buyout firms tend to have a better ability to raise larger funds after they have successfully raised their first funds[a]	■ Venture capital firms tend to be less scalable relative to buyout firms; the increase in size of subsequent funds tend to be less significant[b]
■ Variable revenue to the general partner (GP) at buyout firms generally comprise the following three sources: carried interest, transaction fees, and monitoring fees[c]	■ Carried interest (participation in profits) is generally the main source of variable revenue to the general partner at venture capital firms; transaction and monitoring fees are rare in practice[d]

[a] Andrew Metrick and Ayako Yasuda, "The Economics of Private Equity Funds." University of Pennsylvania, The Wharton School (September 9, 2007).
[b] Ibid.
[c] Ibid.
[d] Ibid.

2.4 Valuation Issues in Buyout Transactions

A buyout is a form of private equity transaction in which the buyer acquires from the seller a controlling stake in the equity capital of a target company. The generic term "buyout" thus refers explicitly to the notion of acquiring control. It comprises a wide range of techniques, including but not limited to, management buyouts (MBOs), leveraged buyouts (LBOs), or takeovers. Our focus in this reading will be on LBOs, which consist in the acquisition of a company using borrowed money to finance a significant portion of the acquisition price.

Typically, the structuring of LBO transactions involves a negotiation between the providers of equity capital, senior debt, high yield bonds, and mezzanine finance. Mezzanine finance[6] is a hybrid form of financing that may be perceived as a bridge between equity and debt. It is generally structured flexibly and tailored to fit the specific requirements of every transaction.

2.4.1 The LBO Model

The LBO model is not a separate valuation technique, but rather a way of determining the impact of the capital structure, purchase price, and various other parameters on the returns expected by the private equity fund from the deal.

The LBO model has three main input parameters: the cash flow forecasts of the target company, the expected return from the providers of financing (equity, senior debt, high yield bonds, mezzanine), and the amount of financing available for the transaction. The free cash flow forecasts of the target company are generally prepared by the management of the target company and are subject to an extensive due diligence process (strategic, commercial, financial, legal, and environmental) to determine the reliability of such forecasts. These forecasts are prepared on the basis of an explicit forecast horizon that generally corresponds to the expected holding horizon of the private equity firm in the equity capital of the target company.

The exit year is typically considered as a variable with the objective to determine the expected IRR sensitivity on the equity capital around the anticipated exit date. The exit value is determined most frequently by reference to an expected range of exit multiples determined on the basis of a peer group of comparable companies (Enterprise Value-to-EBITDA).

On the basis of the input parameters, the LBO model provides the maximum price that can be paid to the seller while satisfying the target returns for the providers of financing. This is why the LBO model is not a valuation methodology per se. It is a negotiation tool that helps develop a range of acceptable prices to conclude the transaction.

Exhibit 4 is a "value creation chart," summarizing the sources of the additional value between the exit value and the original cost. Value creation comes from a combination of factors: earnings growth arising from operational improvements and enhanced corporate governance; multiple expansion depending on pre-identified potential exits; and optimal financial leverage and repayment of part of the debt with operational cash flows before the exit. Each component of the value creation chart should be carefully considered and backed by supporting analyses, frequently coming from the lengthy due diligence process (especially commercial, tax, and financial) and also from a strategic review with the objective to quantify the range of plausible value creation.

---

6 For a more comprehensive discussion of mezzanine finance, refer to "Mezzanine Finance—A Hybrid Instrument with a Future," *Economic Briefing No 42*, Credit Suisse (2006).

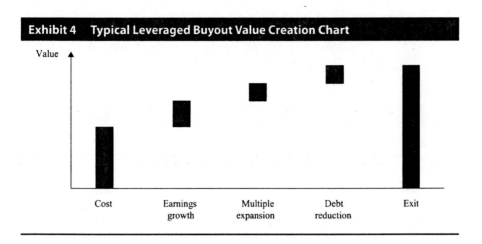

Exhibit 4 Typical Leveraged Buyout Value Creation Chart

Exhibit 5 provides an example of a €5,000 (amounts in millions) investment in a private equity transaction. The transaction is financed with 50 percent debt and 50 percent equity. The €2,500 equity investment is further broken into €2,400 of preference shares owned by the private equity fund, €95 of equity owned by the private equity fund, and €5 of management equity. The preference shares are promised a 12 percent annual return (paid at exit). The private equity firm equity is promised 95 percent of the residual value of the firm after creditors and preference shares are paid, and management equity holders are promised the remaining 5 percent.

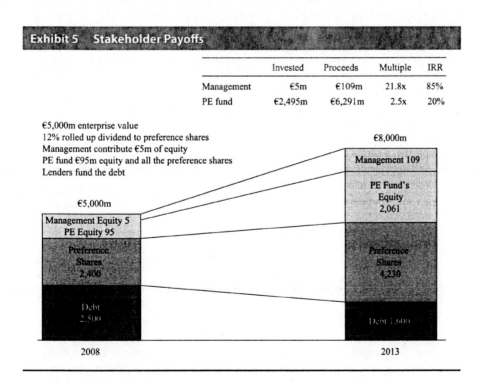

Exhibit 5 Stakeholder Payoffs

	Invested	Proceeds	Multiple	IRR
Management	€5m	€109m	21.8x	85%
PE fund	€2,495m	€6,291m	2.5x	20%

Assume that the exit value, five years after investment, is 1.6 times the original cost. The initial investment of €5,000 has an exit value of €8,000. The specific payoffs for the four claimants are as follows:

- Senior debt has been partially retired with operational cash flows, reducing debt from €2,500 to €1,600. So debtholders get €1,600.

- Preference shares are paid a 12 percent return for 5 years, so they receive €2,400$(1.12)^5$ = €4,230.
- PE Fund equity receives 95 percent of the terminal equity value, or 0.95[8000 − (4230 + 1600)] = €2,061.
- Management equity receives 5 percent of the terminal equity value, or 0.05[8000 − (4230 + 1600)] = €109.

As you can see, preference shares increase in value over time as a result of their preferred dividend being capitalized, and the equity held by the PE fund and by the management is expected to increase significantly depending on the total enterprise value upon exit. Both the equity sold to managers, frequently known as the management equity program (MEP), and the equity held by the private equity firm are most sensitive to the level of the exit. The larger the exit multiple, the larger the upside potential for both the MEP and the equity held by the private equity firm. In the example, assuming that an exit of 1.6 times cash may be achieved at the anticipated exit date (2013), the management would realize an IRR of 85 percent per annum on its investment and the private equity fund equity holders an IRR of 20 percent per annum. The private equity firm also earns 12 percent per annum on its preference shares.

This chart also demonstrates the critical importance of leverage in buyout transactions. A reduction in financial leverage over time is instrumental in magnifying returns available to shareholders. Note that the bulk of financial leverage in LBOs consists of senior debt, much of which will be amortizing. Therefore, the reduction in financial leverage gradually increases over time as a proportion of principal is paid back to senior lenders on an annual or semi-annual basis depending on the terms of senior debt. As a result of senior debt gradual repayment over time, a larger proportion of operating cash flows becomes available to equity holders. Of course, this mechanism works well as long as no significant adverse economic factors negatively impact the business of the target LBO company and also provided that a successful exit can be handled in the foreseeable future. It should be remembered, however, that these high levels of debt increase significantly the risks borne by the equity investors, and such increased risk should be taken into account when comparing the realized returns with alternative investment classes (such as investments in the stock market).

Typically, a series of scenarios with varying levels of cash exits, growth assumptions, and debt levels are engineered with the use of an LBO model, using as inputs the required rate of return from each stakeholder (equity, mezzanine, senior debt holders), to gain a sound understanding of the buyout firm's flexibility in conducting the deal.

2.5 Valuation Issues in Venture Capital Transactions

In venture capital, pre-money valuation and post-money valuation are two fundamental concepts. Pre-money valuation (PRE) refers to the agreed value of a company prior to a round of financing or investment (I). Post-money valuation (POST) is the value of a company after the financing or investing round. Therefore:

POST = PRE + I

The proportionate ownership of the venture capital investor is determined by I/POST.

EXAMPLE 1

Investment and Ownership Interest of a VC Firm

A venture capital firm invests £1 million on a £1.5 million pre-money valuation and the VC firm obtains 40 percent of shares. In this case, PRE is £1.5 million, POST is £2.5 million, and the proportion financed by venture capital is £1 million/£2.5 million. The parties agreed that the VC firm would retain 40 percent of the shares and have that proportion of the rights of shareholders should dividends be paid or the firm sold.

Typically, both pre-money valuation and the level of the venture capital investment are subject to intense negotiations between the founders and the venture capital firm, bearing in mind the fundamental issue of dilution of ownership. Dilution of ownership is the reduction in the proportional ownership of a shareholder in the capital of a company resulting from the issuance of additional shares and/or of securities convertible into shares at some stage in the future. Additional financing rounds and the issuance of stock options to the management of a company are examples of dilution of ownership.

In VC transactions, there is typically significant uncertainty surrounding the projected future cash flows. Consequently, the discounted cash flow methodology is rarely used as the first method to determine value. Similarly, there are challenges applying the comparable companies approach as start-ups generally have unique features and it may be extremely difficult to find comparable quoted companies operating in the same field. Alternative valuation methodologies including the venture capital approach[7] or the real option methodology are also used to determine value. Traditional valuation methodologies typically comprise the income approach (discounted cash flow valuation), the relative value or market approach (information relative to a group of comparable companies is gathered and normalized relative to the EBITDA, EBIT, and revenue of the company being valued), and the cost approach (cost to recreate or replace the asset or company). Generally speaking, the appraisal of intangible assets, comprising the founder's know-how, experience, licenses, patents, and in progress research and development (IPRD), along with an assessment of the expected market potential of the company's product or products in development form the basis for assessing a pre-money valuation. Because of the significant level of uncertainty surrounding the business, it is not infrequent to observe a cap on the pre-money valuation (i.e., €3 million, €5 million, etc.).

In buyouts, given the significant predictability of cash flows, the income-based approach (discounted cash flows, adjusted present value, LBO model, target IRR) is frequently used as a primary method to determine the value of equity, considering the expected change in leverage until the time of exit of the investment. The initial high and declining financial leverage is the main technical valuation issue that needs to be adequately factored into the income approach when applied to a buyout valuation. The value is also frequently corroborated by an analysis of the peer group of comparable publicly traded companies.

2.6 Exit Routes: Returning Cash to Investors

The exit is among the most critical mechanisms to unlock value in private equity. Most private equity firms consider their exit options prior to investing and factor their assessment of the exit outcome into their analysis of target and expected internal rate of return.

Private equity investors generally have access to the following four exit routes for their investments:

- *Initial Public Offering (IPO)*: going public offers significant advantages including higher valuation multiples as a result of an enhanced liquidity, access to large amounts of capital, and the possibility to attract higher caliber managers. But an

---

7 Discussed in "A Note on Valuation of Venture Capital Deals."

IPO comes at the expense of a cumbersome process, less flexibility, and significant costs. Therefore, an IPO is an appropriate exit route for private companies with an established operating history, excellent growth prospects, and having a sufficient size. Timing of the IPO is also an important consideration. After the internet bubble collapse in March 2000, the number of successful IPOs plummeted in the subsequent years, forcing venture capital firms to change their exit plans for many of their investments.

▪ *Secondary Market*: sale of stake held by a financial investor to other financial investors or to strategic investors (companies operating or willing to establish in the same sector or market of the portfolio company). With the increased segmentation of private equity, secondary market transactions tend to occur within each segment, i.e., buyout firms tend to sell to other buyout firms (secondary buyouts) and venture firms to other venture firms (secondary venture capital transactions). These secondary market transactions are very common in practice and currently account for a significant proportion of exits, especially in the buyout segment. Venture capital exits by means of a buyout are also possible but rare in practice as buyout firms are reluctant to finance development stage companies with a significant amount of leverage. The two main advantages of secondary market transactions are 1) the possibility to achieve the highest valuation multiples in the absence of an IPO, and 2) with the segmentation of private equity firms, specialized firms have the skill to bring their portfolio companies to the next level (restructuring, merger, new market) and sell either to a strategic investor seeking to exploit synergies or to another private equity firm having another set of skills and the ability to further add value to the portfolio company.

▪ *Management Buyout (MBO)*: takeover by the management group using significant amounts of leverage to finance the acquisition of the company. Alignment of interest is optimal under this exit scenario but may come at the expense of an excessive leverage that may significantly reduce the company's flexibility.

▪ *Liquidation*: controlling shareholders have the power to liquidate the company if the company is no longer viable. This exit mechanism generally results in a floor value for the portfolio company but may come at a cost of very negative publicity for the private equity firm if the portfolio company is large and the employee count is significant.

Timing the exit and determining the optimal exit route are important investment management decisions to be made by private equity firms. Although the exit may be carefully planned, the unexpected can cause changes to the exit plan. This may mean that the exit could be delayed or accelerated depending on the market or purely opportunistic circumstances. Suppose, for example, that an LBO firm is planning an exit of one of its portfolio companies but the public market and economic conditions have collapsed, rendering any exit via a trade sale or an IPO unprofitable. The LBO firm may instead conduct another acquisition at depressed prices, merge this acquisition with the portfolio company with the objective to strengthen its market position or product range, and wait for better market conditions before conducting the sale. Flexibility is thus critical in private equity during harder times and underlines the importance for a private equity firm to have sufficient financial strength.

There seems to be no boundaries to the size of the largest buyout transactions as expectations have been consistently exceeded over the past few years and the $50 billion threshold appears now to be in sight for the largest buyout firms. The three largest buyout transactions in history, HCA Inc., Equity Office, and TXU Corporation, were all undertaken over the eighteen months before this reading was written. Private equity firms appear to be moving into uncharted territory in regards to managing exits at that level. The central question about these mega buyout transactions is how the exit will take place given that the extent of the exit possibilities is much more limited relative to smaller deals. IPOs, for example, raise significantly more challenges, such as the need for a gradual exit over time because only a single block of shares can be sold initially, and may prove excessively risky if market conditions are suboptimal. Some large companies may be viewed as holding companies of a portfolio of real assets. Such companies may be sold in tranches to prospective buyers. The real challenge will be for unified companies for which an exit will need to take place for the entire entity.

Understanding the anticipated exit provides clues as to what valuation methodologies or IRR models to employ. Timing of the exit will influence the way stress testing is conducted on the expected exit multiple. When the exit is anticipated in the near future (one to two years), the prevailing valuation multiples extracted from comparable quoted firms provide good guidance on the expected exit multiple. Stress tests on that value may be conducted for small incremental changes and on the basis of market knowledge. If the exit is anticipated in a much longer time horizon, the current valuation multiples are less relevant and stress tests may need to be conducted on a wider range of values to determine the anticipated exit multiple. Stress testing in this context consists of simulating incremental changes in the input variables of the valuation model (such as components of the discount factor, terminal growth rates, etc.) and to financial forecasts (sales growth, assumed future operating margins, etc.) in order to determine the range of value outcomes and to assess the stability of the valuation methodology.

2.7 Summary

Valuation is the most critical aspect of private equity transactions. The investment decision-making process typically flows from the screening of investment opportunities to preparing a proposal, appraising the investment, structuring the deal, and finally to the negotiating phase. Because of the difficulties in valuing private companies, a variety of alternative valuation methods are typically used to provide guidance on the appropriate range. Along with the various due diligence investigations (commercial or strategic, financial, legal, tax, environmental) generally conducted on private equity investment opportunities, valuation serves a dual purpose: assessing a company's ability to generate superior cash flows from a distinctive competitive advantage and serving as a benchmark for negotiations with the seller. After all, although seeing opportunities for adding value is important, it is also essential—for the investors in the private equity fund—that the seller does not appropriate all the potential gains by extracting a high price during the transaction.

Post-investment, valuation of private equity investments is also very important, as investors expect to be fully informed about the performance of the portfolio companies. This raises a separate set of issues, which are considered in the next section.

PRIVATE EQUITY FUND STRUCTURES AND VALUATION

3

When analyzing and evaluating financial performance of a private equity fund from the perspective of an investor, a solid grasp of private equity fund structures, terms of investment, private equity fund valuation, and due diligence are an absolute prerequisite. The distinctive characteristics of private equity relative to public equities raise many more challenges when interpreting financial performance. Two of the main differentiating characteristics of private equity, in addition to the structure and terms, relate to the nature of subscriptions made by investors in private equity structures and to the "J" curve effect. Investors commit initially a certain amount to the private equity fund that is subsequently drawn by the fund as the fund's capital is deployed in target portfolio companies. This contrasts with public market investing in which investment orders typically are disbursed fully at the time the orders are settled on the markets. The "J-curve" effect refers to the typical time profile of reported returns by private equity funds, whereby low or negative returns are reported in the early years of a private equity fund (in large part as a result of the fees' impact on net returns), followed by increased returns thereafter as the private equity firm manages portfolio companies toward the exit.

3.1 Understanding Private Equity Fund Structures

The limited partnership has emerged as the dominant form for private equity structures in most jurisdictions. Funds that are structured as limited partnerships are governed by a limited partnership agreement between the fund manager, called the general partner (GP), and the fund's investors, called limited partners (LPs). Whereas the GP has management control over the fund and is jointly liable for all debts, LPs have limited liability, i.e., they do not risk more than the amount of their investment in the fund. The other main alternative to the limited partnership is a corporate structure, called company limited by shares, which mirrors in its functioning the limited partnership but offers a better legal protection to the GP and to some extent the LPs, depending on the jurisdictions. Some fund structures, especially the Luxembourg-based private equity fund vehicle SICAR (société d'investissement en capital à risque), are subject to a light regulatory oversight offering enhanced protection to LPs. The vast majority of these private equity fund structures are "closed end," which restricts existing investors from redeeming their shares over the lifetime of the fund and limiting new investors to entering the fund only at predefined time periods, at the discretion of the GP.

Private equity firms operate effectively in two businesses: the business of managing private equity investments and the business of raising funds. Therefore, private equity firms tend to plan their marketing efforts well in advance of the launch of their funds to ensure that the announced target fund size will be met successfully once the fund is effectively started. The premarketing phase of a private equity fund, depending on whether it is a first fund or a following fund, may take between one to two years. Once investors effectively commit their investments in the fund, private equity managers draw on investors' commitments as the fund is being deployed and invested in portfolio companies. Private equity funds tend to have a duration of 10–12 years, generally extendable to an additional 2–3 years. Exhibit 6 illustrates the funding stages for a private equity fund.

Exhibit 6 Funding Stages for a Private Equity Fund

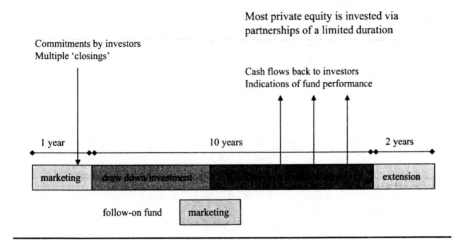

How are private equity funds structured?

Fund terms are contractually defined in a fund prospectus or limited partnership agreement available to qualified prospective investors. The definition of qualified investors depends on the jurisdiction. Typically, wealth criteria (exceeding US$1 million, for example) and/or a minimum subscription threshold (minimum €125,000, for example) apply. The nature of the terms are frequently the result of the balance of negotiation power between GPs and LPs. Although the balance of negotiation power used to be in favor of LPs, it has now turned in favor of GPs, at least among the oversubscribed funds. Any significant downturn in private equity may change the balance of power in favor of LPs. Negotiation of terms has the objective to ensure alignment of interests between the GP and LPs and defining the GP's incentives (transaction fees, profit shares, etc.) The most significant terms may be categorized into economic and corporate governance terms.

Economic Terms

- *Management fees* represent a percentage of committed capital paid annually to the GP during the lifetime of the fund. Fees in the region of 1.5 percent to 2.5 percent are fairly common. Although less frequent, management fees may also be calculated on the basis of the net asset value or on invested capital.

- *Transaction fees* are fees paid to GPs in their advisory capacity when they provide investment banking services for a transaction (mergers and acquisitions, IPOs) benefiting the fund. These fees may be subject to sharing agreements with LPs, typically according to a 50/50 split between the GP and LPs. When such fee-sharing agreements apply, they generally come as a deduction to the management fees.

- *Carried interest* represents the general partner's share of profits generated by a private equity fund. Carried interest is frequently in the region of 20 percent of the fund's profits (after management fees).

- *Ratchet* is a mechanism that determines the allocation of equity between share-holders and the management team of the private equity controlled company. A ratchet enables the management team to increase its equity allocation depending on the company's actual performance and the return achieved by the private equity firm.

- *Hurdle rate* is the internal rate of return that a private equity fund must achieve before the GP receives any carried interest. The hurdle rate is typically in the range of 7 percent to 10 percent. The objective is to align the interests of the GP with those of LPs by giving additional incentives to the GP to outperform traditional investment benchmarks.

EXAMPLE 2

Calculation of Carried Interest

Suppose that a LBO fund has committed capital of US$100 million, carried interest of 20 percent, and a hurdle rate of 8 percent. The fund called 75 percent of its commitments from investors at the beginning of year 1, which was invested at the beginning of year 1 in target company A for $40 million and target company B for $35 million. Suppose that at the end of year 2, a profit of $5 million has been realized by the GP upon exit of the investment in company A, and the value of the investment in company B has remained unchanged. Suppose also that the GP is entitled to carried interest on a deal-by-deal basis, i.e., the IRR used to calculate carried interest is calculated for each investment upon exit. A theoretical carried interest of $1 million (20 percent of $5 million) could be granted to the GP, but the IRR upon exit of investment in company A is only 6.1 percent. Until the IRR exceeds the hurdle rate, no carried interest may be paid to the GP.

- *Target fund size* is expressed as an absolute amount in the fund prospectus or information memorandum. This information is critical as it provides a signal both about the GP's capacity to manage a portfolio of a predefined size and also in terms of fund raising. A fund that closed with a significantly lower size relative to the target size would raise questions about the GP's ability to raise funds on the market and would be perceived as a negative signal.

- *Vintage year* is the year the private equity fund was launched. Reference to vintage year allows performance comparison of funds of the same stage and industry focus.

- *Term of the fund* is typically 10 years, extendable for additional shorter periods (by agreement with the investors). Although infrequently observed, funds can also be of unlimited duration, and in this case are often quoted on stock markets (such as investment trusts).

Corporate Governance Terms

- *Key man clause.* Under the key man clause, a certain number of key named executives are expected to play an active role in the management of the fund. In case of the departure of such a key executive or insufficient time spent in the management of the fund, the "key man" clause provides that the GP may be prohibited from making any new investments until a new key executive is appointed.

- *Disclosure and confidentiality.* Private equity firms have no obligations to disclose publicly their financial performance. A court ruling[8] requiring California Public Employees Retirement System (CalPERS) to report publicly its returns on private equity investments, the Freedom of Information Act (FOIA) in the United States, and similar legislation in other European countries have led public pension funds to report information about their private equity investments. Disclosable information relates to financial performance of the underlying funds but does not extend to information on the companies in which the funds invest. This latter information is not typically disclosed. The reporting by CalPERS is a prominent example of the application of this clause.[9] Some private equity fund terms may be more restrictive on confidentiality and information disclosure and effectively limit information available to investors subject to FOIA.

- *Clawback provision.* A clawback provision requires the GP to return capital to LPs in excess of the agreed profit split between the GP and LPs. This provision ensures that, when a private equity firm exits from a highly profitable investment early in the fund's life but subsequent exits are less profitable, the GP pays back capital contributions, fees, and expenses to LPs to ensure that the profit split is in line with the fund's prospectus. The clawback is normally due on termination of the fund but may be subject to an annual reconciliation (or "true-up").

- *Distribution waterfall.* A distribution waterfall is a mechanism providing an order of distributions to LPs first before the GP receives carried interest. Two distinct distribution mechanisms are predominant: deal-by-deal waterfalls allowing earlier distribution of carried interest to the GP after each individual deal (mostly employed in the United States) and total return waterfalls resulting in earlier distributions to LPs as carried interest is calculated on the profits of the entire portfolio (mostly employed in Europe and for funds-of-funds). Under the total return method, two alternatives are possible to calculate carried interest. In the first alternative, the GP receives carried interest only after the fund has returned the entire committed capital to LPs. In the second alternative, the GP receives carried interest on any distribution as long as the value of the investment portfolio exceeds a certain threshold (usually 20 percent) above invested capital.

EXAMPLE 3

Distribution Waterfalls

Suppose a private equity fund has a committed capital totaling £300 million and a carried interest of 20 percent. After a first investment of £30 million, the fund exits the investment 9 months later with a £15 million profit. Under the deal-by-deal method, the GP would be entitled to 20 percent of the deal profit, i.e., £3 million. In the first alternative of the total return method, the entire proceeds of the sale, i.e., £45 million, are entitled to the LPs and nothing (yet) to the GP. In the second alternative, the exit value of £45 million exceeds by more than 20 percent the invested value of £30 million. The GP would thus be entitled to £3 million.

---

8 S. Chaplinsky and S. Perry, "CalPERS vs. Mercury News: Disclosure comes to private equity," Darden Business Publishing.
9 Information about CalPERS' private equity holdings is available from the company's website, www.calpers.ca.gov.

Continuing the above example with a clawback provision with an annual true-up, suppose that the deal-by-deal method applies and that a second investment of £25 million is concluded with a loss of £5 million 1 year later. Therefore, at the annual true-up, the GP would have to pay back £1 million to LPs. In practice, an escrow account is used to regulate these fluctuations until termination of the fund.

- *Tag-along, drag along rights* are contractual provisions in share purchase agreements that ensure any potential future acquirer of the company may not acquire control without extending an acquisition offer to all shareholders, including the management of the company.
- *No-fault divorce.* A GP may be removed without cause, provided that a super majority (generally above 75 percent) of LPs approve that removal.
- *Removal for "cause"* is a clause that allows either a removal of the GP or an earlier termination of the fund for "cause." Such "cause" may include gross negligence of the GP, a "key person" event, a felony conviction of a key management person, bankruptcy of the GP, or a material breach of the fund prospectus.
- *Investment restrictions* generally impose a minimum level of diversification of the fund's investments, a geographic and/or sector focus, or limits on borrowing.
- *Co-investment.* LPs generally have a first right of co-investing along with the GP. This can be advantageous for the LPs as fees and profit share are likely to be lower (or zero) on co-invested capital. The GP and affiliated parties are also typically restricted in their co-investments to prevent conflicts of interest with their LPs. Crossover co-investments are a classic example of a conflict of interest. A crossover co-investment occurs when a subsequent fund launched by the same GP invests in a portfolio company that has received funding from a previous fund.

3.2 What Are the Risks and Costs of Investing in Private Equity?

Private equity investing is typically restricted by laws and regulations in most jurisdictions to "qualified investors" comprising institutions and high-net-worth individuals meeting certain wealth criteria. These restrictions are motivated by the high levels of risks incurred in private equity investing, and are generally subject to disclosure in the private equity fund prospectus. Such risks may be categorized as general private equity risk factors, investment strategy specific risk factors (buyout, venture capital, mezzanine), industry specific risk factors, risk factors specific to the investment vehicle, and sometimes regional or emerging market risks when applicable.

Following are some general private equity risk factors:

- *Illiquidity of investments*: Because private equity investments are generally not traded on any securities market, the exit of investments may not be conducted on a timely basis.
- *Unquoted investments*: Investing in unquoted securities may be risky relative to investing in securities quoted on a regulated securities exchange.
- *Competition for attractive investment opportunities*: Competition for finding investment opportunities on attractive terms may be high.

- *Reliance on the management of investee companies (agency risk)*: There is no assurance that the management of the investee companies will run the company in the best interests of the private equity firm, particularly in earlier stage deals in which the management may retain a controlling stake in the company and enjoy certain private benefits of control.

- *Loss of capital*: High business and financial risks may result in substantial loss of capital.

- *Government regulations*: Investee companies' product and services may be subject to changes in government regulations that adversely impact their business model.

- *Taxation risk*: Tax treatment of capital gains, dividends, or limited partnerships may change over time.

- *Valuation of investments*: Valuation of private equity investments is subject to significant judgment. When valuations are not conducted by an independent party, they may be subject to biases.

- *Lack of investment capital*: Investee companies may require additional future financing that may not be available.

- *Lack of diversification*: Investment portfolios may be highly concentrated and may, therefore, be exposed to significant losses. Investors generally want to invest in a mix of private equity funds of different vintages, different stages of developments for underlying investments in portfolio companies, and achieve a certain level of diversification across various private equity strategies (large and mid-market buyout, venture capital, mezzanine, restructuring).

- *Market risk*: Changes in general market conditions (interest rates, currency exchange rates) may adversely affect private equity investments. The impact of market risk is, however, long term in nature given the long-term horizon of private equity firms. Temporary short-term market fluctuations are generally irrelevant.

Costs associated with private equity investing are substantially more significant relative to public market investing. These costs may be broken down as follows:

- *Transaction fees*: Corresponding to due diligence, bank financing costs, legal fees for arranging acquisition, and sale transactions in investee companies.

- *Investment vehicle fund setup costs*: Comprises mainly legal costs for the setup of the investment vehicle. Such costs are typically amortized over the life of the investment vehicle.

- *Administrative costs*: Custodian, transfer agent, and accounting costs generally charged yearly as a fraction of the investment vehicle's net asset value.

- *Audit costs*: A fixed annual fee.

- *Management and performance fees*: These are generally more significant relative to plain investment funds. A 2 percent management fee and a 20 percent performance fee are common in the private equity industry.

- *Dilution*: A more subtle source of cost, dilution may come from stock option plans granted to the management and to the private equity firm and from additional rounds of financing.

- *Placement fees*: Fundraising fees may be charged up front or by means of a trailer fee by the fund raiser. A trailer fee is generally charged annually, corresponding to a fraction of the amount invested by limited partners as long as these amounts remain invested in the investment vehicle. An up front placement fee of 2 percent is not uncommon in private equity.

3.3 Due Diligence Investigations by Potential Investors

Prior to investing in a private equity fund, prospective investors generally conduct a thorough due diligence on the fund. Several fundamental characteristics of private equity funds underline the importance of the due diligence process.

- Private equity funds tend to exhibit a strong persistence of returns over time. This means that top performing funds tend to continue to outperform and poor performing funds also tend to continue to perform poorly or disappear.

- The performance range between funds is extremely large. For example, the difference between top quartile and third quartile fund IRRs can be about 20 percentage points.

- Liquidity in private equity is typically very limited and thus LPs are locked for the long term. On the other hand, when private equity funds exit an investment, they return the cash to the investors immediately. Therefore, the "duration" of an investment in private equity is typically shorter than the maximum life of the fund.

The European Venture Capital association (EVCA) has issued an "Illustrative due diligence questionnaire—Venture capital funds," that may serve as a guide, but not as a substitute, for the due diligence process conducted by LPs before investing in a venture capital or private equity fund.

3.4 Private Equity Fund Valuation

The description of private equity valuation[10] in a fund prospectus is generally associated with the fund's calculation of net asset value (NAV). The NAV is generally defined as the value of the fund assets less liabilities corresponding to the accrued fund expenses. The fund's assets are frequently valued by GPs, depending on their valuation policies, in the following ways:[11]

1 at cost with significant adjustments for subsequent financing events or deterioration

2 at lower of cost or market value

3 by a revaluation of a portfolio company whenever a new financing round involving new investors takes place

4 at cost with no interim adjustment until the exit

5 with a discount for restricted securities[12]

6 more rarely, marked to market by reference to a peer group of public comparables and applying illiquidity discounts.

Private equity industry valuation standards, such as those originally produced by the British, French, and European industry associations (latest revisions can be found at www.privateequityvaluation.com), have increasingly been adopted by funds operating in many jurisdictions.

Industry practices suggest that because a valuation is adjusted with a new round of financing, the NAV may be more stale in down markets when there is a long gap between funding rounds. This mechanism is similar to the valuation of investment funds of publicly quoted securities. There is thus a fundamental implicit break-up

---

10 For a comprehensive discussion of this topic, refer to Thomas Meyer and Pierre-Yves Mathonet, *Beyond the J Curve: Managing a Portfolio of Venture Capital and Private Equity Funds*, Wiley, (2004).

11 Foster Center for Entrepreneurship and Private Equity, Dartmouth College.

12 Example: Reg. 144 securities.

assumption whereby the fund may be broken up at any time, the funds underlying investments may be liquidated individually and immediately, and the proceeds returned to LPs. Whereas this fundamental break-up assumption may hold for publicly traded securities, which are marked to market, this assumption may be more questionable for private equity investment portfolios typically held over a long period of time. The fundamental question facing investors is: At what value should investments in portfolio companies be reported, prior to the private equity fund exiting the investment and returning the proceeds to the LPs? There is no straight answer to that question as there is no market for securities issued by private equity companies.

Undrawn LP commitments raise additional challenges for private equity fund valuation. Although undrawn commitments represent a LP's legal obligations to meet capital calls in the future, they are not accounted for in the NAV calculation. The value of such undrawn commitments largely depends on the expected cash flows that will be generated by future investments made by the GP. Although undrawn commitments are not part of the NAV, they should be viewed as unfunded liabilities. McGrady[13] suggested to "gauge the reaction to the unfunded portion, a seller may consider the ease with which a general partnership could raise another fund in the current market."

Comparisons between private equity funds following different investment strategies require a careful analysis of their respective valuation policies in order to avoid biases. Whereas, for example, an early stage venture capital fund may keep its investments at cost, a late stage development capital fund may mark its portfolio companies by reference to public market comparables. At times when a market bubble is forming in certain sectors, such as the technology bubble in 2000, such reference to public market comparables may distort the valuation of portfolio companies and thus reported fund returns.

Another important aspect of private equity valuations is that they are mostly performed by GPs. Under the pressure from LPs, an increasing number of annual or semi-annual valuations are performed by independent valuers that are mandated by GPs.

The above discussion on private equity valuation emphasizes both the qualitative and quantitative issues that need to be taken into consideration.

3.5 Evaluating Fund Performance

Because each private equity fund is unique, the assessment of financial performance needs to be made with a good knowledge of the specific fund structure, terms, valuation policies, and the outcome of the due diligence. Typically, an analysis of a private equity fund's financial performance includes the following.

3.5.1 *Analysis of IRR and Multiples Gross and Net of Fees since Inception*

Here, net of fees means net of management fees, carried interest, or of any other financial arrangements that accrue to the GP. The IRR, a cash-flow-weighted rate of return, is deemed the most appropriate measure of private equity performance by the Global Investment Performance Standards (GIPS), Venture Capital and Private Equity Valuation Principles, and by other venture capital and private equity standards. The interpretation of IRR in private equity should, however, be subject to caution because an implicit assumption behind the IRR calculation is that the fund is fully liquid, whereas a significant portion of the NAV is illiquid during a substantial part of a private equity fund's life. Therefore, valuation of portfolio companies according to industry standards is important to ensure the quality of the IRR figures.

---

13 C. McGrady, Pricing private equity secondary transactions, Dallas, TX, Cogent Partners (2002).

The distinction between gross and net IRR is also important. Gross IRR relates cash flows between the private equity fund and its portfolio companies and is often considered a good measure of the investment management team's track record in creating value. Net IRR relates cash flows between the private equity fund and LPs, and so captures the returns enjoyed by investors. Fees and profit shares create significant deviations between gross and net IRRs. IRR analysis is often combined with a benchmark IRR analysis, i.e., the median IRR for the relevant peer group of comparable private equity funds operating with a similar investment strategy and vintage year. This is particularly important because there are clear trends over time in private equity returns, with some vintage years producing much higher returns than others.

In addition to IRR, multiples are used frequently as a measure of performance. Multiples simply measure the total return to investors relative to the total sum invested. Although multiples ignore the time value of money, their ease of calculation and their ability to differentiate between "realized" actual proceeds from divestments and "unrealized" portfolio subject to GP valuation make these ratios very popular among LPs. The multiples used most frequently by LPs and also defined by GIPS that provide additional information about private equity funds performance are as follows:

- PIC (paid in capital): the ratio of paid in capital to date divided by committed capital. This ratio provides information about the proportion of capital called by a GP.

- DPI (distributed to paid in): cumulative distributions paid out to LPs as a proportion of the cumulative invested capital. This ratio is often called "cash-on-cash return." It provides an indication of the private equity fund's realized return on investment. DPI is presented net of management fees and carried interest.

- RVPI (residual value to paid in): value of LPs' shareholding held with the private equity fund as a proportion of the cumulative invested capital. The numerator is measured as the remaining portfolio companies as valued by the GP. This ratio is a measure of the private equity fund's unrealized return on investment. RVPI is presented net of management fees and carried interest.

- TVPI (total value to paid in): the portfolio companies' distributed and undistributed value as a proportion of the cumulative invested capital. TVPI is the sum of DPI and RVPI. TVPI is presented net of management fees and carried interest.

In addition to quantitative measures of return, an analysis of a private equity fund financial performance also includes:

- an analysis of realized investments since inception, commenting on all successes and failures;

- an analysis of unrealized investments, highlighting all red flags in the portfolio and the expected time to exit per portfolio company;

- a cash flow forecast at the portfolio company level and for the aggregate portfolio; and

- an analysis of portfolio valuation, audited financial statements, and the NAV.

EXAMPLE 4

Calculating and Interpreting a Private Equity Fund Performance

Suppose that a private equity fund has a DPI of 0.07 and a RVPI of 0.62 after 5 years. IRR is –17 percent. The fund follows a venture capital strategy in high technology, has a vintage year of 1999, and a term of 10 years. A DPI of 7 percent indicates that few successful exits were made. A RVPI of 62 percent points to an extended J-curve effect for the fund as TVPI amounts to 69 percent at the midlife of the fund. A vintage year of 1999 provides hints that the fund was actually started before the technology market crash of 2000 and that the routes to exit for portfolio companies have been dramatically changed. During the technology market crash, the investment portfolio probably suffered a number of complete write-offs. In this situation, an LP should thus consider the state of the existing portfolio to examine the number of write-offs and other signals of ailing companies in the fund portfolio. The risk of not recovering the invested amount at termination of the fund is significant. Compliance with valuation policies by the GP should also be closely monitored by LPs to ensure that the GP's expectations are not excessive given the current state of the portfolio.

Note that with the increased allocations to private equity, performance comparisons across asset classes are often misinterpreted. IRR, the standard measure of private equity returns, is cash-flow-weighted, whereas performance of most other asset classes is measured in terms of time-weighted rate of return. In an attempt to solve these performance comparison issues, new performance measurement techniques have been developed. One of them, called the Public Market Equivalent (PME), was proposed by Austin Long and Craig Nickles in the mid-1990s. It provides a solution to this benchmarking issue, but its reliability poses, at times, serious problems.[14] Put simply, PME is the cash-flow-weighted rate of return of an index (S&P 500 or any other index) assuming the same cash flow pattern as a private equity fund. It is thus an index return measure.

CONCEPT IN ACTION: EVALUATING A PRIVATE EQUITY FUND

4

This section illustrates the use of many of the concepts above to evaluate the performance of a private equity fund.

Michael Hornsby, CFA, is a Senior Investment Officer at Icarus, a UK-based institutional investor in private equity. He is contemplating an investment in Europa Venture Partners III, a new late stage technology venture capital fund, after a thorough due diligence performed on the fund and an updated due diligence on the GP. Icarus has been an investor in Europa Venture Partners' (EVP) previous two funds, EVP I and EVP II. Icarus has been satisfied with the performance of EVP so far and is seeking to further expand its relationship with this GP because Icarus considers it a niche venture capital firm operating in a less crowded segment of the pan-European technology markets. As a result of its success, EVP decided to increase its carried interest for the third fund to 25 percent from 20 percent for the previous two funds.

---

14 Christophe Rouvinez, "Private Equity Benchmarking with PME +," *Venture Capital Journal* (August 2003).

Hornsby has received the information about the fund's financial performance and is seeking assistance in calculating and interpreting financial performance for a number of specific queries as outlined below.

Europa Venture Partners (EVP)

General Partner   Europa Venture Partners (EVP) was established to provide equity financing to later stage technology companies in need of development capital across Europe. The GP seeks to provide strategic support to seasoned entrepreneurial teams and bring proven new technologies to the market. The GP targets investment in portfolio companies between €2 million and €10 million.

Fund	Vintage	Established in 1999 Actual Fund Size (€ Millions)	Capital Called (%)	Mgmt Fees (%)	Type: Development Capital Carried Interest (%)	Hurdle Rate (%)	Term	Report Date
EVP I	2001	125	92	2	20	8	2009	31 Dec 2006
EVP II	2003	360	48	2	20	8	2012	31 Dec 2006

Financial performance for investments by Icarus in EVP funds

Fund	Committed Capital (€ Millions)	Capital Called Down	Gross IRR (%)	Net IRR (%)	DPI (X)	RVPI (X)	TVPI (X)	Quartile
EVP I	10	9.2	16.1	11.3	1.26	1.29	2.55	1
EVP II	25	12.0	1.6	(0.4)	0.35	1.13	1.48	2

Hornsby also is interested in verifying management fees, carried interest, and the NAV of EVP I. He has the following information about yearly capital calls, operating results, and distributions.

Calls, Operating Results, and Distributions (€ Million)						
	2001	2002	2003	2004	2005	2006
Called-down	50	15	10	25	10	5
Realized results	0	0	10	35	40	80
Unrealized results	–5	–15	15	10	15	25
Distributions	—	—	—	25	45	75

Operating results correspond to the sum of realized results from exits of portfolio companies and of unrealized results from the revaluation of investments held in portfolio companies. In addition to the information available on EVP I, Hornsby also knows from the fund prospectus that the distribution waterfall is calculated according to the total return method following the first alternative, i.e., the GP receives carried interest only after the fund has returned the entire committed capital to LPs. Management fees are calculated on the basis of the paid-in capital. Hornsby also wants to calculate DPI, RVPI, and TVPI of EVP I for 2006 and is interested in understanding how to calculate gross and net IRRs.

1 Interpret and compare the financial performance of EVP I and EVP II.

2 Based on the information given, calculate the management fees, carried interest, and the NAV of EVP I. Also calculate DPI, RVPI, and TVPI of EVP I for 2006. Explain on the basis of EVP I how gross and net IRRs are calculated, and calculate the gross and net IRRs.

Solution to 1:

In the table above, the first venture capital fund (EVP I) made its first capital call in 2001 and returned €1.26 (all amounts in millions) for every €1 that had been drawn down to LPs two years ahead of the termination of the fund. EVP I residual value remains high at 1.29 times capital drawn down, which is a good signal about the profitability of the fund at termination. The fund ranks in the first quartile, which means that it belongs to the best performing funds of that category and vintage year. Gross IRR of 16.1 percent after 6 years of operations, and 11.3 percent net of fees represents a good performance.

The second fund exhibits, to date, very modest performance in terms of gross and net IRR, which indicates that the fund is still experiencing the J-curve effect. EVP II has returned 35 percent of capital drawn down to LPs and a residual value of 113 percent of capital drawn down, which indicates that despite the fund being in its early years, the GP has already managed a number of profitable exits and increased the value of the investment portfolio half way through the termination of the fund. Actual fund size significantly exceeds previous fund size and is an indication that the GP is gaining momentum in terms of fund raising, probably partly attributable to the strong performance of the first fund.

Solution to 2:

Cash Flows and Distributions (€ Million)								
Year	Called-down (1)	Paid-in Capital (2)	Mgmt Fees (3)	Operating Results (4)	NAV before Distributions (5)	Carried Interest (6)	Distributions (7)	NAV after Distributions (8)
2001	50	50	1.0	−5	44.0			44.0
2002	15	65	1.3	−15	42.7			42.7
2003	10	75	1.5	25	76.2			76.2
2004	25	100	2.0	45	144.2	3.8	25	115.4
2005	10	110	2.2	55	178.2	6.8	45	126.4
2006	5	115	2.3	105	234.1	11.2	75	147.9

Based on this table, the calculations of DPI, RVPI, and TVPI can be derived as follows:

■ Paid-in capital = Cumulative capital called-down (shown in Column 2)

■ Management fees = (2 Percent) × (Column 2)

- Carried interest: The first year that NAV is higher than committed capital (€125m), carried interest is 20 percent of the excess, or (20 Percent) ([NAV in Column 5] – €125m). Thereafter, provided that NAV before distribution exceeds committed capital, carried interest is (20 Percent)(increase in NAV before distributions). For example, carried interest in 2006 is calculated as follows: (20 Percent)(234.1 – 178.2)
- NAV before distributions = NAV after distributions$_{t-1}$ + (Column 1) – (Column 3) + (Column 4)
- NAV after distributions = (Column 5) – (Column 6) – (Column 7)
- DPI = (25 + 45 + 75)/115 or 1.26x
- RVPI = 147.9/115 or 1.29x
- TVPI = 1.26 + 1.29 = 2.55x

The IRRs may be developed as follows:

- Gross IRRs are estimated by calculating the internal rate of return between the following cash flows: called down capital at the beginning of period (Column 1) and the previous year's operating results (Column 4).
- Net IRRs are estimated by calculating the internal rate of return between the following cash flows: called down capital at the beginning of period (Column 1) and the previous year's operating results (Column 4) net of management fees (Column 3) and carried interest (Column 6). The calculated IRRs are in the bottom row of the following table.

Year End	Cash Flows for Gross IRR	Cash Flows for Net IRR
2000	–50	–50.0
2001	–20	–21.0
2002	–25	–26.3
2003	0	–1.5
2004	35	29.2
2005	50	41.0
2006	105	91.5
IRR	16.1%	11.3%

5   PREFATORY COMMENTS ON THE CASE STUDY

The case study that follows is a complement to this private equity valuation reading and is included to show the reader how to apply in context valuation methodologies in a private equity setting.

A Note on Valuation of Venture Capital Deals

This technical note on the valuation of venture capital deals is meant to explain the foundations of the venture capital method for valuing venture capital investments, the specific issues and diligences that must be addressed, and illustrate the concept in action with a case study.

SUMMARY

This reading focuses on valuation issues confronting investors in a private equity fund and the methods that the funds use to make investment decisions.

- Private equity funds seek to add value by various means, including optimizing financial structures, incentivizing management, and creating operational improvements.

- Private equity can be thought of as an alternative system of governance for corporations: rather than ownership and control being separated as in most publicly quoted companies, private equity concentrates ownership and control. Many view this governance arbitrage as a fundamental source of the returns earned by the best private equity funds.

- A critical role for the GP is valuation of potential investments. But because these investments are usually privately owned, valuation encounters a myriad of challenges, some of which have been discussed in this reading.

- Valuation techniques differ according to the nature of the investment. Early stage ventures require very different techniques than leveraged buyouts. Private equity professionals tend to use multiple techniques when performing a valuation, and they explore many different scenarios for the future development of the business.

- In buyouts the availability of debt financing can have a big impact on the scale of private equity activity and also seems to impact the valuations observed in the market.

- Because private equity funds have incentives to acquire, add value, and then exit within the lifetime of the fund, they are considered buy-to-sell investors. Planning the exit route for the investment is a critical role for the GP, and a well-timed and executed investment can be a significant source of realized value.

- In addition to the problems encountered by the private equity funds in valuing potential portfolio investments, many challenges exist in valuing the investment portfolio on an ongoing basis. This is because the investments have no easily observed market value, and there is a high element of judgment involved in valuing each of the portfolio companies prior to their sale by the fund.

- The two main metrics for measuring the ongoing and ultimate performance of private equity funds are IRR and multiples. Comparisons of the observed returns from private equity across funds and with other assets are demanding because it is important to control for the timing of cash flows, differences in risk, portfolio composition, and vintage year effects.

APPENDIX: A NOTE ON VALUATION OF VENTURE CAPITAL DEALS

When times are mysterious serious numbers are eager to please.

—Musician, Paul Simon, in the lyrics to his song *When Numbers Get Serious*

In this note, I discuss some of the fundamental issues of valuation in venture capital deals. The topics discussed are not necessarily limited to venture capital-backed companies, but they frequently surface in entrepreneurial companies that are financed either by venture capitalists or other private equity investors.

In Section 1, I introduce the so-called venture capital method. This is really a simple net present value (NPV) method that takes the perspective of the investor instead of the firm. This method has the advantage of extreme simplicity, but it makes many strong assumptions that limit its usefulness. I focus on three main issues in the remaining sections. In Section 2, I examine the problem of determining the terminal value. In Section 3, I examine the treatment of risk. In Section 4, I examine how to determine the funding requirements and I examine a number of ways of dealing with multiple financing rounds. In Section 5, I briefly cover the use of these methods in actual negotiations.

1 The Basic Venture Capital Method

1.1 An Example

There exists a simple approach to valuation that is sometimes referred to as the venture capital method. The method is sometimes explained in the language of internal rates of return (IRR) and sometimes in terms of NPV. Since most of you have been more exposed to the NPV framework, I will use that language. I will then show that it is in fact *identical* to the IRR framework.

To illustrate my method I will use a fictional start-up company called "SpiffyCalc," which is seeking financing from a venture capital fund by the name of "Vulture Ventures." Studying their crystal ball, the founders of SpiffyCalc expect to be able to sell the company for $25 million in four years.[15] At this point they need to raise $3 million. Vulture Ventures considers this a risky business and wants to apply a discount rate of 50 percent to be adequately compensated for the risk they will bear.[16] The entrepreneurs also decided that whatever valuation they would get, they wanted to own 1 million shares, which they thought would be a cool number to brag about.

---

15 In Section 2, I discuss how one might replace the crystal ball by a liquid crystal display screen, as a slight improvement in the art of future telling.

16 In Section 3, I discuss discount rates in more detail.

This note was prepared by Thomas Hellmann, Assistant Professor of Strategic Management, Stanford University, as the basis for class discussion rather than to illustrate either effective or ineffective handling of an administrative situation. "A Note on Valuation of Venture Capital Deals," by Thomas Hellmann, revised April 20, 2006. Copyright © 2001 by the Board of Trustees of Leland Stanford Junior University. All rights reserved. Used with permission from the Stanford University Graduate School of Business.

It is useful to define variables for the key assumptions we have made.

V = terminal value (at time of exit) = $25 million (in four years)

t = time to exit event = 4 years

I = amount of investment = $3 million

r = discount return used by investors = 50 percent

x = number of existing shares (owned by the entrepreneurs) = 1 million

Step 1   *Determine the Post-Money Valuation*

The only positive cash flow in this model occurs at the time of exit (typically an IPO or an acquisition), where we measure the terminal value of the company, denoted by V = $25 million. This means that after receiving the required $3 million, the initial value of the company is simply the discounted terminal value in 4 years' time. If Vulture Ventures is using a discount rate of 50 percent, the NPV of the terminal value in four years is $V/(1 + r)^t$ = $25 million/$(1.5)^4$ = $4,938,272 = POST. This is called the post-money valuation, i.e., the value of the company once the initial investment has been made. Intuitively, this is the value that is being placed on the entire company. This value is obviously not realized at the time of financing, as it depends on the belief that there will be great financial returns in the future.

Step 2   *Determine the Pre-Money Valuation*

Subtracting the cost of the investment of $3 million from the post-money valuation yields PRE = $1,938,272. This is called the pre-money valuation.

Step 3   *Determine the Ownership Fraction*

Vulture Ventures is investing $3 million in a venture valued at $4,938,272. In order to get back its money it therefore needs to own a sufficient fraction of the company. If they own a fraction F = $3 million/$4,938,272 = 60.75 percent, they get their required rate of return on their investment.

Step 4   *Obtain the Number of Shares*

The founders want to hold 1 million shares. When Vulture Ventures makes its investment it needs to calculate the number of shares required to achieve its desired ownership fraction. In order to obtain a 60.75 percent ownership share, Vulture Venture makes the following calculation: let x be the number of shares owned by the founders (x = 1 million) and y be the number of shares that Vulture Ventures requires, then $y/(1,000,000 + y) = F$ = 60.75 percent. After some algebraic transformation we get y = 1,000,000 [0.6075/(1−0.6075)] = 1,547,771. Vulture Ventures thus needs 1,547,771 shares to obtain their desired 60.75 percent of the company.

Step 5   *Obtain the Price of Shares*

The price of shares is thus given by $3 million/1,547,771 = $1.94.

1.2 The General Case

We can calculate all important variables of a deal in a simple five step procedure:

Step 1   POST = $V/(1 + r)^t$

POST is the post-money valuation.

Step 2   PRE = POST − I

PRE is the pre-money valuation.

Step 3 $F = I/POST$

F is the required ownership fraction for the investor.

Step 4 $y = x\,[F/(1 - F)]$

y is the number of shares the investors require to achieve their desired ownership fraction.

Step 5 $p_1 = I/y$

p_1 is the price per share.

1.3 Sensitivity Analysis with the Basic Venture Capital Method

It is interesting to do some sensitivity analysis. How will the value of the company change if we change our assumptions? We will examine the effect of changing the following assumptions:

Variation 1   reduce the terminal value by 10 percent

Variation 2   increase the discount rate by an absolute 10 percent

Variation 3   increase investment by 10 percent

Variation 4   increase time to exit by 10 percent

Variation 5   increase the number of exiting shares: this has no effect on any real values!

Single Period NPV Method		Base Model	Variation 1	Variation 2
Exit Value	V	$25,000,000	**$22,500,000**	$25,000,000
Time to exit	t	4	4	4
Discount rate	r	50.00%	50.00%	**60.00%**
Investment amount	I	$3,000,000	$3,000,000	$3,000,000
Number of existing shares	x	1,000,000	1,000,000	1,000,000
Post-Money	POST	$4,938,272	$4,444,444	$3,814,697
Pre-Money	PRE	$1,938,272	$1,444,444	$814,697
Ownership fraction of investors	F	60.75%	67.50%	78.64%
Ownership fraction of entrepreneurs	1 – F	39.25%	32.50%	21.36%
Number of new shares	y	1,547,771	2,076,923	3,682,349
Price per share	p	$1.94	$1.44	$0.81
Final wealth of investors		$15,187,500	$15,187,500	$19,660,800
Final wealth of entrepreneurs		$9,812,500	$7,312,500	$5,339,200
NPV of investors' wealth		$3,000,000	$3,000,000	$3,000,000
NPV of entrepreneurs' wealth		$1,938,272	$1,444,444	$814,697

Single Period NPV Method		Variation 3	Variation 4	Variation 5
Exit Value	V	$25,000,000	$25,000,000	$25,000,000
Time to exit	t	4	**4.4**	4
Discount rate	r	50.00%	50.00%	50.00%
Investment amount	I	**$3,300,000**	$3,000,000	$3,000,000
Number of existing shares	x	1,000,000	1,000,000	**2,000,000**
Post-Money	POST	$4,938,272	$4,198,928	$4,938,272

Single Period NPV Method		Variation 3	Variation 4	Variation 5
Pre-Money	PRE	$1,638,272	$1,198,928	$1,938,272
Ownership fraction of investors	F	66.83%	71.45%	60.75%
Ownership fraction of entrepreneurs	1 – F	33.18%	28.55%	39.25%
Number of new shares	y	2,014,318	2,502,235	3,095,541
Price per share	p	$1.64	$1.20	$0.97
Final wealth of investors		$16,706,250	$17,861,700	$15,187,500
Final wealth of entrepreneurs		$8,293,750	$7,138,300	$9,812,500
NPV of investors' wealth		$3,300,000	$3,000,000	$3,000,000
NPV of entrepreneurs' wealth		$1,638,272	$1,198,928	$1,938,272

1.4 The Treatment of Option Pools

One subtle point in this calculation is the treatment of an employee option pool. Most venture capital deals include a nontrivial amount of shares for the option pool. This option pool will be depleted over time as the company hires executives and other employees. How do we account for the option pool in these calculations? The norm is that the entrepreneurs' shares and the option pool are lumped into one. Consider an example where the entrepreneurs receive 2 million shares, the investors receive 2 million shares, and there is an option pool of 1 million shares. Investors are investing $2 million at $1 per share. We then say that the post-money valuation is $5 million and the pre-money valuation is $3 million. Note, however, that from the entrepreneurs' perspective they are getting only $2 million of the pre-money valuation. The other $1 million is reserved for the option pool.

1.5 An Alternative Phrasing of the Venture Capital Method in Terms of IRR

The so-called venture capital method is often explained in the language of IRRs. While the IRR is often a problematic method in finance, our venture capital method is sufficiently simple that the IRR and the NPV method give *exactly the same answer*. Below I use the above example to walk you through the logic of the IRR calculation in the way it is sometimes presented as the venture capital method.

Step 1 *Determine the future wealth that Vulture Ventures needs to obtain in order to achieve their desired IRR.*

When Vulture Ventures decides to invest in a company, it formulates a "desired rate of return." Suppose that Vulture Ventures is asking for 50 percent IRR. Also, SpiffyCalc needs an investment of $3 million. We can then determine how much money Vulture Ventures needs to accumulate in order to achieve its desired return. Vulture Ventures would want to make $3 million $\times (1.5)^4$ = $15,187,500 in four years.

Step 2 *Determine the fraction of shares that Vulture Ventures needs to hold in order to achieve the desired IRR.*

To find out the required percentage of shares that Vulture Ventures needs to achieve a 50 percent IRR, we simply divide its required wealth by the estimated value of the company, i.e., $15,187,500/$25 million = 0.6075. Vulture Ventures would thus need 60.75 percent of the shares.

Step 3 *Determine the number of shares.*

When Vulture Ventures makes its investment it needs to calculate the number of shares required to achieve its desired ownership fraction. We assume that the founders of SpiffyCalc issued themselves 1,000,000 shares, and nobody else owns any other shares. We then calculate how many shares Vulture Ventures needs to obtain a 60.75 percent ownership share in the company. Using the same reasoning as before let x be the number of shares owned by the founders (x = 1,000,000) and y be the number of shares that Vulture Ventures requires, then $y/(1,000,000 + y) = 0.6075$. After some algebraic transformation we have $y = 1,000,000 [0.6075/(1 - 0.6075)] = 1,547,771$. Vulture Ventures thus needs 1,547,771 shares to obtain their desired 60.75 percent of the company.

Step 4   *Determine the price of shares.*

Given that Vulture Ventures is investing $3 million, the price of a share is $3 million/1,547,771 = $1.94.

Step 5   *Determine post-money valuation.*

The post-money valuation can actually be calculated in a number of ways. First, if an investment of $3 million buys 60.75 percent of the company, then it must be that 60.75 percent × post-money valuation = $3 million. It follows that the post-money valuation is given by $3 million/0.6075 = $4,938,272. Another way to obtain the post-money valuation is to note that there are 2,547,771 shares in the company that are valued at $1.94, so the post-money valuation is 2,547,771 × $1.94 ≈ $4.94 million (allowing for rounding error).

Step 6   *Determine pre-money valuation.*

To calculate the pre-money valuation we simply subtract the value of the VC's investment from the post-money valuation. This is $4,938,272 − $3 million = $1,938,272. Another way of calculating the pre-money valuation is to evaluate the existing shares at the new price, i.e., 1,000,000 × $1.94 ≈ $1.94 million (again allowing for rounding error).

We note that all the values are exactly the same as for the NPV method. The only difference is that one additional step was needed in the IRR method, namely to calculate the required wealth of the investors at a future point in time.[17]

Again, we can write down the general case:

Step 1 $W = I (1 + r)^t$

W is the amount of wealth investors expect to accumulate.

Step 2 $F = W/V$

F is the fraction of share ownership required by investors.

Step 3 $y = x [F/(1 - F)]$

y is the number of shares the investors require to achieve their desired ownership fraction.

Step 4 $p_1 = I/y$

p_1 is the price per share.

Step 5   POST = I/For POST = $p_1 \times (x + y)$

POST is the post-money valuation.

Step 6   PRE = POST − I or PRE = $p_1 \times x$

---

17 In the spreadsheet that accompanies the case, future wealth is also discounted back into the present to obtain the NPV of the stakes for the entrepreneurs and investors.

PRE is the pre-money valuation.

2 Estimating the Terminal Value

Conceptually the terminal value represents the value of the company at the time of an exit event, be it an IPO or an acquisition.[18] Probably the most frequently used method to determine the terminal value is to take a multiple of earnings at the time of exit. Typically an estimate is taken of what the earnings are before tax, and then an industry multiple is taken. The difficulty is obviously to come up with a good estimate of the earnings and to find an appropriate industry multiple. This is particularly difficult for highly innovative ventures that operate in new or emerging industries.

Instead of taking a multiple of earnings, one might also consider taking multiples of sales or assets, or indeed of whatever other accounting measure is meaningful in that specific industry. The common methodology of all these multiples calculations is to look at comparable firms in the industry. One problem is that it is often difficult to find truly comparable companies. Another problem is that one typically looks at recent comparable deals. If a company is financed at a time when the stock market peaks and it uses recent IPOs as a basis of comparison, it will obtain large multiples. But these multiples may not reflect the multiples that it will be able to obtain when it plans to go public several years later.[19]

In principle, better methods of estimating terminal value would be to use NPV, CAPM, APT, or whatever equilibrium valuation model we think fits the data best. The problem, however, is that it is exceedingly difficult to come up with reasonable cash flow projections. And indeed, again one would look at comparable firms in the industry to come up with these estimates. These calculations may therefore not be much more accurate than the rough estimates using the multiples method.

Note that the implicit assumption for these estimates of the terminal value is typically that they measure the value of the company in case of success. This leads us to examine the issue of risk more carefully.

3 Accounting for Risk

In the venture capital method of valuation, the estimate of the terminal value is typically based on some kind of success scenario. Because there is considerable risk involved in a typical venture capital deal, venture capitalists usually apply a very high discount risk "to compensate for the risk." It is not hard to see why they use this method. Venture capitalists are negotiating with entrepreneurs who are often overconfident and have a strong tendency to overstate the prospects of their new ventures. Venture capitalists can argue with them for some time, but rather than having a long and aggravating debate about these estimates, the VCs can simply deflate them by applying a higher discount rate. I therefore suspect that the venture capital method is simply a victim of bargaining dynamics. The method, however, is rather confusing, as it combines two distinct reasons for discounting. One of the reasons is that VCs need to be compensated for holding significant (and typically nondiversifiable) risk. The second is that VCs do not believe that the venture will necessarily succeed. The problem here is that the earnings estimate does not represent the *expected* earnings, but the earnings in case of success.[20] There are two closely related ways of dealing with this.

---

18 To be precise, the relevant value is the pre-money valuation at the exit event.
19 While one would think that venture capitalists take this effect into account (and indeed they typically use that argument to talk multiples down) it is still true that venture capital valuations appreciate in times of rising stock markets.
20 Technically speaking, the first aspect is true risk as measured in terms of the variance (or covariance) of returns. The second aspect does not concern the variance, but the overestimation of the mean.

The first method is to simply recognize the fact that the discount rate incorporates a "risk of failure" component, as well as a true risk–diversification component. Since venture capitalists are not diversified, they may use a high discount rate to account for the variability of returns around their expected value.[21] Suppose, for example, that the risk–aversion of the VC fund implies an approximate risk-adjusted discount rate of 20 percent. If it was certain that this company would succeed, then the post-money valuation would simply be given by $25 million/ $(1.2)^4$ = \$12,056,327. But suppose now that the investors actually believe that the company might simply falter (with no value left) and that the probability of that event happening is 20 percent each year. The probability of getting the terminal valuation is only $(80 \text{ percent})^4$ = 40.96 percent, so that that the expected postmoney valuation is only 0.4096 × \$12,056,327 = \$4,938,272. We chose those numbers such that we get the same post-money valuation as before. This can be seen from the following: Let π be the probability of failure in any one year, then

$$\text{POST} = \frac{(1-\pi)^t X}{(1+r)^t} = \left(\frac{1-\pi}{1+r}\right)^t X = \frac{X}{(1+\tilde{r})^t} \text{ where } \tilde{r} = \frac{1+r}{1-\pi} - 1$$

$$= \frac{r+\pi}{1-\pi}$$

In our case $\tilde{r} = \dfrac{1+0.2}{1-0.2} - 1 = 0.5$: a 20 percent failure rate, combined with a 20 percent discount rate, have the combined effect of a 50 percent discount rate. Note that these numbers do not simply add up, so we need to go through the above formulas.

The second method is to allow for a variety of scenarios to generate a less biased estimate of expected returns. Typically we would try to adjust the terminal value to better reflect our true expectations. For example, SpiffyCalc's estimate of \$25 million may have been based on an estimated earnings of \$2.5 million and a multiple of 10. Suppose now that \$2.5 million earnings is in fact an optimistic estimate. Suppose that there is a possibility that SpiffyCalc's product won't work, in which case the company will have no earnings. Or it may work, but the opportunity is smaller than originally hoped for, so that earnings in year 3 are only \$1 million and the multiple is only 5, reflecting a lower growth potential. Suppose now that each of these three scenarios are equally likely. The expected terminal value is not \$25 million but only 1/3 × \$0 + 1/3 × 5 × \$1 million + 1/3 × 10 × \$2.5 million = \$10 million.

When valuing the company, the VC may now use a lower discount rate that reflects only the true amount of risk in the venture. Using the corrected estimate of \$10 million and applying a 20 percent discount rate as before leads to a post-money valuation of \$4,822,531. The VC would need to own 62.21 percent of the company.

4 Investment Amounts and Multiple Rounds of Finance

How do we determine the amount of money that needs to be raised? Again, there are a variety of methods. A simple and powerful method is to go to the entrepreneurs' financial projections and look at their cash flow statement, which tracks the expected cash balances of the company over time. An important insight that comes out of this method is that it is often better to raise money in several rounds. We illustrate this with our hypothetical example of SpiffyCalc.

---

21 The limited partners of the VC funds, however, tend to be very diversified. This can lead to some conflicts of interest, which we will not dwell on here.

4.1 An Example

Starting with a cash balance of $0, the company projects the following cash balances:

End of Year 1	End of Year 2	End of Year 3	End of Year 4	End of Year 5
$(1,600,000)	$(2,700,000)	$(4,600,000)	$(2,600,000)	$1,200,000

Looking at these numbers, SpiffyCalc realized that raising $3 million would get the company through its first two years. But after two years the company would need some additional money to survive. Indeed, SpiffyCalc estimated that the lowest cash balance would occur at the end of year 3, and that it would generate positive cash flows thereafter. The company therefore recognized that it needed to raise a total of $4.6 million. It also thought that it was more prudent to leave itself with some safety cushion, so it decided to raise a total of $5 million dollars. When it put those numbers into its spreadsheet, however, the numbers demonstrated that investors needed to receive 101.25 percent of the company and that its pre-money valuation was –$61,728. This obviously means that at $5 million, the project was a negative NPV project.

But SpiffyCalc also noticed that it didn't need to raise the entire $5 million right from the start. For example, it could initially raise $3 million, and then raise the remaining $2 million after two years. In this case, the valuation method needs to take into account that the equity that first-round investors put into the business will be diluted in future rounds. This is a difficult problem, as it requires that we make assumptions about the terms of financing of these future rounds. While these assumptions may be difficult to get by, ignoring them will almost certainly lead to an inaccurate valuation. Indeed, ignoring future dilution will lead the venture capitalist to pay too much. The NPV framework is the most flexible and powerful method to account for future dilution.[22]

Suppose now that SpiffyCalc has already identified "Slowtrain Investors" as a potential investor for that second round. Suppose also that all investors apply a 50 percent discount rate through the four years before SpiffyCalc expects to be acquired. At the end of the second year, when "Slowtrain Investors" makes the second round investment, it would be doing the same calculation as we did above. It would use $POST_2$ = $25 million/$(1.5)^2$ = $11,111,111 as the postmoney valuation. It would ask for a $2,000,000/11,111,111 = 18.00$ percent ownership stake. This means that the existing owners of the firm (the founders) and the first round investors (Vulture Ventures) would jointly only retain 82 percent of the company, or $0.82 \times \$11,111,111 = \$9,111,111$. This is also the pre-money valuation at the time of this second round of financing, and no coincidence, since the pre-money valuation measures precisely the value for the existing owners of the firm.

For the first round investment, Vulture Ventures can then expect the company to be worth $9,111,111 at the time of the second round, i.e., in two years' time. It then uses the same method as above to calculate the post-money valuation at the time of the first round, i.e., $POST_1$ = $9,111,111/$(1.5)^2$ = $4,049,383. This implies that it will ask for $3,000,000/\$4,049,383 = 74.09$ percent of the shares of the company. Note, however, that Vulture Ventures will not own 74.09 percent after four years. Instead, it expects a future dilution that will bring its ownership down to $f_1 = 0.82 \times 0.7409 =$

---

22 It is sometimes argued that future dilution does not matter in efficient markets, but we have to be careful with this argument. In a typical venture capital situation the company can only meet its financial projections if it manages to raise additional capital. In that sense the future dilution applies not to new investment opportunities of the company, but to the realization of the current investment opportunity. As an early round investor we therefore want to take account of the future dilution. This is different from the scenario in which future dilution relates to raising money for future investment opportunities that are additively separable from the current investment.

60.75 percent (the lower case notation indicates final ownership, after dilution). This is obviously a familiar number, as we have seen before that Vulture Ventures needs exactly 60.75 percent to get their required return on their investment of $3 million.

So far we haven't said anything about the number of shares and the price of shares for either the first or second round. In fact, we cannot calculate the price and number of shares for the second round before we calculate the price and number of shares for the first round. For this first round, we use the usual method, i.e., $y_1 = x_1 F_1/(1 - F_1) = 1,000,000 \times 0.7409/(1 - 0.7409) = 2,858,824$ and thus $p_1 = 3,000,000/2,858,824 = \$1.05$. For the second round we repeat the exercise. The important step, however, is to use the correct number of shares, namely the total number of existing shares (irrespective of whether they are owned by the entrepreneur or the investor). We have $x_2 = (x_1 + y_1) = 1,000,000 + 2,858,824 = 3,858,824$ as the number of existing shares at the time of the second round. The new number of shares required is thus $y_2 = x_2 F_2/(1 - F_2) = 3,858,824(0.18)/(1 - 0.18) = 847,059$. The price of the second round shares is then given by $\$2,000,000/847,059 = \$2.36$.

The following table summarizes these assumptions and results.

NPV Method with Two Rounds of Financing	Time of Exit	Second Round	First Round
Exit Value	$25,000,000		
Compound discount rate		2.25	2.25
Investment amount		2,000,000	3,000,000
Number of existing shares		3,858,824	1,000,000
Post-Money		$11,111,111	$4,049,383
Pre-Money		$9,111,111	$1,049,383
Ownership Fraction		18.00%	74.09%
Number of new shares		847,059	2,858,824
Price per share		$2.36	$1.05
Ownership shares of entrepreneurs	21.25%		
Wealth of entrepreneurs	$5,312,500	$2,361,111	$1,049,383
Ownership shares of first round investors	60.75%		
Wealth of first round investors	$15,187,500	$6,750,000	$3,000,000
Ownership shares of second round investors	18.00%		
Wealth of second round investors	$4,500,000	$2,000,000	

4.2 The General Case with Multiple Rounds of Financing

We are now in a position to examine the general case. We show the formulas for the case where there are two rounds of financing. All variables pertaining to round 1 (2) will have the subscript $_{1 (2)}$. The case with an arbitrary number of rounds is a straightforward extension discussed at the end of the section.

Step 1   *Define appropriate compound interest rates.*

Suppose that the terminal value is expected to occur at some date T_3, the second round at some date T_2, and the first round is happening at date T_1. Define $(1 + R_2)$ as the compound discount rate between time T_2 and T_3. If, for example, there are three years between the second round and the exit time, and if the discount rate for these three years is 40 percent, 35 percent, and 30 percent, respectively, then $(1 + R_2) = 1.4 \times 1.35 \times 1.3$. The compound discount rate $(1 + R_1)$ is defined similarly for the time between dates T_1 and T_2 (not T_3!!!).

Step 2 $POST_2 = V/(1 + R_2)$

Where $POST_2$ is the post-money valuation at the time of the second round, V is the terminal value and R_2 is the compound discount rate between the time of the second round and the time of exit.

Step 3 $PRE_2 = POST_2 - I_2$

PRE_2 is the pre-money valuation at the time of the second round of financing and I_2 is the amount raised in the second round.

Step 4 $POST_1 = PRE_2/(1 + R_1)$

Where $POST_1$ is the post-money valuation at the time of the first round and R_1 is the compound discount rate between the time of the first and second rounds.

Step 5 $PRE_1 = POST_1 - I_1$

PRE_1 is the pre-money valuation at the time of the first round of financing, and I_1 is the amount raised in the first round.

Step 6 $F_2 = I_2/POST_2$

F_2 is the required ownership fraction for the investors in the second round.

Step 7 $F_1 = I_1/POST_1$

F_1 is the required ownership fraction for the investors in the first round (this is not their final ownership share, as they will get diluted by a factor of $(1 - F_2)$ in the second round).

Step 8 $y_1 = x_1 [F_1/(1 - F_1)]$

y_1 is the number of new shares that the investors in the first round require to achieve their desired ownership fraction, and x_1 is the number of existing shares.[23]

Step 9 $p_1 = I_1/y_1$

p_1 is the price per share in the first round.

Step 10 $x_2 = x_1 + y_1$

x_2 is the number of existing shares at the time of the second round.

Step 11 $y_2 = x_2 [F_2/(1 - F_2)]$

y_2 is the number of new shares that the investors in the second round require to achieve their desired ownership fraction.

Step 12 $p_2 = I_2/y_2$

p_2 is the price per share in the second round.

The general case is a straightforward extension of the case with two rounds. First we need to define the compound discount rates between all the rounds. Then we find the post- and pre-money valuations working backwards from the terminal value to each round of financing, all the way back to the first round of financing. For each round we discount the pre-money valuation of the subsequent round to get the post-money valuation of the round. Once we have the post-money valuations for all rounds we can calculate all the required ownership shares. To get the number and prices of shares we begin with the usual formula for the first round and then count up for each round.

---

23 If there are no pre-existing shares, one may also fix a total number of shares and then simply allocate them according to the fractions F_1 and $(1 - F_1)$.

4.3 Some Further Examples

Consider a first variation of the model. Suppose that the discount rate is highest in the early years and becomes lower after a while. For example, assume that the discount rate is 60 percent in the first year, stays at 50 percent in years two and three, and falls to 40 percent in the fourth year. This changes our compound discount rates: we have $(1 + R_2) = 1.5 \times 1.4 = 2.1$ and $(1 + R_1) = 1.6 \times 1.5 = 2.4$

Variation 1	Time of Exit	Second Round	First Round
Exit Value	$25,000,000		
Compound discount rate		2.1	2.4
Investment amount		2,000,000	3,000,000
Number of existing shares		3,661,972	1,000,000
Post-Money		$11,904,762	$4,126,984
Pre-Money		$9,904,762	$1,126,984
Ownership Fraction		16.80%	72.69%
Number of new shares		739,437	2,661,972
Price per share		$2.70	$1.13
Ownership shares of entrepreneurs	22.72%		
Wealth of entrepreneurs	$5,680,000	$2,704,762	$1,126,984
Ownership shares of first round investors	60.48%		
Wealth of first round investors	$15,120,000	$7,200,000	$3,000,000
Ownership shares of second round investors	16.80%		
Wealth of second round investors	$4,200,000	$2,000,000	

There are many other variations that we can examine in this model. A second variation of particular interest is to examine the role of the timing of the second round. Suppose, for example, that SpiffyCalc might be able to delay the timing of the second round by one year. In this case the compound discount rates are given by $(1 + R_2) = 1.4$ and $(1 + R_1) = 1.6 \times 1.5 \times 1.5 = 3.6$. Delaying the second round of financing would improve the valuation of the company.

Variation 2	Time of Exit	Second Round	First Round
Exit Value	$25,000,000		
Compound discount rate		1.4	3.6
Investment amount		2,000,000	3,000,000
Number of existing shares		3,135,593	1,000,000
Post-Money		$17,857,143	$4,404,762
Pre-Money		$15,857,143	$1,404,762
Ownership Fraction		11.20%	68.11%
Number of new shares		395,480	2,135,593
Price per share		$5.06	$1.40
Ownership shares of entrepreneurs	28.32%		
Wealth of entrepreneurs	$7,080,000	$5,057,143	$1,404,762
Ownership shares of first round investors	60.48%		
Wealth of first round investors	$15,120,000	$10,800,000	$3,000,000
Ownership shares of second round investors	11.20%		
Wealth of second round investors	$2,800,000	$2,000,000	

5 The Determinants of Valuation: Looking beyond the Numbers

To put things in perspective, it should be said that any method of valuation depends critically on the assumptions we make. Indeed, any valuation number can be justified by an appropriate choice of the discount rates and the terminal value. There is a more fundamental point here. A valuation method is a sophisticated tool for determining how entrepreneurs and venture capitalists should split the returns of the new venture. But the actual split, i.e., the actual deal, is not really driven by the valuation method, but rather by the outcome of the bargaining between the entrepreneurs and the venture capitalists. The relative bargaining power is thus the true economic determinant of the valuation that entrepreneurs will obtain for their companies. The valuation method, however, is an important tool to master for all parties involved, as it often provides the quantitative basis for the negotiation.

PRACTICE PROBLEMS

1 Jo Ann Ng is a senior analyst at SING INVEST, a large regional mid-market buyout manager in Singapore. She is considering the exit possibilities for an existing investment in a mature automotive parts manufacturer that was acquired 3 years ago at a multiple of 7.5 times EBITDA. SING INVEST originally anticipated exiting its investment in China Auto Parts, Inc. within 3 to 6 years. Ng noted that current market conditions have deteriorated and that companies operating in a similar business trade at an average multiple of 5.5 times EBITDA. She deemed, however, based on analyst reports and industry knowledge that the market is expected to recover strongly within the next two years because of the fast increasing demand for cars in emerging markets. Upon review of market opportunities, Ng also noted that China Gear Box, Inc., a smaller Chinese auto parts manufacturer presenting potential strong synergies with China Auto Parts, Inc., is available for sale at an EBITDA multiple of 4.5. Exits by means of an IPO or a trade sale to a financial or strategic (company) buyer are possible in China. How would you advise Ng to enhance value upon exit of China Auto Parts?

2 Wenda Lee, CFA, is a portfolio manager at a UK-based private equity institutional investor. She is considering an investment in a mid-market European buyout fund to achieve a better diversification of her firm's existing private equity portfolio. She short listed two funds that she deemed to have a similar risk return profile. Before deciding which one to invest in, she is carefully reviewing and comparing the terms of each fund.

	Mid-Market Fund A	Mid-Market Fund B
Management fees	2.5%	1.5%
Transaction fees	100% to the GP	50–50% split
Carried interest	15%	20%
Hurdle rate	6%	9%
Clawback provision	No	Yes
Distribution waterfall	Deal-by-deal	Total return

Based on the analysis of terms, which fund would you recommend to Lee?

3 Jean Pierre Dupont is the CIO of a French pension fund allocating a substantial portion of its assets to private equity. The existing private equity portfolio comprises mainly large buyout funds, mezzanine funds, and a limited allocation to a special situations fund. The pension fund decided to further increase its allocation to European venture capital. The investment committee of the pension fund requested Dupont present an analysis of five key investment characteristics specific to venture capital relative to buyout investing. Can you assist Dupont in this request?

4 Discuss the ways that private equity funds can create value.

5 What problems are encountered when using comparable publicly traded companies to value private acquisition targets?

6 What are the main ways in which the performance of private equity limited partnerships can be measured A) during the life of the fund, and B) once all investments have been exited?

The following information relates to Questions 7–12

Martha Brady is the chief investment officer (CIO) of the Upper Darby County (UDC) public employees' pension system. Brady is considering an allocation of a portion of the pension system's assets to private equity. She has asked two of her analysts, Jennifer Chau, CFA, and Matthew Hermansky, to provide more information about the workings of the private equity market.

Brady recognizes that the private equity asset class covers a broad spectrum of equity investments that are not traded in public markets. She asks Chau to describe the major differences between assets that constitute this asset class. Chau notes that the private equity class ranges from venture capital financing of early stage companies to complete buyouts of large publicly traded or even privately held companies. Chau describes some of the characteristics of venture capital and buyout investments.

Chau mentions that private equity firms take care to align the economic interests of the managers of the investments they control with the interests of the private equity firms. Various contractual clauses are inserted in the compensation contracts of the management team in order to reward or punish managers who do not meet agreed on target objectives.

One concern is the illiquidity of private equity investments over time. But some funds are returned to investors over the life of the fund because a number of investment opportunities are exited early. A number of provisions describe the distribution of returns to investors, some of which favor the limited partners. One such provision is the distribution waterfall mechanism that provides distributions to limited partners (LP) before the general partner (GP) receives the carried interest. This distribution mechanism is called the total return waterfall.

Chau prepares the following data to illustrate the distribution waterfall mechanism and the funds provided to limited partners when a private equity fund with a zero hurdle rate exits from its first three projects during a three-year period.

Exhibit 1	Investment Returns and Distribution Waterfalls
Private equity committed capital	$400 million
Carried interest	20%
First project investment capital	$20 million
Second project investment capital	$45 million
Third project investment capital	$50 million
Proceeds from first project	$25 million
Proceeds from second project	$35 million
Proceeds from third project	$65 million

Chau cautions that investors must understand the terminology used to describe the performance of private equity funds. Interpretation of performance numbers should be made with the awareness that much of the fund assets are illiquid during a substantial part of the fund's life. She provides the latest data in Exhibit 2 for Alpha, Beta, and Gamma Funds—diversified high-technology venture capital funds formed five years ago and each with five years remaining to termination.

Chau studies the data and comments: "Of the three funds, the Alpha Fund has the best chance to outperform over the remaining life. First, because the management has earned such a relatively high residual value on capital and will be able to earn a high return on the remaining funds called down. At termination, the RVPI will earn double the '0.65' value when the rest of the funds are called down. Second, its 'cash on cash' return as measured by DPI is already as high as that of the Beta Fund. PIC, or paid-in capital, provides information about the proportion of capital called by the GP. The PIC of Alpha is relatively low relative to Beta and Gamma."

Exhibit 2	Financial Performance of Alpha, Beta, and Gamma Funds		
Fund	**PIC**	**DPI**	**RVPI**
Alpha	0.30	0.10	0.65
Beta	0.85	0.10	1.25
Gamma	0.85	1.25	0.75

Hermansky notes that a private equity fund's ability to properly plan and execute its exit from an investment is vital for the fund's success. Venture funds such as Alpha, Beta, and Gamma take special care to plan for exiting from investments. Venture funds tend to focus on certain types of exits, especially when equity markets are strong.

Brady then asks the analysts what procedures private equity firms would use to value investments in their portfolios as well as any other investments that might be added to the portfolio. She is concerned about buying into a fund with existing assets that do not have public market prices to ascertain value. In such cases, the GP may overvalue the assets and new investors in the fund will pay a higher NAV for the fund assets than they are worth.

Hermansky makes three statements regarding the valuation methods used in private equity transactions during the early stages of selling a fund to investors.

Statement 1   For venture capital investment in the early stages of analysis, emphasis is placed on the discounted cash flow approach to valuation.

Statement 2   For buyout investments, income-based approaches are used frequently as a primary method of valuation.

Statement 3   If a comparable group of companies exist, multiples of revenues or earnings are used frequently to derive a value for venture capital investments.

7   The characteristic that is *most likely* common to both the venture capital and buyout private equity investment is:

A   measurable and assessable risk.

B   the extensive use of financial leverage.

C   the strength of the individual track record and ability of members of management.

8 The contractual term enabling management of the private equity controlled company to be rewarded with increased equity ownership as a result of meeting performance targets is called:

   A   a ratchet.

   B   the tag-along right.

   C   the clawback provision.

9 For the projects described in Exhibit 1, under a deal-by-deal method with a clawback provision and true-up every three years, the cumulative dollar amount the GP receives by the end of the three years is equal to:

   A   one million.

   B   two million.

   C   three million.

10 Are Chau's two reasons for interpreting Alpha Fund as the best performing fund over the remaining life correct?

   A   No.

   B   Yes.

   C   The first reason is correct, but the second reason is incorrect.

11 The exit route for a venture capital investment is *least likely* to be in the form of a(n):

   A   initial public offering (IPO).

   B   sale to other venture funds targeting the same sector.

   C   buyout by the management of the venture investment.

12 Which statement by Hermansky is the *least* valid?

   A   Statement 1.

   B   Statement 2.

   C   Statement 3.

SOLUTIONS

1   The exit strategies available to SING INVEST to divest their holding in China Auto Parts, Inc. will largely depend on the following two factors:

- Time remaining until the fund's term expires. If the time remaining is sufficiently long, the fund's manager has more flexibility to work out an exit at more favorable market circumstances and terms.

- Amount of undrawn commitments from LPs in the fund. If sufficient LP commitments can be drawn, the fund manager may take advantage of current market investment opportunities at depressed market prices with the objective to enhance returns upon exit in an expected more favorable market environment.

In the case of China Auto Parts Inc., depending on an analysis of the above, Ng could advise the acquisition of China Gear Box, Inc. subject to an indepth analysis of potential synergies with China Auto Parts, Inc. The objective here may thus be twofold: benefit from short-term market conditions and enhance the value of existing investments by reinforcing their market potential with a strategic merger.

2   Assuming that both funds have similar risk return characteristics, a closer analysis of economic and corporate governance terms should be instrumental in determining which fund to select.

In economic terms, Mid-Market Fund B has a higher carried interest relative to Mid-Market Fund A, but Mid-Market Fund B has a fee structure that is better aligned with the interests of LPs. A larger proportion of Mid-Market Fund B's fees will be on achieving successful exits (through the carried interest), whereas Mid-Market Fund A will earn relatively larger fees on running the fund (management fees and transaction fees) without necessarily achieving high performance. In addition, the 9 percent hurdle rate of Mid-Market Fund B is indicative of a stronger confidence of the fund manager to achieve a minimum compounded 9 percent return to LPs under which no carried interest will be paid.

In corporate governance terms, Mid-Market Fund B is far better aligned with the interests of LPs as a result of a clawback provision and a more favorable distribution waterfall to LPs that will allow payment of carried interest on a total return basis instead of deal-by-deal.

The conclusion is that Mid-Market Fund B appears better aligned with the interests of LPs.

3

Venture Capital	Buyout
Primarily equity funded. Use of leverage is rare and very limited.	Extensive use of leverage consisting of a large proportion of senior debt and a significant layer of junior and/or mezzanine debt.
Returns of investment portfolios are generally characterized by very high returns from a limited number of highly successful investments and a significant number of write-offs from low performing investments or failures.	Returns of investment portfolios are generally characterized by lower variance across returns from underlying investments. Bankruptcies are rare events.

Venture Capital	Buyout
Venture capital firm monitors achievement of milestones defined in business plan and growth management.	Buyout firm monitors cash flow management and strategic and business planning.
Expanding capital requirement if in the growth phase.	Low working capital requirement.
Assessment of risk is difficult because of new technologies, new markets, and lack of operating history.	Risk is measurable (e.g., mature businesses, long operating history, etc.).

4 The main ways that private equity funds can create value include the following:

- Operational improvements and clearly defined strategies. In the case of later stage companies and buyouts, private equity owners can often create value by focusing the business on its most profitable opportunities and providing new strategic direction for the business. In the case of venture capital deals, the private equity funds can provide valuable business experience, mentor management, and offer access to their network of contacts and other portfolio companies.

- Creating incentives for managers and aligning their goals with the investors. This is often achieved by providing significant monetary rewards to management if the private equity fund secures a profitable exit. In the case of buyouts, the free cash flow available to management is minimized by taking on significant amounts of debt financing.

- Optimizing the financial structure of the company. In the case of buyouts, the use of debt can reduce the tax payments made by the company and reduce the cost of capital. There may also be opportunities in certain market conditions to take advantage of any mispricing of risk by lenders, which can allow the private equity funds to take advantage of interest rates that do not fully reflect the risks being carried by the lenders. Many would point to the period from mid-2006 to mid-2007 as a period when such conditions prevailed.

5 There are many complexities in using comparable companies to value private targets, including the following:

- The lack of public comparison companies operating in the same business, facing the same risks, and at the same stage of development. It is often possible to identify "approximate" comparisons but very rare to find an exact match. It is essential, therefore, to use judgment when using comparison company information, rather than just taking the average multiples derived from a sample of disparate companies.

- Comparison companies may have different capital structures, so estimated beta coefficients and some financial ratios should be adjusted accordingly.

- Reported accounting numbers for earnings must be chosen carefully and adjusted for any exceptional items, atypical revenues, and costs in the reference year. Care must also be taken to decide which earnings figures to compare—the main choices are trailing earnings (the last 12 months), earnings from the last audited accounts, or prospective year-ahead earnings.

6 In the early years of a fund, all measures of returns are of little relevance because fees drag down the reported returns and investments are initially valued at cost. This produces the J-curve effect. After a few years (longer in the case of venture capital investments), performance measures become more meaningful and the two main measures used by investors are IRR and return

multiples (of the initial sum invested). During the life of the fund it is necessary to value the non-exited investments and add them to the realized returns. The former inevitably involves an element of judgment on the part of the General Partner, especially when it is difficult to estimate the likely market value of the investment. Once all the investments have been exited, the multiples and IRR can be estimated easily, taking account of the exact timing of the cash flows into and out of the fund. The most relevant measures for investors are computed net of management fees and any carried interest earned by the General Partner.

7 C is correct. Members of both the firm being bought out and the venture capital investment usually have strong individual management track records. Extensive financial leverage is common in buyouts but not venture capital investments, whereas measurable risk is more common in buyouts than in venture capital situations.

8 A is correct.

9 B is correct. On a cumulative basis for three years, the fund earns $10 million, of which $2 million goes to the GP. The $2 million earned by the GP corresponds to 20 percent of the difference between total three-year proceeds and three-year invested capital, or 0.2[(25 + 35 + 65) − (20 + 45 + 50)].

10 A is correct. Chau misinterprets DPI, RVPI, and PIC. The returns earned to date are for each dollar of invested capital, that which has been drawn down, not total returns. Chau mistakenly believes (assuming the same management skill) the result for Alpha Fund at termination will be on the order of 3 × 0.65 = 1.95 instead of 0.65. In both cases, Alpha Fund has underperformed relative to the other two funds.

11 C is correct. Leverage needed to finance a management buyout is not readily available to firms with limited history.

12 A is correct. Statement 1 is the least likely to be valid.

A Primer on Commodity Investing

by Frank J. Fabozzi, PhD, CPA, CFA, Roland Füss, PhD, and
Dieter G. Kaiser, PhD

*Frank J. Fabozzi, PhD, CPA, CFA, is at EDHEC Business School (France). Roland Füss,
PhD, is at the University of St. Gallen (Switzerland). Dieter G. Kaiser, PhD (Germany).*

LEARNING OUTCOMES

Mastery	The candidate should be able to:
☐	a. describe types of market participants in commodity futures markets;
☐	b. explain storability and renewability in the context of commodities and determine whether a commodity is storable and/or renewable;
☐	c. explain the convenience yield and how it relates to the stock (inventory level) of a commodity;
☐	d. distinguish among capital assets, store-of-value assets, and consumable or transferable assets and explain implications for valuation;
☐	e. compare ways of participating in commodity markets, including advantages and disadvantages of each;
☐	f. explain backwardation and contango in terms of spot and futures prices;
☐	g. describe the components of return to a commodity futures and a portfolio of commodity futures;
☐	h. explain how the sign of the roll return depends on the term structure of futures prices;
☐	i. compare the insurance perspective, the hedging pressure hypothesis, and the theory of storage and their implications for futures prices and expected future spot prices.

Commodities are currently enjoying a renaissance due to institutional investors such as pension funds and traditional portfolio managers. Many market participants attribute the recent dramatic price increases in commodities to increased demand for consumer goods, particularly from the populous countries of India and China. Demand from Brazil and Russia, two of the fastest-growing economies currently, has undoubtedly also played a part. (Collectively, these four countries are referred to as the *BRIC countries*.)

Globalization and economic and political convergence have been behind the stimulated growth in these economies to a large extent. Besides increased investment on an enterprise level, increasing state investment in infrastructure in China has also led to enormous demand for commodities. This has caused a shock to the worldwide supply and demand dynamics, leading to at least short-term price increases.

Such dramatic increases in commodity prices are often explained by the *commodity super cycle theory*. According to Heap, a *super cycle* is a lasting boom in real commodity prices, usually brought on by urbanization and industrialization in a major economy.[1] Hence, super cycles are driven by demand caused by an expansion of material-based production due to intense economic activity. The economic situation in China is of crucial importance to the commodity markets. China has greatly increased its share of global commodity consumption over the past few years, and is seen as the major driver of the current commodity boom.

For example, between 2001 and 2005, China's demand for copper, aluminum, and iron increased by 78%, 85%, and 92%, respectively. This clearly shows China's considerable influence on commodity pricing. This super cycle, however, is not characterized by a continuous growth phase, as the events of May 2006 show. Many commodities were under pressure during that time, and actually lost about one-fourth of their value.

Under market conditions like these, the question inevitably arises as to whether this is a temporary price correction or a general trend change. Following the super cycle theory, a long-lasting upward trend in commodities in the future is likely, as most remain far below their historic highs when adjusted for inflation.

Compared to foreign exchange or equity markets, there is almost no way to intervene in commodity markets. Because the production side reacts very sluggishly to market distortions, short-term supply and demand shocks are compensated for only by price movements.[2] These inherent asset class volatilities are the main reason many investors have refrained from investing in commodities, despite the fact they can provide valuable diversification benefits to traditional security portfolios because of their low correlation with bonds and stocks.[3]

This chapter first discusses the basics of commodity markets by describing the market participants, the commodity subsectors, and the different kinds of commodity investment vehicles available to investors. Subsequently, we illustrate the return components of index-based, that is, passive long-only, commodity futures investments in the context of the price discovery process, and we investigate the risk/

---

[1] Alan Heap, "China—The Engine of Commodities Super Cycle," *Citigroup Global Equity Research* (March 2005). The past 200 years have seen several such upswings, lasting from between 15 and 25 years. For example, in the late nineteenth century, industrialization in the United States triggered such a boom. The postwar period of 1945 to 1975, when enormous resources were needed to rebuild Europe, can also be characterized as a super cycle.

[2] In contrast, central banks possess a variety of money market instruments to maintain the value and stability of their currency. At the same time, central banks can control—at least to some extent—the economic development of an economy through changes in interest rates to avoid inflationary or deflationary tendencies.

[3] Kenneth A. Froot, "Hedging Portfolios with Real Assets," *Journal of Portfolio Management* (Summer 1995), pp. 60-77.

return characteristics of commodity futures indexes. Following this, we provide an empirical analysis of portfolio allocation of traditional security portfolios, explicitly taking commodity futures into account.

MARKET PARTICIPANTS

Futures market participants are normally classified into hedgers, speculators (traders), and arbitrageurs. Commodity producers pass on the price risk that results from highly volatile and difficult to forecast commodity futures markets to speculators, and therefore pay a premium. Commodity producers have a distinct interest in hedging the price of their product in advance (a short hedge).

For example, consider the situation in the classic agricultural market. Farmers face a weather-dependent, volatile supply that is met by a relatively stable demand. Contrary to the maintenance cost for cattle breeding or the purchase cost of seed, the selling price generally is known only upon completion.

We see the opposite in the manufacturing industry: As the manufacturing industry hedges increasing commodity prices (a long hedge), the contrarian position to the commodity producers' short positions is taken. Airline companies, for example, often appear as long hedgers to guard against increasing fuel prices, the underlying in which the airline companies are short. If an existing or expected cash position is compensated for via an opposite future, the market participant is classified as a *hedger*. Hence, for the commodity producer, there is a fixed net profit; for the commodity manufacturer, there is a fixed purchase price.

Speculators represent the largest group in the futures markets. Their main task is to provide liquidity on the one hand, while balancing the long and short hedges on the other hand. Contrary to the commodity producers or the manufacturing industry, which try to avoid susceptibility to unfavorable price developments, the intention of speculators is to take a distinct market position and speculate for a price change. To make a profit, speculators deliberately take on risk by betting on rising or falling prices. As opposed to hedging, speculation is subject to both huge gains and huge losses, since speculators do not hold compensating cash positions.

The third and smallest group of market participants is the *arbitrageurs*, who try to take advantage of time- or location-based price differences in commodity futures markets, or between spot and futures markets, in order to generate riskless profits. Clearly, this group also intends to make profits, but their trading activity does not involve taking risky positions. Moreover, they use economic and financial data to detect existing price differences with respect to time and location. If these price differences exceed interlocal or intertemporal transfer costs such as shipping, interest rates, warehouse costs, or insurance costs, riskless profits can be realized. Consequently, price differences among the markets are adjusted, price relationships among the markets are restored, and arbitrageurs guarantee market balancing.

In the case of cash and carry arbitrage, the resale price of today's leveraged spot position is simultaneously set by selling the commodity futures. This short futures position implies an unconditional commitment to purchase the underlying at maturity. At maturity of the futures, the specified commodities are tendered against the maturing short futures. If the profit from the spot trade of the physical commodity exceeds the value of the futures plus the cost of debt financing, the arbitrageur will realize a profit from what is known as a *basis trade*.

COMMODITY SECTORS

Investments in international commodity markets differ greatly from other investments in several important ways. First, commodities are real assets—primarily consumption and not investment goods. They have an intrinsic value, and provide utility by use in industrial manufacturing or in consumption. Furthermore, supply is limited because in any given period, commodities have only a limited availability. For example, renewable commodities like grains can be produced virtually without limitation. However, their yearly harvest is strictly limited. In addition, the supply of certain commodities shows a strong seasonal component. While metals can be mined almost all year, agricultural commodities like soybeans depend on the harvesting cycle.

Another important aspect of commodities as an asset class is heterogeneity. The quality of commodities is not standardized; every commodity has its own specific properties. A common way to classify them is to distinguish between soft and hard commodities. *Hard commodities* are products from the energy, precious metals, and industrial metals sectors. *Soft commodities* are usually weather-dependent, perishable commodities for consumption from the agricultural sector, such as grains, soybeans, or livestock, such as cattle or hogs. Exhibit 1 shows the classification of commodity sectors.

Exhibit 1   Classification of Commodity Sectors

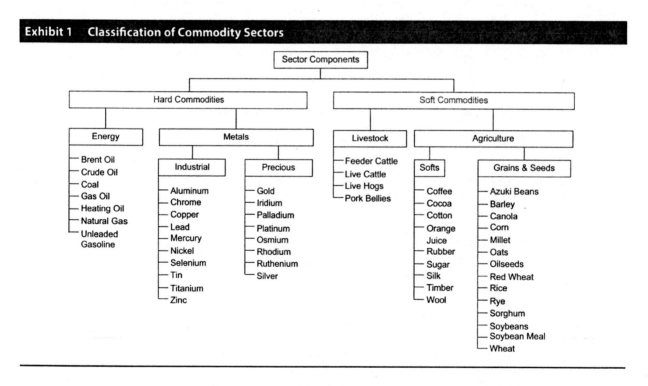

Storability and availability (or renewability) are also important features of commodities. However, because storability plays a decisive role in pricing, we distinguish between storable and nonstorable commodities. A commodity is said to have a high degree of storability if it is not perishable and the cost of storage remains low with respect to its total value. Industrial metals such as aluminum or copper are prime examples: They fulfill both criteria to a high degree. In contrast, livestock is storable to only a limited degree, as it must be continuously fed and housed at current costs, and is only profitable in a specific phase of its life cycle.

Commodities such as silver, gold, crude oil, and aluminum are nonrenewable. The supply of nonrenewable commodities depends on the ability of producers to mine raw material in both sufficient quantity and sufficient quality.

The availability of commodity manufacturing capacities also influences supply. For some metals (excluding precious metals) and crude oil, the discovery and exploration of new reserves of raw materials is still an important issue. The price of nonrenewable resources depends strongly on current investor demand, while the price of renewable resources depends more on estimated future production costs.[4] The monetary benefit from holding a commodity physically instead of being long the respective futures is called the *convenience yield*. The convenience yield reflects market participants' expectations regarding a possible future scarcity of a short-term nonrenewable commodity.

COMMODITIES AS AN ASSET CLASS OF THEIR OWN

There is a broad consensus among academics and practitioners that commodities compared to other alternative assets can be considered—in a portfolio context—as an asset class of their own.[5] By definition, an asset class consists of similar assets that show a homogeneous risk-return profile (a high internal correlation), and a heterogeneous risk-return profile toward other asset classes (a low external correlation). The key properties are common value drivers, and not necessarily common price patterns. This is based on the idea that a separate asset class contains a unique risk premium that cannot be replicated by combining other asset classes.[6] Furthermore, it is generally required that the long-term returns and liquidity from an asset class are significant to justify an allocation.

To describe existing asset classes, Greer explains the decomposition into so-called super classes: *capital assets, store of value assets,* and *consumable or transferable assets.*[7] Continuous performance is a characteristic of capital assets. Equity capital like stocks provides a continuous stream of dividend payments, while fixed income guarantees regular interest payments in the absence of the default of the obligor. Redemption of invested loan capital can then be allocated among other investments.

Common to all capital assets is that their valuation follows the net present value method by discounting expected future cash flows. In contrast, real estate as an asset class has a hybrid classification. On the one hand, real estate can be classified as a capital asset because it promises a continuous rental stream and has market value. On the other hand, some features of real estate assets can justify their classification as store of value assets (for example, if the real estate is used for the owner's own purpose). Such store of value assets cannot be consumed, nor do they generate income; classic examples are foreign exchange, art, and antiquities.

Commodities belong to the third super class—*consumable or transferable* (C/T) assets. In contrast to stocks and bonds, C/T assets, physical commodities like energy, grains, or livestock, do not generate continuous cash flows, but rather have an economic

---

4 The events following Hurricane Katrina in 2005 clearly illustrated the insufficiency of the refinery capacities for crude oil and natural gas. Declining investment in this sector over the years has led to a bottleneck. The absence of investment in the industrial metals sector is also an issue for the supply side.
5 In reality, most alternative investments such as hedge funds or private equity are not an asset class in their own, but are considered alternative investment strategies within an existing asset class.
6 Bernd Scherer, "Commodities as an Asset Class: Testing for Mean Variance Spanning under Arbitrary Constraints," *Deutsche Bank—An Investors' Guide to Commodities* (April 2005), pp. 35–42.
7 Robert J. Greer, "What is an Asset Class, Anyway?" *Journal of Portfolio Management* (Winter 1997), pp. 86–91.

value. Grains, for example, can be consumed or used as input goods; crude oil is manufactured into a variety of products. This difference is what makes commodities a unique asset class.

Hence, it is obvious that commodity prices cannot be determined by the net present value method or by discounting future cash flows. Thus, interest rates have only a minor influence on the value of commodities. Moreover, commodity prices are the result of the interaction between supply and demand on specific markets.[8] In this context, it is not surprising that the *capital asset pricing model* (CAPM) cannot adequately explain commodity futures returns. As we have noted, commodities are not capital assets.[9]

The line between the super classes is blurred in the case of gold. On the one hand, gold as a commodity is used in such things as electrical circuitry because of its excellent conductivity. On the other hand, gold as a store of value asset is a precious metal and is used for investment, similarly to currencies. The rising demand of commodities since the stock market downturn in 2002 clearly demonstrates this characteristic. Because gold can be leased, Anson has even classified it as a capital asset.[10]

Another specific criterion that differentiates commodities from capital assets is that commodities are denominated worldwide in US dollars, while the value of a specific commodity is determined through global rather than regional supply and demand. In comparison, equity markets reflect the respective economic development within a country or a region.

Prospects for Commodity Market Participation

In general, there are several ways to participate in commodity markets via a number of different kinds of financial instruments. The most important are (1) direct investment in the physical good; (2) indirect investment in stocks of natural resource companies or (3) commodity mutual funds; (4) an investment in commodity futures, or (5) an investment in structured products on commodity futures indexes.

Buying the Physical Good

First, it seems obvious to invest directly in commodities by purchasing the physical goods at the spot market. However, immediate or within-two-days delivery is frequently not practical for investors. According to Geman, precious metals such as gold, silver, or platinum are an exception, as they do not have high current costs and do not require storage capacity.[11] However, a portfolio consisting solely of precious metals would not be a sufficiently diversified portfolio for investors to hold.

---

8 James H. Scott, "Managing Asset Classes," *Financial Analysts Journal* (January-February 1994), pp. 62–69.
9 The two components of risk, systematic (market) and unsystematic (company-specific), are considered within the CAPM framework. Since unsystematic risk is eliminated in a broadly diversified portfolio, investors are only compensated for systematic risk. The risk premium is then the product of systematic risk (beta) multiplied by the market price of risk, defined as the difference between the expected return of the market portfolio and the riskless interest rate. In the CAPM, the market portfolio is composed only of stocks and bonds, so commodity returns cannot be represented by financial market returns. Thus, it is not possible to distinguish between systematic and unsystematic risk. Finally, commodity prices depend on global supply and demand and not on the perception of the market regarding an adequate risk premium for a specific asset class. See Claude Erb and Campbell R. Harvey, "The Tactical and Strategic Value of Commodity Futures," *Financial Analysts Journal* (April/May 2006), pp. 69–97; and Zvi Bodie and Victor I. Rosansky, "Risk and Return in Commodity Futures," *Financial Analysts Journal* (May/June 1980), pp. 27–39.
10 Precious metals such as gold, silver, or platinum can generate a lucrative stream of income by being leased at market leasing rates. See Mark J. P. Anson, *The Handbook of Alternative Assets*, 2nd ed. (Hoboken, NJ: John Wiley & Sons, 2006).
11 Hélyette Geman, *Commodities and Commodity Derivatives: Modeling and Pricing for Agriculturals, Metals and Energy* (Chichester: John Wiley & Sons, 2005).

Commodity Stocks

An investment in commodity stocks (*natural resource companies*), which generate a majority of their profits by buying and selling physical commodities, may conceivably be considered an alternative investment strategy. In general, the term "commodity stock" cannot be clearly differentiated. It consists of listed companies that are related to commodities (i.e., those that explore, mine, refine, manufacture, trade, or supply commodities to other companies). Such an indirect investment in commodities (e.g., the purchase of petrochemical stocks) is only an insufficient substitute for a direct investment. By investing in such stocks, investors do not receive direct exposure to commodities because listed natural resource companies all have their own characteristics and inherent risks.

Georgiev shows that these sector-specific stocks are only slightly correlated with commodity prices, and hence prices of commodity stocks do not completely reflect the performance of the underlying market.[12] This is because stocks reflect other price-relevant factors such as the strategic position of the company, management quality, capital structure (the debt/equity ratio), the expectations and ratings of company and profit growth, risk sensitivity, as well as information transparency and information credibility.[13]

Stock markets also show quick and more sensible reactions to expected developments that can impact company value. Hence, other causes of independent price discovery exist that differ from a pure commodity investment. Moreover, there may be temporary market disequilibriums, especially for stocks with low free float, where few buy and sell transactions can already cause major price reactions. Finally, natural resource companies are subject to operational risk caused by human or technical failure, internal regulations, or external events. This means that when investing in a company listed on the stock exchange, both the associated market risk as well as any idiosyncratic risk must be considered carefully.[14]

However, the risk of commodity stocks is not completely reflected in the price volatility. First, particularly in the energy and metal sectors, there is the paradox that companies threaten their own business fundamentals by extracting exhaustible resources. On the one hand, long-term decreasing total reserves mean rising prices and a positive prospective for investors and commodity producers. On the other hand, commodity producers suffer when resources are depleted.

Second, there is always the risk of a total loss if prices decrease below total production costs and the extraction of a commodity is stopped. By constructing an index consisting of commodity stocks, Gorton and Rouwenhorst show empirically that observed return correlations with commodity futures are even lower than those with the S&P 500.[15] Furthermore, the commodity stock index exhibits lower historical returns than a direct commodity investment.[16]

---

12 Georgi Georgiev, Benefits of Commodity Investment, Working Paper, 2005.

13 For example, consider the poor information policy of Shell in the matter of the Brent Spar oil platform in 1995, which led to a massive stock price decline.

14 Note that the majority of large oil and energy companies hedge the risk associated with buying and selling oil products in order to smooth yearly profits.

15 Gary Gorton and K. Geert Rouwenhorst, "Facts and Fantasies about Commodity Futures," *Financial Analysts Journal* (April–May 2006), pp. 47–68.

16 For example, the returns of European oil companies covary strongly with Euro-Stoxx, but less with oil price returns. Exceptions are gold and silver stocks, whose beta to the domestic stock index is smaller than the beta to the gold and silver price.

Commodity Funds

Finally, in contrast to an investment in commodity stocks, one can actively invest in commodity funds, realizing an adequate diversification benefit with moderate transaction costs. Commodity funds differ in terms of management style, allocation strategy, geographic, and temporal investment horizon in the denominated currency, and investment behavior. It is also important for investors to distinguish between active and passive funds (i.e., index tracking funds). Commodity stock indexes (e.g., the MSCI World Materials, the FTSE World Mining, the HSBC Global Mining, the Morgan Stanley Commodity Related Index, the FTSE World Oil, and Gas, or the FTSE Goldmines) and commodity futures indexes can be used to benchmark actively managed commodity funds. *Commodity trading advisors* (CTAs) also present an alternative to actively managed investment products. Today, there are also about 450 hedge funds with energy- and commodity-related trading strategies.

Commodity Futures Indexes

Nowadays, investors can choose from an increasing number of investible commodity futures indexes as a *passive* form of investing in commodities (see Exhibit 2). Commodities have an exceptional position among alternative investments because they provide investible indexes for a broad universe of commodity sectors. According to Doyle, Hill, and Jack, between US $55 billion and $60 billion were invested in the Goldman Sachs Commodity Index (GSCI) in March 2007, and another US $15 billion was linked to the Dow Jones-AIG Commodity Index.[17] Estimates for December 2006 state that about US $90 billion of invested capital from pension and mutual funds are invested in commodity-based indexes or products.[18]

Exhibit 2	Commodity Futures Indexes		
	Reuters/Jefferies Commodity Research Bureau (RJ/CRB)	**Goldman Sachs Commodity Index (GSCI)**	**DowJones/AIG Commodity Index (DJ-AIGCI)**
Introduced in	2005	1991	1998
Historical data available since	1982	1970	1991
Number of commodities	19	24	19
Weighting scheme	Within a graduated system of four groups, based on liquidity and economic relevance	Rolling five-year average of world production	Liquidity data, in conjunction with dollar-weighted production from the past five years
Rebalancing frequency	Monthly	Yearly	Yearly
Allocation restrictions	None	None	33% maximum per sector; 2% market minimum per commodity
Relevant futures price on which the index calculation is based	Next futures contract/delivery month	Next month with sufficient liquidity	Next futures contract/delivery month

---

17 Emmet Doyle, Jonathan Hill, and Ian Jack, Growth in Commodity Investment: Risks and Challenges for Commodity Market Participants, Financial Services Authority, Working Paper, 2007.
18 In 2001, the total invested capital in the GSCI was between $4 billion and $5 billion. At the beginning of 2007, Standard & Poor's acquired the GSCI Commodity Index, which was subsequently renamed the S&P GSCI Commodity Index.

	Reuters/Jefferies Commodity Research Bureau (RJ/CRB)	Goldman Sachs Commodity Index (GSCI)	DowJones/AIG Commodity Index (DJ-AIGCI)
Exhibit 2 (Continued)			
Roll period	4 Days	5 Days	5 Days
Calculation method	Arithmetic	Arithmetic	Arithmetic

For the majority of investors, an index-oriented investment represents the most reasonable way to obtain exposure to commodities or an individual commodity sector. Such an investment can be done cost-effectively using the following two types of financial products:

- Exchange-traded funds (ETFs) on commodity indexes.
- Commodity index certificates closely tied to commodity indexes.

Index funds have the advantage of being relatively easy to trade and reasonably priced. Another advantage of funds over certificates is the nonexisting credit risk of the issuer. Because ETFs represent special assets, investor deposits are safe even if the investment company goes bankrupt.

Certificates constitute legal obligations that can be quickly and fairly cheaply issued by banks. In the case of commodity index certificates, the issuing institution invests in futures markets and rolls the futures contracts for a fee. The term of a certificate is normally restricted to a fixed date (e.g., rainbow certificates, whose underlyings are different subindexes or asset classes, or discount and bonus certificates). But there are also open-end certificates.

However, because the indexes, like the commodities themselves, are denominated in US dollars, investors are exposed to currency risk. Quanto certificates, discount certificates with a currency hedge, can be used to mitigate this risk.

The main disadvantage of index certificates is that they often use excess return indexes as the underlying instrument. These indexes do not consider all the return components, in contrast to total return indexes, which may lead to lower returns during periods of high interest rates. Investing in a low performance excess return index compared to a total return index can nevertheless be an advantage because the latter bears little or no initial costs and no yearly management fees. Hence, for investors with short-term investment horizons, certificates on excess return indexes with lower returns can be a smart choice during periods of low interest rates.

Another disadvantage of index-based commodity investments is that due to their construction, they can only consider short-term futures contracts. Commodity funds not linked to commodity indexes, however, can freely determine their optimal term by investing directly in commodity futures contracts. And similarly to purchasing rainbow certificates on different asset classes, there is also the possibility of purchasing commodity funds that do not invest exclusively in commodity indexes, but also include commodity stocks to a certain extent.

Commodity Futures

In addition to options and other derivatives, commodity products are based primarily on futures contracts. A futures contract is a mutual binding agreement between two parties to deliver or accept and pay (or undertake a cash settlement): (1) a qualitative explicitly determined underlying (in this case commodities); (2) in a certain quantity; (3) at a fixed date; and (4) at a fixed, already at conclusion of the contract determined price. Futures can be described as mutually binding, exchange-traded "unconditional" forward contracts, since the conclusion of a futures contract leads to a legally binding accomplishment in the future if there is no compensating contrary transaction.[19]

Contract sizes in the commodity market are standardized. The smallest tradable unit represents a contract, and the smallest possible price change of a futures is called a *tick*. The value of the minimum price change is the US dollar and cent-denominated tick, multiplied by the contract size (also known as the *point value*) of the commodity. It is common practice to deposit a margin for every futures contract. The amount is determined by the exchange, but it is usually between 2% and 10% of the contract.[20] However, the margin changes according to the price and volatility of the contract.

In this context, we also distinguish between the initial margin, the minimum deposit required to invest in a futures contract, and the maintenance margin, the minimum deposit required to be on account at the exchange as long as the futures position is held. If the capital deposit on the account falls to or below the value of the maintenance margin due to price variations, the broker issues a margin call to recoup the initial value of the clients' capital. If an investor does not want to increase the margin, he can also close part of or the entire position, and accept a loss. For collateral in terms of the initial margin, investors in futures receive interest income from money market interest.

Generally, for commodity futures, there are two forms of settlement: delivery of the commodity at maturity, which happens in about 2% of the cases, and closing the futures position (i.e., buying or selling the same amount of contracts before maturity). Daily price limits are a specific characteristic of commodity futures markets. They were established to allow the market to stabilize during times of extreme movements (e.g., a cooling-off phase).[21] Hence, daily price limits, again determined by the exchange, represent the maximum possible increase or decrease of a commodity price from the settlement price of the preceding trading day. In the case of limit up (limit down), the sellers (buyers) are outnumbered by buyers (sellers) who are willing to buy (sell) at the upper (lower) price limit. At this price limit, there may still be trading activity, but it may not exceed (limit up) or fall short of (limit down) the price limit.

The following are the contract specifications published regularly by the futures exchanges:

- *The type and quality of the futures underlying.* The type of commodity, abbreviation, and futures exchange.
- *The contract size.* The amount and units of the underlying asset per futures contract.
- *Price determination.* The formal notation of futures prices at the futures exchange.
- *Trading hours.*
- *The tick.* The minimum permissible price fluctuation.
- *The currency* in which the futures contract is quoted.
- *The daily price limit.*
- *The last trading date.*
- *Delivery regulations* (e.g., delivery month, type of settlement).

---

19 In contrast, in the case of conditional forward contracts such as options, the option holder has no obligation to exercise his option right, and can thus abandon the option at maturity.
20 However, futures commission merchants may charge higher margins than the exchanges.
21 Franklin R. Edwards and Salih Neftci, "Extreme Price Movements and Margin Levels in Futures Markets," *Journal of Futures Markets* (December 1988), pp. 639-655.

Investors in commodity futures can profit from price movements of the underlying commodity without having to fulfill the logistical or storage requirements connected with a direct purchase. However, this is only possible if the position is closed before maturity. The advantages of futures investments lie especially in the tremendous flexibility and leveraged nature of the futures position due to the low capital requirements. Thus, a shift of an existing futures position is possible at any time, even in the short term. By holding long or short positions, investors can profit from rising and falling markets. Furthermore, the futures markets are characterized by a high degree of liquidity and low transaction costs.

Despite the numerous advantages of an active investment in commodity futures, it is not always advisable for a private investor to take futures positions in such volatile commodities. Even if diversification by a large number of different futures contracts were guaranteed, the investor would still face the problem of maintaining an exposure to commodity prices without the liability of physical delivery of the underlying contract. This requires continuously closing existing futures positions and reestablishing new positions by opening more futures contracts. This is referred to as *rolling of futures contracts*, and it may be quite costly depending on the forward curve of the futures market.[22] In addition, falling futures prices may constantly trigger margin calls (although margins can be withdrawn if the futures prices increase). Overall, however, compared to traditional assets, managing futures positions requires a great deal of time and effort.[23]

COMMODITY EXCHANGES

The trading of commodity futures takes place at specialized exchanges that function as public marketplaces, where commodities are purchased and sold at a fixed price for a fixed delivery date. Commodity futures exchanges are mostly structured as membership associations, and operate for the benefit of their members. Transactions must be made as standardized futures contracts by a broker who is also a member of the exchange. Only members are allowed to trade.[24] The main task of a commodity exchange is to provide an organized marketplace with uniform rules and standardized contracts.

The first commodity exchange was founded by Japanese farmers trading rice futures contracts in Osaka. In the United States, the Chicago Board of Trade, founded in 1848, was the first institution. Even today, most commodities are still traded there.[25] The British London Metal Exchange was founded in 1877.

Energy futures trading, however, only began with the foundation of the International Petroleum Exchange (IPE) in London in 1980.[26] Trading of WTI crude oil at the New York Mercantile Exchange (NYMEX) began in 1983; trading of Brent crude oil began in 1988. In terms of traded volume, the Chicago Mercantile Exchange (CME), founded in 1998, is the world's most important futures exchange. There are about 30

---

22 An active, indirect investment in commodities can be achieved by purchasing futures contracts and closing them prior to maturity. In order to keep an exposure to commodities, investors must buy another futures contract with a later maturity date (this is called *rolling*, and must be repeated before each maturity date).
23 It is also possible to invest in commodity swaps and forwards. These instruments, however, are of minor liquidity since they are tailor-made for individual investors. Furthermore, these derivatives are not traded at the exchange, and commodity investment strategies of individual investors cannot be publicly observed.
24 Membership in commodity exchanges is restricted to individuals who often act in the name of investment banks, brokers, or producers.
25 According to Geman, in the United States most futures exchanges still function as open outcry trading systems, although many exchanges around the world operate on an electronic platform. See Geman, *Commodities and Commodity Derivatives: Modeling and Pricing for Agriculturals, Metals and Energy*, p. 11.
26 Since 2005, the IPE operates under the name ICE Futures.

commodity exchanges worldwide; the most important are listed in Exhibit 3. Based on traded volume, the majority of commodity futures trading takes place in the United States, United Kingdom, Japan, and China.

Exhibit 3   Major Commodity Exchanges

Exchange Name	Abbreviation	Country	Traded Futures	Web Site
Chicago Board of Trade	CBOT	United States	Agricultural products and oil	cbot.com
Chicago Mercantile Exchange	CME	Unites States	Agricultural products and livestock	cme.com
New York Mercantile Exchange	NYMEX	United States	Energy and metals	nymex.com
Intercontinental Exchange	ICE	United Kingdom	Energy	theice.com
London Metal Exchange	LME	United Kingdom	Metals	lme.co.uk
Winnipeg Commodity Exchange	WCE	Canada	Agricultural products	wce.ca
Tokyo Commodity Exchange	TOCOM	Japan	Energy and metals	tocom.or.jp
Shanghai Metal Exchange	SHME	China	Metals	shme.com
Dalian Commodity Exchange	DCE	China	Agricultural products and oil	dce.com.cn
Brazilian Mercantile and Futures Exchange	BM&F	Brazil	Agricultural products	bmf.com.br
Risk Management Exchange	RMX	Germany	Agricultural products and livestock	wtb-hannover.de
National Commodity and Derivatives Exchange	NCDEX	India	Agricultural products and metals	ncdex.com

PRICES AT THE COMMODITY FUTURES EXCHANGES

Backwardation and Contango

One of the primary questions regarding commodity futures is the existence of risk premiums in commodity markets.[27] In this context, we refer to the price discovery and the related term structure of commodity futures markets. Assuming that the spot futures arbitrage relationship holds, the valid futures price of a commodity at time t and the remaining time to maturity T, $F(t,T)$ equals the cash price $S(t)$, multiplied by the continuously compounded riskless interest rate r (storage cost is neglected here):

$$F_0 = S_0 e^{rT} \tag{1}$$

In contrast to financial securities, commodities, however, do involve storage costs. Let U_t denote the cash value of storage costs, which are assumed to be proportional to the commodities' price and can thus be interpreted as a negative return:

$$F_0 = S_0 e^{(r+U)T} \tag{2}$$

However, the aforementioned arbitrage relationship does not hold for commodities. Note that the spot futures parity varies from the future parity, which states that the futures price observed today is an undistorted estimate of the cash price $E_t[S(T)]$

---

[27] See Kat and Oomen, "What Every Investor Should Know About Commodities: Part I."

at maturity. If we consider the forward curve of a specific commodity displaying the future price at different maturity dates of the contract, we observe two different trends: In the case of *backwardation*, the term structure curve has a negative trend (i.e., futures prices with longer time to maturity are lower than current spot prices, $F_{t,T} < S_t$ for increasing T). Hence, the investment return lies on average above the forward premium (i.e., an investor can generate profits by holding long positions in the respective futures contracts). In the case of *contango*, however, the opposite holds, based on the assumption of rational expectations. In a *contangoed* situation, the futures price lies above the actual spot price—hence the forward curve displays a positive slope.

In the literature, there are numerous explanations for this, but each sheds light on only a fraction of the complex "futures puzzle."[28] Lewis attributes the varying term structures between commodity sectors to the *theory of storage cost*, and to the existence of a *convenience yield* (Y).[29] Considering the futures price of consumption goods, we must adjust equation 2 for the physical ownership of a scarce commodity:

$$F_0 = S_0 e^{(r+U-Y)T} \tag{3}$$

The convenience yield varies over time (e.g., in the case of an unexpected increase or decrease in commodity supply). Commodities exposed to strong stock price variations from sudden supply or demand shocks are likely to exhibit a change or even a reversion in the term structure. The slope of the term structure curve thus indicates the stock of a commodity, and reflects market expectations for its availability in the future.[30]

Backwardation and contango depend strongly on the respective supply and demand situation of global commodity markets. Anson distinguishes between markets that offer price risk hedges for producers on the one hand, and hedges for commodity consumers on the other.[31] According to the theory of normal backwardation, the demand for short hedges greatly exceeds that for long hedges—hence, speculators have incentives to take these excessive positions. In order to compensate speculators, the short hedgers provide a risk premium that constitutes a deduction from the expected spot price. A contangoed market may arise when buyers depend on delivery schedules (e.g., in the manufacturing industry). Thus, there may be a surplus of long hedgers, which may lead to a rising term structure curve.

The theory of backwardation is confirmed by the empirical evidence that the slope of the term structure curve is determined by the storability of the individual commodity (the *storage hypothesis*). Eagleeye and Till conclude that the key to a

---

28 For a review of the different approaches, see Claude Erb and Campbell R. Harvey, "The Tactical and Strategic Value of Commodity Futures," *Financial Analysts Journal* (April–May 2006), pp. 69–97; and Barry Feldman and Hilary Till, "Separating the Wheat from the Chaff: Backwardation as the Long-Term Driver of Commodity Futures Performance; Evidence from Soy, Corn and Wheat Futures from 1950 to 2004," Working Paper, 2007.

29 According to Kaldor's theory of storage, the convenience yield reflects the utility of holding the physical commodity, in contrast to a pure contractual agreement about the delivery of the specific commodity. The utility results from the prevention of costs associated with disruptions in the production process. See Hélyette Geman, "Energy Commodity Prices: Is Mean-Reversion Dead?" *Journal of Alternative Investments* (Fall 2005), pp. 31–45; and Nicolas Kaldor, "Speculation and Economic Stability," *Review of Economic Studies* (October 1939), pp. 1–27.

30 The theory of *normal backwardation*, which dates to Keynes, is closely linked to the theory of convenience yield. Normal backwardation states that the futures price is lower than the expected spot price in the future, $F(t,T) < E[S(T)]$. Keynes argued that in commodity markets, backwardation does not describe an abnormal market situation, but is due to the fact that commodity producers hedge their price risk more frequently than commodity consumers. See John M. Keynes, *A Treatise on Money* (London: Macmillan, 1930). This argument has set off an academic discussion lasting until today. See, for example, Colin A. Carter, Gordon C. Rausser, and Andrew Schmitz, "Efficient Asset Portfolios and the Theory of Normal Backwardation," *Journal of Political Economy* (April 1983), pp. 319–331; Lester Telser, "Futures Trading and the Storage of Cotton and Wheat," *Journal of Political Economy* (June 1958), pp. 233-255; and Paul Cootner, "Returns to Speculators: Telser versus Keynes," *Journal of Political Economy* (August 1960), pp. 398–404.

31 Anson, *The Handbook of Alternative Assets*.

successful long-term investment lies in choosing an index that gives more weight to sectors with low storage capacity. They refer to the GSCI due to its high proportion of energy (74.57% as of January 2006).[32]

To verify the storage hypothesis, we analyze the individual subindexes of the GSCI. We thus determine the monthly share in percent of backwardation and contango over our observation period (January 1970–December 2006) for the agricultural, energy, industrial metals, livestock, and precious metals sectors.[33] We choose the GSCI because of its availability and its long data history. Its subindexes are available in all three index versions (total return, excess return, and spot return), and it provides the longest actually calculated index series since 1992.

As Exhibit 4 shows, backwardation is no temporary phenomenon. The energy sector and the livestock sector, which contain the majority of nonstorable commodities, are characterized by a high percentage of backwardation. The precious metals sector, on the other hand, has been almost exclusively in contango due to its low storage costs.

Exhibit 4   Backwardation in Commodities

| Sector | Observation Period | Number of Observations (in months) | | | Percentage of Backwardation |
		Total	In Contango	In Backwardation	
Agricultural	1970–2006	444	281	69	15.54%
Energy	1983–2006	288	275	140	48.61%
Industrial Metals	1977–2006	360	236	66	18.33%
Livestock	1970–2006	444	275	150	33.78%
Precious Metals	1973–2006	408	264	14	3.43%

Return Components of Commodity Futures Investments

To compare the long-term performance of commodities and other asset classes, we assume a fully collateralized commodity futures investment. Such diversified long-term passive commodity portfolios are characterized by long-only positions in commodity futures. In comparison to futures investments, which may require a margin depending on capital invested, the futures position is fully collateralized with cash. This means that, for such an unleveraged total return index, the initial and maintenance margins, as well as the entire outstanding cash, are invested at the riskless interest rate. Hence, the return of such an investible index can be decomposed into the following three return components:[34] the spot return, the roll return (generated by switching from the maturing futures contract into the next closest futures contract), and the collateral

---

32 Joseph Eagleeye and Hilary Till, "Commodities—Active Strategies for Enhanced Return," in *The Handbook of Inflation Hedging Investments*, edited by Robert J. Greer (Hoboken, NJ: John Wiley & Sons, 2005), pp. 127–158.

33 For this purpose, we compare the monthly returns of the spot and the excess return indexes. If the excess return exceeds the spot return, the market is backwardated, and vice versa; months with a spread of less than 0.1% are not considered.

34 For example, Ernest M. Ankrim and Chris R. Hensel, "Commodities in Asset Allocation: Real-Asset Alternative to Real Estate?" *Financial Analysts Journal*, (May/June 1993), pp. 20–29; Erb and Harvey, "The Tactical and Strategic Value of Commodity Futures," and Robert J. Greer, "The Nature of Commodity Index Returns," *Journal of Alternative Investments* (Summer 2000), pp. 45–52.

return (the interest payment on the cash position). If we consider a commodity futures portfolio instead of an individual futures contract, an additional component may exist, the so-called rebalancing (diversification) return:

Total return = Spot return + Roll return + Collateral return

+ Rebalancing return

$$\text{(4)}$$

The majority of investors focus on an increase in physical commodity prices, that is, the *spot return*, R_S, defined as the percentage change of the spot price S_t of the respective commodity:

$$R_S = \frac{S_t - S_{t-1}}{S_{t-1}} \qquad \text{(5)}$$

The spot price is influenced by fundamental factors like changes in supply, global demand variations, or unexpected price changes.[35] These price changes at the spot market are immediately reflected at the futures market.

Theoretically, the spot return is the component of the commodity futures return that is most strongly correlated with unexpected inflation.[36]

Forecasting spot prices is difficult because their factors are unpredictable. The prices of the respective commodities can vary greatly due to differences in commodity type, extraction method, production, and use. Industrial metals, for example, are used in manufacturing. Thus, their demand depends strongly on worldwide economic development. In contrast, the supply of agricultural products is determined mainly by the harvest,[37] which in turn depends on other factors (similarly to the energy sector). Extreme drought, frost, or thunderstorms can reduce the harvest or even destroy it entirely. In addition, all commodities are dependent on political factors. Besides numerous market barriers, which are known ex ante, other factors like political instability or war can lead to volatility in commodity prices.

The *roll return R_r* results from the extension of the futures contract and the shape of the term structure curve. The roll return reflects the profit from the convergence of the futures price toward the spot price over time, and the subsequent rolling of the maturing futures into the next nearest month's futures contract. If the commodity market is in backwardation (contango), the rolling from the maturing to the next shortest futures contract generates positive (negative) income.[38] Given that the futures price $F_{t-1,t}$ and the spot price S_t are equal at contract maturity, the selling price of the near month futures contracts prior to expiration varies from the new futures contract, $F_{t,T}$, by the amount of backwardation (contango) (see Exhibit 5). This means we can express the roll return at time t as:

$$R_r = \frac{F_{t,T} - F_{t-1,t}}{F_{t-1,t}} = \frac{F_{t,T} - S_t}{S_t} \qquad \text{(6)}$$

where a negative (positive) value corresponds to a positive (negative) roll return and thus to backwardation (contango).

---

35 Adam De Chiara and Daniel M. Raab, "The Benefits of Real Asset Portfolio Diversification," *Euromoney International Commodities Review* (2002), pp. 3–10.

36 Ankrim and Hensel, "Commodities in Asset Allocation: Real-Asset Alternative to Real Estate?"

37 Supply exhibits a strong seasonal component. Agricultural commodities can only be produced at specific times, and in amounts that may fluctuate.

38 Note that the futures contract is rolled before maturity. Thus the roll return results from selling the maturing future and investing the returns into the next nearest futures contract. The roll return is positive when the market is in backwardation, and negative when it is in contango. In a contangoed situation, the spot price to which the initial futures contract converges is lower than the price of the new futures contract.

Exhibit 5   Return Components of Commodity Futures

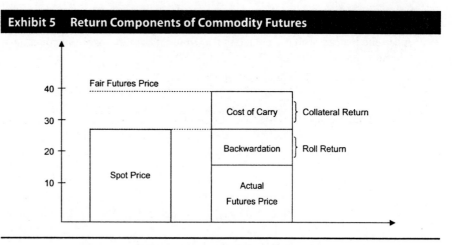

Generally, when investing in a futures contract, it is only necessary to deposit a margin payment (a fixed percentage of the underlying capital), and not the total position. In contrast, a collateral return is based on the assumption that the whole futures position is collateralized by cash. Interest is thus paid on this capital at the US Treasury bill rate, which is explicitly considered in the total return index.

Booth and Fama introduced the *rebalancing return* as a fourth return component by stating that a significant return portion of a value-weighted commodity index stems from the reallocation of the sectors or commodities in the index.[39] This is because the individual commodities are only marginally correlated, or not correlated at all.[40] If the price movements follow a random walk or in contrast return to their long-term average level—that is, production costs (mean reversion)—the construction of a value-weighted commodity index can generate a surplus in this asset class.[41] As a result of spot price volatility, there is a regular shift in index composition. If a commodity in the portfolio shows continuous appreciation, this commodity's share of total portfolio value will increase as well.

According to their construction principles, the commodity indexes we describe here constitute a fixed weight for all commodities with respect to relative index value. Thus they must be rebalanced on a regular basis: Futures that have increased in value are sold; those that have decreased in value are purchased.

Unlike a pure buy-and-hold strategy, where the value of the portfolio increases linearly with market value, such a dynamic asset allocation strategy enables investors to participate strongly in booming markets.[42] Thus, a "free lunch" may be obtained via the lower systematic risk achieved by reducing the standard deviation of the portfolio,

39 The rebalancing return is often called the diversification return. See, for example, David G. Booth and Eugene F. Fama, "Diversification Returns and Asset Contributions," *Financial Analysts Journal* (January/February 1992), pp. 26–32.

40 Based on a comparison between the Dow Jones-AIG Commodity Index and a self-constructed index with constant weights, Chiara and Raab show that a yearly rebalanced index leads to higher returns as long as the underlying commodities are not perfectly correlated. See Chiara and Raab, "The Benefits of Real Asset Portfolio Diversification."

41 Greer, "The Nature of Commodity Index Returns."

42 André F. Perold and William F. Sharpe, "Dynamic Strategies for Asset Allocation," *Financial Analysts Journal* (January/February 1988), pp. 16–27.

without any effect on arithmetic return.[43] According to this, the rebalancing approach[44] mentioned above leads to significantly higher returns, especially in volatile, trendless markets like the commodity market.

Exhibit 6 decomposes the annualized monthly total returns of the sector indexes into their individual return components and corresponding standard deviations. Over our entire sample period, all subindexes show positive total returns.[45] The industrial metals, precious metals, and agricultural sectors show on average negative roll returns, while energy and livestock commodities generate positive returns from the roll procedure. This coincides with the *theory of storage*.

Exhibit 6 also clearly shows that the *collateral yield*, at about 6%, constitutes a relatively large part of the total return, thus explaining the tremendous difference between the returns of the total and excess return indexes. Furthermore, the average spot return, which is highly volatile, is of special interest and is positive for all individual sectors. Hence, the majority of total return variation is based on the spot price. This result concurs significantly with the studies of Ankrim and Hensel[46] as well as Erb and Harvey.[47]

Exhibit 6 Return Components of the Goldman Sachs Subindexes

Sector	Spot Return μ (%)	Spot Return σ (%)	Roll Return μ (%)	Roll Return σ (%)	Collateral Return μ (%)	Collateral Return σ (%)	Total Return μ (%)	Total Return σ (%)
Agricultural	4.60	19.68	−3.86	5.60	6.15	0.87	6.89	19.44
Energy	7.87	31.14	2.55	7.64	5.26	2.03	15.68	31.54
Industrial metals	7.52	22.62	−1.07	6.31	6.21	0.93	12.65	23.74
Livestock	4.02	19.41	1.20	8.26	6.17	0.95	11.38	18.30
Precious metals	8.96	23.13	−6.22	2.49	6.24	0.91	8.98	23.15

The following section takes a closer look at the different types of futures indexes that can be used for performance measurement. These indexes are closely linked with the sources of futures return. The total return index as a performance index results from the actual futures return plus the interest rate payment on the collateral. The futures return itself is composed of the spot and roll return, and is called the excess return:

Total return = Collateral return + Futures return

= Collateral return + Spot return + Roll return   (7)

Excess return = Spot return + Roll return = Futures return   (8)

A *spot return index* does not represent the prices at the spot market, but rather measures the price movements at the futures market, since reliable prices are not immediately available for all commodities. Hence, we can calculate the spot return

---

43 John Y. Campbell, "Diversification: A Bigger Free Lunch," *Canadian Investment Review* (Winter 2000), pp. 14–15.
44 The literature often mentions a constant-mix strategy in the context of fixed portions relative to the total portfolio.
45 The periods under consideration for the individual subindexes follow those in Exhibit 4.
46 Ankrim and Hensel, "Commodities in Asset Allocation: Real-Asset Alternative to Real Estate?"
47 Erb and Harvey, "The Tactical and Strategic Value of Commodity Futures."

index by using the *near-month contract* or *spot month contract* as a proxy for the spot price of each individual commodity.[48] Just before maturity, the calculation is related to the next contract. The replacement is done without considering any discrepancies in value between the shortest and the second-shortest future.[49] Thus, the spot return index is a general indicator of existing price trends in commodity markets, and cannot be used as a performance measure or for comparison with other financial asset returns.

In the case of the *excess return index*, by switching from a maturing to a new contract (which is actually done from the fifth to the ninth working day of the month), a futures contract is rolled. The roll performance is captured in the index, so that the performance of the excess return index is composed of the spot return on the one hand, and the roll performance on the other (e.g., see the GSCI Energy Index in Exhibit 7). Because investors might hold and roll the underlying commodity futures themselves, the index is theoretically replicable, and can thus serve as a basis for financial instruments. According to its construction, the underlying of the excess return index is assumed to be an *un*collateralized futures instrument (i.e., a leveraged spot position).

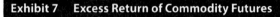

Exhibit 7   Excess Return of Commodity Futures

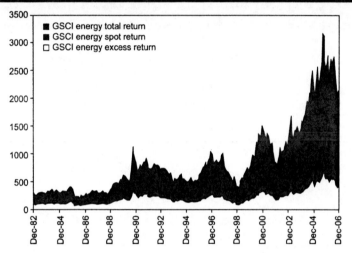

In contrast to the excess return indexes, the total return index is based on a fully cash-collateralized commodity investment. Hence, in the long run, tremendous return differences can arise between the total and the excess return indexes.[50] However, we cannot compare the excess return index directly with the total return index; that is, the excess return plus Treasury bill rate does not equal the total return. We must consider the influence of the reinvestment of the Treasury bill collateral income into commodity futures, as well as the deposit of the profits (withdrawal of losses) from the futures contracts into (out of) the Treasury bills.

---

48 Viola Markert, Commodities as Assets and Consumption Goods: Implications for the Valuation of Commodity Futures, Doctoral Dissertation, University of St. Gallen and Basel (2005); and Gorton and Rouwenhorst, "Facts and Fantasies about Commodity Futures."
49 As a result of the roll procedure, there is an increase or decrease in the index depending on the forward curve of the underlying commodity.
50 It can be advisable to invest in, for example, a certificate on a total return index in comparison to an underperforming excess return index, because there are no initial up-front payments and no yearly management fees. Thus, it may be sensible to purchase certificates on the seemingly worse excess return index during times of low interest rates. Note also that there are opportunity costs from investing in total return indexes, since the entire capital must be invested in Treasury bills and cannot be allocated more efficiently.

MODELS OF EXPECTED RETURNS

The literature contains several models that can be used to arrive at commodity futures returns expectations. In this context, Erb and Harvey mention four:[51]

- The capital asset pricing model (CAPM)
- The insurance perspective
- The hedging pressure hypothesis
- The theory of storage

Under the CAPM framework, the market beta drives the prospective capital asset returns. However, as we discussed earlier, commodity futures are not considered capital assets. Thus, application of the CAPM model is of limited use.

The insurance perspective argues that risk premiums are available if hedgers use commodity futures to avoid commodity price risk. Hedgers (producers) hold commodities in stock, and therefore must have a short position in commodity futures. To attract speculators, hedgers must offer an insurance premium. Therefore, the futures price for a commodity is less than the expected spot price in the future ("normal backwardation").[52] Unfortunately, expected futures spot prices are unobservable. This theory suggests that all long positions in commodity futures have a positive expected excess return, which consequently justifies "long-only" investments. But this model implicitly assumes that hedgers hold commodities in stocks, and seek to mitigate price risk by selling commodity futures.

We can consider the hedging pressure hypothesis as a continuation of the insurance perspective. It also highlights the fact that consumers who demand commodities may want to hedge their risk. Anson uses the example of Boeing as a consumer of aluminum.[53] The airplane producer is short in aluminum because it does not own any aluminum mining interests and can therefore eliminate the risk of higher futures prices by taking a long position in aluminum futures. This causes the futures price to be higher than the expected spot price in the future. Under these circumstances, investors seeking to earn an insurance premium will choose to short the commodity futures. The hedging pressure hypothesis argues that investors will receive a risk premium that is a positive excess return for going short in a "normal contangoed" commodity futures market.

The theory of storage emphasizes the role of inventories, and conceptually links inventories with commodity futures prices. The difference between futures prices and spot prices can be explained by storage costs and the so-called *convenience yield* of holding specific commodities in inventory. The underlying idea is that the holder of a storable commodity has a consumption option that is implicitly embedded in a convenience yield. Inventories act as a damper on price volatility because they provide an additional way to balance supply and demand. This theory predicts an inverse relationship between the level of inventories and the convenience yield—the lower the inventories, the higher the convenience yield. Difficult-to-store commodities should therefore have lower inventory levels and higher convenience yields than easy-to-store commodities. According to Till, examples of difficult-to-store commodities include heating oil, live cattle, and live hogs.[54]

---

51 Erb and Harvey, "The Tactical and Strategic Value of Commodity Futures."

52 John M. Keynes, *A Treatise on Money* (London: Macmillan, 1930).

53 Anson, *The Handbook of Alternative Assets.*

54 Hilary Till, "Two Types of Systematic Return Available in the Futures Markets," *Commodities Now* (September 2000), pp. 1–5.

RISK AND PERFORMANCE CHARACTERISTICS

Based on their historical return, risk, and correlation performance, commodity investments have an advantage over traditional assets, but they exhibit some similarities to
stocks. Kaplan and Lummer, for example, conclude in their empirical investigation that
commodities show an equity-like performance over the long run.[55] This finding is also
supported by many other studies such as Greer, who concludes that the performance
of unleveraged commodity indexes from 1970 to 1999 was on average positive, and
comparable to equities with regard to return and volatility.[56]

Bodie and Rosansky[57] analyze an equally weighted commodity futures portfolio
between 1949 and 1976, and Gorton and Rouwenhorst[58] between 1959 and 2004.
Both studies confirm equity-like returns for commodities. In addition, during the high
inflation period of the 1970s, commodities had the highest real returns by far of all
the asset classes. Gorton and Rouwenhorst found differences with traditional assets.
They show that commodity returns exhibit positive skewness, in contrast to stocks,
which have negative skewness and thus include higher downside risk.[59]

Exhibit 8 shows the performance of both traditional and alternative assets starting
with a reference basis of 100 in December 1993. After consolidating in 2006, the GSCI,
which is heavily invested in energy, currently shows very strong performance, along
with indirect real estate and hedge funds. In contrast, equity investments in emerging
markets show the smallest price increases.

**Exhibit 8   Performance of the Goldman Sachs Commodity Index Compared
to Other Financial Assets**

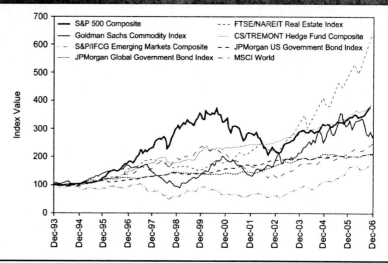

---

55 Paul D. Kaplan and Scott L. Lummer, GSCI Collateralized Futures as a Hedging and Diversification
Tool for Institutional Portfolios: An Update, Working Paper, 1997.
56 Greer, "The Nature of Commodity Index Returns."
57 Bodie and Rosansky, "Risk and Return in Commodity Futures."
58 Gorton and Rouwenhorst, "Facts and Fantasies about Commodity Futures."
59 Gorton and Rouwenhorst, "Facts and Fantasies about Commodity Futures."

During the January 1994–December 2006 period, commodities had an annualized return of 9.64%, with a volatility of 20.25% (see Exhibit 9).[60] Thus, compared to other observed asset classes, commodities have a high average volatility. However, note that the downside risk of the S&P 500 Composite, the S&P/IFCG Emerging Markets, and the FTSE/NAREIT Real Estate Index are higher because of their negative skewness; commodities possess positive skewness.

Exhibit 9   Annualized Average Monthly Return and Volatility (January 1994–December 2006)

	r_{ann}	σ_{ann}	r_{Min}	r_{Max}	Skewness	Excess Kurtosis	Sharpe Ratio
GSCI Composite	9.64%	20.25%	−14.41%	16.88%	0.063	0.024	0.281
S&P 500 Composite	11.43%	14.27%	−14.46%	9.78%	−0.622	0.838	0.524
MSCI World	7.91%	13.43%	−13.45%	8.91%	−0.658	0.890	0.294
Emerging Markets	6.76%	20.62%	−25.56%	12.37%	−0.765	1.877	0.136
Hedge Funds Composite	10.71%	7.66%	−7.55%	8.53%	0.099	2.465	0.882
Real Estate Index	14.99%	13.04%	−14.58%	10.39%	−0.510	1.472	0.846
JPMorgan US Govt. Bonds	5.91%	4.65%	−4.68%	3.71%	−0.509	1.084	0.421
JPMorgan Global Bonds	5.98%	6.23%	−4.30%	5.65%	0.320	0.336	0.325
T-bill rate	3.96%	0.49%	0.07%	0.53%	−0.644	−1.049	—

The most beneficial investment in terms of the Sharpe ratio is the CS/Tremont Hedge Fund Index. However, hedge fund investors also face high excess kurtosis. When considering only return and volatility, an indirect investment in real estate also seems less favorable due to negative skewness and positive excess kurtosis. Furthermore, the poor performance of emerging market equities seen in Exhibit 8 is also confirmed by the descriptive statistics, especially considering the exorbitant volatility.

As mentioned above, commodities serve an important diversification function in asset allocation due to their long-term low correlation with stocks, bonds, real estate, hedge funds, and, to a lesser extent, their absolute performance characteristics. According to Greer, commodity indexes have a negative correlation with stocks and bonds and a positive correlation with the inflation rate, especially unexpected changes in inflation. There are, however, significant differences among the individual commodity sectors: Energy, metals, livestock, and sugar show the best inflation hedging potential. Greer also finds very high correlation coefficients among different kinds of commodity sectors.[61]

According to Kat and Oomen, commodity futures and traditional assets like stocks and bonds are uncorrelated.[62] In specific phases, the correlation admittedly increases—therefore not all commodities are useful for portfolio diversification in

---

60 The high variability can be explained by the GSCI's large share in energy. The energy sector currently represents over 70% of the total index (as at end 2006), and is itself composed of 40% crude oil, which has experienced extreme volatility over the last few years.
61 Greer, "The Nature of Commodity Index Returns."
62 Harry M. Kat and Roel C. A. Oomen, "What Every Investor Should Know About Commodities, Part II: Multivariate Return Analysis," *Journal of Investment Management* (Third Quarter 2007).

every market phase. However, even in down markets, commodities as a group do not lose their diversification potential. According to Anson, there are three reasons for low or negative correlations between commodities and stocks/bonds.[63] First, inflation has a positive effect on commodity prices, but a negative effect on equity and bond markets. Second, investor expectations in commodity markets are different from those in equity and bond markets. Finally, a trade-off between capital return and commodity return exists in industrial production.

Exhibit 10 shows the return correlation structure between the total return indexes of various asset classes. As can be seen, correlation is only significant at the 5% level between commodities and hedge funds, which turn out to be relatively low at 0.167. This can be traced back to the commodity trading advisors and managed futures funds included in the CS/Tremont Hedge Fund Composite Index.

On the other hand, the return correlation between the money market and the commodity market is negative. Hence, the results of several academic studies[64] are confirmed for our sample period: Commodities show a high diversification potential in traditional *and* alternative security portfolios. Chong and Miffre support the findings that the conditional correlations between commodity futures and the S&P 500 decrease during times of down markets, that is, exactly when market risk increases and diversification is strongly needed.[65] The conditional correlations between commodities and fixed income, on the other hand, increase during times of increased bond volatility.

PORTFOLIO OPTIMIZATION WITH COMMODITIES

In this section, we analyze whether an allocation in commodities yields any diversification benefits for a portfolio consisting of US and global stocks, fixed income, and a riskless asset represented by the Treasury bill rate (i.e., whether the efficient frontier shifts into the upperleft corner in the expected return-standard deviation diagram). According to Markowitz,[66] these portfolios are considered from the set of all efficient portfolios (efficient in the sense that no others exhibit a superior risk-return combination). These efficient portfolios are located on the borderline formed by the set of all portfolios between the *minimum variance portfolio* (MVP) and the *maximum return portfolio* (MaxEP).

Exhibit 11 shows how portfolio efficiency can be improved by including commodities in a traditional portfolio, thus rotating the efficient frontier counterclockwise around the MVP (the Treasury bill rate). The upward shift of the efficient frontier also provides higher risk-adjusted returns. The efficient frontier of the traditional portfolio is limited by a 98% investment in Treasury bills for the MVP, and 100% in the S&P 500 for the MaxEP.

---

63 Anson, *The Handbook of Alternative Assets.*

64 See, for example, Kat and Oomen, "What Every Investor Should Know About Commodities: Part I"; Hilary Till, "Taking Full Advantage of the Statistical Properties of Commodity Investments," *Journal of Alternative Investments* (Summer 2001), pp. 63–66; Evert B. Vrugt, Rob Bauer, Roderick Molenaar, and Tom Molenaar, Dynamic Commodity Timing Strategies, Working Paper, 2004; and Gorton and Rouwenhorst, "Facts and Fantasies about Commodity Futures."

65 James Chong and Joelle Miffre, Conditional Risk Premia and Correlations in Commodity Futures Markets, Working Paper, 2006.

66 Harry M. Markowitz, "Portfolio Selection," *Journal of Finance* (March 1952), pp. 77–91.

Exhibit 10   Correlation Matrix

	GSCI Commodity Index	S&P 500 Composite	MSCI World	S&P/IFCG Emerging Markets	CS/Tremont Hedge Fund Comp.	FTSE/NAREIT Real Estate	JPMorgan US Govt. Bonds	JPMorgan Global Govt. Bonds	US Treasury Bill Rate
GSCI Commodity Index	1								
S&P 500 Composite	0.003	1							
MSCI World	0.068	0.937[b]	1						
S&P/IFCG Emerging Markets	0.136	0.643[b]	0.724[b]	1					
CS/Tremont Hedge Fund Comp.	0.167[a]	0.487[b]	0.493[b]	0.503[b]	1				
FTSE/NAREIT Real Estate	0.005	0.299[b]	0.314[b]	0.350[b]	0.223[b]	1			
JPMorgan US Govt. Bonds	0.079	−0.098	−0.159[a]	−0.216[b]	0.098	0.032	1		
JPMorgan Global Govt. Bonds	0.156	−0.016	0.064	−0.069	−0.050	0.118	0.597[b]	1	
US Treasury bill rate	−0.063	0.084	0.008	−0.180[a]	0.102	−0.066	0.105	−0.084	1

[a,b] Denote significance of the correlation coefficient at the 95% and 99% confidence levels, respectively.

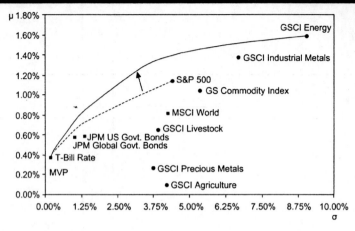

Exhibit 11   Expected Return-Standard Deviation (μ – σ) Portfolio Optimization (monthly returns in percent)

Starting from the MVP and incorporating individual commodity sectors, the share of global bonds initially increases to 69% (see Exhibit 12). Subsequently, the proportions of the energy and industrial metals sectors increase continuously, together with the share of US stocks. At a monthly return level of about 1%, livestock is represented with a share of about 4% to 5%. However, agricultural and precious metals are excluded entirely from the allocation. At a monthly return level of about 1.4%, the portfolio only consists of an allocation in the S&P 500 (28%), the energy sector (37%), and the industrial metals sector (35%).

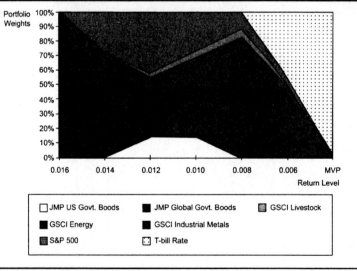

Exhibit 12   μ-σ-Portfolio Allocation (monthly returns in percent)

Thus, with an increasing return level, the proportion of commodities in the portfolio expands as the allocation in US stocks increases. It is remarkable that the GSCI Composite is not included in any allocations. It seems advisable to invest directly in the respective individual subsectors.

CONCLUSION

In an environment of historically low interest rates, markedly reduced upward potential, and continuously decreasing risk premiums for traditional asset classes, there is growing demand from institutional and private investors for alternative investments. An allocation to commodities offers not only a hedge against inflation, but also effective diversification because of its low correlation with traditional asset classes.

In the long run, commodity investments show equity-like returns, but are accompanied by lower volatility and shortfall risk. The advantages hold for passive investment in commodity futures indexes, which are considered indicators of commodity market price movements. However, the futures indexes of individual providers differ with regard to sector weights, index construction, and calculation method—hence there are tremendous variations in risk-return characteristics.

In a total and excess return index, an important return component results from the risk premium connected with the roll yield. This results from rolling commodity futures positions with a backwardated term structure. A direct investment in commodities generates positive roll returns in certain backwardated markets. Investors in passive commodity futures indexes must take into account that, independent from the term structure curve, only long positions can be held. According to Akey, one solution may be to use an active and tactical benchmark in the form of a commodity trading advisor index (a CTA index).[67]

In view of current global market demand, we assume that the growth of commodity consumption, particularly in the BRIC countries (Brazil, India, Russia, and China) will continue to generate high demand for commodities in all sectors. But because low commodity prices over the last two decades did not lead to sufficient investment in increased production capacity, we expect that pricing pressure on the commodity markets will intensify. In addition, we expect to see short-run scarcity in the commodity supply due to increasing inventories. In light of this tremendous development and according to the commodity super cycle theory, we predict a lasting boom in the commodity markets in the near future.

---

67 Rian P. Akey, "Commodities: A Case for Active Management," *Journal of Alternative Investments* (Fall 2005), pp. 8–30.

PRACTICE PROBLEMS

The following information relates to Questions 1–7

Horizon Yield, Inc. is a commodities trading firm. Horizon's most important clients are pension plans seeking diversification by gaining exposure to commodities. Albert Billingsley specializes in agricultural markets and recently joined Horizon as head trader.

On 1 September 2012, Billingsley, anticipating an increase in the spot prices of corn and wheat, considers purchasing corn and wheat futures contracts for delivery on 15 December 2012. Price data for corn and wheat are presented in Exhibit 1.

Exhibit 1	Corn and Wheat Spot and Futures Prices
	Price per Bushel as of 1 September 2012
Spot corn	$2.65
Spot wheat	$4.20
December 2012 corn	$2.85
December 2012 wheat	$3.70

Billingsley takes a long position in 100 December 2012 wheat futures contracts. One month later, on 1 October, a hail storm causes significant destruction to wheat crops, resulting in a temporary shortage in the supply of wheat.

On 14 December, one day before the wheat futures contracts mature, Billingsley decides to maintain his exposure to wheat, so he sells his December wheat futures contracts and purchases March wheat futures contracts for delivery on 15 March 2013. Price data for wheat is presented in Exhibit 2:

Exhibit 2	Wheat Spot and Futures Prices
	Price per Bushel as of 14 December 2012
Spot wheat	$4.50
March 2013 wheat	$4.20

Horizon Yield's management wants to expand the firm's products by offering a precious metals fund. An internal committee proposes two possible investment strategies for the new fund:

Strategy 1: Invest in a portfolio of mining stocks.

Strategy 2: Actively manage a portfolio of precious metals futures.

The managers ask Billingsley to review the advantages and disadvantages of each possible strategy and make a recommendation.

1 Billingsley's activities in the wheat market would *most likely* classify him as a(n):

  A hedger.

  B speculator.

  C arbitrageur.

2 Which of the following factors had the *most* influence on the value of the futures contracts Billingsley purchased on 1 September?

  A Interest rates

  B Expected cash flows

  C Global supply and demand

3 Based on Exhibit 1, the forward curve of wheat can *best* be described as being:

  A flat.

  B in contango.

  C in backwardation.

4 The events on 1 October *most likely* caused December wheat's convenience yield to:

  A increase.

  B decrease.

  C remain the same.

5 Based on Exhibit 2, Billingsley's roll return on his investment in wheat futures contracts on 14 December is:

  A zero.

  B positive.

  C negative.

6 The forward curve of the commodity for Strategy 2 of the new fund offering is *most likely* to experience:

  A contango.

  B backwardation.

  C a negative trend.

7 A potential disadvantage of implementing Strategy 2 for the new precious metals fund is that the:

  A fund would have less financial flexibility than if Strategy 1 was implemented.

  B strategy would require more time and effort in monitoring positions than Strategy 1.

  C fund's securities would exhibit lower correlation with commodity prices than Strategy 1.

SOLUTIONS

1   B is correct. A speculator's goal is to take distinct market positions, deliberately taking on risk by betting on rising or falling prices. Billingsley took a long position in wheat futures, expecting to profit from an increase in the price of wheat. Billingsley may achieve the expected gains if the price of wheat increases, but he is also exposed to significant losses if the price of wheat falls. Therefore, Billingsley is a speculator.

A is incorrect because a market participant is classified as a hedger if an existing or expected cash position is compensated for via an opposite future. Billingsley did not enter into the wheat futures contracts to offset an existing or expected cash position.

C is incorrect because an arbitrageur tries to take advantage of time- or location-based price differences in commodity futures markets, or between spot and futures markets, in order to generate riskless profits. Billingsley's trades in wheat were long-only and were not riskless.

2   C is correct. Wheat is a consumable asset and thus has its value determined primarily through global supply and demand factors.

A is incorrect because consumable assets do not generate income. As a result, interest rates have only a minor effect on their values.

B is incorrect because, in contrast to stocks and bonds, consumable assets do not generate continuous cash flows. As a result, cash flows are not a material factor in determining the value of consumable assets.

3   C is correct. Backwardation describes a term structure curve that has a negative trend (i.e., future prices with longer time to maturity are lower than current spot prices). Exhibit 1 shows that the wheat price for delivery in December is lower than that of the spot price on 1 September. As a result, the forward curve is in backwardation.

A is incorrect because Exhibit 1 shows that wheat for delivery in December is lower than the spot price on 1 September. As a result, the forward curve is in backwardation and not flat.

B is incorrect because in a contangoed situation, the futures price lies above the spot price. Exhibit 1 shows that wheat for delivery in December is lower than the spot price on 1 September.

4   A is correct. Convenience yield is the monetary benefit from holding a commodity physically instead of being long the respective futures, and is affected in large part by inventory levels. Supply shortages increase the spot price and provide profit opportunities for holders of the commodities, thus increasing the convenience yield. Supply surpluses, on the other hand, decrease the spot price and the convenience yield.

B is incorrect because supply shortages increase the spot price and provide profit opportunities for holders of the commodities, thus increasing the convenience yield.

C is incorrect because a short-term change in the supply of a commodity would affect the convenience yield either positively or negatively; it would not remain the same.

5   B is correct. The roll return reflects the profit from the convergence of the futures price toward the spot price over time, and the subsequent rolling of the maturing futures into the next nearest month's futures contract. If the

commodity market is in backwardation, the rolling from the maturing to the next shortest futures contract generates positive income. Because Billingsley is selling at the spot price ($4.50) and is buying at the lower futures price ($4.20), the roll return will be positive.

A is incorrect because the spot price ($4.50) is higher than the futures price ($4.20), so that the roll return will be positive, not zero.

C is incorrect because the spot price ($4.50) is higher than the futures price ($4.20), so that the roll return will be positive, not negative.

6 A is correct. Empirical evidence has shown that the slope of the term structure curve is determined by the storability of the individual commodity. Nonstorable commodities are characterized by a high percentage of backwardation, while commodities with low storage costs, such as precious metals, are almost exclusively in contango.

B is incorrect because empirical evidence has verified the storage hypothesis, demonstrating that low-storage-cost commodities are in contango the majority of the time.

C is incorrect because a negative trending forward curve is indicative of a commodity in backwardation, not contango.

7 B is correct. Maintaining a diversified exposure to commodity futures (Strategy 2) requires constantly monitoring positions and rolling over contracts to avoid physical delivery of the commodity. Compared to investing in a portfolio of traditional assets like stocks (Strategy 1), actively managing a portfolio of futures contracts requires a great deal of time and effort.

A is incorrect because the advantages of futures investments (Strategy 2) lie especially in the tremendous flexibility and leveraged nature of the futures position due to the low capital requirements.

C is incorrect because sector-specific stocks (Strategy 1) are often only slightly correlated with commodity prices. This low correlation between stocks and commodity prices reflects other company-relevant factors such as management quality, capital structure, etc. Futures prices (Strategy 2) are generally more correlated with commodity prices.

Fixed Income

TOPIC LEVEL LEARNING OUTCOME

The candidate should be able to estimate the risks and expected returns for fixed income instruments, analyze the term structure of interest rates and yield spreads, and evaluate fixed income instruments with embedded options and unique features.

14

Fixed Income

Valuation Concepts

This study session covers essential knowledge and skills needed for the valuation of fixed income investments. It begins with a discussion of the term structure of interest rates and interest rate dynamics. The next reading addresses arbitrage-free valuation of fixed-income securities. The study session concludes with an introduction to the valuation and analysis of bonds with embedded options.

READING ASSIGNMENTS

The Term Structure and Interest Rate Dynamics

by Thomas S.Y. Ho, PhD, Sang Bin Lee, PhD, and
Stephen E. Wilcox, PhD, CFA

Thomas S.Y. Ho, PhD, is at Thomas Ho Company Ltd (USA). Sang Bin Lee, PhD, is at Hanyang University (Korea). Stephen E. Wilcox, PhD, CFA, is at Minnesota State University, Mankato (USA).

LEARNING OUTCOMES

Mastery	The candidate should be able to:
☐	a. describe relationships among spot rates, forward rates, yield to maturity, expected and realized returns on bonds, and the shape of the yield curve;
☐	b. describe the forward pricing and forward rate models and calculate forward and spot prices and rates using those models;
☐	c. describe how zero-coupon rates (spot rates) may be obtained from the par curve by bootstrapping;
☐	d. describe the assumptions concerning the evolution of spot rates in relation to forward rates implicit in active bond portfolio management;
☐	e. describe the strategy of riding the yield curve;
☐	f. explain the swap rate curve and why and how market participants use it in valuation;
☐	g. calculate and interpret the swap spread for a given maturity;
☐	h. describe the Z-spread;
☐	i. describe the TED and Libor–OIS spreads;
☐	j. explain traditional theories of the term structure of interest rates and describe the implications of each theory for forward rates and the shape of the yield curve;
☐	k. describe modern term structure models and how they are used;
☐	l. explain how a bond's exposure to each of the factors driving the yield curve can be measured and how these exposures can be used to manage yield curve risks;
☐	m. explain the maturity structure of yield volatilities and their effect on price volatility.

1   INTRODUCTION

Interest rates are both a barometer of the economy and an instrument for its control. The term structure of interest rates—market interest rates at various maturities—is a vital input into the valuation of many financial products. The goal of this reading is to explain the term structure and interest rate dynamics—that is, the process by which the yields and prices of bonds evolve over time.

A spot interest rate (in this reading, "spot rate") is a rate of interest on a security that makes a single payment at a future point in time. The forward rate is the rate of interest set today for a single-payment security to be issued at a future date. Section 2 explains the relationship between these two types of interest rates and why forward rates matter to active bond portfolio managers. Section 2 also briefly covers other important return concepts.

The swap rate curve is the name given to the swap market's equivalent of the yield curve. Section 3 describes in more detail the swap rate curve and a related concept, the swap spread, and describes their use in valuation.

Sections 4 and 5 describe traditional and modern theories of the term structure of interest rates, respectively. Traditional theories present various largely qualitative perspectives on economic forces that may affect the shape of the term structure. Modern theories model the term structure with greater rigor.

Section 6 describes yield curve factor models. The focus is a popular three-factor term structure model in which the yield curve changes are described in terms of three independent movements: level, steepness, and curvature. These factors can be extracted from the variance–covariance matrix of historical interest rate movements.

A summary of key points concludes the reading.

2   SPOT RATES AND FORWARD RATES

In this section, we will first explain the relationships among spot rates, forward rates, yield to maturity, expected and realized returns on bonds, and the shape of the yield curve. We will then discuss the assumptions made about forward rates in active bond portfolio management.

At any point in time, the price of a risk-free single-unit payment (e.g., $1, €1, or £1) at time T is called the **discount factor** with maturity T, denoted by $P(T)$. The yield to maturity of the payment is called a **spot rate**, denoted by $r(T)$. That is,

$$P(T) = \frac{1}{\left[1 + r(T)\right]^T} \qquad\qquad \textbf{(1)}$$

The discount factor, $P(T)$, and the spot rate, $r(T)$, for a range of maturities in years $T > 0$ are called the **discount function** and the **spot yield curve** (or, more simply, **spot curve**), respectively. The spot curve represents the term structure of interest rates at any point in time. Note that the discount function completely identifies the spot curve and vice versa. The discount function and the spot curve contain the same set of information about the time value of money.

The spot curve shows, for various maturities, the annualized return on an option-free and default-risk-free **zero-coupon bond** (**zero** for short) with a single payment of principal at maturity. The spot rate as a yield concept avoids the complications associated with the need for a reinvestment rate assumption for coupon-paying securities. Because the spot curve depends on the market pricing of these option-free zero-coupon bonds at any point in time, the shape and level of the spot yield curve are dynamic—that is, continually changing over time.

As Equation 1 suggests, the default-risk-free spot curve is a benchmark for the time value of money received at any future point in time as determined by the market supply and demand for funds. It is viewed as the most basic term structure of interest rates because there is no reinvestment risk involved; the stated yield equals the actual realized return if the zero is held to maturity. Thus, the yield on a zero-coupon bond maturing in year T is regarded as the most accurate representation of the T-year interest rate.

A **forward rate** is an interest rate that is determined today for a loan that will be initiated in a future time period. The term structure of forward rates for a loan made on a specific initiation date is called the **forward curve**. Forward rates and forward curves can be mathematically derived from the current spot curve.

Denote the forward rate of a loan initiated T^* years from today with tenor (further maturity) of T years by $f(T^*,T)$. Consider a forward contract in which one party to the contract, the buyer, commits to pay the other party to the contract, the seller, a forward contract price, denoted by $F(T^*,T)$, at time T^* years from today for a zero-coupon bond with maturity T years and unit principal. This is only an agreement to do something in the future at the time the contract is entered into; thus, no money is exchanged between the two parties at contract initiation. At T^*, the buyer will pay the seller the contracted forward price value and will receive from the seller at time $T^* + T$ the principal payment of the bond, defined here as a single currency unit.

The **forward pricing model** describes the valuation of forward contracts. The no-arbitrage argument that is used to derive the model is frequently used in modern financial theory; the model can be adopted to value interest rate futures contracts and related instruments, such as options on interest rate futures.

The no-arbitrage principle is quite simple. It says that tradable securities with identical cash flow payments must have the same price. Otherwise, traders would be able to generate risk-free arbitrage profits. Applying this argument to value a forward contract, we consider the discount factors—in particular, the values $P(T^*)$ and $P(T^* + T)$ needed to price a forward contract, $F(T^*,T)$. This forward contract price has to follow Equation 2, which is known as the forward pricing model.

$$P(T^* + T) = P(T^*)F(T^*,T) \tag{2}$$

To understand the reasoning behind Equation 2, consider two alternative investments: (1) buying a zero-coupon bond that matures in $T^* + T$ years at a cost of $P(T^* + T)$, and (2) entering into a forward contract valued at $F(T^*,T)$ to buy at T^* a zero-coupon bond with maturity T at a cost today of $P(T^*)F(T^*,T)$. The payoffs for the two investments at time $T^* + T$ are the same. For this reason, the initial costs of the investments have to be the same, and therefore, Equation 2 must hold. Otherwise, any trader could sell the overvalued investment and buy the undervalued investment with the proceeds to generate risk-free profits with zero net investment.

Working the problems in Example 1 should help confirm your understanding of discount factors and forward prices. Please note that the solutions in the examples that follow may be rounded to two or four decimal places.

EXAMPLE 1

Spot and Forward Prices and Rates (1)

Consider a two-year loan ($T = 2$) beginning in one year ($T^* = 1$). The one-year spot rate is $r(T^*) = r(1) = 7\% = 0.07$. The three-year spot rate is $r(T^* + T) = r(1 + 2) = r(3) = 9\% = 0.09$.

1   Calculate the one-year discount factor: $P(T^*) = P(1)$.

2   Calculate the three-year discount factor: $P(T^* + T) = P(1 + 2) = P(3)$.

3   Calculate the forward price of a two-year bond to be issued in one year: $F(T^*,T) = F(1,2)$.

4   Interpret your answer to Problem 3.

Solution to 1:

Using Equation 1,

$$P(1) = \frac{1}{(1 + 0.07)^1} = 0.9346$$

Solution to 2:

$$P(3) = \frac{1}{(1 + 0.09)^3} = 0.7722$$

Solution to 3:

Using Equation 2,

$$0.7722 = 0.9346 \times F(1,2).$$

$$F(1,2) = 0.7722 \div 0.9346 = 0.8262.$$

Solution to 4:

The forward contract price of $F(1,2) = 0.8262$ is the price, agreed on today, that would be paid one year from today for a bond with a two-year maturity and a risk-free unit-principal payment (e.g., \$1, €1, or £1) at maturity. As shown in the solution to 3, it is calculated as the three-year discount factor, $P(3) = 0.7722$, divided by the one-year discount factor, $P(1) = 0.9346$.

2.1 The Forward Rate Model

This section uses the forward rate model to establish that when the spot curve is upward sloping, the forward curve will lie above the spot curve, and that when the spot curve is downward sloping, the forward curve will lie below the spot curve.

The forward rate $f(T^*,T)$ is the discount rate for a risk-free unit-principal payment $T^* + T$ years from today, valued at time T^*, such that the present value equals the forward contract price, $F(T^*,T)$. Then, by definition,

$$F(T^*,T) = \frac{1}{\left[1 + f(T^*,T)\right]^T} \tag{3}$$

By substituting Equations 1 and 3 into Equation 2, the forward pricing model can be expressed in terms of rates as noted by Equation 4, which is the **forward rate model**:

$$\left[1 + r(T^* + T)\right]^{(T^*+T)} = \left[1 + r(T^*)\right]^{T^*}\left[1 + f(T^*,T)\right]^T \tag{4}$$

Thus, the spot rate for $T^* + T$, which is $r(T^* + T)$, and the spot rate for T^*, which is $r(T^*)$, imply a value for the T-year forward rate at T^*, $f(T^*,T)$. Equation 4 is important because it shows how forward rates can be extrapolated from spot rates; that is, they are implicit in the spot rates at any given point in time.[1]

---

1 An approximation formula that is based on taking logs of both sides of Equation 4 and using the approximation $\ln(1 + x) \approx x$ for small x is $f(T^*,T) \approx [(T^* + T)r(T^* + T) - T^*r(T^*)]/T$. For example, $f(1,2)$ in Example 2 could be approximated as $(3 \times 11\% - 1 \times 9\%)/2 = 12\%$, which is very close to 12.01%.

Equation 4 suggests two interpretations or ways to look at forward rates. For example, suppose $f(7,1)$, the rate agreed on today for a one-year loan to be made seven years from today, is 3%. Then 3% is the

- reinvestment rate that would make an investor indifferent between buying an eight-year zero-coupon bond or investing in a seven-year zero-coupon bond and at maturity reinvesting the proceeds for one year. In this sense, the forward rate can be viewed as a type of breakeven interest rate.

- one-year rate that can be locked in today by buying an eight-year zero-coupon bond rather than investing in a seven-year zero-coupon bond and, when it matures, reinvesting the proceeds in a zero-coupon instrument that matures in one year. In this sense, the forward rate can be viewed as a rate that can be locked in by extending maturity by one year.

Example 2 addresses forward rates and the relationship between spot and forward rates.

EXAMPLE 2

Spot and Forward Prices and Rates (2)

The spot rates for three hypothetical zero-coupon bonds (zeros) with maturities of one, two, and three years are given in the following table.

Maturity (T)	1	2	3
Spot rates	$r(1) = 9\%$	$r(2) = 10\%$	$r(3) = 11\%$

1 Calculate the forward rate for a one-year zero issued one year from today, $f(1,1)$.

2 Calculate the forward rate for a one-year zero issued two years from today, $f(2,1)$.

3 Calculate the forward rate for a two-year zero issued one year from today, $f(1,2)$.

4 Based on your answers to 1 and 2, describe the relationship between the spot rates and the implied one-year forward rates.

Solution to 1:

$f(1,1)$ is calculated as follows (using Equation 4):

$$\left[1 + r(2)\right]^2 = \left[1 + r(1)\right]^1\left[1 + f(1,1)\right]^1$$

$$(1 + 0.10)^2 = (1 + 0.09)^1\left[1 + f(1,1)\right]^1$$

$$f(1,1) = \frac{(1.10)^2}{1.09} - 1 = 11.01\%$$

Solution to 2:

$f(2,1)$ is calculated as follows:

$$\left[1 + r(3)\right]^3 = \left[1 + r(2)\right]^2\left[1 + f(2,1)\right]^1$$

$$(1 + 0.11)^3 = (1 + 0.10)^2\left[1 + f(2,1)\right]^1$$

$$f(2,1) = \frac{(1.11)^3}{(1.10)^2} - 1 = 13.03\%$$

Solution to 3:

$f(1,2)$ is calculated as follows:

$$\left[1 + r(3)\right]^3 = \left[1 + r(1)\right]^1 \left[1 + f(1,2)\right]^2$$

$$(1 + 0.11)^3 = (1 + 0.09)^1 \left[1 + f(1,2)\right]^2$$

$$f(1,2) = \sqrt[2]{\frac{(1.11)^3}{1.09}} - 1 = 12.01\%$$

Solution to 4:

The upward-sloping zero-coupon yield curve is associated with an upward-sloping forward curve (a series of increasing one-year forward rates because 13.03% is greater than 11.01%). This point is explained further in the following paragraphs.

The analysis of the relationship between spot rates and one-period forward rates can be established by using the forward rate model and successive substitution, resulting in Equations 5a and 5b:

$$\left[1 + r(T)\right]^T = \left[1 + r(1)\right]\left[1 + f(1,1)\right]\left[1 + f(2,1)\right]\left[1 + f(3,1)\right]\ldots$$
$$\left[1 + f(T - 1,1)\right]$$

(5a)

$$r(T) =$$

$$\left\{\left[1 + r(1)\right]\left[1 + f(1,1)\right]\left[1 + f(2,1)\right]\left[1 + f(3,1)\right]\ldots\left[1 + f(T - 1,1)\right]\right\}^{(1/T)} - 1$$

(5b)

Equation 5b shows that the spot rate for a security with a maturity of $T > 1$ can be expressed as a geometric mean of the spot rate for a security with a maturity of $T = 1$ and a series of $T - 1$ forward rates.

Whether the relationship in Equation 5b holds in practice is an important consideration for active portfolio management. If an active trader can identify a series of short-term bonds whose actual returns will exceed today's quoted forward rates, then the total return over his or her investment horizon would exceed the return on a maturity-matching, buy-and-hold strategy. Later, we will use this same concept to discuss dynamic hedging strategies and the local expectations theory.

Examples 3 and 4 explore the relationship between spot and forward rates.

EXAMPLE 3

Spot and Forward Prices and Rates (3)

Given the data and conclusions for $r(1)$, $f(1,1)$, and $f(2,1)$ from Example 2:

   $r(1) = 9\%$

   $f(1,1) = 11.01\%$

   $f(2,1) = 13.03\%$

Show that the two-year spot rate of $r(2) = 10\%$ and the three-year spot rate of $r(3)$ = 11% are geometric averages of the one-year spot rate and the forward rates.

Solution:

Using Equation 5a,

$$\left[1 + r(2)\right]^2 = \left[1 + r(1)\right]\left[1 + f(1,1)\right]$$

$$r(2) = \sqrt[2]{(1 + 0.09)(1 + 0.1101)} - 1 \approx 10\%$$

$$\left[1 + r(3)\right]^3 = \left[1 + r(1)\right]\left[1 + f(1,1)\right]\left[1 + f(2,1)\right]$$

$$r(3) = \sqrt[3]{(1 + 0.09)(1 + 0.1101)(1 + 0.1303)} - 1 \approx 11\%$$

We can now consolidate our knowledge of spot and forward rates to explain important relationships between the spot and forward rate curves. The forward rate model (Equation 4) can also be expressed as Equation 6.

$$\left\{\frac{\left[1 + r(T^* + T)\right]}{\left[1 + r(T^*)\right]}\right\}^{\frac{T^*}{T}}\left[1 + r(T^* + T)\right] = \left[1 + f(T^*,T)\right] \tag{6}$$

To illustrate, suppose $T^* = 1$, $T = 4$, $r(1) = 2\%$, and $r(5) = 3\%$; the left-hand side of Equation 6 is

$$\left(\frac{1.03}{1.02}\right)^{\frac{1}{4}}(1.03) = (1.0024)(1.03) = 1.0325$$

so $f(1,4) = 3.25\%$. Given that the yield curve is upward sloping—so, $r(T^* + T) > r(T^*)$—Equation 6 implies that the forward rate from T^* to T is greater than the long-term $(T^* + T)$ spot rate: $f(T^*,T) > r(T^* + T)$. In the example given, 3.25% > 3%. Conversely, when the yield curve is downward sloping, then $r(T^* + T) < r(T^*)$ and the forward rate from T^* to T is lower than the long-term spot rate: $f(T^*,T) < r(T^* + T)$. Equation 6 also shows that if the spot curve is flat, all one-period forward rates are equal to the spot rate. For an upward-sloping yield curve—$r(T^* + T) > r(T^*)$—the forward rate rises as T^* increases. For a downward-sloping yield curve—$r(T^* + T) < r(T^*)$—the forward rate declines as T^* increases.

EXAMPLE 4

Spot and Forward Prices and Rates (4)

Given the spot rates $r(1) = 9\%$, $r(2) = 10\%$, and $r(3) = 11\%$, as in Examples 2 and 3:

1 Determine whether the forward rate $f(1,2)$ is greater than or less than the long-term rate, $r(3)$.

2 Determine whether forward rates rise or fall as the initiation date, T^*, for the forward rate is increased.

Solution to 1:

The spot rates imply an upward-sloping yield curve, $r(3) > r(2) > r(1)$, or in general, $r(T^* + T) > r(T^*)$. Thus, the forward rate will be greater than the long-term rate, or $f(T^*,T) > r(T^* + T)$. Note from Example 2 that $f(1,2) = 12.01\% > r(1 + 2) = r(3) = 11\%$.

Solution to 2:

The spot rates imply an upward-sloping yield curve, $r(3) > r(2) > r(1)$. Thus, the forward rates will rise with increasing T^*. This relationship was shown in Example 2, in which $f(1,1) = 11.01\%$ and $f(2,1) = 13.03\%$.

These relationships are illustrated in Exhibit 1, using actual data. The spot rates for US Treasuries as of 31 July 2013 are represented by the lowest curve in the exhibit, which was constructed using interpolation between the data points, shown in the table following the exhibit. Note that the spot curve is upward sloping. The spot curve and the forward curves for the end of July 2014, July 2015, July 2016, and July 2017 are also presented in Exhibit 1. Because the yield curve is upward sloping, the forward curves lie above the spot curve and increasing the initiation date results in progressively higher forward curves. The highest forward curve is that for July 2017. Note that the forward curves in Exhibit 1 are progressively flatter at later start dates because the spot curve flattens at the longer maturities.

Exhibit 1   Spot Curve vs. Forward Curves, 31 July 2013

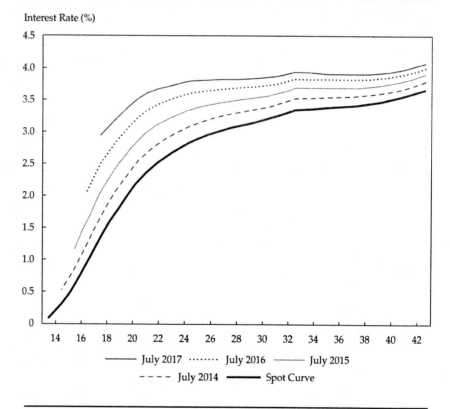

Interest Rate (%)

July 2017 ········ July 2016 ———— July 2015
– – – – July 2014 ———— Spot Curve

Maturity (years)	1	2	3	5	7	10	20	30
Spot rate (%)	0.11	0.33	0.61	1.37	2.00	2.61	3.35	3.66

When the spot yield curve is downward sloping, the forward yield curve will be below the spot yield curve. Spot rates for US Treasuries as of 31 December 2006 are presented in the table following Exhibit 2. We used linear interpolation to construct the spot curve based on these data points. The yield curve data were also somewhat modified to make the yield curve more downward sloping for illustrative purposes. The spot curve and the forward curves for the end of December 2007, 2008, 2009, and 2010 are presented in Exhibit 2.

Exhibit 2   Spot Curve vs. Forward Curves, 31 December 2006 (Modified for Illustrative Purposes)

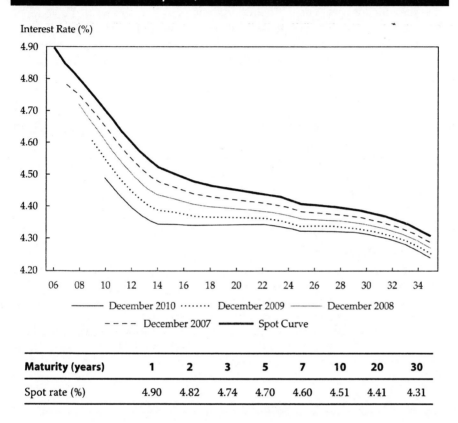

Maturity (years)	1	2	3	5	7	10	20	30
Spot rate (%)	4.90	4.82	4.74	4.70	4.60	4.51	4.41	4.31

The highest curve is the spot yield curve, and it is downward sloping. The results show that the forward curves are lower than the spot curve. Postponing the initiation date results in progressively lower forward curves. The lowest forward curve is that dated December 2010.

An important point that can be inferred from Exhibit 1 and Exhibit 2 is that forward rates do not extend any further than the furthest maturity on today's yield curve. For example, if yields extend to 30 years on today's yield curve, then three years hence, the most we can model prospectively is a bond with 27 years to final maturity. Similarly, four years hence, the longest maturity forward rate would be $f(4,26)$.

In summary, when the spot curve is upward sloping, the forward curve will lie above the spot curve. Conversely, when the spot curve is downward sloping, the forward curve will lie below the spot curve. This relationship is a reflection of the basic mathematical truth that when the average is rising (falling), the marginal data point must be above (below) the average. In this case, the spot curve represents an average over a whole time period and the forward rates represent the marginal changes between future time periods.[2]

We have thus far discussed the spot curve and the forward curve. Another curve important in practice is the government par curve. The **par curve** represents the yields to maturity on coupon-paying government bonds, priced at par, over a range of maturities. In practice, recently issued ("on the run") bonds are typically used to create the par curve because new issues are typically priced at or close to par.

The par curve is important for valuation in that it can be used to construct a zero-coupon yield curve. The process makes use of the fact that a coupon-paying bond can be viewed as a portfolio of zero-coupon bonds. The zero-coupon rates are determined by using the par yields and solving for the zero-coupon rates one by one, in order from earliest to latest maturities, via a process of forward substitution known as **bootstrapping**.

WHAT IS BOOTSTRAPPING?

The practical details of deriving the zero-coupon yield are outside the scope of this reading. But the meaning of bootstrapping cannot be grasped without a numerical illustration. Suppose the following yields are observed for annual coupon sovereign debt:

Par Rates:

One-year par rate = 5%, Two-year par rate = 5.97%, Three-year par rate = 6.91%, Four-year par rate = 7.81%. From these we can bootstrap zero-coupon rates.

Zero-Coupon Rates:

The one-year zero-coupon rate is the same as the one-year par rate because, under the assumption of annual coupons, it is effectively a one-year pure discount instrument. However, the two-year bond and later-maturity bonds have coupon payments before maturity and are distinct from zero-coupon instruments.

The process of deriving zero-coupon rates begins with the two-year maturity. The two-year zero-coupon rate is determined by solving the following equation in terms of one monetary unit of current market value, using the information that $r(1) = 5\%$:

$$1 = \frac{0.0597}{(1.05)} + \frac{1 + 0.0597}{\left[1 + r(2)\right]^2}$$

In the equation, 0.0597 and 1.0597 represent payments from interest and principal and interest, respectively, per one unit of principal value. The equation implies that $r(2) = 6\%$. We have bootstrapped the two-year spot rate. Continuing with forward substitution, the three-year zero-coupon rate can be bootstrapped by solving the following equation, using the known values of the one-year and two-year spot rates of 5% and 6%:

$$1 = \frac{0.0691}{(1.05)} + \frac{0.0691}{(1.06)^2} + \frac{1 + 0.0691}{\left[1 + r(3)\right]^3}$$

Thus, $r(3) = 7\%$. Finally the four-year zero-coupon rate is determined to be 8% by using

$$1 = \frac{0.0781}{(1.05)} + \frac{0.0781}{(1.06)^2} + \frac{0.0781}{(1.07)^3} + \frac{1 + 0.0781}{\left[1 + r(4)\right]^4}$$

In summary, $r(1) = 5\%$, $r(2) = 6\%$, $r(3) = 7\%$, and $r(4) = 8\%$.

---

2 Extending this discussion, one can also conclude that when a spot curve curve rises and then falls, the forward curves will also rise and then fall.

In the preceding discussion, we considered an upward-sloping (spot) yield curve (Exhibit 1) and an inverted or downward-sloping (spot) yield curve (Exhibit 2). In developed markets, yield curves are most commonly upward sloping with diminishing marginal increases in yield for identical changes in maturity; that is, the yield curve "flattens" at longer maturities. Because nominal yields incorporate a premium for expected inflation, an upward-sloping yield curve is generally interpreted as reflecting a market expectation of increasing or at least level future inflation (associated with relatively strong economic growth). The existence of risk premiums (e.g., for the greater interest rate risk of longer-maturity bonds) also contributes to a positive slope.

An inverted yield curve (Exhibit 2) is somewhat uncommon. Such a term structure may reflect a market expectation of declining future inflation rates (because a nominal yield incorporates a premium for expected inflation) from a relatively high current level. Expectations of declining economic activity may be one reason that inflation might be anticipated to decline, and a downward-sloping yield curve has frequently been observed before recessions.[3] A flat yield curve typically occurs briefly in the transition from an upward-sloping to a downward-sloping yield curve, or vice versa. A humped yield curve, which is relatively rare, occurs when intermediate-term interest rates are higher than short- and long-term rates.

2.2 Yield to Maturity in Relation to Spot Rates and Expected and Realized Returns on Bonds

Yield to maturity (YTM) is perhaps the most familiar pricing concept in bond markets. In this section, our goal is to clarify how it is related to spot rates and a bond's expected and realized returns.

How is the yield to maturity related to spot rates? In bond markets, most bonds outstanding have coupon payments and many have various options, such as a call provision. The YTM of these bonds with maturity T would not be the same as the spot rate at T. But, the YTM should be mathematically related to the spot curve. Because the principle of no arbitrage shows that a bond's value is the sum of the present values of payments discounted by their corresponding spot rates, the YTM of the bond should be some weighted average of spot rates used in the valuation of the bond.

Example 5 addresses the relationship between spot rates and yield to maturity.

EXAMPLE 5

Spot Rate and Yield to Maturity

Recall from earlier examples the spot rates $r(1) = 9\%$, $r(2) = 10\%$, and $r(3) = 11\%$. Let $y(T)$ be the yield to maturity.

1   Calculate the price of a two-year annual coupon bond using the spot rates. Assume the coupon rate is 6% and the face value is $1,000. Next, state the formula for determining the price of the bond in terms of its yield to maturity. Is $r(2)$ greater than or less than $y(2)$? Why?

2   Calculate the price of a three-year annual coupon-paying bond using the spot rates. Assume the coupon rate is 5% and the face value is £100. Next, write a formula for determining the price of the bond using the yield to maturity. Is $r(3)$ greater or less than $y(3)$? Why?

---

3 The US Treasury yield curve inverted in August 2006, more than a year before the recession that began in December 2007. See Haubrich (2006).

Solution to 1:

Using the spot rates,

$$\text{Price} = \frac{\$60}{(1 + 0.09)^1} + \frac{\$1,060}{(1 + 0.10)^2} = \$931.08$$

Using the yield to maturity,

$$\text{Price} = \frac{\$60}{[1 + y(2)]^1} + \frac{\$1,060}{[1 + y(2)]^2} = \$931.08$$

Note that $y(2)$ is used to discount both the first- and second-year cash flows. Because the bond can have only one price, it follows that $r(1) < y(2) < r(2)$ because $y(2)$ is a weighted average of $r(1)$ and $r(2)$ and the yield curve is upward sloping. Using a calculator, one can calculate the yield to maturity $y(2) = 9.97\%$, which is less than $r(2) = 10\%$ and greater than $r(1) = 9\%$, just as we would expect. Note that $y(2)$ is much closer to $r(2)$ than to $r(1)$ because the bond's largest cash flow occurs in Year 2, thereby giving $r(2)$ a greater weight than $r(1)$ in the determination of $y(2)$.

Solution to 2:

Using the spot rates,

$$\text{Price} = \frac{£5}{(1 + 0.09)^1} + \frac{£5}{(1 + 0.10)^2} + \frac{£105}{(1 + 0.11)^3} = £85.49$$

Using the yield to maturity,

$$\text{Price} = \frac{£5}{[1 + y(3)]^1} + \frac{£5}{[1 + y(3)]^2} + \frac{£105}{[1 + y(3)]^3} = £85.49$$

Note that $y(3)$ is used to discount all three cash flows. Because the bond can have only one price, $y(3)$ must be a weighted average of $r(1)$, $r(2)$, and $r(3)$. Given that the yield curve is upward sloping in this example, $y(3) < r(3)$. Using a calculator to compute yield to maturity, $y(3) = 10.93\%$, which is less than $r(3) = 11\%$ and greater than $r(1) = 9\%$, just as we would expect because the weighted yield to maturity must lie between the highest and lowest spot rates. Note that $y(3)$ is much closer to $r(3)$ than it is to $r(2)$ or $r(1)$ because the bond's largest cash flow occurs in Year 3, thereby giving $r(3)$ a greater weight than $r(2)$ and $r(1)$ in the determination of $y(3)$.

Is the yield to maturity the expected return on a bond? In general, it is not, except under extremely restrictive assumptions. The expected rate of return is the return one anticipates earning on an investment. The YTM is the expected rate of return for a bond that is held until its maturity, assuming that all coupon and principal payments are made in full when due and that coupons are reinvested at the original YTM. However, the assumption regarding reinvestment of coupons at the original yield to maturity typically does not hold. The YTM can provide a poor estimate of expected return if (1) interest rates are volatile; (2) the yield curve is steeply sloped, either upward or downward; (3) there is significant risk of default; or (4) the bond has one or more embedded options (e.g., put, call, or conversion). If either (1) or (2) is the case, reinvestment of coupons would not be expected to be at the assumed rate (YTM). Case (3) implies that actual cash flows may differ from those assumed in the YTM calculation, and in case (4), the exercise of an embedded option would, in general, result in a holding period that is shorter than the bond's original maturity.

The realized return is the actual return on the bond during the time an investor holds the bond. It is based on actual reinvestment rates and the yield curve at the end of the holding period. With perfect foresight, the expected bond return would equal the realized bond return.

To illustrate these concepts, assume that $r(1) = 5\%$, $r(2) = 6\%$, $r(3) = 7\%$, $r(4) = 8\%$, and $r(5) = 9\%$. Consider a five-year annual coupon bond with a coupon rate of 10%. The forward rates extrapolated from the spot rates are $f(1,1) = 7.0\%$, $f(2,1) = 9.0\%$, $f(3,1) = 11.1\%$, and $f(4,1) = 13.1\%$. The price, determined as a percentage of par, is 105.43.

The yield to maturity of 8.62% can be determined using a calculator or by solving

$$105.43 = \frac{10}{\left[1 + y(5)\right]} + \frac{10}{\left[1 + y(5)\right]^2} + \cdots + \frac{110}{\left[1 + y(5)\right]^5}$$

The yield to maturity of 8.62% is the bond's expected return assuming no default, a holding period of five years, and a reinvestment rate of 8.62%. But what if the forward rates are assumed to be the future spot rates?

Using the forward rates as the expected reinvestment rates results in the following expected cash flow at the end of Year 5:

$10(1 + 0.07)(1 + 0.09)(1 + 0.111)(1 + 0.131) + 10(1 + 0.09)(1 + 0.011)(1 + 0.131) + 10(1 + 0.111)(1 + 0.131) + 10(1 + 0.131) + 110 \approx 162.2.2$

Therefore, the expected bond return is (162.22 − 105.43)/105.43 = 53.87% and the expected annualized rate of return is 9.00% [solve $(1 + x)^5 = 1 + 0.5387$].

From this example, we can see that the expected rate of return is not equal to the YTM even if we make the generally unrealistic assumption that the forward rates are the future spot rates. Implicit in the determination of the yield to maturity as a potentially realistic estimate of expected return is a flat yield curve; note that in the formula just used, every cash flow was discounted at 8.62% regardless of its maturity.

Example 6 will reinforce your understanding of various yield and return concepts.

EXAMPLE 6

Yield and Return Concepts

1 When the spot curve is upward sloping, the forward curve:
   A lies above the spot curve.
   B lies below the spot curve.
   C is coincident with the spot curve.

2 Which of the following statements concerning the yield to maturity of a default-risk-free bond is *most* accurate? The yield to maturity of such a bond:
   A equals the expected return on the bond if the bond is held to maturity.
   B can be viewed as a weighted average of the spot rates applying to its cash flows.
   C will be closer to the realized return if the spot curve is upward sloping rather than flat through the life of the bond.

3 When the spot curve is downward sloping, an increase in the initiation date results in a forward curve that is:
   A closer to the spot curve.
   B a greater distance above the spot curve.
   C a greater distance below the spot curve.

Solution to 1:

A is correct. Points on a spot curve can be viewed as an average of single-period rates over given maturities whereas forward rates reflect the marginal changes between future time periods.

Solution to 2:

B is correct. The YTM is the discount rate that, when applied to a bond's promised cash flows, equates those cash flows to the bond's market price and the fact that the market price should reflect discounting promised cash flows at appropriate spot rates.

Solution to 3:

C is correct. This answer follows from the forward rate model as expressed in Equation 6. If the spot curve is downward sloping (upward sloping), increasing the initiation date (T^*) will result in a forward curve that is a greater distance below (above) the spot curve. See Exhibit 1 and Exhibit 2.

2.3 Yield Curve Movement and the Forward Curve

This section establishes several important results concerning forward prices and the spot yield curve in anticipation of discussing the relevance of the forward curve to active bond investors.

The first observation is that the forward contract price remains unchanged as long as future spot rates evolve as predicted by today's forward curve. Therefore, a change in the forward price reflects a deviation of the spot curve from that predicted by today's forward curve. Thus, if a trader expects that the future spot rate will be lower than what is predicted by the prevailing forward rate, the forward contract value is expected to increase. To capitalize on this expectation, the trader would buy the forward contract. Conversely, if the trader expects the future spot rate to be higher than what is predicted by the existing forward rate, then the forward contract value is expected to decrease. In this case, the trader would sell the forward contract.

Using the forward pricing model defined by Equation 2, we can determine the forward contract price that delivers a T-year-maturity bond at time T^*, $F(T^*,T)$ using Equation 7 (which is Equation 2 solved for the forward price):

$$F(T^*,T) = \frac{P(T^* + T)}{P(T^*)} \qquad (7)$$

Now suppose that after time t, the new discount function is the same as the forward discount function implied by today's discount function, as shown by Equation 8.

$$P^*(T) = \frac{P(t + T)}{P(t)} \qquad (8)$$

Next, after a lapse of time t, the time to expiration of the contract is $T^* - t$, and the forward contract price at time t is $F^*(t,T^*,T)$. Equation 7 can be rewritten as Equation 9:

$$F^*(t,T^*,T) = \frac{P^*(T^* + T - t)}{P^*(T^* - t)} \qquad (9)$$

Substituting Equation 8 into Equation 9 and adjusting for the lapse of time t results in Equation 10:

$$F^*(t,T^*,T) = \frac{\dfrac{P(t + T^* + T - t)}{P(t)}}{\dfrac{P(t + T^* - t)}{P(t)}} = \frac{P(T^* + T)}{P(T^*)} = F(T^*,T) \qquad \text{(10)}$$

Equation 10 shows that the forward contract price remains unchanged as long as future spot rates are equal to what is predicted by today's forward curve. Therefore, a change in the forward price is the result of a deviation of the spot curve from what is predicted by today's forward curve.

To make these observations concrete, consider a flat yield curve for which the interest rate is 4%. Using Equation 1, the discount factors for the one-year, two-year, and three-year terms are, to four decimal places,

$$P(1) = \frac{1}{(1 + 0.04)^1} = 0.9615$$

$$P(2) = \frac{1}{(1 + 0.04)^2} = 0.9246$$

$$P(3) = \frac{1}{(1 + 0.04)^3} = 0.8890$$

Therefore, using Equation 7, the forward contract price that delivers a one-year bond at Year 2 is

$$F(2,1) = \frac{P(2 + 1)}{P(2)} = \frac{P(3)}{P(2)} = \frac{0.8890}{0.9246} = 0.9615$$

Suppose the future discount function at Year 1 is the same as the forward discount function implied by the Year 0 spot curve. The lapse of time is $t = 1$. Using Equation 8, the discount factors for the one-year and two-year terms one year from today are

$$P^*(1) = \frac{P(1 + 1)}{P(1)} = \frac{P(2)}{P(1)} = \frac{0.9246}{0.9615} = 0.9616$$

$$P^*(2) = \frac{P(1 + 2)}{P(1)} = \frac{P(3)}{P(1)} = \frac{0.8890}{0.9615} = 0.9246$$

Using Equation 9, the price of the forward contract one year from today is

$$F^*(1,2,1) = \frac{P^*(2 + 1 - 1)}{P^*(2 - 1)} = \frac{P^*(2)}{P^*(1)} = \frac{0.9246}{0.9616} = 0.9615$$

The price of the forward contract has not changed. This will be the case as long as future discount functions are the same as those based on today's forward curve.

From this numerical example, we can see that if the spot rate curve is unchanged, then each bond "rolls down" the curve and earns the forward rate. Specifically, when one year passes, a three-year bond will return $(0.9246 - 0.8890)/0.8890 = 4\%$, which is equal to the spot rate. Furthermore, if another year passes, the bond will return $(0.9615 - 0.9246)/0.9246 = 4\%$, which is equal to the implied forward rate for a one-year security one year from today.

2.4 Active Bond Portfolio Management

One way active bond portfolio managers attempt to outperform the bond market's return is by anticipating changes in interest rates relative to the projected evolution of spot rates reflected in today's forward curves.

Some insight into these issues is provided by the forward rate model (Equation 4). By re-arranging terms in Equation 4 and letting the time horizon be one period, T* = 1, we get

$$\frac{[1 + r(T + 1)]^{T+1}}{[1 + f(1,T)]^{T}} = [1 + r(1)] \qquad (11)$$

The numerator of the left hand side of Equation 11 is for a bond with an initial maturity of $T + 1$ and a remaining maturity of T after one period passes. Suppose the prevailing spot yield curve after one period is the current forward curve; then, Equation 11 shows that the total return on the bond is the one-period risk-free rate. The following sidebar shows that the return of bonds of varying tenor over a one-year period is always the one-year rate (the risk-free rate over the one-year period) if the spot rates evolve as implied by the current forward curve at the end of the first year.

WHEN SPOT RATES EVOLVE AS IMPLIED BY THE CURRENT FORWARD CURVE

As in earlier examples, assume the following:

$r(1) = 9\%$

$r(2) = 10\%$

$r(3) = 11\%$

$f(1,1) = 11.01\%$

$f(1,2) = 12.01\%$

If the spot curve one year from today reflects the current forward curve, the return on a zero-coupon bond for the one-year holding period is 9%, regardless of the maturity of the bond. The computations below assume a par amount of 100 and represent the percentage change in price. Given the rounding of price and the forward rates to the nearest hundredth, the returns all approximate 9%. However, with no rounding, all answers would be precisely 9%.

The return of the one-year zero-coupon bond over the one-year holding period is 9%. The bond is purchased at a price of 91.74 and is worth the par amount of 100 at maturity.

$$\left(100 \div \frac{100}{1 + r(1)}\right) - 1 = \left(100 \div \frac{100}{1 + 0.09}\right) - 1 = \frac{100}{91.74} - 1 = 9\%$$

The return of the two-year zero-coupon bond over the one-year holding period is 9%. The bond is purchased at a price of 82.64. One year from today, the two-year bond has a remaining maturity of one year. Its price one year from today is 90.08, determined as the par amount divided by 1 plus the forward rate for a one-year bond issued one year from today.

$$\left(\frac{100}{1 + f(1,1)} \div \frac{100}{[1 + r(2)]^{2}}\right) - 1 = \left(\frac{100}{1 + 0.1101} \div \frac{100}{(1 + 0.10)^{2}}\right) - 1$$

$$= \frac{90.08}{82.64} - 1 = 9\%$$

The return of the three-year zero-coupon bond over the one-year holding period is 9%. The bond is purchased at a price of 73.12. One year from today, the three-year bond has a remaining maturity of two years. Its price one year from today of 79.71 reflects the forward rate for a two-year bond issued one year from today.

$$\left(\frac{100}{\left[1 + f(1,2)\right]^2} \div \frac{100}{\left[1 + r(3)\right]^3} \right) - 1 =$$

$$\left(\frac{100}{(1 + 0.1201)^2} \div \frac{100}{(1 + 0.11)^3} \right) - 1 = \frac{79.71}{73.12} - 1 \cong 9\%$$

This numerical example shows that the return of a bond over a one-year period is always the one-year rate (the risk-free rate over the one period) if the spot rates evolve as implied by the current forward curve.

But if the spot curve one year from today differs from today's forward curve, the returns on each bond for the one-year holding period will not all be 9%. To show that the returns on the two-year and three-year bonds over the one-year holding period are not 9%, we assume that the spot rate curve at Year 1 is flat with yields of 10% for all maturities.

The return on a one-year zero-coupon bond over the one-year holding period is

$$\left(100 \div \frac{100}{1 + 0.09} \right) - 1 = 9\%$$

The return on a two-year zero-coupon bond over the one-year holding period is

$$\left(\frac{100}{1 + 0.10} \div \frac{100}{(1 + 0.10)^2} \right) - 1 = 10\%$$

The return on a three-year zero-coupon bond over the one-year holding period is

$$\left(\frac{100}{(1 + 0.10)^2} \div \frac{100}{(1 + 0.11)^3} \right) - 1 = 13.03\%$$

The bond returns are 9%, 10%, and 13.03%. The returns on the two-year and three-year bonds differ from the one-year risk-free interest rate of 9%.

Equation 11 provides a total return investor with a means to evaluate the cheapness or expensiveness of a bond of a certain maturity. If any one of the investor's expected future spot rates is lower than a quoted forward rate for the same maturity, then (all else being equal) the investor would perceive the bond to be undervalued in the sense that the market is effectively discounting the bond's payments at a higher rate than the investor is and the bond's market price is below the intrinsic value perceived by the investor.

Another example will reinforce the point that if a portfolio manager's projected spot curve is above (below) the forward curve and his or her expectation turns out to be true, the return will be less (more) than the one-period risk-free interest rate.

For the sake of simplicity, assume a flat yield curve of 8% and that a trader holds a three-year bond paying annual coupons based on a 8% coupon rate. Assuming a par value of 100, the current market price is also 100. If today's forward curve turns out to be the spot curve one year from today, the trader will earn an 8% return.

If the trader projects that the spot curve one year from today is above today's forward curve—for example, a flat yield curve of 9%—the trader's expected rate of return is 6.24%, which is less than 8%:

$$\frac{8 + \dfrac{8}{1 + 0.09} + \dfrac{108}{(1 + 0.09)^2}}{100} - 1 = 6.24\%$$

If the trader predicts a flat yield curve of 7%, the trader's expected return is 9.81%, which is greater than 8%:

$$\frac{8 + \dfrac{8}{1 + 0.07} + \dfrac{108}{(1 + 0.07)^2}}{100} - 1 = 9.81\%$$

As the gap between the projected future spot rate and the forward rate widens, so too will the difference between the trader's expected return and the original yield to maturity of 8%.

This logic is the basis for a popular yield curve trade called **riding the yield curve** or **rolling down the yield curve**. As we have noted, when a yield curve is upward sloping, the forward curve is always above the current spot curve. If the trader does not believe that the yield curve will change its level and shape over an investment horizon, then buying bonds with a maturity longer than the investment horizon would provide a total return greater than the return on a maturity-matching strategy. The total return of the bond will depend on the spread between the forward rate and the spot rate as well as the maturity of the bond. The longer the bond's maturity, the more sensitive its total return is to the spread.

In the years following the 2008 financial crisis, many central banks around the world acted to keep short-term interest rates very low. As a result, yield curves subsequently had a steep upward slope (see Exhibit 1). For active management, this provided a big incentive for traders to access short-term funding and invest in long-term bonds. Of course, this trade is subject to significant interest rate risk, especially the risk of an unexpected increase in future spot rates (e.g., as a result of a spike in inflation). Yet, such a carry trade is often made by traders in an upward-sloping yield curve environment.[4]

In summary, when the yield curve slopes upward, as a bond approaches maturity or "rolls down the yield curve," it is valued at successively lower yields and higher prices. Using this strategy, a bond can be held for a period of time as it appreciates in price and then sold before maturity to realize a higher return. As long as interest rates remain stable and the yield curve retains an upward slope, this strategy can continuously add to the total return of a bond portfolio.

Example 7 address how the preceding analysis relates to active bond portfolio management.

---

4 Carry trades can take many forms. Here, we refer to a maturity spread carry trade in which the trader borrows short and lends long in the same currency. The maturity spread carry trade is used frequently by hedge funds. There are also cross-currency and credit spread carry trades. Essentially, a carry trade involves simultaneously borrowing and lending to take advantage of what a trader views as being a favorable interest rate differential.

EXAMPLE 7

Active Bond Portfolio Management

1 The "riding the yield curve" strategy is executed by buying bonds whose maturities are:

 A equal to the investor's investment horizon.

 B longer than the investor's investment horizon.

 C shorter than the investor's investment horizon.

2 A bond will be overvalued if the expected spot rate is:

 A equal to the current forward rate.

 B lower than the current forward rate.

 C higher than the current forward rate.

3 Assume a flat yield curve of 6%. A three-year £100 bond is issued at par paying an annual coupon of 6%. What is the bond's expected return if a trader predicts that the yield curve one year from today will be a flat 7%?

 A 4.19%

 B 6.00%

 C 8.83%

4 A forward contract price will increase if:

 A future spot rates evolve as predicted by current forward rates.

 B future spot rates are lower than what is predicted by current forward rates.

 C future spot rates are higher than what is predicted by current forward rates.

Solution to 1:

B is correct. A bond with a longer maturity than the investor's investment horizon is purchased but then sold prior to maturity at the end of the investment horizon. If the yield curve is upward sloping and yields do not change, the bond will be valued at successively lower yields and higher prices over time. The bond's total return will exceed that of a bond whose maturity is equal to the investment horizon.

Solution to 2:

C is correct. If the expected discount rate is higher than the forward rate, then the bond will be overvalued. The expected price of the bond is lower than the price obtained from discounting using the forward rate.

Solution to 3:

A is correct. Expected return will be less than the current yield to maturity of 6% if yields increase to 7%. The expected return of 4.19% is computed as follows:

$$\frac{6 + \dfrac{6}{1 + 0.07} + \dfrac{106}{(1 + 0.07)^2}}{100} - 1 \approx 4.19\%$$

Solution to 4:

B is correct. The forward rate model can be used to show that a change in the forward contract price requires a deviation of the spot curve from that predicted by today's forward curve. If the future spot rate is lower than what is predicted by the prevailing forward rate, the forward contract price will increase because it is discounted at an interest rate that is lower than the originally anticipated rate.

3 THE SWAP RATE CURVE

Section 2 described the spot rate curve of default-risk-free bonds as a measure of the time value of money. The swap rate curve, or swap curve for short, is another important representation of the time value of money used in the international fixed-income markets. In this section, we will discuss how the swap curve is used in valuation.

3.1 The Swap Rate Curve

Interest rate swaps are an integral part of the fixed-income market. These derivative contracts, which typically exchange, or swap, fixed-rate interest payments for floating-rate interest payments, are an essential tool for investors who use them to speculate or modify risk. The size of the payments reflects the floating and fixed rates, the amount of principal—called the notional amount, or notional—and the maturity of the swap. The interest rate for the fixed-rate leg of an interest rate swap is known as the **swap rate**. The level of the swap rate is such that the swap has zero value at the initiation of the swap agreement. Floating rates are based on some short-term reference interest rate, such as three-month or six-month dollar Libor (London Interbank Offered Rate); other reference rates include euro-denominated Euribor (European Interbank Offered Rate) and yen-denominated Tibor (Tokyo Interbank Offered Rate). Note that the risk inherent in various floating reference rates varies according to the risk of the banks surveyed; for example, the spread between Tibor and yen Libor was positive as of October 2013, reflecting the greater risk of the banks surveyed for Tibor. The yield curve of swap rates is called the **swap rate curve**, or, more simply, the **swap curve**. Because it is based on so-called **par swaps**, in which the fixed rates are set so that no money is exchanged at contract initiation—the present values of the fixed-rate and benchmark floating-rate legs being equal— the swap curve is a type of par curve. When we refer to the "par curve' in this reading, the reference is to the government par yield curve, however.

The swap market is a highly liquid market for two reasons. First, unlike bonds, a swap does not have multiple borrowers or lenders, only counterparties who exchange cash flows. Such arrangements offer significant flexibility and customization in the swap contract's design. Second, swaps provide one of the most efficient ways to hedge interest rate risk. The Bank for International Settlements (BIS) estimated that the notional amount outstanding on interest rate swaps was about US$370 trillion in December 2012.[5]

---

[5] Because the amount outstanding relates to notional values, it represents far less than $370 trillion of default exposure.

Many countries do not have a liquid government bond market with maturities longer than one year. The swap curve is a necessary market benchmark for interest rates in these countries. In countries in which the private sector is much bigger than the public sector, the swap curve is a far more relevant measure of the time value of money than is the government's cost of borrowing.

In Asia, the swap markets and the government bond markets have developed in parallel, and both are used in valuation in credit and loan markets. In Hong Kong and South Korea, the swap markets are active out to a maturity of 10 years, whereas the Japanese swap market is active out to a maturity of 30 years. The reason for the longer maturity in the Japanese government market is that the market has been in existence for much longer than those in Hong Kong and South Korea.

According to the *2013 CIA World Fact Book*, the size of the government bond market relative to GDP is 214.3% for Japan but only 33.7% and 46.9% for Hong Kong and South Korea, respectively. For the United States and Germany, the numbers are 73.6% and 81.7%, and the world average is 64%. Even though the interest rate swap market in Japan is very active, the US interest rate swap market is almost three times larger than the Japanese interest rate swap market, based on outstanding amounts.

3.2 Why Do Market Participants Use Swap Rates When Valuing Bonds?

Government spot curves and swap rate curves are the chief reference curves in fixed-income valuation. The choice between them can depend on multiple factors, including the relative liquidity of these two markets. In the United States, where there is both an active Treasury security market and a swap market, the choice of a benchmark for the time value of money often depends on the business operations of the institution using the benchmark. On the one hand, wholesale banks frequently use the swap curve to value assets and liabilities because these organizations hedge many items on their balance sheet with swaps. On the other hand, retail banks with little exposure to the swap market are more likely to use the government spot curve as their benchmark.

Let us illustrate how a financial institution uses the swap market for its internal operations. Consider the case of a bank raising funds using a certificate of deposit (CD). Assume the bank can borrow $10 million in the form of a CD that bears interest of 1.5% for a two-year term. Another $10 million CD offers 1.70% for a three-year term. The bank can arrange two swaps: (1) The bank receives 1.50% fixed and pays three-month Libor minus 10 bps with a two-year term and $10 million notional, and (2) the bank receives 1.70% fixed and pays three-month Libor minus 15 bps with a three-year term and a notional amount of $10 million. After issuing the two CDs and committing to the two swaps, the bank has raised $20 million with an annual funding cost for the first two years of three-month Libor minus 12.5 bps applied to the total notional amount of $20 million. The fixed interest payments received from the counterparty to the swap are paid to the CD investors; in effect, fixed-rate liabilities have been converted to floating-rate liabilities. The margins on the floating rates become the standard by which value is measured in assessing the total funding cost for the bank.

By using the swap curve as a benchmark for the time value of money, the investor can adjust the swap spread so that the swap would be fairly priced given the spread. Conversely, given a swap spread, the investor can determine a fair price for the bond. We will use the swap spread in the following section to determine the value of a bond.

3.3 How Do Market Participants Use the Swap Curve in Valuation?

Swap contracts are non-standardized and are simply customized contracts between two parties in the over-the-counter market. The fixed payment can be specified by an amortization schedule or to be coupon paying with non-standardized coupon payment dates. For this section, we will focus on zero-coupon bonds. The yields on these bonds determine the swap curve, which, in turn, can be used to determine bond values. Examples of swap par curves are given in Exhibit 3.

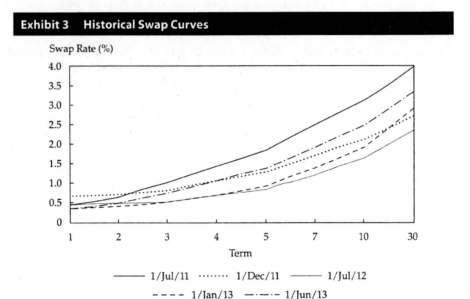

Exhibit 3   Historical Swap Curves

Note: Horizontal axis is not drawn to scale. (Such scales are commonly used as an industry standard because most of the distinctive shape of yield curves is typically observed before 10 years.)

Each forward date has an associated discount factor that represents the value today of a hypothetical payment that one would receive on the forward date, expressed as a fraction of the hypothetical payment. For example, if we expect to receive ₩10,000 (10,000 South Korean won) in one year and the current price of the security is ₩9,259.30, then the discount factor for one year would be 0.92593 (= ₩9,259.30/₩10,000). Note that the rate associated with this discount factor is 1/0.92593 −1 ≈ 8.00%.

To price a swap, we need to determine the present value of cash flows for each leg of the transaction. In an interest rate swap, the fixed leg is fairly straightforward because the cash flows are specified by the coupon rate set at the time of the agreement. Pricing the floating leg is more complex because, by definition, the cash flows change with future changes in interest rates. The forward rate for each floating payment date is calculated by using the forward curves.

Let $s(T)$ stand for the swap rate at time T. Because the value of a swap at origination is set to zero, the swap rates must satisfy Equation 12. Note that the swap rates can be determined from the spot rates and the spot rates can be determined from the swap rates.

$$\sum_{t=1}^{T} \frac{s(T)}{\left[1 + r(t)\right]^{t}} + \frac{1}{\left[1 + r(T)\right]^{T}} = 1 \qquad \text{(12)}$$

The right side of Equation 12 is the value of the floating leg, which is always 1 at origination. The swap rate is determined by equating the value of the fixed leg, on the left-hand side, to the value of the floating leg.

Example 8 addresses the relationship between the swap rate curve and spot curve.

EXAMPLE 8

Determining the Swap Rate Curve

Suppose a government spot curve implies the following discount factors:

$$P(1) = 0.9524$$
$$P(2) = 0.8900$$
$$P(3) = 0.8163$$
$$P(4) = 0.7350$$

Given this information, determine the swap rate curve.

Solution:

Recall from Equation 1 that $P(T) = \dfrac{1}{\left[1 + r(T)\right]^{T}}$. Therefore,

$$r(T) = \left\{\frac{1}{\left[P(T)\right]}\right\}^{(1/T)} - 1$$

$$r(1) = \left(\frac{1}{0.9524}\right)^{(1/1)} - 1 = 5.00\%$$

$$r(2) = \left(\frac{1}{0.8900}\right)^{(1/2)} - 1 = 6.00\%$$

$$r(3) = \left(\frac{1}{0.8163}\right)^{(1/3)} - 1 = 7.00\%$$

$$r(4) = \left(\frac{1}{0.7350}\right)^{(1/4)} - 1 = 8.00\%$$

Using Equation 12, for $T = 1$,

$$\frac{s(1)}{\left[1 + r(1)\right]^{1}} + \frac{1}{\left[1 + r(1)\right]^{1}} = \frac{s(1)}{(1 + 0.05)^{1}} + \frac{1}{(1 + 0.05)^{1}} = 1$$

Therefore, $s(1) = 5\%$.

For $T = 2$,

$$\frac{s(2)}{\left[1 + r(1)\right]^{1}} + \frac{s(2)}{\left[1 + r(2)\right]^{2}} + \frac{1}{\left[1 + r(2)\right]^{2}} = \frac{s(2)}{(1 + 0.05)^{1}} + \frac{s(2)}{(1 + 0.06)^{2}} + \frac{1}{(1 + 0.06)^{2}} = 1$$

Therefore, $s(2) = 5.97\%$.

For $T = 3$,

$$\frac{s(3)}{\left[1+r(1)\right]^1} + \frac{s(3)}{\left[1+r(2)\right]^2} + \frac{s(3)}{\left[1+r(3)\right]^3} + \frac{1}{\left[1+r(3)\right]^3} =$$

$$\frac{s(3)}{(1+0.05)^1} + \frac{s(3)}{(1+0.06)^2} + \frac{s(3)}{(1+0.07)^3} + \frac{1}{(1+0.07)^3} = 1$$

Therefore, $s(3) = 6.91\%$.

For $T = 4$,

$$\frac{s(4)}{\left[1+r(1)\right]^1} + \frac{s(4)}{\left[1+r(2)\right]^2} + \frac{s(4)}{\left[1+r(3)\right]^3} + \frac{s(4)}{\left[1+r(4)\right]^4} + \frac{1}{\left[1+r(4)\right]^4} =$$

$$\frac{s(4)}{(1+0.05)^1} + \frac{s(4)}{(1+0.06)^2} + \frac{s(4)}{(1+0.07)^3} + \frac{s(4)}{(1+0.08)^4} + \frac{1}{(1+0.08)^4} = 1$$

Therefore, $s(4) = 7.81\%$.

Note that the swap rates, spot rates, and discount factors are all mathematically linked together. Having access to data for one of the series allows you to calculate the other two.

3.4 The Swap Spread

The swap spread is a popular way to indicate credit spreads in a market. The **swap spread** is defined as the spread paid by the fixed-rate payer of an interest rate swap over the rate of the "on-the-run" (most recently issued) government security with the same maturity as the swap.[6]

Often, fixed-income prices will be quoted in SWAPS +, for which the yield is simply the yield on an equal-maturity government bond plus the swap spread. For example, if the fixed rate of a five-year fixed-for-float Libor swap is 2.00% and the five-year Treasury is yielding 1.70%, the swap spread is 2.00% − 1.70% = 0.30%, or 30 bps.

For euro-denominated swaps, the government yield used as a benchmark is most frequently bunds (German government bonds) with the same maturity. Gilts (UK government bonds) are used as a benchmark in the United Kingdom. CME Group began clearing euro-denominated interest rate swaps in 2011.

A Libor/swap curve is probably the most widely used interest rate curve because it is often viewed as reflecting the default risk of private entities at a rating of about A1/A+, roughly the equivalent of most commercial banks. (The swap curve can also be influenced by the demand and supply conditions in government debt markets, among other factors.) Another reason for the popularity of the swap market is that it is unregulated (not controlled by governments), so swap rates are more comparable across different countries. The swap market also has more maturities with which to construct a yield curve than do government bond markets. Libor is used for short-maturity yields, rates derived from eurodollar futures contracts are used for mid-maturity

---

6 The term "swap spread" is sometimes also used as a reference to a bond's basis point spread over the interest rate swap curve and is a measure of the credit and/or liquidity risk of a bond. In its simplest form, the swap spread in this sense can be measured as the difference between the yield to maturity of the bond and the swap rate given by a straight-line interpolation of the swap curve. These spreads are frequently quoted as an I-spread, ISPRD, or interpolated spread, which is a reference to a linearly interpolated yield. In this reading, the term "swap spread" refers to an excess yield of swap rates over the yields on government bonds and I-spreads to refer to bond yields net of the swap rates of the same maturities.

yields, and swap rates are used for yields with a maturity of more than one year. The swap rates used are the fixed rates that would be paid in swap agreements for which three-month Libor floating payments are received.[7]

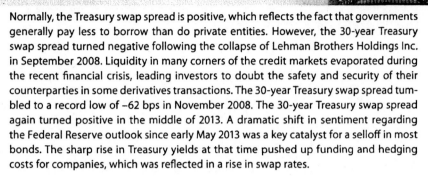

HISTORY OF THE US SWAP SPREAD, 2008–2013

Normally, the Treasury swap spread is positive, which reflects the fact that governments generally pay less to borrow than do private entities. However, the 30-year Treasury swap spread turned negative following the collapse of Lehman Brothers Holdings Inc. in September 2008. Liquidity in many corners of the credit markets evaporated during the recent financial crisis, leading investors to doubt the safety and security of their counterparties in some derivatives transactions. The 30-year Treasury swap spread tumbled to a record low of –62 bps in November 2008. The 30-year Treasury swap spread again turned positive in the middle of 2013. A dramatic shift in sentiment regarding the Federal Reserve outlook since early May 2013 was a key catalyst for a selloff in most bonds. The sharp rise in Treasury yields at that time pushed up funding and hedging costs for companies, which was reflected in a rise in swap rates.

To illustrate the use of the swap spread in fixed-income pricing, consider a US$1 million investment in GE Capital (GECC) notes with a coupon rate of 1 5/8% (1.625%) that matures on 2 July 2015. Coupons are paid semiannually. The evaluation date is 12 July 2012, so the remaining maturity is 2.97 years [= 2 + (350/360)]. The swap rates for two-year and three-year maturities are 0.525% and 0.588%, respectively. By simple interpolation between these two swap rates, the swap rate for 2.97 years is 0.586% [= 0.525% + (350/360)(0.588% – 0.525%)]. If the swap spread for the same maturity is 0.918%, then the yield to maturity on the bond is 1.504% (= 0.918% + 0.586%). Given the yield to maturity, the invoice price (price including accrued interest) for US$1 million face value is

$$\frac{1{,}000{,}000\left(\dfrac{0.01625}{2}\right)}{\left(1+\dfrac{0.01504}{2}\right)^{\left(1-\frac{10}{180}\right)}}+\frac{1{,}000{,}000\left(\dfrac{0.01625}{2}\right)}{\left(1+\dfrac{0.01504}{2}\right)^{\left(2-\frac{10}{180}\right)}}+\cdots+$$

$$\frac{1{,}000{,}000\left(\dfrac{0.01625}{2}\right)}{\left(1+\dfrac{0.01504}{2}\right)^{\left(6-\frac{10}{180}\right)}}+\frac{1{,}000{,}000}{\left(1+\dfrac{0.01504}{2}\right)^{\left(6-\frac{10}{180}\right)}}=US\$1{,}003{,}954.12$$

The left side sums the present values of the semiannual coupon payments and the final principal payment of US$1,000,000. The accrued interest rate amount is US$451.39 [= 1,000,000 × (0.01625/2)(10/180)]. Therefore, the clean price (price not including accrued interest) is US$1,003,502.73 (= 1,003,954.12 – 451.39).

The swap spread helps an investor to identify the time value, credit, and liquidity components of a bond's yield to maturity. If the bond is default free, then the swap spread could provide an indication of the bond's liquidity or it could provide evidence of market mispricing. The higher the swap spread, the higher the return that investors require for credit and/or liquidity risks.

Although swap spreads provide a convenient way to measure risk, a more accurate measure of credit and liquidity is called the zero-spread (Z-spread). The **Z-spread** is the constant basis point spread that would need to be added to the implied spot yield

---

[7] The US dollar market uses three-month Libor, but other currencies may use one-month or six-month Libor.

curve so that the discounted cash flows of a bond are equal to its current market price. This spread will be more accurate than a linearly interpolated yield, particularly with steep interest rate swap curves.

USING THE Z-SPREAD IN VALUATION

Consider again the GECC semi-annual coupon note with a maturity of 2.97 years and a par value of US$1,000,000. The spot yield curve is

$r(0.5) = 0.16\%$

$r(1) = 0.21\%$

$r(1.5) = 0.27\%$

$r(2) = 0.33\%$

$r(2.5) = 0.37\%$

$r(3) = 0.41\%$

The Z-spread is given as 109.6 bps. Using the spot curve and the Z-spread, the invoice price is

$$\frac{1{,}000{,}000\left(\dfrac{0.01625}{2}\right)}{\left(1 + \dfrac{0.0016 + 0.01096}{2}\right)^{\left(1 - \frac{10}{180}\right)}} + \frac{1{,}000{,}000\left(\dfrac{0.01625}{2}\right)}{\left(1 + \dfrac{0.00021 + 0.01096}{2}\right)^{\left(2 - \frac{10}{180}\right)}} + \cdots +$$

$$\frac{1{,}000{,}000\left(\dfrac{0.01625}{2}\right)}{\left(1 + \dfrac{0.0041 + 0.01096}{2}\right)^{\left(6 - \frac{10}{180}\right)}} +$$

$$\frac{1{,}000{,}000}{\left(1 + \dfrac{0.0041 + 0.01096}{2}\right)^{\left(6 - \frac{10}{180}\right)}} = \text{US\$1{,}003{,}954.12}$$

3.5 Spreads as a Price Quotation Convention

We have discussed both Treasury curves and swap curves as benchmarks for fixed-income valuation, but they usually differ. Therefore, quoting the price of a bond using the bond yield net of either a benchmark Treasury yield or swap rate becomes a price quote convention.

The Treasury rate can differ from the swap rate for the same term for several reasons. Unlike the cash flows from US Treasury bonds, the cash flows from swaps are subject to much higher default risk. Market liquidity for any specific maturity may differ. For example, some parts of the term structure of interest rates may be more actively traded with swaps than with Treasury bonds. Finally, arbitrage between these two markets cannot be perfectly executed.

Swap spreads to the Treasury rate (as opposed to the **I-spreads**, which are bond rates net of the swap rates of the same maturities) are simply the differences between swap rates and government bond yields of a particular maturity. One problem in defining swap spreads is that, for example, a 10-year swap matures in exactly 10 years whereas there typically is no government bond with exactly 10 years of remaining maturity. By convention, therefore, the 10-year swap spread is defined as the difference between the 10-year swap rate and the 10-year on-the-run government bond. Swap spreads of other maturities are defined similarly.

To generate the curves in Exhibit 4, we used the constant-maturity Treasury note to exactly match the corresponding swap rate. The 10-year swap spread is the 10-year swap rate less the 10-year constant-maturity Treasury note yield. Because counterparty risk is reflected in the swap rate and US government debt is considered nearly free of default risk, the swap rate is usually greater than the corresponding Treasury note rate and the 10-year swap spread is usually, but not always, positive.

Exhibit 4   10-Year Swap Rate vs. 10-Year Treasury Rate

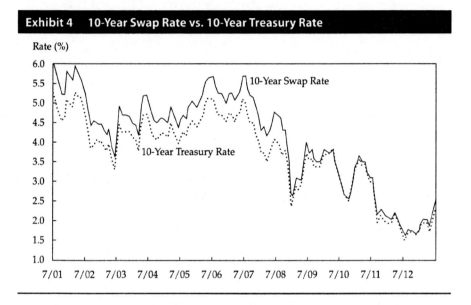

The **TED spread** is an indicator of perceived credit risk in the general economy. TED is an acronym formed from US T-bill and ED, the ticker symbol for the eurodollar futures contract. The TED spread is calculated as the difference between Libor and the yield on a T-bill of matching maturity. An increase (decrease) in the TED spread is a sign that lenders believe the risk of default on interbank loans is increasing (decreasing). Therefore, as it relates to the swap market, the TED spread can also be thought of as a measure of counterparty risk. Compared with the 10-year swap spread, the TED spread more accurately reflects risk in the banking system, whereas the 10-year swap spread is more often a reflection of differing supply and demand conditions.

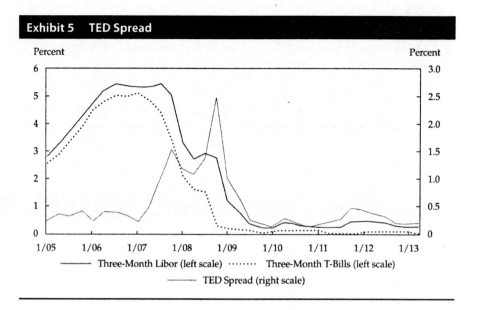

Exhibit 5   TED Spread

Three-Month Libor (left scale) ········ Three-Month T-Bills (left scale)

TED Spread (right scale)

Another popular measure of risk is the **Libor–OIS spread**, which is the difference between Libor and the overnight indexed swap (OIS) rate. An OIS is an interest rate swap in which the periodic floating rate of the swap is equal to the geometric average of an overnight rate (or overnight index rate) over every day of the payment period. The index rate is typically the rate for overnight unsecured lending between banks—for example, the federal funds rate for US dollars, Eonia (Euro OverNight Index Average) for euros, and Sonia (Sterling OverNight Index Average) for sterling. The Libor–OIS spread is considered an indicator of the risk and liquidity of money market securities.

4   TRADITIONAL THEORIES OF THE TERM STRUCTURE OF INTEREST RATES

This section presents four traditional theories of the underlying economic factors that affect the shape of the yield curve.

4.1 Local Expectations Theory

One branch of traditional term structure theory focuses on interpreting term structure shape in terms of investors' expectations. Historically, the first such theory is known as the **unbiased expectations theory** or **pure expectations theory**. It says that the forward rate is an unbiased predictor of the future spot rate; its broadest interpretation is that bonds of any maturity are perfect substitutes for one another. For example, buying a bond with a maturity of five years and holding it for three years has the same expected return as buying a three-year bond or buying a series of three one-year bonds.

The predictions of the unbiased expectations theory are consistent with the assumption of risk neutrality. In a risk-neutral world, investors are unaffected by uncertainty and risk premiums do not exist. Every security is risk free and yields the risk-free rate for that particular maturity. Although such an assumption leads to interesting results, it clearly is in conflict with the large body of evidence that shows that investors are risk averse.

A theory that is similar but more rigorous than the unbiased expectations theory is the **local expectations theory**. Rather than asserting that every maturity strategy has the same expected return over a given investment horizon, this theory instead contends that the expected return for every bond over short time periods is the risk-free rate. This conclusion results from an assumed no-arbitrage condition in which bond pricing does not allow for traders to earn arbitrage profits.

The primary way that the local expectations theory differs from the unbiased expectations theory is that it can be extended to a world characterized by risk. Although the theory requires that risk premiums be nonexistent for very short holding periods, no such restrictions are placed on longer-term investments. Thus, the theory is applicable to both risk-free as well as risky bonds.

Using the formula for the discount factor in Equation 1 and the variation of the forward rate model in Equation 5, we can produce Equation 13, where $P(t,T)$ is the discount factor for a T-period security at time t.

$$\frac{1}{P(t,T)} = \left[1 + r(1)\right]\left[1 + f(1,1)\right]\left[1 + f(2,1)\right]\left[+f(3,1)\right]...\left[1 + f(T-1,1)\right] \qquad \textbf{(13)}$$

Using Equation 13, we can show that if the forward rates are realized, the one-period return of a long-term bond is $r(1)$, the yield on a one-period risk-free security, as shown in Equation 14.

$$\frac{P(t+1,T-1)}{P(t,T)} = 1 + r(1) \qquad \textbf{(14)}$$

The local expectations theory extends this equation to incorporate uncertainty while still assuming risk neutrality in the short term. When we relax the certainty assumption, then Equation 14 becomes Equation 15, where the tilde (~) represents an uncertain outcome. In other words, the one-period return of a long-term risky bond is the one-period risk-free rate.

$$\frac{E\left[\tilde{P}(t+1,T-1)\right]}{P(t,T)} = 1 + r(1) \qquad \textbf{(15)}$$

Although the local expectations theory is economically appealing, it is often observed that short-holding-period returns on long-dated bonds do exceed those on short-dated bonds. The need for liquidity and the ability to hedge risk essentially ensure that the demand for short-term securities will exceed that for long-term securities. Thus, both the yields and the actual returns for short-dated securities are typically lower than those for long-dated securities.

4.2 Liquidity Preference Theory

Whereas the unbiased expectations theory leaves no room for risk aversion, liquidity preference theory attempts to account for it. **Liquidity preference theory** asserts that **liquidity premiums** exist to compensate investors for the added interest rate risk they face when lending long term and that these premiums increase with maturity.[8] Thus, given an expectation of unchanging short-term spot rates, liquidity preference theory predicts an upward-sloping yield curve. The forward rate provides an estimate of the expected spot rate that is biased upward by the amount of the liquidity premium, which invalidates the unbiased expectations theory.

---

8 The wording of a technical treatment of this theory would be that these premiums increase monotonically with maturity. A sequence is said to be monotonically increasing if each term is greater than or equal to the one before it. Define $LP(T)$ as the liquidty premium at maturity T. If premiums increase monotonically with maturity, then $LP(T+t) \geq LP(T)$ for all $t > 0$.

For example, the US Treasury offers bonds that mature in 30 years. However, the majority of investors have an investment horizon that is shorter than 30 years.[9] For investors to hold these bonds, they would demand a higher return for taking the risk that the yield curve changes and that they must sell the bond prior to maturity at an uncertain price. That incrementally higher return is the liquidity premium. Note that this premium is not to be confused with a yield premium for the lack of liquidity that thinly traded bonds may bear. Rather, it is a premium applying to all long-term bonds, including those with deep markets.

Liquidity preference theory fails to offer a complete explanation of the term structure. Rather, it simply argues for the existence of liquidity premiums. For example, a downward-sloping yield curve could still be consistent with the existence of liquidity premiums if one of the factors underlying the shape of the curve is an expectation of deflation (i.e., a negative rate of inflation due to monetary or fiscal policy actions). Expectations of sharply declining spot rates may also result in a downward-sloping yield curve if the expected decline in interest rates is severe enough to offset the effect of the liquidity premiums.

In summary, liquidity preference theory claims that lenders require a liquidity premium as an incentive to lend long term. Thus, forward rates derived from the current yield curve provide an upwardly biased estimate of expected future spot rates. Although downward-sloping or hump-shaped yield curves may sometimes occur, the existence of liquidity premiums implies that the yield curve will typically be upward sloping.

4.3 Segmented Markets Theory

Unlike expectations theory and liquidity preference theory, **segmented markets theory** allows for lender and borrower preferences to influence the shape of the yield curve. The result is that yields are not a reflection of expected spot rates or liquidity premiums. Rather, they are solely a function of the supply and demand for funds of a particular maturity. That is, each maturity sector can be thought of as a segmented market in which yield is determined independently from the yields that prevail in other maturity segments.

The theory is consistent with a world where there are asset/liability management constraints, either regulatory or self-imposed. In such a world, investors might restrict their investment activity to a maturity sector that provides the best match for the maturity of their liabilities. Doing so avoids the risks associated with an asset/liability mismatch.

For example, because life insurers sell long-term liabilities against themselves in the form of life insurance contracts, they tend to be most active as buyers in the long end of the bond market. Similarly, because the liabilities of pension plans are long term, they typically invest in long-term securities. Why would they invest short term given that those returns might decline while the cost of their liabilities stays fixed? In contrast, money market funds would be limited to investing in debt with maturity of one year or less, in general.

In summary, the segmented markets theory assumes that market participants are either unwilling or unable to invest in anything other than securities of their preferred maturity. It follows that the yield of securities of a particular maturity is determined entirely by the supply and demand for funds of that particular maturity.

---

9 This view can be confirmed by examining typical demand for long-term versus short-term Treasuries at auctions.

4.4 Preferred Habitat Theory

The **preferred habitat theory** is similar to the segmented markets theory in proposing that many borrowers and lenders have strong preferences for particular maturities but it does not assert that yields at different maturities are determined independently of each other.

However, the theory contends that if the expected additional returns to be gained become large enough, institutions will be willing to deviate from their preferred maturities or habitats. For example, if the expected returns on longer-term securities exceed those on short-term securities by a large enough margin, money market funds will lengthen the maturities of their assets. And if the excess returns expected from buying short-term securities become large enough, life insurance companies might stop limiting themselves to long-term securities and place a larger part of their portfolios in shorter-term investments.

The preferred habitat theory is based on the realistic notion that agents and institutions will accept additional risk in return for additional expected returns. In accepting elements of both the segmented markets theory and the unbiased expectations theory, yet rejecting their extreme polar positions, the preferred habitat theory moves closer to explaining real-world phenomena. In this theory, both market expectations and the institutional factors emphasized in the segmented markets theory influence the term structure of interest rates.

PREFERRED HABITAT AND QE

The term "quantitative easing" (QE) refers to an unconventional monetary policy used by central banks to increase the supply of money in an economy when central bank and/or interbank interest rates are already close to zero. The first of three QE efforts by the US Federal Reserve began in late 2008, following the establishment of a near-zero target range for the federal funds rate. Since then, the Federal Reserve has greatly expanded its holdings of long-term securities via a series of asset purchase programs, with the goal of putting downward pressure on long-term interest rates thereby making financial conditions even more accommodative. Exhibit 6 presents information regarding the securities held by the Federal Reserve on 20 September 2007 (when all securities held by the Fed were US Treasury issuance) and 19 September 2013 (one year after the third round of QE was launched).

Exhibit 6	Securities Held by the US Federal Reserve	
(US$ millions)	**20 Sept. 2007**	**19 Sept. 2013**
Securities held outright	779,636	3,448,758
US Treasury	779,636	2,047,534
Bills	267,019	0
Notes and bonds, nominal	472,142	1,947,007
Notes and bonds, inflation indexed	35,753	87,209
Inflation compensation	4,723	13,317
Federal agency	0	63,974
Mortgage-backed securities	0	1,337,520

As Exhibit 6 shows, the Federal Reserve's security holdings on 20 September 2007 consisted entirely of US Treasury securities and about 34% of those holdings were short term in the form of T-bills. On 19 September 2013, only about 59% of the Federal

Reserve's security holdings were Treasury securities and none of those holdings were T-bills. Furthermore, the Federal Reserve held well over US$1.3 trillion of mortgage-backed securities (MBS), which accounted for almost 39% of all securities held.

Prior to the QE efforts, the yield on MBS was typically in the 5%–6% range. It declined to less than 2% by the end of 2012. Concepts related to preferred habitat theory could possibly help explain that drop in yield.

The purchase of MBS by the Federal Reserve essentially reduced the supply of these securities that was available for private purchase. Assuming that many MBS investors are either unwilling or unable to withdraw from the MBS market because of their investment in gaining expertise in managing interest rate and repayment risks of MBS, MBS investing institutions would have a "preferred habitat" in the MBS market. If they were unable to meet investor demand without bidding more aggressively, these buyers would drive down yields on MBS.

The case can also be made that the Federal Reserve's purchase of MBS helped reduced prepayment risk, which also resulted in a reduction in MBS yields. If a homeowner pre-pays on a mortgage, the payment is sent to MBS investors on a pro-rata basis. Although investors are uncertain about when such a prepayment will be received, prepayment is more likely in a declining interest rate environment.

Use Example 9 to test your understanding of traditional term structure theories.

EXAMPLE 9

Traditional Term Structure Theories

1 In 2010, the Committee of European Securities Regulators created guide-lines that restricted weighted average life (WAL) to 120 days for short-term money market funds. The purpose of this restriction was to limit the ability of money market funds to invest in long-term, floating-rate securities. This action is *most* consistent with a belief in:

   A the preferred habitat theory.

   B the segmented markets theory.

   C the local expectations theory.

2 The term structure theory that asserts that investors cannot be induced to hold debt securities whose maturities do not match their investment horizon is *best* described as the:

   A preferred habitat theory.

   B segmented markets theory.

   C unbiased expectations theory.

3 The unbiased expectations theory assumes investors are:

   A risk averse.

   B risk neutral.

   C risk seeking.

4 Market evidence shows that forward rates are:

   A unbiased predictors of future spot rates.

   B upwardly biased predictors of future spot rates.

   C downwardly biased predictors of future spot rates.

5 Market evidence shows that short holding-period returns on short-maturity bonds *most* often are:

   A less than those on long-maturity bonds.

B about equal to those on long-maturity bonds.

C greater than those on long-maturity bonds.

Solution to 1:

A is correct. The preferred habitat theory asserts that investors are willing to move away from their preferred maturity if there is adequate incentive to do so. The proposed WAL guideline was the result of regulatory concern about the interest rate risk and credit risk of long-term, floating-rate securities. An inference of this regulatory action is that some money market funds must be willing to move away from more traditional short-term investments if they believe there is sufficient compensation to do so.

Solution to 2:

B is correct. Segmented markets theory contends that asset/liability management constraints force investors to buy securities whose maturities match the maturities of their liabilities. In contrast, preferred habitat theory asserts that investors are willing to deviate from their preferred maturities if yield differentials encourage the switch. The unbiased expectations theory makes no assumptions about maturity preferences. Rather, it contends that forward rates are unbiased predictors of future spot rates.

Solution to 3:

B is correct. The unbiased expectations theory asserts that different maturity strategies, such as rollover, maturity matching, and riding the yield curve, have the same expected return. By definition, a risk-neutral party is indifferent about choices with equal expected payoffs, even if one choice is riskier. Thus, the predictions of the theory are consistent with the existence of risk-neutral investors.

Solution to 4:

B is correct. The existence of a liquidity premium ensures that the forward rate is an upwardly biased estimate of the future spot rate. Market evidence clearly shows that liquidity premiums exist, and this evidence effectively refutes the predictions of the unbiased expectations theory.

Solution to 5:

A is correct. Although the local expectations theory predicts that the short-run return for all bonds will be equal to the risk-free rate, most of the evidence refutes that claim. Returns from long-dated bonds are generally higher than those from short-dated bonds, even over relatively short investment horizons. This market evidence is consistent with the risk–expected return trade-off that is central to finance and the uncertainty surrounding future spot rates.

MODERN TERM STRUCTURE MODELS

5

Modern term structure models provide quantitatively precise descriptions of how interest rates evolve. A model provides a sometimes simplified description of a real-world phenomenon on the basis of a set of assumptions; models are often used to solve particular problems. These assumptions cannot be completely accurate in depicting the real world, but instead, the assumptions are made to explain real-world phenomena sufficiently well to solve the problem at hand.

Interest rate models attempt to capture the statistical properties of interest rate movements. The detailed description of these models depends on mathematical and statistical knowledge well outside the scope of the investment generalist's technical preparation. Yet, these models are very important in the valuation of complex fixed-income instruments and bond derivatives. Thus, we provide a broad overview of these models in this reading. Equations for the models and worked examples are given for readers who are interested.

5.1 Equilibrium Term Structure Models

Equilibrium term structure models are models that seek to describe the dynamics of the term structure using fundamental economic variables that are assumed to affect interest rates. In the modeling process, restrictions are imposed that allow for the derivation of equilibrium prices for bonds and interest rate options. These models require the specification of a drift term (explained later) and the assumption of a functional form for interest rate volatility. The best-known equilibrium models are the **Cox–Ingersoll–Ross model**[10] and the **Vasicek model**,[11] which are discussed in the next two sections.

Equilibrium term structure models share several characteristics:

- *They are one-factor or multifactor models.* One-factor models assume that a single observable factor (sometimes called a state variable) drives all yield curve movements. Both the Vasicek and CIR models assume a single factor, the short-term interest rate, *r*. This approach is plausible because empirically, parallel shifts are often found to explain more than 90% of yield changes. In contrast, multifactor models may be able to model the curvature of a yield curve more accurately but at the cost of greater complexity.

- *They make assumptions about the behavior of factors.* For example, if we focus on a short-rate single-factor model, should the short rate be modeled as mean reverting? Should the short rate be modeled to exhibit jumps? How should the volatility of the short rate be modeled?

- *They are, in general, more sparing with respect to the number of parameters that must be estimated compared with arbitrage-free term structure models.* The cost of this relative economy in parameters is that arbitrage-free models can, in general, model observed yield curves more precisely.[12]

An excellent example of an equilibrium term structure model is the Cox–Ingersoll–Ross (CIR) model discussed next.

5.1.1 *The Cox–Ingersoll–Ross Model*

The CIR model assumes that every individual has to make consumption and investment decisions with their limited capital. Investing in the productive process may lead to higher consumption in the following period, but it requires sacrificing today's consumption. The individual must determine his or her optimal trade-off assuming that he or she can borrow and lend in the capital market. Ultimately, interest rates will reach a market equilibrium rate at which no one needs to borrow or lend. The CIR model can explain interest rate movements in terms of an individual's preferences for investment and consumption as well as the risks and returns of the productive processes of the economy.

---

10 Cox, Ingersoll, and Ross (1985).
11 Vasicek (1977).
12 Other contrasts are more technical. They include that equilibrium models use real probabilities whereas arbitrage-free models use so-called risk-neutral probabilities. See footnote 9 for another contrast.

As a result of this analysis, the model shows how the short-term interest rate is related to the risks facing the productive processes of the economy. Assuming that an individual requires a term premium on the long-term rate, the model shows that the short-term rate can determine the entire term structure of interest rates and the valuation of interest rate–contingent claims. The CIR model is presented in Equation 16.

In Equation 16, the terms "dr" and "dt" mean, roughly, an infinitely small increment in the (instantaneous) short-term interest rate and time, respectively; the CIR model is an instance of a so-called continuous-time finance model. The model has two parts: (1) a deterministic part (sometimes called a "drift term"), the expression in dt, and (2) a stochastic (i.e., random) part, the expression in dz, which models risk.

$$dr = a(b - r)dt + \sigma\sqrt{r}dz \tag{16}$$

The way the deterministic part, $a(b - r)dt$, is formulated in Equation 16 ensures mean reversion of the interest rate toward a long-run value b, with the speed of adjustment governed by the strictly positive parameter a. If a is high (low), mean reversion to the long-run rate b would occur quickly (slowly). In Equation 16, for simplicity of presentation we have assumed that the **term premium** of the CIR model is equal to zero.[13] Thus, as modeled here, the CIR model assumes that the economy has a constant long-run interest rate that the short-term interest rate converges to over time.

Mean reversion is an essential characteristic of the interest rate that sets it apart from many other financial data series. Unlike stock prices, for example, interest rates cannot rise indefinitely because at very high levels, they would hamper economic activity, which would ultimately result in a decrease in interest rates. Similarly, with rare historical exceptions, nominal interest rates are non-negative. As a result, short-term interest rates tend to move in a bounded range and show a tendency to revert to a long-run value b.

Note that in Equation 16, there is only one stochastic driver, dz, of the interest rate process; very loosely, dz can be thought of as an infinitely small movement in a "random walk." The stochastic or volatility term, $\sigma\sqrt{r}dz$, follows the random normal distribution for which the mean is zero, the standard deviation is 1, and the standard deviation factor is $\sigma\sqrt{r}$. The standard deviation factor makes volatility proportional to the square root of the short-term rate, which allows for volatility to increase with the level of interest rates. It also avoids the possibility of non-positive interest rates for all positive values of a and b.[14]

Note that a, b, and σ are model parameters that have to be specified in some manner.

AN ILLUSTRATION OF THE CIR MODEL

Assume again that the current short-term rate is $r = 3\%$ and the long-run value for the short-term rate is $b = 8\%$. As before, assume that the speed of the adjustment factor is $a = 0.40$ and the annual volatility is $\sigma = 20\%$. Using Equation 16, the CIR model provides the following formula for the change in short-term interest rates, dr:

$$dr = 0.40(8\% - r)dt + (20\%)\sqrt{r}dz$$

Assume that a random number generator produced standard normal random error terms, dz, of 0.50, –0.10, 0.50, and –0.30. The CIR model would produce the evolution of interest rates shown in Exhibit 7. The bottom half of the exhibit shows the pricing of bonds consistent with the evolution of the short-term interest rate.

---

13 Equilibrium models, but not arbitrage-free models, assume that a term premium is required on long-term interest rates. A term premium is the additional return required by lenders to invest in a bond to maturity net of the expected return from continually reinvesting at the short-term rate over that same time horizon.
14 As long as $2ab > \sigma^2$, per Yan (2001, p. 65).

$t = 0$

$dr = 0.4 \times (8\% - r)dt + (20\%)\sqrt{r}\,dz$

$= 0.4 \times (8\% - 3\%) \times 1 +$

$\quad 20\% \times \sqrt{3\%} \times 0.5$

$= 3.7324\%$

Exhibit 7   Evolution of the Short-Term Rate in the CIR Model

			Time		
Parameter	**t = 0**	**t = 1**	**t = 2**	**t = 3**	**t = 4**
r	3.000%	6.732%	6.720%	9.825%	7.214%
$a(b - r) = 0.40(8\% - r)$	2.000%	0.507%	0.512%	-0.730%	
dz	0.500	-0.100	0.500	-0.300	
$\sigma\sqrt{r}\,dz = 20\%\sqrt{r}\,dz$	1.732%	-0.519%	2.592%	-1.881%	
dr	3.732%	-0.012%	3.104%	-2.611%	
$r(t + 1) = r + dr$	6.732%	6.720%	9.825%	7.214%	

YTM for Zero-Coupon Bonds Maturing in					
1 Year	3.862%	6.921%	6.911%	9.456%	7.316%
2 Years	4.499%	7.023%	7.015%	9.115%	7.349%
5 Years	5.612%	7.131%	7.126%	8.390%	7.327%
10 Years	6.333%	7.165%	7.162%	7.854%	7.272%
30 Years	6.903%	7.183%	7.182%	7.415%	7.219%

The simulation of interest rates starts with an interest rate of 3%, which is well below the long-run value of 8%. Interest rates generated by the model quickly move toward this long-run value. Note that the standard normal variable dz is assumed to be 0.50 in time periods $t = 0$ and $t = 2$ but the volatility term, $\sigma\sqrt{r}\,dz$, is much higher in $t = 2$ than in $t = 0$ because volatility increases with the level of interest rates in the CIR model.

This example is stylized and intended for illustrative purposes only. The parameters used in practice typically vary significantly from those used here.

5.1.2 The Vasicek Model

Although not developed in the context of a general equilibrium of individuals seeking to make optimal consumption and investment decisions, as was the case for the CIR model, the Vasicek model is viewed as an equilibrium term structure model. Similar to the CIR model, the Vasicek model captures mean reversion.

Equation 17 presents the Vasicek model:

$$dr = a(b - r)dt + \sigma dz \tag{17}$$

The Vasicek model has the same drift term as the CIR model and thus tends toward mean reversion in the short rate, r. The stochastic or volatility term, σdz, follows the random normal distribution for which the mean is zero and the standard deviation is 1. Unlike the CIR Model, interest rates are calculated assuming that volatility remains constant over the period of analysis. As with the CIR model, there is only one stochastic driver, dz, of the interest rate process and a, b, and σ are model parameters that have to be specified in some manner. The main disadvantage of the Vasicek model is that it is theoretically possible for the interest rate to become negative.

V

AN ILLUSTRATION OF THE VASICEK MODEL

Assume that the current short-term rate is $r = 3\%$ and the long-run value for the short-term rate is $b = 8\%$. Also assume that the speed of the adjustment factor is $a = 0.40$ and the annual volatility is $\sigma = 2\%$. Using Equation 17, the Vasicek model provides the following formula for the change in short-term interest rates, dr:

$$dr = 0.40(8\% - r)dt + (2\%)dz$$

The stochastic term, dz, is typically drawn from a standard normal distribution with a mean of zero and a standard deviation of 1. Assume that a random number generator produced standard normal random error terms of 0.45, 0.18, −0.30, and 0.25. The Vasicek model would produce the evolution of interest rates shown in Exhibit 8.

Exhibit 8   Evolution of the Short-Term Rate in the Vasicek Model

Parameter	Time				
	$t = 0$	$t = 1$	$t = 2$	$t = 3$	$t = 4$
r	3.000%	5.900%	7.100%	6.860%	7.816%
$a(b - r)$	2.000%	0.840%	0.360%	0.456%	
dz	0.450	0.180	-0.300	0.250	
σdz	0.900%	0.360%	-0.600%	0.500%	
dr	2.900%	1.200%	-0.240%	0.956%	
$r(t + 1) = r + dr$	5.900%	7.100%	6.860%	7.816%	
YTM for Zero-Coupon Bonds Maturing in					
1 Year	3.874%	6.264%	7.253%	7.055%	7.843%
2 Years	4.543%	6.539%	7.365%	7.200%	7.858%
5 Years	5.791%	7.045%	7.563%	7.460%	7.873%
10 Years	6.694%	7.405%	7.670%	7.641%	7.876%
30 Years	7.474%	7.716%	7.816%	7.796%	7.875%

[Handwritten annotation:]
$$\tau = 0$$
$$dr = 0.4 \times (8\% - 3\%) \times 1 + 2\% \times 0.45 = 2.9\%$$
$$r_{t=1} = 3\% + 2.9\% = 5.9\%$$

Note that the simulation of interest rates starts with an interest rate of 3%, which is well below the long-run value of 8%. Interest rates generated by the model move quickly toward this long-run value despite declining in the third time period, which reflects the mean reversion built into the model via the drift term $a(b - r)dt$.

This example is stylized and intended for illustrative purposes only. The parameters used in practice typically vary significantly from those used here.

Note that because both the Vasicek model and the CIR model require the short-term rate to follow a certain process, the estimated yield curve may not match the observed yield curve. But if the parameters of the models are believed to be correct, then investors can use these models to determine mispricings.

5.2 Arbitrage-Free Models: The Ho–Lee Model

In **arbitrage-free models**, the analysis begins with the observed market prices of a reference set of financial instruments and the underlying assumption is that the reference set is correctly priced. An assumed random process with a drift term and volatility factor is used for the generation of the yield curve. The computational process that determines the term structure is such that the valuation process generates the market prices of the reference set of financial instruments. These models are called "arbitrage-free" because the prices they generate match market prices.

The ability to calibrate models to market data is a desirable feature of any model, and this fact points to one of the main drawbacks of the Vasicek and CIR models: They have only a finite number of free parameters, and so it is not possible to specify these parameter values in such a way that model prices coincide with observed market prices. This problem is overcome in arbitrage-free models by allowing the parameters to vary deterministically with time. As a result, the market yield curve can be modeled with the accuracy needed for such applications as valuing derivatives and bonds with embedded options.

The first arbitrage-free model was introduced by Ho and Lee.[15] It uses the relative valuation concepts of the Black–Scholes–Merton option-pricing model. Thus, the valuation of interest rate contingent claims is based solely on the yield curve's shape and its movements. The model assumes that the yield curve moves in a way that is consistent with a no-arbitrage condition.

In the **Ho–Lee model**, the short rate follows a normal process, as shown in Equation 18:

$$dr_t = \theta_t dt + \sigma dz_t \qquad\qquad (18)$$

The model can be calibrated to market data by inferring the form of the time-dependent drift term, θ_t, from market prices, which means the model can precisely generate the current term structure. This calibration is typically performed via a binomial lattice-based model in which at each node the yield curve can move up or down with equal probability. This probability is called the "implied risk-neutral probability." Often it is called the "risk-neutral probability," which is somewhat misleading because arbitrage-free models do not assume market professionals are risk neutral as does the local expectations theory. This is analogous to the classic Black–Scholes–Merton option model insofar as the pricing dynamics are simplified because we can price debt securities "as if" market investors were risk neutral.

To make the discussion concrete, we illustrate a two-period Ho-Lee model. Assume that the current short-term rate is 4%. The time step is monthly, and the drift terms, which are determined using market prices, are $\theta_1 = 1\%$ in the first month and $\theta_2 = 0.80\%$ in the second month. The annual volatility is 2%. Below, we create a two-period binomial lattice-based model for the short-term rate. Note that the monthly volatility is

$$\sigma\sqrt{\frac{1}{t}} = 2\%\sqrt{\frac{1}{12}} = 0.5774\%$$

and the time step is

$$dt = \frac{1}{12} = 0.0833$$

$$dr_t = \theta_t dt + \sigma dz_t = \theta_t(0.0833) + (0.5774)dz_t$$

If the rate goes up in the first month,

$$r = 4\% + (1\%)(0.0833) + 0.5774\% = 4.6607\%$$

If the rate goes up in the first month and up in the second month,

$$r = 4.6607\% + (0.80\%)(0.0833) + 0.5774\% = 5.3047\%$$

If the rate goes up in the first month and down in the second month,

$$r = 4.6607\% + (0.80\%)(0.0833) - 0.5774\% = 4.1499\%$$

---

15 Ho and Lee (1986).

If the rate goes down in the first month,

r = 4% + (1%)(0.0833) − 0.5774% = 3.5059%

If the rate goes down in the first month and up in the second month,

r = 3.5059% + (0.80%)(0.0833) + 0.5774% = 4.1499

If the rate goes down in the first month and down in the second month,

r = 3.5059% + (0.80%)(0.0833) − 0.5774% = 2.9951%

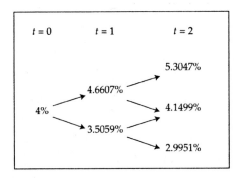

The interest rates generated by the model can be used to determine zero-coupon bond prices and the spot curve. By construction, the model output is consistent with market prices. Because of its simplicity, the Ho–Lee model is useful for illustrating most of the salient features of arbitrage-free interest rate models. Because the model generates a symmetrical ("bell-shaped" or normal) distribution of future rates, negative interest rates are possible. Note that although the volatility of the one-period rate is constant at each node point in the illustration, time-varying volatility—consistent with the historical behavior of yield curve movements—can be modeled in the Ho–Lee model because sigma (interest rate volatility) can be specified as a function of time. A more sophisticated example using a term structure of volatilities as inputs is outside the scope of this reading.

As mentioned before, models are assumptions made to describe certain phenomena and to provide solutions to problems at hand. Modern interest rate theories are proposed for the most part to value bonds with embedded options because the values of embedded options are frequently contingent on interest rates. The general equilibrium models introduced here describe yield curve movement as the movement in a single short-term rate. They are called one-factor models and, in general, seem empirically satisfactory. Arbitrage-free models do not attempt to explain the observed yield curve. Instead, these models take the yield curve as given. For this reason, they are sometimes labeled as **partial equilibrium models**.

The basic arbitrage-free concept can be used to solve much broader problems. These models can be extended to value many bond types, allowing for a term structure of volatilities, uncertain changes in the shape of the yield curve, adjustments for the credit risk of a bond, and much more. Yet, these many extensions are still based on the concept of arbitrage-free interest rate movements. For this reason, the principles of these models form a foundation for much of the modern progress made in financial modeling.

Example 10 addresses several basic points about modern term structure models.

EXAMPLE 10

Modern Term Structure Models

1 Which of the following would be expected to provide the *most* accurate modeling with respect to the observed term structure?

   A CIR model

   B Ho–Lee model

   C Vasicek model

2 Which of the following statements about the Vasicek model is *most* accurate? It has:

   A a single factor, the long rate.

   B a single factor, the short rate.

   C two factors, the short rate and the long rate.

3 The CIR model:

   A assumes interest rates are not mean reverting.

   B has a drift term that differs from that of the Vasicek model.

   C assumes interest rate volatility increases with increases in the level of interest rates.

Solution to 1:

B is correct. The CIR model and the Vasicek model are examples of equilibrium term structure models, whereas the Ho–Lee model is an example of an arbitrage-free term structure model. A benefit of arbitrage-free term structure models is that they are calibrated to the current term structure. In other words,the starting prices ascribed to securities are those currently found in the market. In contrast, equilibrium term structure models frequently generate term structures that are inconsistent with current market data.

Solution to 2:

B is correct. Use of the Vasicek model requires assumptions for the short-term interest rate, which are usually derived from more general assumptions about the state variables that describe the overall economy. Using the assumed process for the short-term rate, one can determine the yield on longer-term bonds by looking at the expected path of interest rates over time.

Solution to 3:

C is correct. The drift term of the CIR model is identical to that of the Vasicek model, and both models assume that interest rates are mean reverting. The big difference between the two models is that the CIR model assumes that interest rate volatility increases with increases in the level of interest rates. The Vasicek model assumes that interest rate volatility is a constant.

---

6   YIELD CURVE FACTOR MODELS

The effect of yield volatilities on price is an important consideration in fixed-income investment, particularly for risk management and portfolio evaluation. In this section, we will describe measuring and managing the interest rate risk of bonds.

6.1 A Bond's Exposure to Yield Curve Movement

Shaping risk is defined as the sensitivity of a bond's price to the changing shape of the yield curve. The shape of the yield curve changes continually, and yield curve shifts are rarely parallel. For active bond management, a bond investor may want to base trades on a forecasted yield curve shape or may want to hedge the yield curve risk on a bond portfolio. Shaping risk also affects the value of many options, which is very important because many fixed-income instruments have embedded options.

Exhibits 9 through 11 show historical yield curve movements for US, Japanese, and South Korean government bonds from August 2005 to July 2013. The exhibits show that the shape of the yield curve changes considerably over time. In the United States and South Korea, central bank policies in response to the Great Recession led to a significant decline in short-term yields during the 2007–2009 time period. Long-term yields eventually followed suit, resulting in a flattening of the yield curve. Short-term Japanese yields have been low for quite some time, and recent long-term yields are the lowest of any developed market. Note that the vertical axis values of the three exhibits differ.

Exhibit 9   Historical US Yield Curve Movements

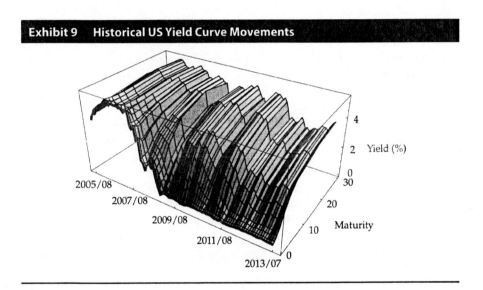

Exhibit 10   Historical Japanese Yield Curve Movements

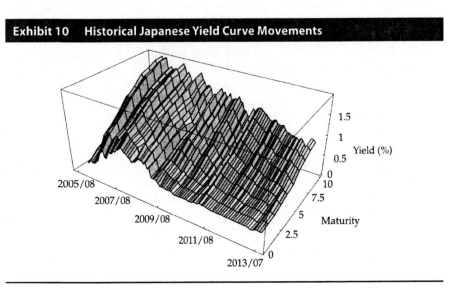

Exhibit 11   Historical Korean Yield Curve Movements

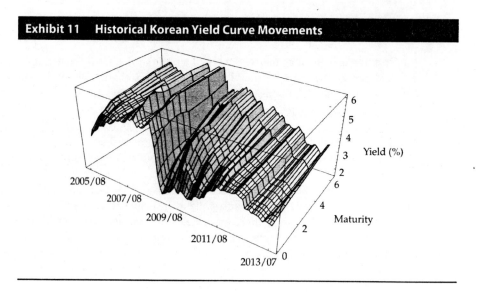

6.2 Factors Affecting the Shape of the Yield Curve

The previous section showed that the yield curve can take nearly any shape. The challenge for a fixed-income manager is to implement a process to manage the yield curve shape risk in his or her portfolio. One approach is to find a model that reduces most of the possible yield curve movements to a probabilistic combination of a few standardized yield curve movements. This section presents one of the best-known yield curve factor models.

A **yield curve factor model** is defined as a model or a description of yield curve movements that can be considered realistic when compared with historical data. Research shows that there are models that can describe these movements with some accuracy. One specific yield curve factor model is the three-factor model of Litterman and Scheinkman (1991), who found that yield curve movements are historically well described by a combination of three independent movements, which they interpreted as **level, steepness,** and **curvature.** The level movement refers to an upward or downward shift in the yield curve. The steepness movement refers to a non-parallel shift in the yield curve when either short-term rates change more than long-term rates or long-term rates change more than short-term rates. The curvature movement is a reference to movement in three segments of the yield curve: the short-term and long-term segments rise while the middle-term segment falls or vice versa.

The method to determine the number of factors—and their economic interpretation—begins with a measurement of the change of key rates on the yield curve, in this case 10 different points along the yield curve, as shown in Exhibits 12 and 13. The historical variance/covariance matrix of these interest rate movements is then obtained. The next step is to try to discover a number of independent factors (not to exceed the number of variables—in this case, selected points along the yield curve) that can explain the observed variance/covariance matrix. The approach that focuses on identifying the factors that best explain historical variances is known as **principal components analysis** (PCA). PCA creates a number of synthetic factors defined as (and calculated to be) statistically independent of each other; how these factors may be interpreted economically is a challenge to the researcher that can be addressed by relating movements in the factors (as we will call the principal components in this discussion) to movements in observable and easily understood variables.

In applying this analysis to historical data for the period of August 2005–July 2013, very typical results were found, as expressed in Exhibit 12 and graphed in Exhibit 13. The first principal component explained about 77% of the total variance/covariance, and the second and third principal components (or factors) explained 17% and 3%, respectively. These percentages are more commonly recognized as R^2s, which, by the underlying assumptions of principal components analysis, can be simply summed to discover that a linear combination of the first three factors explains almost 97% of the total yield curve changes in the sample studied.

Exhibit 12	The First Three Yield Curve Factors, US Treasury Securities, August 2005–July 2013 (Entries are percents)									
Time to Maturity (Years)	**0.25**	**0.5**	**1**	**2**	**3**	**5**	**7**	**10**	**20**	**30**
Factor 1 "Level"	−0.2089	−0.2199	−0.2497	−0.2977	−0.3311	−0.3756	−0.3894	−0.3779	−0.3402	−0.3102
Factor 2 "Steepness"	0.5071	0.4480	0.3485	0.2189	0.1473	−0.0371	−0.1471	−0.2680	−0.3645	−0.3514
Factor 3 "Curvature"	0.4520	0.2623	0.0878	−0.3401	−0.4144	−0.349	−0.1790	0.0801	0.3058	0.4219

Note that in Exhibit 13, the x-axis represents time to maturity in years.

Exhibit 13	The First Three Yield Curve Factors for US Treasury Securities, August 2005–July 2013

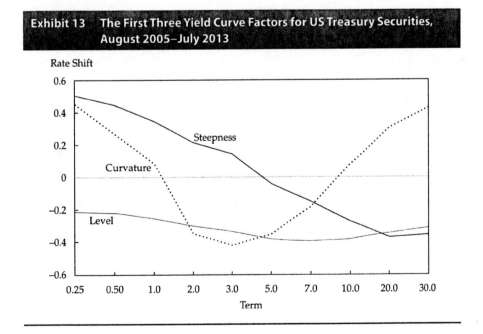

How should Exhibit 12 be interpreted? Exhibit 12 shows that for a one standard deviation positive change in the first factor (normalized to have unit standard deviation), the yield for a 0.25-year bond would decline by 0.2089%, a 0.50-year bond by 0.2199%, and so on across maturities, so that a 30-year bond would decline by 0.3102%.

Because the responses are in the same direction and by similar magnitudes, a reasonable interpretation of the first factor is that it describes (approximately) parallel shifts up and down the entire length of the yield curve.

Examining the second factor, we notice that a unitary positive standard deviation change appears to raise rates at shorter maturities (e.g., +0.5071% for 0.25-year bonds) but lowers rates at longer maturities (e.g., −0.3645% and −0.3514% for 20- and 30-year bonds, respectively). We can reasonably interpret this factor as one that causes changes in the steepness or slope of the yield curve. We note that the R^2 associated with this factor of 17% is much less important than the 77% R^2 associated with the first factor, which we associated with parallel shifts in the yield curve.

The third factor contributes a much smaller R^2 of 3%, and we associate this factor with changes in the curvature or "twist" in the curve because a unitary positive standard deviation change in this factor leads to positive yield changes at both short and long maturities but produces declines at intermediate maturities.

PCA shows similar results when applied to other government bond markets during the August 2005–July 2013 time period. Exhibits 14 and 15 reflect the results graphically for the Japanese and South Korean markets. In these instances, results can also be well explained by factors that appear to be associated, in declining order of importance, with parallel shifts, changes in steepness, and changes in curvature. Note that in Exhibits 14 and 15, as in Exhibit 13, the x-axis represents time to maturity in years.

Exhibit 14   The First Three Yield Curve Factors for Japanese Government Securities, August 2005–July 2013

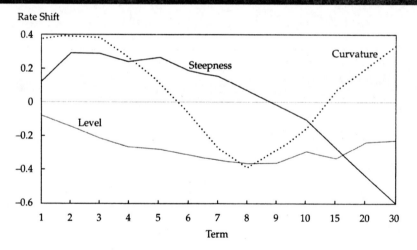

Exhibit 15   The First Three Yield Curve Factors for South Korean Government Securities, August 2005–July 2013

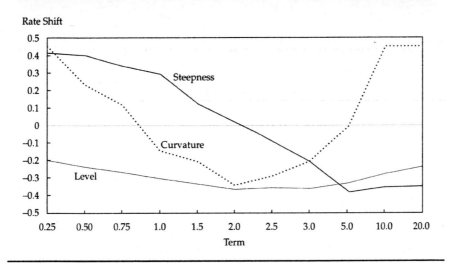

As in any other time series or regression model, the impact of the factors may change depending on the time period selected for study. However, if the reader selects any date within the sample period used to estimate these factors, a linear combination of the factors should explain movements of the yield curve on that date well.

6.3 The Maturity Structure of Yield Curve Volatilities

In modern fixed-income management, quantifying interest rate volatilities is important for at least two reasons. First, most fixed-income instruments and derivatives have embedded options. Option values, and hence the values of the fixed-income instrument, crucially depend on the level of interest rate volatilities. Second, fixed-income interest rate risk management is clearly an important part of any management process, and such risk management includes controlling the impact of interest rate volatilities on the instrument's price volatility.

The term structure of interest rate volatilities is a representation of the yield volatility of a zero-coupon bond for every maturity of security. This volatility curve (or "vol") or volatility term structure measures yield curve risk.

Interest rate volatility is not the same for all interest rates along the yield curve. On the basis of the typical assumption of a lognormal model, the uncertainty of an interest rate is measured by the annualized standard deviation of the proportional change in a bond yield over a specified time interval. For example, if the time interval is a one-month period, then the specified time interval equals 1/12 years. This measure is called interest rate volatility, and it is denoted $\sigma(t,T)$, which is the volatility of the rate for a security with maturity T at time t. The term structure of volatilities is given by Equation 19:

$$\sigma(t,T) = \frac{\sigma\left[\Delta r(t,T)/r(t,T)\right]}{\sqrt{\Delta t}} \tag{19}$$

In Exhibit 16, to illustrate a term structure of volatility, the data series is deliberately chosen to end before the 2008 financial crisis, which was associated with some unusual volatity magnitudes.

Exhibit 16	Historical Volatility Term Structure: US Treasuries, August 2005–December 2007									
Maturity (years)	0.25	0.50	1	2	3	5	7	10	20	30
$\sigma(t,T)$	0.3515	0.3173	0.2964	0.2713	0.2577	0.2154	0.1885	0.1621	0.1332	0.1169

For example, the 35.15% standard deviation for the three-month T-bill in Exhibit 16 is based on a monthly standard deviation of 0.1015 = 10.15%, which annualizes as

$$0.1015 \div \sqrt{\frac{1}{12}} = 0.3515 = 35.15\%$$

The volatility term structure typically shows that short-term rates are more volatile than long-term rates. Research indicates that short-term volatility is most strongly linked to uncertainty regarding monetary policy whereas long-term volatility is most strongly linked to uncertainty regarding the real economy and inflation. Furthermore, most of the co-movement between short-term and long-term volatilities appears to depend on the ever-changing correlations between these three determinants (monetary policy, the real economy, and inflation). During the period of August 2005–December 2007, long-term volatility was lower than short-term volatility, falling from 35.15% for the 0.25-year rate to 11.69% for the 30-year rate.

6.4 Managing Yield Curve Risks

Yield curve risk—risk to portfolio value arising from unanticipated changes in the yield curve—can be managed on the basis of several measures of sensitivity to yield curve movements. Management of yield curve risk involves changing the identified exposures to desired values by trades in security or derivative markets (the details fall under the rubric of fixed-income portfolio management and thus are outside the scope of this reading).

One available measure of yield curve sensitivity is effective duration, which measures the sensitivity of a bond's price to a small parallel shift in a benchmark yield curve. Another is based on key rate duration, which measures a bond's sensitivity to a small change in a benchmark yield curve at a specific maturity segment. A further measure can be developed on the basis of the factor model developed in Section 6.3. Using one of these last two measures allows identification and management of "shaping risk"—that is, sensitivity to changes in the shape of the benchmark yield curve—in addition to the risk associated with parallel yield curve changes, which is addressed adequately by effective duration.

To make the discussion more concrete, consider a portfolio of 1-year, 5-year, and 10-year zero-coupon bonds with $100 value in each position; total portfolio value is therefore $300. Also consider the hypothetical set of factor movements shown in the following table:

Year	1	5	10
Parallel	1	1	1
Steepness	−1	0	1
Curvature	1	0	1

In the table, a parallel movement or shift means that all the rates shift by an equal amount—in this case, by a unit of 1. A steepness movement means that the yield curve steepens with the long rate shifting up by one unit and the short rate shifting down by one unit. A curvature movement means that both the short rate and the long rate shift up by one unit whereas the medium-term rate remains unchanged. These movements need to be defined, as they are here, such that none of the movements can be a linear combination of the other two movements. Next, we address the calculation of the various yield curve sensitivity measures.

Because the bonds are zero-coupon bonds, the effective duration of each bond is the same as the maturity of the bonds.[16] The portfolio's effective duration is the weighted sum of the effective duration of each bond position; for this equally weighted portfolio, effective duration is $0.333(1 + 5 + 10) = 5.333$.

To calculate **key rate durations**, consider various yield curve movements. First, suppose that the one-year rate changes by 100 bps while the other rates remain the same; the sensitivity of the portfolio to that shift is $1/[(300)(0.01)] = 0.3333$. We conclude that the key rate duration of the portfolio to the one-year rate, denoted D_1, is 0.3333. Likewise, the key rate durations of the portfolio to the 5-year rate, D_5, and the 10-year rate, D_{10}, are 1.6667 and 3.3333, respectively. Note that the sum of the key rate durations is 5.333, which is the same as the effective duration of the portfolio. This fact can be explained intuitively. Key rate duration measures the portfolio risk exposure to each key rate. If all the key rates move by the same amount, then the yield curve has made a parallel shift, and as a result, the proportional change in value has to be consistent with effective duration. The related model for yield curve risk based on key rate durations would be

$$\left(\frac{\Delta P}{P}\right) \approx -D_1 \Delta r_1 - D_5 \Delta r_5 - D_{10} \Delta r_{10} \qquad (20)$$
$$= -0.3333 \Delta r_1 - 1.6667 \Delta r_5 - 3.3333 \Delta r_{10}$$

Next, we can calculate a measure based on the decomposition of yield curve movements into parallel, steepness, and curvature movements made in Section 6.3. Define D_L, D_S, and D_C as the sensitivities of portfolio value to small changes in the level, steepness, and curvature factors, respectively. Based on this factor model, Equation 21 shows the proportional change in portfolio value that would result from a small change in the level factor (Δx_L), the steepness factor (Δx_S), and the curvature factor (Δx_C).

$$\left(\frac{\Delta P}{P}\right) \approx -D_L \Delta x_L - D_S \Delta x_S - D_C \Delta x_C \qquad (21)$$

Because D_L is by definition sensitivity to a parallel shift, the proportional change in the portfolio value per unit shift (the line for a parallel movement in the table) is $5.3333 = 16/[(300)(0.01)]$. The sensitivity for steepness movement can be calculated as follows (see the line for steepness movement in the table). When the steepness makes an upward shift of 100 bps, it would result in a downward shift of 100 bps for the 1-year rate, resulting in a gain of \$1, and an upward shift for the 10-year rate, resulting in a loss of \$10. The change in value is therefore $(1 - 10)$. D_S is the negative of the proportional change in price per unit change in this movement and in this case is $3.0 = -(1 - 10)/[(300)(0.01)]$. Considering the line for curvature movement in the table, $D_C = 3.6667 = (1 + 10)/[(300)(0.01)]$. Thus, for our hypothetical bond portfolio, we can analyze the portfolio's yield curve risk using

$$\left(\frac{\Delta P}{p}\right) \approx -5.3333 \Delta x_L - 3.0 \Delta x_S - 3.6667 \Delta x_C \qquad (22)$$

---

16 Exactly so under continuous compounding.

For example, if $\Delta x_L = -0.0050$, $\Delta x_S = 0.002$, and $\Delta x_C = 0.001$, the predicted change in portfolio value would be +1.7%. It can be shown that key rate durations are directly related to level, steepness, and curvature in this example and that one set of sensitivities can be derived from the other. One can use the numerical example to verify that[17]

$$D_L = D_1 + D_5 + D_{10}$$

$$D_S = -D_1 + D_{10}$$

$$D_C = D_1 + D_{10}$$

Example 11 reviews concepts from this section and the preceding sections.

EXAMPLE 11

Term Structure Dynamics

1   The most important factor in explaining changes in the yield curve has been found to be:

   A   level.

   B   curvature.

   C   steepnesss.

2   A movement of the yield curve in which the short rate decreases by 150 bps and the long rate decreases by 50 bps would *best* be described as a:

   A   flattening of the yield curve resulting from changes in level and steepness.

   B   steepening of the yield curve resulting from changes in level and steepness.

   C   steepening of the yield curve resulting from changes in steepness and curvature.

3   A movement of the yield curve in which the short- and long-maturity sectors increase by 100 bps and 75 bps, respectively, but the intermediate-maturity sector increases by 10 bps, is *best* described as involving a change in:

   A   level only.

   B   curvature only.

   C   level and curvature.

4   Typically, short-term interest rates:

   A   are less volatile than long-term interest rates.

   B   are more volatile than long-term interest rates.

   C   have about the same volatility as long-term rates.

---

17 To see this, decompose Δr_1, Δr_5, and Δr_{10} into three factors—parallel, steepness, and curvature—based on the hypothetical movements in the table.

$\Delta r_1 = \Delta x_L - \Delta x_s + \Delta x_C$

$\Delta r_5 = \Delta x_L$

$\Delta r_{10} = \Delta x_L + \Delta x_S + \Delta x_C$

When we plug these equations into the expression for portfolio change based on key rate duration and simplify, we get

$$\frac{\Delta P}{P} = -D_1(\Delta x_L - \Delta x_S + \Delta x_C) - D_5(\Delta x_L) - D_{10}(\Delta x_L + \Delta x_S + \Delta x_C)$$

$$= -(D_1 + D_5 + D_{10})\Delta x_L - (-D_1 + D_{10})\Delta x_S - (D_1 + D_{10})\Delta x_C$$

5 Suppose for a given portfolio that key rate changes are considered to be changes in the yield on 1-year, 5-year, and 10-year securities. Estimated key rate durations are $D_1 = 0.50$, $D_2 = 0.70$, and $D_3 = 0.90$. What is the percentage change in the value of the portfolio if a parallel shift in the yield curve results in all yields declining by 50 bps?

A −1.05%.

B +1.05%

C +2.10%.

Solution to 1:

A is correct. Research shows that upward and downward shifts in the yield curve explain more than 75% of the total change in the yield curve.

Solution to 2:

B is correct. Both the short-term and long-term rates have declined, indicating a change in the level of the yield curve. Short-term rates have declined more than long-term rates, indicating a change in the steepness of the yield curve.

Solution to 3:

C is correct. Both the short-term and long-term rates have increased, indicating a change in the level of the yield curve. However, intermediate rates have increased less than both short-term and long-term rates, indicating a change in curvature.

Solution to 4:

B is correct. A possible explanation is that expectations for long-term inflation and real economic activity affecting longer-term interest rates are slower to change than those related to shorter-term interest rates.

Solution to 5:

B is correct. A decline in interest rates would lead to an increase in bond portfolio value: $-0.50(-0.005) - 0.70(-0.005) - 0.90(-0.005) = 0.0105 = 1.05\%$.

SUMMARY

- The spot rate for a given maturity can be expressed as a geometric average of the short-term rate and a series of forward rates.

- Forward rates are above (below) spot rates when the spot curve is upward (downward) sloping, whereas forward rates are equal to spot rates when the spot curve is flat.

- If forward rates are realized, then all bonds, regardless of maturity, will have the same one-period realized return, which is the first-period spot rate.

- If the spot rate curve is upward sloping and is unchanged, then each bond "rolls down" the curve and earns the forward rate that rolls out of its pricing (i.e., a T^*-period zero-coupon bond earns the T^*-period forward rate as it rolls down to be a $T^* - 1$ period security). This implies an expected return in excess of short-maturity bonds (i.e., a term premium) for longer-maturity bonds if the yield curve is upward sloping.

- Active bond portfolio management is consistent with the expectation that today's forward curve does not accurately reflect future spot rates.

- The swap curve provides another measure of the time value of money.

- The swap markets are significant internationally because swaps are frequently used to hedge interest rate risk exposure.

- The swap spread, the I-spread, and the Z-spread are bond quoting conventions that can be used to determine a bond's price.

- Swap curves and Treasury curves can differ because of differences in their credit exposures, liquidity, and other supply/demand factors.

- The local expectations theory, liquidity preference theory, segmented markets theory, and preferred habitat theory provide traditional explanations for the shape of the yield curve.

- Modern finance seeks to provide models for the shape of the yield curve and the use of the yield curve to value bonds (including those with embedded options) and bond-related derivatives. General equilibrium and arbitrage-free models are the two major types of such models.

- Arbitrage-free models are frequently used to value bonds with embedded options. Unlike equilibrium models, arbitrage-free models begin with the observed market prices of a reference set of financial instruments, and the underlying assumption is that the reference set is correctly priced.

- Historical yield curve movements suggest that they can be explained by a linear combination of three principal movements: level, steepness, and curvature.

- The volatility term structure can be measured using historical data and depicts yield curve risk.

- The sensitivity of a bond value to yield curve changes may make use of effective duration, key rate durations, or sensitivities to parallel, steepness, and curvature movements. Using key rate durations or sensitivities to parallel, steepness, and curvature movements allows one to measure and manage shaping risk.

REFERENCES

Cox, John C., Jonathan E. Ingersoll, and Stephen A. Ross. 1985. "An Intertemporal General Equilibrium Model of Asset Prices." *Econometrica*, March:363–384.

Haubrich, Joseph G. 2006. "Does the Yield Curve Signal Recession?" Federal Reserve Bank of Cleveland (15 April).

Ho, Thomas S.Y., and Sang Bin Lee. 1986. "Term Structure Movements and Pricing Interest Rate Contingent Claims." *Journal of Finance*, December:1011–1029.

Litterman, Robert, and José Scheinkman. 1991. "Common Factors Affecting Bond Returns." *Journal of Fixed Income*, vol. 1, no. 1 (June):54–61.

Vasicek, Oldrich. 1977. "An Equilibrium Characterization of the Term Structure." *Journal of Financial Economics*, November:177–188.

Yan, Hong. 2001. "Dynamic Models of the Term Structure." *Financial Analysts Journal*, vol. 57, no. 4 (July/August):60–76.

PRACTICE PROBLEMS

1 Given spot rates for one-, two-, and three-year zero coupon bonds, how many forward rates can be calculated?

2 Give two interpretations for the following forward rate: The two-year forward rate one year from now is 2%.

3 Describe the relationship between forward rates and spot rates if the yield curve is flat.

4 **A** Define the yield to maturity for a coupon bond.

   B Is it possible for a coupon bond to earn less than the yield to maturity if held to maturity?

5 If a bond trader believes that current forward rates overstate future spot rates, how might he or she profit from that conclusion?

6 Explain the strategy of riding the yield curve.

7 What are the advantages of using the swap curve as a benchmark of interest rates relative to a government bond yield curve?

8 Describe how the Z-spread can be used to price a bond.

9 What is the TED spread and what type of risk does it measure?

10 According to the local expectations theory, what would be the difference in the one-month total return if an investor purchased a five-year zero-coupon bond versus a two-year zero-coupon bond?

11 Compare the segmented market and the preferred habitat term structure theories.

12 **A** List the three factors that have empirically been observed to affect Treasury security returns and explain how each of these factors affects returns on Treasury securities.

   B What has been observed to be the most important factor in affecting Treasury returns?

   C Which measures of yield curve risk can measure shaping risk?

13 Which forward rate cannot be computed from the one-, two-, three-, and four-year spot rates? The rate for a:

   A one-year loan beginning in two years.

   B two-year loan beginning in two years.

   C three-year loan beginning in two years.

14 Consider spot rates for three zero-coupon bonds: $r(1) = 3\%$, $r(2) = 4\%$, and $r(3) = 5\%$. Which statement is correct? The forward rate for a one-year loan beginning in one year will be:

   A less than the forward rate for a one-year loan beginning in two-years.

   B greater than the forward rate for a two-year loan beginning in one-year.

   C greater than the forward rate for a one-year loan beginning in two-years.

15 If one-period forward rates are decreasing with maturity, the yield curve is *most likely*:

   A flat.

B   upward-sloping.

C   downward sloping.

The following information relates to Questions 16–29

A one-year zero-coupon bond yields 4.0%. The two- and three-year zero-coupon bonds yield 5.0% and 6.0% respectively.

16 The rate for a one-year loan beginning in one year is *closest* to:

    A   4.5%.

    B   5.0%.

    C   6.0%.

17 The forward rate for a two-year loan beginning in one year is *closest* to:

    A   5.0%

    B   6.0%

    C   7.0%

18 The forward rate for a one-year loan beginning in two years is *closest* to:

    A   6.0%

    B   7.0%

    C   8.0%

19 The five-year spot rate is not given above; however, the forward price for a two-year zero-coupon bond beginning in three years is known to be 0.8479. The price today of a five-year zero-coupon bond is *closest* to:

    A   0.7119.

    B   0.7835.

    C   0.9524.

20 The one-year spot rate $r(1) = 4\%$, the forward rate for a one-year loan beginning in one year is 6%, and the forward rate for a one-year loan beginning in two years is 8%. Which of the following rates is *closest* to the three-year spot rate?

    A   4.0%

    B   6.0%

    C   8.0%

21 The one-year spot rate $r(1) = 5\%$ and the forward price for a one-year zero-coupon bond beginning in one year is 0.9346. The spot price of a two-year zero-coupon bond is *closest* to:

    A   0.87.

    B   0.89.

    C   0.93.

22 In a typical interest rate swap contract, the swap rate is *best* described as the interest rate for the:

    A   fixed-rate leg of the swap.

    B   floating-rate leg of the swap.

    C   difference between the fixed and floating legs of the swap.

23 A two-year fixed-for-floating Libor swap is 1.00% and the two-year US Treasury bond is yielding 0.63%. The swap spread is *closest* to:

  A   37 bps.

  B   100 bps.

  C   163 bps.

24 The swap spread is quoted as 50 bps. If the five-year US Treasury bond is yielding 2%, the rate paid by the fixed payer in a five-year interest rate swap is *closest* to:

  A   0.50%.

  B   1.50%.

  C   2.50%.

25 If the three-month T-bill rate drops and the Libor rate remains the same, the relevant TED spread:

  A   increases.

  B   decreases.

  C   does not change.

26 Given the yield curve for US Treasury zero-coupon bonds, which spread is *most* helpful pricing a corporate bond? The:

  A   Z-Spread.

  B   TED spread.

  C   Libor–OIS spread.

27 A four-year corporate bond with a 7% coupon has a Z-spread of 200 bps. Assume a flat yield curve with an interest rate for all maturities of 5% and annual compounding. The bond will *most likely* sell:

  A   close to par.

  B   at a premium to par.

  C   at a discount to par.

28 The Z-spread of Bond A is 1.05% and the Z-spread of Bond B is 1.53%. All else equal, which statement *best* describes the relationship between the two bonds?

  A   Bond B is safer and will sell at a lower price.

  B   Bond B is riskier and will sell at a lower price.

  C   Bond A is riskier and will sell at a higher price.

29 Which term structure model can be calibrated to closely fit an observed yield curve?

  A   The Ho–Lee Model

  B   The Vasicek Model

  C   The Cox–Ingersoll–Ross Model

SOLUTIONS

1 Three forward rates can be calculated from the one-, two- and three-year spot rates. The rate on a one-year loan that begins at the end of Year 1 can be calculated using the one- and two-year spot rates; in the following equation one would solve for $f(1,1)$:

$$[1 + r(2)]^2 = [1 + r(1)]^1[1 + f(1,1)]^1$$

The rate on a one-year loan that starts at the end of Year 2 can be calculated from the two- and three-year spot rates; in the following equation one would solve for $f(2,1)$:

$$[1 + r(3)]^3 = [1 + r(2)]^2[1 + f(2,1)]^1$$

Additionally, the rate on a two-year loan that begins at the end of Year 1 can be computed from the one- and three-year spot rates; in the following equation one would solve for $f(1,2)$:

$$[1 + r(3)]^3 = [1 + r(1)]^1[1 + f(1,2)]^2$$

2 For the two-year forward rate one year from now of 2%, the two interpretations are as follows:

● 2% is the rate that will make an investor indifferent between buying a three-year zero-coupon bond or investing in a one-year zero-coupon bond and when it matures reinvesting in a zero-coupon bond that matures in two years.

● 2% is the rate that can be locked in today by buying a three-year zero-coupon bond rather than investing in a one-year zero-coupon bond and when it matures reinvesting in a zero-coupon bond that matures in two years.

3 A flat yield curve implies that all spot interest rates are the same. When the spot rate is the same for every maturity, successive applications of the forward rate model will show all the forward rates will also be the same and equal to the spot rate.

4 A The yield to maturity of a coupon bond is the expected rate of return on a bond if the bond is held to maturity, there is no default, and the bond and all coupons are reinvested at the original yield to maturity.

   B Yes, it is possible. For example, if reinvestment rates for the future coupons are lower than the initial yield to maturity, a bond holder may experience lower realized returns.

5 If forward rates are higher than expected future spot rates the market price of the bond will be lower than the intrinsic value. This is because, everything else held constant, the market is currently discounting the bonds cash flows at a higher rate than the investor's expected future spot rates. The investor can capitalize on this by purchasing the undervalued bond. If expected future spot rates are realized, then bond prices should rise, thus generating gains for the investor.

6 The strategy of riding the yield curve is one in which a bond trader attempts to generate a total return over a given investment horizon that exceeds the return to bond with maturity matched to the horizon. The strategy involves buying a bond with maturity more distant than the investment horizon. Assuming an upward sloping yield curve, if the yield curve does not change level or shape, as

the bond approaches maturity (or rolls down the yield curve) it will be priced at successively lower yields. So as long as the bond is held for a period less than maturity, it should generate higher returns because of price gains.

7   Some countries do not have active government bond markets with trading at all maturities. For those countries without a liquid government bond market but with an active swap market, there are typically more points available to construct a swap curve than a government bond yield curve. For those markets, the swap curve may be a superior benchmark.

8   The Z-spread is the constant basis point spread added to the default-free spot curve to correctly price a risky bond. A Z-spread of 100bps for a particular bond would imply that adding a fixed spread of 100bps to the points along the spot yield curve will correctly price the bond. A higher Z-spread would imply a riskier bond.

9   The TED spread is the difference between a Libor rate and the US T-Bill rate of matching maturity. It is an indicator of perceived credit risk in the general economy. I particular, because sovereign debt instruments are typically the benchmark for the lowest default risk instruments in a given market, and loans between banks (often at Libor) have some counterparty risk, the TED spread is considered to at least in part reflect default (or counterparty) risk in the banking sector.

10 The local expectations theory asserts that the total return over a one-month horizon for a five-year zero-coupon bond would be the same as for a two-year zero-coupon bond.

11 Both theories attempt to explain the shape of any yield curve in terms of supply and demand for bonds. In segmented market theory, bond market participants are limited to purchase of maturities that match the timing of their liabilities. In the preferred habitat theory, participants have a preferred maturity for asset purchases, but may deviate from it if they feel returns in other maturities offer sufficient compensation for leaving their preferred maturity segment.

12 **A**   Studies have shown that there have been three factors that affect Treasury returns: (1) changes in the level of the yield curve, (2) changes in the slope of the yield curve, and (3) changes in the curvature of the yield curve. Changes in the level refer to upward or downward shifts in the yield curve. For example, an upward shift in the yield curve is likely to result in lower returns across all maturities. Changes in the slope of the yield curve relate to the steepness of the yield curve. Thus, if the yield curve steepens it is likely to result in higher returns for short maturity bonds and lower returns for long maturity bonds. An example of a change in the curvature of the yield curve is a situation where rates fall at the short and long end of the yield curve while rising for intermediate maturities. In this situation returns on short and long maturities are likely to rise to rise while declining for intermediate maturity bonds.

B   Empirically, the most important factor is the change in the level of interest rates.

C   Key rate durations and a measure based on sensitivities to level, slope, and curvature movements can address shaping risk, but effective duration cannot.

13 C is correct. There is no spot rate information to provide rates for a loan that terminates in five years. That is $f(2,3)$ is calculated as follows:

$$f(2,3) = \sqrt[3]{\frac{[1+r(5)]^5}{[1+r(2)]^2}}$$

The equation above indicates that in order to calculate the rate for a three-year loan beginning at the end of two years you need the five year spot rate $r(5)$ and the two-year spot rate $r(2)$. However $r(5)$ is not provided.

14 A is correct. The forward rate for a one-year loan beginning in one-year $f(1,1)$ is $1.04^2/1.03 - 1 = 5\%$. The rate for a one-year loan beginning in two-years $f(2,1)$ is $1.05^3/1.04^2 - 1 = 7\%$. This confirms that an upward sloping yield curve is consistent with an upward sloping forward curve.

15 C is correct. If one-period forward rates are decreasing with maturity then the forward curve is downward sloping. This turn implies a downward sloping yield curve where longer term spot rates $r(T + T^*)$ are less than shorter term spot rates $r(T)$.

16 C is correct. From the forward rate model, we have

$$[1 + r(2)]^2 = [1 + r(1)]^1[1 + f(1,1)]^1$$

Using the one- and two-year spot rates, we have

$$(1 + .05)^2 = (1 + .04)^1[1 + f(1,1)]^1, \text{ so } \frac{(1 + .05)^2}{(1 + .04)^1} - 1 = f(1,1) = 6.010\%$$

17 C is correct. From the forward rate model,

$$[1 + r(3)]^3 = [1 + r(1)]^1[1 + f(1,2)]^2$$

Using the one and three-year spot rates, we find

$$(1 + 0.06)^3 = (1 + 0.04)^1[1 + f(1,2)]^2, \text{ so } \sqrt{\frac{(1 + 0.06)^3}{(1 + 0.04)^1}} - 1 = f(1,2) = 7.014\%$$

18 C is correct. From the forward rate model,

$$[1 + r(3)]^3 = [1 + r(2)]^2[1 + f(2,1)]^1$$

Using the two and three-year spot rates, we find

$$(1 + 0.06)^3 = (1 + 0.05)^2[1 + f(2,1)]^1, \text{ so } \frac{(1 + 0.06)^3}{(1 + 0.05)^2} - 1 = f(2,1) = 8.029\%$$

19 A is correct. We can convert spot rates to spot prices to find $P(3) = \dfrac{1}{(1.06)^3} = 0.8396$. The forward pricing model can be used to find the price of the five-year zero as $P(T^* + T) = P(T^*)F(T^*,T)$, so $P(5) = P(3)F(3,2) = 0.8396 \times 0.8479 = 0.7119$.

20 B is correct. Applying the forward rate model, we find

$$[1 + r(3)]^3 = [1 + r(1)]^1[1 + f(1,1)]^1[1 + f(2,1)]^1$$

So $[1 + r(3)]^3 = (1 + 0.04)^1(1 + 0.06)^1(1 + 0.08)^1$, $\sqrt[3]{1.1906} - 1 = r(3) = 5.987\%$.

21 B is correct. We can convert spot rates to spot prices and use the forward pricing model, so have $P(1) = \dfrac{1}{(1.05)^1} = 0.9524$. The forward pricing model is $P(T^* + T) = P(T^*)F(T^*,T)$ so $P(2) = P(1)F(1,1) = 0.9524 \times 0.9346 = 0.8901$.

22 A is correct. The swap rate is the interest rate for the fixed-rate leg of an interest rate swap.

23 A is correct. The swap spread = 1.00% – 0.63% = 0.37% or 37 bps.

24 C is correct. The fixed leg of the five-year fixed-for-floating swap will be equal to the five-year Treasury rate plus the swap spread: 2% + 0.5% = 2.5%.

25 A is correct. The TED spread is the difference between the three-month Libor rate and the three-month Treasury bill rate. If the T-bill rate falls and Libor does not change, the TED spread will increase.

26 A is correct. The Z-spread is the single rate which, when added to the rates of the spot yield curve, will provide the correct discount rates to price a particular risky bond.

27 A is correct. The 200bps Z-spread can be added to the 5% rates from the yield curve to price the bond. The resulting 7% discount rate will be the same for all of the bond's cash-flows, since the yield curve is flat. A 7% coupon bond yielding 7% will be priced at par.

28 B is correct. The higher Z-spread for Bond B implies it is riskier than Bond A. The higher discount rate will make the price of Bond B lower than Bond A.

29 A is correct. The Ho–Lee model is arbitrage-free and can be calibrated to closely match the observed term structure.

The Arbitrage-Free Valuation Framework

by Steven V. Mann, PhD

Steven V. Mann, PhD, is at the University of South Carolina (USA).

LEARNING OUTCOMES

Mastery	The candidate should be able to:
☐	a. explain what is meant by arbitrage-free valuation of a fixed-income instrument;
☐	b. calculate the arbitrage-free value of an option-free, fixed-rate coupon bond;
☐	c. describe a binomial interest rate tree framework;
☐	d. describe the backward induction valuation methodology and calculate the value of a fixed-income instrument given its cash flow at each node;
☐	e. describe the process of calibrating a binomial interest rate tree to match a specific term structure;
☐	f. compare pricing using the zero-coupon yield curve with pricing using an arbitrage-free binomial lattice;
☐	g. describe pathwise valuation in a binomial interest rate framework and calculate the value of a fixed-income instrument given its cash flows along each path;
☐	h. describe a Monte Carlo forward-rate simulation and its application.

INTRODUCTION

1

The idea that market prices will adjust until there are no opportunities for arbitrage underpins the valuation of fixed-income securities, derivatives, and other financial assets. It is as intuitive as it is well-known. For a given investment, if the net proceeds are zero (e.g., buying and selling the same dollar amount of stocks) and the risk is zero, the return should be zero. Valuation tools must produce a value that is arbitrage free. The purpose of this reading is to develop a set of valuation tools for bonds that are consistent with this notion.

The reading is organized around the learning objectives. After this brief introduction, Section 2 defines an arbitrage opportunity and discusses the implications of no arbitrage for the valuation of fixed-income securities. Section 3 presents some essential ideas and tools from yield curve analysis needed to introduce the binomial interest rate tree. In this section, the binomial interest rate tree framework is developed and used to value an option-free bond. The process used to calibrate the interest rate tree to match the current yield curve is introduced. This step ensures that the interest rate tree is consistent with pricing using the zero-coupon (i.e., spot) curve. The final topic presented in the section is an introduction of pathwise valuation. Section 4 describes a Monte Carlo forward-rate simulation and its application. A summary of the major results is given in Section 5.

2   THE MEANING OF ARBITRAGE-FREE VALUATION

Arbitrage-free valuation refers to an approach to security valuation that determines security values that are consistent with the absence of an **arbitrage opportunity**, which is an opportunity for trades that earn riskless profits without any net investment of money. In well-functioning markets, prices adjust until there are no arbitrage opportunities, which is the **principle of no arbitrage** that underlies the practical validity of arbitrage-free valuation. This principle itself can be thought of as an implication of the idea that identical assets should sell at the same price.

These concepts will be explained in greater detail shortly, but to indicate how they arise in bond valuation, consider first an imaginary world in which financial assets are free of risk and the benchmark yield curve is flat. A flat yield curve implies that the relevant yield is the same for all cash flows regardless of when the cash flows are delivered in time.[1] Accordingly, the value of a bond is the present value of its certain future cash flows. In discounting those cash flows—determining their present value—investors would use the risk-free interest rate because the cash flows are certain; because the yield curve is assumed to be flat, one risk-free rate would exist and apply to all future cash flows. This is the simplest case of bond valuation one can envision. When we exit this imaginary world and enter more realistic environs, bonds' cash flows are risky (i.e., there is some chance the borrower will default) and the benchmark yield curve is not flat. How would our approach change?

A fundamental principle of valuation is that the value of any financial asset is equal to the present value of its expected future cash flows. This principle holds for any financial asset from zero-coupon bonds to interest rate swaps. Thus, the valuation of a financial asset involves the following three steps:

Step 1   Estimate the future cash flows.

Step 2   Determine the appropriate discount rate or discount rates that should be used to discount the cash flows.

Step 3   Calculate the present value of the expected future cash flows found in Step 1 by applying the appropriate discount rate or rates determined in Step 2.

The traditional approach to valuing bonds is to discount all cash flows with the same discount rate as if the yield curve were flat. However, a bond is properly thought of as a package or portfolio of zero-coupon bonds. Each zero-coupon bond in such a package can be valued separately at a discount rate that depends on the shape of the

---

1 The terms yield, interest rate, and discount rate will be used interchangeably.

yield curve and when its single cash flow is delivered in time. The term structure of these discount rates is referred to as the spot curve. Bond values derived by summing the present values of the individual zeros (cash flows) determined by such a procedure can be shown to be arbitrage free.[2] Ignoring transaction costs for the moment, if the bond's value was much less than the sum of the values of its cash flows individually, a trader would perceive an arbitrage opportunity and buy the bond while selling claims to the individual cash flows and pocketing the excess value. Although the details bear further discussion (see Section 2.3), the valuation of a bond as a portfolio of zeros based on using the spot curve is an example of arbitrage-free valuation. Regardless of the complexity of the bond, each component must have an arbitrage-free value. A bond with embedded options can be valued in parts as the sum of the arbitrage-free bond without options (that is, a bond with no embedded options) and the arbitrage-free value of each of the options.

2.1 The Law of One Price

The central idea of financial economics is that market prices will adjust until there are no opportunities for arbitrage. We will define shortly what is meant by an arbitrage opportunity, but for now think of it as "free money." Prices will adjust until there is no free money to be acquired. Arbitrage opportunities arise as a result of violations of the **law of one price**. The law of one price states that two goods that are perfect substitutes must sell for the same current price in the absence of transaction costs. Two goods that are identical, trading side by side, are priced the same. Otherwise, if it were costless to trade, one would simultaneously buy at the lower price and sell at the higher price. The riskless profit is the difference in the prices. An individual would repeat this transaction without limit until the two prices converge. An implication of these market forces is deceptively straightforward and basic. If you do not put up any of your own money and take no risk, your expected return should be zero.

2.2 Arbitrage Opportunity

With this background, let us define arbitrage opportunity more precisely. An arbitrage opportunity is a transaction that involves no cash outlay that results in a riskless profit. There are two types of arbitrage opportunities. The first type of arbitrage opportunity is often called **value additivity** or, put simply, the value of the whole equals the sum of the values of the parts. Consider two risk-free investments with payoffs one year from today and the prices today provided in Exhibit 1. Asset A is a simple risk-free zero-coupon bond that pays off one dollar and is priced today at 0.952381 ($1/1.05). Asset B is a portfolio of 105 units of Asset A that pays off $105 one year from today and is priced today at $95. The portfolio does not equal the sum of the parts. The portfolio (Asset B) is cheaper than buying 105 units of Asset A at a price of $100 and then combining. An astute investor would sell 105 units of Asset A for 105 × $0.952381 = $100 while simultaneously buying one portfolio Asset B for $95. This position generates a certain $5 today ($100-95) and generates net $0 one year from today because cash inflow for Asset B matches the amount for the 105 units of Asset A sold. An investor would engage in this trade over and over again until the prices adjust.

The second type of arbitrage opportunity is often called **dominance**. A financial asset with a risk-free payoff in the future must have a positive price today. Consider two assets, C and D, that are risk-free zero-coupon bonds. Payoffs in one year and prices today are displayed in Exhibit 1. On careful review, it appears that Asset D is cheap relative to Asset C. If both assets are risk-free, they should have the same

---

2 A zero is a zero-coupon bond or discount instrument.

discount rate. To make money, sell two units of Asset C at a price of $200 and use the proceeds to purchase one unit of Asset D for $200. The construction of the portfolio involves no net cash outlay today. Although it requires zero dollars to construct today, the portfolio generates $10 one year from today. Asset D will generate a $220 cash inflow whereas the two units of Asset C sold will produce a cash outflow of $210.

Exhibit 1	Price Today and Payoffs in One Year for Sample Assets	
Asset	Price Today	Payoff in One Year
A	$0.952381	$1
B	$95	$105
C	$100	$105
D	$200	$220

This existence of both types of arbitrage opportunities is transitory. Investors aware of this mispricing will demand the securities in question in unlimited quantities. Something must change in order to restore stability. Prices will adjust until there are no arbitrage opportunities.

EXAMPLE 1

Arbitrage Opportunities

Which of the following investment alternatives includes an arbitrage opportunity?

Bond A: The yield for a 3% coupon 10-year annual-pay bond is 2.5% in New York City. The same bond sells for $104.376 per $100 face value in Chicago.

Bond B: The yield for a 3% coupon 10-year annual-pay bond is 3.2% in Hong Kong. The same bond sells for RMB97.220 per RMB100 face value in Shanghai.

Solution:

Bond B is correct. Bond B's arbitrage-free price is $3/1.032 + 3/1.032^2 + ... + 103/1.032^{10} = 98.311$, which is higher than the price in Shanghai. Therefore, an arbitrage opportunity exists. Buy bonds in Shanghai for RMB97.220 and sell them in Hong Kong for RMB98.311. You make RMB1.091 per RMB100 of bonds traded.

Bond A's arbitrage-free price is $3/1.025 + 3/1.025^2 + ... + 103/1.025^{10} = 104.376$, which matches the price in Chicago. Therefore, no arbitrage opportunity exists in this market.

2.3 Implications of Arbitrage-Free Valuation for Fixed-Income Securities

Using the arbitrage-free approach, any fixed-income security should be thought of as a package or portfolio of zero-coupon bonds. Thus, a five-year 2% coupon Treasury issue should be viewed as a package of eleven zero-coupon instruments (10 semiannual coupon payments, one of which is made at maturity, and one principal value payment at maturity) The market mechanism for US Treasuries that enables this approach is the dealer's ability to separate the bond's individual cash flows and trade them as zero-coupon securities. This process is called **stripping**. In addition, dealers can recombine the appropriate individual zero-coupon securities and reproduce the underlying coupon Treasury. This process is called **reconstitution**. Dealers in sovereign debt markets around the globe are free to engage in the same process.

Arbitrage profits are possible when value additivity does not hold. The arbitrage-free valuation approach does not allow a market participant to realize an arbitrage profit through stripping and reconstitution. By viewing any security as a package of zero-coupon securities, a consistent and coherent valuation framework can be developed. Viewing a security as a package of zero-coupon bonds means that two bonds with the same maturity and different coupon rates are viewed as different packages of zero-coupon bonds and valued accordingly. Moreover, two cash flows that have identical risks delivered at the same time will be valued using the same discount rate even though they are attached to two different bonds.

INTEREST RATE TREES AND ARBITRAGE-FREE VALUATION

3

The goal of this section is to develop a method to produce an arbitrage-free value for an option-free bond and to provide a framework—based on interest rate trees–that is rich enough to be applied to the valuation of bonds with embedded options.

For bonds that are option-free, the simplest approach to arbitrage-free valuation involves determining the arbitrage-free value as the sum of the present values of expected future values using the benchmark spot rates. Benchmark securities are liquid, safe securities whose yields serve as building blocks for other interest rates in a particular country or currency. Sovereign debt is the benchmark in many countries. For example, on-the-run Treasuries serve as benchmark securities in the United States. Par rates derived from the Treasury yield curve can be used to obtain spot rates by means of bootstrapping. Gilts serve as a benchmark in the United Kingdom. In markets where the sovereign debt market is not sufficiently liquid, the swaps curve is a viable alternative.

In this reading, benchmark bonds are assumed to be correctly priced by the market. The valuation model we develop will be constructed so as to reproduce exactly the prices of the benchmark bonds.

EXAMPLE 2

The Arbitrage-Free Value of an Option-Free Bond

The yield to maturity ("par rate") for a benchmark one-year annual-pay bond is 2%, for a benchmark two-year annual-pay bond is 3%, and for a benchmark three-year annual-pay bond is 4%. A three year, 5% coupon, annual-pay bond with the same risk and liquidity as the benchmarks is selling for $102.7751 today (time zero) to yield 4%. Is this value correct for the bond given the current term structure?

Solution:

The first step in the solution is to find the correct spot rate (zero-coupon rates) for each year's cash flow.[3] The spot rates may be determined using bootstrapping, which is an iterative process. Using the bond valuation equation below, one can solve iteratively for the spot rates, z_t (rate on a zero-coupon bond of maturity t), given the periodic payment, PMT, on the relevant benchmark bond.

$$100 = \frac{PMT}{(1+z_1)^1} + \frac{PMT}{(1+z_2)^2} + \cdots + \frac{PMT+100}{(1+z_N)^N}$$

A revised equation, which uses the par rate rather than PMT, may also be used to calculate the spot rates. The revised equation is:

$$1 = \frac{\text{Par rate}}{[1+r(1)]^1} + \frac{\text{Par rate}}{[1+r(2)]^2} + \cdots + \frac{\text{Par rate}+1}{[1+r(N)]^N}$$

where par rate is PMT divided by 100 and represents the par rate on the benchmark bond and $r(t)$ is the t-period zero-coupon rate.

In this example, the one-year spot rate, $r(1)$, is 2%, which is the same as the one-year par rate. To solve for $r(2)$:

$$1 = \frac{0.03}{[1+r(1)]^1} + \frac{0.03+1}{[1+r(2)]^2} = \frac{0.03}{(1+0.02)^1} + \frac{0.03+1}{[1+r(2)]^2}$$

$r(2) = 3.015\%$

To solve for $r(3)$:

$$1 = \frac{0.04}{(1+0.02)^1} + \frac{0.04}{(1+0.03015)^2} + \frac{0.04+1}{[1+r(3)]^3}$$

$r(3) = 4.055\%$

The spot rates are 2%, 3.015%, and 4.055%. The correct arbitrage-free price for the bond, then, is

$P_0 = 5/1.02 + 5/1.03015^2 + 105/1.04055^3 = \$102.8102$

To be arbitrage-free, each cash flow of a bond must be discounted by the spot rate for zero-coupon bonds maturing on the same date as the cash flow. Discounting early coupons by the bond's yield to maturity gives too much discounting with an upward sloping yield curve and too little discounting for a downward sloping yield curve. The bond is mispriced by $0.0351 per $100 of par value.

For option-free bonds, performing valuation discounting with spot rates produces an arbitrage-free valuation. For bonds that have embedded options, we need a different approach. The challenge one faces when developing a framework for valuing bonds with embedded options is that their expected future cash flows are interest rate dependent. If the bonds are option-free, changes in interest rates have no impact on the size and timing of the bond's cash flows. For bonds with options attached, changes in future interest rates impact the likelihood the option will be exercised and in so doing impact the cash flows. Therefore, in order to develop a framework that values both bonds without and with embedded options, we must allow interest rates to take on different potential values in the future based on some assumed level of volatility. The vehicle to portray this information is an interest rate "tree" representing possible future interest rates consistent with the assumed volatility. Because the interest rate

---

3 Par, spot, and forward interest rates were discussed in Level I.

tree resembles a lattice, these models are often called "lattice models." The interest rate tree performs two functions in the valuation process: (1) generate the cash flows that are interest rate dependent and (2) supply the interest rates used to determine the present value of the cash flows. This approach will be used in later readings when considering learning outcome statements involving callable bonds.

An interest rate model seeks to identify the elements or *factors* that are believed to explain the dynamics of interest rates. These factors are random or *stochastic* in nature, so we cannot predict the path of any particular factor. An interest rate model must, therefore, specify a statistical process that describes the stochastic property of these factors in order to arrive at a reasonably accurate representation of the behavior of interest rates. What is important to understand is that the interest rate models commonly used are based on how short-term interest rates can evolve (i.e., change) over time. Consequently, these interest rate models are referred to as one-factor models because only one interest rate is being modeled over time. More complex models consider how more than one interest rate changes over time (e.g., the short rate and the long rate) and are referred to as two-factor models.

Our task at hand is to describe the binomial interest rate tree framework. The valuation model we are attempting to build is the binomial lattice model. It is so named because the short interest rate can take on one of two possible values consistent with the volatility assumption and an interest rate model. As we will soon discover, the two possible interest rates next period will be consistent with the following three conditions: (1) an interest rate model that governs the random process of interest rates, (2) the assumed level of interest rate volatility, and (3) the current benchmark yield curve. We take the prices of the benchmark bonds as given such that when these bonds are valued in our model we recover the market values for each benchmark bond. In this way, we tie the model to the current yield curve that reflects the underlying economic reality.

3.1 The Binomial Interest Rate Tree

The first stop for demonstrating the binomial valuation method is to present the benchmark par curve by using bonds of a particular country or currency. For simplicity in our illustration, we will use US dollars. The same principles hold with equal force regardless of the country or currency. The benchmark par curve is presented in Exhibit 2. For simplicity, we assume that all bonds have annual coupon payments. Benchmark bonds are conveniently priced at par so the yields to maturity and the coupon rates on the bonds are the same. From these par rates, we use the bootstrapping methodology to uncover the underlying spot rates shown in Exhibit 3. Because the par curve is upward sloping, it comes as no surprise that after Year 1 the spot rates are higher than the par rates. In Exhibit 4 we present the one-year implied forward rates derived from the spot curve using no arbitrage. Because the par, spot, and forward curves reflect the same information about interest rates, if one of the three curves is known, it is possible to generate the other two curves. The three curves are only identical if the yield curve is flat.

Exhibit 2	Benchmark Par Curve	
Maturity (Years)	**Par Rate**	**Bond Price**
1	1.00%	100
2	1.20%	100
3	1.25%	100

(continued)

Exhibit 2	(Continued)	
Maturity (Years)	**Par Rate**	**Bond Price**
4	1.40%	100
5	1.80%	100

Exhibit 3	Underlying One-Year Spot Rates of Par Rates
Maturity (Years)	**One-Year Spot Rate**
1	1.000%
2	1.201%
3	1.251%
4	1.404%
5	1.819%

Exhibit 4	One-Year Implied Forward Rates
Maturity (Years)	**Forward Rate**
Current one-year rate	1.000%
One-year rate, one year forward	1.400%
One-year rate, two years forward	1.350%
One-year rate, three years forward	1.860%
One-year rate, four years forward	3.500%

Recall from our earlier discussion that if we value the benchmark bonds using rates derived from these curves, we will recover the market price of par for all five bonds in Exhibit 2. Specifically, par rates represent the single interest applied to all the cash flows that will produce the market prices. Discounting each cash flow separately with the set of spot rates will also give the same answer. Finally, forward rates are the discount rates of a single cash flow over a single period. If we discount each cash flow with the appropriate discount rate for each period, the computed values will match the observed prices.

When we approach the valuation of bonds with cash flows that are interest rate dependent, we must explicitly allow interest rates to change. We accomplish this task by introducing interest rate volatility and generating an interest rate tree (see Section 3.2 for a discussion of interest rate volatility). An interest rate tree is simply a visual representation of the possible values of interest rates based on an interest rate model and an assumption about interest rate volatility.

A binomial interest rate tree is presented in Exhibit 5. Our goal is to learn how to populate this structure with interest rates. Notice the i's, which represent different potential values one-year interest rates may take over time. As we move from left to right on the tree, the number of possible interest rates increases. The first is the current time (in years), or formally Time 0. The interest rate displayed at Time 0 is the discount rate that converts Time 1 payments to Time 0 present values. At the bottom of the graph, time is the unit of measurement. Notice that there is one year between possible interest rates. This is called the "time step" and, in our illustration, it matches the frequency of the annual cash flows. The i's in Exhibit 5 are called nodes. The first node is called the root of the tree and is simply the current one-year rate at Time 0.

Exhibit 5   Binomial Interest Rate Tree

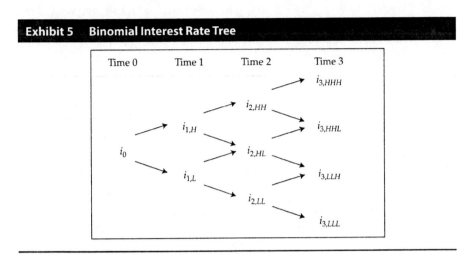

We now turn to the question of how to obtain the two possible values for the one-year interest rate one year from today. Two assumptions are required: an interest rate model and a volatility of interest rates. Recall an interest rate model puts structure on the randomness. We are going to use the lognormal random walk, and the resulting tree structure is often referred to as a lognormal tree. A lognormal model of interest rates insures two appealing properties: (1) non-negativity of interest rates and (2) higher volatility at higher interest rates. At each node, there are two possible rates one year forward at Time 1. We will assume for the time being that each has an equal probability of occurring. The two possible rates we will calculate are going to be higher and lower than the one-year forward rate at Time 1 one year from now.

We denote i_L to be the rate lower than the implied forward rate and i_H to be the higher forward rate. The lognormal random walk posits the following relationship between $i_{1,L}$ and $i_{1,H}$:

$$i_{1,H} = i_{1,L}e^{2\sigma}$$

where σ is the standard deviation and e is Euler's number, the base of natural logarithms, which is a constant 2.7183.[4] The random possibilities each period are (nearly) centered on the forward rates calculated from the benchmark curve. The intuition of this relationship is deceptively quick and simple. Think of the one-year forward implied interest rate from the yield curve as the average of possible values for the one-year rate at Time 1. The lower of the two rates, i_L, is one standard deviation below the mean (one-year implied forward rate) and i_H is one standard deviation above the mean. Thus, the higher and lower values (i_L and i_H) are multiples of each other and the multiplier is $e^{2\sigma}$. Note that as the standard deviation (i.e., volatility) increases, the multiplier increases and the two rates will grow farther apart but will still be (nearly) centered on the implied forward rate derived from the spot curve. We will demonstrate this soon.

---

4 The number e is transcendental and continues infinitely without repeating.

We use the following notation to describe the tree at Time 1. Let

σ = assumed volatility of the one-year rate,

$i_{1,L}$ = the lower one-year forward rate one year from now at Time 1, and

$i_{1,H}$ = the higher one-year forward rate one year from now at Time 1.

For example, suppose that $i_{1,L}$ is 1.194% and σ is 15% per year, then $i_{1,H}$ = $1.194\%(e^{2\times0.15})$ = 1.612%.

At Time 2, there are three possible values for the one-year rate, which we will denote as follows:

$i_{2,LL}$ = one-year forward rate at Time 2 assuming the lower rate at Time 1 and the lower rate at Time 2

$i_{2,HH}$ = one-year forward rate at Time 2 assuming the higher rate at Time 1 and the higher rate at Time 2

$i_{2,HL}$ = one-year forward rate at Time 2 assuming the higher rate at Time 1 and the lower rate at Time 2, or equivalently, the lower rate at Time 1 and the higher rate at Time 2

The middle rate will be close to the implied one-year forward rate one year from now derived from the spot curve, whereas the other two rates are two standard deviations above and below this value. (Recall that the multiplier for adjacent rates on the tree differs by a multiple of e raised to the 2σ.) This type of tree is called a recombining tree because there are two paths to get to the middle rate. This feature of the model results in faster computation because the number of possible outcomes each period grows linearly rather than exponentially.

The relationship between $i_{2,LL}$ and the other two one-year rates is as follows:

$i_{2,HH}$ = $i_{2,LL}(e^{4\sigma})$ and $i_{2,HL}$ = $i_{2,LL}(e^{2\sigma})$

In a given period, adjacent possible outcomes in the tree are two standard deviations apart. So, for example, if $i_{2,LL}$ is 0.980%, and assuming once again that σ is 15%, we calculate

$i_{2,HH}$ = $0.980\%(e^{4\times0.15})$ = 1.786%

and

$i_{2,HL}$ = $0.980\%(e^{2\times0.15})$ = 1.323%.

There are four possible values for the one-year forward rate at Time 3. These are represented as follows: $i_{3,HHH}$, $i_{3,HHL}$, $i_{3,LLH}$ and $i_{3,LLL}$. Once again all the forward rates in the tree are multiples of the lowest possible rates each year. The lowest possible forward rate at Time 3 is $i_{3,LLL}$ and is related to the other three as given below:

$i_{3,HHH}$ = $(e^{6\sigma})i_{3,LLL}$

$i_{3,HHL}$ = $(e^{4\sigma})i_{3,LLL}$

$i_{3,LLH}$ = $(e^{2\sigma})i_{3,LLL}$

Exhibit 6 shows the notation for a four-year binomial interest rate tree. We can simplify the notation by centering the one-year rates on the tree on implied forward rates on the benchmark yield curve and letting i_t be the one-year rate t years from now be the centering rates. The subscripts indicate the rates at the end of the year, so in the second year, it is the rate at the end of Time 2 to the end of Time 3. Exhibit 6 uses this uniform notation. Note that adjacent forward rates in the tree are two standard deviations (σs) apart.

Exhibit 6	Four-Year Binomial Tree

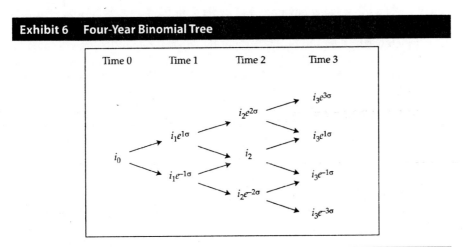

Before we attempt to build an interest rate tree, two additional tools are needed. These tools are introduced in the next two sections.

3.2 What Is Volatility and How Is It Estimated?

Recall that variance is a measure of dispersion of a probability distribution. The standard deviation is the square root of the variance and it is a statistical measure of volatility in the same units as the mean. With a simple lognormal distribution, the changes in interest rates are proportional to the level of the one-period interest rates each period. Volatility is measured relative to the current level of rates. It can be shown that for a lognormal distribution the standard deviation of the one-year rate is equal to $i_0\sigma$.[5] For example, if σ is 10% and the one-year rate (i_0) is 2%, then the standard deviation of the one-year rate is 2% × 10% = 0.2% or 20 bps. As a result, interest rate moves are larger when interest rates are high and are smaller when interest rates are low. One of the benefits of a lognormal distribution is that if interest rates get too close to zero, the absolute change in interest rates becomes smaller and smaller. Negative interest rates are not possible.

There are two methods commonly used to estimate interest rate volatility. The first method is by estimating historical interest rate volatility; volatility is calculated by using data from the recent past with the assumption that what has happened recently is indicative of the future. A second method to estimate interest rate volatility is based on observed market prices of interest rate derivatives (e.g., swaptions, caps, floors). This approach is called implied volatility.

3.3 Determining the Value of a Bond at a Node

To find the value of the bond at a particular node, we use the backward induction valuation methodology. Barring default, we know that at maturity the bonds will be valued at par. So, we start at maturity, fill in those values, and work back from right to left to find the bond's value at the desired node. Suppose we want to determine the bond's value at the lowest node at Time 1. To find this value, we must first calculate the bond's value at the two nodes to the right of the node we selected. The bond's value at the two nodes immediately to the right must be available.

---

5 Given that $e^{2\sigma} \approx 1 + 2\sigma$, the standard deviation of the one-year rate is $\dfrac{re^{2\sigma} - r}{2} \approx \dfrac{r + 2\sigma r - r}{2} = \sigma r$.

A bond's value at any node will depend on the future cash flows. For a coupon-paying bond, the cash flows are the periodic coupon payments one period from now, which will not depend on the level of the interest rate or the bond's value one year from now. Unlike the coupon payment, the bond's value one year from now will depend on the one-year rate chance selects. Specifically, the bond's value depends on whether the one-year rate is the higher or lower rate. At any given node at which the valuation is sought, these cash flows are reported in the two nodes immediately to the right of that node. The bond's value depends on whether the rate is the higher or lower rate and its value reported at the two nodes to the right of the node at which we are valuing the bond. This is illustrated in Exhibit 7.

Exhibit 7   Finding a Bond's Value at Any Node

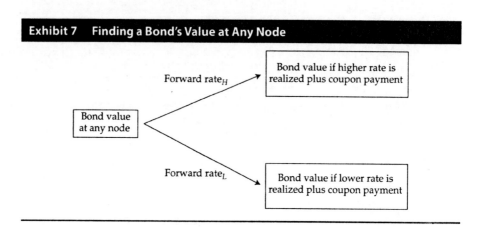

Now that we have specified the cash flows, the next step is to determine the present value of those cash flows. The relevant discount rate to use is the one-year forward rate at the node. Because there are two possible interest rates one year from today, there are two present values to calculate. The two states of the world are whether chance selects the higher or lower one-year forward rate one year hence. Because it is assumed that either outcome is equally likely, the average of the two present values is computed. This same procedure holds for any node with forward rates discounting cash flows moving from node to node.

Let us make this process more complete by introducing some notation. Assume that the one-year forward rate is i at a particular node and let

VH = the bond's value if the higher forward rate is realized one year hence,
VL = the bond's value if the lower forward rate is realized one year hence, and
C = coupon payment that is not dependent on interest rates.

At any node, the cash flows one year from today are the coupon payment plus the bond's value if chance chooses the higher one-year forward rate ($C + VH$) and the coupon payment plus the bond's value if chance chooses the lower forward rate ($C + VL$). A bond's value at any node is determined by the following expression:

$$\text{Bond value at a node} = 0.50 \times \left[\frac{VH + C}{(1 + i)} + \frac{VL + C}{(1 + i)} \right] \qquad \text{(1)}$$

EXAMPLE 3

Pricing a Bond Using a Binomial Tree

Using the interest rate tree below, find the correct price for a three-year, annual-pay bond with a coupon rate of 5%.

Exhibit 8   Three-Year Binomial Interest Rate Tree

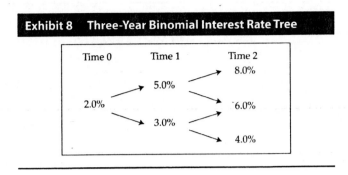

Solution:

Calculating the bond's value includes being careful with the timing of cash flows. A three-year bond pays coupons and returns principal at the *end* of each year. When we state an annual interest rate, that rate is effective as of the *beginning* of that year.

Exhibit 9   Three-Year Binomial Tree

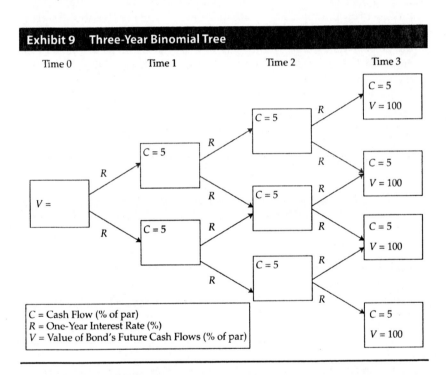

C = Cash Flow (% of par)
R = One-Year Interest Rate (%)
V = Value of Bond's Future Cash Flows (% of par)

No matter what level interest rates move to at Time 3, the cash flow from a three-year bond at Time 3 will be the same: par plus a final coupon payment. In addition, a coupon payment will be made at Time 2. Consequently, Time 2 values will be:

Time 0	Time 1	Time 2
		$0.5 \times [(105/1.08 + 105/1.08)] + 5 = 102.2222$
		$0.5 \times [(105/1.06 + 105/1.06)] + 5 = 104.0566$
		$0.5 \times [(105/1.04 + 105/1.04)] + 5 = 105.9615$

Time 1 values will be the average of Time 2 discounted plus the coupon payment:

Time 0	Time 1
	$0.5 \times [(102.2222/1.05 + 104.0566/1.05)] + 5 = 103.2280$
	$0.5 \times [(104.0566/1.03 + 105.9615/1.03)] + 5 = 106.9506$

Finally, we bring the price back to Time 0. Because no time has elapsed, there is no coupon payment at Time 0, making the Time 0 value the average of the Time 1 values discounted to today:

Time 0
$0.5 \times [(103.2280/1.02 + 106.9506/1.02)] = 103.0287$

3.4 Constructing the Binomial Interest Rate Tree

The construction of a binomial interest rate tree requires multiple steps, but keep in mind what we are trying to accomplish. We are making an assumption about the process that generates interest rates and volatility. The first step is to describe the process of calibrating a binomial interest rate tree to match a specific term structure. We do this to ensure that the model is arbitrage free. We fit the interest rate tree to the current yield curve by choosing interest rates so that the model produces the benchmark bond values reported in Section 3.1. By doing this, we tie the model to the underlying economic reality.

Recall from Exhibits 2, 3, and 4 the benchmark bond price information and the relevant par, spot, and forward curves. We will assume that volatility, σ, is 15% and construct a two-year tree using the two-year bond that carries a coupon rate of 1.2%. A complete four-year binomial interest rate tree is presented in Exhibit 10. We will demonstrate how these rates are determined. The current one-year rate is 1%, i_0.

Exhibit 10	Four-Year Binomial Interest Rate Tree		
Time 0	Time 1	Time 2	Time 3
1.0000%	1.6121%	1.7862%	2.8338%
	1.1943%	1.3233%	2.0994%
		0.9803%	1.5552%
			1.1521%

Finding the rates in the tree is an iterative process, and the interest rates are found numerically. There are two possible rates that will discount cash flows from Time 2 to Time 1—the higher rate and the lower rate. We observe these rates one year from today. These two rates must be consistent with the volatility assumption, the interest rate model, and the observed market value of the benchmark bond. Assume that the interest rate volatility is 15%. From our discussion earlier, we know that at Time 1 the lower one-year rate is lower than the implied one-year forward rate and the higher rate is a multiple of the lower rate. We iterate to a solution with constraints in mind. Once we select these rates, how will we know the rates are correct? The answer is when we discount the cash flows using the tree and produce a value that matches the price of the two-year benchmark bond. If the model does not produce the correct price with this result, we need to select another forward rate and repeat the process. The process of calibrating a binomial interest rate tree to match a specific term structure is illustrated in the following paragraphs.

Suppose we use an analytic tool, such as Solver in Excel, to carry out this calculation and it produces a value for $i_{1,L}$ of 1.1943%. This is the lower one-year rate. The higher one-year rate is 1.6121% [= $1.1943\%(e^{2\times0.15})$]. Recall from the information on the benchmark bonds, that the two-year bond will pay its maturity value of $100 in Time 2 and an annual coupon payment of $1.20. The bond's value at Time 2 is $101.20. The present value of the coupon payment plus the bond's maturity value if the higher one-year rate is realized, VH, is $99.59444 (= $101.20/1.016121). Alternatively, the present value of the coupon payment plus the bond's maturity value if the lower one-year rate is realized, VL, is $100.00563 (= $101.20/1.011943). These two calculations determine the bond's value one year forward. Effectively, the forward rates move the bond's value from Time 2 to Time 1.

100	99.59444 + 1.20	100 + 1.20
	100.00563 + 1.20	100 + 1.20
		100 + 1.20

To find the value today, we discount the coupon payment and bond values just obtained (VH and VL). Including the coupon payment, we obtain $100.79444 ($99.59444 + $1.20) as the cash flow for the higher rate and $101.20563 ($100.00563 + $1.20) as the cash flow for the lower rate. We use the current one year rate to obtain the present value of the two cash flows as follows:

$$\frac{VH + C}{1 + i} = \frac{\$100.79444}{1.01000} = \$99.79647$$

and

$$\frac{VL + C}{1 + i} = \frac{\$101.20563}{1.01} = 100.20360$$

Multiplying each present value by 0.5, we obtain a bond value of $100, which is the price of the two-year benchmark bond. The model produces the same value as the market, so we take rates 1.1943% and 1.6121% as the forward rates at Time 1.

1%	1.6122%
	1.1943%

To build out the tree one more year, we repeat the same process, this time using a three-year benchmark bond with a coupon rate of 1.25%. Now, we are looking for three forward rates that are consistent with (1) the interest rate model assumed, (2) the assumed volatility of 15%, (3) a current one-year rate of 1.0%, and (4) the two possible forward rates one year from now (at Time 1) of 1.1943% (the lower rate) and 1.6121% (the higher rate), as shown in Exhibit 11.

Exhibit 11   Finding Forward Rates for Binomial Tree

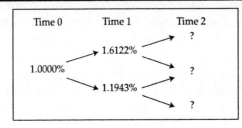

At Time 3, we receive the final coupon payment and maturity value. In Exhibit 12, we see these values filled in for the three-year benchmark bond and three forward rates we must find. These are the rates from previous calculations. We simply work backward from right to left to obtain these values.

Exhibit 12	Working Backward to Find Forward Rates		
Time 0	**Time 1**	**Time 2**	**Time 3**
100	?	?	101.25
	?	?	101.25
		?	101.25
			101.25

We selected a value for $i_{2,LL}$, which is 0.9803% and is below the implied one-year forward rate, two years hence. All of the other forward rates are multiples of this rate. The corresponding rates for $i_{2,HL}$ and $i_{2,HH}$ would be 1.3233% and 1.7863%, respectively. To demonstrate that these are the correct values, we simply work backward from the four nodes at Time 3 of the tree in Exhibit 12. The same procedure is used to obtain the values at the other nodes. The completed tree is shown in Exhibit 13.

Exhibit 13	Completed Binomial Tree with Calculated Forward Rates

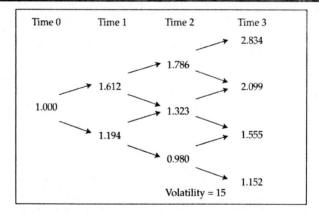

Let us focus on the impact of volatility on the possible forward rates in the tree. If we were to use a higher estimate of volatility, say 20%, the possible forward rates should spread out on the tree. If we were to use a lower estimate of volatility, say 0.01%, the rates should collapse to the implied forward rates from the current yield curve. Exhibits 14 and 15 depict the interest rate trees for the volatilities of 20% and 0.01%, respectively, and confirm the expected outcome.

Exhibit 14	Completed Tree with σ = 20%		
Time 0	**Time 1**	**Time 2**	**Time 3**
1.0000%	1.6806%	1.9415%	3.2134%
	1.1265%	1.3014%	2.1540%

Exhibit 14   (Continued)

Time 0	Time 1	Time 2	Time 3
		0.8724%	1.4439%
			0.9678%

Exhibit 15   Completed Tree with σ = 0.01%

Time 0	Time 1	Time 2	Time 3
1.0000%	1.4029%	1.3523%	1.8653%
	1.4026%	1.3521%	1.8649%
		1.3518%	1.8645%
			1.8641%

EXAMPLE 4

Calibrating a Binomial Tree to Match a Specific Term Structure

As in Example 2, the one-year par rate is 2.0%, the two-year par rate is 3.0%, and the three-year par rate is 4.0%. Consequently, the spot rates are $S_1 = 2.0\%$, $S_2 = 3.015\%$ and $S_3 = 4.055\%$. Zero-coupon bond prices are $P_1 = 1/1.020 = 0.9804$, $P_2 = 1/(1.03015)^2 = 0.9423$, and $P_3 = 1/(1.04055)^3 = 0.8876$. Interest volatility is 15% for all years.

Calibrate the binomial tree in Exhibit 16.

Exhibit 16   Binomial Tree to Calibrate

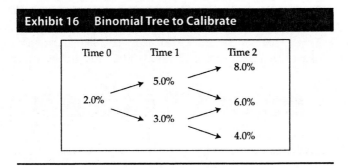

Solution:

Time 0

The par, spot, and forward rates are all the same for the first period in a binomial tree. Consequently, $Y_0 = S_0 = F_0 = 2.0\%$.

Time 1

Because the two-year spot rate is the geometric average of the one-year forward rate at Time 0 and the one-year forward rate at Time 1, we can infer the average forward rate for Time 2. $1.03015^2 = (1.02)(1+F_{1,1})$ implies $F_{1,1}$ = 4.040%. In addition, because we have chosen to impose a lognormal model on interest rate changes, $F_{1,1u} = (F_{1,1d})(e^{2\sigma})$. So, the two numbers average to 4.040% and one is $e^{2\sigma}$ greater than the other.

Beginning at $F_{1,1d}$ = (4.040%)($e^{-0.15}$) = 3.477% and $F_{1,1u}$ = (4.040%)($e^{0.15}$) = 4.694% gives a price for the two-year zero of [(0.5)(1/1.03477) + (0.5) (1/1.04694)]/1.02 = 0.9419. Notice that the price is quite close to the correct value of 0.9423. By using numeric methods (in this case, Excel's Solver), we find that the actual number for $F_{1,1d}$ = 3.442% instead of 3.477%, making $F_{1,1u}$ = 4.646% instead of 4.694%.

Exhibit 17   Calibration of Time 1

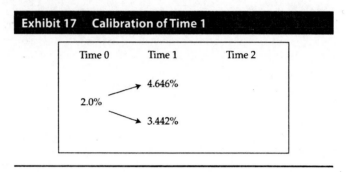

Time 2

We will begin with the average forward rate for Time 2, $F_{2,1} = (1.04055^3/1.03015^2)$ – 1= 6.167% as the middle value with (6.167%)($e^{-0.3}$) = 4.569% and (6.167%)($e^{0.3}$) = 8.325% as the lower and upper values. Those values give a price for a three-year zero-coupon bond of 0.8866, which is close to the correct price of 0.8876. Using numerical methods (again, Excel's Solver), we find that the three correct one-year forwards are 4.482%, 6.051%, and 8.167%.

Working backward through the tree, we find values at Time 2 to be 1/1.08167 = 0.9245, 1/1.06051 = 0.9429, and 1/1.04482 = 0.9571. Coming back to Time 1, the tree values are (0.5)(0.9245)/1.04602 + (0.5)(0.9429)/1.04602 = 0.8923 and (05) (0.9429)/1.03409 + (0.5)(0.9571)/1.03409 = 0.9188. Finally, coming back to the beginning of Time 0, we find (0.5)(0.8923)/1.02 + (0.5)(0.9188)/1.02 = 0.88778876.

Exhibit 18   Calibration of Time 2

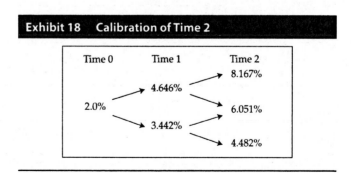

Exhibit 19 Working Backward to Calculate Tree Values

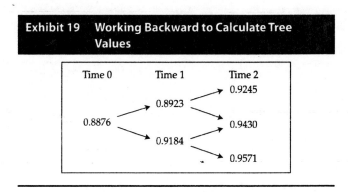

Now that our tree gives the correct prices for zero-coupon bonds maturing in one, two, and three years, we say that our tree is calibrated to be arbitrage free. It will price option-free bonds correctly, including par prices for the par bonds used to find the spot rates and, to the extent that we have chosen an appropriate interest rate process and interest rate volatility, it will provide insights into the value of bonds with embedded options and their risk parameters.

3.5 Valuing an Option-Free Bond with the Tree

Our next task is twofold. First, we calculate the arbitrage-free value of an option-free, fixed-rate coupon bond. Second, we compare the pricing using the zero-coupon yield curve with the pricing using an arbitrage-free binomial lattice. Because these two valuation methods are arbitrage-free, these two values must be the same.

Now, consider an option-free bond with four years remaining to maturity and a coupon rate of 2%. Note that this is not a benchmark bond and it carries a higher coupon than the four-year benchmark bond, which is priced at par. The value of this bond can be calculated by discounting the cash flow at the spot rates in Exhibit 3 as shown in the following equation:

$$\frac{\$2}{(1.01)^1} + \frac{\$2}{(1.01201)^2} + \frac{\$2}{(1.01251)^3} + \frac{\$100 + \$2}{(1.01404)^4} = \$102.33$$

The binomial interest rate tree should produce the same value as discounting the cash flows with the spot rates. An option-free bond that is valued by using the binomial interest rate tree should have the same value as discounting by the spot rates, which is true because the binomial interest rate tree is arbitrage-free.

Let us give the tree a test run and use the 2% option-free bond with four years remaining to maturity. Also assume that the issuer's benchmark yield curve is the one given in Exhibit 2, hence the appropriate binomial interest rate tree is the one in Exhibit 13. Exhibit 20 shows the various values in the discounting process and produces a bond value of $102.3254. The tree produces the same value for the bond as the spot rates and is therefore consistent with our standard valuation model.[6]

Exhibit 20 Sample Valuation for an Option-Free Bond using a Binomial Tree

Time 0	Time 1	Time 2	Time 3	Time 4
102.3254	102.6769	101.7639	101.1892	102
	104.0204	102.8360	101.9027	102

(continued)

---

6 There is a slight difference in price due to rounding at intermediate steps.

Exhibit 20	(Continued)			
Time 0	Time 1	Time 2	Time 3	Time 4
		103.6417	102.4380	102
			102.8382	102
				102

EXAMPLE 5

Confirming the Arbitrage-Free Value of a Bond

Using the par curve from Example 2 and Example 4, the yield to maturity for a one-year annual-pay bond is 2%, for a two-year annual-pay bond is 3%, and for a three-year annual-pay bond is 4%. Because this is the same curve as that used in Example 4, we can use the calibrated tree from that example to price a bond. Let us use a three-year annual-pay bond with a 5% coupon, just as we did in Example 2. We know that if the calibrated tree was built correctly and we perform calculations to value the bond with that tree (Exhibit 18, shown here again), its price should be $102.8102.

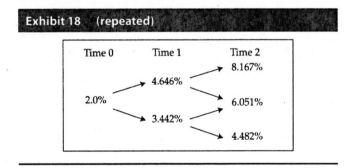

Exhibit 18   (repeated)

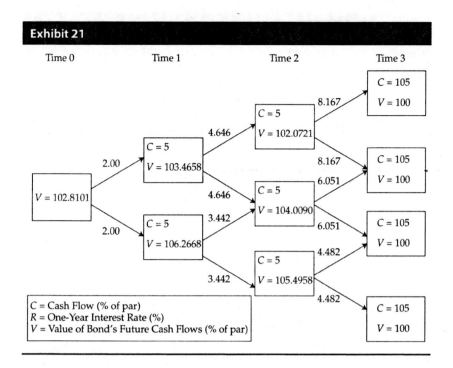

Exhibit 21

Time 0   Time 1   Time 2   Time 3

C = Cash Flow (% of par)
R = One-Year Interest Rate (%)
V = Value of Bond's Future Cash Flows (% of par)

Because the tree was calibrated to the same par curve (and spot curve) that was used to price this option-free bond using spot rates only, the tree gives the same price as the spot rate pricing.

3.6 Pathwise Valuation

An alternative approach to backward induction in a binomial tree is called pathwise valuation. The binomial interest rate tree specifies all potential rate paths in the model, whereas an interest rate path is the route an interest rate takes from the current time to the security's maturity. Pathwise valuation calculates the present value of a bond for each possible interest rate path and takes the average of these values across paths. We will use the pathwise valuation approach to produce the same value as the backward induction method for an option-free bond. Pathwise valuation involves the following steps: (1) specify a list of all potential paths through the tree, (2) determine the present value of a bond along each potential path, and (3) calculate the average across all possible paths.

Determining all potential paths is just like the following experiment. Suppose you are tossing a fair coin and are keeping track of the number of ways heads and tails can be combined. We will use a device called Pascal's Triangle, displayed in Exhibit 22. Pascal's Triangle can be built as follows: Start with the number 1 at the top of the triangle. The numbers in the boxes below are the sum of the two numbers above it except that the edges on each side are all 1. The shaded numbers show that 3 is the sum of 2 and 1. Now toss the coin while keeping track of the possible outcomes. The possible groupings are listed in Exhibit 23 where H stands for heads and T stands for tails.

Exhibit 22

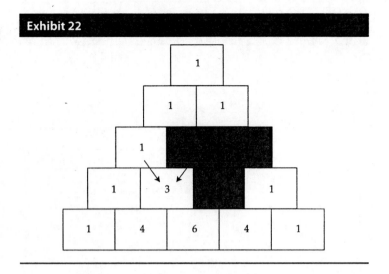

Exhibit 23

Number of Tosses	Outcomes	Pascal's Triangle
1	H T	1, 1
2	HH HT TH TT	1,2,1
3	HHH HHT HTH THH HTT THT TTH TTT	1, 3, 3, 1

This experiment mirrors exactly the number of interest rate paths in our binomial interest rate tree. The total number of paths for each period/year can be easily determined by using Pascal's Triangle. Let us work through an example for a three-year zero-coupon bond. From Pascal's Triangle, there are four possible paths to arrive at Year 3: HH, HT, TH, TT. Using the same binomial tree from Section 3.4, we specify the four paths as well as the possible forward rates along those paths. In Exhibit 24, the last column on the right shows the present value for each path. In the bottom right corner is the average present value across all paths.

Exhibit 24   Four Interest Rate Paths for a Three-Year Zero-Coupon Bond

Path	Forward Rate Year 1	Forward Rate Year 2	Forward Rate Year 3	Present Value
1	1.0000%	1.6122%	1.7663%	95.74780
2	1.0000%	1.6122%	1.323%	96.16670
3	1.0000%	1.1943%	1.323%	96.56384
4	1.0000%	1.1943%	0.9803%	96.89155
				96.34250

Now, we can use the binomial tree to confirm our calculations for the three-year zero-coupon bond, to within a small rounding error (0.0045, less than half a cent). The analysis is presented in Exhibit 25. The interest rate tree does indeed produce the same value.

Exhibit 25	Binomial Tree to Confirm Bond's Value		
Time 0	**Time 1**	**Time 2**	**Time 3**
96.338	96.907	98.245	100.000
	97.695	98.694	100.000
		99.029	100.000
			100.000

EXAMPLE 6

Pathwise Valuation Based on a Binomial Interest Rate Tree

Using the par curve from Example 2, Example 4, and Example 5, the yield to maturity for a one-year annual-pay bond is 2%, for a two-year annual-pay bond is 3%, and for a three-year annual-pay bond is 4%. We know that if we generate the paths in the tree correctly and discount the cash flows directly, the three-year, annual-pay, 5% coupon bond should still be priced at $102.8102.

There are eight paths through the three-year tree, four of which are unique. We discount the cash flows along each of the eight paths and take their average, as shown in Exhibits 26, 27, and 28.

Exhibit 26	Cash Flows			
Path	**Time 0**	**Time 1**	**Time 2**	**Time 3**
1	0	5	5	105
2	0	5	5	105
3	0	5	5	105
4	0	5	5	105
5	0	5	5	105
6	0	5	5	105
7	0	5	5	105
8	0	5	5	105

Exhibit 27	Discount Rates			
Path	**Time 0**	**Time 1**	**Time 2**	**Time 3**
1	2%	4.646%	8.167%	
2	2%	4.646%	8.167%	

(continued)

Exhibit 27	(Continued)			
Path	Time 0	Time 1	Time 2	Time 3
3	2%	4.646%	6.051%	
4	2%	4.646%	6.051%	
5	2%	3.442%	6.051%	
6	2%	3.442%	6.051%	
7	2%	3.442%	4.482%	
8	2%	3.442%	4.482%	

Exhibit 28	Present Values
Path	Time 0
1	100.5296
2	100.5296
3	102.3449
4	102.3449
5	103.4792
6	103.4792
7	104.8876
8	104.8876
Average	**102.8103**

4   MONTE CARLO METHOD

The Monte Carlo method is an alternative method for simulating a sufficiently large number of potential interest rate paths in an effort to discover how a value of a security is affected. This method involves randomly selecting paths in an effort to approximate the results of a complete pathwise valuation. Monte Carlo methods are often used when a security's cash flows are path dependent. Cash flows are path dependent when the cash flow to be received in a particular period depends on the path followed to reach its current level as well as the current level itself. For example, the valuation of mortgage-backed securities depends to a great extent on the level of prepayments, which are interest rate path dependent. Interest rate paths are generated based on some probability distribution, an assumption about volatility, and the model is fit to the current benchmark term structure of interest rates. The benchmark term structure is represented by the current spot rate curve such that the average present value across all scenario interest rate paths for each benchmark bond equals its actual market value. By using this approach, the model is rendered arbitrage free, which is equivalent to calibrating the interest rate tree as discussed in Section 3.

Suppose we intend to value a 30-year bond with the Monte Carlo method. For simplicity, assume the bond has monthly coupon payments (e.g., mortgage-backed securities). The following steps are taken: (1) simulate numerous (say, 500) paths of one-month interest rates under some volatility assumption and probability distribution, (2) generate spot rates from the simulated future one-month interest rates, (3) determine the cash flow along each interest rate path, (4) calculate the present value for each path, and (5) calculate the average present value across all interest rate paths.

Using the procedure just described, the model will produce benchmark bond values equal to the market prices only by chance. We want to ensure this is the case, otherwise the model will neither fit the current spot curve nor be arbitrage free. A constant is added to all interest rates on all paths such that the average present value for each benchmark bond equals its market value. The constant added to all short interest rates is called a drift term. When this technique is used, the model is said to be drift adjusted.

A question that arises concerns how many paths are appropriate for the Monte Carlo method. Increasing the number of paths increases the accuracy of the estimate in a statistical sense. It does not mean the model is closer to the true fundamental value of the security. The Monte Carlo method is only as good as the valuation model used and the accuracy of the inputs.

One other element that yield curve modelers often include in their Monte Carlo estimation is mean reversion. Mean reversion starts with the common-sense notion that history suggests that interest rates almost never get "too high" or "too low." What is meant by "too high" and "too low" is left to the discretion of the modeler. We implement mean reversion by implementing upper and lower bounds on the random process generating future interest rates. Mean reversion has the effect of moving the interest rate toward the implied forward rates from the yield curve.

EXAMPLE 7

The Application of Monte Carlo Simulation to Bond Pricing

Replace the interest rate paths from Example 6 with randomly generated paths that have been calibrated to the same initial par and spot curves, as shown in Exhibit 29.

Exhibit 29	Discount Rates			
Path	Time 0	Time 1	Time 2	Time 3
1	2%	2.500%	4.548%	
2	2%	3.600%	6.116%	
3	2%	4.600%	7.766%	
4	2%	5.500%	3.466%	
5	2%	3.100%	8.233%	
6	2%	4.500%	6.116%	
7	2%	3.800%	5.866%	
8	2%	4.000%	8.233%	

Exhibit 30	Present Values
Path	**Time 0**
1	105.7459
2	103.2708
3	100.91064
4	103.8543
5	101.9075
6	102.4236
7	103.3020
8	101.0680
Average	**102.8103**

Because we continue to get $102.8103, as shown in Exhibit 30, as the price for our three-year, annual-pay, 5% coupon bond, we know that the Monte Carlo simulation has been calibrated correctly. The paths are now different enough such that path dependent securities, such as mortgage-backed securities, can be analyzed in ways that provide insights not possible in binomial trees.

SUMMARY

This reading presents the principles and tools for arbitrage valuation of fixed-income securities. Much of the discussion centers on the binomial interest rate tree, which can be used extensively to value both option-free bonds and bonds with embedded options. The following are the main points made in the reading:

- A fundamental principle of valuation is that the value of any financial asset is equal to the present value of its expected future cash flows.
- A fixed-income security is a portfolio of zero-coupon bonds.
- Each zero-coupon bond has its own discount rate that depends on the shape of the yield curve and when the cash flow is delivered in time.
- In well-functioning markets, prices adjust until there are no opportunities for arbitrage.
- The law of one price states that two goods that are perfect substitutes must sell for the same current price in the absence of transaction costs.
- An arbitrage opportunity is a transaction that involves no cash outlay yet results in a riskless profit.
- Using the arbitrage-free approach, viewing a security as a package of zero-coupon bonds means that two bonds with the same maturity and different coupon rates are viewed as different packages of zero-coupon bonds and valued accordingly.
- For bonds that are option free, an arbitrage-free value is simply the present value of expected future values using the benchmark spot rates.

- A binomial interest rate tree permits the short interest rate to take on one of two possible values consistent with the volatility assumption and an interest rate model.

- An interest rate tree is a visual representation of the possible values of interest rates (forward rates) based on an interest rate model and an assumption about interest rate volatility.

- The possible interest rates for any following period are consistent with the following three assumptions: (1) an interest rate model that governs the random process of interest rates, (2) the assumed level of interest rate volatility, and (3) the current benchmark yield curve.

- From the lognormal distribution, adjacent interest rates on the tree are multiples of e raised to the 2σ power.

- One of the benefits of a lognormal distribution is that if interest rates get too close to zero, then the absolute change in interest rates becomes smaller and smaller.

- We use the backward induction valuation methodology that involves starting at maturity, filling in those values, and working back from right to left to find the bond's value at the desired node.

- The interest rate tree is fit to the current yield curve by choosing interest rates that result in the benchmark bond value. By doing this, the bond value is arbitrage free.

- An option-free bond that is valued by using the binomial interest rate tree should have the same value as discounting by the spot rates.

- Pathwise valuation calculates the present value of a bond for each possible interest rate path and takes the average of these values across paths.

- The Monte Carlo method is an alternative method for simulating a sufficiently large number of potential interest rate paths in an effort to discover how the value of a security is affected and involves randomly selecting paths in an effort to approximate the results of a complete pathwise valuation.

PRACTICE PROBLEMS

The following information relates to Questions 1–6

Katrina Black, portfolio manager at Coral Bond Management, Ltd., is conducting a training session with Alex Sun, a junior analyst in the fixed income department. Black wants to explain to Sun the arbitrage-free valuation framework used by the firm. Black presents Sun with Exhibit 1, showing a fictitious bond being traded on three exchanges, and asks Sun to identify the arbitrage opportunity of the bond. Sun agrees to ignore transaction costs in his analysis.

Exhibit 1	Three-Year, €100 par, 3.00% Coupon, Annual Pay Option-Free Bond		
	Eurex	**NYSE Euronext**	**Frankfurt**
Price	€103.7956	€103.7815	€103.7565

Black shows Sun some exhibits that were part of a recent presentation. Exhibit 3 presents most of the data of a binomial lognormal interest rate tree fit to the yield curve shown in Exhibit 2. Exhibit 4 presents most of the data of the implied values for a four-year, option-free, annual pay bond with a 2.5% coupon based on the information in Exhibit 3.

Exhibit 2	Yield to Maturity Par Rates for One-, Two-, and Three-Year Annual Pay Option-Free Bonds	
One-year	**Two-year**	**Three-year**
1.25%	1.50%	1.70%

Exhibit 3	Binomial Interest Rate Tree Fit to the Yield Curve (Volatility = 10%)			
Current	**Year 1**	**Year 2**	**Year 3**	**Year 4**
1.2500%	1.8229%	1.8280%	2.6241%	Node 4–1
	1.4925%	Node 2–2	Node 3–2	4.2009%
		1.2254%	1.7590%	3.4394%
			Node 3–4	2.8159%
				Node 4–5

Exhibit 4	Implied Values (in Euros) for a 2.5%, Four-Year, Option-Free, Annual Pay Bond Based on Exhibit 3			
Year 0	Year 1	Year 2	Year 3	Year 4
103.4960	104.2876	103.2695	102.3791	102.5000
	Node 1–2	104.0168	102.8442	102.5000
		104.6350	103.2282	102.5000
			103.5448	102.5000
				102.5000

Black asks about the missing data in Exhibits 3 and 4 and directs Sun to complete the following tasks related to those exhibits:

Task 1   Test that the binomial interest tree has been properly calibrated to be arbitrage-free.

Task 2   Develop a spreadsheet model to calculate pathwise valuations. To test the accuracy of the spreadsheet, use the data in Exhibit 3 and calculate the value of the bond if it takes a path of lowest rates in Year 1 and Year 2 and the second lowest rate in Year 3.

Task 3   Identify a type of bond where the Monte Carlo calibration method should be used in place of the binomial interest rate method.

Task 4   Update Exhibit 3 to reflect the current volatility, which is now 15%.

1   Based on Exhibit 1, the *best* action that an investor should take to profit from the arbitrage opportunity is to:

A   buy on Frankfurt, sell on Eurex.

B   buy on NYSE Euronext, sell on Eurex.

C   buy on Frankfurt, sell on NYSE Euronext.

2   Based on Exhibits 1 and 2, the exchange that reflects the arbitrage-free price of the bond is:

A   Eurex.

B   Frankfurt.

C   NYSE Euronext.

3   Which of the following statements about the missing data in Exhibit 3 is correct?

A   Node 3–2 can be derived from Node 2–2.

B   Node 4–1 should be equal to Node 4–5 multiplied by $e^{0.4}$.

C   Node 2–2 approximates the implied one-year forward rate one year from now.

4   Based on the information in Exhibits 3 and 4, the bond price in euros at Node 1–2 in Exhibit 4 is *closest* to:

A   102.7917.

B   104.8640.

C   105.2917.

5   A benefit of performing Task 1 is that it:

A   enables the model to price bonds with embedded options.

B   identifies benchmark bonds that have been mispriced by the market.

    C allows investors to realize arbitrage profits through stripping and reconstitution.

6 If the assumed volatility is changed as Black requested in Task 4, the forward rates shown in Exhibit 3 will *most likely*:

    A spread out.

    B remain unchanged.

    C converge to the spot rates.

The following information relates to Questions 7–10

Betty Tatton is a fixed income analyst with the hedge fund Sailboat Asset Management (SAM). SAM invests in a variety of global fixed-income strategies, including fixed-income arbitrage. Tatton is responsible for pricing individual investments and analyzing market data to assess the opportunity for arbitrage. She uses two methods to value bonds:

    Method 1   Discount each year's cash flow separately using the appropriate interest rate curve.

    Method 2   Build and use a binomial interest rate tree.

    Tatton compiles pricing data for a list of annual pay bonds (Exhibit 1). Each of the bonds will mature in two years, and Tatton considers the bonds as being risk-free; both the one-year and two-year benchmark spot rates are 2%. Tatton calculates the arbitrage-free prices and identifies an arbitrage opportunity to recommend to her team.

Exhibit 1	Market Data for Selected Bonds	
Asset	**Coupon**	**Market Price**
Bond A	1%	98.0584
Bond B	3%	100.9641
Bond C	5%	105.8247

    Next, Tatton uses the benchmark yield curve provided in Exhibit 2 to consider arbitrage opportunities of both option-free corporate bonds and corporate bonds with embedded options. The benchmark bonds in Exhibit 2 pay coupons annually, and the bonds are priced at par.

Exhibit 2	Benchmark Par Curve
Maturity (years)	**Yield to Maturity (YTM)**
1	3.0%
2	4.0%
3	5.0%

Tatton then identifies three mispriced three-year annual-pay bonds and compiles data on the bonds (see Exhibit 3).

Exhibit 3   Market Data of Annual-Pay Corporate Bonds

Company	Coupon	Market Price	Yield	Embedded Option?
Hutto-Barkley Inc.	3%	94.9984	5.6%	No
Luna y Estrellas Intl.	0%	88.8996	4.0%	Yes
Peaton Scorpio Motors	0%	83.9619	6.0%	No

Lastly, Tatton identifies two mispriced Swiss bonds, Bond X, a three-year bond, and Bond Y, a five-year bond. Both are annual-pay bonds with a coupon rate of 6%. To calculate the bonds' values, Tatton devises the first three years of the interest rate lognormal tree presented in Exhibit 4 using historical interest rate volatility data. Tatton considers how this data would change if implied volatility, which is higher than historical volatility, were used instead.

Exhibit 4   Interest Rate Tree; Forward Rates Based on Swiss Market

Year 1	Year 2	Year 3
	4%	6%
1%		5%
	2%	3%

7   Based on Exhibit 1, which of the following bonds *most likely* includes an arbitrage opportunity?

   A   Bond A

   B   Bond B

   C   Bond C

8   Based on Exhibits 2 and 3 and using Method 1, the amount (in absolute terms) by which the Hutto-Barkley corporate bond is mispriced is *closest* to:

   A   0.3368 per 100 of par value.

   B   0.4682 per 100 of par value.

   C   0.5156 per 100 of par value.

9   Method 1 would *most likely* **not** be an appropriate valuation technique for the bond issued by:

   A   Hutto-Barkley Inc.

   B   Luna y Estrellas Intl.

   C   Peaton Scorpio Motors.

10 Based on Exhibit 4 and using Method 2, the correct price for Bond X is *closest* to:

   A   97.2998.

   B   109.0085.

   C   115.0085.

SOLUTIONS

1 A is correct. This is the same bond being sold at three different prices so an arbitrage opportunity exists by buying the bond from the exchange where it is priced lowest and immediately selling it on the exchange that has the highest price. Accordingly, an investor would maximize profit from the arbitrage opportunity by buying the bond on the Frankfurt exchange (which has the lowest price of €103.7565) and selling it on the Eurex exchange (which has the highest price of €103.7956) to generate a risk-free profit of €0.0391 (as mentioned, ignoring transaction costs) per €100 par.

B is incorrect because buying on NYSE Euronext and selling on Eurex would result in an €0.0141 profit per €100 par (€103.7956 – €103.7815 = €0.0141), which is not the maximum arbitrage profit available. A greater profit would be realized if the bond were purchased in Frankfurt and sold on Eurex.

C is incorrect because buying on Frankfurt and selling on NYSE Euronext would result in an €0.0250 profit per €100 par (€103.7815 – €103.7565 = €0.0250). A greater profit would be realized if the bond were purchased in Frankfurt and sold on Eurex.

2 C is correct. The bond from Exhibit 1 is selling for its calculated value on the NYSE Euronext exchange. The arbitrage-free value of a bond is the present value of its cash flows discounted by the spot rate for zero coupon bonds maturing on the same date as each cash flow. The value of this bond, 103.7815, is calculated as follows:

	Year 1	Year 2	Year 3	Total PV
Yield to maturity	1.2500%	1.500%	1.700%	
Spot rate[1]	1.2500%	1.5019%	1.7049%	
Cash flow	3.00	3.00	103.00	
Present value of payment[2]	2.9630	2.9119	97.9066	103.7815

	Eurex	NYSE Euronext	Frankfurt
Price	€103.7956	€103.7815	€103.7565
Mispricing (per 100 par value)	0.141	0	–0.025

Notes:

1 Spot rates calculated using bootstrapping; for example: Year 2 spot rate (z_2): $100 = 1.5/1.0125 + 101.5/(1+z_2)^2 = 0.015019$.

2 Present value calculated using the formula $PV = FV/(1+r)^n$, where n = number of years until cash flow, FV=cash flow amount, and r = spot rate.

A is incorrect because the price on the Eurex exchange, €103.7956, was calculated using the yield to maturity rate to discount the cash flows when the spot rates should have been used. C is incorrect because the price on the Frankfurt exchange, €103.7565, uses the Year 3 spot rate to discount all the cash flows.

3 C is correct. Because Node 2–2 is the middle node rate in Year 2, it will be close to the implied one-year forward rate one year from now (as derived from the spot curve). Node 4–1 should be equal to the product of Node 4–5 and $e^{0.8}$.

Lastly, Node 3–2 cannot be derived from Node 2–2; it can be derived from any other Year 3 node; for example, Node 3–2 can be derived from Node 3–4 (equal to the product of Node 3–4 and $e^{4\sigma}$).

4 C is correct. The value of a bond at a particular node, in this case Node 1–2, can be derived by working backwards from the two nodes to the right of that node on the tree. In this case, those two nodes are the middle node in Year 2, equal to 104.0168, and the lower node in Year 2, equal to 104.6350. The bond value at Node 1–2 is calculated as follows:

$$\text{Value} = 0.5 \times [\,(104.0168/1.014925 + 104.6350/1.014925)\,] + 2.5$$
$$= 0.5 \times [102.4872 + 103.0963] + 2.5$$
$$= 105.2917$$

A is incorrect because the calculation does not include the coupon payment. B is incorrect because the calculation incorrectly uses the Year 0 and Year 1 node values.

5 A is correct. Calibrating a binomial interest rate tree to match a specific term structure is important because we can use the known valuation of a benchmark bond from the spot rate pricing to verify the accuracy of the rates shown in the binomial interest rate tree. Once its accuracy is confirmed, the interest rate tree can then be used to value bonds with embedded options. While discounting with spot rates will produce arbitrage-free valuations for option-free bonds, this spot rate method will not work for bonds with embedded options where expected future cash flows are interest-rate dependent (as rate changes impact the likelihood of options being exercised). The interest rate tree allows for the alternative paths that a bond with embedded options might take.

B is incorrect because calibration does not identify mispriced benchmark bonds. In fact, benchmark bonds are employed to prove the accuracy of the binomial interest rate tree, as they are assumed to be correctly priced by the market.

C is incorrect because the calibration of the binomial interest rate tree is designed to produce an arbitrage-free valuation approach and such an approach does not allow a market participant to realize arbitrage profits though stripping and reconstitution.

6 A is correct. Volatility is one of the two key assumptions required to estimate rates for the binomial interest rate tree. Increasing the volatility from 10% to 15% would cause the possible forward rates to spread out on the tree as it increases the exponent in the relationship multiple between nodes ($e^{x\sigma}$, where $x = 2$ times the number of nodes above the lowest node in a given year in the interest rate tree). Conversely, using a lower estimate of volatility would cause the forward rates to narrow or converge to the implied forward rates from the prevailing yield curve.

B is incorrect because volatility is a key assumption in the binomial interest rate tree model. Any change in volatility will cause a change in the implied forward rates.

C is incorrect because increasing the volatility from 10% to 15% causes the possible forward rates to spread out on the tree, not converge to the implied forward rates from the current yield curve. Rates will converge to the implied forward rates when lower estimates of volatility are assumed.

7 B is correct. Bond B's arbitrage-free price is calculated as follows:

$$\frac{3}{1.02} + \frac{103}{1.02^2} = 101.9416$$

which is higher than the bond's market price of 100.9641. Therefore, an arbitrage opportunity exists. Since the bond's value (100.9641) is less than the sum of the values of its discounted cash flows individually (101.9416), a trader would perceive an arbitrage opportunity and could buy the bond while selling claims to the individual cash flows (zeros), capturing the excess value. The arbitrage-free prices of Bond A and Bond C are equal to the market prices of the respective bonds, so there is no arbitrage opportunity for these two bonds:

$$\text{Bond A: } \frac{1}{1.02} + \frac{101}{1.02^2} = 98.0584$$

$$\text{Bond C: } \frac{5}{1.02} + \frac{105}{1.02^2} = 105.8247$$

8 C is correct. The first step in the solution is to find the correct spot rate (zero-coupon rates) for each year's cash flow. The benchmark bonds in Exhibit 2 are conveniently priced at par so the yields to maturity and the coupon rates on the bonds are the same. Because the one-year issue has only one cash flow remaining, the YTM equals the spot rate of 3% (or $z_1 = 3\%$). The spot rates for Year 2 (z_2) and Year 3 (z_3) are calculated as follows:

$$100 = \frac{4}{1.0300} + \frac{104}{(1+z_2)^2}; z_2 = 4.02\%$$

$$100 = \frac{5}{1.0300} + \frac{5}{(1.0402)^2} + \frac{105}{(1+z_3)^3}; z_3 = 5.07\%$$

The correct arbitrage-free price for the Hutto-Barkley Inc. bond is:

$$P_0 = \frac{3}{(1.0300)} + \frac{3}{(1.0402)^2} + \frac{103}{(1.0507)^3} = 94.4828$$

Therefore, the bond is mispriced by 94.4828 − 94.9984 = −0.5156 per 100 of par value.

A is incorrect because the correct spot rates are not calculated and instead the Hutto-Barkley Inc. bond is discounted using the respective YTM for each maturity. Therefore, this leads to an incorrect mispricing of 94.6616 − 94.9984 = −0.3368 per 100 of par value.

B is incorrect because the spot rates are derived using the coupon rate for Year 3 (maturity) instead of using each year's respective coupon rate to employ the bootstrap methodology. This leads to an incorrect mispricing of 94.5302 − 94.9984 = −0.4682 per 100 of par value.

9 B is correct. The Luna y Estrellas Intl. bond contains an embedded option. Method 1 will produce an arbitrage-free valuation for option-free bonds; however, for bonds with embedded options, changes in future interest rates impact the likelihood the option will be exercised and so impact future cash flows. Therefore, to develop a framework that values bonds with embedded options, interest rates must be allowed to take on different potential values in the future based on some assumed level of volatility (Method 2).

A and C are incorrect because the Hutto-Barkley Inc. bond and the Peaton Scorpio Motors bond are both option-free bonds and can be valued using either Method 1 or Method 2 to produce an arbitrage-free valuation.

10 B is correct. The first step is to identify the cash flows:

Time 0	Time 1	Time 2	Time 3
			106
		6	
	6		106
0		6	
	6		106
		6	
			106

Next, calculate the cash flows for each year beginning with Year 3 and move backwards to Year 1:

Year 3:

$$0.5 \times \left[\left(\frac{106}{1.06} \right) + \left(\frac{106}{1.06} \right) \right] + 6 = 106.0000$$

$$0.5 \times \left[\left(\frac{106}{1.05} \right) + \left(\frac{106}{1.05} \right) \right] + 6 = 106.9524$$

$$0.5 \times \left[\left(\frac{106}{1.03} \right) + \left(\frac{106}{1.03} \right) \right] + 6 = 108.9126$$

Year 2:

$$0.5 \times \left[\left(\frac{106.0000}{1.04} \right) + \left(\frac{106.9524}{1.04} \right) \right] + 6 = 108.3810$$

$$0.5 \times \left[\left(\frac{106.9524}{1.02} \right) + \left(\frac{108.9126}{1.02} \right) \right] + 6 = 111.8162$$

Year 1:

$$0.5 \times \left[\left(\frac{108.3810}{1.01} \right) + \left(\frac{111.8162}{1.01} \right) \right] = 109.0085$$

A is incorrect because the coupon payment is not accounted for at each node calculation. C is incorrect because it assumes that a coupon is paid in Year 1 (time zero) when no coupon payment is paid at time zero.

Valuation and Analysis: Bonds with Embedded Options

by Leslie Abreo, MFE, Ioannis Georgiou, CFA, and Andrew Kalotay, PhD

Leslie Abreo, MFE, is at Andrew Kalotay Associates, Inc. (USA). Ioannis Georgiou, CFA (Cyprus). Andrew Kalotay, PhD, is at Andrew Kalotay Associates, Inc. (USA).

LEARNING OUTCOMES

Mastery	The candidate should be able to:
☐	a. describe fixed-income securities with embedded options;
☐	b. explain the relationships between the values of a callable or putable bond, the underlying option-free (straight) bond, and the embedded option;
☐	c. describe how the arbitrage-free framework can be used to value a bond with embedded options;
☐	d. explain how interest rate volatility affects the value of a callable or putable bond;
☐	e. explain how changes in the level and shape of the yield curve affect the value of a callable or putable bond;
☐	f. calculate the value of a callable or putable bond from an interest rate tree;
☐	g. explain the calculation and use of option-adjusted spreads;
☐	h. explain how interest rate volatility affects option-adjusted spreads;
☐	i. calculate and interpret effective duration of a callable or putable bond;
☐	j. compare effective durations of callable, putable, and straight bonds;
☐	k. describe the use of one-sided durations and key rate durations to evaluate the interest rate sensitivity of bonds with embedded options;
☐	l. compare effective convexities of callable, putable, and straight bonds;
☐	m. describe defining features of a convertible bond;
☐	n. calculate and interpret the components of a convertible bond's value;

(continued)

1 INTRODUCTION

The valuation of a fixed-rate option-free bond generally requires determining its future cash flows and discounting them at the appropriate rates. Valuation becomes more complicated when a bond has one or more embedded options because the values of embedded options are typically contingent on interest rates.

Understanding how to value and analyze bonds with embedded options is important for practitioners. Issuers of bonds often manage interest rate exposure with embedded options such as call provisions. Investors in callable bonds must appreciate the risk of being called. The perception of this risk is collectively represented by the premium, in terms of increased coupon or yield, that the market demands for callable bonds relative to otherwise identical option-free bonds. Issuers and investors must also understand how other types of embedded options, such as put provisions, conversion options, caps, and floors, affect bond values and the sensitivity of these bonds to interest rate movements.

We begin this reading with a brief overview in Section 2 of various types of embedded options. We then discuss bonds that include a call or put provision. Taking a building-block approach, we show in Section 3 how the arbitrage-free valuation framework discussed in a previous reading can be applied to the valuation of callable and putable bonds, first in the absence of interest rate volatility and then when interest rates fluctuate. We also discuss how option-adjusted spreads are used to value risky callable and putable bonds. Section 4 covers interest rate sensitivity. It highlights the need to use effective duration, including one-sided durations and key rate durations, as well as effective convexity to assess the effect of interest rate movements on the value of callable and putable bonds.

We then turn to bonds that include other familiar types of embedded options. Section 5 focuses on the valuation of capped and floored floating-rate bonds (floaters). Convertible bonds are discussed in Section 6. The valuation of convertible bonds, which are typically callable and may also be putable, is complex because it depends not only on interest rate movements but also on future price movements of the issuer's underlying common stock.

Section 7 briefly highlights the importance of analytics software in bond valuation and analysis. Section 8 summarizes the reading.

2 OVERVIEW OF EMBEDDED OPTIONS

The term "embedded bond options" or **embedded options** refers to contingency provisions found in the bond's indenture or offering circular. These options represent rights that enable their holders to take advantage of interest rate movements. They can be exercised by the issuer or the bondholder, or they may be exercised automatically depending on the course of interest rates. For example, a call option allows the issuer to benefit from lower interest rates by retiring the bond issue early and refinancing at a lower cost. In contrast, a put option allows the bondholder to benefit from higher interest rates by putting back the bonds to the issuer and reinvesting the proceeds of the retired bond at a higher yield. These options are not independent of the bond and thus cannot be traded separately—hence the adjective "embedded." In this section, we provide a review of familiar embedded options.

Corresponding to every embedded option, or combination of embedded options, is an underlying bond with a specified issuer, issue date, maturity date, principal amount and repayment structure, coupon rate and payment structure, and currency denomination. In this reading, this underlying option-free bond is also referred to as the **straight bond**. The coupon of an underlying bond can be fixed or floating. Fixed-coupon bonds may have a single rate for the life of the bond, or the rate may step up or step down according to a coupon schedule. The coupons of floaters are reset periodically according to a formula based on a reference rate plus a credit spread—for example, six-month Libor + 100 basis points (bps). Except when we discuss capped and floored floaters, this reading focuses on fixed-coupon, single-rate bonds, also referred to as fixed-rate bonds.

2.1 Simple Embedded Options

Call and put options are standard examples of embedded options. In fact, the vast majority of bonds with embedded options are callable, putable, or both. The call provision is by far the most prevalent type of embedded option.

2.1.1 Call Options

A **callable bond** is a bond that includes an embedded call option. The call option is an issuer option—that is, the right to exercise the option is at the discretion of the bond's issuer. The call provision allows the issuer to redeem the bond issue prior to maturity. Early redemption usually happens when the issuer has the opportunity to replace a high-coupon bond with another bond that has more favorable terms, typically when interest rates have fallen or when the issuer's credit quality has improved.

Until the 1990s, most long-term corporate bonds in the United States were callable after either five or 10 years. The initial call price (exercise price) was typically at a premium above par, the premium depended on the coupon, and the call price gradually declined to par a few years prior to maturity. Today, most investment-grade corporate bonds are essentially non-refundable. They may have a "make-whole call," so named because the call price is such that the bondholders are more than "made whole" (compensated) in exchange for surrendering their bonds. The call price is calculated at a narrow spread to a benchmark security, usually an on-the-run sovereign bond such as Treasuries in the United States or gilts in the United Kingdom. Thus, economical refunding is virtually out of question, and investors need have no fear of receiving less than their bonds are worth.

Most callable bonds include a **lockout period** during which the issuer cannot call the bond. For example, a 10-year callable bond may have a lockout period of three years, meaning that the first potential call date is three years after the bond's issue date. Lockout periods may be as short as one month or extend to several years. For example, high-yield corporate bonds are often callable a few years after issuance. Holders of such bonds are usually less concerned about early redemption than about possible default. Of course, this perspective can change over the life of the bond—for example, if the issuer's credit quality improves.

Callable bonds include different types of call features. The issuer of a European-style callable bond can only exercise the call option on a single date at the end of the lockout period. An American-style callable bond is continuously callable from the end of the lockout period until the maturity date. A Bermudan-style call option can be exercised only on a predetermined schedule of dates after the end of the lockout period. These dates are specified in the bond's indenture or offering circular.

With a few exceptions, bonds issued by government-sponsored enterprises in the United States (e.g., Fannie Mae, Freddie Mac, Federal Home Loan Banks, and Federal Farm Credit Banks) are callable. These bonds tend to have relatively short maturities (5–10 years) and very short lockout periods (three months to one year). The call price is almost always at 100% of par, and the call option is often Bermudan style.

Tax-exempt municipal bonds (often called "munis"), a type of non-sovereign (local) government bond issued in the United States, are almost always callable at 100% of par any time after the end of the 10th year. They may also be eligible for advance refunding—a highly specialized topic that is not discussed here.

Although the bonds of US government-sponsored enterprises and municipal issuers account for most of the callable bonds issued and traded globally, bonds that include call provisions are also found in other countries in Asia Pacific, Europe, Canada, and Central and South America. The vast majority of callable bonds are denominated in US dollars or euros because of investors' demand for securities issued in these currencies. Australia, the United Kingdom, Japan, and Norway are examples of countries where there is a market for callable bonds denominated in local currency.

2.1.2 *Put Options and Extension Options*

A **putable bond** is a bond that includes an embedded put option. The put option is an investor option—that is, the right to exercise the option is at the discretion of the bondholder. The put provision allows the bondholders to put back the bonds to the issuer prior to maturity, usually at par. This usually happens when interest rates have risen and higher-yielding bonds are available.

Similar to callable bonds, most putable bonds include lockout periods. They can be European or, rarely, Bermudan style, but there are no American-style putable bonds.

Another type of embedded option that resembles a put option is an extension option: At maturity, the holder of an **extendible bond** has the right to keep the bond for a number of years after maturity, possibly with a different coupon. In this case, the terms of the bond's indenture or offering circular are modified, but the bond remains outstanding. Examples of extendible bonds can be found among Canadian issuers such as Royal Bank of Canada, which, as of July 2013, has a 1.125% semi-annual coupon bond outstanding that matures on 22 July 2016 but is extendible to 21 July 2017. We will discuss the resemblance between a putable and an extendible bond in Section 3.5.2.

2.2 Complex Embedded Options

Although callable and putable bonds are the most common types of bonds with embedded options, there are bonds with other types of options or combinations of options.

For instance, a bond can be both callable and putable. For example, as of July 2013, DIC Asset AG, a German corporate issuer, has a 5.875% annual coupon bond outstanding that matures on 16 May 2016. This bond can be either called by the issuer or put by the bondholders.

Convertible bonds are another type of bond with an embedded option. The conversion option allows bondholders to convert their bonds into the issuer's common stock. Convertible bonds are usually also callable by the issuer; the call provision enables the issuer to take advantage of lower interest rates or to force conversion. We will discuss convertible bonds thoroughly in Section 6.

Another layer of complexity is added when the option is contingent on some particular event. An example is the estate put or survivor's option that may be available to retail investors. For example, as of July 2013, GE Capital, a US corporate issuer, has a 5% semi-annual coupon callable bond outstanding that matures on 15 March 2018. In the event of its holder's death, this bond can be put at par by his or her heirs. Because the estate put comes into play only in the event of the bondholder's death, the value of a bond with an estate put is contingent on the life expectancy of its holder, which is uncertain.

BONDS WITH ESTATE PUTS

Colloquially known as "death-put" bonds, bonds with an estate put or survivor's option can be redeemed at par by the heirs of a deceased bondholder. The bonds should be put only if they sell at a discount—that is, if the prevailing price is below par. Otherwise, they should be sold in the market at a premium.

There is usually a ceiling on the principal amount of the bond the issuer is required to accept in a given year, such as 1% of the original principal amount. Estates giving notice of a put that would result in exceeding this ceiling go into a queue in chronological order.

The value of the estate put depends on the bondholder's life expectancy. The shorter the life expectancy, the greater the value of the estate put. A complicating factor is that most bonds with an estate put are also callable, usually at par and within five years of the issue date. If the issuer calls the bond early, the estate put is extinguished. Needless to say, valuing a callable bond with an estate put requires specialized tools. The key concept to keep in mind is that the value of such a bond depends not only on interest rate movements, like any bond with an embedded option, but also on the investor's life expectancy.

Bonds may contain several interrelated issuer options without any investor option. A prime example is a **sinking fund bond** (sinker), which requires the issuer to set aside funds over time to retire the bond issue, thus reducing credit risk. Such a bond may be callable and may also include options unique to sinking fund bonds, such as an acceleration provision and a delivery option.

SINKING FUND BONDS

The underlying bond has an amortizing structure—for example, a 30-year maturity with level annual principal repayments beginning at the end of the 11th year. In this case, each payment is 5% of the original principal amount. A typical sinking fund bond may include the following options:

- A standard *call option* above par, with declining premiums, starting at the end of Year 10. Thus, the entire bond issue could be called from Year 10 onward.

- An *acceleration provision*, such as a "triple up." Such a provision allows the issuer to repurchase at par three times the mandatory amount, or in this case 15% of the original principal amount, on any scheduled sinking fund date. Assume that the issuer wants to retire the bonds at the end of Year 11. Instead of calling the entire outstanding amount at a premium, it would be more cost effective to "sink" 15% at par and call the rest at a premium. Thus, the acceleration provision provides an additional benefit to the issuer if interest rates decline.

■ A *delivery option*, which allows the issuer to satisfy a sinking fund payment by delivering bonds to the bond's trustee in lieu of cash.[1] If the bonds are currently trading below par, say at 90% of par, it is more cost effective for the issuer to buy back bonds from investors to meet the sinking fund requirements than to pay par. The delivery option benefits the issuer if interest rates rise. Of course, the benefit can be materialized only if there is a liquid market for the bonds. Investors can take defensive action by accumulating the bonds and refusing to sell them at a discount.

From the issuer's perspective, the combination of the call option and the delivery option is effectively a "long straddle."[2] As a consequence, a sinking fund bond benefits the issuer not only if interest rates decline but also if they rise. Determining the combined value of the underlying bond and the three options is quite challenging.

EXAMPLE 1

Types of Embedded Options

1 Investors in putable bonds *most likely* seek to take advantage of:

   A   interest rate movements.

   B   changes in the issuer's credit rating.

   C   movements in the price of the issuer's common stock.

2 The decision to exercise the option embedded in an extendible bond is made by:

   A   the issuer.

   B   the bondholder.

   C   either the issuer or the bondholder.

3 The conversion option in a convertible bond is a right held by:

   A   the issuer.

   B   the bondholders.

   C   jointly by the issuer and the bondholders.

Solution to 1:

A is correct. A putable bond offers the bondholder the ability to take advantage of a rise in interest rates by putting back the bond to the issuer and reinvesting the proceeds of the retired bond in a higher-yielding bond.

---

1 A bond's trustee is typically a financial institution with trust powers. It is appointed by the issuer, but it acts in a fiduciary capacity with the bondholders. In public offerings, it is the trustee that determines, usually by lot, which bonds are to be retired.

2 A long straddle is an option strategy involving the purchase of a put option and a call option on the same underlying with the same exercise price and expiration date. At expiration, if the underlying price is above the exercise price, the put option is worthless but the call option is in the money. In contrast, if the underlying price is below the exercise price, the call option is worthless but the put option is in the money. Thus, a long straddle benefits the investor when the underlying price moves up or down. The greater the move up or down (i.e., the greater the volatility), the greater the benefit for the investor.

Solution to 2:

B is correct. An extendible bond includes an extension option that gives the bondholder the right to keep the bond for a number of years after maturity, possibly with a different coupon.

Solution to 3:

B is correct. A conversion option is a call option that gives the bondholders the right to convert their bonds into the issuer's common stock.

The presence of embedded options affects a bond's value. To quantify this effect, financial theory and financial technology come into play. The following section presents basic valuation and analysis concepts for bonds with embedded options.

VALUATION AND ANALYSIS OF CALLABLE AND PUTABLE BONDS

3

Under the arbitrage-free framework, the value of a bond with embedded options is equal to the sum of the arbitrage-free values of its parts. We first identify the relationships between the values of a callable or putable bond, the underlying option-free (straight) bond, and the call or put option, and then discuss how to value callable and putable bonds under different risk and interest rate volatility scenarios.

3.1 Relationships between the Values of a Callable or Putable Bond, Straight Bond, and Embedded Option

The value of a bond with embedded options is equal to the sum of the arbitrage-free value of the straight bond and the arbitrage-free values of the embedded options.

For a callable bond, the decision to exercise the call option is made by the issuer. Thus, the investor is long the bond but short the call option. From the investor's perspective, therefore, the value of the call option *decreases* the value of the callable bond relative to the value of the straight bond.

Value of callable bond = Value of straight bond − Value of issuer call option

The value of the straight bond can be obtained by discounting the bond's future cash flows at the appropriate rates, as described in Section 3.2. The hard part is valuing the call option because its value is contingent on future interest rates—specifically, the issuer's decision to call the bond depends on its ability to refinance at a lower cost. In practice, the value of the call option is often calculated as the difference between the value of the straight bond and the value of the callable bond:

Value of issuer call option
= Value of straight bond − Value of callable bond   **(1)**

For a putable bond, the decision to exercise the put option is made by the investor. Thus, the investor has a long position in both the bond and the put option. As a consequence, the value of the put option *increases* the value of the putable bond relative to the value of the straight bond.

Value of putable bond = Value of straight bond + Value of investor put option

It follows that

> Value of investor put option
> = Value of putable bond − Value of straight bond   **(2)**

Although most investment professionals do not need to be experts in bond valuation, they should have a solid understanding of the basic analytical approach, presented in the following sections.

3.2 Valuation of Default-Free and Option-Free Bonds: A Refresher

An asset's value is the present value of the cash flows the asset is expected to generate in the future. In the case of a default-free and option-free bond, the future cash flows are, by definition, certain. Thus, the question is, at which rates should these cash flows be discounted? The answer is that each cash flow should be discounted at the spot rate corresponding to the cash flow's payment date. Although spot rates might not be directly observable, they can be inferred from readily available information, usually from the market prices of actively traded on-the-run sovereign bonds of various maturities. These prices can be transformed into spot rates, par rates (i.e., coupon rates of hypothetical bonds of various maturities selling at par), or forward rates. Recall from Level I that spot rates, par rates, and forward rates are equivalent ways of conveying the same information; knowing any one of them is sufficient to determine the others.

Suppose we want to value a three-year 4.25% annual coupon bond. Exhibit 1 provides the equivalent forms of a yield curve with maturities of one, two, and three years.

Exhibit 1	Equivalent Forms of a Yield Curve		
Maturity (year)	**Par Rate (%)**	**Spot Rate (%)**	**One-Year Forward Rate (%)**
1	2.500	2.500	0 years from now 2.500
2	3.000	3.008	1 year from now 3.518
3	3.500	3.524	2 years from now 4.564

We start with the par rates provided in the second column of Exhibit 1. Because we are assuming annual coupons and annual compounding, the one-year spot rate is simply the one-year par rate. The hypothetical one-year par bond implied by the given par rate has a single cash flow of 102.500 (principal plus coupon) in Year 1.[3] In order to have a present value of par, this future cash flow must be divided by 1.025. Thus, the one-year spot rate or discount rate is 2.500%.

A two-year 3.000% par bond has two cash flows: 3 in Year 1 and 103 in Year 2. By definition, the sum of the two discounted cash flows must equal 100. We know that the discount rate appropriate for the first cash flow is the one-year spot rate (2.500%). We now solve the following equation to determine the two-year spot rate (S_2):

$$\frac{3}{(1.025)} + \frac{103}{\left(1 + S_2\right)^2} = 100$$

---

[3] In this reading, all cash flows and values are expressed as a percentage of par.

We can follow a similar approach to determine the three-year spot rate (S_3):

$$\frac{3.500}{(1.02500)} + \frac{3.500}{(1.03008)^2} + \frac{103.500}{(1 + S_3)^3} = 100$$

The one-year forward rates are determined by using indifference equations. Assume an investor has a two-year horizon. She could invest for two years either at the two-year spot rate, or at the one-year spot rate for one year and then reinvest the proceeds at the one-year forward rate one year from now ($F_{1,1}$). The result of investing using either of the two approaches should be the same. Otherwise, there would be an arbitrage opportunity. Thus,

$$(1 + 0.03008)^2 = (1 + 0.02500) \times (1 + F_{1,1})$$

Similarly, the one-year forward rate two years from now ($F_{2,1}$) can be calculated using the following equation:

$$(1 + 0.03524)^3 = (1 + 0.03008)^2 \times (1 + F_{2,1})$$

The three-year 4.25% annual coupon bond can now be valued using the spot rates:[4]

$$\frac{4.25}{(1.02500)} + \frac{4.25}{(1.03008)^2} + \frac{104.25}{(1.03524)^3} = 102.114$$

An equivalent way to value this bond is to discount its cash flows one year at a time using the one-year forward rates:

$$\frac{4.25}{(1.02500)} + \frac{4.25}{(1.02500)(1.03518)} + \frac{104.25}{(1.02500)(1.03518)(1.04564)} = 102.114$$

3.3 Valuation of Default-Free Callable and Putable Bonds in the Absence of Interest Rate Volatility

When valuing bonds with embedded options, the approach relying on one-period forward rates provides a better framework than that relying on the spot rates because we need to know the value of the bond at different points in time in the future to determine whether the embedded option will be exercised at those points in time.

3.3.1 *Valuation of a Callable Bond at Zero Volatility*

Let us apply this framework to the valuation of a Bermudan-style three-year 4.25% annual coupon bond that is callable at par one year and two years from now. The decision to exercise the call option is made by the issuer. Because the issuer borrowed money, it will exercise the call option when the value of the bond's future cash flows is higher than the call price (exercise price). Exhibit 2 shows how to calculate the value of this callable bond using the one-year forward rates calculated in Exhibit 1.

---

4 The examples in this reading were created in Microsoft Excel. Numbers may differ from the results obtained using a calculator because of rounding.

Exhibit 2	Valuation of a Default-Free Three-Year 4.25% Annual Coupon Bond Callable at Par One Year and Two Years from Now at Zero Volatility			
	Today	**Year 1**	**Year 2**	**Year 3**
Cash Flow		4.250	4.250	104.250
Discount Rate		2.500%	3.518%	4.564%
Value of the Callable Bond	$\dfrac{100 + 4.250}{1.02500} = 101.707$	$\dfrac{99.700 + 4.250}{1.03518} = \cancel{100.417}$	$\dfrac{104.250}{1.04564} = 99.700$	
		Called at 100	Not called	

We start by discounting the bond's cash flow at maturity (104.250) to Year 2 using the one-year forward rate two years from now (4.564%). The present value at Year 2 of the bond's future cash flows is 99.700. This value is lower than the call price of 100, so a rational borrower will not call the bond at that point in time. Next, we add the cash flow in Year 2 (4.250) to the present value of the bond's future cash flows at Year 2 (99.700) and discount the sum to Year 1 using the one-year forward rate one year from now (3.518%). The present value at Year 1 of the bond's future cash flows is 100.417. Here, a rational borrower will call the bond at 100 because leaving it out-standing would be more expensive than redeeming it. Last, we add the cash flow in Year 1 (4.250) to the present value of the bond's future cash flows at Year 1 (100.000), and we discount the sum to today at 2.500%. The result (101.707) is the value of the callable bond.

We can apply Equation 1 to calculate the value of the call option embedded in this callable bond. The value of the straight bond is the value of the default-free and option-free three-year 4.25% annual coupon bond calculated in Section 3.2 (102.114). Thus,

Value of issuer call option = 102.114 – 101.707 = 0.407

Recall from the earlier discussion about the relationships between the value of a callable bond, straight bond, and call option that the investor is long the bond and short the call option. Thus, the value of the call option decreases the value of the callable bond relative to that of an otherwise identical option-free bond.

3.3.2 Valuation of a Putable Bond at Zero Volatility

We now apply this framework to the valuation of a Bermudan-type three-year 4.25% annual coupon bond that is putable at par one year and two years from now. The decision to exercise the put option is made by the investor. Because the investor lent money, he will exercise the put option when the value of the bond's future cash flows is lower than the put price (exercise price). Exhibit 3 shows how to calculate the value of the three-year 4.25% annual coupon bond putable at par one year and two years from today.

Exhibit 3	Valuation of a Default-Free Three-Year 4.25% Annual Coupon Bond Putable at Par One Year and Two Years from Now at Zero Volatility			
	Today	**Year 1**	**Year 2**	**Year 3**
Cash Flow		4.250	4.250	104.250
Discount Rate		2.500%	3.518%	4.564%
Value of the Putable Bond	$\dfrac{100.707 + 4.250}{1.02500} = 102.397$	$\dfrac{100 + 4.250}{1.03518} = 100.707$	$\dfrac{104.250}{1.04564} = \cancel{99.700}$	
		Not put	Put at 100	

We can apply Equation 2 to calculate the value of the put option:

Value of investor put option = 102.397 − 102.114 = 0.283

Because the investor is long the bond and the put option, the value of the put option increases the value of the putable bond relative to that of an otherwise identical option-free bond.

OPTIMAL EXERCISE OF OPTIONS

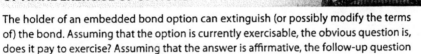

The holder of an embedded bond option can extinguish (or possibly modify the terms of) the bond. Assuming that the option is currently exercisable, the obvious question is, does it pay to exercise? Assuming that the answer is affirmative, the follow-up question is whether it is better to exercise the option at present or to wait.

Let us consider the first question: Would it be profitable to exercise the option? The answer is usually straightforward: Compare the value of exercising with the value of not exercising. For example, suppose that a bond is currently putable at 100. If the bond's market price is above 100, putting the bond makes no sense because the cash value from selling the bond would exceed 100. In contrast, if the bond's market price is 100, putting the bond should definitely be considered. Note that the market price of the bond cannot be less than 100 because such a situation creates an arbitrage opportunity: Buy the bond below 100 and immediately put it at 100.

The logic of a call decision by the issuer is similar. If a bond's market price is significantly less than the call price, calling is foolish because the bonds could be simply repurchased in the market at a lower price. Alternatively, if the price is very close to the call price, calling may make sense.

Assume that we have determined that exercising the option would be profitable. If the option under consideration is European style, it is obvious that it should in fact be exercised: There is no justification for not doing so. But if it is an American-style or Bermudan-style option, the challenge is to determine whether it is better to act now or to wait for a better opportunity in the future. The problem is that although circumstances may become more favorable, they may also get worse. So, option holders must consider the odds and decide to act or wait, depending on their risk preference.

The approach presented in this reading for valuing bonds with embedded options assumes that the option holders, be they issuers or investors, are risk neutral. They exercise if, and only if, the benefit from exercise exceeds the expected benefit from waiting. In reality, option holders may be risk averse and may exercise early even if the option is worth more alive than dead.

EXAMPLE 2

Valuation of Default-Free Callable and Putable Bonds

George Cahill, a portfolio manager, has identified three five-year annual coupon bonds issued by a sovereign government. The three bonds have identical characteristics, except that Bond A is an option-free bond, Bond B is callable at par in two years and three years from today, and Bond C is callable and putable at par two years and three years from today.

1   Relative to the value of Bond A, the value of Bond B is:

   A   lower.

   B   the same.

   C   higher.

2   Relative to the value of Bond B, the value of Bond C is:

   A   lower.

   B   the same.

   C   higher.

3   Under a steeply upward-sloping yield curve scenario, Bond C will *most likely*:

   A   be called by the issuer.

   B   be put by the bondholders.

   C   mature without exercise of any of the embedded options.

Solution to 1:

A is correct. Bond B is a callable bond, and Bond A is the underlying option-free (straight) bond. The call option embedded in Bond B is an issuer option that decreases the bond's value for the investor. If interest rates decline, bond prices usually increase, but the price appreciation of Bond B will be capped relative to the price appreciation of Bond A because the issuer will call the bond to refinance at a lower cost.

Solution to 2:

C is correct. Relative to Bond B, Bond C includes a put option. A put option is an investor option that increases the bond's value for the investor. Thus, the value of Bond C is higher than that of Bond B.

Solution to 3:

B is correct. As interest rates rise, bond prices decrease. Thus, the bondholders will have an incentive to exercise the put option so that they can reinvest the proceeds of the retired bond at a higher yield.

Exhibits 2 and 3 show how callable and putable bonds are valued in the absence of interest rate volatility. In real life, however, interest rates do fluctuate. Thus, the option holder must consider possible evolutions of the yield curve over time.

3.4 Effect of Interest Rate Volatility on the Value of Callable and Putable Bonds

In this section, we discuss the effects of interest rate volatility as well as the level and shape of the yield curve on the value of embedded options.

3.4.1 *Interest Rate Volatility*

The value of any embedded option, regardless of the type of option, increases with interest rate volatility. The greater the volatility, the more opportunities exist for the embedded option to be exercised. Thus, it is critical for issuers and investors to understand the effect of interest rate volatility on the value of bonds with embedded options.

The effect of interest rate volatility is represented in an interest rate tree or lattice, as illustrated in Exhibit 4. From each node on the tree starting from today, interest rates could go up or down. From these two states, interest rates could again go up or down. The dispersion between these up and down states anywhere on the tree is determined by the process generating interest rates based on a given yield curve and interest rate volatility assumptions.

Exhibit 4   Building an Interest Rate Tree

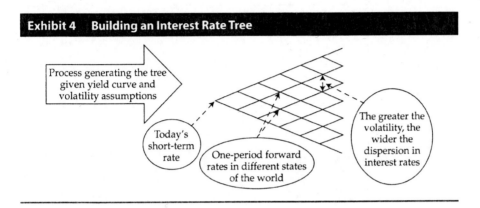

Exhibits 5 and 6 show the effect of interest rate volatility on the value of a callable bond and putable bond, respectively.

Exhibit 5   Value of a 30-Year 4.50% Bond Callable at Par in 10 Years under Different Volatility Scenarios Assuming a 4% Flat Yield Curve

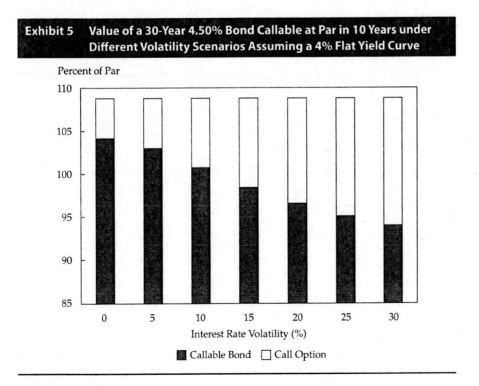

The stacked bars in Exhibit 5 represent the value of the straight bond, which is unaffected by interest rate volatility. The white component is the value of the call option which, when taken away from the value of the straight bond, gives the value of the callable bond—the shaded component. All else being equal, the call option increases in value with interest rate volatility. At zero volatility, the value of the call option is 4.60% of par; at 30% volatility, it is 14.78% of par. Thus, as interest rate volatility increases, the value of the callable bond decreases.

Exhibit 6　Value of a 30-Year 3.75% Bond Putable at Par in 10 Years under Different Volatility Scenarios Assuming a 4% Flat Yield Curve

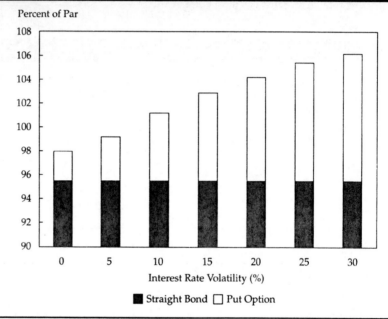

In Exhibit 6, the shaded component is the value of the straight bond, the white component is the value of the put option, and, thus, the stacked bars represent the value of the putable bond. All else being equal, the put option increases in value with interest rate volatility. At zero volatility, the value of the put option is 2.30% of par; at 30% volatility, it is 10.54% of par. Thus, as interest rate volatility increases, the value of the putable bond increases.

3.4.2 Level and Shape of the Yield Curve

The value of a callable or putable bond is also affected by changes in the level and shape of the yield curve.

3.4.2.1 Effect on the Value of a Callable Bond　Exhibit 7 shows the value of the same callable bond as in Exhibit 5 under different flat yield curve levels assuming an interest rate volatility of 15%.

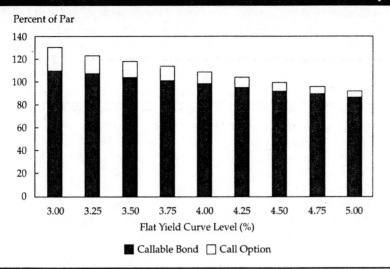

Exhibit 7   Value of a 30-Year 4.50% Bond Callable at Par in 10 Years under Different Flat Yield Curve Levels at 15% Interest Rate Volatility

Exhibit 7 shows that as interest rates decline, the value of the straight bond rises, but the rise is partially offset by the increase in the value of the call option. For example, if the yield curve is 5% flat, the value of the straight bond is 92.27% of par and the value of the call option is 5.37% of par, so the value of the callable bond is 86.90% of par. If the yield curve declines to 3% flat, the value of the straight bond rises by 40% to 129.54% of par, but the value of the callable bond only increases by 27% to 110.43% of par. Thus, the value of the callable bond rises less rapidly than the value of the straight bond, limiting the upside potential for the investor.

The value of a call option, and thus the value of a callable bond, is also affected by changes in the shape of the yield curve, as illustrated in Exhibit 8.

Exhibit 8   Value of a Call Option Embedded in a 30-Year 4.50% Bond Callable at Par in 10 Years under Different Yield Curve Shapes at 15% Interest Rate Volatility

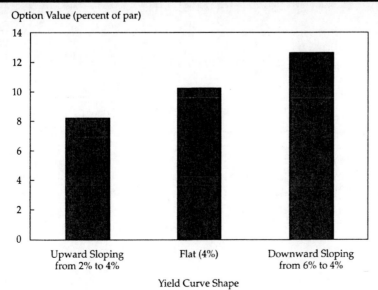

All else being equal, the value of the call option increases as the yield curve flattens. If the yield curve is upward sloping with short-term rates at 2% and long-term rates at 4% (the first bar), the value of the call option represents approximately 8% of par. It rises to approximately 10% of par if the yield curve flattens to 4% (the second bar). The value of the call option increases further if the yield curve actually inverts. Exhibit 8 shows that it exceeds 12% of par if the yield curve is downward sloping with short-term rates at 6% and long-term rates at 4% (the third bar). An inverted yield curve is rare but does happen from time to time.

The intuition to explain the effect of the shape of the yield curve on the value of the call option is as follows. When the yield curve is upward sloping, the one-period forward rates on the interest rate tree are high and opportunities for the issuer to call the bond are fewer. When the yield curve flattens or inverts, many nodes on the tree have lower forward rates, thus increasing the opportunities to call.

Assuming a normal, upward-sloping yield curve at the time of issue, the call option embedded in a callable bond issued at par is out of the money. It would not be called if the arbitrage-free forward rates at zero volatility prevailed. Callable bonds issued at a large premium, as happens frequently in the municipal sector in the United States, are in the money. They will be called if the arbitrage-free forward rates prevail.

3.4.2.2 Effect on the Value of a Putable Bond   Exhibits 9 and 10 show how changes in the level and shape of the yield curve affect the value of the putable bond used in Exhibit 6.

Exhibit 9   Value of a 30-Year 3.75% Bond Putable at Par in 10 Years under Different Flat Yield Curve Levels at 15% Interest Rate Volatility

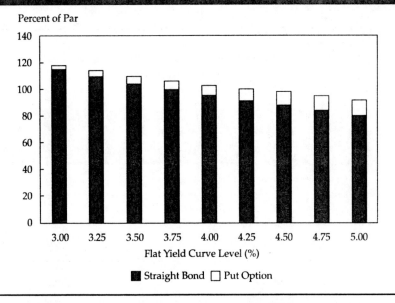

Exhibit 9 illustrates why the put option is considered a hedge against rising interest rates for investors. As interest rates rise, the value of the straight bond declines, but the decline is partially offset by the increase in the value of the put option. For example, if the yield curve moves from 3% flat to 5% flat, the value of the straight bond falls by 30%, but the fall in the value of the putable bond is limited to 22%.

Exhibit 10   Value of the Put Option Embedded in a 30-Year 3.75% Bond Putable at Par in 10 Years under Different Yield Curve Shapes at 15% Interest Rate Volatility

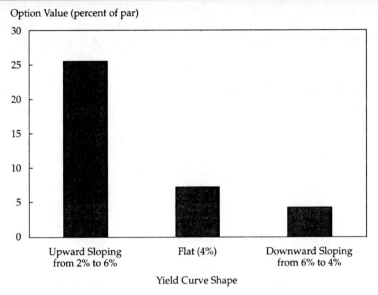

All else being equal, the value of the put option decreases as the yield curve moves from being upward sloping, to flat, to downward sloping. When the yield curve is upward sloping, the one-period forward rates in the interest rate tree are high, which creates more opportunities for the investor to put the bond. As the yield curve flattens or inverts, the number of opportunities declines.

3.5 Valuation of Default-Free Callable and Putable Bonds in the Presence of Interest Rate Volatility

The procedure to value a bond with an embedded option in the presence of interest rate volatility is as follows:

- Generate a tree of interest rates based on the given yield curve and interest rate volatility assumptions.

- At each node of the tree, determine whether the embedded options will be exercised.

- Apply the backward induction valuation methodology to calculate the bond's present value. This methodology involves starting at maturity and working back from right to left to find the bond's present value.

Let us return to the default-free three-year 4.25% annual coupon bonds discussed in Sections 3.3.1 (callable) and 3.3.2 (putable) to illustrate how to apply this valuation procedure. The bonds' characteristics are identical. The yield curve given in Exhibit 1 remains the same with one-year, two-year, and three-year par yields of 2.500%, 3.000%, and 3.500%, respectively. But we now assume an interest rate volatility of 10% instead of 0%. The resulting binomial interest rate tree showing the one-year forward rates zero, one, and two years from now is shown in Exhibit 11. The branching from each node to an up state and a down state is assumed to occur with equal probability.

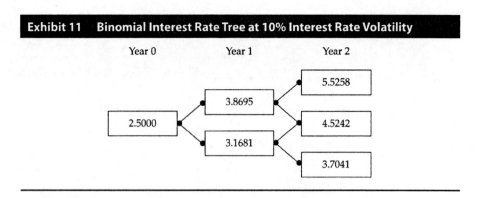

Exhibit 11   Binomial Interest Rate Tree at 10% Interest Rate Volatility

The calibration of a binomial interest rate tree was discussed in a previous reading. As mentioned before, the one-year par rate, the one-year spot rate, and the one-year forward rate zero years from now are identical (2.500%). Because there is no closed-form solution, the one-year forward rates one year from now in the two states are determined iteratively by meeting the following two constraints:

1 The rate in the up state (R_u) is given by

$$R_u = R_d \times e^{2\sigma\sqrt{t}}$$

where R_d is the rate in the down state, σ is the interest rate volatility (10% here), and t is the time in years between "time slices" (a year, so here $t = 1$).

2 The discounted value of a two-year par bond (bearing a 3.000% coupon rate in this example) equals 100.

In Exhibit 11, at the one-year time slice, R_d is 3.1681% and R_u is 3.8695%. Having established the rates that correctly value the one-year and two-year par bonds implied by the given par yield curve, we freeze these rates and proceed to iterate the rates in the next time slice to determine the one-year forward rates in the three states two years from now. The same constraints as before apply—that is, (1) each rate must be related to its neighbor by the factor $e^{2\sigma\sqrt{t}}$, and (2) the rates must discount a three-year par bond (bearing a 3.500% coupon rate in this example) to a value of 100.

Now that we have determined all the one-year forward rates, we can value the three-year 4.25% annual coupon bonds that are either callable or putable at par one year and two years from now.

3.5.1 *Valuation of a Callable Bond with Interest Rate Volatility*

Exhibit 12 depicts the valuation of a callable bond at 10% volatility.

Exhibit 12   Valuation of a Default-Free Three-Year 4.25% Annual Coupon Bond Callable at Par One Year and Two Years from Now at 10% Interest Rate Volatility

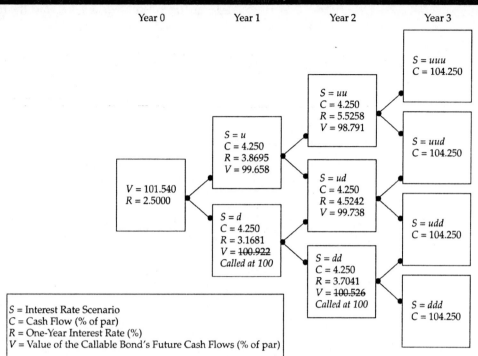

S = Interest Rate Scenario
C = Cash Flow (% of par)
R = One-Year Interest Rate (%)
V = Value of the Callable Bond's Future Cash Flows (% of par)

From the one-year rate, the two interest rate scenario branches in the tree are labeled *u* for an up state and *d* for a down state. Because this is a recombining binomial tree, the interest rate scenarios can be both the up state from the previous down state, and the down state from the previous up state. We use a single designation from the alternatives, if any. Thus, in Year 1, the states are *u* and *d*; in Year 2, *uu*, *ud*, and *dd*; and in Year 3, *uuu*, *uud*, *udd*, and *ddd*.

Starting from Year 3, we note that the bond's cash flow at maturity is 104.250 in the four states of the world. Each of the four cash flows in Year 3 is simply discounted at the appropriate one-year forward rate to Year 2. For example, the 104.250 in the state *uuu* is discounted at the one-year forward rate two years from now (5.5258%), which gives a value of 98.791. Because the bond is callable at par in Year 2, we check each scenario to determine whether the present value of the future cash flows is higher than the call price, in which case the issuer calls the bond. Exercise happens only in state *dd*, and so we reset the value from 100.526 to 100 in that state.

The value in each state of Year 1 is calculated by discounting the values in the two future states emanating from the present state plus the coupon at the appropriate rate in the present state. The probability-weighted average of these two discounted values is the value in the present state in Year 1. Because we assume equal probability for the two branches from any state, we simply divide the sum of the two discounted values by two. For example, the value in state *d* of Year 1 is given by

$$\frac{1}{2} \times \left(\frac{99.738 + 4.250}{1.031681} + \frac{100 + 4.250}{1.031681} \right) = 100.922$$

Finally, in Year 0, the value of the callable bond is 101.540. The value of the call option, obtained by taking the difference between the value of the straight bond and the value of the callable bond, is now 0.574 (102.114 − 101.540). The fact that the value of the call option is larger at 10% volatility than at 0% volatility (0.407) is consistent with our earlier discussion that option value increases with interest rate volatility.

Valuation of a Callable Bond Assuming Interest Rate Volatility

Return to the valuation of the Bermudan-style three-year 4.25% annual coupon bond callable at par in one year and two years from now as depicted in Exhibit 12. The one-year, two-year, and three-year par yields are 2.500%, 3.000%, and 3.500%, respectively, and the interest rate volatility is 10%.

1 Assume that nothing changes relative to the initial setting except that the interest rate volatility is now 15% instead of 10%. The new value of the callable bond is:

   A less than 101.540.

   B equal to 101.540.

   C more than 101.540.

2 Assume that nothing changes relative to the initial setting except that the bond is now callable at 102 instead of 100. The new value of the callable bond is *closest to*:

   A 100.000.

   B 102.000.

   C 102.114.

Solution to 1:

A is correct. A higher interest rate volatility increases the value of the call option. Because the value of the call option is subtracted from the value of the straight bond to obtain the value of the callable bond, a higher value for the call option leads to a lower value for the callable bond. Thus, the value of the callable bond at 15% volatility is less than that at 10% volatility—that is, less than 101.540.

Solution to 2:

C is correct. Looking at Exhibit 12, the call price is too high for the call option to be exercised in any scenario. Thus, the value of the call option is zero, and the value of the callable bond is equal to the value of the straight bond—that is, 102.114.

3.5.2 *Valuation of a Putable Bond with Interest Rate Volatility*

The valuation of the three-year 4.25% annual coupon bond putable at par in one year and two years from now at 10% volatility is depicted in Exhibit 13. The procedure for valuing a putable bond is very similar to that described earlier for valuing a callable bond, except that in each state, the bond's value is compared with the put price. The investor puts the bond only when the present value of the bond's future cash flows is lower than the put price. In this case, the value is reset to the put price (100). It happens twice in Year 2, in states *uu* and *ud*.

Exhibit 13 Valuation of a Default-Free Three-Year 4.25% Annual Coupon Bond Putable at Par One Year and Two Years from Now at 10% Interest Rate Volatility

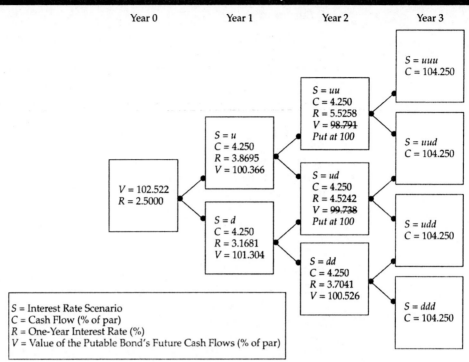

The value of the putable bond is 102.522. The value of the put option, obtained by taking the difference between the value of the putable bond and the value of the straight bond, is now 0.408 (102.522 – 102.114). As expected, the value of the put option is larger at 10% volatility than at 0% volatility (0.283).

EXAMPLE 4

Valuation of a Putable Bond Assuming Interest Rate Volatility

Return to the valuation of the Bermudan-style three-year 4.25% annual coupon bond putable at par in one year and two years from now, as depicted in Exhibit 13. The one-year, two-year, and three-year par yields are 2.500%, 3.000%, and 3.500%, respectively, and the interest rate volatility is 10%.

1 Assume that nothing changes relative to the initial setting except that the interest rate volatility is now 20% instead of 10%. The new value of the putable bond is:

   A less than 102.522.

   B equal to 102.522.

   C more than 102.522.

2 Assume that nothing changes relative to the initial setting except that the bond is now putable at 95 instead of 100. The new value of the putable bond is *closest to*:

   A 97.522.

    B   102.114.

    C   107.522.

Solution to 1:

C is correct. A higher interest rate volatility increases the value of the put option. Because the value of the put option is added to the value of the straight bond to obtain the value of the putable bond, a higher value for the put option leads to a higher value for the putable bond. Thus, the value of the putable bond at 20% volatility is more than that at 10% volatility—that is, more than 102.522.

Solution to 2:

B is correct. Looking at Exhibit 13, the put price is too low for the put option to be exercised in any scenario. Thus, the value of the put option is zero, and the value of the putable bond is equal to the value of the straight bond—that is, 102.114.

PUTABLE VS. EXTENDIBLE BONDS

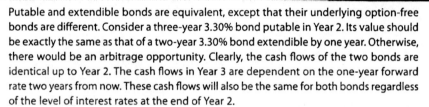

Putable and extendible bonds are equivalent, except that their underlying option-free bonds are different. Consider a three-year 3.30% bond putable in Year 2. Its value should be exactly the same as that of a two-year 3.30% bond extendible by one year. Otherwise, there would be an arbitrage opportunity. Clearly, the cash flows of the two bonds are identical up to Year 2. The cash flows in Year 3 are dependent on the one-year forward rate two years from now. These cash flows will also be the same for both bonds regardless of the level of interest rates at the end of Year 2.

    If the one-year forward rate at the end of Year 2 is higher than 3.30%, the putable bond will be put because the bondholder can reinvest the proceeds of the retired bond at a higher yield, and the extendible bond will not be extended for the same reason. So, both bonds pay 3.30% for two years and are then redeemed. Alternatively, if the one-year forward rate at the end of Year 2 is lower than 3.30%, the putable bond will not be put because the bondholder would not want to reinvest at a lower yield, and the extendible bond will be extended to hold onto the higher interest rate. Thus, both bonds pay 3.30% for three years and are then redeemed.

EXAMPLE 5

Valuation of Bonds with Embedded Options Assuming Interest Rate Volatility

Sidley Brown, a fixed income associate at KMR Capital, is analyzing the effect of interest rate volatility on the values of callable and putable bonds issued by Weather Analytics (WA). WA is owned by the sovereign government, so its bonds are considered default free. Brown is currently looking at three of WA's bonds and has gathered the following information about them:

Characteristic	Bond X	Bond Y	Bond Z
Times to maturity	Three years from today	Three years from today	Three years from today
Coupon	5.2% annual	Not available	4.8% annual

Characteristic	Bond X	Bond Y	Bond Z
Type of bond	Callable at par one year and two years from today	Callable at par one year and two years from today	Putable at par two years from today
Price (as a % of par)	Not available	101.325	Not available

The one-year, two-year, and three-year par rates are 4.400%, 4.700%, and 5.000%, respectively. Based on an estimated interest rate volatility of 15%, Brown has constructed the following binomial interest rate tree:

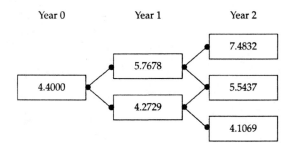

1   The price of Bond X is *closest to*:

   A   96.057% of par.

   B   99.954% of par.

   C   100.547% of par.

2   The coupon rate of Bond Y is *closest to*:

   A   4.200%.

   B   5.000%.

   C   6.000%.

3   The price of Bond Z is *closest to*:

   A   99.638% of par.

   B   100.340% of par.

   C   100.778% of par.

Brown is now analyzing the effect of interest rate volatility on the price of WA's bonds.

4   Relative to its price at 15% interest rate volatility, the price of Bond X at a lower interest rate volatility will be:

   A   lower.

   B   the same.

   C   higher.

5   Relative to its price at 15% interest rate volatility, the price of Bond Z at a higher interest rate volatility will be:

   A   lower.

   B   the same.

   C   higher.

Solution to 1:

B is correct.

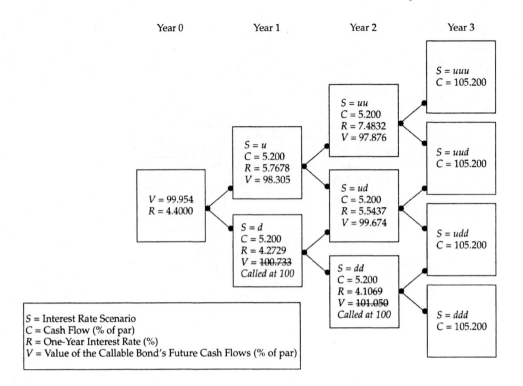

Solution to 2:

C is correct.

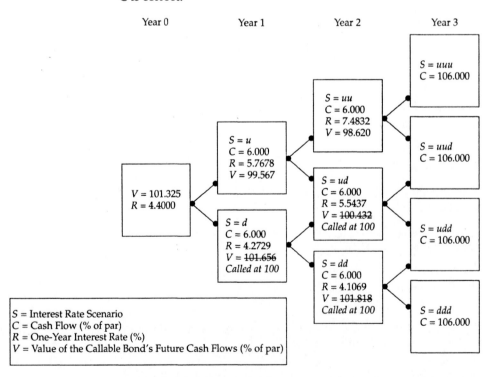

Although the correct answer can be found by using the interest rate tree depicted, it is possible to identify it by realizing that the other two answers are clearly incorrect. The three-year 5% straight bond is worth par given that the three-year par rate is 5%. Because the presence of a call option reduces the price of a callable bond, a three-year 5% bond callable at par can only be worth less than par, and certainly less than 101.325 given the yield curve and interest rate volatility assumptions, so B is incorrect. The value of a bond with a coupon rate of 4% is even less, so A is incorrect. Thus, C must be the correct answer.

Solution to 3:

B is correct.

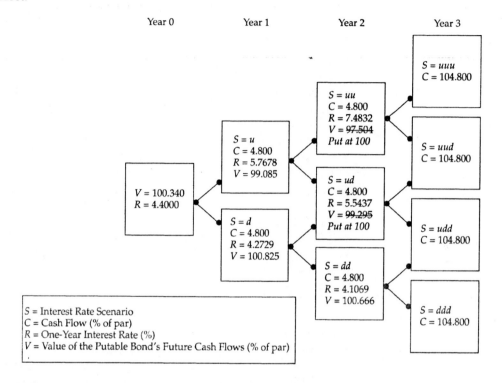

S = Interest Rate Scenario
C = Cash Flow (% of par)
R = One-Year Interest Rate (%)
V = Value of the Putable Bond's Future Cash Flows (% of par)

Solution to 4:

C is correct. Bond X is a callable bond. As shown in Equation 1, the value of the call option decreases the value of Bond X relative to the value of the underlying option-free bond. As interest rate volatility decreases, the value of the call option decreases, and thus the value of Bond X increases.

Solution to 5:

C is correct. Bond Z is a putable bond. As shown in Equation 2, the value of the put option increases the value of Bond Z relative to the value of the underlying option-free bond. As interest rate volatility increases, the value of the put option increases, and thus the value of Bond Z increases.

3.6 Valuation of Risky Callable and Putable Bonds

Although the approach described earlier for default-free bonds may apply to securities issued by sovereign governments in their local currency, the fact is that most bonds are subject to default. Accordingly, we have to extend the framework to the valuation of risky bonds.

There are two distinct approaches to valuing bonds that are subject to default risk. The industry-standard approach is to increase the discount rates above the default-free rates to reflect default risk. Higher discount rates imply lower present values, and thus the value of a risky bond will be lower than that of an otherwise identical default-free bond. How to obtain an appropriate yield curve for a risky bond is discussed in Section 3.6.1.

The second approach to valuing risky bonds is by making the default probabilities explicit—that is, by assigning a probability to each time period going forward. For example, the probability of default in Year 1 may be 1%; the probability of default in Year 2, conditional on surviving Year 1, may be 1.25%; and so on. This approach requires specifying the recovery value given default (e.g., 40% of par). Information about default probabilities and recovery values may be accessible from credit default swaps. This important topic is covered in another reading.

3.6.1 Option-Adjusted Spread

Depending on available information, there are two standard approaches to construct a suitable yield curve for a risky bond. The more satisfactory but less convenient one is to use an issuer-specific curve, which represents the issuer's borrowing rates over the relevant range of maturities. Unfortunately, most bond professionals do not have access to such a level of detail. A more convenient and relatively satisfactory alternative is to uniformly raise the one-year forward rates derived from the default-free benchmark yield curve by a fixed spread, which is estimated from the market prices of suitable bonds of similar credit quality. This fixed spread is known as the zero-volatility spread, or Z-spread.

To illustrate, we return to the three-year 4.25% option-free bond introduced in Section 3.2, but we now assume that it is a risky bond and that the appropriate Z-spread is 100 bps. To calculate the arbitrage-free value of this bond, we have to increase each of the one-year forward rates given in Exhibit 1 by the Z-spread of 100 bps:

$$\frac{4.25}{(1.03500)} + \frac{4.25}{(1.03500)(1.04518)} + \frac{104.25}{(1.03500)(1.04518)(1.05564)} = 99.326$$

As expected, the value of this risky bond (99.326) is considerably lower than the value of an otherwise identical but default-free bond (102.114).

The same approach can be applied to the interest rate tree when valuing risky bonds with embedded options. In this case, an **option-adjusted spread** (OAS) is used. As depicted in Exhibit 14, the OAS is the constant spread that, when added to all the one-period forward rates on the interest rate tree, makes the arbitrage-free value of the bond equal to its market price. Note that the Z-spread for an option-free bond is simply its OAS at zero volatility.

Exhibit 14   Interest Rate Tree and OAS

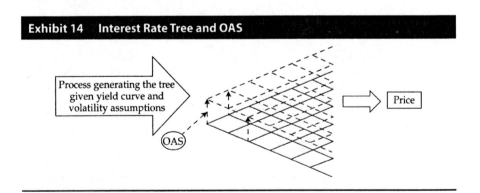

If the bond's price is given, the OAS is determined by trial and error. For example, suppose that the market price of a three-year 4.25% annual coupon bond callable in one year and two years from now, identical to the one valued in Exhibit 12 except that it is risky instead of default-free, is 101.000. To determine the OAS, we try shifting all the one-year forward rates in each state by adding a constant spread. For example, when we add 30 bps to all the one-year forward rates, we obtain a value for the callable bond of 100.973, which is lower than the bond's price. Because of the inverse relationship between a bond's price and its yield, this result means that the discount rates are too high, so we try a slightly lower spread. Adding 28 bps results in a value for the callable bond of 101.010, which is slightly too high. As illustrated in Exhibit 15, the constant spread added uniformly to all the one-period forward rates that justifies the given market price of 101.000 is 28.55 bps; this number is the OAS.

Exhibit 15   OAS of a Risky Three-Year 4.25% Annual Coupon Bond Callable at Par One Year and Two Years from Now at 10% Interest Rate Volatility

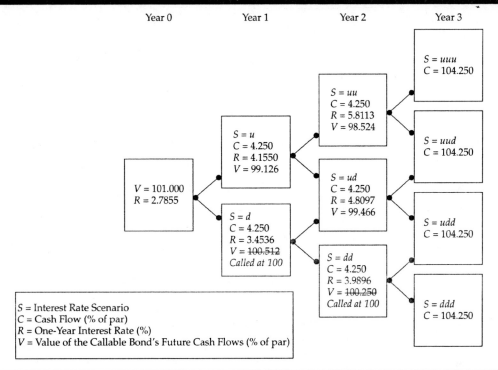

As illustrated in Exhibit 15, the value at each node is adjusted based on whether the call option is exercised. Thus, the OAS removes the amount that results from the option risk, which is why this spread is called "option adjusted."

OAS is often used as a measure of value relative to the benchmark. An OAS lower than that for a bond with similar characteristics and credit quality indicates that the bond is likely overpriced (rich) and should be avoided. A larger OAS than that of a bond with similar characteristics and credit quality means that the bond is likely under-priced (cheap). If the OAS is close to that of a bond with similar characteristics and credit quality, the bond looks fairly priced. In our example, the OAS at 10% volatility is 28.55 bps. This number should be compared with the OAS of bonds with similar characteristics and credit quality to make a judgment about the bond's attractiveness.

3.6.2 Effect of Interest Rate Volatility on Option-Adjusted Spread

The dispersion of interest rates on the tree is volatility dependent, and so is the OAS. Exhibit 16 shows the effect of volatility on the OAS for a callable bond. The bond is a 5% annual coupon bond with 23 years left to maturity, callable in three years, priced at 95% of par, and valued assuming a flat yield curve of 4%.

Exhibit 16   Effect of Interest Rate Volatility on the OAS for a Callable Bond

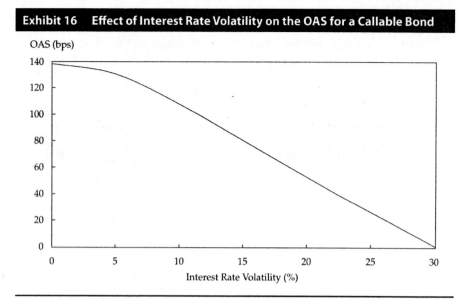

Exhibit 16 shows that as interest rate volatility increases, the OAS for the callable bond decreases. The OAS drops from 138.2 bps at 0% volatility to 1.2 bps at 30% volatility. This exhibit clearly demonstrates the importance of the interest rate volatility assumption. Returning to the example in Exhibit 15, the callable bond may look underpriced at 10% volatility. If an investor assumes a higher volatility, however, the OAS and thus relative cheapness will decrease.

EXAMPLE 6

Option-Adjusted Spread

Robert Jourdan, a portfolio manager, has just valued a 7% annual coupon bond that was issued by a French company and has three years remaining until maturity. The bond is callable at par one year and two years from now. In his valuation, Jourdan used the yield curve based on the on-the-run French government bonds. The one-year, two-year, and three-year par rates are 4.600%, 4.900%, and 5.200%, respectively. Based on an estimated interest rate volatility of 15%, Jourdan constructed the following binomial interest rate tree:

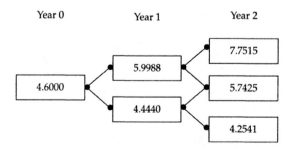

Jourdan valued the callable bond at 102.294% of par. However, Jourdan's colleague points out that because the corporate bond is more risky than French government bonds, the valuation should be performed using an OAS of 200 bps.

1 To update his valuation of the French corporate bond, Jourdan should:

   A subtract 200 bps from the bond's annual coupon rate.

    B add 200 bps to the rates in the binomial interest rate tree.

    C subtract 200 bps from the rates in the binomial interest rate tree.

2 All else being equal, the value of the callable bond at 15% volatility is *closest to*:

    A 99.198% of par.

    B 99.247% of par.

    C 104.288% of par.

3 Holding the price calculated in the previous question, the OAS for the callable bond at 20% volatility will be:

    A lower.

    B the same.

    C higher.

Solution to 1:

B is correct. The OAS is the constant spread that must be *added* to all the one-period forward rates given in the binomial interest rate tree to justify a bond's given market price.

Solution to 2:

B is correct.

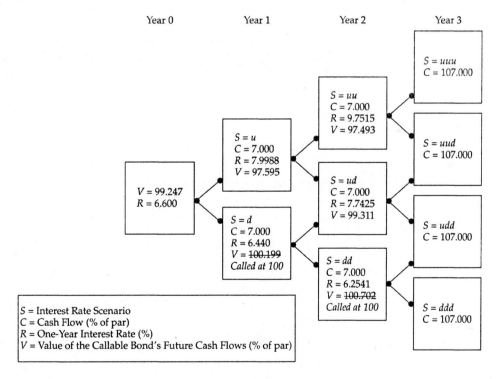

Solution to 3:

A is correct. If interest rate volatility increases from 15% to 20%, the OAS for the callable bond will decrease.

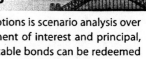

SCENARIO ANALYSIS OF BONDS WITH OPTIONS

Another application of valuing bonds with embedded options is scenario analysis over a specified investment horizon. In addition to reinvestment of interest and principal, option valuation comes into play in that callable and putable bonds can be redeemed and their proceeds reinvested during the holding period. Making scenario-dependent, optimal option-exercise decisions involves computationally intensive use of OAS technology because the call or put decision must be evaluated considering the evolution of interest rate scenarios during the holding period.

Performance over a specified investment horizon entails a trade-off between reinvestment of cash flows and change in the bond's value. Let us take the example of a 4.5% bond with five years left to maturity and assume that the investment horizon is one year. If the bond is option free, higher interest rates increase the reinvestment income but result in lower principal value at the end of the investment horizon. Because the investment horizon is short, reinvestment income is relatively insignificant, and performance will be dominated by the change in the value of the principal. Accordingly, lower interest rates will result in superior performance.

If the bond under consideration is callable, however, it is not at all obvious how the interest rate scenario affects performance. Suppose, for example, that the bond is first callable six months from now and that its current market price is 99.74. Steeply rising interest rates would depress the bond's price, and performance would definitely suffer. But steeply declining interest rates would also be detrimental because the bond would be called and *both interest and principal* would have to be reinvested at lower interest rates. Exhibit 17 shows the return over the one-year investment horizon for the 4.5% bond first callable in six months with five years left to maturity and valued on a 4% flat yield curve.

Exhibit 17 Effect of Interest Rate Changes on a Callable Bond's Total Return

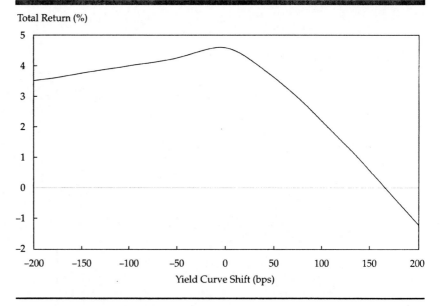

Exhibit 17 clearly shows that lower interest rates do not guarantee higher returns for callable bonds. The point to keep in mind is that the bond may be called long before the end of the investment horizon. Assuming that it is called on the horizon date would overestimate performance. Thus, a realistic prediction of option exercise is essential when performing scenario analysis of bonds with embedded options.

INTEREST RATE RISK OF BONDS WITH EMBEDDED OPTIONS

4

Measuring and managing exposure to interest rate risk are two essential tasks of fixed-income portfolio management. Applications range from hedging a portfolio to asset–liability management of financial institutions. Portfolio managers, whose performance is often measured against a benchmark, also need to monitor the interest rate risk of both their portfolio and the benchmark. In this section, we cover two key measures of interest rate risk: duration and convexity.

4.1 Duration

The duration of a bond measures the sensitivity of the bond's full price (including accrued interest) to changes in the bond's yield to maturity (in the case of *yield* duration measures) or to changes in benchmark interest rates (in the case of yield-curve or *curve* duration measures). Yield duration measures, such as modified duration, can be used only for option-free bonds because these measures assume that a bond's expected cash flows do not change when the yield changes. This assumption is in general false for bonds with embedded options because the values of embedded options are typically contingent on interest rates. Thus, for bonds with embedded options, the only appropriate duration measure is the curve duration measure known as effective (or option-adjusted) duration. Because effective duration works for straight bonds as well as for bonds with embedded options, practitioners tend to use it regardless of the type of bond being analyzed.

4.1.1 *Effective Duration*

Effective duration indicates the sensitivity of the bond's price to a 100 bps parallel shift of the benchmark yield curve—in particular, the government par curve—assuming no change in the bond's credit spread.[5] The formula for calculating a bond's effective duration is

$$\text{Effective duration} = \frac{(PV_-) - (PV_+)}{2 \times (\Delta\text{Curve}) \times (PV_0)} \tag{3}$$

where

  ΔCurve = the magnitude of the parallel shift in the benchmark yield curve (in decimal);

  PV_- = the full price of the bond when the benchmark yield curve is shifted down by ΔCurve;

  PV_+ = the full price of the bond when the benchmark yield curve is shifted up by ΔCurve; and

  PV_0 = the current full price of the bond (i.e., with no shift).

How is this formula applied in practice? Without a market price, we would need an issuer-specific yield curve to compute PV_0, PV_-, and PV_+. But practitioners usually have access to the bond's current price and thus use the following procedure:

1 Given a price (PV_0), calculate the implied OAS to the benchmark yield curve at an appropriate interest rate volatility.

---

5 Although it is possible to explore how arbitrary changes in interest rates affect the bond's price, in practice, the change is usually specified as a parallel shift of the benchmark yield curve.

2 Shift the benchmark yield curve down, generate a new interest rate tree, and then revalue the bond using the OAS calculated in Step 1. This value is PV_-.

3 Shift the benchmark yield curve up by the same magnitude as in Step 2, generate a new interest rate tree, and then revalue the bond using the OAS calculated in Step 1. This value is PV_+.

4 Calculate the bond's effective duration using Equation 3.

Let us illustrate using the same three-year 4.25% bond callable at par one year and two years from now, the same par yield curve (i.e., one-year, two-year, and three-year par yields of 2.500%, 3.000%, and 3.500%, respectively), and the same interest rate volatility (10%) as before. As in Section 3.6, we assume that the bond's current full price is 101.000. We apply the procedure just described:

1 As shown in Exhibit 15, given a price (PV_0) of 101.000, the OAS at 10% volatility is 28.55 bps.

2 We shift the par yield curve down by, say, 30 bps, generate a new interest rate tree, and then revalue the bond at an OAS of 28.55 bps. As shown in Exhibit 18 below, PV_- is 101.599.

3 We shift the par yield curve up by the same 30 bps, generate a new interest rate tree, and then revalue the bond at an OAS of 28.55 bps. As shown in Exhibit 19 below, PV_+ is 100.407.

4 Thus,

$$\text{Effective duration} = \frac{101.599 - 100.407}{2 \times 0.003 \times 101.000} = 1.97$$

An effective duration of 1.97 indicates that a 100-bps increase in interest rate would reduce the value of the three-year 4.25% callable bond by 1.97%.

Exhibit 18   Valuation of a Three-Year 4.25% Annual Coupon Bond Callable at Par One Year and Two Years from Now at 10% Interest Rate Volatility with an OAS of 28.55 bps When Interest Rates Are Shifted Down by 30 bps

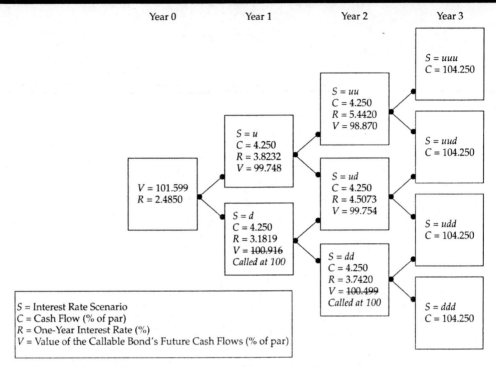

| Year 0 | Year 1 | Year 2 | Year 3 |

S = Interest Rate Scenario
C = Cash Flow (% of par)
R = One-Year Interest Rate (%)
V = Value of the Callable Bond's Future Cash Flows (% of par)

Exhibit 19   Valuation of a Three-Year 4.25% Annual Coupon Bond Callable at Par One Year and Two Years from Now at 10% Interest Rate Volatility with an OAS of 28.55 bps When Interest Rates Shifted Are Shifted Up by 30 bps

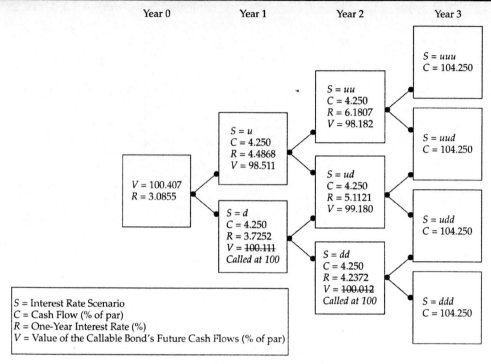

The effective duration of a callable bond cannot exceed that of the straight bond. When interest rates are high relative to the bond's coupon, the call option is out of the money, so the bond is unlikely to be called. Thus, the effect of an interest rate change on the price of a callable bond is very similar to that on the price of an otherwise identical option-free bond—the callable and straight bonds have very similar effective durations. In contrast, when interest rates fall, the call option moves into the money. Recall that the call option gives the issuer the right to retire the bond at the call price and thus limits the price appreciation when interest rates decline. As a consequence, the call option reduces the effective duration of the callable bond relative to that of the straight bond.

The effective duration of a putable bond also cannot exceed that of the straight bond. When interest rates are low relative to the bond's coupon, the put option is out of the money, so the bond is unlikely to be put. Thus, the effective duration of the putable bond is in this case very similar to that of an otherwise identical option-free bond. In contrast, when interest rates rise, the put option moves into the money and limits the price depreciation because the investor can put the bond and reinvest the proceeds of the retired bond at a higher yield. Thus, the put option reduces the effective duration of the putable bond relative to that of the straight bond.

When the embedded option (call or put) is deep in the money, the effective duration of the bond with an embedded option resembles that of the straight bond maturing on the first exercise date, reflecting the fact that the bond is highly likely to be called or put on that date.

Exhibit 20 compares the effective durations of option-free, callable, and putable bonds. All bonds are 4% annual coupon bonds with a maturity of 10 years. Both the call option and the put option are European-like and exercisable two months from now. The bonds are valued assuming a 4% flat yield curve and an interest rate volatility of 10%.

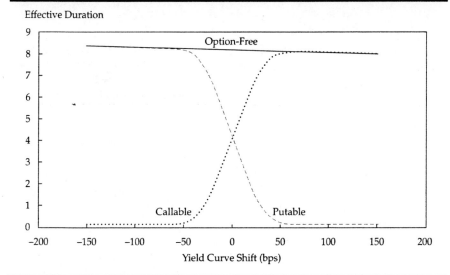

Exhibit 20 Comparison of the Effective Durations of Option-Free, Callable, and Putable Bonds

Exhibit 20 shows that the effective duration of an option-free bond changes very little in response to interest rate movements. As expected, when interest rates rise, the put option moves into the money, which limits the price depreciation of the putable bond and shortens its effective duration. In contrast, the effective duration of the callable bond shortens when interest rates fall, which is when the call option moves into the money, limiting the price appreciation of the callable bond.

EFFECTIVE DURATION IN PRACTICE

Effective duration is a concept most practically used in the context of a portfolio. Thus, an understanding of the effective durations of various types of instruments helps manage portfolio duration. In the following table, we show some properties of the effective duration of cash and the common types of bonds:[6]

Type of Bond	Effective Duration
Cash	0
Zero-coupon bond	≈ Maturity
Fixed-rate bond	< Maturity
Callable bond	≤ Duration of straight bond
Putable bond	≤ Duration of straight bond
Floater (Libor flat)	≈ Time (in years) to next reset

In general, a bond's effective duration does not exceed its maturity. There are a few exceptions, however, such as tax-exempt bonds when analyzed on an after-tax basis.

Knowing the effective duration of each type of bond is useful when one needs to change portfolio duration. For example, if a portfolio manager wants to shorten the effective duration of a portfolio of fixed-rate bonds, he or she can add floaters. For the

---

6 Because the curve shift unit in the denominator of the effective duration formula in Equation 3 is expressed per year, it turns out that the unit of effective duration is in years. In practice, however, effective duration is not viewed as a time measure but as an interest rate risk measure—that is, it reflects the percentage change in price per 100-bps change in interest rates.

debt manager of a company or other issuing entity, another way of shortening effective duration is to issue callable bonds. The topic of changing portfolio duration is covered thoroughly in Level III.

4.1.2 *One-Sided Durations*

Effective durations are normally calculated by averaging the changes resulting from shifting the benchmark yield curve up and down by the same amount. This calculation works well for option-free bonds but in the presence of embedded options, the results can be misleading. The problem is that when the embedded option is in the money, the price of the bond has limited upside potential if the bond is callable or limited downside potential if the bond is putable. Thus, the price sensitivity of bonds with embedded options is not symmetrical to positive and negative changes in interest rates of the same magnitude.

Consider, for example, a 4.5% bond maturing in five years, which is currently callable at 100. On a 4% flat yield curve at 15% volatility, the value of this callable bond is 99.75. If interest rates declined by 30 bps, the price would rise to 100. In fact, no matter how far interest rates decline, the price of the callable bond cannot exceed 100 because no investor will pay more than the price at which the bond can be immediately called. In contrast, there is no limit to the price decline if interest rates rise. Thus, the average price response to up- and down-shifts of interest rates (effective duration) is not as informative as the price responses to the up-shift (one-sided up-duration) and the down-shift (one-sided down-duration) of interest rates.

Exhibits 21 and 22 illustrate why **one-sided durations**—that is, the effective durations when interest rates go up or down—are better at capturing the interest rate sensitivity of a callable or putable bond than the (two-sided) effective duration, particularly when the embedded option is near the money.

Exhibit 21	Durations for a 4.5% Annual Coupon Bond Maturing in Five Years and Immediately Callable at Par on a 4% Flat Yield Curve at 15% Interest Rate Volatility		
	At a 4% **Flat Yield Curve**	**Interest Rate** **up by 30 bps**	**Interest Rate** **down by 30 bps**
Value of the Bond	99.75	99.17	100.00
Duration Measure	Effective duration 1.39	One-sided up-duration 1.94	One-sided down-duration 0.84

Exhibit 21 shows that a 30 bps increase in the interest rate has a greater effect on the value of the callable bond than a 30 bps decrease in the interest rate. The fact that the one-sided up-duration is higher than the one-sided down-duration confirms that the callable bond is more sensitive to interest rate rises than to interest rate declines.

Exhibit 22   Durations for a 4.1% Annual Coupon Bond Maturing in Five Years and Immediately Putable at Par on a 4% Flat Yield Curve at 15% Interest Rate Volatility

	At a 4% Flat Yield Curve	Interest Rate up by 30 bps	Interest Rate down by 30 bps
Value of the Bond	100.45	100.00	101.81
Duration Measure	Effective duration 3.00	One-sided up-duration 1.49	One-sided down-duration 4.51

The one-sided durations in Exhibit 22 indicate that the putable bond is more sensitive to interest rate declines than to interest rate rises.

4.1.3 *Key Rate Durations*

Effective duration is calculated by assuming parallel shifts in the benchmark yield curve. In reality, however, interest rate movements are not as neat. Many portfolio managers and risk managers like to isolate the price responses to changes in the rates of key maturities on the benchmark yield curve. For example, how would the price of a bond be expected to change if only the two-year benchmark rate moved up by 5 bps? The answer is found by using **key rate durations** (also known as partial durations), which reflect the sensitivity of the bond's price to changes in specific maturities on the benchmark yield curve. Thus, key rate durations help portfolio managers and risk managers identify the "shaping risk" for bonds—that is, the bond's sensitivity to changes in the shape of the yield curve (e.g., steepening and flattening).

The valuation procedure and formula applied in the calculation of key rate durations are identical to those used in the calculation of effective duration, but instead of shifting the entire benchmark yield curve, only key points are shifted, one at a time. Thus, the effective duration for each maturity point shift is calculated in isolation.

Exhibits 23, 24, and 25 show the key rate durations for bonds valued at a 4% flat yield curve. Exhibit 23 examines option-free bonds, and Exhibits 24 and 25 extend the analysis to callable and putable bonds, respectively.

Exhibit 23   Key Rate Durations of 10-Year Option-Free Bonds Valued at a 4% Flat Yield Curve

Coupon (%)	Price (% of par)	Key Rate Durations				
		Total	2-Year	3-Year	5-Year	10-Year
0	67.30	9.81	−0.07	−0.34	−0.93	11.15
2	83.65	8.83	−0.03	−0.13	−0.37	9.37
4	100.00	8.18	0.00	0.00	0.00	8.18
6	116.35	7.71	0.02	0.10	0.27	7.32
8	132.70	7.35	0.04	0.17	0.47	6.68
10	149.05	7.07	0.05	0.22	0.62	6.18

As shown in Exhibit 23, for option-free bonds not trading at par (the white rows), shifting any par rate has an effect on the value of the bond, but shifting the maturity-matched (10-year in this example) par rate has the greatest effect. This is simply because the largest cash flow of a fixed-rate bond occurs at maturity with the payment of both the final coupon and the principal.

For an option-free bond trading at par (the shaded row), the maturity-matched par rate is the only rate that affects the bond's value. It is a definitional consequence of "par" rates. If the 10-year par rate on a curve is 4%, then a 4% 10-year bond valued on that curve at zero OAS will be worth par, regardless of the par rates of the other maturity points on the curve. In other words, shifting any rate other than the 10-year rate on the par yield curve will not change the value of a 10-year bond trading at par. Shifting a par rate up or down at a particular maturity point, however, respectively increases or decreases the *discount rate* at that maturity point. These facts will be useful to remember in the following paragraph.

As illustrated in Exhibit 23, key rate durations can sometimes be negative for maturity points that are shorter than the maturity of the bond being analyzed if the bond is a zero-coupon bond or has a very low coupon. We can explain why this is the case by using the zero-coupon bond (the first row of Exhibit 23). As discussed in the previous paragraph, if we increase the five-year par rate, the value of a 10-year bond trading at par must remain unchanged because the 10-year par rate has not changed. But the five-year zero-coupon rate has increased because of the increase in the five-year par rate. Thus, the value of the five-year coupon of the 10-year bond trading at par will be lower than before the increase. But because the value of the 10-year bond trading at par must remain par, the remaining cash flows, including the cash flow occurring in Year 10, must be discounted at slightly *lower* rates to compensate. This results in a lower 10-year zero-coupon rate, which makes the value of a 10-year zero-coupon bond (whose only cash flow is in Year 10) *rise* in response to an *upward* change in the five-year par rate. Consequently, the five-year key rate duration for a 10-year zero-coupon bond is negative (−0.93).

Unlike for option-free bonds, the key rate durations of bonds with embedded options depend not only on the *time to maturity* but also on the *time to exercise*. Exhibits 24 and 25 illustrate this phenomenon for 30-year callable and putable bonds. Both the call option and the put option are European-like exercisable 10 years from now, and the bonds are valued assuming a 4% flat yield curve and a volatility of 15%.

Exhibit 24	Key Rate Durations of 30-Year Bonds Callable in 10 Years Valued at a 4% Flat Yield Curve with 15% Interest Rate Volatility						
Coupon (%)	Price (% of par)	Key Rate Durations					
		Total	2-Year	3-Year	5-Year	10-Year	30-Year
2	64.99	19.73	−0.02	−0.08	−0.21	−1.97	22.01
4	94.03	13.18	0.00	0.02	0.05	3.57	9.54
6	114.67	9.11	0.02	0.10	0.29	6.00	2.70
8	132.27	7.74	0.04	0.17	0.48	6.40	0.66
10	148.95	7.14	0.05	0.22	0.62	6.06	0.19

The bond with a coupon of 2% (the first row of Exhibit 21) is unlikely to be called, and thus it behaves more like a 30-year option-free bond, whose effective duration depends primarily on movements in the 30-year par rate. Therefore, the rate that has the highest effect on the value of the callable bond is the maturity-matched (30-year) rate. As the bond's coupon increases, however, so does the likelihood of the bond being called. Thus, the bond's total effective duration shortens, and the rate that has the highest effect on the callable bond's value gradually shifts from the 30-year rate to the 10-year rate. At the very high coupon of 10%, because of the virtual certainty of being called, the callable bond behaves like a 10-year option-free bond; the 30-year key rate duration is negligible (0.19) relative to the 10-year key rate duration (6.06).

Coupon (%)	Price (% of par)	Key Rate Durations					
		Total	2-Year	3-Year	5-Year	10-Year	30-Year
2	83.89	9.24	−0.03	−0.14	−0.38	8.98	0.81
4	105.97	12.44	0.00	−0.01	−0.05	4.53	7.97
6	136.44	14.75	0.01	0.03	0.08	2.27	12.37
8	169.96	14.90	0.01	0.06	0.16	2.12	12.56
10	204.38	14.65	0.02	0.07	0.21	2.39	11.96

Exhibit 25   Key Rate Durations of 30-Year Bonds Putable in 10 Years Valued at a 4% Flat Yield Curve with 15% Interest Rate Volatility

If the 30-year bond putable in 10 years has a high coupon, its price is more sensitive to the 30-year rate because it is unlikely to be put and thus behaves like an otherwise identical option-free bond. The 10% putable bond (the last row of Exhibit 25), for example, is most sensitive to changes in the 30-year rate, as illustrated by a 30-year key rate duration of 11.96. At the other extreme, a low-coupon bond is most sensitive to movements in the 10-year rate. It is almost certain to be put and so behaves like an option-free bond maturing on the put date.

4.2 Effective Convexity

Duration is an approximation of the expected bond price responses to changes in interest rates because actual changes in bond prices are not linear, particularly for bonds with embedded options. Thus, it is useful to measure **effective convexity**—that is, the sensitivity of duration to changes in interest rates—as well. The formula to calculate a bond's effective convexity is

$$\text{Effective convexity} = \frac{(PV_-) + (PV_+) - \left[2 \times (PV_0)\right]}{(\Delta\text{Curve})^2 \times (PV_0)} \qquad \textbf{(4)}$$

where

ΔCurve = the magnitude of the parallel shift in the benchmark yield curve (in decimal);

PV_- = the full price of the bond when the benchmark yield curve is shifted down by ΔCurve;

PV_+ = the full price of the bond when the benchmark yield curve is shifted up by ΔCurve; and

PV_0 = the current full price of the bond (i.e., with no shift).

Let us return to the three-year 4.25% bond callable at par in one year and two years from now. We still use the same par yield curve (i.e., one-year, two-year, and three-year par yields of 2.500%, 3.000%, and 3.500%, respectively) and the same interest rate volatility (10%) as before, but we now assume that the bond's current full price is 100.785 instead of 101.000. Thus, the implied OAS is 40 bps. Given 30 bps shifts in the benchmark yield curve, the resulting PV_- and PV_+ are 101.381 and 100.146, respectively. Using Equation 4, the effective convexity is:

$$\frac{101.381 + 100.146 - 2 \times 100.785}{(0.003)^2 \times 100.785} = -47.41$$

Exhibit 20 in Section 4.1.1, although displaying effective durations, also illustrates the effective convexities of option-free, callable, and putable bonds. The option-free bond exhibits low positive convexity—that is, the price of an option-free bond rises slightly more when interest rates move down than it declines when interest rates move up by the same amount.

When interest rates are high and the value of the call option is low, the callable and straight bond experience very similar effects from changes in interest rates. They both have positive convexity. However, the effective convexity of the callable bond turns negative when the call option is near the money, as in the example just presented, which indicates that the upside for a callable bond is much smaller than the downside. The reason is because when interest rates decline, the price of the callable bond is capped by the price of the call option if it is near the exercise date.

Conversely, putable bonds always have positive convexity. When the option is near the money, the upside for a putable bond is much larger than the downside because the price of a putable bond is floored by the price of the put option if it is near the exercise date.

Compared side by side, putable bonds have more upside potential than otherwise identical callable bonds when interest rates decline. In contrast, when interest rates rise, callable bonds have more upside potential than otherwise identical putable bonds.

EXAMPLE 7

Interest Rate Sensitivity

Erna Smith, a portfolio manager, has two fixed-rate bonds in her portfolio: a callable bond (Bond X) and a putable bond (Bond Y). She wants to examine the interest rate sensitivity of these two bonds to a parallel shift in the benchmark yield curve. Assuming an interest rate volatility of 10%, her valuation software shows how the prices of these bonds change for 30-bps shifts up or down:

	Bond X	Bond Y
Time to maturity	Three years from today	Three years from today
Coupon	3.75% annual	3.75% annual
Type of bond	Callable at par one year from today	Putable at par one year from today
Current price (% of par)	100.594	101.330
Price (% of par) when shifting the benchmark yield curve down by 30 bps	101.194	101.882
Price (% of par) when shifting the benchmark yield curve up by 30 bps	99.860	100.924

1 The effective duration for Bond X is *closest* to:

A 0.67.

B 2.21.

C 4.42.

2 The effective duration for Bond Y is *closest* to:

A 0.48.

B 0.96.

      C 1.58.

3 When interest rates rise, the effective duration of:

    A Bond X shortens.

    B Bond Y shortens.

    C the underlying option-free (straight) bond corresponding to Bond X lengthens.

4 When the option embedded in Bond Y is in the money, the one-sided durations *most likely* show that the bond is:

    A more sensitive to a decrease in interest rates.

    B more sensitive to an increase in interest rates.

    C equally sensitive to a decrease or to an increase in interest rates.

5 The price of Bond X is affected:

    A only by a shift in the one-year par rate.

    B only by a shift in the three-year par rate.

    C by all par rate shifts but is most sensitive to shifts in the one-year and three-year par rates.

6 The effective convexity of Bond X:

    A cannot be negative.

    B turns negative when the embedded option is near the money.

    C turns negative when the embedded option moves out of the money.

7 Which of the following statements is *most* accurate?

    A Bond Y exhibits negative convexity.

    B For a given decline in interest rate, Bond X has less upside potential than Bond Y.

    C The underlying option-free (straight) bond corresponding to Bond Y exhibits negative convexity.

Solution to 1:

B is correct. The effective duration for Bond X is

$$\text{Effective duration} = \frac{101.194 - 99.860}{2 \times 0.003 \times 100.594} = 2.21$$

A is incorrect because the duration of a bond with a single cash flow one year from now is approximately one year, so 0.67 is too low, even assuming that the bond will be called in one year with certainty. C is incorrect because 4.42 exceeds the maturity of Bond X (three years).

Solution to 2:

C is correct. The effective duration for Bond Y is

$$\text{Effective duration} = \frac{101.882 - 100.294}{2 \times 0.003 \times 101.330} = 1.58$$

Solution to 3:

B is correct. When interest rates rise, a put option moves into the money, and the putable bond is more likely to be put. Thus, it behaves like a shorter-maturity bond, and its effective duration shortens. A is incorrect because when interest rates rise, a call option moves out of the money, so the callable bond is less likely to be called. C is incorrect because the effective duration of an option-free bond changes very little in response to interest rate movements.

Solution to 4:

A is correct. If interest rates rise, the investor's ability to put the bond at par limits the price depreciation. In contrast, there is no limit to the increase in the bond's price when interest rates decline. Thus, the price of a putable bond whose embedded option is in the money is more sensitive to a decrease in interest rates.

Solution to 5:

C is correct. The main driver of the call decision is the two-year forward rate one year from now. This rate is most significantly affected by changes in the one-year and three-year par rates.

Solution to 6:

B is correct. The effective convexity of a callable bond turns negative when the call option is near the money because the price response of a callable bond to lower interest rates is capped by the call option. That is, in case of a decline in interest rates, the issuer will call the bonds and refund at lower rates, thus limiting the upside potential for the investor.

Solution to 7:

B is correct. As interest rates decline, the value of a call option increases whereas the value of a put option decreases. The call option embedded in Bond X limits its price appreciation, but there is no such cap for Bond Y. Thus, Bond X has less upside potential than Bond Y. A is incorrect because a putable bond always has positive convexity—that is, Bond Y has more upside than downside potential. C is incorrect because an option-free bond exhibits low positive convexity.

5 VALUATION AND ANALYSIS OF CAPPED AND FLOORED FLOATING-RATE BONDS

Options in floating-rate bonds (floaters) are exercised automatically depending on the course of interest rates—that is, if the coupon rate rises or falls below the threshold, the cap or floor automatically applies. Similar to callable and putable bonds, capped and floored floaters can be valued by using the arbitrage-free framework.

5.1 Valuation of a Capped Floater

The cap provision in a floater prevents the coupon rate from increasing above a specified maximum rate. As a consequence, a **capped floater** protects the issuer against rising interest rates and is thus an issuer option. Because the investor is long the bond but short the embedded option, the value of the cap decreases the value of the capped floater relative to the value of the straight bond:

Value of capped floater
    = Value of straight bond − Value of embedded cap   (5)

To illustrate how to value a capped floater, consider a floating-rate bond that has a three-year maturity. The floater's coupon pays the one-year Libor annually, set in arrears, and is capped at 4.500%. The term "set in arrears" means that the coupon rate is set at the beginning of the coupon period—that is, the coupon to be paid in one year is determined now. For simplicity, we assume that the issuer's credit quality closely matches the Libor swap curve (i.e., there is no credit spread) and that the

Libor swap curve is the same as the par yield curve given in Exhibit 1 (i.e., one-year, two-year, and three-year par yields of 2.500%, 3.000%, and 3.500%, respectively). We also assume that the interest rate volatility is 10%.

The valuation of the capped floater is depicted in Exhibit 26.

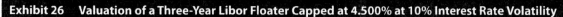

Exhibit 26   Valuation of a Three-Year Libor Floater Capped at 4.500% at 10% Interest Rate Volatility

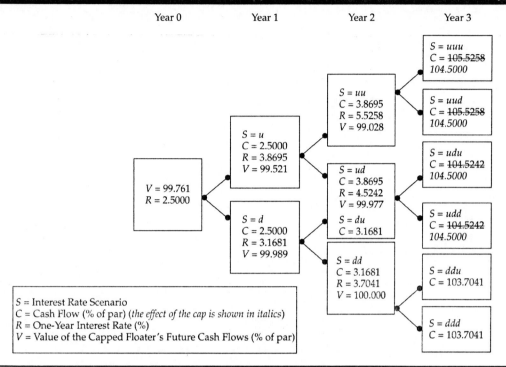

	Year 0	Year 1	Year 2	Year 3

S = uuu
C = ~~105.5258~~
104.5000

S = uu
C = 3.8695
R = 5.5258
V = 99.028

S = uud
C = ~~105.5258~~
104.5000

S = u
C = 2.5000
R = 3.8695
V = 99.521

S = udu
C = ~~104.5242~~
104.5000

S = ud
C = 3.8695
R = 4.5242
V = 99.977

V = 99.761
R = 2.5000

S = du
C = 3.1681

S = udd
C = ~~104.5242~~
104.5000

S = d
C = 2.5000
R = 3.1681
V = 99.989

S = dd
C = 3.1681
R = 3.7041
V = 100.000

S = ddu
C = 103.7041

S = ddd
C = 103.7041

S = Interest Rate Scenario
C = Cash Flow (% of par) (*the effect of the cap is shown in italics*)
R = One-Year Interest Rate (%)
V = Value of the Capped Floater's Future Cash Flows (% of par)

Without a cap, the value of this floater would be 100 because in every scenario, the coupon paid would be equal to the discount rate. But because the coupon rate is capped at 4.500%, which is lower than the highest interest rates in the tree, the value of the capped floater will be lower than the value of the straight bond.

For each scenario, we check whether the cap applies, and if it does, the cash flow is adjusted accordingly. For example, in state *uuu*, Libor is higher than the 4.500% cap. Thus, the coupon is capped at the 4.500 maximum amount, and the cash flow is adjusted downward from the uncapped amount (105.5258) to the capped amount (104.5000). The coupon is also capped for three other scenarios in Year 3.

As expected, the value of the capped floater is lower than 100 (99.761). The value of the cap can be calculated by using Equation 5:

Value of embedded cap = 100 − 99.761 = 0.239

RATCHET BONDS: DEBT MANAGEMENT ON AUTOPILOT

Ratchet bonds are floating-rate bonds with both issuer and investor options. As with conventional floaters, the coupon is reset periodically according to a formula based on a reference rate and a credit spread. A capped floater protects the issuer against rising interest rates. Ratchet bonds offer extreme protection: At the time of reset, the coupon can only decline; it can never exceed the existing level. So, over time, the coupon "ratchets down."

The Tennessee Valley Authority (TVA) was the first issuer of ratchet bonds. In 1998, it issued $575 million 6.75% "PARRS" due 1 June 2028. The coupon rate was resettable on 1 June 2003 and annually thereafter. Exhibit 27 shows annual coupon resets since 2003:[7]

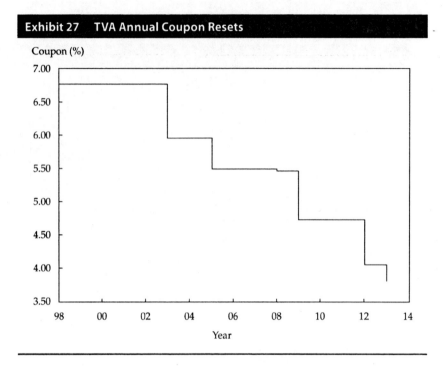

Exhibit 27   TVA Annual Coupon Resets

This ratchet bond has allowed TVA to reduce its borrowing rate by 292 bps without refinancing. You may wonder why anyone would buy such a bond. The answer is that at issuance, the coupon of a ratchet bond is much higher than that of a standard floater. In fact, the initial coupon is set well above the issuer's long-term option-free borrowing rate in order to compensate investors for the potential loss of interest income over time. In this regard, a ratchet bond is similar to a conventional callable bond: When the bond is called, the investor must purchase a replacement in the prevailing lower rate environment. The initial above-market coupon of a callable bond reflects this possibility.

A ratchet bond can be thought of as the lifecycle of a callable bond through several possible calls, in which the bond is replaced by one that is itself callable, to the original maturity. The appeal for the issuer is that these "calls" entail no transaction cost, and the call decision is on autopilot.

Ratchet bonds also contain investor options. Whenever a coupon is reset, the investor has the right to put the bonds back to the issuer at par. The embedded option is called a "contingent put" because the right to put is available to the investor *only* if the coupon is reset. The coupon reset formula of ratchet bonds is designed to assure that the market price at the time of reset is above par, provided that the issuer's credit quality does not deteriorate. Therefore, the contingent put offers investors protection against an adverse credit event. Needless to say, the valuation of a ratchet bond is rather complex.

---

7 See A. Kalotay and L. Abreo, "Ratchet Bonds: Maximum Refunding Efficiency at Minimum Transaction Cost," *Journal of Applied Corporate Finance*, vol. 12, no. 1 (Spring 1999):40–47.

5.2 Valuation of a Floored Floater

The floor provision in a floater prevents the coupon rate from decreasing below a specified minimum rate. As a consequence, a **floored floater** protects the investor against declining interest rates and is thus an investor option. Because the investor is long both the bond and the embedded option, the value of the floor increases the value of the floored floater relative to the value of the straight bond:

Value of floored floater
= Value of straight bond + Value of embedded floor **(6)**

To illustrate how to value a floored floater, we return to the example we used for the capped floater but assume that the embedded option is now a 3.500% floor instead of a 4.500% cap. The other assumptions remain the same. The valuation of the floored floater is depicted in Exhibit 28.

Exhibit 28   Valuation of a Three-Year Libor Floater Floored at 3.500% at 10% Interest Rate Volatility

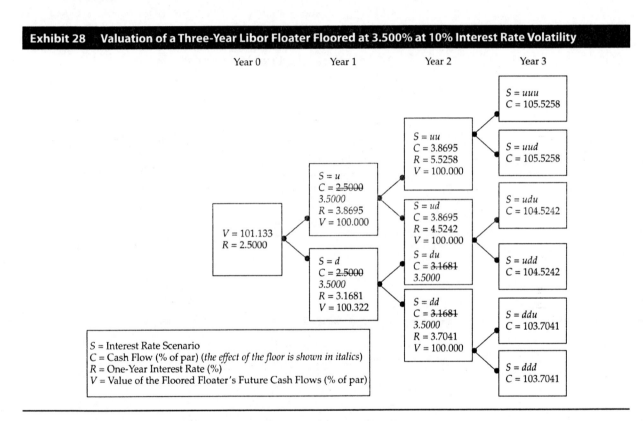

Recall from the discussion about the capped floater that if there were no cap, the value of the floater would be 100 because the coupon paid would equal the discount rate. The same principle applies here: If there were no floor, the value of this floater would be 100. Because the presence of the floor potentially increases the cash flows, however, the value of the floored floater must be equal to or higher than the value of the straight bond.

Exhibit 28 shows that the floor applies in four scenarios in Years 1 and 2, thus increasing the cash flows to the minimum amount of 3.500. As a consequence, the value of the floored floater exceeds 100 (101.133). The value of the floor can be calculated by using Equation 6:

Value of embedded floor = 101.133 − 100 = 1.133

EXAMPLE 8

Valuation of Capped and Floored Floaters

1 A three-year floating rate bond pays annual coupons of one-year Libor (set in arrears) and is capped at 5.600%. The Libor swap curve is as given in Exhibit 1 (i.e., the one-year, two-year, and three-year par yields are 2.500%, 3.000%, and 3.500%, respectively), and interest rate volatility is 10%. The value of the capped floater is *closest to*:

   A 100.000.

   B 105.600.

   C 105.921.

2 A three-year floating-rate bond pays annual coupons of one-year Libor (set in arrears) and is floored at 3.000%. The Libor swap curve is as given in Exhibit 1 (i.e., the one-year, two-year, and three-year par yields are 2.500%, 3.000%, and 3.500%, respectively), and interest rate volatility is 10%. The value of the floored floater is *closest to*:

   A 100.000.

   B 100.488.

   C 103.000.

3 An issuer in the Eurozone wants to sell a three-year floating-rate note at par with an annual coupon based on the 12-month Euribor + 300 bps. Because the 12-month Euribor is currently at an historic low and the issuer wants to protect itself against a sudden increase in interest cost, the issuer's advisers recommend increasing the credit spread to 320 bps and capping the coupon at 5.50%. Assuming an interest rate volatility of 8%, the advisers have constructed the following binomial interest rate tree:

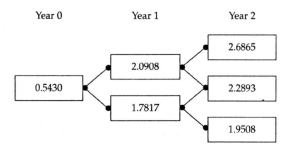

   The value of the capped floater is *closest to*:

   A 92.929.

   B 99.916.

   C 109.265.

Solution to 1:

A is correct. As illustrated in Exhibit 26, the cap is higher than any of the rates at which the floater is reset on the interest rate tree. Thus, the value of the bond is the same as if it had no cap—that is, 100.

Solution to 2:

B is correct. One can eliminate C because as illustrated in Exhibit 28, all else being equal, the bond with a higher floor (3.500%) has a value of 101.133. The value of a bond with a floor of 3.000% cannot be higher. Intuitively, B is the likely correct answer because the straight bond is worth 100. However, it is still necessary to calculate the value of the floored floater because if the floor is low enough, it could be worthless.

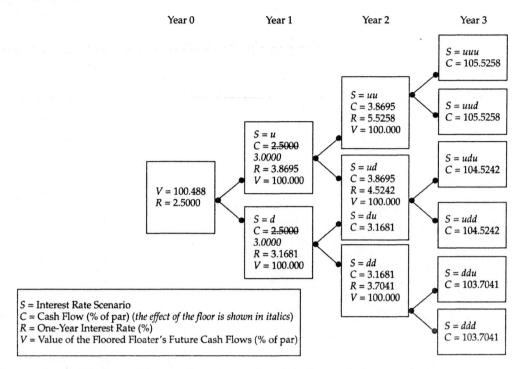

Here, it turns out that the floor adds 0.488 in value to the straight bond. Had the floor been 2.500%, the floored floater and the straight bond would both be worth par.

Solution to 3:

B is correct.

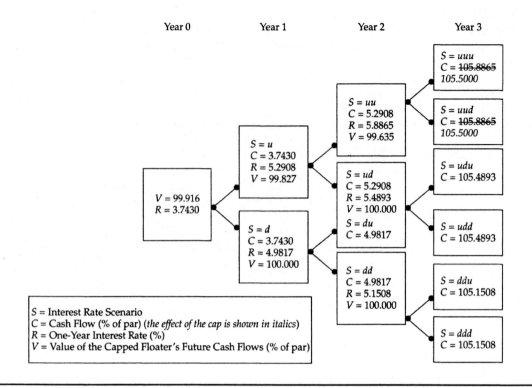

S = Interest Rate Scenario
C = Cash Flow (% of par) (*the effect of the cap is shown in italics*)
R = One-Year Interest Rate (%)
V = Value of the Capped Floater's Future Cash Flows (% of par)

6   VALUATION AND ANALYSIS OF CONVERTIBLE BONDS

So far, we have discussed bonds for which the exercise of the option is at the discretion of the issuer (callable bond), at the discretion of the bondholder (putable bond), or set through a pre-defined contractual arrangement (capped and floored floaters). What distinguishes a convertible bond from the bonds discussed earlier is that exercising the option results in the change of the security from a bond to a common stock. This section describes defining features of convertible bonds and discusses how to analyze and value these bonds.

6.1 Defining Features of a Convertible Bond

A **convertible bond** is a hybrid security. In its traditional form, it presents the characteristics of an option-free bond and an embedded conversion option. The conversion option is a call option on the issuer's common stock, which gives bondholders the right to convert their debt into equity during a pre-determined period (known as the **conversion period**) at a pre-determined price (known as the **conversion price**).

Convertible bonds have been issued and traded since the 1880s. They offer benefits to both the issuer and the investors. Investors usually accept a lower coupon for convertible bonds than for otherwise identical non-convertible bonds because they can participate in the potential upside through the conversion mechanism—that is, if the share price of the issuer's common stock (underlying share price) exceeds the conversion price, the bondholders can convert their bonds into shares at a cost lower than market value. The issuer benefits from paying a lower coupon. In case of conversion, an added benefit for the issuer is that it no longer has to repay the debt that was converted into equity.

However, what might appear as a win–win situation for both the issuer and the investors is not a "free lunch" because the issuer's existing shareholders face dilution in case of conversion. In addition, if the underlying share price remains below the conversion price and the bond is not converted, the issuer must repay the debt or refinance it, potentially at a higher cost. If conversion is not achieved, the bondholders will have lost interest income relative to an otherwise identical non-convertible bond that would have been issued with a higher coupon and would have thus offered investors an additional spread.

We will use the information provided in Exhibit 29 to describe the features of a convertible bond and then illustrate how to analyze it. This exhibit refers to a callable convertible bond issued by Waste Management Utility PLC (WMU), a company listed on the London Stock Exchange.

Exhibit 29 WMU £100,000,000 4.50% Callable Convertible Bonds Due 3 April 2017

Excerpt from the Bond's Offering Circular

- **Issue Date:** 3 April 2012
- **Status:** Senior unsecured, unsubordinated
- **Interest:** 4.50% of nominal value (par) per annum payable annually in arrears, with the first interest payment date on 3 April 2013 unless prior redeemed or converted
- **Issue Price:** 100% of par denominated into bonds of £100,000 each and integral multiples of £1,000 each thereafter
- **Conversion Period:** 3 May 2012 to 5 March 2017
- **Initial Conversion Price:** £6.00 per share
- **Conversion Ratio:** Each bond of par value of £100,000 is convertible to 16,666.67 ordinary shares
- **Threshold Dividend:** £0.30 per share
- **Change of Control Conversion Price:** £4.00 per share
- **Issuer Call Price:** From the second anniversary of issuance: 110%; from the third anniversary of issuance: 105%; from the fourth anniversary of issuance: 103%

Market Information

- **Convertible Bond Price on 4 April 2013:** £127,006
- **Share Price on Issue Date:** £4.58
- **Share Price on 4 April 2013:** £6.23
- **Dividend per Share:** £0.16
- **Share Price Volatility per annum as of 4 April 2013:** 25%

The applicable share price at which the investor can convert the bonds into ordinary (common) shares is called the conversion price. In the WMU example provided in Exhibit 29, the conversion price was set at £6 per share.

The number of shares of common stock that the bondholder receives from converting the bonds into shares is called the **conversion ratio**. In the WMU example, bondholders who have invested the minimum stipulated of £100,000 and convert their bonds into shares will receive 16,666.67 shares each (£100,000/£6) per £100,000 of nominal value. The conversion may be exercised during a particular period or at set intervals during the life of the bond. To accommodate share price volatility and technical settlement requirements, it is not uncommon to see conversion periods similar to the one in Exhibit 29—that is, beginning shortly after the issuance of the convertible bond and ending shortly prior to its maturity.

The conversion price in Exhibit 29 is referred to as the *initial* conversion price because it reflects the conversion price *at issuance*. Corporate actions, such as stock splits, bonus share issuances, and rights or warrants issuances, affect a company's share price and may reduce the benefit of conversion for the convertible bondholders. Thus, the terms of issuance of the convertible bond contain detailed information defining how the conversion price and conversion ratio are adjusted should such a corporate action occur during the life of the bond. For example, suppose that WMU performs a 2:1 stock split to its common shareholders. In this case, the conversion price would be adjusted to £3.00 per share and the conversion ratio would then be adjusted to 33,333.33 shares per £100,000 of nominal value.

As long as the convertible bond is still outstanding and has not been converted, the bondholders receive interest payments (annually in the WMU example). Meanwhile, if the issuer declares and pays dividends, common shareholders receive dividend payments. The terms of issuance may offer no compensation to convertible bondholders for dividends paid out during the life of the bond at one extreme, or they may offer full protection by adjusting the conversion price downward for any dividend payments at the other extreme. Typically, a threshold dividend is defined in the terms of issuance (£0.30 per share in the WMU example). Annual dividend payments below the threshold dividend have no effect on the conversion price. In contrast, the conversion price is adjusted downward for annual dividend payments above the threshold dividend to offer compensation to convertible bondholders.

Should the issuer be acquired by or merged with another company during the life of the bond, bondholders might no longer be willing to continue lending to the new entity. Change-of-control events are defined in the prospectus or offering circular and, if such an event occurs, convertible bondholders usually have the choice between

- a put option that can be exercised during a specified period following the change-of-control event and that provides full redemption of the nominal value of the bond; or
- an adjusted conversion price that is lower than the initial conversion price. This downward adjustment gives the convertible bondholders the opportunity to convert their bonds into shares earlier and at more advantageous terms, and thus allows them to participate in the announced merger or acquisition as common shareholders.

In addition to a put option in case of a change-of-control event, it is not unusual for a convertible bond to include a put option that convertible bondholders can exercise during specified periods. Put options can be classified as "hard" puts or "soft" puts. In the case of a hard put, the issuer must redeem the convertible bond for cash. In the case of a soft put, the investor has the right to exercise the put but the issuer chooses how the payment will be made. The issuer may redeem the convertible bond for cash, common stock, subordinated notes, or a combination of the three.

It is more frequent for convertible bonds to include a call option that gives the issuer the right to call the bond during a specified period and at specified times. As discussed earlier, the issuer may exercise the call option and redeem the bond early if interest rates are falling or if its credit rating is revised upward, thus enabling the issuance of debt at a lower cost. The issuer may also believe that its share price will increase significantly in the future because of its performance or because of events that will take place in the economy or in its sector. In this case, the issuer may try to maximize the benefit to its existing shareholders relative to convertible bondholders and call the bond. To offer convertible bondholders protection against early repayment, convertible bonds usually have a lockout period. Subsequently, they can be called but at a premium, which decreases as the maturity of the bond approaches. In the WMU example, the convertible bond is not callable until its second anniversary, when it is callable at a premium of 10% above par value. The premium decreases to 5% at its third anniversary and 3% at its fourth anniversary.

If a convertible bond is callable, the issuer has an incentive to call the bond when the underlying share price increases above the conversion price in order to avoid paying further coupons. Such an event is called **forced conversion** because it forces bondholders to convert their bonds into shares. Otherwise, the redemption value that bondholders would receive from the issuer calling the bond would result in a disadvantageous position and a loss compared with conversion. Even if interest rates have not fallen or the issuer's credit rating has not improved, thus not allowing refinancing at a lower cost, the issuer might still proceed with calling the bond when the underlying share price exceeds the conversion price. Doing so allows the issuer to take advantage of the favorable equity market conditions and force the bondholders to convert their bonds into shares. The forced conversion strengthens the issuer's capital structure and eliminates the risk that a subsequent correction in equity prices prevents conversion and requires redeeming the convertible bonds at maturity.

6.2 Analysis of a Convertible Bond

There are a number of investment metrics and ratios that help in analyzing and valuing a convertible bond.

6.2.1 Conversion Value

The **conversion value** or parity value of a convertible bond indicates the value of the bond if it is converted at the market price of the shares.

Conversion value = Underlying share price × Conversion ratio

Based on the information provided in Exhibit 29, we can calculate the conversion value for WMU's convertible bonds at the issuance date and on 4 April 2013:

Conversion value at the issuance date = £4.58 × 16,666.67 = £76,333.33

Conversion value on 4 April 2013 = £6.23 × 16,666.67 = £103,833.33

6.2.2 Minimum Value of a Convertible Bond

The minimum value of a convertible bond is equal to the greater of

- the conversion value and
- the value of the underlying option-free bond. Theoretically, the value of the straight bond (straight value) can be estimated by using the market value of a non-convertible bond of the issuer with the same characteristics as the convertible bond but without the conversion option. In practice, such a bond rarely exists. Thus, the straight value is found by using the arbitrage-free framework and by discounting the bond's future cash flows at the appropriate rates.

The minimum value of a convertible bond can also be described as a floor value. It is a *moving* floor, however, because the straight value is not fixed; it changes with fluctuations in interest rates and credit spreads. If interest rates rise, the value of the straight bond falls, making the floor fall. Similarly, if the issuer's credit spread increases as a result, for example, of a downgrade of its credit rating from investment grade to non-investment grade, the floor value will fall too.

Using the conversion values calculated in Section 6.2.1, the minimum value of WMU's convertible bonds at the issuance date is

$$\text{Minimum value at the issuance date} = \text{Maximum}(£76,333.33;£100,000)$$
$$= £100,000$$

The straight value at the issuance date is £100,000 because the issue price is set at 100% of par. But after this date, this value will fluctuate. Thus, to calculate the minimum value of WMU's convertible bond on 4 April 2013, it is first necessary to calculate the value of the straight bond that day using the arbitrage-free framework. From Exhibit 29, the coupon is 4.50%, paid annually. Assuming a 2.5% flat yield curve, the straight value on 4 April 2013 is:

$$\frac{£4,500}{(1.02500)} + \frac{£4,500}{(1.02500)^2} + \frac{£4,500}{(1.02500)^3} + \frac{£100,000 + £4,500}{(1.02500)^4} = £107,523.95$$

It follows that the minimum value of WMU's convertible bonds on 4 April 2013 is

$$\text{Minimum value on 4 April 2013} = \text{Maximum}(£103,833.33;£107,523.95)$$
$$= £107,523.95$$

If the value of the convertible bond were lower than the greater of the conversion value and the straight value, an arbitrage opportunity would ensue. Two scenarios help illustrate this concept. Returning to the WMU example, suppose that the convertible bond is selling for £103,833.33 on 4 April 2013—that is, at a price that is lower than the straight value of £107,523.95. In this scenario, the convertible bond is cheap relative to the straight bond; put another way, the convertible bond offers a higher yield than an otherwise identical non-convertible bond. Thus, investors will find the convertible bond attractive, buy it, and push its price up until the convertible bond price returns to the straight value and the arbitrage opportunity disappears.

Alternatively, assume that on 4 April 2013, the yield on otherwise identical non-convertible bonds is 5.00% instead of 2.50%. Using the arbitrage-free framework, the straight value is £98,227.02. Suppose that the convertible bond is selling at this straight value—that is, at a price that is lower than its conversion value of £103,833.33. In this case, an arbitrageur can buy the convertible bond for £98,227.02, convert it into 16,666.67 shares, and sell the shares at £4.58 each or £103,833.33 in total. The arbitrageur makes a profit equal to the difference between the conversion value and the straight value—that is, £5,606.31 (£103,833.33 – £98,227.02). As more arbitrageurs follow the same strategy, the convertible bond price will increase until it reaches the conversion value and the arbitrage opportunity disappears.

6.2.3 *Market Conversion Price, Market Conversion Premium per Share, and Market Conversion Premium Ratio*

Many investors do not buy a convertible bond at issuance on the primary market but instead buy such a bond later in its life on the secondary market. The **market conversion premium per share** allows investors to identify the premium or discount payable when buying the convertible bond rather than the underlying common stock.[8]

$$\text{Market conversion premium per share} = \text{Market conversion price} - \text{Underlying share price}$$

where

$$\text{Market conversion price} = \frac{\text{Convertible bond price}}{\text{Conversion ratio}}$$

The market conversion price represents the price that investors effectively pay for the underlying common stock if they buy the convertible bond and then convert it into shares. It can be viewed as a break-even price. Once the underlying share price exceeds the market conversion price, any further rise in the underlying share price is certain to increase the value of the convertible bond by at least the same percentage (we will discuss why this is the case in Section 6.4).

Based on the information provided in Exhibit 29,

$$\text{Market conversion price on 4 April 2013} = \frac{£127,006}{£16,666.67} = £7.62$$

and

$$\text{Market conversion premium per share on 4 April 2013} = £7.62 - £6.23 = £1.39$$

The **market conversion premium ratio** expresses the premium or discount investors have to pay as a percentage of the current market price of the shares:

$$\text{Market conversion premium ratio} = \frac{\text{Market conversion premium per share}}{\text{Underlying share price}}$$

In the WMU example,

$$\text{Market conversion premium ratio on 4 April 2013} = \frac{£1.39}{£6.23} = 22.32\%$$

Why would investors be willing to pay a premium to buy the convertible bond? Recall that the straight value acts as a floor for the convertible bond price. Thus, as the underlying share price falls, the convertible bond price will not fall below the straight value. Viewed in this context, the market conversion premium per share resembles the price of a call option. Investors who buy a call option limit their downside risk to the price of the call option (premium). Similarly, the premium paid when buying a convertible bond allows investors to limit their downside risk to the straight value. There is a fundamental difference, however, between the buyers of a call option and the buyers of a convertible bond. The former know exactly the amount of the downside risk, whereas the latter know only that the most they can lose is the difference between the convertible bond price and the straight value because the straight value is not fixed.

---

8 Although discounts are rare, they can theoretically happen given that the convertible bond and the underlying common stock trade in different markets with different types of market participants. For example, highly volatile share prices may result in the market conversion price being lower than the underlying share price.

6.2.4 *Downside Risk with a Convertible Bond*

Many investors use the straight value as a measure of the downside risk of a convertible bond, and calculate the following metric:

$$\text{Premium over straight value} = \frac{\text{Convertible bond price}}{\text{Straight value}} - 1$$

All else being equal, the higher the premium over straight value, the less attractive the convertible bond. In the WMU example,

$$\text{Premium over straight value} = \frac{£127,006}{£107,523.95} - 1 = 18.11\%$$

Despite its use in practice, the premium over straight value is a flawed measure of downside risk because, as mentioned earlier, the straight value is not fixed but rather fluctuates with changes in interest rates and credit spreads.

6.2.5 *Upside Potential of a Convertible Bond*

The upside potential of a convertible bond depends primarily on the prospects of the underlying common stock. Thus, convertible bond investors should be familiar with the techniques used to value and analyze common stocks. These techniques are covered in other readings.

6.3 Valuation of a Convertible Bond

Historically, the valuation of convertible bonds has been challenging because these securities combine characteristics of bonds, stocks, and options, thus requiring an understanding of what affects the value of fixed income, equity, and derivatives. The complexity of convertible bonds has also increased over time as a result of market innovations as well as additions to the terms and conditions of these securities. For example, convertible bonds have evolved into contingent convertible bonds and convertible contingent convertible bonds, which are even more complex to value and analyze.[9]

The fact that many bond's prospectuses or offering circulars frequently provide for an independent financial valuer to determine the conversion price (and in essence the value of the convertible bond) under different scenarios is evidence of the complexity associated with valuing convertible bonds. Because of this complexity, convertible bonds in many markets come with selling restrictions. They are typically offered in very high denominations and only to professional or institutional investors. Regulators perceive them as securities that are too risky for retail investors to invest in directly.

As with any fixed-income instrument, convertible bond investors should perform a diligent risk–reward analysis of the issuer, including its ability to service the debt and repay the principal, as well as a review of the bond's terms of issuance (e.g., collateral, credit enhancements, covenants, and contingent provisions). In addition, convertible bond investors must analyze the factors that typically affect bond prices, such as interest rate movements. Because most convertible bonds have lighter covenants than otherwise similar non-convertible bonds and are frequently issued as subordinated securities, the valuation and analysis of some convertible bonds can be complex.

---

9 Contingent convertible bonds, or "CoCos," pay a higher coupon than otherwise identical non-convertible bonds, but they are usually deeply subordinated and may be converted into equity or face principal write-downs if regulatory capital ratios are breached. Convertible contingent convertible bonds, or "CoCoCos," combine a traditional convertible bond and a CoCo. They are convertible at the discretion of the investor, thus offering upside potential if the share price increases, but they are also converted into equity or face principal write-downs in the event of a regulatory capital breach. CoCos and CoCoCos are usually issued by financial institutions, particularly in Europe.

The investment characteristics of a convertible bond depend on the underlying share price, so convertible bond investors must also analyze factors that may affect the issuer's common stock, including dividend payments and the issuer's actions (e.g., acquisitions or disposals, rights issues). Even if the issuer is performing well, adverse market conditions might depress share prices and prevent conversion. Thus, convertible bond investors must also identify and analyze the exogenous reasons that might ultimately have a negative effect on convertible bonds.

Academics and practitioners have developed advanced models to value convertible bonds, but the most commonly used model remains the arbitrage-free framework. A traditional convertible bond can be viewed as a straight bond and a call option on the issuer's common stock, so

Value of convertible bond = Value of straight bond
+ Value of call option on the issuer's stock

Many convertible bonds include a call option that gives the issuer the right to call the bond during a specified period and at specified times. The value of such bonds is

Value of callable convertible bond = Value of straight bond + Value of call option on the issuer's stock − Value of issuer call option

Suppose that the callable convertible bond also includes a put option that gives the bondholder the right to require that the issuer repurchases the bond. The value of such a bond is

Value of callable putable convertible bond = Value of straight bond + Value of call option on the issuer's stock − Value of issuer call option + Value of investor put option

No matter how many options are embedded into a bond, the valuation procedure remains the same. It relies on generating a tree of interest rates based on the given yield curve and interest rate volatility assumptions, determining at each node of the tree whether the embedded options will be exercised, and then applying the backward induction valuation methodology to calculate the present value of the bond.

6.4 Comparison of the Risk–Return Characteristics of a Convertible Bond, the Straight Bond, and the Underlying Common Stock

In its simplest form, a convertible bond can be viewed as a straight bond and a call option on the issuer's common stock. When the underlying share price is well below the conversion price, the convertible bond is described as "busted convertible" and exhibits mostly bond risk–return characteristics—that is, the risk–return characteristics of the convertible bond resemble those of the underlying option-free (straight) bond. In this case, the call option is out of the money, so share price movements do not significantly affect the price of the call option and, thus, the price of the convertible bond. Consequently, the price movement of the convertible bond closely follows that of the straight bond, and such factors as interest rate movements and credit spreads significantly affect the convertible bond price. The convertible bond exhibits even stronger bond risk–return characteristics when the call option is out of the money and the conversion period is approaching its end because the time value component of the option decreases toward zero, and it is highly likely that the conversion option will expire worthless.

In contrast, when the underlying share price is above the conversion price, a convertible bond exhibits mostly stock risk–return characteristics—that is, the risk–return characteristics of the convertible bond resemble those of the underlying common stock. In this case, the call option is in the money, so the price of the call option and thus the price of the convertible bond is significantly affected by share price movements but mostly unaffected by factors driving the value of an otherwise identical option-free bond, such as interest rate movements. When the call option is in the money, it is more likely to be exercised by the bondholder and the value of the shares resulting from the conversion is higher than the redemption value of the bond. Such convertible bonds trade at prices that follow closely the conversion value of the convertible bond, and their price exhibits similar movements to that of the underlying stock.

In between the bond and the stock extremes, the convertible bond trades like a hybrid instrument. It is important to note the risk–return characteristics of convertible bonds (1) when the underlying share price is below the conversion price and increases toward it and (2) when the underlying share price is above the conversion price but decreases toward it.

In the first case, the call option component increases significantly in value as the underlying share price approaches the conversion price. The return on the convertible bond during such periods increases significantly but at a lower rate than the increase in the underlying share price because the conversion price has not been reached yet. When the share price exceeds the conversion price and goes higher, the change in the convertible bond price converges toward the change in the underlying share price—this is why we noted in Section 6.2.4 that when the underlying share price exceeds the market conversion price, any further rise in the underlying share price is certain to increase the value of the convertible bond by at least the same percentage.

In the second case (that is, when the underlying share price is above the conversion price but decreases toward it), the relative change in the convertible bond price is less than the change in the underlying share price because the convertible bond has a floor. As mentioned earlier, this floor is the minimum value of the convertible bond, which in this case is equal to the value of the underlying option-free bond.

Exhibit 30 illustrates graphically the price behavior of a convertible bond and the underlying common stock.

Exhibit 30   Price Behavior of a Convertible Bond and the Underlying Common Stock

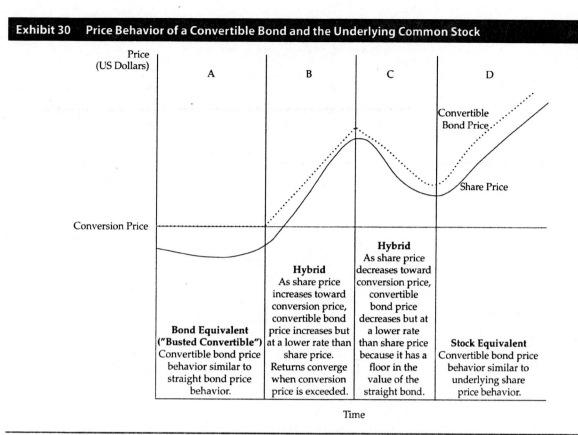

Why would an investor not exercise the conversion option when the underlying share price is above the conversion price, as in areas B, C, and D? The call option on the issuer's common stock may be a European-style option that cannot be exercised now but only at the end of a pre-determined period. Even if the call option is an American-style option, making it possible to convert the bond into equity, it may not be optimal for the convertible bondholder to exercise prior to the expiry of the conversion period; as discussed in Section 3.3.2, it is sometimes better to wait than to exercise an option that is in the money. The investor may also prefer to sell the convertible bond instead of exercising the conversion option.

Except for busted convertibles, the most important factor in the valuation of convertible bonds is the underlying share price. However, it is worth mentioning that large movements in interest rates or in credit spreads may significantly affect the value of convertible bonds. For a convertible bond with a fixed coupon, all else being equal, a significant fall in interest rates would result in an increase in its value and price, whereas a significant rise in interest rates would lead in a decrease in its value and price. Similarly, all else being equal, a significant improvement in the issuer's credit quality would result in an increase in the value and price of its convertible bonds, whereas a deterioration of the issuer's credit quality would lead to a decrease in the value and price of its convertible bonds.

EXAMPLE 9

Valuation of Convertible Bonds

Nick Andrews, a fixed-income investment analyst, has been asked by his supervisor to prepare an analysis of the convertible bond issued by Heavy Element Inc., a chemical industry company, for presentation to the investment committee. Andrews has gathered the following data from the convertible bond's prospectus and market information:

> **Issuer:** Heavy Element Inc.
> **Issue Date:** 15 September 2010
> **Maturity Date:** 15 September 2015
> **Interest:** 3.75% payable annually
> **Issue Size:** $100,000,000
> **Issue Price:** $1,000 at par
> **Conversion Ratio:** 23.26
> **Convertible Bond Price on 16 September 2012:** $1,230
> **Share Price on 16 September 2012:** $52

1 The conversion price is *closest to*:

  A $19.

  B $43.

  C $53.

2 The conversion value on 16 September 2012 is *closest to*:

  A $24.

  B $230.

  C $1,209.

3 The market conversion premium per share on 16 September 2012 is *closest to*:

  A $0.88.

  B $2.24.

  C $9.00.

4 The risk–return characteristics of the convertible bond on 16 September 2012 *most likely* resemble that of:

  A   a busted convertible.

  B   Heavy Element's common stock.

  C   a bond of Heavy Element that is identical to the convertible bond but without the conversion option.

5 As a result of favorable economic conditions, credit spreads for the chemical industry narrow, resulting in lower interest rates for the debt of companies such as Heavy Element. All else being equal, the price of Heavy Element's convertible bond will *most likely*:

  A   decrease significantly.

  B   not change significantly.

  C   increase significantly.

6   Suppose that on 16 September 2012, the convertible bond is available in the secondary market at a price of $1,050. An arbitrageur can make a risk-free profit by:

   A   buying the underlying common stock and shorting the convertible bond.

   B   buying the convertible bond, exercising the conversion option, and selling the shares resulting from the conversion.

   C   shorting the convertible bond and buying a call option on the underlying common stock exercisable at the conversion price on the conversion date.

7   A few months have passed. Because of chemical spills in lake water at the site of a competing facility, the government has introduced very costly environmental legislation. As a result, share prices of almost all publicly traded chemical companies, including Heavy Element, have decreased sharply. Heavy Element's share price is now $28. Now, the risk–return characteristics of the convertible bond *most likely* resemble that of:

   A   a bond.

   B   a hybrid instrument.

   C   Heavy Element's common stock.

Solution to 1:

B is correct. The conversion price is equal to the par value of the convertible bond divided by the conversion ratio—that is, $1,000/23.26 = $43 per share.

Solution to 2:

C is correct. The conversion value is equal to the underlying share price multiplied by the conversion ratio—that is, $52 × 23.26 = $1,209.

Solution to 3:

A is correct. The market conversion premium per share is equal to the convertible bond price divided by the conversion ratio, minus the underlying share price—that is, ($1,230/23.26) – $52 = $52.88 – $52 = $0.88.

Solution to 4:

B is correct. The underlying share price ($52) is well above the conversion price ($43). Thus, the convertible bond exhibits risk–return characteristics that are similar to those of the underlying common stock. A is incorrect because a busted convertible is a convertible bond for which the underlying common stock trades at a significant discount relative to the conversion price. C is incorrect because it describes a busted convertible.

Solution to 5:

B is correct. The underlying share price ($52) is well above the conversion price ($43). Thus, the convertible bond exhibits mostly stock risk–return characteristics, and its price is mainly driven by the underlying share price. Consequently, the decrease in credit spreads will have little effect on the convertible bond price.

Solution to 6:

B is correct. The convertible bond price ($1,050) is lower than its minimum value ($1,209). Thus, the arbitrageur can buy the convertible bond for $1,050; convert it into 23.26 shares; and sell the shares at $52 each, or $1,209 in total, making a profit of $159. A and C are incorrect because in both scenarios, the arbitrageur is short the underpriced asset (convertible bond) and long an overpriced asset, resulting in a loss.

Solution to 7:

A is correct. The underlying share price ($28) is now well below the conversion price ($43), so the convertible bond is a busted convertible and exhibits mostly bond risk–return characteristics. B is incorrect because the underlying share price would have to be close to the conversion price for the risk–return characteristics of the convertible bond to resemble that of a hybrid instrument. C is incorrect because the underlying share price would have to be in excess of the conversion price for the risk–return characteristics of the convertible bond to resemble that of the company's common stock.

7   BOND ANALYTICS

The introduction of OAS analysis in the mid-1980s marked the dawn of modern bond valuation theory. The approach is mathematically elegant, robust, and widely applicable. The typical implementation, however, relies heavily on number crunching. Whether it involves calculating the OAS corresponding to a price, valuing a bond with embedded options, or estimating key rate durations, computers are essential to the process. Needless to say, practitioners must have access to systems that can execute the required calculations correctly and in a timely manner. Most practitioners rely on commercially available systems, but some market participants, in particular financial institutions, may develop analytics in-house.

How can a practitioner tell if such a system is adequate? First, the system should be able to report the correct cash flows, discount rates, and present value of the cash flows. The discount rates can be verified by hand or on a spreadsheet. In practice, it is impossible to examine every calculation, but there are a few relatively simple tests that can be useful, and we present three of these tests below. Also, even if it is difficult to verify that a result is correct, it may be possible to establish that it is wrong.

Check that the put–call parity holds. A simple test for option valuation is to check for put–call parity—that is, the important relationship for European-type options discussed in a previous reading on derivatives. According to put–call parity,

Value(C) – Value(P) = PV(Forward price of bond on exercise date – Exercise price)

C and P refer to the European-type call option and put option on the same underlying bond and have the same exercise date and the same exercise price, respectively. If the system fails this test, look for an alternative.

Check that the value of the underlying option-free bond does not depend on interest rate volatility. To test the integrity of the interest rate tree calibration, set up and value a callable bond with a very high call price, say 150% of par. This structure should have the same value as that of the straight bond independent of interest rate volatility. The same should be true for a putable bond with a very low put price, say 50% of par.

Check that the volatility term structure slopes downward. As discussed earlier, the specified interest rate volatility is that of the short-term rate. This volatility, in turn, implies the volatilities of longer-term rates. In order for the interest rate process to be stable, the implied volatilities should decline as the term lengthens.

SUMMARY

This reading covers the valuation and analysis of bonds with embedded options. The following are the main points made in this reading:

- An embedded option represents a right that can be exercised by the issuer, by the bondholder, or automatically depending on the course of interest rates. It is attached to, or embedded in, an underlying option-free bond called a straight bond.

- Simple embedded option structures include call options, put options, and extension options. Callable and putable bonds can be redeemed prior to maturity, at the discretion of the issuer in the former case and of the bondholder in the latter case. An extendible bond gives the bondholder the right to keep the bond for a number of years after maturity. Putable and extendible bonds are equivalent, except that the underlying option-free bonds are different.

- Complex embedded option structures include bonds with other types of options or combinations of options. For example, a convertible bond includes a conversion option that allows the bondholders to convert their bonds into the issuer's common stock. A bond with an estate put can be put by the heirs of a deceased bondholder. Sinking fund bonds make the issuer set aside funds over time to retire the bond issue and are often callable, may have an acceleration provision, and may also contain a delivery option. Valuing and analyzing bonds with complex embedded option structures is challenging.

- According to the arbitrage-free framework, the value of a bond with an embedded option is equal to the arbitrage-free values of its parts—that is, the arbitrage-free value of the straight bond and the arbitrage-free values of each of the embedded options.

- Because the call option is an issuer option, the value of the call option decreases the value of the callable bond relative to an otherwise identical but non-callable bond. In contrast, because the put option is an investor option, the value of the put option increases the value of the putable bond relative to an otherwise identical but non-putable bond.

- In the absence of default and interest rate volatility, the bond's future cash flows are certain. Thus, the value of a callable or putable bond can be calculated by discounting the bond's future cash flows at the appropriate one-period forward rates, taking into consideration the decision to exercise the option. If a bond is callable, the decision to exercise the option is made by the issuer, which will exercise the call option when the value of the bond's future cash flows is higher than the call price. In contrast, if the bond is putable, the decision to exercise the option is made by the bondholder, who will exercise the put option when the value of the bond's future cash flows is lower than the put price.

- In practice, interest rates fluctuate, and interest rate volatility affects the value of embedded options. Thus, when valuing bonds with embedded options, it is important to consider the possible evolution of the yield curve over time.

- Interest rate volatility is modeled using a binomial interest rate tree. The higher the volatility, the lower the value of the callable bond and the higher the value of the putable bond.

■ Valuing a bond with embedded options assuming an interest rate volatility requires three steps: (1) Generate a tree of interest rates based on the given yield curve and volatility assumptions; (2) at each node of the tree, determine whether the embedded options will be exercised; and (3) apply the backward induction valuation methodology to calculate the present value of the bond.

■ The most commonly used approach to valuing risky bonds is to add a spread to the one-period forward rates used to discount the bond's future cash flows.

■ The option-adjusted spread is the single spread added uniformly to the one-period forward rates on the tree to produce a value or price for a bond. OAS is sensitive to interest rate volatility: The higher the volatility, the lower the OAS for a callable bond.

■ For bonds with embedded options, the best measure to assess the sensitivity of the bond's price to a parallel shift of the benchmark yield curve is effective duration. The effective duration of a callable or putable bond cannot exceed that of the straight bond.

■ The effective convexity of a straight bond is negligible, but that of bonds with embedded options is not. When the option is near the money, the convexity of a callable bond is negative, indicating that the upside for a callable bond is much smaller than the downside, whereas the convexity of a putable bond is positive, indicating that the upside for a putable bond is much larger than the downside.

■ Because the prices of callable and putable bonds respond asymmetrically to upward and downward interest rate changes of the same magnitude, one-sided durations provide a better indication regarding the interest rate sensitivity of bonds with embedded options than (two-sided) effective duration.

■ Key rate durations show the effect of shifting only key points, one at a time, rather than the entire yield curve.

■ The arbitrage-free framework can be used to value capped and floored floaters. The cap provision in a floater is an issuer option that prevents the coupon rate from increasing above a specified maximum rate. Thus, the value of a capped floater is equal to or less than the value of the straight bond. In contrast, the floor provision in a floater is an investor option that prevents the coupon from decreasing below a specified minimum rate. Thus, the value of a floored floater is equal to or higher than the value of the straight bond.

■ The characteristics of a convertible bond include the conversion price, which is the applicable share price at which the bondholders can convert their bonds into common shares, and the conversion ratio, which reflects the number of shares of common stock that the bondholders receive from converting their bonds into shares. The conversion price is adjusted in case of corporate actions, such as stock splits, bonus share issuances, and rights and warrants issuances. Convertible bondholders may receive compensation when the issuer pays dividends to its common shareholders, and they may be given the opportunity to either put their bonds or convert their bonds into shares earlier and at more advantageous terms in the case of a change of control.

■ There are a number of investment metrics and ratios that help analyze and value convertible bonds. The conversion value indicates the value of the bond if it is converted at the market price of the shares. The minimum value of a convertible bond sets a floor value for the convertible bond at the greater of the conversion value or the straight value. This floor is moving, however, because the straight value is not fixed. The market conversion premium represents the price investors effectively pay for the underlying shares if they buy the convertible bond and then convert it into shares. Scaled by the market price of the shares, it represents the premium payable when buying the convertible bond rather than the underlying common stock.

■ Because convertible bonds combine characteristics of bonds, stocks, and options, as well as potentially other features, their valuation and analysis is challenging. Convertible bond investors should consider the factors that affect not only bond prices but also the underlying share price.

■ The arbitrage-free framework can be used to value convertible bonds, including callable and putable ones. Each component (straight bond, call option of the stock, and call and/or put option on the bond) can be valued separately.

■ The risk–return characteristics of a convertible bond depend on the underlying share price relative to the conversion price. When the underlying share price is well below the conversion price, the convertible bond is "busted" and exhibits mostly bond risk–return characteristics. Thus, it is mainly sensitive to interest rate movements. In contrast, when the underlying share price is well above the conversion price, the convertible bond exhibits mostly stock risk–return characteristics. Thus, its price follows similar movements to the price of the underlying stock. In between these two extremes, the convertible bond trades like a hybrid instrument.

PRACTICE PROBLEMS

The following information relates to Questions 1–10

Samuel & Sons is a fixed-income specialty firm that offers advisory services to invest‐ment management companies. On 1 October 20X0, Steele Ferguson, a senior analyst at Samuel, is reviewing three fixed-rate bonds issued by a local firm, Pro Star, Inc. The three bonds, whose characteristics are given in Exhibit 1, carry the highest credit rating.

Exhibit 1	Fixed-Rate Bonds Issued by Pro Star, Inc.		
Bond	**Maturity**	**Coupon**	**Type of Bond**
Bond #1	1 October 20X3	4.40% annual	Option-free
Bond #2	1 October 20X3	4.40% annual	Callable at par on 1 October 20X1 and on 1 October 20X2
Bond #3	1 October 20X3	4.40% annual	Putable at par on 1 October 20X1 and on 1 October 20X2

The one-year, two-year, and three-year par rates are 2.250%, 2.750%, and 3.100%, respectively. Based on an estimated interest rate volatility of 10%, Ferguson constructs the binomial interest rate tree shown in Exhibit 2.

Exhibit 2	Binomial Interest Rate Tree

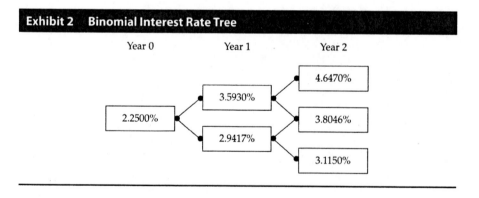

On 19 October 20X0, Ferguson analyzes the convertible bond issued by Pro Star given in Exhibit 3. That day, the market prices of Pro Star's convertible bond and common stock are $1,060 and $37.50, respectively.

Exhibit 3	Convertible Bond Issued by Pro Star, Inc.
Issue Date:	**6 December 20X0**
Maturity Date:	6 December 20X4
Coupon Rate:	2%
Issue Price:	$1,000
Conversion Ratio:	31

1 The call feature of Bond #2 is *best* described as:

A European style.

B American style.

C Bermudan style.

2 The bond that would *most likely* protect investors against a significant increase in interest rates is:

A Bond #1.

B Bond #2.

C Bond #3.

3 A fall in interest rates would *most likely* result in:

A a decrease in the effective duration of Bond #3.

B Bond #3 having more upside potential than Bond #2.

C a change in the effective convexity of Bond #3 from positive to negative.

4 The value of Bond #2 is *closest* to:

A 102.103% of par.

B 103.121% of par.

C 103.744% of par.

5 The value of Bond #3 is *closest* to:

A 102.103% of par.

B 103.688% of par.

C 103.744% of par.

6 All else being equal, a rise in interest rates will *most likely* result in the value of the option embedded in Bond #3:

A decreasing.

B remaining unchanged.

C increasing.

7 All else being equal, if Ferguson assumes an interest rate volatility of 15% instead of 10%, the bond that would *most likely* increase in value is:

A Bond #1.

B Bond #2.

C Bond #3.

8 All else being equal, if the shape of the yield curve changes from upward sloping to flattening, the value of the option embedded in Bond #2 will *most likely*:

A decrease.

B remain unchanged.

C increase.

9 The conversion price of the bond in Exhibit 3 is *closest* to:

   A $26.67.

   B $32.26.

   C $34.19.

10 If the market price of Pro Star's common stock falls from its level on 19 October 20X0, the price of the convertible bond will *most likely*:

   A fall at the same rate as Pro Star's stock price.

   B fall but at a slightly lower rate than Pro Star's stock price.

   C be unaffected until Pro Star's stock price reaches the conversion price.

The following information relates to Question 11–19

Rayes Investment Advisers specializes in fixed-income portfolio management. Meg Rayes, the owner of the firm, would like to add bonds with embedded options to the firm's bond portfolio. Rayes has asked Mingfang Hsu, one of the firm's analysts, to assist her in selecting and analyzing bonds for possible inclusion in the firm's bond portfolio.

Hsu first selects two corporate bonds that are callable at par and have the same characteristics in terms of maturity, credit quality and call dates. Hsu uses the option adjusted spread (OAS) approach to analyse the bonds, assuming an interest rate volatility of 10%. The results of his analysis are presented in Exhibit 1.

Exhibit 1	Summary Results of Hsu's Analysis Using the OAS Approach
Bond	**OAS (in bps)**
Bond #1	25.5
Bond #2	30.3

Hsu then selects the four bonds issued by RW, Inc. given in Exhibit 2. These bonds all have a maturity of three years and the same credit rating. Bonds #4 and #5 are identical to Bond #3, an option-free bond, except that they each include an embedded option.

Exhibit 2	Bonds Issued by RW, Inc.	
Bond	**Coupon**	**Special Provision**
Bond #3	4.00% annual	
Bond #4	4.00% annual	Callable at par at the end of years 1 and 2
Bond #5	4.00% annual	Putable at par at the end of years 1 and 2
Bond #6	One-year Libor annually, set in arrears	

To value and analyze RW's bonds, Hsu uses an estimated interest rate volatility of 15% and constructs the binomial interest rate tree provided in Exhibit 3.

Exhibit 3   Binomial Interest Rate Tree Used to Value RW's Bonds

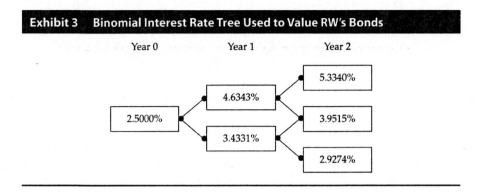

Rayes asks Hsu to determine the sensitivity of Bond #4's price to a 20 bps parallel shift of the benchmark yield curve. The results of Hsu's calculations are shown in Exhibit 4.

Exhibit 4   Summary Results of Hsu's Analysis about the Sensitivity of Bond #4's Price to a Parallel Shift of the Benchmark Yield Curve

	+20 bps	−20 bps
Magnitude of the Parallel Shift in the Benchmark Yield Curve	+20 bps	−20 bps
Full Price of Bond #4 (% of par)	100.478	101.238

Hsu also selects the two floating-rate bonds issued by Varlep, plc given in Exhibit 5. These bonds have a maturity of three years and the same credit rating.

Exhibit 5   Floating-Rate Bonds Issued by Varlep, plc

Bond	Coupon
Bond #7	One-year Libor annually, set in arrears, capped at 5.00%
Bond #8	One-year Libor annually, set in arrears, floored at 3.50%

To value Varlep's bonds, Hsu constructs the binomial interest rate tree provided in Exhibit 6.

Exhibit 6   Binomial Interest Rate Tree Used to Value Varlep's Bonds

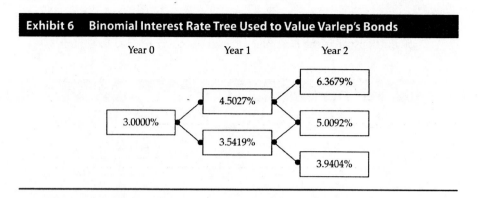

Last, Hsu selects the two bonds issued by Whorton, Inc. given in Exhibit 7. These bonds are close to their maturity date and are identical, except that Bond #9 includes a conversion option. Whorton's common stock is currently trading at $30 per share.

Exhibit 7   Bonds Issued by Whorton, Inc.

Bond	Type of Bond
Bond #9	Convertible bond with a conversion price of $50
Bond #10	Identical to Bond #9 except that it does not include a conversion option

11 Based on Exhibit 1, Rayes would *most likely* conclude that relative to Bond #1, Bond #2 is:

  A overpriced.

  B fairly priced.

  C underpriced.

12 The effective duration of Bond #6 is:

  A lower than or equal to 1.

  B higher than 1 but lower than 3.

  C higher than 3.

13 In Exhibit 2, the bond whose effective duration will lengthen if interest rates rise is:

  A Bond #3.

  B Bond #4.

  C Bond #5.

14 The effective duration of Bond #4 is *closest* to:

  A 0.76.

  B 1.88.

  C 3.77.

15 The value of Bond #7 is *closest* to:

  A 99.697% of par.

  B 99.936% of par.

  C 101.153% of par.

16 The value of Bond #8 is *closest* to:

  A 98.116% of par.

B 100.000% of par.

C 100.485% of par.

17 The value of Bond #9 is equal to the value of Bond #10:

A plus the value of a put option on Whorton's common stock.

B plus the value of a call option on Whorton's common stock.

C minus the value of a call option on Whorton's common stock.

18 The minimum value of Bond #9 is equal to the *greater* of:

A the conversion value of Bond #9 and the current value of Bond #10.

B the current value of Bond #10 and a call option on Whorton's common stock.

C the conversion value of Bond #9 and a call option on Whorton's common stock.

19 The factor that is currently *least likely* to affect the risk-return characteristics of Bond #9 is:

A Interest rate movements.

B Whorton's credit spreads.

C Whorton's common stock price movements.

SOLUTIONS

1   C is correct. The call option embedded in Bond #2 can be exercised only at two predetermined dates: 1 October 20X1 and 1 October 20X2. Thus, the call feature is Bermudan style.

2   C is correct. The bond that would most likely protect investors against a significant increase in interest rates is the putable bond, i.e., Bond #3. When interest rates have risen and higher-yield bonds are available, a put option allows the bondholders to put back the bonds to the issuer prior to maturity and to reinvest the proceeds of the retired bonds in higher-yielding bonds.

3   B is correct. A fall in interest rates results in a rise in bond values. For a callable bond such as Bond #2, the upside potential is capped because the issuer is more likely to call the bond. In contrast, the upside potential for a putable bond such as Bond #3 is uncapped. Thus, a fall in interest rates would result in a putable bond having more upside potential than an otherwise identical callable bond. Note that A is incorrect because the effective duration of a putable bond increases, not decreases, with a fall in interest rates—the bond is less likely to be put and thus behaves more like an option-free bond. C is also incorrect because the effective convexity of a putable bond is always positive. It is the effective convexity of a callable bond that will change from positive to negative if interest rates fall and the call option is near the money.

4   A is correct:

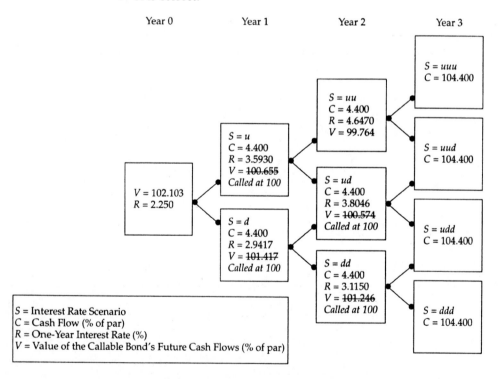

5 C is correct:

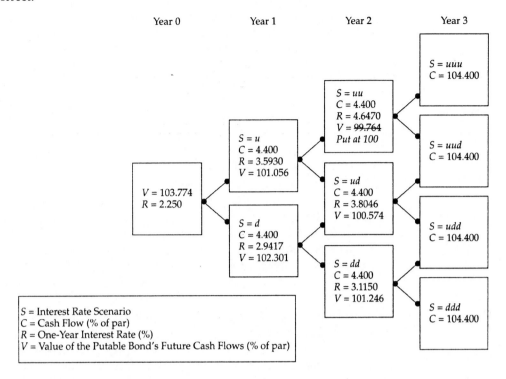

| | Year 0 | Year 1 | Year 2 | Year 3 |

S = uuu
C = 104.400

S = uu
C = 4.400
R = 4.6470
V = 99.764
Put at 100

S = u
C = 4.400
R = 3.5930
V = 101.056

S = uud
C = 104.400

V = 103.774
R = 2.250

S = ud
C = 4.400
R = 3.8046
V = 100.574

S = d
C = 4.400
R = 2.9417
V = 102.301

S = udd
C = 104.400

S = dd
C = 4.400
R = 3.1150
V = 101.246

S = ddd
C = 104.400

S = Interest Rate Scenario
C = Cash Flow (% of par)
R = One-Year Interest Rate (%)
V = Value of the Putable Bond's Future Cash Flows (% of par)

6 C is correct. Bond #3 is a putable bond, and the value of a put option increases as interest rates rise. At higher interest rates, the value of the underlying option-free bond (straight bond) declines, but the decline is offset partially by the increase in the value of the embedded put option, which is more likely to be exercised.

7 C is correct. Regardless of the type of option, an increase in interest rate volatility results in an increase in option value. Because the value of a putable bond is equal to the value of the straight bond *plus* the value of the embedded put option, Bond #3 will increase in value if interest rate volatility increases. Put another way, an increase in interest rate volatility will most likely result in more scenarios where the put option is exercised, which increases the values calculated in the interest rate tree and, thus, the value of the putable bond.

8 C is correct. Bond #2 is a callable bond, and the value of the embedded call option increases as the yield curve flattens. When the yield curve is upward sloping, the one-period forward rates on the interest rate tree are high and opportunities for the issuer to call the bond are fewer. When the yield curve flattens or inverts, many nodes on the tree have lower forward rates, which increases the opportunities to call and, thus, the value of the embedded call option.

9 B is correct. The conversion price of a convertible bond is equal to the par value divided by the conversion ratio—that is, $1,000/31= $32.26 per share.

10 B is correct. The market price on 19 October 20X0 ($37.50) is above the conversion price of $1,000/31 = $32.26 per share. Thus, the convertible bond exhibits mostly stock risk-return characteristics, and a fall in the stock price will result in a fall in the convertible bond price. However, the change in the convertible bond price is less than the change in the stock price because the convertible bond has a floor—that floor is the value of the straight bond.

11 C is correct. The option-adjusted spread (OAS) is the constant spread added to all the one-period forward rates that makes the arbitrage-free value of a risky bond equal to its market price. The OAS approach is often used to assess bond relative values. If two bonds have the same characteristics and credit quality, they should have the same OAS. If this is not the case, the bond with the largest OAS (i.e., Bond #2) is likely to be underpriced (cheap) relative to the bond with the smallest OAS (Bond #1).

12 A is correct. The effective duration of a floating-rate bond is close to the time to next reset. As the reset for Bond #6 is annual, the effective duration of this bond is lower than or equal to 1.

13 B is correct. Effective duration indicates the sensitivity of a bond's price to a 100 bps parallel shift of the benchmark yield curve assuming no change in the bond's credit spread. The effective duration of an option-free bond such as Bond #3 changes very little in response to interest rate movements. As interest rates rise, a call option moves out of the money, which increases the value of the callable bond and lengthens its effective duration. In contrast, as interest rates rise, a put option moves into the money, which limits the price depreciation of the putable bond and shortens its effective duration. Thus, the bond whose effective duration will lengthen if interest rates rise is the callable bond, i.e., Bond #4.

14 B is correct. The effective duration of Bond #4 can be calculated using Equation 3 from the reading, where ΔCurve is 20 bps, PV_ is 101.238, and PV_+ is 100.478. PV_0, the current full price of the bond (i.e., with no shift), is not given but it can be calculated using Exhibit 3 as follows:

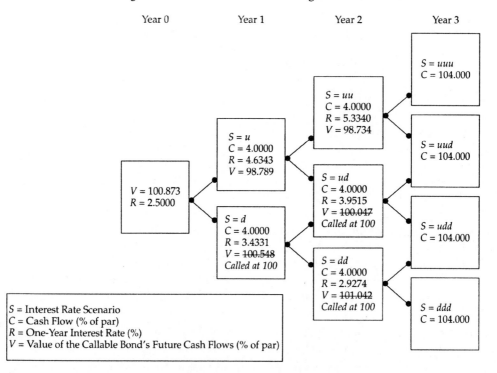

S = Interest Rate Scenario
C = Cash Flow (% of par)
R = One-Year Interest Rate (%)
V = Value of the Callable Bond's Future Cash Flows (% of par)

Thus, the effective duration of Bond #4 is:

$$\text{Effective duration} = \frac{101.238 - 100.478}{2 \times (0.0020) \times (100.873)} = 1.88$$

15 A is correct:

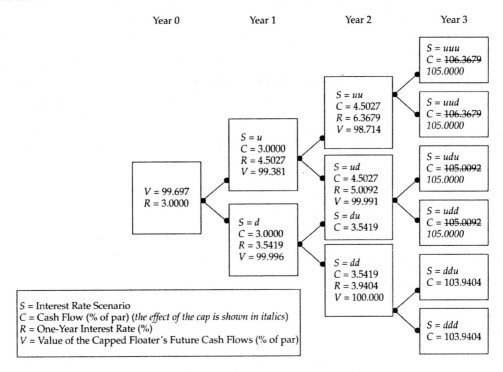

16 C is correct:

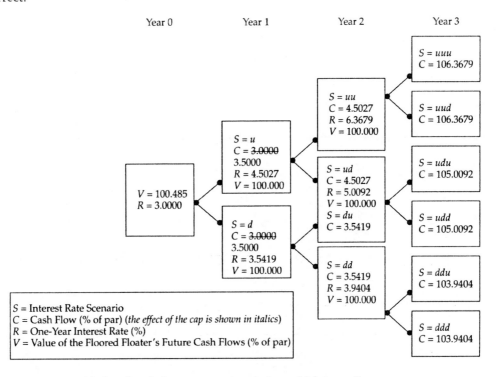

17 B is correct. A convertible bond includes a conversion option, which is a call option on the issuer's common stock. This conversion option gives the bond-holders the right to convert their debt into equity. Thus, the value of Bond #9, the convertible bond, is equal to the value of Bond #10, the underlying option-free bond (straight bond), plus the value of a call option on Whorton's common stock.

18 A is correct. The minimum value of a convertible bond is equal to the greater of the conversion value of the convertible bond (i.e., Bond #9) and the current value of the straight bond (i.e., Bond #10).

19 C is correct. The risk-return characteristics of a convertible bond depend on the market price of the issuer's common stock (underlying share price) relative to the bond's conversion price. When the underlying share price is well below the conversion price, the convertible bond exhibits mostly bond risk-return characteristics. In this case, the price of the convertible bond is mainly affected by interest rate movements and the issuer's credit spreads. In contrast, when the underlying share price is above the conversion price, the convertible bond exhibits mostly stock risk-return characteristics. In this case, the price of the convertible bond is mainly affected by the issuer's common stock price movements. The underlying share price ($30) is lower than the conversion price of Bond #9 ($50). Thus, Bond #9 exhibits mostly bond risk-return characteristics and is least affected by Whorton's common stock price movements.

15

Fixed Income

Topics in Fixed Income Analysis

This study session consists of a discussion of credit analysis and how credit standards affect liquidity.

READING ASSIGNMENTS

Reading 46   Credit Analysis Models
                      by Robert A. Jarrow, PhD, and Donald R. van Deventer, PhD

Credit Analysis Models

by Robert A. Jarrow, PhD, and Donald R. van Deventer, PhD

Robert A. Jarrow, PhD (USA). Donald R. van Deventer, PhD, is at Kamakura Corporation (USA).

LEARNING OUTCOMES

Mastery	The candidate should be able to:
☐	**a.** explain probability of default, loss given default, expected loss, and present value of the expected loss and describe the relative importance of each across the credit spectrum;
☐	**b.** explain credit scoring and credit ratings, including why they are called ordinal rankings;
☐	**c.** explain strengths and weaknesses of credit ratings;
☐	**d.** explain structural models of corporate credit risk, including why equity can be viewed as a call option on the company's assets;
☐	**e.** explain reduced form models of corporate credit risk, including why debt can be valued as the sum of expected discounted cash flows after adjusting for risk;
☐	**f.** explain assumptions, strengths, and weaknesses of both structural and reduced form models of corporate credit risk;
☐	**g.** explain the determinants of the term structure of credit spreads;
☐	**h.** calculate and interpret the present value of the expected loss on a bond over a given time horizon;
☐	**i.** compare the credit analysis required for asset-backed securities to analysis of corporate debt.

1 INTRODUCTION

Since 1990, credit-related financial crises have spurred developments in credit risk analysis. These crises include the following:

- The collapse of the Japanese bubble and its aftermath (1989–present), which originated with overvalued Japanese real estate and equity prices. The collapse was a slow process, lasting for over a decade, and resulted in sluggish growth in the Japanese economy for years to follow.

- The Mexican "tequila crisis" of 1994–1995, which originated with the devaluation of the Mexican peso in December 1994, causing significant losses on Mexican government bonds.

- The Asian crisis, also known as the Asian contagion (1997–1998), which originated with the crash of the Thai baht in July 1997 and spread to equity markets globally.

- The Russian debt crisis (1998), which originated with Russia defaulting on its debt in August 1998, causing significant losses on Russian securities that spread to equity markets globally.

- The 2008 global financial crisis, which was first identified as such in 2008 although it lasted beyond 2008. It originated in part with a decline in housing prices and resulted in significant losses on securitized instruments based on home mortgages. It spread globally to other markets, including equity markets.

Dramatic shifts in key macroeconomic factors caused a wide array of countries', companies', and individuals' default risk to increase during these crises. Traditional credit ratings were only partially effective in capturing the changes in these correlated default risks. As a result, additional tools to quantify and manage risks have been developed. These tools include methods for estimating correlated default probabilities and recovery rates based on macroeconomic factors. These new models are purposefully constructed to incorporate systemic default risk similar to that experienced in the recent financial crisis. This reading describes different approaches to credit risk analysis, the strengths and weaknesses of each approach, and the application of the approaches to credit risk evaluation.

Section 2 presents an overview of four basic measures relevant to credit risk: the probability of default, the loss given default, the expected loss, and the present value of the expected loss. Section 3 discusses two traditional approaches to credit risk management: credit scoring and credit ratings. Both approaches are still widely used. Credit scoring provides an ordinal ranking of the credit risk for retail borrowers (small owner-operated businesses and individuals). Credit ratings provide an ordinal ranking of a borrower's credit riskiness. Credit ratings are used for securities issued by financial and non-financial companies (corporate issuers), sovereigns, and sub-sovereign governments, for the companies and governments themselves, and for asset-backed securities.

Sections 4 and 5 discuss structural and reduced form approaches or models for analyzing credit risk. The structural model is based on insights obtained from option pricing methodology.[1] The reduced form model overcomes limitations inherent in the structural approach and enables the inclusion of systemic default risk into the modeling methodology.[2]

---

1 Merton (1974).

2 The reduced form model of Jarrow and Turnbull (1992, 1995) is based on the Heath–Jarrow–Morton (1992) model for pricing interest rate derivatives. Useful explanatory references include Jarrow (2009) for credit risk models and Chava and Jarrow (2004) for the estimation of the reduced form model's parameters.

How to use structural and reduced form models to price risky debt and to determine the probability of default and the expected loss is shown. For practical applications, the estimation of each models' parameters is described. Strengths and weaknesses of both the structural and reduced form credit risk models are also described.

Section 6 discusses the term structure of credit spreads and shows how to use credit spreads to estimate the present value of the expected loss. Numerous examples are provided to help the reader understand this procedure. Section 7 discusses credit analysis of asset-backed securities (ABS). A summary and practice problems conclude the reading.

MEASURES OF CREDIT RISK

2

This section discusses, in an intuitive fashion, some basic credit risk measures for fixed-income securities: the probability of default, the loss given default, the expected loss, and the present value of the expected loss.

For the purposes of this discussion, consider a bond issued by Company XYZ with a principal of F dollars, a fixed coupon of c% of the principal paid semiannually, and a maturity of T years. The bond is in default if any of the bond's covenants (promises) are violated. The most common cause of default is the omission of a coupon or principal payment. Credit risk is the risk that such a default may occur and result in the partial or total loss of the remaining coupon and principal payments.

To quantify this credit risk, four measures are often estimated. The first is the probability that the bond will default before maturity, called the **probability of default** or **default probability**. Obviously, the higher the probability of default, the more risky the bond, everything else held constant. The second measure is the **loss given default**, the amount of the remaining coupon and principal payments lost in the event of default. The loss given default is often expressed as a percentage of the position or exposure. A related measure is the **recovery rate**, which is the percentage of the position received or recovered in default. The loss given default plus the expected recovery rate when each is expressed as a percentage of the position equals 100%. In the simplest and most extreme case, the loss given default is 100%. In other words, there is no amount recovered.

The third measure is the **expected loss** on the bond. The expected loss is equal to the probability of default multiplied by the loss given default. Calculation of the expected loss is complicated for various reasons, but an important reason is that both the probability of default and the loss given default can depend on the health of the economy, in addition to company-specific balance sheet considerations. Indeed, in a healthy and growing economy, one would expect that the probability of default would be smaller and that if default occurs, the loss given default would be smaller as well. In such a situation, when computing the expected loss, both the default probability and loss given default need to be made dependent on the state of the economy and the weighted average of these state-dependent expected losses need to be calculated. The weights used in this average correspond to the probabilities that the different possible states of the economy occur.

The fourth credit risk measure is the **present value of the expected loss**. The present value of the expected loss is conceptually the largest price one would be willing to pay on a bond to a third party (e.g., an insurer) to entirely remove the credit risk of purchasing and holding the bond. Paying this fee transforms a "credit risky" bond to a "riskless bond," assuming, of course, that the third-party insurer is free of default risk.

The present value of the expected loss is the most complex credit risk measure to calculate because it involves two modifications to the expected loss. The first modification is to explicitly adjust the probabilities to account for the risk of the cash flows (the risk premium). Recall from your studies of option pricing that an option can be valued using "risk-neutral valuation," where one takes the expected value of the option's payoffs discounted to the present by the risk-free rate. In taking this expectation, "risk-neutral" probabilities are used instead of the actual probabilities. The difference between the actual and risk-neutral probabilities is that the risk-neutral probabilities adjust for risk. The actual probabilities are those from "nature." The second modification is to include the time value of money in the calculation—that is, the discounting of the future cash flows to the present. Of course, the loss of the bond's principal 10 years from now has a smaller present value than the loss of the bond's principal 1 year from now. These two adjustments—using the risk-neutral probabilities and discounting—can either decrease or increase the present value of the expected loss relative to the expected loss itself. Of the credit risk measures considered, the present value of the expected loss is perhaps the most important. This is because when one considers the purchase or sale of the bond, one is interested in the exact dollar difference one should pay or receive on the bond, relative to an otherwise identical and riskless government bond. This difference is the single measure that most succinctly captures the credit risk in the bond.

EXAMPLE 1

A bond portfolio manager has $500,000 to invest in a bond portfolio. From his credit risk analysis department he collects the following information on four (hypothetical) debt issues:

Name of Company	Probability of Default (% per year)	Expected Loss (dollars per 100 par)	Present Value of the Expected Loss (dollars per 100 par)
Green Company	1.15	$15.00	$13.50
Sleepy Company	0.85	$20.00	$14.00
Red Fruit Corp.	2.25	$37.00	$32.00
Slot Machines Inc.	0.05	$1.00	$0.75

Rank the companies in terms of the different credit risk measures. Do they give the same ranking? Which measure would you use and why?

Solution:

The rankings are as follows:

Ranking	Probability of Default (% per year)	Expected Loss (dollars per 100 par)	Present Value of the Expected Loss (dollars per 100 par)
Least Risky	Slot Machines Inc.	Slot Machines Inc.	Slot Machines Inc.
.	Sleepy Company	Green Company	Green Company
.	Green Company	Sleepy Company	Sleepy Company
Most Risky	Red Fruit Corp.	Red Fruit Corp.	Red Fruit Corp.

The probability of default gives a different ranking from either the expected loss or the present value of the expected loss. The difference in rankings based on these two measures is due to the loss given default. It is higher for Green Company than it is for Sleepy Company. This can only be true if Sleepy Company's loss given default is smaller than it is for Green Company. Note that the expected loss and the present value of the loss give the same rankings.

A simple example clarifies this distinction. Consider a company, called XYZ, whose one-year default probability is 1. Hence, XYZ is sure to default over the next year. For the purpose of this example, let us also suppose that its loss given default is zero. That is, when XYZ defaults, the debt holders incur no losses. Hence, its expected loss and the present value of the expected loss are zero as well. Then, when ranking XYZ according to the probability of default, it is the most risky company possible; however, according to its expected loss or the present value of the expected loss, it is the least risky company possible. The key difference, of course, between these different measures is due to the loss given default. The present value of the expected loss is the preferred measure because it includes the probability of default, the loss given default, the time value of money, and the risk premium in its computation. The expected loss is second best, including both the default probability and loss given default. The default probability is the least inclusive measure.

The difference between a risky bond's yield to maturity and the yield to maturity of a government bond with similar features is the credit spread. This implies that the credit spread includes within its value the probability of default, the loss given default, and the time value of money, including adjusting for the risk of the cash flows lost in default (the risk premium). The larger the credit spread on a bond, the larger at least one of these underlying components is. To determine which of these components explains the credit spread, one needs a model. Using a model, one can compute which of these components is the largest. To understand credit risk, therefore, one needs to understand credit risk models.

Traditional credit models—credit scoring and credit ratings—can be viewed as a methodology for summarizing credit risk measures into a single measure. Structural and reduced form models are quantitative approaches constructed to enable the computation of the credit risk measures. We discuss each of these approaches next, starting with the traditional credit models.

TRADITIONAL CREDIT MODELS

3

Credit scoring and credit ratings, two traditional approaches to credit risk analysis, apply to different types of borrowers. Credit scoring is used for small owner-operated businesses and individuals. These small borrowers are often referred to as retail borrowers. Credit ratings are used for companies, sovereigns, sub-sovereigns, and those entities' securities, as well as asset-backed securities. An understanding of the traditional approaches to credit risk is useful because

- they are widely used and
- they provide a link between the traditional, financial statement–based credit analysis methods covered in Level I of the CFA Program and the structural and reduced form credit risk models, which are the primary focus of this reading.

Credit scoring ranks a borrower's credit riskiness. It does not provide an estimate of a borrower's default probability. It is called an *ordinal ranking* because it only orders borrowers' riskiness from highest to lowest. Credit scoring is not capable of determining whether Borrower A is twice as risky as Borrower B, a *cardinal ranking*. Probabilities of default provide a cardinal ranking of credit: For example, if Borrower A has a default probability of 2% and Borrower B has a default probability of 4%, then Borrower B is twice as risky as Borrower A.

Credit scoring is performed in most countries around the world, and it is typically applied to individuals and very small businesses where the owner-manager provides his personal guarantee on any borrowings. A retail borrower's credit score from a credit bureau or a financial institution may not be representative of the borrower's credit worthiness. The retail borrower may be borrowing from many institutions in many forms, including credit cards, auto loans, first mortgage loans, second mortgage loans, and home equity lines of credit. Because there are no *cross-default*[3] clauses for retail borrowers, it is possible for a retail borrower to be more likely to default on one type of loan than on another. That means credit scores have different implications for an individual's default probability on different types of loans.

A credit score has the following characteristics:

- Credit scores provide an ordinal ranking of a borrower's credit risk. The higher the score, the less risky the borrower. If Borrower A has a credit score of 800 and Borrower B has a credit score of 400, Borrower A is less likely to default than Borrower B, but it does not mean that Borrower A is half as likely to default as Borrower B.

- Credit scores do not explicitly depend on current economic conditions. For example, if Borrower A has a credit score of 800 and the economy deteriorates, Borrower A's credit score does not adjust unless Borrower A's behavior or financial circumstances change.

- Credit scores are not percentile rankings of the borrower among a universe of borrowers. There can be many borrowers with the same credit score, and the percentage of borrowers with a particular score can change over time. The following chart is based on information from www.creditscoring.com. It summarizes the distribution of credit scores from the US credit specialist FICO as of 8 August 2011. This distribution is representative of credit scores available from credit agencies around the world, including Equifax, Experian, and TransUnion. The delinquency rate is the probability of being more than 90 days past due in the next 24 months:

Percentile	Percentage of People	Score	Delinquency Rate
2nd	2%	300–499	87%
7th	5%	500–549	71%
15th	8%	550–599	51%
27th	12%	600–649	31%
42nd	15%	650–699	15%
60th	18%	700–749	5%
87th	27%	750–799	2%
100th	13%	800–850	1%

---

3 A cross-default clause states that the borrower is in default on Loan 1 if the borrower is in default on any other loan or form of borrowing, say, Loan 2. This is a standard provision for most corporate lending that is intended to prevent the borrower from treating lenders differently when the borrower is in financial distress. Cross-default clauses are rare in sovereign lending, but that is changing rapidly. The clauses are very rare in retail lending.

- Many lenders prefer stability in credit scores over accuracy, so there is some pressure on credit bureaus to take this into account when generating credit scores.

- Credit scores have different implications for the probability of default depending on the borrower and the nature of the loan that has been extended. For example, a retail borrower in financial distress may pay on her home mortgage and default on credit card debt because the consequences for credit card default are less serious. The default probabilities for a given credit score are therefore likely higher on credit card lending than they are on home mortgages.

Credit scores are used in many countries in the world, but scoring varies considerably across countries. In some countries, only negative information, such as a default, is reported. Therefore, no score or information is positive because it means no news has been reported about the borrower. In other countries, factors such as payment history and debt outstanding are used to develop a credit score, but the weighting of the factors can differ across countries. Assuming you are a borrower in the United States, the Federal Trade Commission identifies the following factors that affect your credit score in the United States.[4]

- Have you paid your bills on time? Payment history is a significant factor. If you have paid bills late, had an account referred to collections, or declared bankruptcy, it is likely to affect your score negatively.

- Are you maxed out? Many scoring systems evaluate the amount of debt you have compared with your credit limits. If the amount you owe is close to your credit limit, it's likely to have a negative effect on your score.

- How long have you had credit? The length of your credit track record is important. A short credit history may affect your score negatively, but such factors as timely payments and low balances can offset that.

- Have you applied for new credit lately? Many scoring systems consider whether you have applied for credit recently. If you have applied for too many new accounts recently, it could have a negative effect on your score.

- How many credit accounts do you have and what kinds of accounts are they? Although it is generally considered a plus to have established credit accounts, too many credit card accounts or certain types of loans may have a negative effect on your score.

EXAMPLE 2

A bank analyst is considering the loan applications of three individuals. Each is requesting a personal loan of $55,000. The bank can lend to only one of them. The bank's criteria emphasize the FICO score. Which individual is the bank analyst *most likely* to recommend lending to?

A Individual A has a salary of $157,000, a net worth of $300,000, five credit cards, and a FICO score of 550.

B Individual B has a salary of $97,000, a net worth of $105,000, two credit cards, and a FICO score of 700.

C Individual C has a salary of $110,000, a net worth of $300,000, no credit cards, and a FICO score of 600.

---

4 See www.ftc.gov.

Solution:

The bank analyst is most likely to recommend lending to Individual B. Individual B has the highest FICO score, 700. Individual C appears to be an attractive candidate for a loan but has not built up a credit score by judicious use of credit and repayment, as evidenced by no credit cards.

Credit ratings rank the credit risk of a company, government (sovereign), quasi-government, or asset-backed security. Credit ratings do not provide an estimate of the loan's default probability. Credit ratings have a history that dates back more than a century. Standard & Poor's (S&P) was established in 1860, and Moody's Investors Service was founded in 1909. As of August 2012, 10 credit-rating agencies are recognized by the US Securities and Exchange Commission as "nationally recognized statistical rating organizations." The 10 credit-rating agencies are A.M. Best Company, Inc., DBRS Ltd., Egan-Jones Rating Company, Fitch, Inc., Japan Credit Rating Agency, LACE Financial Corp., Moody's Investors Service, Rating and Investment Information, Inc., RealPoint LLC, and Standard & Poor's Rating Services. Many non-US-based credit-rating agencies are included in the list. As of October 2011, the UK Financial Services Authority[5] had registered the following credit-rating agencies: A.M. Best Europe Rating Services Ltd., DBRS Ratings Limited, Fitch Ratings Limited, Fitch Ratings CIS Limited, Moody's Investors Service Ltd., and Standard & Poor's Credit Market Services Europe Ltd. Regulators around the world have established similar lists of recognized credit-rating agencies.

In addition to the credit ratings issued by third-party rating agencies, **internal ratings** are also created and heavily used by financial institutions to control their credit risk. The number of rating grades and their definitions vary among third-party rating agencies and among financial services firms, but their objective is the same: to create an ordinal ranking of borrowers by riskiness as an aid to portfolio selection and risk management.

Rating agencies like Standard & Poor's and Moody's Investors Service use more than 20 rating grades. Exhibit 1 shows the ratings assigned by these two agencies to debt issues. For Standard & Poor's ratings, *investment-grade* bonds are those rated BBB– and above. All other rating classes are considered *non-investment-grade*, *speculative-grade*, or *junk bonds*. For Moody's Investors Service, investment-grade bonds are those rated Baa3 and above. Large financial institutions define their own rating scales, but 10–20 risk levels are common.

Exhibit 1   Sample Rating Scales Ranked from Best to Worst Rating

Rating Category	Moody's Investors Service	Standard & Poor's	Example of a Bank Internal Rating
1	Aaa	AAA	20
2	Aa1	AA+	19
3	Aa2	AA	18
4	Aa3	AA–	17
5	A1	A+	16
6	A2	A	15
7	A3	A–	14

5 In 2013, the Financial Services Authority was replaced by two new regulatory authorities, the Financial Conduct Authority (FCA) and the Prudential Regulation Authority (PRA).

Rating Category	Moody's Investors Service	Standard & Poor's	Example of a Bank Internal Rating
8	Baa1	BBB+	13
9	Baa2	BBB	12
10	Baa3	BBB−	11
11	Ba1	BB+	10
12	Ba2	BB	9
13	Ba3	BB−	8
14	B1	B+	7
15	B2	B	6
16	B3	B−	5
17	Caa1	CCC+	4
18	Caa2	CCC	3
19	Caa3	CCC−	2
20	Ca	CC	1
21	C	D	

Exhibit 1 (Continued)

Both third-party and internal credit ratings are measures that summarize an extensive analysis of a borrower's credit history. For example, a bank's credit file on a typical corporate borrower may have 100 pages of history and analysis on the borrower's relationship with the bank. Saying that the borrower is BBB+ or rated a 9 is an efficient way to communicate the conclusions of this extensive analysis with respect to the borrower's credit risk in relation to other potential borrowers.

Rating agencies arose because there are economies of scale in the collection of credit-related information. Indeed, there are large fixed costs in obtaining financial information, but fewer costs in distributing the collected information to others. Collecting financial information requires significant time and resources. This was especially true before the advent of the internet, when information was available only in paper form and had to be obtained by visiting companies one by one. Even today, however, credit-rating agencies still profit by reducing the costs of obtaining and analyzing credit information to the eventual end-user, the lender. This is the economic basis of their business franchise.

Some rating agencies, such as Egan-Jones Rating Company, are compensated by subscribers. However, rating agencies are often compensated using an *issuer-pays model*, where the issuer (borrower) pays the credit-rating agency to rate their debt. The rating is then distributed free of charge to potential lenders. If detail is desired on the underlying analysis, an investor/lender has to subscribe. Potential investors/lenders may rely on credit ratings rather than doing their own credit analyses or in conjunction with their own credit analyses. A high credit rating may result in more funds being potentially available to a borrower. The problem with an issuer-pays model is that there is an incentive conflict. To obtain more business, credit-rating agencies have an incentive to give higher ratings than may be deserved. Recent events associated with the 2008 global financial crisis have drawn attention to the potential seriousness of this problem; ratings that were subsequently judged to be higher than justified have resulted in regulators questioning the wisdom of relying on and referring to credit-rating agencies in financial regulations.

Another issue is that rating agencies may be motivated to keep their ratings stable over time to reduce unnecessary volatility in debt market prices. Unfortunately, there is an inherent conflict between stability and accuracy. Stable ratings can only be accurate "on average" because, by design, they change infrequently while information arrives incrementally and continuously with the changing business cycle. This desire for stability in the ratings gives rise to a non-constant relationship over time between credit ratings and default probabilities. To see this phenomenon, consider Exhibit 2 showing historical annual default rate percentages from Standard & Poor's for companies rated CCC.

Exhibit 2	Actual Default Rate on Companies Rated CCC by Standard & Poor's, 1981–2010		
Year	Default Rate (%)	Year	Default Rate (%)
1981	0	1996	4.17
1982	21.43	1997	12.00
1983	6.67	1998	42.86
1984	25.00	1999	32.35
1985	15.38	2000	34.12
1986	23.08	2001	44.55
1987	12.28	2002	44.12
1988	20.37	2003	32.93
1989	33.33	2004	15.33
1990	31.25	2005	8.94
1991	33.87	2006	12.38
1992	30.19	2007	15.09
1993	13.33	2008	26.26
1994	16.67	2009	48.68
1995	28.00	2010	22.27

Source: Standard & Poor's Corporation, *Default, Transition, and Recovery: 2010 Annual Global Corporate Default Study and Rating Transitions* (30 March 2011).

As shown in Exhibit 2, although the credit rating is constant, at CCC, over time, the actual percentage of defaults is not. For example, when the economy was healthy in 1981, the default rate was 0%, but in the recession of 2009, it was 48.68%. The default probability of a CCC company appears to change over time with the business cycle, whereas the rating does not.

Strengths and weaknesses of the traditional credit ratings (both traditional third-party and internal ratings) can be summarized as follows.

Rating Strengths

■ They provide a simple statistic that summarizes a complex credit analysis of a potential borrower.

■ They tend to be stable over time and across the business cycle, which reduces debt market price volatility.

Rating Weaknesses

- They tend to be stable over time, which reduces the correspondence to a debt offering's default probability.

- They do not explicitly depend on the business cycle, whereas a debt offering's default probability does.

- The issuer-pays model for compensating credit-rating agencies has a potential conflict of interest that may distort the accuracy of credit ratings. (This weakness applies to third-party ratings only.)

EXAMPLE 3

A bond portfolio manager has $500,000 to invest in two bonds. He collects the S&P credit ratings and yields to maturity on four hypothetical debt issues:

- Green Company, AA−, 5%

- Sleepy Company, B−, 7%

- Red Fruit Corp, BBB+, 6.5%

- Slot Machines Incorporated, CCC, 9%

Rank the companies in terms of their credit risk. Which companies are investment grade?

Solution:

Using Exhibit 1, the ranking is Green Company, Red Fruit Corp, Sleepy Company, and Slot Machines Inc. The investment-grade bonds are Green Company and Red Fruit Corp.

Traditional credit ratings are applied to corporate debt, government debt, quasi-government debt, and asset-backed securities. Asset-backed securities have some unique characteristics and are discussed in Section 7 of this reading.

STRUCTURAL MODELS

4

Credit-rating agencies use a number of analytical tools to develop their ratings. Structural models underlie the default probabilities and credit analytics provided by Moody's KMV and other vendors, including Kamakura Corporation. **Structural models** were originated to understand the economics of a company's liabilities and build on the insights of option pricing theory. They are called structural models because they are based on the *structure* of a company's balance sheet.

To understand structural models, it is easiest to start with a company with a simple financing structure. The balance sheet of this hypothetical company is shown in Exhibit 3.

Exhibit 3 Balance Sheet of a Simple Company at Time t	
Assets A_t	Debt $D(t,T)$
	Zero-coupon bond

(continued)

Exhibit 3   (Continued)

• maturity T
• face value K

Equity S_t

The company illustrated in Exhibit 3 has assets, liabilities, and equity on its balance sheet. The assets have a time t value of A_t dollars. The liabilities consist of a single debt issue, which is a zero-coupon bond with a face value of K dollars that matures at time T. The time t value of the zero-coupon bond is denoted $D(t,T)$. Finally, the time t value of the company's equity is denoted S_t. The value of the company's assets must equal the total value of its liabilities and equity:

$$A_t = D(t,T) + S_t$$

The company's owners (equity holders) have *limited liability*; the equity holders' liability to the debt holders extends only to the company's assets and not their personal wealth. Alternatively stated, if the equity holders default on the debt payment at time T, the debt holders' only recourse is to take over the company and assume ownership of the company's assets. They have no additional claim on the equity holders' personal wealth. This limited liability is the basis for the analogy between the company's equity and a call option.

4.1 The Option Analogy

To illustrate the option analogy, let us consider the equity holders' decision to pay off the debt at time T. The equity holders will pay off the debt at time T only if it is in their best interests to do so. Because at time T the value of the company's assets is A_T, the equity holders will pay off the debt only if the value of the assets at time T exceeds what is owed—that is, $A_T \geq K$. After the payment, they keep what's left over $(A_T - K)$. If $A_T < K$, the equity holders will default on the debt issue. Consequently, the time T value of the equity is:

$$S_T = \begin{cases} A_T - K & \text{if} \quad A_T \geq K \\ 0 & \text{if} \quad A_T < K \end{cases} = \max[A_T - K, 0]$$

It is now easy to see the *call option analogy* for equity. The company's equity has the same payoff as a European call option on the company's assets with strike price K and maturity T. Hence, holding the company's equity is economically equivalent to owning a European call option on the company's assets. This is the key insight of the structural model.

The time T value of the company's debt is:

$$D(T,T) = \begin{cases} K & \text{if} \quad A_T \geq K \\ A_T & \text{if} \quad A_T < K \end{cases} = \min[K, A_T]$$

This expression states that the debt holders get the face value, K, back if the time T asset value exceeds this payment. Otherwise, the equity holders default and the bondholders take over the company and collect the value of the company's assets. The implication is that:

- the probability that the debt defaults at time T is equal to the probability that the asset's value falls below the face value of the debt—that is, $\text{prob}(A_T < K)$—and

- the loss given default is the quantity $K - A_T$.

To determine these quantities for practical usage, we need to make some assumptions, which are discussed in Section 4.2. Before doing this, we can express $D(T,T)$ in an alternative way by adding K before the bracket and subtracting K inside the bracket on the right side of the previous expression. Doing so gives:

$$D(T,T) = K - \begin{cases} 0 & \text{if} \quad A_T \geq K \\ K - A_T & \text{if} \quad A_T < K \end{cases} = K - \max[K - A_T, 0]$$

In this equation, we see that the debt's time T payoff is equivalent to getting K dollars with certainty less the payoff to a European put option on the company's assets with strike price K and maturity T. We now have a *debt option analogy*:

> Owning the company's debt is economically equivalent to owning a riskless bond that pays K dollars with certainty at time T, and simultaneously selling a European put option on the assets of the company with strike price K and maturity T.

The debt option analogy explains why risky debt is less valuable than riskless debt. The difference in value is equal to the short put option's price. In essence, the debt holders lend the equity holders K dollars and simultaneously sell them an insurance policy for K dollars on the value of their assets. If the assets fall below K, the debt holders take the assets in exchange for their loan. This possibility creates the credit risk.

4.2 Valuation

To use the structural model to determine a company's credit risk, we need to add assumptions that enable us to explicitly value the implied call and put options. To do this, the standard application of the structural model imposes the same assumptions used in option pricing models. These assumptions are

1   the company's assets trade in frictionless markets that are arbitrage free,

2   the riskless rate of interest, r, is constant over time, and

3   the time T value of the company's assets has a lognormal distribution with mean uT and variance $\sigma^2 T$.

The first assumption implies that there are no transaction costs and states that the company's assets are traded in markets that are arbitrage free. "Frictionless markets" means that the markets are *liquid*, with no bid–ask spreads and no quantity impact of a trade on the market price. It also implies that the company's asset value is observable at all times. This implication is significant, and we will return to its importance later in the reading. The no-arbitrage argument is needed to price the option.

The second assumption is that the riskless rate of interest is a constant over time. In other words, there is no interest rate risk in the model. When studying fixed-income securities whose values change with movements in interest rates, this assumption is unrealistic. Because this assumption is not satisfied in actual markets, it is a weakness of this model's formulation.

The third assumption states that the company's asset value evolves over time according to a lognormal distribution with an expected return equal to u% per year and a volatility equal to σ% per year. Consequently, the expected return and volatility of the company's assets over the time period $[0,T]$ are uT and $\sigma^2 T$, respectively.

These three assumptions are identical to those for stock price behavior in the original Black–Scholes option pricing model. Hence, the Black–Scholes option pricing formula applies to the equity's time t value because it is a European call option on the company's assets. The formula is:

$$S_t = A_t N(d_1) - Ke^{-r(T-t)}N(d_2)$$

where

$$d_1 = \frac{\ln\left(\dfrac{A_t}{K}\right) + r(T-t) + \dfrac{1}{2}\sigma^2(T-t)}{\sigma\sqrt{T-t}}$$

$$d_2 = d_1 - \sigma\sqrt{T-t}$$

$N(.)$ = the cumulative standard normal distribution function with mean 0 and variance 1.

The value of the debt can be obtained using the accounting identity $A_t = D(t,T) + S_t$. Substitution of the formula for S_t into this accounting identity gives:

$$D(t,T) = A_t N(-d_1) + Ke^{-r(T-t)}N(d_2)$$

The first term in this expression, $A_t N(-d_1)$, corresponds to the present value of the payoff on the company's debt if default occurs. The second term in this expression, $Ke^{-r(T-t)}N(d_2)$, corresponds to the present value of the payoff on the company's debt if default does not occur. A close examination of the second term shows that the risk-neutral probability of the company's debt not defaulting, prob($A_T \geq K$), is equal to $N(d_2)$. The sum of these two terms, therefore, gives the present value of the company's debt.

This valuation formula is useful for understanding the probability of default, the expected loss, and the present value of the expected loss as shown in the next section.

4.3 Credit Risk Measures

For the evaluation of credit risk, the structural model enables one to explicitly calculate the credit risk measures discussed in Section 2. The following formulas are obtained from the formula for the company's debt, $D(t,T)$, as given in the previous expression.

▪ The probability of the debt defaulting is:

$$\text{prob}(A_T < K) = 1 - \text{prob}(A_T \geq K) = 1 - N(e_2),$$

where

$$e_1 = \frac{\ln\left(\dfrac{A_t}{K}\right) + u(T-t) + \dfrac{1}{2}\sigma^2(T-t)}{\sigma\sqrt{T-t}}$$

$$e_2 = e_1 - \sigma\sqrt{T-t}$$

This expression follows from noting that prob($A_T \geq K$) = $N(e_2)$.

▪ The expected loss is:

$$KN(-e_2) - A_t e^{u(T-t)}N(-e_1)$$

- The present value of the expected loss is obtained by subtracting the value of the debt, $D(t,T)$, from the value of a default-free (riskless) zero-coupon bond:

$$KP(t,T) - D(t,T) = Ke^{-r(T-t)}N(-d_2) - A_tN(-d_1)$$

where $P(t,T) = e^{-r(T-t)}$ is the time t price of a default-free zero-coupon bond paying a dollar at time T.

It is important for the reader to note the following facts about the formulas in this section:

- The present value of the expected loss is the difference between the value of a riskless zero-coupon bond paying K dollars at maturity and the value of the risky debt:

$$Ke^{-r(T-t)} - D(t,T)$$

Alternatively, the present value of the expected loss is also given by the risk-neutral expected discounted loss:

$$\tilde{E}\left(K - D(T,T)\right)e^{-r(T-t)}$$

where $\tilde{E}()$ denotes taking an expectation using the risk-neutral probabilities.

- In this computation, the riskless rate is used to discount the future cash flows. The cash flows' risks are captured in this computation by replacing the actual probabilities with the risk-neutral probabilities. The difference between the use of $\{d_1,d_2\}$ in the present value of the loss and $\{e_1,e_2\}$ in the probability of a loss is due to the difference between the risk-neutral and the actual probabilities. The risk-neutral probabilities are determined by assuming that the asset value's expected return is the riskless rate r (see $\{d_1,d_2\}$), whereas the actual probabilities use the asset value's real expected return of $u\%$ per year (see $\{e_1,e_2\}$).

- The probability of default depends explicitly on the company's assumed liability structure. We mention this fact here for subsequent comparison with the reduced form model. This explicit dependency of the probability of default on the company's liability structure is a limitation of the structural model.

These credit risk measures can be calculated given the inputs $\{A_t, u, r, \sigma, K, T\}$.

EXAMPLE 4

Interpreting Structural Model Credit Risk Measures

Assume a company has the following values:

- Time t asset value: A_t = $1000.
- Expected return on assets: u = 0.03 per year.
- Risk-free rate: r = 0.01 per year.
- Face value of debt: K = $700.
- Time to maturity of debt: $T - t$ = 1 year.
- Asset return volatility: σ = 0.30 per year.

The company's credit risk measures can now be computed. We first need to compute some intermediate quantities:

$$d_1 = \frac{\ln\left(\frac{1,000}{700}\right) + 0.01(1) + \frac{1}{2}(0.3)^2(1)}{0.3\sqrt{1}} = 1.37225$$

$$d_2 = 1.37225 - 0.3\sqrt{1} = 1.07225$$

$$N(-d_1) = 0.0850$$

$$N(-d_2) = 0.1418$$

$$e_1 = \frac{\ln\left(\frac{1,000}{700}\right) + 0.03(1) + \frac{1}{2}(0.3)^2(1)}{0.3\sqrt{1}} = 1.43892$$

$$e_2 = 1.43892 - 0.3\sqrt{1} = 1.13892$$

$$N(-e_1) = 0.0751$$

$$N(-e_2) = 0.1274$$

The probability of default is $\text{prob}(A_T < K) = N(-e_2) = 0.1274$, or 12.74% over the debt's time to maturity, which is one year.

The expected loss is:

$$KN(-e_2) - A_t e^{\mu(T-t)}N(-e_1) = 700(0.1274) - 1,000e^{0.03}(0.0751) = \$11.78$$

The present value of the expected loss is:

$$KP(t,T) - D(t,T) = Ke^{-r(T-t)}N(-d_2) - A_t N(-d_1)$$
$$= 700e^{-0.01(1)}(0.1418) - 1,000(0.0850) = \$13.28$$

In this example, the present value of the expected loss on the $700 bond is $13.28. This value is how much an investor would pay to a third party (an insurer) to remove the risk of default from holding this bond. The expected loss itself is only $11.78.

The difference between the expected loss and the present value of the expected loss includes:

A   a premium for the risk of credit loss only.

B   a discount for the time value of money only.

C   both a discount for the time value of money and a premium for the risk of credit loss.

Solution:

C is correct. The $1.50 difference includes both a discount for the time value of money and the risk premium required by the market to bear the risk of credit loss. In this case, the present value of the expected loss exceeds the expected loss. This means that the risk premium must dominate the difference because the time-value-of-money discount will reduce the present value of the expected loss compared with the expected loss. In other words, in the absence of a risk premium, the present value of the expected loss will be less than the expected loss.

We now discuss estimating the inputs to the model.

4.4 Estimation

Before discussing the estimation of these inputs to the structural model, it is helpful to discuss parameter estimation in option pricing models more generally. There are two ways to estimate the parameters of any option pricing model: *historical* and *implicit*.

Historical estimation is where one uses past time-series observations of the underlying asset's price and standard statistical procedures to estimate the parameters. For example, to estimate the asset's expected return and volatility in the structural model using historical estimation, one obtains past time-series observations of the asset's value, A_t, (say, daily prices for one year) and then computes the mean return over the year and the return's standard deviation.

Implicit estimation, also called *calibration*, uses market prices of the options themselves to find the value of the parameter that equates the market price to the formula's price. In other words, calibration finds the implied value of the parameter. For example, consider using the standard Black-Scholes call option pricing model for a stock option. To estimate the underlying stock's volatility using implicit estimation, one would observe the market value of the call option and find the volatility that equates the Black-Scholes formula to the call's market price, called the *implied volatility*. This procedure is standard in equity option markets. As illustrated by this example, implicit estimation always involves solving an equation, or a set of equations, for an unknown—in this case, the implied volatility.

For the structural model, one cannot use historical estimation. The reason is that the company's assets (which include buildings and non-traded investments), in contrast to our initial assumption, do not trade in frictionless markets. Consequently, the company's asset value is *not observable*. Because one cannot observe the company's asset value, one cannot use standard statistics to compute a mean return or the asset return's standard deviation.

This leaves implicit estimation as the only alternative for the structural model. Implicit estimation is a complex estimation procedure and underlies some commercial vendors' default probability estimates, including Moody's KMV. This procedure requires that the company's equity be actively traded so that a time series of market prices for the company's equity is available, which enables the computation of the company's asset value parameters using the company's debt-to-equity ratio. Here is a step-by-step description of the procedure for computing the company's asset value parameters $\{A_t, \sigma\}$.

- Collect a time series of equity market prices, S_t, for $t = 1, ..., n$ (for example, daily prices over the last year).

- From these equity prices, compute the equity's volatility, which is the sample standard derivation, denoted $\sqrt{var\left(\dfrac{dS}{S}\right)}$.

- For each time t, set up the following two equations:

$$S_t = A_t N(d_1) - Ke^{-r(T-t)}N(d_2)$$

and

$$\sqrt{var\left(\frac{dS}{S}\right)} = N(d_1)\frac{A_t}{S_t}$$

- Solve these $2n$ equations for the $(n + 1)$ unknowns: $\{A_t$ for $t = 1, ..., n$; and $\sigma\}$.

The only remaining parameter to estimate is the company's asset expected return per year, u. Standard practice is to use an equilibrium capital asset pricing model (CAPM) in conjunction with an estimate for the riskless rate, r, to determine u. In the simplest CAPM (a static one-period model), one can write the company's asset return as equal to the risk-free rate plus a risk premium determined by the company's asset beta:

$$u = r + \beta(u_m - r)$$

where β is the beta of the company's asset, u_m is the expected return per year on the market portfolio, and $(u_m - r)$ is the market's equity risk premium. Of course, to use this estimate, one must first determine the company's asset beta and the expected return on the market portfolio. Modern portfolio theory provides the methods for doing this. Standard statistics can be used to estimate the market portfolio's mean return, and linear regression can be used to estimate the company's equity beta. Given an estimate of the company's equity beta, the company's asset beta can be deduced by unlevering the company's equity beta. Estimation of the market's equity risk premium is more challenging because there is no observable expected return on the market portfolio. There is no agreement in the financial community on which method to use to estimate the market's equity risk premium. Many finance professionals advocate the use of a more realistic multi-period CAPM that includes multiple risk factors in the risk premium rather than a single-factor CAPM. However, there is no consensus on how many and which risk factors to include.

A positive attribute of the Black–Scholes model is that it does not require an estimate of a risk premium. It made the formula usable in practice. The fact that one needs to estimate the market's equity risk premium in the computation of the company's default probability is a weakness of the structural model.

A well-known problem with implicit estimation, or calibration more generally, is that if the model's assumptions are not reasonable approximations of the market's actual structure, then the implicit estimate will incorporate the model's error and not represent the true parameter. This bias will, in turn, introduce error into the resulting probability of default and the expected loss, thereby making the resulting estimates unreliable. Unfortunately, this criticism applies to the structural model because its assumptions are not a good representation of reality. This is true for the following reasons:

- A typical company's balance sheet will have a liability structure much more complex than just the simple zero-coupon bond structure represented in Exhibit 3.
- Interest rates are not constant over time. This issue is serious because when dealing with fixed-income securities that involve significant interest rate risk, assuming that interest rates are constant is equivalent to assuming interest rate risk is irrelevant.
- The assumed lognormal distribution for asset prices implies a "thin" tail for the company's loss distribution. There is significant evidence that a company's loss distribution has a left tail "fatter" than those implied by a lognormal distribution.
- It is assumed that the asset's return volatility is constant over time, independent of changing economic conditions and business cycles.
- In contrast to a key assumption, the company's assets do not trade in frictionless markets; examples include buildings and non-traded investments.

The strength of the structural model is the useful economic intuition it provides for understanding the risks involved in a company's debt and equity, which is a primary value of learning this model. Although the structural model underlies some credit risk estimates used in practice, the implausibility of the assumptions underlying structural models brings the models into question. Although many of the structural model's assumptions can be relaxed or modified, the assumption that assets trade in frictionless markets is a defining characteristic of structural models and cannot be relaxed. Generalizing the frictionless market assumption generates the reduced form model discussed in the next section.

Structural Model Strengths

- It provides an option analogy for understanding a company's default probability and recovery rate.
- It can be estimated using only current market prices.

Structural Model Weaknesses

- The default probability and recovery rate depend crucially on the assumed balance sheet of the company, and realistic balance sheets cannot be modeled.
- Its credit risk measures can be estimated only by using implicit estimation procedures because the company's asset value is unobservable.
- Its credit risk measures are biased because implicit estimation procedures inherit errors in the model's formulation.
- The credit risk measures do not explicitly consider the business cycle.

REDUCED FORM MODELS

5

Reduced form models were originated to overcome a key weakness of the structural model—the assumption that the company's assets trade. Reduced form models replace this assumption with a more robust one—that some of the company's debt trades. They are called reduced form models because they impose their assumptions on the outputs of a structural model—the probability of default and the loss given default—rather than on the balance sheet structure itself. Unlike structural models, this change in perspective gives reduced form models tremendous flexibility in matching actual market conditions.

To understand reduced form models, it is easiest to start with a company where one of the liabilities is a zero-coupon bond with face value K and maturity T. For easy comparison with the structural model in the previous section, we denote the time t value of this debt as $D(t,T)$. We divide the time period $[0,T]$ up into the time intervals $0, \Delta, 2\Delta, ..., T - \Delta$ of length Δ.

Reduced form models make the following assumptions:

1 The company's zero-coupon bond trades in frictionless markets that are arbitrage free;

2 The riskless rate of interest, r_t, is stochastic;

3 The state of the economy can be described by a vector of stochastic variables X_t that represent the *macroeconomic* factors influencing the economy at time t;

4 The company defaults at a random time t, where the probability of default over $[t,t + \Delta]$ when the economy is in state X_t is given by $\lambda(X_t)\Delta$;

5 Given the vector of macroeconomic state variables X_t, a company's default represents idiosyncratic risk; and

6 Given default, the percentage loss on the company's debt is $0 \le \iota(X_t) \le 1$.

The first assumption requires only that one of the company's liabilities, a zero-coupon bond, trades in frictionless and arbitrage-free markets. Reduced form models do not assume that the company's assets trade. They also do not assume that the company's remaining liabilities or even its equity trades. Other liabilities could be used in place of a zero-coupon bond. Finally, markets are assumed to be liquid, with no transaction costs or bid–ask spreads, and markets are assumed to be arbitrage free.

The second assumption allows interest rates to be stochastic. Allowing for this possibility is essential to capture the interest rate risk inherent in the pricing of fixed-income securities. Only the term structure evolution must be arbitrage free.

The third assumption is that the relevant state of the economy can be described by a vector of macroeconomic state variables X_t. For example, this set of state variables might include the riskless rate, the inflation rate, the level of unemployment, the growth rate of gross domestic product, and so forth. This set of macroeconomic state variables is stochastic, and its evolution is completely arbitrary. This assumption is not very restrictive.

The fourth, fifth, and sixth assumptions are imposed on the outputs of a structural model, which are the probability of default and the loss given default. The fourth assumption is that the default time can be modeled as a Cox process, with a *default intensity* of $\lambda(X_t)$. Given a company that has not yet defaulted, the **default intensity** gives the probability of default over the next instant $[t, t + \Delta]$ when the economy is in state X_t. The key advantage of this assumption is that the default probability explicitly depends on the business cycle through the macroeconomic state variables X_t. This allows, for example, for the probability that default increases in a recession and declines in a healthy economy. This is a very general method of modeling default over time. In fact, this formulation allows for systemic defaults across companies.

The fifth assumption states that, given the state of the economy, whether a particular company defaults depends only on company-specific considerations. For example, suppose that in a recession, the probability of default increases. Now consider two car companies, General Motors and Ford. In a recession, the probability that each car company defaults will increase. This happens via the dependence of the default intensity on the macroeconomic state variables X_t. The idiosyncratic risk assumption is different. It states that whether either of these two companies actually defaults in a recession depends on each company's actions and not the macroeconomic factors. A company-specific action could be that the company's management made an error in their debt choice in years past, which results in their defaulting now. Management error is idiosyncratic risk, not economy-wide or systematic risk.

An open research question is whether, conditioned on the state of the economy, default risk is idiosyncratic. Although this assumption can be easily relaxed, relaxing it introduces the necessity of estimating a default risk premium. Although it can be done, it introduces additional complexity into the estimation process. We include this assumption here because it is a reasonable first approximation and because it simplifies both the notation and subsequent explanations.

The sixth assumption states that if default occurs, debt is worth only $[1 - t(X_t)]$ of its face value. Here, $[1 - t(X_t)]$ is the percentage recovery rate on the debt in the event of default. The loss given default, $t(X_t)$, explicitly depends on the business cycle through the macroeconomic state variables. This allows, for example, that in a recession the loss given default is larger than it is in a healthy economy. This assumption is also very general and not restrictive.

These six assumptions underlying the reduced form model are very general, allowing the default probability and the loss given default to depend on the business cycle, as reflected in the macroeconomic state variables X_t. Given a proper specification of the functional forms for the default intensity and loss given default and stochastic processes for the spot rate of interest and the macroeconomic variables, they provide a reasonable approximation of actual debt markets.

5.1 Valuation

Under the assumption of no arbitrage, it can be shown that option pricing methodology when applied to a reduced form model implies that risk-neutral probabilities
exist such that the debt's price is equal to the expected discounted payoff to the debt
at maturity—that is,

$$D(t,T) = \tilde{E}\left[\frac{K}{(1 + r_t\Delta)(1 + r_{t+\Delta}\Delta)...(1 + r_{T-\Delta}\Delta)}\right]$$

where $\tilde{E}(.)$ denotes taking an expectation using the risk-neutral probabilities.

The expression shows that the debt's value is given by the expected discounted
value of the K dollars promised at time t. The discounting is done using the risk-free
rate over the time intervals 0, Δ, ..., $T - \Delta$. The adjustment for the risk of the debt's
cash flows occurs through the use of the risk-neutral probabilities when taking the
expectation.

Although the lengthy and challenging proof is not shown here, this expression
can be written as:

$$D(t,T) = \tilde{E}\left\langle\frac{K}{\{1 + [r_t + \lambda(X_t)]\Delta\}\{1 + [r_{t+\Delta} + \lambda(X_{t+\Delta})]\}...\{1 + [r_{T-\Delta} + \lambda(X_{T-\Delta})]\Delta\}}\right\rangle +$$

$$\sum_{i=t}^{T-\Delta}\tilde{E}\left\langle\frac{K[1 - \iota(X_i)]}{\{1 + [r_t + \lambda(X_t)]\Delta\}\{1 + [r_{t+\Delta} + \lambda(X_{t+\Delta})]\}...\{1 + [r_i + \lambda(X_i)]\Delta\}}\lambda(X_i)\Delta\right\rangle$$

This expression decomposes the value of the company's debt into two parts. The first
term on the right side of this expression represents the debt's expected discounted
payoff K given that *there is no default* on the company's debt. Note that the discount
rate on the right side of this expression, $[r_u + \lambda(X_u)]$ has been increased for the risk
of default. The second term on the right side of this expression represents the debt's
expected discounted payoff *if default occurs*. This is equal to the payoff if default
occurs *at time i*, $K[1 - i(X_i)]$, multiplied by the probability of default at time i, $\lambda(X_i)$
Δ, discounted, and then summed across all the times 0, Δ, ..., $T - \Delta$. In this last term,
observe that the loss is subtracted from the debt's promised face value. In conjunction,
these observations prove that the valuation formula explicitly incorporates both the
loss given default and the intensity process.

This form of the debt's price is very abstract and very general. In any application,
a particular evolution for both the interest rate and macroeconomic state variable
vector needs to be specified. Many such structures have been used in the literature
and practice. We illustrate one useful choice later in this section as an example. The
study of more complex specifications is outside the scope of this reading and left for
independent reading.

For this reading, we are especially interested in quantifying the credit risk measures
discussed in Section 2.

5.2 Credit Risk Measures

In the reduced form model, the credit risk measures are quantified as follows:

- The probability of the debt defaulting over $[0,T]$ is:

$$\text{prob}(\tau \leq T) = 1 - E\left\{\frac{1}{[1 + \lambda(X_0)\Delta][1 + \lambda(X_\Delta)]...[1 + \lambda(X_{T-\Delta})\Delta]}\right\}$$

where $E(.)$ denotes taking an expectation using the actual probabilities.

■ The expected loss is:

$$
\sum_{i=0}^{T-\Delta} E\left\{ \frac{\iota(X_i)K}{\left[1 + \lambda(X_0)\Delta\right]\left[1 + \lambda(X_\Delta)\right]\dots\left[1 + \lambda(X_i)\Delta\right]} \lambda(X_i)\Delta \right\}
$$

■ The present value of the expected loss is:

$$
KP(t,T) - D(t,T)
$$

where $D(t,T)$ is given in the formula in section 5.1.

All of these quantities can be easily computed given the required inputs and the probability distribution for the macroeconomic state variables and interest rates. Note that, unlike the structural model, the company's probability of default does not explicitly depend on the company's balance sheet. The same default probability applies to all of the company's liabilities because of the existence of cross-default clauses in corporate debt. In the event of default, reduced form models allow the company's different liabilities to have different loss rates. These are significant advantages of using a reduced form model.

Before discussing the estimation of these inputs, we discuss a simple scenario (constant default probability and loss given default) to illustrate the interpretation of these formulas. This discussion will also prove useful in a subsequent section to understand the term structure of credit spreads.

5.2.1 *Constant Default Probability and Loss Given Default Formulas*

This section illustrates the reduced form pricing formulas for a zero-coupon bond under the following special (and unrealistic) assumptions.

■ The default probability is a constant—that is, $\lambda(X_t) = \lambda$.

> This assumption implies that the probability of default does not depend on the macroeconomic state of the economy.

■ The dollar loss given default is a constant percentage of the zero-coupon bond's value just before default—that is, $\iota(X_\tau)K = \gamma D(\tau-,T)$.

> Here, the symbol $\tau-$ means the instant just before default. Note that, as with the probability of default, the loss given default also does not depend on the macroeconomic state of the economy under this assumption.

Combined, these two additional assumptions imply that the zero-coupon bond's price takes the following special form (see Jarrow 2009):

$$
D(t,T) = Ke^{-\lambda\gamma(T-t)}P(t,T)
$$

where $P(t,T)$ is the time t value of a default-free zero-coupon bond paying one dollar at time T.

The risky zero-coupon bond's price is equal to the fraction $0 < e^{-\lambda\gamma(T-t)} < 1$ of an otherwise equivalent, but riskless, zero-coupon bond's price $KP(t,T)$. The risky company's expected percentage loss per unit of time appears in the exponent of the fraction. To see this, note that

$\lambda\gamma$ = (Probability of default per year) × (Percentage loss given default)

= Expected percentage loss per yearUnder this structure, one can also show that the three credit risk measures are:

■ the probability of the debt defaulting over $[0,T]$:

$$
\text{prob}(\tau \le T) = 1 - e^{-\lambda(T-t)}
$$

- the expected loss:

    $K[1 - e^{-\lambda\gamma(T-t)}]$ and

- the present value of the loss given default:

    $KP(t,T) - D(t,T) = KP(t,T)[1 - e^{-\lambda\gamma(T-t)}]$

Note that in the expected loss and the present value of the expected loss, because the default probability does not depend on the macroeconomic state of the economy, the actual and risk-neutral default probabilities are equal and depend only on λ. Later in this reading, we will use these simple formulas to help understand the term structure of credit spreads and to provide a simple method to estimate expected losses.

EXAMPLE 5

Interpreting Reduced Form Model Credit Risk Measures

Assume a company has the following values for its debt issue:

- Face value: $K = \$700$,
- Time to maturity: $T - t = 1$ year,
- Default intensity (the approximate probability of default per year): $\lambda = 0.01$, and
- Loss given default: $\gamma = 0.4$ (40%).

Let the one-year default-free zero-coupon bond's price, $P(t,T)$, equal 0.96.

The company's probability of default, expected loss, and present value of the expected loss using the constant intensity and loss given default formulas are as follows:

Probability of default:

$\text{prob}(\tau \le T) = 1 - e^{-0.01(1)} = 0.00995$

Expected loss:

$K[1 - e^{-\lambda\gamma(T-t)}] = 700[1 - e^{-0.004(1)}] = \$2.79$

Present value of the expected loss:

$KP(t,T) - D(t,T) = 700(0.96)[1 - e^{-0.004(1)}] = \$2.68$

The probability of default over the life of the bond is 0.995%. The expected loss on the $700 bond is $2.79. The present value of the expected loss is $2.68.

1 The largest amount a bondholder would pay to a third party (an insurer) to remove the credit risk of the bond is:

A $0.11.

B $2.68.

C $2.79.

2 In this case, the premium for the risk of credit loss:

A dominates the discount for the time value of money.

B balances out the discount for the time value of money.

C is dominated by the discount for the time value of money.

Solution to 1:

B is correct. The present value of the expected loss is $2.68. This is the largest amount one would pay to a third party (an insurer) to remove the credit risk from the bond.

Solution to 2:

In this case, the present value of the expected loss is less than the expected loss. The time value of money dominates the risk premium. In other words, the risk premium is dominated by the time value of money.

5.3 Estimation

As explained in the previous section, there are two approaches that can be used to estimate a model's parameters: historical and implicit. As with structural models, implicit estimation is possible. Unlike with structural models, however, historical estimation can be used for a reduced form model because the economy's macroeconomic state variables and the company's debt prices are both observable. This ability to use historical estimation with a reduced form model is a significant advantage of this approach to credit modeling. This section studies both approaches to estimating the parameters of a reduced form model.

5.3.1 *Implicit Estimation*

To use implicit estimation, one must completely specify the inputs to the reduced form model and the probability distributions for the macroeconomic state variables. Many such choices are possible. An illustration of such a choice is given in the previous example. Once a choice is made, the resulting formula for the zero-coupon bond's price will depend on a set of parameters θ—that is, $D(t,T \mid \theta)$. Using this price formula, the goal is to estimate the parameters θ. For example, in the previous example, the parameters θ equal the constant recovery rate and default probability.

For the moment, let us assume that we can directly observe the risky company's zero-coupon bond prices. Although these zero-coupon bonds may not trade in practice, we will show in the next section how to estimate these zero-coupon bond prices from observable risky coupon bond prices, which do trade.

Following is a step-by-step description of the procedure for computing the reduced form model's parameters:

- Collect a time series of risky debt market prices, $D_{market}(t,T)$ for $t = 1, 2, ..., n$ (for example, daily prices over the last year).
- For each time t, set up the equation $D_{market}(t,T) = D(t,T \mid \theta)$.
- Solve these n equations for the parameters θ.

The problem with implicit estimation, of course, is that if one uses a misspecified model—a model that is inconsistent with the market structure—then the resulting estimates will be biased. For example, in the previous illustration, *by assumption*, the default probability and loss given default do not depend on the macroeconomic state of the economy. This is not true in practice. If one uses this model to estimate these parameters, one will get different estimates depending on the state of the economy—economic expansion or recession—in contradiction to the model's assumptions. This contradiction implies that the parameter estimates obtained by this procedure are unreliable. This problem can be avoided by historical estimation, which we discuss next.

5.3.2 *Historical Estimation*

Estimating a reduced form model's parameters using historical estimation is an application of **hazard rate estimation**. Hazard rate estimation is a technique for estimating the probability of a binary event, like default/no default, mortality/no mortality, car crash/no car crash, prepay/no prepay, and so on. It is widely used in medical research and is applicable to enterprise risk management for the full spectrum of insurance-type events. Credit risk is one of those applications.

In theory, default can occur continuously in time. In practice, however, we have default data corresponding only to discrete time intervals. Hence, reduced form credit models must be estimated and implemented using discrete time statistical procedures. We will now illustrate how to estimate the default probability using a hazard rate estimation procedure.

Exhibit 4 shows typical default data for corporate debt. The first column gives the name of a company. In this example, we only list two: Citigroup and Lehman Brothers. Of course in the actual database, all existing companies need to be included. The second column gives the *default flag*, which equals 1 if the given company defaults during the time period indicated and 0 if no default occurred. The time period under consideration is given in the third column. Here, the time period corresponds to a month. Note that Lehman Brothers defaulted on its debt in September 2008, whereas Citigroup did not default over this sample period.

The remaining columns give the macroeconomic state variables X_t, augmented to include company-specific measures, collectively called the *explanatory variables*. They can include borrower-specific balance sheet items, dummy variables for calendar year effects, or other variables. In Exhibit 4, the explanatory variables are market leverage, the stock's return less the riskless rate (called the excess return), the stock's volatility, the Chicago Board Options Exchange Volatility Index (VIX, an index that measures the implied volatility of the S&P 500 Index), the net income to total assets ratio, and the unemployment rate. Other variables could have been included.

Once the default database has been assembled, as in Exhibit 4, the next step is to select a functional form for the intensity process. A convenient choice is the logistic function:

$$\text{prob}(t) = \frac{1}{1 + e^{-\alpha - \sum_{i=1}^{N} b_i X_t^i}}$$

where prob(t) is the probability of default over $[t, t + \Delta]$, $X_t = \left(X_t^1, ..., X_t^N\right)$ represents the N state variables, and $\{\alpha, b_i \text{ for } i = 1, ..., N\}$ are constants.

Exhibit 4	Sample Default Data for Public Company Default Database							
	Dependent Variable		**Explanatory Variables**					
Company	**Default Flag**	**Date**	**Market Leverage**	**Excess Return**	**Stock Volatility**	**VIX**	**Net Income/ Total Assets**	**Unemployment Rate**
Citigroup	0	6/30/2010	0.944985	0.144827	0.571061	34.54	0.002212	9.7
Citigroup	0	7/30/2010	0.937445	0.18934	0.511109	23.5	0.001392	9.5
Citigroup	0	8/31/2010	0.943071	−0.28633	0.43267	26.05	0.001392	9.5
Citigroup	0	9/30/2010	0.940171	−0.27173	0.353897	23.7	0.001392	9.6
Citigroup	0	10/29/2010	0.937534	−0.14237	0.343142	21.2	0.001093	9.6

(continued)

Exhibit 4   (Continued)

Company	Dependent Variable: Default Flag	Date	Market Leverage	Excess Return	Stock Volatility	VIX	Net Income/ Total Assets	Unemployment Rate
Citigroup	0	11/30/2010	0.937113	−0.05561	0.371965·	23.54	0.001093	9.6
Citigroup	0	12/31/2010	0.929734	0.301176	0.369208	17.75	0.001093	9.8
Citigroup	0	1/31/2011	0.925846	0.254157	0.355727	19.53	0.000684	9.4
Citigroup	0	2/28/2011	0.927821	0.174812	0.322558	18.35	0.000684	9.0
Citigroup	0	3/31/2011	0.931556	−0.04238	0.312913	17.74	0.000684	8.9
Citigroup	0	4/29/2011	0.929757	−0.12338	0.254542	14.75	0.00154	8.8
Citigroup	0	5/31/2011	0.936565	−0.19566	0.244869	15.45	0.00154	9.0
Citigroup	0	6/30/2011	0.935858	−0.17385	0.293736	16.52	0.00154	9.1
Lehman	0	1/31/2008	0.984411	−0.30473	0.376592	28.655	0.0012528	6.8
Lehman	0	2/28/2008	0.983969	−0.17537	0.362842	26.07	0.0012528	6.7
Lehman	0	3/31/2008	0.976221	−0.08861	0.329009	23.32	0.0012528	6.7
Lehman	0	4/30/2008	0.972138	0.268176	0.319171	25.894	0.0009837	6.7
Lehman	0	5/31/2008	0.974212	0.221157	0.259633	19.525	0.0009837	6.7
Lehman	0	6/30/2008	0.978134	0.141812	0.249766	21.483	0.0009837	6.7
Lehman	0	7/31/2008	0.976245	−0.07538	0.299611	20.185	0.0006156	6.9
Lehman	1	8/31/2008	0.983393	−0.15638	0.384124	19.514	0.0006156	6.6

In this equation, prob(t) represents the probability of default over the time period $[t, t + \Delta]$ and $\{\alpha, b_i \text{ for } i = 1, ..., N\}$ are the parameters to be estimated. The time period Δ is measured in years, so a month corresponds to $\Delta = 1/12$.

The parameters can be estimated using maximum likelihood estimation.[6] This can be a complex computational exercise. It can be shown that this maximum likelihood estimation is equivalent to running the following simple *linear regression* to estimate the coefficients:

$$\ln\left(\frac{d_t}{1 - d_t}\right) = \alpha + \sum_{i=1}^{N} b_i X_t^i$$

where the dependent variable (the left side of the regression) includes the default flag

$d_t = \{1 \text{ if default}, 0 \text{ if no default}\}$.

This is called a *logistic regression* because of the function on the left side of this expression. Exhibit 5 shows the outputs from running a logistic regression based on data similar to those given in Exhibit 4 but using only four explanatory variables. The first one, unemployment, is a macroeconomic variable that is the same for all companies. The last three variables—the market leverage ratio (accounting liabilities divided by the market value of equity), the net income to assets ratio, and the cash to assets ratio—are specific to the company.

---

6 The maximum likelihood estimator is the estimator that maximizes the probability (the "likelihood") that the observed data was generated by the model. In addition to intuitive appeal, maximum likelihood estimators have good statistical properties.

Exhibit 5	Sample Logistic Regression Results		
Coefficient Name	Coefficient Value	Input Value	Input Name
Alpha	−3		
b1	0.8	0.072	Unemployment (decimal)
b2	1.5	0.9	Market leverage ratio (decimal)
b3	−2	0.01	Net income/assets (decimal)
b4	−1	0.05	Cash/assets (decimal)

Given the coefficients in Exhibit 5, for any time period t, one can substitute the explanatory variables in the logistic function equation to get an estimate of the default probability, prob(t), for the time period considered. In Exhibit 4, we used monthly observation periods, so the default probability given is an estimate for the default probability over the next month. For example, substituting the specific input values shown in Exhibit 5 in the logistic function produces a monthly default probability estimate of

$$\text{prob}(t) = \frac{1}{1 + e^{3-0.8(0.072)-1.5(0.9)+2(0.01)+1(0.05)}} = 0.1594, \text{ or } 15.94\%$$

EXAMPLE 6

Assume that the credit analysis department has derived a new logistic regression model for the one-year default probability. The coefficients of the model and the inputs for Easy Company are given in Exhibit 6.

Exhibit 6	Logistic Regression		
Coefficient Name	Coefficient Value	Input Value	Input Name
Alpha	−4		Constant term
b1	0.07	0.091	Unemployment (decimal)
b2	1.3	0.93	Market leverage ratio (decimal)
b3	−1.96	0.0045	Net income/Assets (decimal)
b4	0.5	0.0315	US Treasury 10-year (decimal)
b5	−0.93	0.043	Cash/Assets (decimal)

What is the one-year probability of default for Easy Company?

Solution:

$$\text{prob}(t) = \frac{1}{1 + e^{4-0.07(0.091)-1.3(0.93)+1.96(0.0045)-0.5(0.0315)+0.93(0.043)}}$$
$$= 0.05638, \text{ or } 5.638\%$$

Estimation of the default probability using the hazard rate estimation methodology is very flexible. The default probabilities generated correspond to default over the next time period, and they depend explicitly on the state of the economy and the company, as represented by the choice of the explanatory variables included in the estimation. The default probabilities are for all of the company's liabilities because of the cross-default clauses present in corporate debt.

To estimate the loss given default process $\{\iota(X_s)\}$, one can use a similar procedure. First, one needs to specify the function form of $\iota(X_s)$. For example, one could assume that

$$\iota(X_t) = c_0 + \sum_{i=1}^{N} c_i X_t^i$$

where $\{c_i$ for $i = 1, ..., N\}$ are constants.

Other functional forms are also possible. To estimate such an equation, one needs historical observations of losses on defaulted debt issues (the left side of the equation). These losses are often available internally within a financial institution's records. The independent variables on the right side correspond to the relevant explanatory variables; for example, they could be the same state variables used in the hazard rate estimation. Given these data, the coefficients of the regression are obtained and the state conditional losses given default are estimated.

Reduced Form Model Strengths

- The model's inputs are observable, so historical estimation procedures can be used for the credit risk measures.
- The model's credit risk measures reflect the changing business cycle.
- The model does not require a specification of the company's balance sheet structure.

Reduced Form Model Weakness

- Hazard rate estimation procedures use past observations to predict the future. For this to be valid, the model must be properly formulated and back tested.

5.4 Comparison of Credit Risk Models

The previous sections have introduced three approaches for evaluating a debt's credit risk: credit ratings, structural models, and reduced form models. All three models have been empirically evaluated with respect to their accuracy in measuring a debt issue's default probability. Of the three approaches, credit ratings are the least accurate predictors. This is because credit ratings tend to lag changes in a debt issue's credit risk because of rating agencies' desire to keep ratings relatively stable over time, and consequently, they are relatively insensitive to changes in the business cycle.

Reduced form models perform better than structural models because structural models are computed using implicit estimation procedures whereas reduced form models are computed using historical estimation (hazard rate procedures). The improved performance is due to the flexibility of hazard rate estimation procedures—that is, both their ability to incorporate changes in the business cycle and their independence of a particular model specifying a company's balance sheet structure.

THE TERM STRUCTURE OF CREDIT SPREADS

6

This section covers the term structure of credit risk spreads, its composition, and how to use **credit spreads** to estimate the present value of the expected loss and the expected percentage loss per year. These estimates are used regularly by financial institutions in their fixed-income investment decisions and computation of their risk management measures. In practice, because risky coupon bonds trade, credit risk spreads are inferred from coupon bond prices. To understand this calculation, we must first understand the valuation of credit risky coupon bonds.

6.1 Coupon Bond Valuation

In this section, we discuss the arbitrage-free pricing theory for coupon bonds. First, consider a default-free coupon bond with coupons equal to C dollars paid at times $i = 1, 2, ..., T$, a face value of F dollars, and a maturity of time T. It is well known that under the assumptions of no arbitrage and frictionless markets, the price of this coupon bond can be written as:

$$B_G(t) = \sum_{i=1}^{T-1} CP(t,i) + (C + F)P(t,T)$$

where $B_G(t)$ is the time t price of the default-free coupon bond.

Unfortunately, for an otherwise credit risky coupon bond—with *promised* coupons equal to C dollars paid at times $i = 1, 2, ..., T$, a face value of F dollars, and a maturity of time T—and the corresponding risky zero-coupon bonds, a similar relation need not hold. The reason is that although the coupon and zero-coupon bonds may come from the same company, they can differ in their seniority and the percentage loss given default. To avoid this situation, we need to impose the following condition on the risky debt issued by the same company:

$B_G(t)$ and $D(t,T)$ for all T must be of *equal priority* in the event of default

where $D(t,T)$ is the time t price of a zero-coupon bond issued by the company. By "equal priority," we mean that in the event of default, the remaining promised cash flows on all these bonds have equal proportionate losses, where the equal proportionality loss factors across bonds can depend on the date of the promised payments. Under this equal priority condition, the following condition holds:

$$B_C(t) = \sum_{i=1}^{T-1} CD(t,i) + (C + F)D(t,T)$$

where $B_C(t)$ is the time t price of the risky coupon bond.

The proof of this pricing formula is straightforward. Because of equal priority, the coupon bond on the left side of this expression and the portfolio of zero-coupon bonds represented by the right side of this expression always have the same cash flows, regardless of default. Consequently, these two methods of obtaining the same future cash flows must have the same price at time t or an arbitrage opportunity exists. This completes the proof.

This sufficient condition is not very restrictive. When computing credit spreads, one wants to hold constant for credit risk. Because different seniority bonds from the same company can have different credit risk, one should always partition bonds into equal seniority before starting any credit risk computation.

6.2 The Term Structure of Credit Spreads

The term structure of credit spreads corresponds to the spread between the yields on default-free and credit risky zero-coupon bonds. In practice, because coupon bonds (rather than zero-coupon bonds) often trade for any given company, to compute the credit spreads one first needs to estimate the zero-coupon bond prices implied by the coupon bond prices. This estimation is done using the previous equations. The typical step-by-step procedure is as follows:

▪ At a given time t, collect N coupon bond prices $\{B_C(t)\}$ for a set of distinct bonds where the maximum-maturity bond in the collection has maturity $T_{max} < N$. This guarantees that there are more bonds than unknowns in the dataset.

▪ For each distinct bond, we have an equation:

$$B_C(t) = \sum_{i=1}^{T-1} CD(t,i) + (C + F)D(t,T)$$

The unknowns $\{D(t,i)$ for $t = 1, ..., T_{max}\}$ are the same across all N equations.

▪ Solve the N equations for the T_{max} unknowns, $\{D(t,i)$ for $t = 1, ..., T_{max}\}$.

For the remainder of this section, without loss of generality, we will assume that at time t, we observe both the term structure of default-free and risky zero-coupon bond prices $\{P(t,T), D(t,T)$ for all $T\}$.

The next step is to compute the yields on these zero-coupon bonds. The yields on the risky $[y_D(t,T)]$ and riskless $[y_P(t,T)]$ zero-coupon bonds are defined by the following expressions:

$$D(t,T) = Ke^{-y_D(t,T)(T-t)} \text{ and }$$

$$P(t,T) = e^{-y_P(t,T)(T-t)}$$

Using these formulas, one generates a set of yields for a discrete set of maturities $\{T = 1, ..., T_{max}\}$, where T_{max} is the largest maturity of all the zero-coupon bonds considered.

The credit spread is defined by *Credit spread*$(t) = y_D(t,T) - y_P(t,T)$.

From these discrete observations, one can obtain a smoothed yield curve using standard smoothing procedures.[7] A smoothed credit spread is illustrated in Exhibit 7. This credit spread is for Treasuries versus swaps (that have the risk of a highly rated European bank). For this exhibit, we used US Treasuries to illustrate these computations, although any sovereign's bonds could have been used instead.

---

7 van Deventer, Imai, and Mesler (2004).

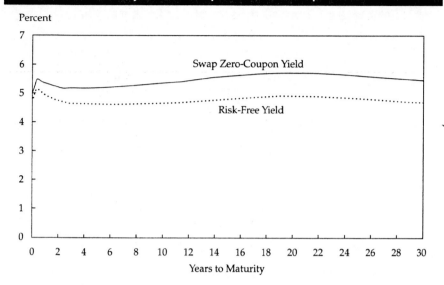

Exhibit 7   US Treasury and ABC Corporation Zero-Coupon Yields

Note: US Treasury and ABC Corporation zero-coupon yields are derived from the Federal Reserve H15 Statistical Release using maximum smoothness forward rate smoothing.
Sources: Kamakura Corporation; Board of Governors of the Federal Reserve.

Using either the structural or reduced form model, *under the frictionless market assumption*, the credit spread is entirely due to credit risk. To see this, it is easiest to use the constant default probability and loss given default formulas of Section 5.2.1.

Recall that the risky zero-coupon bond's price in this example is given by:

$$D(t,T) = Ke^{-\lambda\gamma(T-t)}P(t,T)$$

Performing some algebraic adjustments in the previous equation gives:

$$-\frac{\ln\left(\dfrac{d(t,T)}{K}\right)}{(T-t)} = \lambda\gamma - \frac{\ln[P(t,T)]}{(T-t)}$$

Using the definition of the yields, we see that the credit spread equals:

$$y_D(t,T) - y_P(t,T) = \lambda\gamma$$

Here, the credit spread is equal to the expected percentage loss per year on the risky zero-coupon bond. It is equal to difference between the average yields on the risky zero-coupon bond and the riskless zero-coupon bond.

This example enables us to estimate the expected percentage loss per year implied by the credit spread. It is a rough estimate because the assumption that the default probability and loss given default are constants is not true in practice.

The following is a basic description of the procedure for computing the "back-of-the-envelope" estimate of the expected percentage loss per year.

- Collect a time series of zero-coupon bond yields $\{y_D(t,T), y_P(t,T)\}$ for $t = 1, ..., n$.
- Compute the average yield spread, which gives the estimate:

$$\frac{\sum_{t=1}^{n} y_D(t,T) - y_P(t,T)}{n} = \lambda\gamma$$

Estimate of Expected Percentage Loss per Year

An analyst finds that the one-year yields on HandSoap Corporation (a Japanese company) and Japanese bonds over the past week are as shown below:

Japanese Bonds	HandSoap Corp.
0.0115	0.0357
0.0116	0.0358
0.0116	0.0359
0.0117	0.0360
0.0118	0.0360
Avg.: 0.01164	Avg.: 0.03588

Compute the expected percentage loss per year implied by these yields.

Solution:

$\lambda\gamma = 0.03588 - 0.01164 = 0.02424$.

6.3 Present Value of the Expected Loss

This section shows how to compute the present value of the expected loss using the term structure of credit spreads. From the term structure of credit spreads, one needs to compute the term structure of default-free and risky zero-coupon bond prices $\{P(t,T), D(t,T)$ for all $T\}$. The method for computing these zero-coupon bond prices was discussed in the previous section.

Consider a risky company that has a *promised* cash flow of X_T dollars at time T. The present value of the expected loss is given by:

$$[P(t,T) - D(t,T)]X_T$$

This represents the present value of the cash flow, if riskless, less the present value of the cash flow considering credit risk. Using this simple formula, it is easy to calculate the present value of the expected loss.

Present Value of the Expected Loss

1 Consider Powder Corporation, a German manufacturer, which has promised to pay investors 25 euros on 30 September 2014. Today is 11 August 2011. The risk-free zero-coupon yield on German bonds is 0.3718%. The Powder Corporation credit spread for payment due 30 September 2014 is 0.2739%. For convenience, we have made the assumption that the bonds of the German government are risk free and that there are 365 days in each year. All yields and spreads are continuously compounded.

What is the present value of Powder Corporation's promise to pay both on a credit risky basis and a risk-free basis? What is the present value of the expected loss implied by the credit spread?

Payment Date	Risk-Free Zero-Coupon Yields (%)	Credit Spread (%)	Total Yield (%)	Years to Maturity	Discount Factor	Cash Flow	Present Value	Risk-Free Discount Factor	Risk-Free Present Value	Present Value Difference
9/30/2014	0.3718	0.2739	0.6457	3.1397	0.979930	25	24.4983	0.9884	24.7099	−0.2116

Solution to 1:

The promise to pay 25.00 euros on 30 September 2014 is worth 24.4983 euros considering credit risk. It is worth 24.7099 on a risk-free basis, so the present value of the expected loss due to credit risk is 0.2116.

2 Suppose that Powder Corporation has also promised to pay 25 euros on 31 March 2016. Today is 11 August 2011. The risk-free yield from 11 August 2011 to that date is 0.8892%, and the credit spread is 0.5688%.

What are the credit-adjusted valuation, the risk-free valuation, and the present value of the expected loss due to credit risk?

Payment Date	Risk-Free Zero-Coupon Yields (%)	Credit Spread (%)	Total Yield (%)	Years to Maturity	Discount Factor	Cash Flow	Present Value	Risk-Free Discount Factor	Risk-Free Present Value	Present Value Difference
3/31/2016	0.8892	0.5688	1.4580	4.6411	0.934571	25	23.3643	0.9596	23.9893	−0.6250

Solution to 2:

The credit-adjusted valuation is 23.3643 euros, derived using the continuously compounded total yield. The value on a risk-free basis is 23.9893 euros, so the present value of the expected loss due to credit risk is 0.6250 euro.

3 Suppose now that Powder Corporation has made a promise to pay 1,025 euros on 30 September 2017. Today is 11 August 2011. The risk-free yield from 11 August 2011 to that date is 1.4258%, and the credit spread is 0.8747%. What are the credit-adjusted valuation, the risk-free valuation, and the present value of the expected loss due to credit risk?

Payment Date	Risk-Free Zero-Coupon Yields (%)	Credit Spread (%)	Total Yield (%)	Years to Maturity	Discount Factor	Cash Flow	Present Value	Risk-Free Discount Factor	Risk-Free Present Value	Present Value Difference
9/30/2017	1.4258	0.8747	2.3004	6.1425	0.868226	1025	889.9319	0.9161	939.0528	−49.1209

Solution to 3:

The credit-adjusted present value is 889.9319 euros, and the risk-free valuation is 939.0528 euros. The expected loss due to credit risk is 49.1209 euros.

4 Suppose now that Powder Corporation issues a ten-year 5% coupon bond with semi-annual payment dates and principal of 1,000 euros. The value of this bond at time t when there are n payments remaining is:

$$B_C(t) = \sum_{i=1}^{n} 25D(t,i) + (1,025)D(t,n)$$

The value if this bond were risk free is:

$$B_G(t) = \sum_{i=1}^{n} 25P(t,i) + (1,025)P(t,n)$$

The loss in value due to credit risk is $B_G(t) - B_C(t)$.

Today is 11 August 2011. Let the two payment dates be 30 September and 31 March. The bond, which was originally issued in 2007, matures on 30 September 2017. Using the risk-free yields and credit spreads prevailing on 11 August 2011, what are the credit-adjusted values, risk-free values, and present value of the expected loss due to credit risk on this bond? (Note that valuations will be net present values and accrued interest (an accounting concept) should be ignored.)

Coupon Rate	5.00%
Coupon Payments	Semi-annual
Principal Amount	1000

Payment Dates	Risk-Free Zero-Coupon Yields (%)	Credit Spread (%)	Total Yield (%)	Years to Maturity	Discount Factor	Cash Flow	Present Value	Risk-Free Discount Factor	Risk-Free Present Value	Present Value Difference
9/30/2011	0.0134	0.0696	0.0830	0.1370	0.999886	25	24.9972	1.0000	24.9995	−0.0024
3/31/2012	0.0947	0.1160	0.2107	0.6384	0.998565	25	24.9664	0.9994	24.9849	−0.0185
9/30/2012	0.1033	0.1209	0.2242	1.1397	0.997448	25	24.9362	0.9988	24.9706	−0.0344
3/31/2013	0.1463	0.1454	0.2917	1.6384	0.995233	25	24.8808	0.9976	24.9402	−0.0593
9/30/2013	0.2061	0.1795	0.3856	2.1397	0.991783	25	24.7946	0.9956	24.8900	−0.0954
3/31/2014	0.2723	0.2172	0.4895	2.6384	0.987167	25	24.6792	0.9928	24.8210	−0.1418
9/30/2014	0.3718	0.2739	0.6457	3.1397	0.979930	25	24.4983	0.9884	24.7099	−0.2116
3/31/2015	0.5160	0.3561	0.8722	3.6384	0.968765	25	24.2191	0.9814	24.5350	−0.3159
9/30/2015	0.6953	0.4583	1.1536	4.1397	0.953368	25	23.8342	0.9716	24.2907	−0.4565
3/31/2016	0.8892	0.5688	1.4580	4.6411	0.934571	25	23.3643	0.9596	23.9893	−0.6250
9/30/2016	1.0808	0.6781	1.7589	5.1425	0.913520	25	22.8380	0.9459	23.6484	−0.8104
3/31/2017	1.2597	0.7800	2.0397	5.6411	0.891310	25	22.2828	0.9314	23.2851	−1.0024
9/30/2017	1.4258	0.8747	2.3004	6.1425	0.868226	1025	889.9319	0.9161	939.0528	−49.1209
Total Value							1180.2228		1233.1174	−52.8945

Solution to 4:

Note that three of the payments on this bond were analyzed previously in Questions 1, 2, and 3.

The sum of all credit-adjusted values gives us the total net present value of the bond, 1,180.2228 euros. On a risk-free basis, the bond is worth 1,233.1174 euros, so the present value of the expected loss from credit risk is 52.8945 euros.

5 Consider XYZ Corporation (based in France), which issues a 20-year bond in euros in 2003. The bond has a 6% coupon, payable annually. The bond matures on 30 November 2023, and interest payments are due on 30 November of each year.

What is the credit-adjusted value, the risk-free value, and the present value of the expected loss on this bond if one uses the risk-free yields and credit spreads prevailing on XYZ bonds as of 11 August 2011?

Note that these yields are continuously compounded yields and we are assuming for simplicity that there are 365 days in each year.

Coupon Rate	6.00%
Coupon Payments	Annual
Principal Amount	1000

Payment Dates	Risk-Free Zero-Coupon Yields (%)	Credit Spread (%)	Total Yield (%)	Years to Maturity	Discount Factor	Cash Flow	Present Value	Risk-Free Discount Factor	Risk-Free Present Value	Present Value Difference
11/30/2011	0.0413	0.1323	0.1736	0.3041	0.9995	60	59.9683	0.9999	59.9925	−0.0241
11/30/2012	0.1132	0.2024	0.3156	1.3068	0.9959	60	59.7530	0.9985	59.9113	−0.1583
11/30/2013	0.2265	0.3128	0.5393	2.3068	0.9876	60	59.2582	0.9948	59.6874	−0.4291
11/30/2014	0.4153	0.4969	0.9123	3.3068	0.9703	60	58.2170	0.9864	59.1816	−0.9646
11/30/2015	0.7592	0.8322	1.5915	4.3068	0.9338	60	56.0252	0.9678	58.0698	−2.0446
11/30/2016	1.1423	1.2057	2.3480	5.3096	0.8828	60	52.9673	0.9412	56.4691	−3.5018
11/30/2017	1.4873	1.5333	3.0116	6.3096	0.8269	60	49.6165	0.9109	54.6566	−5.0401
11/30/2018	1.7705	1.8183	3.5888	7.3096	0.7693	60	46.1557	0.8786	52.7164	−6.5608
11/30/2019	2.0358	2.0770	4.1128	8.3096	0.7105	60	42.6313	0.8444	50.6619	−8.0306
11/30/2020	2.2786	2.3136	4.5922	9.3123	0.6520	60	39.1226	0.8088	48.5286	−9.4060
11/30/2021	2.4950	2.5247	5.0197	10.3123	0.5959	60	35.7553	0.7731	46.3884	−10.6331
11/30/2022	2.6842	2.7091	5.3934	11.3123	0.5433	60	32.5973	0.7381	44.2872	−11.6899
11/30/2023	2.8474	2.8682	5.7156	12.3123	0.4947	1060	524.4249	0.7043	746.5366	−222.1117
Total Value							1116.4926		1397.0873	−280.5947

Solution to 5:

XYZ Corporation's bond is analyzed in exactly the same way as the Powder Corporation bond analyzed in Example 4.

The credit-adjusted value is 1,116.4926 euros, and the risk-free value is 1,397.0873 euros. The expected loss due to credit losses is 280.5947 euros.

When considering the decomposition of the credit spread in either the structural or reduced form models, the assumption was made that markets are frictionless. This assumption implies, of course, that there is no quantity impact of a purchase or sale on the price of the security. Such a quantity impact on the purchase or sale price introduces *liquidity risk*, which was assumed away in both of these models. In reality, of course, markets are not frictionless and liquidity risk plays an important role.

In practical applications, one must recognize that the "true" credit spread will consist of both the expected percentage loss (as in the structural and reduced form models) and a liquidity risk premium—that is, $y_D(t,T) - y_P(t,T) = E(\text{Percentage loss}) + \text{Liquidity premium}$.

The liquidity premium will be positive in practice because sovereign government bonds trade in more liquid markets than do most corporate bonds.

7   ASSET-BACKED SECURITIES

In this section, we introduce **asset-backed securities** (ABS). They are discussed separately because they are distinct from either corporate or sovereign debt in the structure of their future cash flows. ABS can appear deceptively similar to corporate debt with similar stated provisions: coupon payments, face value, and maturity date. However, ABS are complex fixed-income instruments created through a process known as securitization.

An asset-backed security is a type of bond issued by a legal entity called a special purpose entity (SPE) or special purpose vehicle (SPV). An SPE is formed to own the pool of securitized assets from which the cash flows will be generated. The pool of securitized assets is typically referred to as the collateral for the ABS. The collateral usually consists of a collection of loans or receivables of a particular type. ABS are classified by the loans or receivables that are the collateral. For example, residential mortgage–backed securities (RMBS) have residential mortgages as their collateral, commercial mortgage–backed securities (CMBS) have commercial mortgages as their collateral, credit card receivables ABS have credit card receivables as their collateral, collateralized debt obligations (CDOs) hold a variety of asset types (corporate bonds, residential mortgages, commercial mortgages, or other ABS) as their collateral, and so forth. The loans and receivables in the pool of securitized assets generate cash flows from interest payments and scheduled and early repayments of principal. The pool of securitized assets can also incur losses if any of the loans or receivables default.

Similar to a company, an SPE is created by the equity holders. To finance the purchase of the collateral, the equity holders issue debt. The structure of the debt for an SPE is different from that of typical corporate debt. An SPE's debt is issued in various bond tranches. The bonds usually have a stated maturity, face value, and coupon payment. The bond tranches are differentiated by their seniority with respect to their receipt of the collateral's cash flows and losses.

The cash flows are paid first to the most senior bond tranches, then to the next senior, and so forth until all coupon payments are paid. Any residual cash flows go to the equity holders. The losses due to defaulting loans go in reverse order. Any losses are first covered by the equity holders, then the least senior bond tranche, and so forth up to the most senior bond tranche. This allocation of cash flows and losses is called the *waterfall*. In practice, the waterfall is often more complex, containing triggers based on the characteristics of the collateral to divert more cash flows to the most senior bond tranches if the collateral's cash flows decline significantly. These triggers are essentially embedded options. A typical SPE is illustrated in Exhibit 8.

Exhibit 8 A Typical Asset-Backed Security SPV			
Assets	Liabilities	Waterfall	
	Senior bond tranche		
Collateral pool (loans)	Mezzanine bond tranche	Cash flows ↓	Losses ↑
	Junior bond tranche		
	.		
	.		
	.		
	Equity		

Unlike corporate debt, an ABS does not go into default when an interest payment is missed. A default in the pool of securitized assets does not cause a default to either the SPE or a bond tranche. For an ABS, the bond continues to trade until either its maturity date or all of its face value is eliminated because of the accumulated losses in the pool of securitized assets or through early loan prepayments. An ABS may be better characterized as a credit derivative than a simple bond because of the complexity of the cash flows.

To value the ABS bond tranches, as with the valuation of any credit derivative, either a structural model or a reduced form model can be used. The valuation must necessarily start with modeling the composition of the collateral pool and the cash flow waterfall. In practice, this exercise is very difficult and complex because different SPEs have different waterfalls. Monte Carlo simulation procedures are often used in practice. The valuation and hedging of ABS, and more generally credit derivatives, are left to future readings.

With respect to credit risk, the credit risk measures used for corporate or sovereign bonds can be applied: probability of loss, expected loss, and present value of the expected loss. As mentioned previously, in this case, the probability of default does not apply, so it is replaced by the probability of a loss. To calculate these measures, a model analogous to those used for corporate and sovereign debt is used. However, the calculations are much more complex.

With respect to the credit ratings of ABS, the credit-rating agencies use the same rating scale as that used for corporate and sovereign debt, although the fact that they are distinct in the structure of their future cash flows is always noted; they may be referred to as structured finance *debt* securities or structured debt. Given the complexity of ABS, the use of the same credit-rating scales may be inappropriate. Some have argued that the credit agencies mis-rated ABS prior to 2007 and that this mis-rating contributed to the 2008 global financial crisis and the subsequent losses.[8] The alleged mis-ratings of structured debt has raised questions about the validity and use of credit ratings. New regulatory reforms have since been introduced by governments around the world, and credit-rating companies have positively responded with changes to their rating methodologies.

SUMMARY

Credit risk analysis is extremely important to a well-functioning economy. Financial crises often originate in the mis-measuring of, and changes in, credit risk. Mis-rating can result in mispricing and misallocation of resources. This reading discusses a variety of approaches to credit risk analysis: credit scoring, credit rating, structural models, and reduced form models. In addition, the reading discusses asset-backed securities and explains why using approaches designed for credit risk analysis of debt may result in problematic measures. Key points of the reading include the following:

- There are four credit risk measures of a bond: the probability of default, the loss given default, the expected loss, and the present value of the expected loss. Of the four, the present value of the expected loss is the most important because it represents the highest price one is willing to pay to own the bond and, as such, it incorporates an adjustment for risk and the time value of money.

---

8 See "Wall Street and the Financial Crisis: Anatomy of a Financial Collapse," Majority and Minority Staff Report, US Senate Committee on Special Investigations (13 April 2011).

- Credit scoring and credit ratings are traditional approaches to credit risk assessment, used to rank retail borrowers.

- During the financial crisis, credit-rating agencies mis-rated debt issues, generating concern over the method in which credit-rating agencies are paid for their services.

- Structural models of credit risk assume a simple balance sheet for the company consisting of a single liability, a zero-coupon bond. Structural models also assume the assets of the company trade and are observable.

- In a structural model, the company's equity can be viewed as a European call option on the assets of the company, with a strike price equal to the debt's face value. This analogy is useful for understanding the debt's probability of default, its loss given default, its expected loss, and the present value of the expected loss.

- The structural model's inputs can only be estimated using calibration, where the inputs are inferred from market prices of the company's equity.

- Reduced form models of credit risk consider a company's traded liabilities. Reduced form models also assume a given process for the company's default time and loss given default. Both of these quantities can depend on the state of the economy as captured by a collection of macroeconomic factors.

- Using option pricing methodology, reduced form models provide insights into the debt's expected loss and the present value of the expected loss.

- The reduced form model's inputs can be estimated using either calibration or historical estimation. Historical estimation is the preferred methodology; it incorporates past time-series observations of company defaults, macroeconomic variables, and company balance sheet characteristics. Hazard rate estimation techniques are used in this regard.

- The term structure of credit spreads is the difference between yields on risky bonds versus default-free zero-coupon bonds. These yields can be estimated from the market prices of traded coupon bonds of both types.

- The present value of the expected loss on any bond can be estimated using the term structure of credit spreads.

- Asset-backed securities (ABS) are issued by a special purpose entity (SPE). The SPE's assets, called the collateral, consist of a collection of loans or receivables. To finance its assets, the SPE issues bonds (the ABS) in tranches that have different priorities with respect to cash flows and losses, called the waterfall.

- ABS do not default, but they can lose value as the SPE's pool of securitized assets incurs defaults. Modeling an ABS's credit risk—the probability of loss, the loss given default, the expected loss, and the present value of the loss—is a complex exercise.

REFERENCES

Chava, S., and R. Jarrow. 2004. "Bankruptcy Prediction with Industry Effects." *Review of Finance*, vol. 8, no. 4:537–569.

Heath, D., R. Jarrow, and A. Morton. 1992. "Bond Pricing and the Term Structure of Interest Rates: A New Methodology for Contingent Claims Valuation." *Econometrica: Journal of the Econometric Society*, vol. 60, no. 1 (January):77–105.

Jarrow, R. 2009. "Credit Risk Models." *Annual Review of Financial Economics*, vol. 1, no. December:37–68.

Jarrow, R., and S. Turnbull. 1992. "Credit Risk: Drawing the Analogy." *Risk Magazine*, 5 (9).

Jarrow, R., and S. Turnbull. 1995. "Pricing Derivatives on Financial Securities Subject to Credit Risk." *Journal of Finance*, vol. 50, no. 1 (March):53–85.

Merton, R.C. 1974. "On the Pricing of Corporate Debt: The Risk Structure of Interest Rates." *Journal of Finance*, vol. 29, no. 2 (May):449–470.

van Deventer, D.R., K. Imai, and M. Mesler. 2004. *Advanced Financial Risk Management: Tools and Techniques for Integrated Credit Risk and Interest Rate Risk Management.* Hoboken, NJ: John Wiley & Sons.

PRACTICE PROBLEMS

Campbell Fixed Income Analytics provides credit analysis services on a consulting basis to fixed income managers. A new hire, Liam Cassidy, has been asked by his supervisor, Malcolm Moriarty, to answer some questions and to analyze a corporate bond issued by Dousing Dragons (DD). Moriarty is trying to assess Cassidy's level of knowledge. Moriarty asks Cassidy:

> "Why are clients willing to pay for structural and reduced form model analytics when they can get credit ratings for free?"

Cassidy identifies the following limitations of credit ratings:

Limitation A	The issuer-pays model may distort the accuracy of credit ratings.
Limitation B	Credit ratings tend to vary across time and across the business cycle.
Limitation C	Credit ratings do not provide an estimate of a bond's default probability.

Cassidy is asked to consider the use of a structural model of credit risk to analyze DD's bonds. Cassidy knows that holding DD's equity is economically equivalent to owning a type of security that is linked to DD's assets. However, Cassidy cannot remember the type of security or why this is true. Moriarty provides a hint:

> "It is true because equity shareholders have limited liability."

Moriarty asks Cassidy to analyze one of DD's bonds using data presented in Exhibit 1 and a reduced form model.

Exhibit 1 Dousing Dragons, Inc. Credit Analysis Worksheet

Coupon rate:	0.875%	Coupon Payments:	Semiannual
Face value:	1,000		
Today's date:	August 15, 2014	Maturity date:	August 15, 2018

Payment dates:	Risk-free Zero Coupon Yields (Percent)	Credit Spread (Percent)	Total Yield (Percent)	Years to Maturity	Discount Factor	Cash Flow	Present Value	Risk-free Discount Factor	Risk-free Present Value
2/15/2015	0.13	0.12	0.25	0.50	0.99880	4.38	4.3747	0.9994	4.3774
8/15/2015	0.20	0.24	0.44	1.00	0.99560	4.38	4.3607	0.9980	4.3712
2/15/2016	0.23	0.31	0.54	1.50	0.99200	4.38	4.3450	0.9966	4.3651
8/15/2016	0.28	0.37	0.65	2.00	0.98710	4.38	4.3235	0.9944	4.3555
2/15/2017	0.32	0.38	0.70	2.50	0.98270	4.38	4.3042	0.9920	4.3450
8/15/2017	0.35	0.39	0.74	3.00	0.97810	4.38	4.2841	0.9896	4.3344
2/15/2018	0.44	0.43	0.87	3.50	0.97010	4.38	4.2490	0.9848	4.3134
8/15/2018	0.47	0.46	0.93	4.00	0.96370	1,004.38	967.9210	0.9814	985.6985
Total value:							998.1623		1,016.1606

Moriarty also asks Cassidy to discuss the similarities and differences in the analysis of asset-backed securities (ABS) and corporate debt. Cassidy states that:

Statement 1   Credit analysis for ABS and corporate bonds incorporates the same credit measures: probability of default, expected loss, and present value of expected loss.

Statement 2   Credit analysis for ABS and corporate bonds is different due to their future cash flow structures.

Statement 3   Credit analysis for ABS and corporate bonds can be done using either a structural or a reduced form model.

1   Which of Cassidy's stated limitations of credit ratings is *incorrect*?

A   Limitation A

B   Limitation B

C   Limitation C

2   Given Moriarty's hint, Cassidy should *most likely* identify the type of security as a European:

A   put option.

B   call option.

C   debt option.

3   The model chosen by Moriarty to analyze one of DD's bonds requires that:

A   the equity of DD is traded.

B   the assets of DD are traded.

C   some of the debt of DD is traded.

4   Compared to a structural model, which of the following estimation approaches will Moriarty's choice of credit model allow him to use?

A   Implicit

B   Historical

C   Calibration

5   Compared to a structural model, an advantage of the model chosen by Moriarty to analyze DD's bond is *most likely* that:

A   its measures reflect the changing business cycle.

B   it requires a specification of the company's balance sheet.

C   it is possible to estimate the expected present value of expected loss.

6   Based on Exhibit 1, the present value of the expected loss due to credit risk on the bond is *closest* to:

A   1.84.

B   16.16.

C   18.00.

7   Based on Exhibit 1, the present value of the expected loss due to credit risk relating to the single promised payment scheduled on February 15, 2017, is *closest* to:

A   0.04.

B   0.08.

C   0.11.

8   Which of Cassidy's statements relating to the similarities and differences between the credit analysis of ABS and corporate bonds is *incorrect*?

A   Statement 1
B   Statement 2
C   Statement 3

SOLUTIONS

1   B is correct. Limitation B is incorrect. Credit ratings tend to be stable, not variable, across time and across the business cycle. Rating agencies may be motivated to keep their ratings stable across time to reduce unnecessary volatility in debt market prices. Credit ratings do not explicitly depend on the business cycle.

The issuer-pays model for compensating credit rating agencies has a potential conflict of interest that may distort the accuracy of credit ratings. Credit ratings do not provide an estimate of default probability. They are ordinal rankings. There is no constant relationship between credit ratings and default probabilities.

2   B is correct. Holding the company's equity is economically equivalent to owning a European call option on the firm's assets. Holding the company's equity has the same payoff as a European call option on the company's assets with a strike price equivalent to the face value of the company's debt.

3   C is correct. The reduced form model assumes that some of the company's debt is traded. Reduced form models do not assume that the company's assets, equity, or all its debt are traded. The structural model assumes that the company's assets trade.

4   B is correct. The ability to use historical estimation is a significant advantage of the reduced form model. Both structural and reduced form models can use implicit estimation (or calibration).

5   A is correct. The reduced form model produces credit risk measures that reflect the changing business cycle. The credit risk measures from structural models do not explicitly depend on the business cycle. Credit ratings are also generally insensitive to changes in the business cycle. The reduced form model requires a specification of the company's balance sheet. Both reduced form and structural models can be used to estimate the expected present value of expected loss.

6   C is correct. The present value of the expected loss due to credit risk is closest to 18.00. It is the difference between the credit-adjusted valuation (present value) of 998.1623 and the risk free valuation (risk-free present value) of 1,016.1606. [1,016.1606 − 998.1623 = 17.9983 ≈ 18.00]

7   A is correct. The present value of the expected loss due to credit risk is 0.04 and is calculated as the risk-free present value of 4.3450 less the risk-adjusted present value of 4.3042, or 0.0408, or approximately 0.04. [4.3450 − 4.3042 = 0.0408 ≈ 0.04]

8   A is correct. Statement 1 is incorrect. The probability of default does not apply to ABS because asset-backed securities do not default when an interest payment is not made. Probability of loss is used in place of default. Credit analysis for both ABS and corporate bonds is different due to their future cash flow structures. Both structural and reduced form models can be used to analyze ABS and corporate bonds.

Glossary

Abandonment option The ability to terminate a project at some future time if the financial results are disappointing.

Abnormal earnings See *residual income*.

Abnormal return The return on an asset in excess of the asset's required rate of return; the risk-adjusted return.

Absolute convergence The idea that developing countries, regardless of their particular characteristics, will eventually catch up with the developed countries and match them in per capita output.

Absolute valuation model A model that specifies an asset's intrinsic value.

Absolute version of PPP The extension of the law of one price to the broad range of goods and services that are consumed in different countries.

Accounting estimates Estimates used in calculating the value of assets or liabilities and in the amount of revenue and expense to allocate to a period. Examples of accounting estimates include, among others, the useful lives of depreciable assets, the salvage value of depreciable assets, product returns, warranty costs, and the amount of uncollectible receivables.

Acquirer The company in a merger or acquisition that is acquiring the target.

Acquiring company The company in a merger or acquisition that is acquiring the target.

Acquisition The purchase of some portion of one company by another; the purchase may be for assets, a definable segment of another entity, or the purchase of an entire company.

Active factor risk The contribution to active risk squared resulting from the portfolio's different-than-benchmark exposures relative to factors specified in the risk model.

Active return The return on a portfolio minus the return on the portfolio's benchmark.

Active risk The standard deviation of active returns.

Active risk squared The variance of active returns; active risk raised to the second power.

Active specific risk The contribution to active risk squared resulting from the portfolio's active weights on individual assets as those weights interact with assets' residual risk.

Add-on interest A procedure for determining the interest on a bond or loan in which the interest is added onto the face value of a contract.

Adjusted funds from operations Funds from operations (FFO) adjusted to remove any non-cash rent reported under straight-line rent accounting and to subtract maintenance-type capital expenditures and leasing costs, including leasing agents' commissions and tenants' improvement allowances.

Adjusted present value (APV) As an approach to valuing a company, the sum of the value of the company, assuming no use of debt, and the net present value of any effects of debt on company value.

Adjusted R^2 A measure of goodness-of-fit of a regression that is adjusted for degrees of freedom and hence does not automatically increase when another independent variable is added to a regression.

Administrative regulations or administrative law Rules issued by government agencies or other regulators.

Agency costs Costs associated with the conflict of interest present when a company is managed by non-owners. Agency costs result from the inherent conflicts of interest between managers and equity owners.

Agency costs of equity The smaller the stake that managers have in the company, the less is their share in bearing the cost of excessive perquisite consumption or not giving their best efforts in running the company.

Agency issues Conflicts of interest that arise when the agent in an agency relationship has goals and incentives that differ from the principal to whom the agent owes a fiduciary duty. Also called *agency problems* or *principal–agent problems*.

Agency problem A conflict of interest that arises when the agent in an agency relationship has goals and incentives that differ from the principal to whom the agent owes a fiduciary duty.

Alpha The return on an asset in excess of the asset's required rate of return; the risk-adjusted return.

American Depositary Receipt A negotiable certificate issued by a depositary bank that represents ownership in a non-US company's deposited equity (i.e., equity held in custody by the depositary bank in the company's home market).

American option An option that can be exercised at any time until its expiration date.

Amortizing and accreting swaps A swap in which the notional principal changes according to a formula related to changes in the underlying.

Analysis of variance (ANOVA) The analysis of the total variability of a dataset (such as observations on the dependent variable in a regression) into components representing different sources of variation; with reference to regression, ANOVA provides the inputs for an *F*-test of the significance of the regression as a whole.

Arbitrage 1) The simultaneous purchase of an undervalued asset or portfolio and sale of an overvalued but equivalent asset or portfolio, in order to obtain a riskless profit on the price differential. Taking advantage of a market inefficiency in a risk-free manner. 2) The condition in a financial market in which equivalent assets or combinations of assets sell for two different prices, creating an opportunity to profit at no risk with no commitment of money. In a well-functioning financial market, few arbitrage opportunities are possible. 3) A risk-free operation that earns an expected positive net profit but requires no net investment of money.

Arbitrage-free models Term structure models that project future interest rate paths that emanate from the existing term structure. Resulting prices are based on a no-arbitrage condition.

Arbitrage-free valuation An approach to valuation that determines security values that are consistent with the absence of arbitrage opportunities.

Arbitrage opportunity An opportunity to conduct an arbitrage; an opportunity to earn an expected positive net profit without risk and with no net investment of money.

Arbitrage portfolio   The portfolio that exploits an arbitrage opportunity.

Arrears swap   A type of interest rate swap in which the floating payment is set at the end of the period and the interest is paid at that same time.

Asset-backed securities   A type of bond issued by a legal entity called a *special purpose vehicle* (SPV), on a collection of assets that the SPV owns. Also, securities backed by receivables and loans other than mortgage loans.

Asset-based approach   Approach that values a private company based on the values of the underlying assets of the entity less the value of any related liabilities.

Asset-based valuation   An approach to valuing natural resource companies that estimates company value on the basis of the market value of the natural resources the company controls.

Asset beta   The unlevered beta; reflects the business risk of the assets; the asset's systematic risk.

Asset purchase   An acquisition in which the acquirer purchases the target company's assets and payment is made directly to the target company.

Asymmetric information   The differential of information between corporate insiders and outsiders regarding the company's performance and prospects. Managers typically have more information about the company's performance and prospects than owners and creditors.

At-the-money   An option in which the underlying value equals the exercise price.

Autocorrelation   The correlation of a time series with its own past values.

Autoregressive model (AR)   A time series regressed on its own past values, in which the independent variable is a lagged value of the dependent variable.

Available-for-sale investments   Debt and equity securities not classified as either held-to-maturity or fair value through profit or loss securities. The investor is willing to sell but not actively planning to sell. In general, available-for-sale securities are reported at fair value on the balance sheet.

Backward integration   A merger involving the purchase of a target ahead of the acquirer in the value or production chain; for example, to acquire a supplier.

Backwardation   A condition in the futures markets in which the benefits of holding an asset exceed the costs, leaving the futures price less than the spot price.

Bankruptcy   A declaration provided for by a country's laws that typically involves the establishment of a legal procedure that forces creditors to defer their claims.

Basic earnings per share   (EPS) Net earnings available to common shareholders (i.e., net income minus preferred dividends) divided by the weighted average number of common shares outstanding during the period.

Basis swap   1) An interest rate swap involving two floating rates. 2) A swap in which both parties pay a floating rate.

Basis trade   A trade based on the pricing of credit in the bond market versus the price of the same credit in the CDS market. To execute a basis trade, go long the "underpriced" credit and short the "overpriced" credit. A profit is realized when the price of credit between the short and long position converges.

Bear hug   A tactic used by acquirers to circumvent target management's objections to a proposed merger by submitting the proposal directly to the target company's board of directors.

Benchmark   A comparison portfolio; a point of reference or comparison.

Benchmark value of the multiple   In using the method of comparables, the value of a price multiple for the comparison asset; when we have comparison assets (a group), the mean or median value of the multiple for the group of assets.

Bill-and-hold basis   Sales on a bill-and-hold basis involve selling products but not delivering those products until a later date.

Binomial model   A model for pricing options in which the underlying price can move to only one of two possible new prices.

Binomial tree   The graphical representation of a model of asset price dynamics in which, at each period, the asset moves up with probability p or down with probability $(1 - p)$.

Blockage factor   An illiquidity discount that occurs when an investor sells a large amount of stock relative to its trading volume (assuming it is not large enough to constitute a controlling ownership).

Bond indenture   A legal contract specifying the terms of a bond issue.

Bond option   An option in which the underlying is a bond; primarily traded in over-the-counter markets.

Bond yield plus risk premium method   An estimate of the cost of common equity that is produced by summing the before-tax cost of debt and a risk premium that captures the additional yield on a company's stock relative to its bonds. The additional yield is often estimated using historical spreads between bond yields and stock yields.

Bonding costs   Costs borne by management to assure owners that they are working in the owners' best interest (e.g., implicit cost of non-compete agreements).

Book value   Shareholders' equity (total assets minus total liabilities) minus the value of preferred stock; common shareholders' equity.

Book value of equity   Shareholders' equity (total assets minus total liabilities) minus the value of preferred stock; common shareholders' equity.

Book value per share   The amount of book value (also called carrying value) of common equity per share of common stock, calculated by dividing the book value of shareholders' equity by the number of shares of common stock outstanding.

Bootstrapping   A statistical method for estimating a sample distribution based on the properties of an approximating distribution.

Bottom-up approach   With respect to forecasting, an approach that usually begins at the level of the individual company or a unit within the company.

Bottom-up investing   An approach to investing that focuses on the individual characteristics of securities rather than on macroeconomic or overall market forecasts.

Breakup value   The value derived using a sum-of-the-parts valuation.

Breusch–Pagan test   A test for conditional heteroskedasticity in the error term of a regression.

Broker   1) An agent who executes orders to buy or sell securities on behalf of a client in exchange for a commission. 2) *See* Futures commission merchants.

Brokerage   The business of acting as agents for buyers or sellers, usually in return for commissions.

Buy-side analysts Analysts who work for investment management firms, trusts, and bank trust departments, and similar institutions.

Call An option that gives the holder the right to buy an underlying asset from another party at a fixed price over a specific period of time.

Callable bond Bond that includes an embedded call option that gives the issuer the right to redeem the bond issue prior to maturity, typically when interest rates have fallen or when the issuer's credit quality has improved.

Cannibalization Cannibalization occurs when an investment takes customers and sales away from another part of the company.

Cap 1) A contract on an interest rate, whereby at periodic payment dates, the writer of the cap pays the difference between the market interest rate and a specified cap rate if, and only if, this difference is positive. This is equivalent to a stream of call options on the interest rate. 2) A combination of interest rate call options designed to hedge a borrower against rate increases on a floating-rate loan.

Cap rate See *capitalization rate.*

Capital charge The company's total cost of capital in money terms.

Capital deepening An increase in the capital-to-labor ratio.

Capital rationing A capital rationing environment assumes that the company has a fixed amount of funds to invest.

Capital structure The mix of debt and equity that a company uses to finance its business; a company's specific mixture of long-term financing.

Capitalization of earnings method In the context of private company valuation, valuation model based on an assumption of a constant growth rate of free cash flow to the firm or a constant growth rate of free cash flow to equity.

Capitalization rate The divisor in the expression for the value of perpetuity. In the context of real estate, the divisor in the direct capitalization method of estimating value. The cap rate equals net operating income divided by value.

Capitalized cash flow method In the context of private company valuation, valuation model based on an assumption of a constant growth rate of free cash flow to the firm or a constant growth rate of free cash flow to equity. Also called *capitalized cash flow model.*

Capitalized cash flow model In the context of private company valuation, valuation model based on an assumption of a constant growth rate of free cash flow to the firm or a constant growth rate of free cash flow to equity. Also called *capitalized cash flow method.*

Capitalized income method In the context of private company valuation, valuation model based on an assumption of a constant growth rate of free cash flow to the firm or a constant growth rate of free cash flow to equity.

Caplet Each component call option in a cap.

Capped floater Floating-rate bond with a cap provision that prevents the coupon rate from increasing above a specified maximum rate. It protects the issuer against rising interest rates.

Capped swap A swap in which the floating payments have an upper limit.

Carried interest A share of any profits that is paid to the general partner (manager) of an investment partnership, such as a private equity or hedge fund, as a form of compensation designed to be an incentive to the manager to maximize performance of the investment fund.

Carrying costs The costs of holding an asset, generally a function of the physical characteristics of the underlying asset.

Cash available for distribution Funds from operations (FFO) adjusted to remove any non-cash rent reported under straight-line rent accounting and to subtract maintenance-type capital expenditures and leasing costs, including leasing agents' commissions and tenants' improvement allowances.

Cash-generating unit The smallest identifiable group of assets that generates cash inflows that are largely independent of the cash inflows of other assets or groups of assets.

Cash offering A merger or acquisition that is to be paid for with cash; the cash for the merger might come from the acquiring company's existing assets or from a debt issue.

Cash settlement A procedure used in certain derivative transactions that specifies that the long and short parties engage in the equivalent cash value of a delivery transaction.

Catalyst An event or piece of information that causes the marketplace to re-evaluate the prospects of a company.

CDS spread A periodic premium paid by the buyer to the seller that serves as a return over Libor required to protect against credit risk.

Chain rule of forecasting A forecasting process in which the next period's value as predicted by the forecasting equation is substituted into the right-hand side of the equation to give a predicted value two periods ahead.

Cheapest-to-deliver The debt instrument that can be purchased and delivered at the lowest cost yet has the same seniority as the reference obligation.

Clean surplus accounting Accounting that satisfies the condition that all changes in the book value of equity other than transactions with owners are reflected in income. The bottom-line income reflects all changes in shareholders' equity arising from other than owner transactions. In the absence of owner transactions, the change in shareholders' equity should equal net income. No adjustments such as translation adjustments bypass the income statement and go directly to shareholders equity.

Clean surplus relation The relationship between earnings, dividends, and book value in which ending book value is equal to the beginning book value plus earnings less dividends, apart from ownership transactions.

Clientele effect The preference some investors have for shares that exhibit certain characteristics.

Club convergence The idea that only rich and middle-income countries sharing a set of favorable attributes (i.e., are members of the "club") will converge to the income level of the richest countries.

Cobb–Douglas production function A function of the form $Y = K^{\alpha} L^{1-\alpha}$ relating output (Y) to labor (L) and capital (K) inputs.

Cointegrated Describes two time series that have a long-term financial or economic relationship such that they do not diverge from each other without bound in the long run.

Commercial real estate properties Income-producing real estate properties, properties purchased with the intent to let, lease, or rent (in other words, produce income).

Common size statements Financial statements in which all elements (accounts) are stated as a percentage of a key figure such as revenue for an income statement or total assets for a balance sheet.

Company fundamental factors   Factors related to the company's internal performance, such as factors relating to earnings growth, earnings variability, earnings momentum, and financial leverage.

Company share-related factors   Valuation measures and other factors related to share price or the trading characteristics of the shares, such as earnings yield, dividend yield, and book-to-market value.

Comparables   Assets used as benchmarks when applying the method of comparables to value an asset. Also called *comps*, *guideline assets*, or *guideline companies*.

Compiled financial statements   Financial statements that are not accompanied by an auditor's opinion letter.

Comprehensive income   All changes in equity other than contributions by, and distributions to, owners; income under clean surplus accounting; includes all changes in equity during a period except those resulting from investments by owners and distributions to owners; comprehensive income equals net income plus other comprehensive income.

Comps   Assets used as benchmarks when applying the method of comparables to value an asset.

Conditional convergence   The idea that convergence of per capita income is conditional on the countries having the same savings rate, population growth rate, and production function.

Conditional heteroskedasticity   Heteroskedasticity in the error variance that is correlated with the values of the independent variable(s) in the regression.

Conglomerate discount   The discount possibly applied by the market to the stock of a company operating in multiple, unrelated businesses.

Conglomerate merger   A merger involving companies that are in unrelated businesses.

Consolidation   The combining of the results of operations of subsidiaries with the parent company to present financial statements as if they were a single economic unit. The assets, liabilities, revenues and expenses of the subsidiaries are combined with those of the parent company, eliminating intercompany transactions.

Constant dividend payout ratio policy   A policy in which a constant percentage of net income is paid out in dividends.

Constant maturity swap   A swap in which the floating rate is the rate on a security known as a constant maturity treasury or CMT security.

Constant maturity treasury (CMT)   A hypothetical US Treasury note with a constant maturity. A CMT exists for various years in the range of 2 to 10.

Constant returns to scale   The condition that if all inputs into the production process are increased by a given percentage, then output rises by that same percentage.

Contango   A situation in a futures market where the current futures price is greater than the current spot price for the underlying asset.

Contingent consideration   Potential future payments to the seller that are contingent on the achievement of certain agreed on occurrences.

Continuing earnings   Earnings excluding nonrecurring components. Also referred to as *core earnings, persistent earnings*, or *underlying earnings*.

Continuing residual income   Residual income after the forecast horizon.

Continuing value   The analyst's estimate of a stock's value at a particular point in the future.

Continuous time   Time thought of as advancing in extremely small increments.

Control premium   An increment or premium to value associated with a controlling ownership interest in a company.

Convenience yield   The nonmonetary return offered by an asset when the asset is in short supply, often associated with assets with seasonal production processes.

Conventional cash flow   A conventional cash flow pattern is one with an initial outflow followed by a series of inflows.

Conversion factor   An adjustment used to facilitate delivery on bond futures contracts in which any of a number of bonds with different characteristics are eligible for delivery.

Conversion period   For a convertible bond, the period during which bondholders have the right to convert their bonds into shares.

Conversion price   For a convertible bond, the price per share at which the bond can be converted into shares.

Conversion ratio   For a convertible bond, the number of shares of common stock that a bondholder receives from converting the bond into shares.

Conversion value   For a convertible bond, the value of the bond if it is converted at the market price of the shares. Also called *parity value.*

Convertible bond   Bond with an embedded conversion option that gives the bondholder the right to convert their bonds into the issuer's common stock during a pre-determined period at a pre-determined price.

Core earnings   Earnings excluding nonrecurring components. Also referred to as *continuing earnings, persistent earnings*, or *underlying earnings.*

Corporate governance   The system of principles, policies, procedures, and clearly defined responsibilities and accountabilities used by stakeholders to overcome the conflicts of interest inherent in the corporate form.

Corporate raider   A person or organization seeking to profit by acquiring a company and reselling it, or seeking to profit from the takeover attempt itself (e.g., greenmail).

Corporation   A legal entity with rights similar to those of a person. The chief officers, executives, or top managers act as agents for the firm and are legally entitled to authorize corporate activities and to enter into contracts on behalf of the business.

Correlation analysis   The analysis of the strength of the linear relationship between two data series.

Cost approach   Approach that values a private company based on the values of the underlying assets of the entity less the value of any related liabilities. In the context of real estate, this approach estimates the value of a property based on what it would cost to buy the land and construct a new property on the site that has the same utility or functionality as the property being appraised.

Cost of carry   The cost associated with holding some asset, including financing, storage, and insurance costs. Any yield received on the asset is treated as a negative carrying cost.

Cost-of-carry model   A model for pricing futures contracts in which the futures price is determined by adding the cost of carry to the spot price.

Cost of debt   The cost of debt financing to a company, such as when it issues a bond or takes out a bank loan.

Cost of equity   The required rate of return on common stock.

Covariance stationary Describes a time series when its expected value and variance are constant and finite in all periods and when its covariance with itself for a fixed number of periods in the past or future is constant and finite in all periods.

Covered interest arbitrage A transaction executed in the foreign exchange market in which a currency is purchased (sold) and a forward contract is sold (purchased) to lock in the exchange rate for future delivery of the currency. This transaction should earn the risk-free rate of the investor's home country.

Covered interest rate parity Relationship among the spot exchange rate, forward exchange rate, and the interest rates in two currencies that ensures that the return on a hedged (i.e., covered) foreign risk-free investment is the same as the return on a domestic risk-free investment.

Cox–Ingersoll–Ross model A partial equilibrium term structure model that assumes interest rates are mean reverting and interest rate volatility is directly related to the level of interest rates.

Credit correlation The correlation of credits contained in an index CDS.

Credit curve The credit spreads for a range of maturities of a company's debt; applies to non-government borrowers and incorporates credit risk into each rate.

Credit default swap A derivative contract between two parties in which the buyer makes a series of cash payments to the seller and receives a promise of compensation for credit losses resulting from the default.

Credit derivative A derivative instrument in which the underlying is a measure of the credit quality of a borrower.

Credit event The outcome that triggers a payment from the credit protection seller to the credit protection buyer.

Credit protection buyer One party to a credit default swap; the buyer makes a series of cash payments to the seller and receives a promise of compensation for credit losses resulting from the default.

Credit protection seller One party to a credit default swap; the buyer makes a series of cash payments to the seller and receives a promise of compensation for credit losses resulting from the default.

Credit ratings Ordinal rankings of the credit risk of a company, government (sovereign), quasi-government, or asset-backed security.

Credit risk The risk that the borrower will not repay principal and interest. Also called *default risk*.

Credit scoring Ordinal rankings of a retail borrower's credit riskiness. It is called an *ordinal ranking* because it only orders borrowers' riskiness from highest to lowest.

Credit spreads The difference between the yields on default-free and credit risky zero-coupon bonds.

Currency option An option that allows the holder to buy (if a call) or sell (if a put) an underlying currency at a fixed exercise rate, expressed as an exchange rate.

Current credit risk The risk associated with the possibility that a payment currently due will not be made.

Current exchange rate For accounting purposes, the spot exchange rate on the balance sheet date.

Current rate method Approach to translating foreign currency financial statements for consolidation in which all assets and liabilities are translated at the current exchange rate. The current rate method is the prevalent method of translation.

Curvature One of the three factors (the other two are level and steepness) that empirically explain most of the changes in the shape of the yield curve. A shock to the curvature factor affects mid-maturity interest rates, resulting in the term structure becoming either more or less hump-shaped.

Curve trade Buying a CDS of one maturity and selling a CDS on the same reference entity with a different maturity.

Cyclical businesses Businesses with high sensitivity to business- or industry-cycle influences.

Daily settlement See *marking to market*.

Data mining The practice of determining a model by extensive searching through a dataset for statistically significant patterns.

Day trader A trader holding a position open somewhat longer than a scalper but closing all positions at the end of the day.

"Dead-hand" provision A poison pill provision that allows for the redemption or cancellation of a poison pill provision only by a vote of continuing directors (generally directors who were on the target company's board prior to the takeover attempt).

Debt ratings An objective measure of the quality and safety of a company's debt based upon an analysis of the company's ability to pay the promised cash flows, as well as an analysis of any indentures.

Decision rule With respect to hypothesis testing, the rule according to which the null hypothesis will be rejected or not rejected; involves the comparison of the test statistic to rejection point(s).

Deep-in-the-money Options that are far in-the-money.

Deep-out-of-the-money Options that are far out-of-the-money.

Default intensity Gives the probability of default over the next instant $[t, t + \Delta]$ when the economy is in state X_t.

Default probability See *probability of default*.

Default risk See *credit risk*.

Definition of value A specification of how "value" is to be understood in the context of a specific valuation.

Definitive merger agreement A contract signed by both parties to a merger that clarifies the details of the transaction, including the terms, warranties, conditions, termination details, and the rights of all parties.

Delivery A process used in a deliverable forward contract in which the long pays the agreed-upon price to the short, which in turn delivers the underlying asset to the long.

Delivery option The feature of a futures contract giving the short the right to make decisions about what, when, and where to deliver.

Delta The relationship between the option price and the underlying price, which reflects the sensitivity of the price of the option to changes in the price of the underlying.

Dependent variable The variable whose variation about its mean is to be explained by the regression; the left-hand-side variable in a regression equation.

Depository Trust and Clearinghouse Corporation A US-headquartered entity providing post-trade clearing, settlement, and information services.

Depreciated replacement cost In the context of real estate, the replacement cost of a building adjusted different types of depreciation.

Derivative A financial instrument whose value depends on the value of some underlying asset or factor (e.g., a stock price, an interest rate, or exchange rate).

Descriptive statistics The study of how data can be summarized effectively.

Diff swaps A swap in which the payments are based on the difference between interest rates in two countries but payments are made in only a single currency.

Diluted earnings per share (diluted EPS) Net income, minus preferred dividends, divided by the weighted average number of common shares outstanding considering all dilutive securities (e.g., convertible debt and options); the EPS that would result if all dilutive securities were converted into common shares.

Dilution A reduction in proportional ownership interest as a result of the issuance of new shares.

Diminishing marginal productivity When each additional unit of an input, keeping the other inputs unchanged, increases output by a smaller increment.

Direct capitalization method In the context of real estate, this method estimates the value of an income-producing property based on the level and quality of its net operating income.

Direct financing leases A type of finance lease, from a lessor perspective, where the present value of the lease payments (lease receivable) equals the carrying value of the leased asset. The revenues earned by the lessor are financing in nature.

Discount To reduce the value of a future payment in allowance for how far away it is in time; to calculate the present value of some future amount. Also, the amount by which an instrument is priced below its face value.

Discount factor The present value or price of a risk-free single-unit payment when discounted using the appropriate spot rate.

Discount for lack of control An amount or percentage deducted from the pro rata share of 100 percent of the value of an equity interest in a business to reflect the absence of some or all of the powers of control.

Discount for lack of marketability An amount of percentage deducted from the value of an ownership interest to reflect the relative absence of marketability.

Discount function Discount factors for the range of all possible maturities. The spot curve can be derived from the discount function and vice versa.

Discount interest A procedure for determining the interest on a loan or bond in which the interest is deducted from the face value in advance.

Discount rate Any rate used in finding the present value of a future cash flow.

Discounted abnormal earnings model A model of stock valuation that views intrinsic value of stock as the sum of book value per share plus the present value of the stock's expected future residual income per share.

Discounted cash flow (DCF) analysis In the context of merger analysis, it is an estimate of a target company's value found by discounting the company's expected future free cash flows to the present.

Discounted cash flow method Income approach that values an asset based on estimates of future cash flows discounted to present value by using a discount rate reflective of the risks associated with the cash flows. In the context of real estate, this method estimates the value of an income-producing property based by discounting future projected cash flows.

Discounted cash flow model A model of intrinsic value that views the value of an asset as the present value of the asset's expected future cash flows.

Discrete time Time thought of as advancing in distinct finite increments.

Discriminant analysis A multivariate classification technique used to discriminate between groups, such as companies that either will or will not become bankrupt during some time frame.

Diversified REITs REITs that own and operate in more than one type of property; they are more common in Europe and Asia than in the United States.

Divestiture The sale, liquidation, or spin-off of a division or subsidiary.

Dividend coverage ratio The ratio of net income to dividends.

Dividend discount model (DDM) A present value model of stock value that views the intrinsic value of a stock as present value of the stock's expected future dividends.

Dividend displacement of earnings The concept that dividends paid now displace earnings in all future periods.

Dividend imputation tax system A taxation system which effectively assures that corporate profits distributed as dividends are taxed just once, at the shareholder's tax rate.

Dividend payout ratio The ratio of cash dividends paid to earnings for a period.

Dividend policy The strategy a company follows with regard to the amount and timing of dividend payments.

Dividend rate the annualized amount of the most recent dividend.

Dominance An arbitrage opportunity when a financial asset with a risk-free payoff in the future must have a positive price today.

Double taxation system Corporate earnings are taxed twice when paid out as dividends. First, corporate earnings are taxed regardless of whether they will be distributed as dividends or retained at the G-13 corporate level, and second, dividends are taxed again at the individual shareholder level.

DOWNREIT A variation of the UPREIT structure under which the REIT owns more than one partnership and may own properties at both the REIT level and the partnership level.

Downstream A transaction between two related companies, an investor company (or a parent company) and an associate company (or a subsidiary) such that the investor company records a profit on its income statement. An example is a sale of inventory by the investor company to the associate or by a parent to a subsidiary company.

Due diligence Investigation and analysis in support of a recommendation; the failure to exercise due diligence may sometimes result in liability according to various securities laws.

Dummy variable A type of qualitative variable that takes on a value of 1 if a particular condition is true and 0 if that condition is false.

Duration A measure of an option-free bond's average maturity. Specifically, the weighted average maturity of all future cash flows paid by a security, in which the weights are the present value of these cash flows as a fraction of the bond's price. A measure of a bond's price sensitivity to interest rate movements.

Dutch disease A situation in which currency appreciation driven by strong export demand for resources makes other segments of the economy (particularly manufacturing) globally uncompetitive.

Dynamic hedging   A strategy in which a position is hedged by making frequent adjustments to the quantity of the instrument used for hedging in relation to the instrument being hedged.

Earnings surprise   The difference between reported EPS and expected EPS. Also referred to as *unexpected earnings*.

Earnings yield   EPS divided by price; the reciprocal of the P/E ratio.

Economic growth   The expansion of production possibilities that results from capital accumulation and technological change.

Economic obsolescence   In the context of real estate, a reduction in value due to current economic conditions.

Economic profit   See *residual income*.

Economic sectors   Large industry groupings.

Economic value added   (EVA°) A commercial implementation of the residual income concept; the computation of EVA° is the net operating profit after taxes minus the cost of capital, where these inputs are adjusted for a number of items.

Economies of scale   A situation in which average costs per unit of good or service produced fall as volume rises. In reference to mergers, the savings achieved through the consolidation of operations and elimination of duplicate resources.

Edwards–Bell–Ohlson model   A model of stock valuation that views intrinsic value of stock as the sum of book value per share plus the present value of the stock's expected future residual income per share.

Effective convexity   Sensitivity of duration to changes in interest rates.

Effective duration   Sensitivity of the bond's price to a 100 bps parallel shift of the benchmark yield curve, assuming no change in the bond's credit spread.

Embedded options   Contingency provisions found in a bond's indenture or offering circular representing rights that enable their holders to take advantage of interest rate movements. They can be exercised by the issuer, by the bondholder, or automatically depending on the course of interest rates.

Enterprise value   (EV) Total company value (the market value of debt, common equity, and preferred equity) minus the value of cash and investments.

Enterprise value multiple   A valuation multiple that relates the total market value of all sources of a company's capital (net of cash) to a measure of fundamental value for the entire company (such as a pre-interest earnings measure).

Entry price   The price paid to acquire an asset.

Equilibrium   The condition in which supply equals demand.

Equity carve-out   A form of restructuring that involves the creation of a new legal entity and the sale of equity in it to outsiders.

Equity charge   The estimated cost of equity capital in money terms.

Equity forward   A contract calling for the purchase of an individual stock, a stock portfolio, or a stock index at a later date at an agreed-upon price.

Equity options   Options on individual stocks; also known as stock options.

Equity REIT   A REIT that owns, operates, and/or selectively develops income-producing real estate.

Error autocorrelation   The autocorrelation of the error term.

Error term   The portion of the dependent variable that is not explained by the independent variable(s) in the regression.

Estimated parameters   With reference to a regression analysis, the estimated values of the population intercept and population slope coefficient(s) in a regression.

Eurodollar   A dollar deposited outside the United States.

European option   An option that can only be exercised on its expiration date.

Ex ante version of PPP   Hypothesis that expected changes in the spot exchange rate are equal to expected differences in national inflation rates. An extension of relative purchasing power parity to expected future changes in the exchange rate.

Ex-dividend   Trading ex-dividend refers to shares that no longer carry the right to the next dividend payment.

Ex-dividend date   The first date that a share trades without (i.e., "ex") the dividend.

Ex-dividend price   The price at which a share first trades without (i.e., "ex") the right to receive an upcoming dividend.

Excess earnings method   Income approach that estimates the value of all intangible assets of the business by capitalizing future earnings in excess of the estimated return requirements associated with working capital and fixed assets.

Exchange for physicals (EFP)   A permissible delivery procedure used by futures market participants, in which the long and short arrange a delivery procedure other than the normal procedures stipulated by the futures exchange.

Exchange ratio   The number of shares that target stockholders are to receive in exchange for each of their shares in the target company.

Exercise   The process of using an option to buy or sell the underlying. Also called *exercising the option*.

Exercise price   The fixed price at which an option holder can buy or sell the underlying. Also called *strike price, striking price,* or *strike*.

Exercise rate   The fixed rate at which the holder of an interest rate option can buy or sell the underlying. Also called *strike rate*.

Exercise value   The value of an asset given a hypothetically complete understanding of the asset's investment characteristics; the value obtained if an option is exercised based on current conditions. Also called *intrinsic value*.

Exercising the option   The process of using an option to buy or sell the underlying. Also called *exercise*.

Exit price   The price received to sell an asset or paid to transfer a liability.

Expanded CAPM   An adaptation of the CAPM that adds to the CAPM a premium for small size and company-specific risk.

Expected holding-period return   The expected total return on an asset over a stated holding period; for stocks, the sum of the expected dividend yield and the expected price appreciation over the holding period.

Expected loss   The probability of default multiplied by the loss given default; the full amount owed minus the expected recovery.

Expiration date   The date on which a derivative contract expires.

Exposure to foreign exchange risk   The risk of a change in value of an asset or liability denominated in a foreign currency due to a change in exchange rates.

Extendible bond   Bond with an embedded option that gives the bondholder the right to keep the bond for a number of years after maturity, possibly with a different coupon.

External growth   Company growth in output or sales that is achieved by buying the necessary resources externally (i.e., achieved through mergers and acquisitions).

External sustainability approach   An approach to assessing the equilibrium exchange rate that focuses on exchange rate adjustments required to ensure that a country's net foreign-asset/GDP ratio or net foreign-liability/GDP ratio stabilizes at a sustainable level.

Factor   A common or underlying element with which several variables are correlated.

Factor betas   An asset's sensitivity to a particular factor; a measure of the response of return to each unit of increase in a factor, holding all other factors constant.

Factor portfolio   See *pure factor portfolio*.

Factor price   The expected return in excess of the risk-free rate for a portfolio with a sensitivity of 1 to one factor and a sensitivity of 0 to all other factors.

Factor risk premium   The expected return in excess of the risk-free rate for a portfolio with a sensitivity of 1 to one factor and a sensitivity of 0 to all other factors. Also called *factor price*.

Factor sensitivity   See *factor betas*.

Failure to pay   When a borrower does not make a scheduled payment of principal or interest on any outstanding obligations after a grace period.

Fair market value   The market price of an asset or liability that trades regularly.

Fair value   The amount at which an asset (or liability) could be bought (or incurred) or sold (or settled) in a current transaction between willing parties, that is, other than in a forced or liquidation sale; as defined in IFRS and US GAAP, the price that would be received to sell an asset or paid to transfer a liability in an orderly transaction between market participants at the measurement date.

Fiduciary call   A combination of a European call and a risk-free bond that matures on the option expiration day and has a face value equal to the exercise price of the call.

Finance lease   Essentially, the purchase of some asset by the buyer (lessee) that is directly financed by the seller (lessor). Also called *capital lease*.

Financial contagion   A situation where financial shocks spread from their place of origin to other locales; in essence, a faltering economy infects other, healthier economies.

Financial distress   Heightened uncertainty regarding a company's ability to meet its various obligations because of lower or negative earnings.

Financial futures   Futures contracts in which the underlying is a stock, bond, or currency.

Financial risk   The risk that environmental, social, or governance risk factors will result in significant costs or other losses to a company and its shareholders; the risk arising from a company's obligation to meet required payments under its financing agreements.

Financial transaction   A purchase involving a buyer having essentially no material synergies with the target (e.g., the purchase of a private company by a company in an unrelated industry or by a private equity firm would typically be a financial transaction).

First-differencing   A transformation that subtracts the value of the time series in period $t - 1$ from its value in period t.

First-in, first-out (FIFO)   The first in, first out, method of accounting for inventory, which matches sales against the costs of items of inventory in the order in which they were placed in inventory.

First-order serial correlation   Correlation between adjacent observations in a time series.

Fitted parameters   With reference to a regression analysis, the estimated values of the population intercept and population slope coefficient(s) in a regression.

Fixed-rate perpetual preferred stock   Nonconvertible, noncallable preferred stock with a specified dividend rate that has a claim on earnings senior to the claim of common stock, and no maturity date.

Flip-in pill   A poison pill takeover defense that dilutes an acquirer's ownership in a target by giving other existing target company shareholders the right to buy additional target company shares at a discount.

Flip-over pill   A poison pill takeover defense that gives target company shareholders the right to purchase shares of the acquirer at a significant discount to the market price, which has the effect of causing dilution to all existing acquiring company shareholders.

Floor   A combination of interest rate put options designed to hedge a lender against lower rates on a floating-rate loan.

Floor traders   Market makers that buy and sell by quoting a bid and an ask price. They are the primary providers of liquidity to the market.

Floored floater   Floating-rate bond with a floor provision that prevents the coupon rate from decreasing below a specified minimum rate. It protects the investor against declining interest rates.

Floored swap   A swap in which the floating payments have a lower limit.

Floorlet   Each component put option in a floor.

Flotation cost   Fees charged to companies by investment bankers and other costs associated with raising new capital.

Forced conversion   For a convertible bond, when the issuer calls the bond and forces bondholders to convert their bonds into shares, which typically happens when the underlying share price increases above the conversion price.

Foreign currency transactions   Transactions that are denominated in a currency other than a company's functional currency.

Forward contract   An agreement between two parties in which one party, the buyer, agrees to buy from the other party, the seller, an underlying asset at a later date for a price established at the start of the contract.

Forward curve   The term structure of forward rates for loans made on a specific initiation date.

Forward dividend yield   A dividend yield based on the anticipated dividend during the next 12 months.

Forward integration   A merger involving the purchase of a target that is farther along the value or production chain; for example, to acquire a distributor.

Forward P/E   A P/E calculated on the basis of a forecast of EPS; a stock's current price divided by next year's expected earnings.

Forward price or forward rate   The fixed price or rate at which the transaction scheduled to occur at the expiration of a forward contract will take place. This price is agreed on at the initiation date of the contract.

Forward pricing model   The model that describes the valuation of forward contracts.

Forward rate   An interest rate that is determined today for a loan that will be initiated in a future time period.

Forward rate agreement (FRA)   A forward contract calling for one party to make a fixed interest payment and the other to make an interest payment at a rate to be determined at the contract expiration.

Forward rate model   The forward pricing model expressed in terms of spot and forward interest rates.

Forward swap   A forward contract to enter into a swap.

Franking credit   A tax credit received by shareholders for the taxes that a corporation paid on its distributed earnings.

Free cash flow   The actual cash that would be available to the company's investors after making all investments necessary to maintain the company as an ongoing enterprise (also referred to as free cash flow to the firm); the internally generated funds that can be distributed to the company's investors (e.g., shareholders and bondholders) without impairing the value of the company.

Free cash flow hypothesis   The hypothesis that higher debt levels discipline managers by forcing them to make fixed debt service payments and by reducing the company's free cash flow.

Free cash flow method   Income approach that values an asset based on estimates of future cash flows discounted to present value by using a discount rate reflective of the risks associated with the cash flows.

Free cash flow to equity   The cash flow available to a company's common shareholders after all operating expenses, interest, and principal payments have been made, and necessary investments in working and fixed capital have been made.

Free cash flow to equity model   A model of stock valuation that views a stock's intrinsic value as the present value of expected future free cash flows to equity.

Free cash flow to the firm   The cash flow available to the company's suppliers of capital after all operating expenses (including taxes) have been paid and necessary investments in working and fixed capital have been made.

Free cash flow to the firm model   A model of stock valuation that views the value of a firm as the present value of expected future free cash flows to the firm.

Friendly transaction   A potential business combination that is endorsed by the managers of both companies.

Functional currency   The currency of the primary economic environment in which an entity operates.

Functional obsolescence   In the context of real estate, a reduction in value due to a design that differs from that of a new building constructed for the intended use of the property.

Fundamental factor models   A multifactor model in which the factors are attributes of stocks or companies that are important in explaining cross-sectional differences in stock prices.

Fundamentals   Economic characteristics of a business such as profitability, financial strength, and risk.

Funds available for distribution   Funds from operations (FFO) adjusted to remove any non-cash rent reported under straight-line rent accounting and to subtract maintenance-type capital expenditures and leasing costs, including leasing agents' commissions and tenants' improvement allowances.

Funds from operations   Accounting net earnings excluding (1) depreciation charges on real estate, (2) deferred tax charges, and (3) gains or losses from sales of property and debt restructuring.

Futures commission merchants (FCMs)   Individuals or companies that execute futures transactions for other parties off the exchange.

Futures contract   A variation of a forward contract that has essentially the same basic definition but with some additional features, such as a clearinghouse guarantee against credit losses, a daily settlement of gains and losses, and an organized electronic or floor trading facility.

FX carry trade   An investment strategy that involves taking on long positions in high-yield currencies and short positions in low-yield currencies.

Gamma   A numerical measure of how sensitive an option's delta is to a change in the underlying.

Generalized least squares   A regression estimation technique that addresses heteroskedasticity of the error term.

Going-concern assumption   The assumption that the business will maintain its business activities into the foreseeable future.

Going-concern value   A business's value under a going-concern assumption.

Goodwill   An intangible asset that represents the excess of the purchase price of an acquired company over the value of the net identifiable assets acquired.

Gross domestic product   A money measure of the goods and services produced within a country's borders over a stated time period.

Gross lease   A lease under which the tenant pays a gross rent to the landlord who is responsible for all operating costs, utilities, maintenance expenses, and real estate taxes relating to the property.

Growth accounting equation   The production function written in the form of growth rates. For the basic Cobb–Douglas production function, it states that the growth rate of output equals the rate of technological change plus α times the growth rate of capital plus $(1 - \alpha)$ times the growth rate of labor.

Growth capital expenditures   Capital expenditures needed for expansion.

Growth option   The ability to make additional investments in a project at some future time if the financial results are strong. Also called *expansion option*.

Guideline assets   Assets used as benchmarks when applying the method of comparables to value an asset.

Guideline companies   Assets used as benchmarks when applying the method of comparables to value an asset.

Guideline public companies   Public-company comparables for the company being valued.

Guideline public company method   A variation of the market approach; establishes a value estimate based on the observed multiples from trading activity in the shares of public companies viewed as reasonably comparable to the subject private company.

Guideline transactions method   A variation of the market approach; establishes a value estimate based on pricing multiples derived from the acquisition of control of entire public or private companies that were acquired.

Harmonic mean   A type of weighted mean computed by averaging the reciprocals of the observations, then taking the reciprocal of that average.

Hazard rate   The probability that an event will occur, given that it has not already occurred.

Hazard rate estimation   A technique for estimating the probability of a binary event, such as default/no default, mortality/no mortality, and prepay/no prepay.

Health care REITs REITs that invest in skilled nursing facilities (nursing homes), assisted living and independent residential facilities for retired persons, hospitals, medical office buildings, or rehabilitation centers.

Hedge ratio The relationship of the quantity of an asset being hedged to the quantity of the derivative used for hedging.

Hedging A general strategy usually thought of as reducing, if not eliminating, risk.

Held for trading investments Debt or equity securities acquired with the intent to sell them in the near term.

Held-to-maturity investments Debt (fixed-income) securities that a company intends to hold to maturity; these are presented at their original cost, updated for any amortization of discounts or premiums.

Herfindahl–Hirschman Index (HHI) A measure of market concentration that is calculated by summing the squared market shares for competing companies in an industry; high HHI readings or mergers that would result in large HHI increases are more likely to result in regulatory challenges.

Heteroskedastic With reference to the error term of regression, having a variance that differs across observations.

Heteroskedasticity The property of having a nonconstant variance; refers to an error term with the property that its variance differs across observations.

Heteroskedasticity-consistent standard errors Standard errors of the estimated parameters of a regression that correct for the presence of heteroskedasticity in the regression's error term.

Historical exchange rates For accounting purposes, the exchange rates that existed when the assets and liabilities were initially recorded.

Ho–Lee model The first arbitrage-free term structure model. The model is calibrated to market data and uses a binomial lattice approach to generate a distribution of possible future interest rates.

Holding period return The return that an investor earns during a specified holding period; a synonym for total return.

Homoskedasticity The property of having a constant variance; refers to an error term that is constant across observations.

Horizontal merger A merger involving companies in the same line of business, usually as competitors.

Hostile transaction An attempt to acquire a company against the wishes of the target's managers.

Hotel REITs REITs that own hotel properties but, similar to health care REITs, in many countries they must refrain from operating their properties themselves to maintain their tax-advantaged REIT status.

Human capital The accumulated knowledge and skill that workers acquire from education, training, or life experience.

Hybrid approach With respect to forecasting, an approach that combines elements of both top-down and bottom-up analysis.

Hybrid REITs REITs that own and operate income-producing real estate and invest in mortgages as well; REITs that have positions in both real estate assets and real estate debt.

I-spreads Shortened form of "interpolated spreads" and a reference to a linearly interpolated yield.

Illiquidity discount A reduction or discount to value that reflects the lack of depth of trading or liquidity in that asset's market.

Impairment Diminishment in value as a result of carrying (book) value exceeding fair value and/or recoverable value.

Impairment of capital rule A legal restriction that dividends cannot exceed retained earnings.

Implied repo rate The rate of return from a cash-and-carry transaction implied by the futures price relative to the spot price.

Implied volatility The volatility that option traders use to price an option, implied by the price of the option and a particular option-pricing model.

In-sample forecast errors The residuals from a fitted time-series model within the sample period used to fit the model.

In-the-money Options that, if exercised, would result in the value received being worth more than the payment required to exercise.

Income approach Valuation approach that values an asset as the present discounted value of the income expected from it. In the context of real estate, this approach estimates the value of a property based on an expected rate of return; the estimated value is the present value of the expected future income from the property, including proceeds from resale at the end of a typical investment holding period.

Incremental cash flow The cash flow that is realized because of a decision; the changes or increments to cash flows resulting from a decision or action.

Indenture A written contract between a lender and borrower that specifies the terms of the loan, such as interest rate, interest payment schedule, maturity, etc.

Independent projects Independent projects are projects whose cash flows are independent of each other.

Independent regulators Regulators recognized and granted authority by a government body or agency. They are not government agencies per se and typically do not rely on government funding.

Independent variable A variable used to explain the dependent variable in a regression; a right-hand-side variable in a regression equation.

Index amortizing swap An interest rate swap in which the notional principal is indexed to the level of interest rates and declines with the level of interest rates according to a predefined schedule. This type of swap is frequently used to hedge securities that are prepaid as interest rates decline, such as mortgage-backed securities.

Index CDS A type of credit default swap that involves a combination of borrowers.

Indexing An investment strategy in which an investor constructs a portfolio to mirror the performance of a specified index.

Industrial REITs REITs that hold portfolios of single-tenant or multi-tenant industrial properties that are used as warehouses, distribution centers, light manufacturing facilities, and small office or "flex" space.

Industry structure An industry's underlying economic and technical characteristics.

Information ratio (IR) Mean active return divided by active risk; or alpha divided by the standard deviation of diversifiable risk.

Informational frictions Forces that restrict availability, quality, and/or flow of information and its use.

Initial margin requirement The margin requirement on the first day of a transaction as well as on any day in which additional margin funds must be deposited.

Initial public offering (IPO) The initial issuance of common stock registered for public trading by a formerly private corporation.

Inter-temporal rate of substitution the ratio of the marginal utility of consumption *s* periods in the future (the numerator) to the marginal utility of consumption today (the denominator).

Interest rate call An option in which the holder has the right to make a known interest payment and receive an unknown interest payment.

Interest rate cap A series of call options on an interest rate, with each option expiring at the date on which the floating loan rate will be reset, and with each option having the same exercise rate. A cap in general can have an underlying other than an interest rate.

Interest rate collar A combination of a long cap and a short floor, or a short cap and a long floor. A collar in general can have an underlying other than an interest rate.

Interest rate floor A series of put options on an interest rate, with each option expiring at the date on which the floating loan rate will be reset, and with each option having the same exercise rate. A floor in general can have an underlying other than the interest rate. Also called *floor*.

Interest rate option An option in which the underlying is an interest rate.

Interest rate parity A formula that expresses the equivalence or parity of spot and forward rates, after adjusting for differences in the interest rates.

Interest rate put An option in which the holder has the right to make an unknown interest payment and receive a known interest payment.

Interest rate risk Risk that interest rates will change such that the return earned is not commensurate with returns on comparable instruments in the marketplace.

Internal rate of return (IRR) Rate of return that discounts future cash flows from an investment to the exact amount of the investment; the discount rate that makes the present value of an investment's costs (outflows) equal to the present value of the investment's benefits (inflows).

Internal ratings Credit ratings developed internally and used by financial institutions or other entities to manage risk.

International Fisher effect Proposition that nominal interest rate differentials across currencies are determined by expected inflation differentials.

Intrinsic value The value of an asset given a hypothetically complete understanding of the asset's investment characteristics; the value obtained if an option is exercised based on current conditions. The difference between the spot exchange rate and the strike price of a currency.

Inverse price ratio The reciprocal of a price multiple, e.g., in the case of a P/E ratio, the "earnings yield" E/P (where P is share price and E is earnings per share).

Investment objectives Desired investment outcomes; includes risk objectives and return objectives.

Investment strategy An approach to investment analysis and security selection.

Investment value The value to a specific buyer, taking account of potential synergies based on the investor's requirements and expectations.

ISDA Master Agreement A standard or "master" agreement published by the International Swaps and Derivatives Association. The master agreement establishes the terms for each party involved in the transaction.

Judicial law Interpretations of courts.

Justified (fundamental) P/E The price-to-earnings ratio that is fair, warranted, or justified on the basis of forecasted fundamentals.

Justified price multiple The estimated fair value of the price multiple, usually based on forecasted fundamentals or comparables.

Key rate durations Sensitivity of a bond's price to changes in specific maturities on the benchmark yield curve. Also called *partial durations*.

kth order autocorrelation The correlation between observations in a time series separated by *k* periods.

Labor force Everyone of working age (ages 16 to 64) that either is employed or is available for work but not working.

Labor force participation rate The percentage of the working age population that is in the labor force.

Labor productivity The quantity of real GDP produced by an hour of labor. More generally, output per unit of labor input.

Labor productivity growth accounting equation States that potential GDP growth equals the growth rate of the labor input plus the growth rate of labor productivity.

Lack of marketability discount An extra return to investors to compensate for lack of a public market or lack of marketability.

Last-in, first-out (LIFO) The last in, first out, method of accounting for inventory, which matches sales against the costs of items of inventory in the reverse order the items were placed in inventory (i.e., inventory produced or acquired last are assumed to be sold first).

Law of one price Hypothesis that (1) identical goods should trade at the same price across countries when valued in terms of a common currency, or (2) two equivalent financial instruments or combinations of financial instruments can sell for only one price. The latter form is equivalent to the principle that no arbitrage opportunities are possible.

Leading dividend yield Forecasted dividends per share over the next year divided by current stock price.

Leading P/E A P/E calculated on the basis of a forecast of EPS; a stock's current price divided by next year's expected earnings.

Legal risk The risk that failures by company managers to effectively manage a company's environmental, social, and governance risk exposures will lead to lawsuits and other judicial remedies, resulting in potentially catastrophic losses for the company; the risk that the legal system will not enforce a contract in case of dispute or fraud.

Legislative and regulatory risk The risk that governmental laws and regulations directly or indirectly affecting a company's operations will change with potentially severe adverse effects on the company's continued profitability and even its long-term sustainability.

Lessee The party obtaining the use of an asset through a lease.

Lessor The owner of an asset that grants the right to use the asset to another party.

Level One of the three factors (the other two are steepness and curvature) that empirically explain most of the changes in the shape of the yield curve. A shock to the level factor changes the yield for all maturities by an almost identical amount.

Leveraged buyout (LBO) A transaction whereby the target company management team converts the target to a privately held company by using heavy borrowing to finance the purchase of the target company's outstanding shares.

Leveraged recapitalization A post-offer takeover defense mechanism that involves the assumption of a large amount of debt that is then used to finance share repurchases;

the effect is to dramatically change the company's capital structure while attempting to deliver a value to target shareholders in excess of a hostile bid.

Libor–OIS spread   The difference between Libor and the overnight indexed swap (OIS) rate.

Limit down   A limit move in the futures market in which the price at which a transaction would be made is at or below the lower limit.

Limit move   A condition in the futures markets in which the price at which a transaction would be made is at or beyond the price limits.

Limit up   A limit move in the futures market in which the price at which a transaction would be made is at or above the upper limit.

Linear association   A straight-line relationship, as opposed to a relationship that cannot be graphed as a straight line.

Linear regression   Regression that models the straight-line relationship between the dependent and independent variable(s).

Linear trend   A trend in which the dependent variable changes at a constant rate with time.

Liquidation   To sell the assets of a company, division, or subsidiary piecemeal, typically because of bankruptcy; the form of bankruptcy that allows for the orderly satisfaction of creditors' claims after which the company ceases to exist.

Liquidation value   The value of a company if the company were dissolved and its assets sold individually.

Liquidity preference theory   A term structure theory that asserts liquidity premiums exist to compensate investors for the added interest rate risk they face when lending long term.

Liquidity premium   The premium or incrementally higher yield that investors demand for lending long term.

Liquidity risk   The risk that a financial instrument cannot be purchased or sold without a significant concession in price due to the size of the market.

Local currency   The currency of the country where a company is located.

Local expectations theory   A term structure theory that contends the return for all bonds over short time periods is the risk-free rate.

Locals   Market makers that buy and sell by quoting a bid and an ask price. They are the primary providers of liquidity to the market.

Locational obsolescence   In the context of real estate, a reduction in value due to decreased desirability of the location of the building.

Locked limit   A condition in the futures markets in which a transaction cannot take place because the price would be beyond the limits.

Lockout period   Period during which a bond's issuer cannot call the bond.

Log-linear model   With reference to time-series models, a model in which the growth rate of the time series as a function of time is constant.

Log-log regression model   A regression that expresses the dependent and independent variables as natural logarithms.

Logit model   A qualitative-dependent-variable multiple regression model based on the logistic probability distribution.

London interbank offered rate   (Libor) Collective name for multiple rates at which a select set of banks believe they could borrow unsecured funds from other banks in the London interbank market for different currencies and different borrowing periods ranging from overnight to one year.

Long   The buyer of a derivative contract. Also refers to the position of owning a derivative.

Long/short trade   A long position in one CDS and a short position in another.

Long-term equity anticipatory securities   (LEAPS) Options originally created with expirations of several years.

Look-ahead bias   A bias caused by using information that was not available on the test date.

Loss given default   The amount that will be lost if a default occurs.

Lower bound   The lowest possible value of an option.

Macroeconomic balance approach   An approach to assessing the equilibrium exchange rate that focuses on exchange rate adjustments needed to close the gap between the medium-term expectation for a country's current account balance and that country's normal (or sustainable) current account balance.

Macroeconomic factor model   A multifactor model in which the factors are surprises in macroeconomic variables that significantly explain equity returns.

Macroeconomic factors   Factors related to the economy, such as the inflation rate, industrial production, or economic sector membership.

Maintenance capital expenditures   Capital expenditures needed to maintain operations at the current level.

Maintenance margin requirement   The margin requirement on any day other than the first day of a transaction.

Managerialism theories   Theories that posit that corporate executives are motivated to engage in mergers to maximize the size of their company rather than shareholder value.

Margin   The amount of money that a trader deposits in a margin account. The term is derived from the stock market practice in which an investor borrows a portion of the money required to purchase a certain amount of stock. In futures markets, there is no borrowing so the margin is more of a down payment or performance bond.

Marginal investor   An investor in a given share who is very likely to be part of the next trade in the share and who is therefore important in setting price.

Mark-to-market   The revaluation of a financial asset or liability to its current market value or fair value.

Market approach   Valuation approach that values an asset based on pricing multiples from sales of assets viewed as similar to the subject asset.

Market conversion premium per share   For a convertible bond, the difference between the market conversion price and the underlying share price, which allows investors to identify the premium or discount payable when buying a convertible bond rather than the underlying common stock.

Market conversion premium ratio   For a convertible bond, the market conversion premium per share expressed as a percentage of the current market price of the shares.

Market efficiency   A finance perspective on capital markets that deals with the relationship of price to intrinsic value. The **traditional efficient markets formulation** asserts that an asset's price is the best available estimate of its intrinsic value. The **rational efficient markets formulation** asserts that investors should expect to be rewarded for the costs of information gathering and analysis by higher gross returns.

Market timing   Asset allocation in which the investment in the market is increased if one forecasts that the market will outperform T-bills.

Market value   The estimated amount for which a property should exchange on the date of valuation between a willing buyer and a willing seller in an arm's-length transaction after proper marketing wherein the parties had each acted knowledgeably, prudently, and without compulsion.

Market value of invested capital   The market value of debt and equity.

Marking to market   A procedure used primarily in futures markets in which the parties to a contract settle the amount owed daily. Also known as the *daily settlement*.

Mature growth rate   The earnings growth rate in a company's mature phase; an earnings growth rate that can be sustained long term.

Mean reversion   The tendency of a time series to fall when its level is above its mean and rise when its level is below its mean; a mean-reverting time series tends to return to its long-term mean.

Merger   The absorption of one company by another; two companies become one entity and one or both of the pre-merger companies ceases to exist as a separate entity.

Method based on forecasted fundamentals   An approach to using price multiples that relates a price multiple to forecasts of fundamentals through a discounted cash flow model.

Method of comparables   An approach to valuation that involves using a price multiple to evaluate whether an asset is relatively fairly valued, relatively undervalued, or relatively overvalued when compared to a benchmark value of the multiple.

Minority Interest   The proportion of the ownership of a subsidiary not held by the parent (controlling) company.

Mispricing   Any departure of the market price of an asset from the asset's estimated intrinsic value.

Mixed offering   A merger or acquisition that is to be paid for with cash, securities, or some combination of the two.

Model specification   With reference to regression, the set of variables included in the regression and the regression equation's functional form.

Molodovsky effect   The observation that P/Es tend to be high on depressed EPS at the bottom of a business cycle, and tend to be low on unusually high EPS at the top of a business cycle.

Momentum indicators   Valuation indicators that relate either price or a fundamental (such as earnings) to the time series of their own past values (or in some cases to their expected value).

Monetary assets and liabilities   Assets and liabilities with value equal to the amount of currency contracted for, a fixed amount of currency. Examples are cash, accounts receivable, accounts payable, bonds payable, and mortgages payable. Inventory is not a monetary asset. Most liabilities are monetary.

Monetary/non-monetary method   Approach to translating foreign currency financial statements for consolidation in which monetary assets and liabilities are translated at the current exchange rate. Non-monetary assets and liabilities are translated at historical exchange rates (the exchange rates that existed when the assets and liabilities were acquired).

Monetizing   The conversion of the value of a financial transaction into currency.

Moneyness   The relationship between the price of the underlying and an option's exercise price.

Monitoring costs   Costs borne by owners to monitor the management of the company (e.g., board of director expenses).

Mortgage-backed securities   Asset-backed securitized debt obligations that represent rights to receive cash flows from portfolios of mortgage loans.

Mortgage REITs   REITs that invest the bulk of their assets in interest-bearing mortgages, mortgage securities, or short-term loans secured by real estate.

Mortgages   Loans with real estate serving as collateral for the loans.

Multi-family/residential REITs   REITs that invest in and manage rental apartments for lease to individual tenants, typically using one-year leases.

Multicollinearity   A regression assumption violation that occurs when two or more independent variables (or combinations of independent variables) are highly but not perfectly correlated with each other.

Multiple linear regression   Linear regression involving two or more independent variables.

Multiple linear regression model   A linear regression model with two or more independent variables.

Mutually exclusive projects   Mutually exclusive projects compete directly with each other. For example, if Projects A and B are mutually exclusive, you can choose A or B, but you cannot choose both.

n-Period moving average   The average of the current and immediately prior $n - 1$ values of a time series.

Naked credit default swap   A position where the owner of the CDS does not have a position in the underlying credit.

Negative serial correlation   Serial correlation in which a positive error for one observation increases the chance of a negative error for another observation, and vice versa.

Net asset balance sheet exposure   When assets translated at the current exchange rate are greater in amount than liabilities translated at the current exchange rate. Assets exposed to translation gains or losses exceed the exposed liabilities.

Net asset value   The difference between assets and liabilities, all taken at current market values instead of accounting book values.

Net asset value per share   Net asset value divided by the number of shares outstanding.

Net lease   A lease under which the tenant pays a net rent to the landlord as well as an additional amount based on the tenant's pro rata share of the operating costs, utilities, maintenance expenses, and real estate taxes relating to the property.

Net liability balance sheet exposure   When liabilities translated at the current exchange rate are greater assets translated at the current exchange rate. Liabilities exposed to translation gains or losses exceed the exposed assets.

Net operating income   Gross rental revenue minus operating costs, but before deducting depreciation, corporate overhead, and interest expense. In the context of real estate, a measure of the income from the property after deducting operating expenses for such items as property taxes, insurance, maintenance, utilities, repairs, and insurance but before deducting any costs associated with financing and before deducting federal income taxes. It is similar to earnings before interest, taxes, depreciation, and amortization (EBITDA) in a financial reporting context.

Net operating profit less adjusted taxes (NOPLAT) A company's operating profit with adjustments to normalize the effects of capital structure.

Net present value (NPV) The present value of an investment's cash inflows (benefits) minus the present value of its cash outflows (costs).

Net realisable value Estimated selling price in the ordinary course of business less the estimated costs necessary to make the sale.

Net regulatory burden The private costs of regulation less the private benefits of regulation.

Net rent A rent that consists of a stipulated rent to the landlord and a further amount based on their share of common area costs for utilities, maintenance, and property taxes.

Netting When parties agree to exchange only the net amount owed from one party to the other.

Network externalities The impact that users of a good, a service, or a technology have on other users of that product; it can be positive (e.g., a critical mass of users makes a product more useful) or negative (e.g., congestion makes the product less useful).

No-growth company A company without positive expected net present value projects.

No-growth value per share The value per share of a no-growth company, equal to the expected level amount of earnings divided by the stock's required rate of return.

Node Each value on a binomial tree from which successive moves or outcomes branch.

Non-cash rent An amount equal to the difference between the average contractual rent over a lease term (the straight-line rent) and the cash rent actually paid during a period. This figure is one of the deductions made from FFO to calculate AFFO.

Non-convergence trap A situation in which a country remains relative poor, or even falls further behind, because it fails to t implement necessary institutional reforms and/or adopt leading technologies.

Non-monetary assets and liabilities Assets and liabilities that are not monetary assets and liabilities. Non-monetary assets include inventory, fixed assets, and intangibles, and non-monetary liabilities include deferred revenue.

Non-renewable resources Finite resources that are depleted once they are consumed; oil and coal are examples.

Nonconventional cash flow In a nonconventional cash flow pattern, the initial outflow is not followed by inflows only, but the cash flows can flip from positive (inflows) to negative (outflows) again (or even change signs several times).

Nondeliverable forwards (NDFs) Cash-settled forward contracts, used predominantly with respect to foreign exchange forwards.

Nonearning assets Cash and investments (specifically cash, cash equivalents, and short-term investments).

Nonlinear relation An association or relationship between variables that cannot be graphed as a straight line.

Nonstationarity With reference to a random variable, the property of having characteristics such as mean and variance that are not constant through time.

Normal backwardation The condition in futures markets in which futures prices are lower than expected spot prices.

Normal contango The condition in futures markets in which futures prices are higher than expected spot prices.

Normal EPS The EPS that a business could achieve currently under mid-cyclical conditions. Also called *normalized EPS*.

Normalized earnings The expected level of mid-cycle earnings for a company in the absence of any unusual or temporary factors that affect profitability (either positively or negatively).

Normalized EPS The EPS that a business could achieve currently under mid-cyclical conditions. Also called *normal EPS*.

Normalized P/E P/E based on normalized EPS data.

Notional amount The amount of protection being purchased in a CDS.

NTM P/E Next twelve months P/E: current market price divided by an estimated next twelve months EPS.

Off-market FRA A contract in which the initial value is intentionally set at a value other than zero and therefore requires a cash payment at the start from one party to the other.

Off-the-run A series of securities or indexes that were issued/created prior to the most recently issued/created series.

Office REITs REITs that invest in and manage multi-tenanted office properties in central business districts of cities and suburban markets.

Offsetting A transaction in exchange-listed derivative markets in which a party re-enters the market to close out a position.

On-the-run The most recently issued/created series of securities or indexes.

One-sided durations Effective durations when interest rates go up or down, which are better at capturing the interest rate sensitivity of bonds with embedded options that do not react symmetrically to positive and negative changes in interest rates of the same magnitude.

Operating lease An agreement allowing the lessee to use some asset for a period of time; essentially a rental.

Operating risk The risk attributed to the operating cost structure, in particular the use of fixed costs in operations; the risk arising from the mix of fixed and variable costs; the risk that a company's operations may be severely affected by environmental, social, and governance risk factors.

Operational risk The risk of loss from failures in a company's systems and procedures, or from external events.

Opportunity cost The value that investors forgo by choosing a particular course of action; the value of something in its best alternative use.

Optimal capital structure The capital structure at which the value of the company is maximized.

Option A financial instrument that gives one party the right, but not the obligation, to buy or sell an underlying asset from or to another party at a fixed price over a specific period of time. Also referred to as contingent claims.

Option-adjusted spread (OAS) Constant spread that, when added to all the one-period forward rates on the interest rate tree, makes the arbitrage-free value of the bond equal to its market price.

Option premium The amount of money a buyer pays and seller receives to engage in an option transaction.

Option price The amount of money a buyer pays and seller receives to engage in an option transaction.

Orderly liquidation value The estimated gross amount of money that could be realized from the liquidation sale of an asset or assets, given a reasonable amount of time to find a purchaser or purchasers.

Organic growth Company growth in output or sales that is achieved by making investments internally (i.e., excludes growth achieved through mergers and acquisitions).

Other comprehensive income Changes to equity that bypass (are not reported in) the income statement; the difference between comprehensive income and net income.

Out-of-sample forecast errors The differences between actual and predicted value of time series outside the sample period used to fit the model.

Out-of-the-money Options that, if exercised, would require the payment of more money than the value received and therefore would not be currently exercised.

Overnight index swap (OIS) A swap in which the floating rate is the cumulative value of a single unit of currency invested at an overnight rate during the settlement period.

Pairs trading An approach to trading that uses pairs of closely related stocks, buying the relatively undervalued stock and selling short the relatively overvalued stock.

Par curve A hypothetical yield curve for coupon-paying Treasury securities that assumes all securities are priced at par.

Par swap A swap in which the fixed rate is set so that no money is exchanged at contract initiation.

Parameter instability The problem or issue of population regression parameters that have changed over time.

Partial equilibrium models Term structure models that make use of an assumed form of interest rate process. Underlying risk factors, such as the impact of changing interest rates on the economy, are not incorporated in the model.

Partial regression coefficients The slope coefficients in a multiple regression. Also called *partial slope coefficients*.

Partial slope coefficients The slope coefficients in a multiple regression. Also called *partial regression coefficients*.

Partnership A business owned and operated by more than one individual.

Payer swaption A swaption that allows the holder to enter into a swap as the fixed-rate payer and floating-rate receiver.

Payoff The value of an option at expiration.

Payout amount The payout ratio times the notional.

Payout policy The principles by which a company distributes cash to common shareholders by means of cash dividends and/or share repurchases.

Payout ratio An estimate of the expected credit loss.

Pecking order theory The theory that managers take into account how their actions might be interpreted by outsiders and thus order their preferences for various forms of corporate financing. Forms of financing that are least visible to outsiders (e.g., internally generated funds) are most preferable to managers and those that are most visible (e.g., equity) are least preferable.

PEG The P/E-to-growth ratio, calculated as the stock's P/E divided by the expected earnings growth rate.

Perfect capital markets Markets in which, by assumption, there are no taxes, transactions costs, or bankruptcy costs, and in which all investors have equal ("symmetric") information.

Performance appraisal The evaluation of risk-adjusted performance; the evaluation of investment skill.

Periodic inventory system An inventory accounting system in which inventory values and costs of sales are determined at the end of the accounting period.

Perpetual inventory system An inventory accounting system in which inventory values and costs of sales are continuously updated to reflect purchases and sales.

Perpetuity A perpetual annuity, or a set of never-ending level sequential cash flows, with the first cash flow occurring one period from now.

Persistent earnings Earnings excluding nonrecurring components. Also referred to as *core earnings*, *continuing earnings*, or *underlying earnings*.

Pet projects Projects in which influential managers want the corporation to invest. Often, unfortunately, pet projects are selected without undergoing normal capital budgeting analysis.

Physical deterioration In the context of real estate, a reduction in value due to wear and tear.

Physical settlement Involves actual delivery of the debt instrument in exchange for a payment by the credit protection seller of the notional amount of the contract.

Plain vanilla swap An interest rate swap in which one party pays a fixed rate and the other pays a floating rate, with both sets of payments in the same currency.

Poison pill A pre-offer takeover defense mechanism that makes it prohibitively costly for an acquirer to take control of a target without the prior approval of the target's board of directors.

Poison puts A pre-offer takeover defense mechanism that gives target company bondholders the right to sell their bonds back to the target at a pre-specified redemption price, typically at or above par value; this defense increases the need for cash and raises the cost of the acquisition.

Pooling of interests method A method of accounting in which combined companies were portrayed as if they had always operated as a single economic entity. Called pooling of interests under US GAAP and uniting of interests under IFRS. (No longer allowed under US GAAP or IFRS.)

Portfolio balance approach A theory of exchange rate determination that emphasizes the portfolio investment decisions of global investors and the requirement that global investors willingly hold all outstanding securities denominated in each currency at prevailing prices and exchange rates.

Position trader A trader who typically holds positions open overnight.

Positive serial correlation Serial correlation in which a positive error for one observation increases the chance of a positive error for another observation, and a negative error for one observation increases the chance of a negative error for another observation.

Potential credit risk The risk associated with the possibility that a payment due at a later date will not be made.

Potential GDP The maximum amount of output an economy can sustainably produce without inducing an increase in the inflation rate. The output level that corresponds to full employment with consistent wage and price expectations.

Preferred habitat theory A term structure theory that contends that investors have maturity preferences and require yield incentives before they will buy bonds outside of their preferred maturities.

Premise of value The status of a company in the sense of whether it is assumed to be a going concern or not.

Premium The amount of money a buyer pays and seller receives to engage in an option transaction.

Premium leg The series of payments the credit protection buyer promises to make to the credit protection seller.

Present value model A model of intrinsic value that views the value of an asset as the present value of the asset's expected future cash flows.

Present value of growth opportunities The difference between the actual value per share and the no-growth value per share. Also called *value of growth*.

Present value of the expected loss Conceptually, the largest price one would be willing to pay on a bond to a third party (e.g., an insurer) to entirely remove the credit risk of purchasing and holding the bond.

Presentation currency The currency in which financial statement amounts are presented.

Price limits Limits imposed by a futures exchange on the price change that can occur from one day to the next.

Price momentum A valuation indicator based on past price movement.

Price multiples The ratio of a stock's market price to some measure of value per share.

Price-setting option The operational flexibility to adjust prices when demand varies from forecast. For example, when demand exceeds capacity, the company could benefit from the excess demand by increasing prices.

Priced risk Risk for which investors demand compensation for bearing (e.g., equity risk, company-specific factors, macroeconomic factors).

Principal–agent problem A conflict of interest that arises when the agent in an agency relationship has goals and incentives that differ from the principal to whom the agent owes a fiduciary duty.

Principal components analysis (PCA) A non-parametric method of extracting relevant information from high-dimensional data that uses the dependencies between variables to represent information in a more tractable, lower-dimensional form.

Principle of no arbitrage In well-functioning markets, prices will adjust until there are no arbitrage opportunities.

Prior transaction method A variation of the market approach; considers actual transactions in the stock of the subject private company.

Private market value The value derived using a sum-of-the-parts valuation.

Probability of default The probability that a bond issuer will not meet its contractual obligations on schedule.

Probability of survival The probability that a bond issuer will meet its contractual obligations on schedule.

Probit model A qualitative-dependent-variable multiple regression model based on the normal distribution.

Procedural law The body of law that focuses on the protection and enforcement of the substantive laws.

Production-flexibility The operational flexibility to alter production when demand varies from forecast. For example, if demand is strong, a company may profit from employees working overtime or from adding additional shifts.

Project sequencing To defer the decision to invest in a future project until the outcome of some or all of a current project is known. Projects are sequenced through time, so that investing in a project creates the option to invest in future projects.

Prospective P/E A P/E calculated on the basis of a forecast of EPS; a stock's current price divided by next year's expected earnings.

Protection leg The contingent payment that the credit protection seller may have to make to the credit protection buyer.

Protective put An option strategy in which a long position in an asset is combined with a long position in a put.

Proxy fight An attempt to take control of a company through a shareholder vote.

Proxy statement A public document that provides the material facts concerning matters on which shareholders will vote.

Prudential supervision Regulation and monitoring of the safety and soundness of financial institutions to promote financial stability, reduce system-wide risks, and protect customers of financial institutions.

Purchasing power gain A gain in value caused by changes in price levels. Monetary liabilities experience purchasing power gains during periods of inflation.

Purchasing power loss A loss in value caused by changes in price levels. Monetary assets experience purchasing power loss during periods of inflation.

Purchasing power parity (PPP) The idea that exchange rates move to equalize the purchasing power of different currencies.

Pure expectations theory A term structure theory that contends the forward rate is an unbiased predictor of the future spot rate. Also called the *unbiased expectations theory*.

Pure factor portfolio A portfolio with sensitivity of 1 to the factor in question and a sensitivity of 0 to all other factors.

Put An option that gives the holder the right to sell an underlying asset to another party at a fixed price over a specific period of time.

Put–call–forward parity The relationship among puts, calls, and forward contracts.

Put–call parity An equation expressing the equivalence (parity) of a portfolio of a call and a bond with a portfolio of a put and the underlying, which leads to the relationship between put and call prices.

Putable bond Bond that includes an embedded put option, which gives the bondholder the right to put back the bonds to the issuer prior to maturity, typically when interest rates have risen and higher-yielding bonds are available.

Qualitative dependent variables Dummy variables used as dependent variables rather than as independent variables.

Quality of earnings analysis The investigation of issues relating to the accuracy of reported accounting results as reflections of economic performance; quality of earnings analysis is broadly understood to include not only earnings management, but also balance sheet management.

Random walk A time series in which the value of the series in one period is the value of the series in the previous period plus an unpredictable random error.

Rational efficient markets formulation See *market efficiency*.

Real estate investment trusts (REITS) Tax-advantaged entities (companies or trusts) that typically own, operate, and—to a limited extent—develop income-producing real estate property.

Real estate operating companies Regular taxable real estate ownership companies that operate in the real estate industry in countries that do not have a tax-advantaged REIT regime in place or are engaged in real estate activities of a kind and to an extent that do not fit within their country's REIT framework.

Real exchange rate The relative purchasing power of two currencies, defined in terms of the *real* goods and services that each can buy at prevailing national price levels and nominal exchange rates. Measured as the ratio of national price levels expressed in a common currency.

Real interest rate parity The proposition that real interest rates will converge to the same level across different markets.

Real options Options that relate to investment decisions such as the option to time the start of a project, the option to adjust its scale, or the option to abandon a project that has begun.

Receiver swaption   A swaption that allows the holder to enter into a swap as the fixed-rate receiver and floating-rate payer.

Reconstitution   When dealers recombine appropriate individual zero-coupon securities and reproduce an underlying coupon Treasury.

Recovery rate   The percentage of the loss recovered.

Reduced form models   Models of credit analysis based on the outputs of a structural model but with different assumptions. The model's credit risk measures reflect changing economic conditions.

Reference entity   The borrower on a single-name CDS.

Reference obligation   A particular debt instrument issued by the borrower that is the designated instrument being covered.

Regime   With reference to a time series, the underlying model generating the times series.

Regression coefficients   The intercept and slope coefficient(s) of a regression.

Regulatory arbitrage   Entities identify and use some aspect of regulations that allows them to exploit differences in economic substance and regulatory interpretation or in foreign and domestic regulatory regimes to their (the entities) advantage.

Regulatory burden   The costs of regulation for the regulated entity.

Regulatory capture   Theory that regulation often arises to enhance the interests of the regulated.

Regulatory competition   Regulators may compete to provide a regulatory environment designed to attract certain entities.

Relative-strength indicators   Valuation indicators that compare a stock's performance during a period either to its own past performance or to the performance of some group of stocks.

Relative valuation models   A model that specifies an asset's value relative to the value of another asset.

Relative version of PPP   Hypothesis that changes in (nominal) exchange rates over time are equal to national inflation rate differentials.

Renewable resources   Resources that can be replenished, such as a forest.

Rental price of capital   The cost per unit of time to rent a unit of capital.

Replacement cost   In the context of real estate, the value of a building assuming it was built today using current construction costs and standards.

Replacement value   The market value of a swap.

Reporting unit   For financial reporting under US GAAP, an operating segment or one level below an operating segment (referred to as a component).

Reputational risk   The risk that a company will suffer an extended diminution in market value relative to other companies in the same industry due to a demonstrated lack of concern for environmental, social, and governance risk factors.

Required rate of return   The minimum rate of return required by an investor to invest in an asset, given the asset's riskiness.

Residential properties   Properties that provide housing for individuals or families. Single-family properties may be owner-occupied or rental properties, whereas multi-family properties are rental properties even if the owner or manager occupies one of the units.

Residual autocorrelations   The sample autocorrelations of the residuals.

Residual dividend policy   A policy in which dividends are paid from any internally generated funds remaining after such funds are used to finance positive NPV projects.

Residual income   Earnings for a given time period, minus a deduction for common shareholders' opportunity cost in generating the earnings. Also called *economic profit* or *abnormal earnings*.

Residual income method   Income approach that estimates the value of all intangible assets of the business by capitalizing future earnings in excess of the estimated return requirements associated with working capital and fixed assets.

Residual income model   (RIM) A model of stock valuation that views intrinsic value of stock as the sum of book value per share plus the present value of the stock's expected future residual income per share. Also called *discounted abnormal earnings model* or *Edwards–Bell–Ohlson model*.

Residual loss   Agency costs that are incurred despite adequate monitoring and bonding of management.

Restructuring   Reorganizing the financial structure of a firm.

Retail REITs   REITs that invest in such retail properties as regional shopping malls or community/neighborhood shopping centers.

Return on capital employed   Operating profit divided by capital employed (debt and equity capital).

Return on invested capital   A measure of the after-tax profitability of the capital invested by the company's shareholders and debt holders.

Reviewed financial statements   A type of non-audited financial statements; typically provide an opinion letter with representations and assurances by the reviewing accountant that are less than those in audited financial statements.

Rho   The sensitivity of the option price to the risk-free rate.

Riding the yield curve   A maturity trading strategy that involves buying bonds with a maturity longer than the intended investment horizon. Also called *rolling down the yield curve*.

Risk-neutral probabilities   Weights that are used to compute a binomial option price. They are the probabilities that would apply if a risk-neutral investor valued an option.

Risk-neutral valuation   The process by which options and other derivatives are priced by treating investors as though they were risk neutral.

Risk reversal   An option position that consists of the purchase of an out-of-the-money call and the simultaneous sale of an out-of-the-money put with the same "delta," on the same underlying currency or security, and with the same expiration date.

Robust standard errors   Standard errors of the estimated parameters of a regression that correct for the presence of heteroskedasticity in the regression's error term.

Roll   When an investor moves from one series to a new one.

Rolling down the yield curve   A maturity trading strategy that involves buying bonds with a maturity longer than the intended investment horizon. Also called *riding the yield curve*.

Root mean squared error (RMSE)   The square root of the average squared forecast error; used to compare the out-of-sample forecasting performance of forecasting models.

Sales comparison approach   In the context of real estate, this approach estimates value based on what similar or comparable properties (comparables) transacted for in the current market.

Sales-type leases   A type of finance lease, from a lessor perspective, where the present value of the lease payments (lease receivable) exceeds the carrying value of the leased asset. The revenues earned by the lessor are operating (the profit on the sale) and financing (interest) in nature.

Scaled earnings surprise   Unexpected earnings divided by the standard deviation of analysts' earnings forecasts.

Scalper   A trader who offers to buy or sell futures contracts, holding the position for only a brief period of time. Scalpers attempt to profit by buying at the bid price and selling at the higher ask price.

Scatter plot   A two-dimensional plot of pairs of observations on two data series.

Scenario analysis   Analysis that involves changing multiple assumptions at the same time.

Screening   The application of a set of criteria to reduce a set of potential investments to a smaller set having certain desired characteristics.

Seasonality   A characteristic of a time series in which the data experiences regular and predictable periodic changes, e.g., fan sales are highest during the summer months.

Seats   Memberships in a derivatives exchange.

Securities offering   A merger or acquisition in which target shareholders are to receive shares of the acquirer's common stock as compensation.

Security selection risk   See *active specific risk.*

Segmented markets theory   A term structure theory that contends yields are solely a function of the supply and demand for funds of a particular maturity.

Self-regulating organizations   Private, non-governmental organizations that both represent and regulate their members. Some self-regulating organizations are also independent regulators.

Sell-side analysts   Analysts who work at brokerages.

Sensitivity analysis   Analysis that shows the range of possible outcomes as specific assumptions are changed; involves changing one assumption at a time.

Serially correlated   With reference to regression errors, errors that are correlated across observations.

Settlement   In the case of a credit event, the process by which the two parties to a CDS contract satisfy their respective obligations.

Settlement date   The date on which the parties to a swap make payments. Also called *payment date.*

Settlement period   The time between settlement dates.

Settlement price   The official price, designated by the clearinghouse, from which daily gains and losses will be determined and marked to market.

Shaping risk   The sensitivity of a bond's price to the changing shape of the yield curve.

Shareholders' equity   Total assets minus total liabilities.

Shark repellents   A pre-offer takeover defense mechanism involving the corporate charter (e.g., staggered boards of directors and supermajority provisions).

Shopping center   REITs that invest in such retail properties as regional shopping malls or community/neighborhood shopping centers.

Short   The seller of a derivative contract. Also refers to the position of being short a derivative.

Single-name CDS   Credit default swap on one specific borrower.

Sinking fund bond   A bond which requires the issuer to set aside funds over time to retire the bond issue, thus reducing credit risk.

Sole proprietorship   A business owned and operated by a single person.

Speculative value   The difference between the market price of the option and its intrinsic value, determined by the uncertainty of the underlying over the remaining life of the option. Also called *time value.*

Spin-off   A form of restructuring in which shareholders of a parent company receive a proportional number of shares in a new, separate entity; shareholders end up owning stock in two different companies where there used to be one.

Split-off   A form of restructuring in which shareholders of the parent company are given shares in a newly created entity in exchange for their shares of the parent company.

Split-rate tax system   In reference to corporate taxes, a split-rate system taxes earnings to be distributed as dividends at a different rate than earnings to be retained. Corporate profits distributed as dividends are taxed at a lower rate than those retained in the business.

Spot curve   The term structure of spot rates for loans made today.

Spot rate   The interest rate that is determined today for a risk-free, single-unit payment at a specified future date.

Spot yield curve   The term structure of spot rates for loans made today.

Spurious correlation   A correlation that misleadingly points toward associations between variables.

Stabilized NOI   In the context of real estate, the expected NOI when a renovation is complete.

Stable dividend policy   A policy in which regular dividends are paid that reflect long-run expected earnings. In contrast to a constant dividend payout ratio policy, a stable dividend policy does not reflect short-term volatility in earnings.

Standard deviation   The positive square root of the variance; a measure of dispersion in the same units as the original data.

Standard of value   A specification of how "value" is to be understood in the context of a specific valuation.

Standardized beta   With reference to fundamental factor models, the value of the attribute for an asset minus the average value of the attribute across all stocks, divided by the standard deviation of the attribute across all stocks.

Standardized unexpected earnings   (SUE) Unexpected earnings per share divided by the standard deviation of unexpected earnings per share over a specified prior time period.

Static trade-off theory of capital structure   A theory pertaining to a company's optimal capital structure; the optimal level of debt is found at the point where additional debt would cause the costs of financial distress to increase by a greater amount than the benefit of the additional tax shield.

Statistical factor model   A multifactor model in which statistical methods are applied to a set of historical returns to determine portfolios that best explain either historical return covariances or variances.

Statistically significant   A result indicating that the null hypothesis can be rejected; with reference to an estimated regression coefficient, frequently understood to mean a result indicating that the corresponding population regression coefficient is different from 0.

Statutes   Laws enacted by legislative bodies.

Statutory merger   A merger in which one company ceases to exist as an identifiable entity and all its assets and liabilities become part of a purchasing company.

Steady state rate of growth   The constant growth rate of output (or output per capita) which can or will be sustained indefinitely once it is reached. Key ratios, such as the capital–output ratio, are constant on the steady-state growth path.

Steepness   One of the three factors (the other two are level and curvature) that empirically explain most of the changes in the shape of the yield curve. A shock to the steepness factor changes short-term yields more than long-term yields.

Sterilized intervention   A policy measure in which a monetary authority buys or sells its own currency to mitigate undesired exchange rate movements and simultaneously offsets the impact on the money supply with transactions in other financial instruments (usually money market instruments).

Stock purchase   An acquisition in which the acquirer gives the target company's shareholders some combination of cash and securities in exchange for shares of the target company's stock.

Storage costs   The costs of holding an asset, generally a function of the physical characteristics of the underlying asset.

Storage REITs   REITs that own and operate self-storage properties, sometimes referred to as mini-warehouse facilities.

Straight bond   An underlying option-free bond with a specified issuer, issue date, maturity date, principal amount and repayment structure, coupon rate and payment structure, and currency denomination.

Straight-line rent   The average annual rent under a multi-year lease agreement that contains contractual increases in rent during the life of the lease. For example if the rent is $100,000 in Year 1, $105,000 in Year 2, and $110,000 in Year 3, the average rent to be recognized each year as revenue under straight-line rent accounting is ($100,000 + $105,000 + $110,000)/3 = $105,000.

Straight-line rent adjustment   See *non-cash rent*.

Strategic transaction   A purchase involving a buyer that would benefit from certain synergies associated with owning the target firm.

Strike   See *exercise price*.

Strike price   See *exercise price*.

Strike rate   The fixed rate at which the holder of an interest rate option can buy or sell the underlying. Also called *exercise rate*.

Striking price   See *exercise price*.

Stripping   A dealer's ability to separate a bond's individual cash flows and trade them as zero-coupon securities.

Structural models   Structural models of credit analysis build on the insights of option pricing theory. They are based on the structure of a company's balance sheet.

Subsidiary merger   A merger in which the company being purchased becomes a subsidiary of the purchaser.

Substantive law   The body of law that focuses on the rights and responsibilities of entities and relationships among entities.

Succession event   A change of corporate structure of the reference entity, such as through a merger, divestiture, spinoff, or any similar action, in which ultimate responsibility for the debt in question is unclear.

Sum-of-the-parts valuation   A valuation that sums the estimated values of each of a company's businesses as if each business were an independent going concern.

Sunk cost   A cost that has already been incurred.

Supernormal growth   Above average or abnormally high growth rate in earnings per share.

Survivorship bias   Bias that may result when failed or defunct companies are excluded from membership in a group.

Sustainable growth rate   The rate of dividend (and earnings) growth that can be sustained over time for a given level of return on equity, keeping the capital structure constant and without issuing additional common stock.

Swap curve   The term structure of swap rates.

Swap rate   The interest rate for the fixed-rate leg of an interest rate swap.

Swap rate curve   The term structure of swap rates.

Swap spread   The difference between the fixed rate on an interest rate swap and the rate on a Treasury note with equivalent maturity; it reflects the general level of credit risk in the market.

Swaption   An option to enter into a swap.

Synthetic call   The combination of puts, the underlying, and risk-free bonds that replicates a call option.

Synthetic CDO   Created by combining a portfolio of default-free securities with a combination of credit default swaps undertaken as protection sellers.

Synthetic forward contract   The combination of the underlying, puts, calls, and risk-free bonds that replicates a forward contract.

Synthetic lease   A lease that is structured to provide a company with the tax benefits of ownership while not requiring the asset to be reflected on the company's financial statements.

Synthetic put   The combination of calls, the underlying, and risk-free bonds that replicates a put option.

Systematic risk   Risk that affects the entire market or economy; it cannot be avoided and is inherent in the overall market. Systematic risk is also known as non-diversifiable or market risk.

Systemic risk   The risk of failure of the financial system.

Takeover   A merger; the term may be applied to any transaction, but is often used in reference to hostile transactions.

Takeover premium   The amount by which the takeover price for each share of stock must exceed the current stock price in order to entice shareholders to relinquish control of the company to an acquirer.

Tangible book value per share   Common shareholders' equity minus intangible assets reported on the balance sheet, divided by the number of shares outstanding.

Target   The company in a merger or acquisition that is being acquired.

Target capital structure   A company's chosen proportions of debt and equity.

Target company   The company in a merger or acquisition that is being acquired.

Target payout ratio   A strategic corporate goal representing the long-term proportion of earnings that the company intends to distribute to shareholders as dividends.

Technical indicators   Momentum indicators based on price.

TED spread   A measure of perceived credit risk determined as the difference between Libor and the T-bill yield of matching maturity.

Temporal method   A variation of the monetary/non-monetary translation method that requires not only monetary assets and liabilities, but also non-monetary assets and liabilities that are measured at their current value on the balance sheet date to be translated at the current exchange rate. Assets and liabilities are translated at rates consistent with the timing of their measurement value. This method is typically used when the functional currency is other than the local currency.

Tender offer   A public offer whereby the acquirer invites target shareholders to submit ("tender") their shares in return for the proposed payment.

Term premium   The additional return required by lenders to invest in a bond to maturity net of the expected return from continually reinvesting at the short-term rate over that same time horizon.

Terminal price multiples   The price multiple for a stock assumed to hold at a stated future time.

Terminal share price   The share price at a particular point in the future.

Terminal value of the stock   The analyst's estimate of a stock's value at a particular point in the future. Also called *continuing value of the stock*.

Termination date   The date of the final payment on a swap; also, the swap's expiration date.

Theta   The rate at which an option's time value decays.

Time series   A set of observations on a variable's outcomes in different time periods.

Time to expiration   The time remaining in the life of a derivative, typically expressed in years.

Time value   The difference between the market price of the option and its intrinsic value, determined by the uncertainty of the underlying over the remaining life of the option. Also called *speculative value*.

Time value decay   The loss in the value of an option resulting from movement of the option price towards its payoff value as the expiration day approaches.

Tobin's *q*   The ratio of the market value of debt and equity to the replacement cost of total assets.

Top-down approach   With respect to forecasting, an approach that usually begins at the level of the overall economy. Forecasts are then made at more narrowly defined levels, such as sector, industry, and market for a specific product.

Top-down investing   An approach to investing that typically begins with macroeconomic forecasts.

Total factor productivity (TFP)   A multiplicative scale factor that reflects the general level of productivity or technology in the economy. Changes in total factor productivity generate proportional changes in output for any input combination.

Total invested capital   The sum of market value of common equity, book value of preferred equity, and face value of debt.

Total return swap   A swap in which one party agrees to pay the total return on a security. Often used as a credit derivative, in which the underlying is a bond.

Tracking error   The standard deviation of the differences between a portfolio's returns and its benchmark's returns; a synonym of active risk. Also called *tracking risk*.

Tracking risk   The standard deviation of the differences between a portfolio's returns and its benchmark's returns; a synonym of active risk. Also called *tracking error*.

Trailing dividend yield   Current market price divided by the most recent annualized dividend.

Trailing P/E   A stock's current market price divided by the most recent four quarters of EPS (or the most recent two semi-annual periods for companies that report interim data semi-annually.) Also called *current P/E*.

Tranche CDS   A type of credit default swap that covers a combination of borrowers but only up to pre-specified levels of losses.

Transaction exposure   The risk of a change in value between the transaction date and the settlement date of an asset of liability denominated in a foreign currency.

Trend   A long-term pattern of movement in a particular direction.

Triangular arbitrage   An arbitrage transaction involving three currencies which attempts to exploit inconsistencies among pair wise exchange rates.

Unbiased expectations theory   A term structure theory that contends the forward rate is an unbiased predictor of the future spot rate. Also called the *pure expectations theory*.

Unconditional heteroskedasticity   Heteroskedasticity of the error term that is not correlated with the values of the independent variable(s) in the regression.

Uncovered interest rate parity   The proposition that the expected return on an uncovered (i.e., unhedged) foreign currency (risk-free) investment should equal the return on a comparable domestic currency investment.

Underlying   An asset that trades in a market in which buyers and sellers meet, decide on a price, and the seller then delivers the asset to the buyer and receives payment. The underlying is the asset or other derivative on which a particular derivative is based. The market for the underlying is also referred to as the spot market.

Underlying earnings   Earnings excluding nonrecurring components. Also referred to as *continuing earnings*, *core earnings*, or *persistent earnings*.

Unexpected earnings   The difference between reported EPS and expected EPS. Also referred to as an *earnings surprise*.

Unit root   A time series that is not covariance stationary is said to have a unit root.

Uniting of interests method   A method of accounting in which combined companies were portrayed as if they had always operated as a single economic entity. Called pooling of interests under US GAAP and uniting of interests under IFRS. (No longer allowed under US GAAP or IFRS).

Unlimited funds   An unlimited funds environment assumes that the company can raise the funds it wants for all profitable projects simply by paying the required rate of return.

Unsterilized intervention   A policy measure in which a monetary authority buys or sells its own currency to mitigate undesired exchange rate movements and does not offset the impact on the money supply with transactions in other financial instruments.

Upfront payment   The difference between the credit spread and the standard rate paid by the protection if the standard rate is insufficient to compensate the protection seller. Also called *upfront premium*.

Upfront premium   See *upfront payment*.

UPREITs   An umbrella partnership REIT under which the REIT owns an operating partnership and serves as the general partner of the operating partnership. All or most of the properties are held in the operating partnership.

Upstream   A transaction between two related companies, an investor company (or a parent company) and an associate company (or a subsidiary company) such that the associate company records a profit on its income statement. An example is a sale of inventory by the associate to the investor company or by a subsidiary to a parent company.

Valuation   The process of determining the value of an asset or service on the basis of variables perceived to be related to future investment returns, or on the basis of comparisons with closely similar assets.

Value additivity   An arbitrage opportunity when the value of the whole equals the sum of the values of the parts.

Value at risk (VAR)   A money measure of the minimum value of losses expected during a specified time period at a given level of probability.

Value of growth   The difference between the actual value per share and the no-growth value per share.

Variance   The expected value (the probability-weighted average) of squared deviations from a random variable's expected value.

Variation margin   Additional margin that must be deposited in an amount sufficient to bring the balance up to the initial margin requirement.

Vasicek model   A partial equilibrium term structure model that assumes interest rates are mean reverting and interest rate volatility is a constant.

Vega   The relationship between option price and volatility.

Venture capital investors   Private equity investors in development-stage companies.

Vertical merger   A merger involving companies at different positions of the same production chain; for example, a supplier or a distributor.

Visibility   The extent to which a company's operations are predictable with substantial confidence.

Weighted average cost   An inventory accounting method that averages the total cost of available inventory items over the total units available for sale.

Weighted average cost of capital   (WACC) A weighted average of the after-tax required rates of return on a company's common stock, preferred stock, and long-term debt, where the weights are the fraction of each source of financing in the company's target capital structure.

Weighted harmonic mean   See *harmonic mean.*

White-corrected standard errors   A synonym for robust standard errors.

White knight   A third party that is sought out by the target company's board to purchase the target in lieu of a hostile bidder.

White squire   A third party that is sought out by the target company's board to purchase a substantial minority stake in the target—enough to block a hostile takeover without selling the entire company.

Winner's curse   The tendency for the winner in certain competitive bidding situations to overpay, whether because of overestimation of intrinsic value, emotion, or information asymmetries.

Write-down   A reduction in the value of an asset as stated in the balance sheet.

Yield curve factor model   A model or a description of yield curve movements that can be considered realistic when compared with historical data.

Z-spread   The constant basis point spread that needs to be added to the implied spot yield curve such that the discounted cash flows of a bond are equal to its current market price.

Zero   A bond that does not pay a coupon but is priced at a discount and pays its full face value at maturity.

Zero-cost collar   A transaction in which a position in the underlying is protected by buying a put and selling a call with the premium from the sale of the call offsetting the premium from the purchase of the put. It can also be used to protect a floating-rate borrower against interest rate increases with the premium on a long cap offsetting the premium on a short floor.

Zero-coupon bond   A bond that does not pay a coupon but is priced at a discount and pays its full face value at maturity.

Index